Free
(Revolving Door)

.8
m___der
community
supervision *

PROBATION

Revocation of
Parole or
Probation or
New Conviction

PAROLE

JAIL

PRISON

2.2
million in
custody *

Free
(Revolving Door)

Successful Appeal
(Revolving Door)

* Correctional Populations in the US, 2012
http://www.bjs.gov/content/pub/pdf/cpus12.pdf

AMERICAN CORRECTIONS

AMERICAN CORRECTIONS

CORRECTIONS

Concepts and Controversies

Barry Krisberg
University of California, Berkeley

Susan Marchionna
Criminal Justice Communications Consultant

Christopher Hartney
National Council on Crime and Delinquency

Los Angeles | London | New Delhi
Singapore | Washington DC

Los Angeles | London | New Delhi
Singapore | Washington DC

FOR INFORMATION:

SAGE Publications, Inc.
2455 Teller Road
Thousand Oaks, California 91320
E-mail: order@sagepub.com

SAGE Publications Ltd.
1 Oliver's Yard
55 City Road
London, EC1Y 1SP
United Kingdom

SAGE Publications India Pvt. Ltd.
B 1/I 1 Mohan Cooperative Industrial Area
Mathura Road, New Delhi 110 044
India

SAGE Publications Asia-Pacific Pte. Ltd.
3 Church Street
#10–04 Samsung Hub
Singapore 049483

Printed in the United States of America

Library of Congress Cataloging-in-Publication Data

Krisberg, Barry.

American corrections : concepts and controversies / Barry Krisberg, Susan Marchionna, Christopher Hartney.

pages cm
Includes bibliographical references and index.

ISBN 978-1-4129-7439-4 (pbk. : alk. paper)

1. Corrections—United States. 2. Criminal justice, Administration of—United States. I. Marchionna, Susan. II. Hartney, Christopher III. Title.

HV9471.K75 2014
365'.973—dc23   2014014625

This book is printed on acid-free paper.

SUSTAINABLE FORESTRY INITIATIVE   Certified Sourcing
www.sfiprogram.org
SFI-00993
This Label Applies to Text Stock Only

Acquisitions Editor: Jerry Westby
Associate Editor: Jessica Miller
Assistant Editor: Rachael Leblond
Production Editor: Libby Larson
Copy Editor: Melinda Masson
Typesetter: C&M Digitals (P) Ltd.
Proofreader: WendyJo Dymond
Indexer: Sheila Bodell
Cover Designer: Scott Van Atta
Interior Design: Scott Van Atta
Marketing Manager: Terra Schultz

14 15 16 17 18 10 9 8 7 6 5 4 3 2 1

Brief Contents

Part IV: The Effectiveness and Future of American Corrections

Detailed Contents

Chapter 5: Probation and Alternatives to Incarceration

Chapter 8: Juvenile Corrections   **178**

Chapter 11: Corrections and the Color Line — 254

Chapter 12: Women in the Corrections System — 276

Chapter 13: Challenging and Vulnerable Populations   304

Chapter 14: Death Row and the Death Penalty   324

Part IV: The Effectiveness and Future of American Corrections   345

Chapter 15: The Growth of Privatization in Corrections   346

Chapter 16: The Politics and Future of Mass Incarceration 372

Preface

The goal of this text is to present a contemporary and critical lens through which students can examine and evaluate American corrections. Crime and punishment are poorly understood in our society; perhaps that is true for all societies. In the current educational realm, we find that too many texts do too little to advance students' comprehension of the thorny issues and controversies involved in corrections. Too many do too little to question the conventional wisdom and tilt the system on its side for a better view. It is, therefore, our primary intent to promote a new literacy of corrections—a more thoughtful and more thought-provoking view of a subject matter that is as old as society itself. This is an important time of change in the field of corrections in our nation. We wish for the undergraduate student to achieve more than a superficial grasp of the components and context of the correctional system as we all stand on the threshold of what could be a new paradigm of society's response to crime. To advance the cause of steady system improvement, today's students of corrections need to inquire beyond rote knowledge of the status quo and apply their energies to understanding problems and devising solutions.

Our system processes enormous numbers of individuals through jails, probation departments, prisons, and parole boards—at a rate far greater than almost every other nation. Billions of dollars are spent each year, not on rehabilitation but on doing little more than warehousing and surveilling millions of system-involved individuals. Nearly all the residents of our prisons and jails will eventually return to our neighborhoods and communities. It is, therefore, in society's interest that offenders exit the corrections system in better shape—mentally, socially, and physically—than when they entered that system, and certainly not worse. Only then will we approach a more consistent application of justice for all communities and a more durable public safety. The question remains as to what are the means to this end. The need for change is clear; the means to make those changes are available; and the opportunity for change is here. Most Americans believe in the pursuit of less costly and more effective alternatives. It is the sincere wish of the authors that the students of this text will come away not only with a grasp of the complexity and enormity of the crisis in American corrections, but also with a true sense of hope that a more just and effective correctional system is within our reach.

The reader will notice the point of view of this text—that corrections consumes vast amounts of public resources that could be better used on education, on other aspects of public safety, and to support vulnerable families and communities, and that society would be better served if correctional methods proven to be effective were the norm for holding lawbreakers accountable and for helping to prepare them for a better life.

Major Features and Organization

This book is organized into four main sections: (1) History and Sentencing, (2) Correctional Practice, (3) Critical Issues and Policy Questions, and (4) The Effectiveness and Future of American Corrections. Each section contains two to six chapters. This preface will give professors and students a clear overview of what they can expect to teach or learn, the perspective of the authors, and the techniques and aids used to make the book's information and ideas as comprehensible and relevant as possible. Each of the chapters touches on a key aspect of the American correctional system, providing history, current characteristics, trends, the most current data available, critiques, and (because of the interrelatedness of the subject matter) frequent cross-referencing with other chapters. The authors hope that, by connecting the chapter topics, the reader will gain a deeper and more nuanced appreciation for the complexity of our correctional system and how changes in one area may have positive or negative impacts on another.

Part I: History and Sentencing

The corrections system in the United States has a unique historical foundation, and its current form is remarkable for its size and structure. Many assume that, because American democracy has its roots in equity and freedom, its justice system should be a paragon of civil and individual rights. The authors believe that the best way to protect that ideal of justice is to view it with an unflinching eye and question its trajectory.

Chapter 1: The Corrections System. This introduction presents an overview of our system, explaining its components and structure and how it fits into the entire justice system. The chapter will orient the reader to our critical perspective and make the opening case for the need for constant improvements in the complex, difficult, and troubled system. From the very start, the student will understand that corrections entails issues and controversies, reflections of society's tensions, and competing opinions over policy and practice as well as philosophy.

Chapter 2: A Historical Perspective on Punishment and Social Structure. This chapter begins with the historical foundations of the various components of corrections, through the Middle Ages, colonialism, the Industrial Revolution, and the major periods of modern American history. History allows us to understand the key choices that lawmakers and citizens have made over time. These choices have their roots in Western class structure and have undoubtedly shaped contemporary correctional policy and practice. By examining the theories of important penological thinkers and the innovations of key historical figures and movements, we can better understand the evolution of corrections and imagine the possible alternatives.

Chapter 3: The Purpose of Punishment and Sentencing Trends. This chapter offers an overview of the major rationales for criminal sanctioning and how those fluctuate over time under the influence of social and political movements. The text describes the significant ways that politicians and voters—who typically know too little on the subject—can influence correctional policy. In addition, the chapter covers the major theories of sentencing and a variety of sentencing schemes, such as determinate and indeterminate sentencing. The reader will find, for example, that judges held a great amount of discretion in sentencing decisions until determinate sentencing schemes shifted that discretion to prosecutors. The reader will gain insight into significant legal developments, including three strikes and mandatory minimums, and will explore the key influences of common conventions, such as plea bargaining and presentence investigations.

Part II: Correctional Practice

This section describes the basic components of the American corrections system. The order of the chapters aligns with the typical chronological path of an involved individual moving through the system: jails, probation and alternatives to incarceration, prisons, and parole and reentry. It concludes with chapters on youth in the system and those on the "front lines"—the corrections workforce.

Chapter 4: Jails. The chapter on jails explains the significant, multifaceted role that jails play on the corrections stage. After arrest, most defendants are brought to jails for decisions on release, bail, or extended custody as they await trial. This chapter describes each of the purposes that jails serve, who is held in jails, and the various data that help to measure the jail population. In addition, the reader will learn how jails are administered and staffed, how things work in jail, and the physical characteristics of jails. Beyond the factual side, readers will gain a sense of the difficulty of managing in a single, closed setting an extremely diverse population, including individuals from every type of racial, cultural, and economic background, first-timers and seasoned career criminals, low-level offenders and serious felons, and—perhaps most importantly—those "innocent until proven guilty" and those already convicted. The text also delves into programming in jails and the difficulties in providing services to a population in constant flux.

Chapter 5: Probation and Alternatives to Incarceration. This chapter introduces the reader to community supervision. Probation agencies and probation officers are some of the unsung heroes of the system, being largely underfunded for the enormous role they play supervising millions of Americans annually. After defining probation and its purposes, the chapter discusses its history, who is on probation, the process of probation, and what probation officers do, illuminating the often-conflicting roles of probation officer as both police officer and social worker. The text explains some of probation's complexity—caseload sizes, supervision and investigation, revocations, how agencies are organized and administered, and the differences inherent in the approach to probation, whether it emphasizes law enforcement or rehabilitation. In addition, the text surveys some relatively new types of community-based supervision that are designed to safely supervise more serious offenders in their community, save taxpayer money, and improve rehabilitation. An important aspect of these alternatives is their continuing innovation and the evaluation of their efficacy to improve outcomes for probation clients and public safety.

Chapter 6: Prisons. Prisons are what most people think of when the subject of corrections arises. This chapter includes descriptions of the purpose and design of the various types of prisons and whom they hold and a discussion of prison operations, such as security-level classification, response to discipline issues, and costs. It differentiates prisons from jails and the state system from the federal system, and describes incarceration rates among states. The text describes the stunning growth in the past decades of the incarcerated population, along with the associated challenges of prison crowding, health and safety issues, the de-emphasis of rehabilitative programming, prisoner discipline, the overuse of solitary confinement, the "supermax," and instances of abuse and corruption among the workforce.

Chapter 7: Coming Home: Reentry and Parole. The number of people on parole and reentering society after prison has grown in proportion to those incarcerated. Support for traditional parole as a viable penal sanction among the public and lawmakers has fluctuated over time. In most states, parole in its various forms continues to be a key adjunct to the prison sentence. It is viewed both as a punitive sanction and as an opportunity for prisoners to successfully reenter society and avoid a return to custody. This chapter offers a brief history of parole. It explains how parole is organized, how it functions, the role of the parole board through history and today, and what the parole data say. It also looks at the rise of the "reentry movement," evidence-based practice in community supervision, and assessing promising directions for the future.

Chapter 8: Juvenile Corrections. In recognition of the fundamental differences between adults and youth, the United States has had a separate system of justice for juveniles for over a century. This chapter offers a brief overview of the current status of juvenile corrections, which differs (or should differ) from adult programs in significant ways. The two systems are sadly similar in certain ways, including that both exhibit striking racial disparities. The latest available data illustrate current trends in juvenile corrections, including the recent waves of litigation brought on by abuse scandals and civil rights violations in juvenile facilities. At the same time, litigation has also opened the door to some remarkable opportunities for reform. In surveying what is effective and what is not, the text offers a challenge to assumptions that have bolstered fads for handling youth in the system.

Chapter 9: The Corrections Workforce. The opportunities for correctional reforms mentioned thus far are dependent in large measure on the attitudes and capacities of the staff that work with both adults and juveniles—the correctional workforce. Key to their success or failure is the culture in which they work, including the conditions and interpersonal climate of the workplace, the nature and extent of the training and institutional support they receive, and the policies and practices they follow as dictated by agency leadership. How that workforce is evolving or failing to evolve has a direct impact on all aspects of the system. Employees occupy a wide variety of roles: prison guard, probation or parole officer, administrator, or support staff; each position has its own education and training requirements. The text delves into such topics as studies about the psychological impact of the correctional experience on staff, the need to recruit more women and people of color, and the role of public employee unions within corrections. Leadership is critical to the implementation of changes to the system; the text outlines some of the more promising developments in staffing and leadership.

Part III: Critical Issues and Policy Questions

To delve further into a purposeful and critical analysis of the system, the text presents the ways in which race, ethnicity, class, and gender intersect and manifest in the current corrections system. Individual chapters in this section show how each of these key factors is a contributor to a complex construct and how each helps to shape the contours of American corrections.

Chapter 10: Law and Corrections. Much of what goes on in the world of corrections lies outside of the public's view. Partly due to this lack of transparency, corrections systems have violated laws and constitutional principles in many states and communities. Through the lens of litigation, the text refers to the range and magnitude of problems plaguing state and local prison systems, some of the possible reasons for them, and the administrative and legal strategies intended to reduce such abuses. In particular, this chapter examines the impact of key legislation, including the Prison Litigation Reform Act (PLRA, 1995), the Prison Rape Elimination Act (PREA, 2003), and the Civil Rights of Institutionalized Persons Act (CRIPA, 1980). The text also explores the value of efforts on the part of current professional groups to set standards and to stop abusive practices.

Chapter 11: Corrections and the Color Line. Perhaps the most obvious systemic injustice in the current state of American corrections is the racial disparity in the population of individuals under penal control. This text is dedicated to looking at relevant data as a means of grasping the extent of disparity and how it accumulates as individuals become more deeply entrenched in the system. The chapter explores the issues behind this dynamic and looks at how the overincarceration of racial minorities harms the communities from which most inmates come. The subject of race would not be thoroughly addressed without discussions of immigration, gangs, and the specific sentencing policies that contribute to disparity.

Chapter 12: Women in the Corrections System. In this chapter, the reader will find a discussion of results of research on incarcerated women—the characteristics of women currently in the system, the different pathways that lead girls and women to system involvement compared to those of men, how girls and women are treated in the system, unique challenges that they face, and the prospects for more effective gender-responsive programming. It is becoming more widely understood that women have very different needs in overcoming their system involvement; for example, they are motivated far more than men are by ties to their children, their families, and other important social relationships. The move toward gender-responsive and trauma-informed practice is part of a more general progressive culture shift toward greater efficacy in what works for women.

Chapter 13: Challenging and Vulnerable Populations. This chapter is devoted to exploring the nature and extent of the issues surrounding particularly vulnerable inmates and the special approaches needed for them. The first such groups are those with severe medical or mental health problems, and those with physical and cognitive disabilities. Next is the growing number of elderly prisoners that the corrections system must safely manage and for whom it must provide more intensive levels of care to meet constitutional standards. Another important group is lesbian, gay, bisexual, transgender, and questioning (LGBTQ) inmates, who also have special vulnerabilities and needs. Because of PREA legislation, the courts will be paying increased attention to these individuals going forward. An already strained corrections system will be required to do more for special groups; however, the dominant ideology of punishment in corrections often gets in the way of providing compassionate care and treatment, even when such care is mandated by law. For example, despite strenuous advocacy efforts to ban the practice, many states continue to sentence minors to adult prisons and jails. Safely housing and managing young inmates is a significant dilemma for most adult corrections facilities.

Chapter 14: Death Row and the Death Penalty. Due to its meaning, both literally and symbolically, as society's most extreme punishment, capital punishment (the death penalty) is covered in a separate chapter. The text addresses the changing landscape of capital punishment laws, as they continue to be challenged in courts across the nation. Increasing efforts that advocate for the innocent on death row have resulted in startling revelations about how many persons have been wrongfully convicted and sentenced to die. The text covers the arguments for and against the death penalty (wrongful conviction among them), controversies about methods of execution, the question of deterrence, the costs of death row, the impact of race, the interests of victim families, and the role of the media and popular opinion in defining policy and law as regards this most final response to crime.

Part IV: The Effectiveness and Future of American Corrections

The last section of this book "zooms out" to look at broader questions. We have in this nation created a correctional behemoth with significant flaws; we are continually faced with the challenges of how to reform it. To do that well, one must look critically at what is effective and just policy. In concluding this volume, it is fitting to offer a perspective on how the nation can and should respond to the myriad crises facing the corrections system and to pose the question of how to most effectively structure political strategies to support progressive reform. The readers will examine several key emerging trends in corrections.

Chapter 15: The Growth of Privatization in Corrections. This chapter focuses on one of the most controversial of recent trends, the practice of handing over the operation of prisons and jails or prisoners themselves to private, for-profit companies. Many questions remain unanswered about the role of the private prison in the nation's criminal justice system. Do private prisons save money? Do they produce lower recidivism rates? What are the consequences for prisoners and their families as inmates are shipped out of state to be housed in private facilities? Are the legal safeguards and standards governing inmates in public facilities also applicable to private prisons, and if so, how are they enforced? Is the public interest served when societal needs are linked to common business practices, such as reducing costs through hiring less experienced correctional staff and lobbying for tougher sentencing laws that favor corporate profits? The text outlines the history of prison privatization, the major players, and the impact of privatization on public employee unions, on the quality of the services provided, and on the quality of the work environment. The move toward privatization must be examined in light of community corrections programming and other viable alternatives to incarceration.

Chapter 16: The Politics and Future of Mass Incarceration. This chapter describes the political forces that have contributed to soaring rates of incarceration, such as mandatory sentencing, three-strikes laws, and truth in sentencing. Though the reader will have already been introduced to the subject, in this section the text turns a critical eye to the argument that higher levels of incarceration have led to declines in crime rates and to the political science behind so-called "tough on crime" policies. Recent public opinion polls about punishment and corrections offer some grassroots insights into these issues. By the time the reader arrives as this point in the book, he or she should have a solid basis for thinking critically about this broad question.

Pedagogical Aids

In each of the chapters in this book, the reader will find a range of teaching and learning features that will aid in conveying the breadth and depth of each topic—Learning Objectives, Spotlights, In the Courts, Key Terms, You Decide, and Discussion Questions.

From the start, the student will find a set of **Learning Objectives** that set the stage for the chapter contents and tell the reader what knowledge to expect to gain. They are designed to orient and stimulate the critical thinking perspective that sets this book apart from others.

Included throughout are **Spotlight** features that offer a more in-depth treatment of specific subtopics. For example, a Spotlight in the history chapter delves into the convict lease system, and the sentencing chapter takes a closer look at three-strikes laws. The Spotlights suggest that students might follow their own curiosities and dig deeper into the details they find most intriguing. To do so, each chapter (beginning with Chapter 2) includes its own **Discussion Questions** and additional resources, which are meant to help the student gain a fuller, more nuanced understanding of the subject matter.

One cannot fully understand the operations of the criminal justice system without considering the role of the courts in shaping it. Litigation plays an ever-larger role in holding the corrections system accountable to constitutional principles and to important civil rights laws. Each chapter presents a pivotal legal case—**In the Courts**—that has helped to steer policy and practice in that area—an invitation to students to explore further the many challenges inside the courtroom that continue to shape the world of corrections. For example, the prison chapter presents the case of *Brown v. Plata*, which has helped to usher in one of the most important reform movements of the modern era, shifting responsibility for probation clients and reentering prisoners from the state to the local level.

Whenever a new relevant **Key Term** is introduced, it is highlighted, indicating a glossary term that the student can easily check and integrate into his or her vocabulary. The definition of terms is an important conceptual tool. Integrating vocabulary means integrating new concepts as well.

To further encourage the student to absorb new information and to form educated opinions, the **You Decide** feature offers an opportunity to wrestle with a tricky dilemma. These are real-life situations that real deciders face. Thus, there are no clear-cut answers, right or wrong, just as is often the case in the real world. For example, the jail chapter presents the dilemma that administrators face in determining whether the practice of strip-searching inmates is effective and appropriate—whether the intrusion is legitimately justifiable.

Data

The reader will find a wide variety of graphic representations of the most current data available from reliable national sources, such as the U.S. Bureau of Justice Statistics—a branch of the federal Department of Justice. Also included are results from rigorous research studies on the functioning of different elements of the correctional process. To begin with, graphics help to convey, for example, the stunning growth in the use of incarceration in the United States over the past several decades.

Ancillaries and Technology

SAGE edge offers a robust online environment featuring an impressive array of free tools and resources for review, study, and further exploration, keeping both instructors and students on the cutting edge of teaching and learning. SAGE edge content is open access and available on demand. Learning and teaching has never been easier!

edge.sagepub.com/krisberg

SAGE edge for Students provides a personalized approach to help students accomplish their coursework goals in an easy-to-use learning environment.

- Mobile-friendly **eFlashcards** strengthen understanding of key terms and concepts.
- Mobile-friendly practice **quizzes** allow for independent assessment by students of their mastery of course material.
- Carefully selected chapter-by-chapter video links and multimedia content enhance classroom-based explorations of key topics.
- A customized online **action plan** includes tips and feedback on progress through the course and materials, which allows students to individualize their learning experience.
- **Chapter summaries** with **learning objectives** reinforce the most important material.
- **Interactive exercises** and meaningful web links facilitate student use of internet resources, further exploration of topics, and responses to critical thinking questions.
- EXCLUSIVE! Access is provided to full-text **SAGE journal articles** that have been carefully selected to support and expand on the concepts presented in each chapter.

SAGE edge for Instructors, supports teaching by making it easy to integrate quality content and create a rich learning environment for students.

- **Test banks** provide a diverse range of pre-written options as well as the opportunity to edit any question and/or insert personalized questions to effectively assess students' progress and understanding.
- **Sample course syllabi** for semester and quarter courses provide suggested models for structuring one's course.
- Editable, chapter-specific **PowerPoint® slides** offer complete flexibility for creating a multimedia presentation for the course.
- EXCLUSIVE! Access to full-text **SAGE journal articles** that have been carefully selected to support and expand on the concepts presented in each chapter to encourage students to think critically.
- **Multimedia content** includes original SAGE videos that appeal to students with different learning styles.
- **Lecture notes** summarize key concepts by chapter to ease preparation for lectures and class discussions.
- A **Course cartridge** provides easy LMS integration.

A Word About Language

Throughout this text, authors use a number of terms to refer to individuals under the supervision of correctional authorities. The reader will find such terms as *prisoners, residents, inmates,* and *offenders* used more or less interchangeably to refer to individuals imprisoned in jails or prisons. People who have not yet been sentenced are usually referred to as *defendants*. Frontline jail and prison staff are usually referred to as *correctional officers* but also may be termed the more colloquial *guards*. Those under supervision in the community might be referred to as *clients, probationers,* or *parolees*. The definition of the term *parole* itself is not nearly as clear as it was just a few decades ago. It is used here generally to refer to a variety of approaches to supervision following release from prison, including traditional discretionary parole, mandatory parole, and terms of supervised release. In any case, the word choices are meant to effectively express the range of terminology typically used in the corrections field. They are not intended to communicate a specific value judgment or point of view. However, the authors recognize the importance of these terms and that they often do impart a value judgment, whether intentional or unintentional.

A Note About Race and Ethnicity

There is a great deal of confusion about race and ethnicity, even in the terms we use. In large part, both are referred to as "social constructs," meaning that they are essentially human inventions that we use to denote different groups of people. And both race and ethnicity have been used to justify discriminatory policies and practices. We see slow evolution over time toward a more enlightened view of human variation. For example, during the prelude to World War II, European Jews were labeled as non-White to justify their destruction. Jews are no longer referred to in this way. Needless to say, we have a long way to go to true social justice.

In the most general terms, *race* refers to natural physical characteristics that one is born with, and *ethnicity* refers to cultural attributes that one may adopt, regardless of physical characteristics or origin. A person of Korean descent raised in Italy might speak Italian, eat Italian food, understand Italian history and art, and know nothing about Korean culture.

The terms *Hispanic* and *Latino* are often used interchangeably. *Hispanic* usually refers to descendants of the Iberian Peninsula, contemporary Spain, or nations that speak Spanish. It is the official term of the U.S. Census. *Latino* refers more often to the geographic regions considered Latin America (including Central and South America and the Caribbean) and is more commonly used west of the Mississippi. However, as we tend to see on documentation of various types, *Hispanic* is a term that refers to ethnicity but is often listed as a racial category next to *White, African American,* or *Asian*.

In the corrections field, there are wide discrepancies in the way race and ethnicity are documented. For example, some agencies rely on how defendants identify themselves. Others rely on the observations and subjectivity of the staff person recording the information.

The careful student should realize that terms that relate to race and ethnicity (indeed, the terms themselves) are often imprecisely used and inconsistently defined. In either case, the extent to which these categories are used to apply a different standard of legal protection and result in unjust disadvantages is what concerns us in this text.

Acknowledgments

Barry Krisberg: I would like to thank my life partner, Karen McKie, our children, Moshe, Zaid, and Jessica, for their constant support, their patience for hearing my emerging ideas, and their unconditional love. I also want to acknowledge the Edith Street Irregulars—a collection of children, dogs, cats, and birds that kept my spirits high. Special thanks go to dear friends and colleagues Fred Mills, Richard Tillson, Jeanne Woodford, Frank Zimring, and Yitzhak Bakal, who have taught me so much. A special debt of gratitude goes to Christopher Edley Jr., who made a place for me at the Warren Institute at Berkeley Law.

Susan Marchionna: I would like to thank my friends and family who have supported me throughout this project. My mother, Sara, gave me a quiet place to work and a home-cooked dinner on many, many occasions. My children, Whitney, Aron, and Sara, were always a source of support and encouragement. Barry Krisberg and Jeanne Woodford have been unfailing mentors to me, and their help has been invaluable. Thank you to my co-author, Chris for his careful attention to the data and for locking arms with me during the home stretch. Thanks also to Kate and Charlie for offering me a much-needed haven.

Christopher Hartney: Thank you to all who supported me in this work. Thanks to my co-authors, Barry and Susan, for their wisdom and patience, and for sharing with me the joys of hummingbirds and the A's. To my dear Molly, who continues to help me and plenty of others believe we can do important things. To my incredible sons, Riley, for back rubs and soccer breaks, and Finn, for cappuccinos and snuggles. To my mom, Patricia, and dad, Robert, for, along with so much else, showing me how to both care and write with purpose. To my siblings, Meg—who watches over me today just as she did when I was very young—Tiger, Marko, and Big D, and the extended families we are lucky enough to call our own—how easy to give to others from a position of such love and strength! To the whole NCCD family, current and past, who never fail both to inspire me professionally and to generously support my life away from work. Finally, to a group of friends who may not know how deeply they inspire me, the JoyBoys, of yesteryear and today, thank you, and see you at the start of summer.

ALL OF US:

We would all like to thank all the people at SAGE, for their help. To begin with, we thank Jerry Westby, who has had unflagging vision, enthusiasm, and support for this project, and has been with us for the long haul. The trajectory of this undertaking proved to be longer and more complex than we expected, but Jerry's confidence repeatedly filled our sails when our energies were waning. We want to thank and acknowledge everyone at Sage who participated in formulating this book and in making it become a reality. This includes: Jerry Westby, Libby Larson, Jessica Miller, Rachael Leblond, MaryAnn Vail, and Scott Van Atta. We owe a large debt to the many reviewers who took time to comment thoughtfully about our draft chapters. Their input helped hold us to a high standard and gave us insight into the instructor's mind.

Jack Atherton, Northwestern State University

Kevin M. Beaver, Florida State University

Fran Bernat, Texas A & M International University

Bruce L Bikle, California State University Sacramento

Ashley G. Blackburn, University of Houston - Downtown

Kristie R. Blevins, Eastern Kentucky University

John M. Boal, University of Akron

Michael Botts, Arkansas State University

Michael Braun, Southern Oregon University

Dennis Brewster, Southeastern Oklahoma State University

Jennifer E. Cobbina, Michigan State University

Tom Dempsey, Southern Utah University

Elizabeth Corzine Dretsch, Troy University

Ida Dupont, Pace University

Martha Earwood, University of Alabama at Birmingham

Mary Beth Finn, Herzing University

Michael Fischer, Norfolk State University

Natasha A. Frost, Northeastern University

Jane Garvey, University of Connecticut

Krista S. Gehring, University of Houston-Downtown

Dana Greene, New Mexico State University

Marie L. Griffin, Arizona State University

Michael Hallett, University of North Florida

Mario Hesse, St. Cloud State University

Verna Jones, Jackson State University

S. Kris Kawucha, University of North Texas

John Kramer, Penn State University

Todd M. Krohn, The University of Georgia

Cathryn F. Lavery, Iona College

Dennis W. McLean, Keiser University

Pamela Mertens, Northeastern State University

Kurt Robak, RidgeWater College

James Record, California University of Pennsylvania

Jennie K. Singer, California State University, Sacramento

Hayden P. Smith, University of South Carolina

Larry Spencer, Alabama State University

Jennifer Sumner, Seattle University

Lynn Tankersley, Mercer University

Sheryl L. Van Horne, Arcadia University

Lindsey Vigesaa, Nova Southeastern University

Vanessa Woodward, University of Southern Mississippi

We would also like to thank Morgan Lewis, whose help at a crucial juncture got us through. Thank you to Caroline Glesmann, who coauthored the report that was the basis for the privatization chapter.

Finally, we would like to acknowledge the millions involved in the corrections system—the keepers and the kept—who strive daily and in every corner in search of true justice.

I

History and Sentencing

1 The Corrections System

LEARNING OBJECTIVES

1 To understand the basic purpose and structure of the corrections system and how it relates to the justice system as a whole.

2 To identify some of the societal factors that influence the corrections system and some of the ways that corrections impacts society.

3 To gain a critical perspective and an insight into our complex corrections system and some of the serious issues it faces, with an eye toward what works.

4 To be introduced to the enormous changes in corrections in the past 30 years, including "mass

A Legacy of Crisis and Turmoil

Tom Clements was the director of corrections in Colorado. He was gunned down at his own home in March 2013. The murder of a high-level corrections leader is very rare, but this tragic event points to many all-too-common aspects of the ongoing crisis of American corrections. The assassin was Evan Spencer Ebel, who was 28 years old and had just spent eight years in Colorado prisons, most of that time in solitary confinement. Ebel was a member of a White supremacist prison gang—the 211 Crew. He was nicknamed "Evil Ebel" by fellow inmates and had "HATE" tattooed on his hand. He committed over 28 serious disciplinary infractions while imprisoned, including threats to prison staff and assaults on both staff and other inmates. While in custody, he pled guilty to assaulting a corrections officer in 2008, for which he was to serve an additional four years beyond his original sentence. On the day he shot Director Clements, Ebel first killed a pizza delivery person, whose truck he then used to gain access to Clements's home. In Ebel's car, the police found bomb supplies, surveillance equipment, an assortment of guns, and handwritten directions to Clements's address.[1] Letters of grievance Ebel had written while in custody expressed his growing anger over his long-term solitary confinement. They also showed his frustration that authorities did nothing to prepare him for life in the community after years of imprisonment.[2]

To make matters worse, Ebel was not supposed to be released from the Colorado prison system for another four years. Mistakes on the part of the judge and the court reporter led Colorado prison officials to release him before serving the extra time for assaulting the prison guard.

Director Clements was a well-respected corrections leader who championed the cause of penal reform. During his many years as a high-level correctional administrator in Missouri, he used his position to introduce more humane prison conditions, find additional funding for literacy and rehabilitation programs, and expand efforts to assist prisoners to successfully return home. He also advocated for curtailing solitary confinement in prisons, reducing its use in Colorado by half before his death. Clements was a devoutly religious person who believed that many prisoners could be rehabilitated.[3]

▲ While on parole after years in solitary confinement, convicted murderer Evan Spencer "Evil" Ebel murdered a pizza delivery man and used his truck to gain access to and murder chief of Colorado Department of Corrections Tom Clements.

© Colorado Department of Corrections / Associated Press

Solitary confinement: Special imprisonment where the inmate is isolated from human contact. Solitary is intended as an additional punishment, but is sometimes used for protective custody or suicide watch. Solitary confinement tends to create or exacerbate mental illness.

incarceration" and its associated monetary and societal costs.

 To begin to grasp the ebb and flow of correctional philosophy in the United States, and the balance point between punishment and rehabilitation.

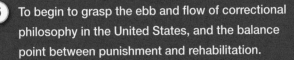 To be introduced to the authors' approach in this book, which encourages readers to ask why the system is the way it is, what works and what does not work to fulfill the system's purposes, and what can be done to improve the system.

▲ Social tensions are present inside prisons just as they are on the outside. Inside, they are often magnified, as they become a stronger part of the inmate's personal and group identity.

© iStockphoto.com / duncan 1890

Grievance: An official statement of complaint about wrong done to a person. Prisoners may file a grievance with officials about infringements on their rights or unfair or inhumane treatment. Facilities must have a policy and procedure in place for processing and responding to inmate grievances.

Prison: Detention facilities operated either by state governments or by the Federal Bureau of Prisons (BOP) that are designed to hold individuals who have been convicted of crimes and who are serving sentences of a year or more.

This tragic series of events illustrates many of the themes that come to light in this book. Social dynamics inside facilities contribute to very dangerous situations for staff and other inmates. **Prisons** continue to be plagued with racial tensions and inequities. The American prison and sentencing system is so overtaxed that errors occur: People are released who should be incarcerated, and other inmates are held illegally past their release dates. Severe mental health issues among inmates compound these challenges, and effective treatment services are all too inadequate to meet the needs of the imprisoned population. Overwhelmed and underfunded corrections officials have come to depend on the extensive use of solitary confinement and other harsh methods to manage these explosively dangerous circumstances. Although popular opinion seems to have shifted since the 2000s, generally the public either has supported this overuse of solitary and other harsh practices as fitting with a tough-on-crime approach to corrections or was simply unaware of it.

Corrections as a System

Criminal Justice and Corrections

The criminal justice system includes law enforcement (police), the criminal courts, and **corrections**. These three systems work in many complementary ways. Each branch of American government is involved. The executive branch runs the agencies, the legislative branch makes laws and allocates funding, and the courts review claims of law violations and sentence those convicted of crimes. Each branch plays a different role, with some overlap. Each influences the system as a whole by interpreting, shaping, and applying laws, regulations, and policies, and by making decisions that ultimately determine who is involved in the system, for how long, and in what setting.

A defendant's case progresses through the bureaucratic steps leading to a "day in court." After being charged with a crime, a defendant may be held in **custody** or sent home. In either case, correctional officers are responsible for ensuring that defendants appear in court for their hearings and avoid further criminal behavior. The police assist with **community supervision**, and the courts make the key decisions about pretrial custody, guilt or innocence, and, if applicable, sentencing. But, the day-to-day responsibility for the defendant falls to corrections. For those convicted of a crime, this responsibility continues as the convicted individual serves his or her sentence—in the community, in jail, or in prison.

Elements of the Corrections System

The American corrections system is not really a single system, but a collection of systems and agencies, governed by laws, administrative policies, and broad constitutional provisions. We commonly use the singular *system* to refer to the whole. But there are actually 50 separate and distinct state systems, a federal system, and hundreds of local county or municipal corrections agencies. Each of these levels of corrections has its own function within the whole.

The U.S. Constitution and U.S. Supreme Court rulings give defendants certain rights—such as the right to legal counsel—as they are processed through each level of the system.

However, federal sentencing guidelines have no bearing in the state systems, except perhaps to set an example that states may adopt on their own. Each state controls its own sentencing laws and practices. The Supreme Court has also ruled that a death sentence for youth under age 18 is unconstitutional, yet capital punishment for adults remains a state decision. To encourage state compliance with laws established by Congress, the government leverages federal funding for state corrections. On a more practical level, individuals under the authority of the federal system may actually be held in a state facility, or vice versa, for reasons such as moving the inmate from one geographical region to another, allowing access to the courts, or providing otherwise unavailable medical care. Corrections also involves often complex relationships between state and local agencies. State laws and practices typically hold sway over those of local jurisdictions.

▲ Corrections officers require adequate training and support to respond to conflicts with an appropriate balance of restraint and force.

© iStockphoto.com / HakuNellies

In addition to law enforcement, the courts, and elected officials, there is a wide range of important corrections system stakeholders. A variety of public and private agencies, both nonprofit and for profit, provide programming and treatment services as well as support services such as laundry, food, and maintenance. Other public agencies for health and human services are important players in corrections. Inmates often receive their medical care in the local community, such as at county hospitals or private clinics. Community groups not only provide services, especially for probationers and parolees and those in alternatives to incarceration, but also do so within facilities. Professional associations establish and promulgate standards for different aspects of the corrections system. Advocacy groups push for reforms from both the political left and right. Private philanthropy funds innovative corrections programs and research to identify and promote promising approaches. Academics and independent researchers write about corrections theory and practice, help train the next generation of correctional workers, and evaluate policy and programs. Volunteers from local communities often serve in various roles, both in community-based corrections and in facilities.

Of course, a crucial group within the corrections system is made up of corrections officers, including facility staff and probation or parole officers in the community. These are the men and women who, on a daily basis, negotiate the myriad laws, policies, and practices of a complicated and imperfect system. In many states, correctional officers have developed powerful unions and strong political lobbies to protect their interests—pay and benefits, training and education, work conditions, and other issues. The corrections workforce is changing and will continue to change into the future, with more women and people of color joining the ranks.

Corrections and Society

The Purpose of Corrections: Society's Response to Crime

Corrections is a tough business. It is not a "feel-good" proposition; on the contrary, it is rooted in basic human conflict. It exists to help society deal with some of its most difficult problems, such as violence. The purpose of corrections is to fulfill society's need to respond to criminal behavior. The goals of the response are to stop the offensive behavior, reduce the likelihood it will happen again, and make the offender pay some price.

Corrections: The punishment, supervision, and treatment of individuals suspected or convicted of criminal or delinquent offenses and the various legal and extralegal entities involved in carrying out that function.

Custody: Detention in a prison or jail or being held under guard of law enforcement.

Community supervision: Various forms of noncustodial supervision where offenders are allowed to live in the community while remaining under the jurisdiction of the court or corrections agency, similar to and including probation and parole, and usually with the condition that failure will entail time behind bars.

Jurisdiction: (1) The authority to make pronouncements on legal matters and administer justice within a defined area of responsibility. (2) The political-geographical region with decision-making authority.

Incapacitation: A method of preventing crime by removing the offender from the community.

Deterrence: The use of punishment, or the threat of punishment, to discourage individuals from committing crime.

Put in more academic terms, the purposes of corrections are incapacitation, deterrence, and retribution.

Incapacitation means removing a person from society and limiting his or her opportunities to commit more crime. The individual is incapacitated through restricted freedoms—usually involving imprisonment in prison or jail, supervision in the community, or both. Fines, community service, and other elements of sentencing are also considered incapacitation, because they limit the ability of the individual to engage as freely in other endeavors.

Deterrence means steering a person away from lawbreaking behavior with the threat of punishment—implicitly or explicitly. The possibilities or the reality of punishment and the denial of freedom are meant to make the criminal or potential criminal avoid future crime.

Retribution, or punishment, means exacting a sacrifice on the part of the offender in payment for the wrong done to victims and to society. Society achieves retribution by demanding that the convicted person give back, in the form of jail or prison time, fines, community service, or compensation to those harmed by the criminal behavior. Practically speaking, when people speak of accountability, they most often mean retribution.

Figure 1.1 Incarceration Rates of World Nations

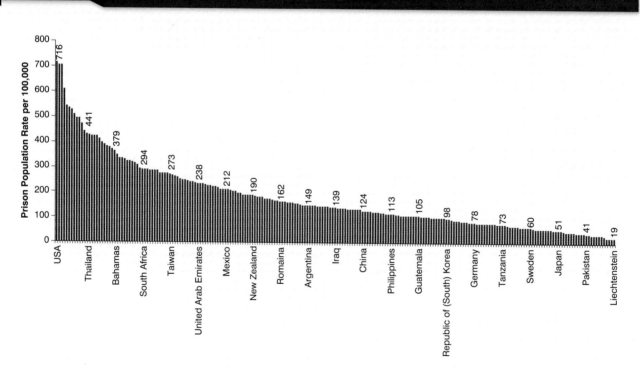

International Perspective. The developments in U.S. corrections fits within a global framework, which lends itself to aid us in comparing and contrasting corrections issues in the United States to those of other nations. Other countries, even those we consider to be less "developed," rely far less on incarceration than our country does to respond to nonviolent crimes. Looking at international statistics, the United States tops both lists—the largest number of incarcerated persons and the highest incarceration rate (716 per 100,000 in the U.S. general population) of all nations on earth. Of the 223 listed nations, all but 34 have incarceration rates below 300. In 2011, nearly 24% of all of the world's prison and jail inmates were locked up in the United States,[4] which had less than 5% of the world's population.[5]

Source: International Centre for Prison Studies, World Prison Brief, 2013.

Rehabilitation, or returning a person to a state of readiness to rejoin and contribute to society, is arguably a fourth purpose of corrections. Some believe that facilitating rehabilitation is a responsibility of the government and of society. Others might not call it a "purpose" but admit that time spent under correctional control provides an opportunity for rehabilitation that should not be wasted. Finally, many believe rehabilitation really has no place in corrections and that it amounts to pampering or special help to unworthy individuals.

The Fiscal Impact of Corrections

After decades of stability, the American corrections system grew at a dizzying rate between 1980 and 2011. As the U.S. general population grew by 37% in that period, the prison population grew by 371%—10 times as much. The number of jail inmates tripled (up 304%), and the number of persons on probation and parole rose by 225% and 287%, respectively. By 2011, there were almost 2.4 million Americans incarcerated in prisons and jails and almost 7 million under all forms of correctional supervision. This equates to 1 in every 34 adult residents of the nation being under some form of correctional supervision.[6] Meanwhile, rates of serious and violent crime have fluctuated somewhat but have generally declined since 1995.

Table 1.1 — Federal, State, and Local Justice System Expenditures, 2010

Activity	Federal ($ in billions)	State ($ in billions)	Local ($ in billions)	Total ($ in billions)
Police Protection	32	14	83	**124**
Judicial and Legal*	14	22	22	**56**
Corrections	9	49	27	80
Total Justice System	54	85	132	**261**

The corrections system costs a lot of money. In 2010, the United States spent $80 billion on corrections—$9 billion in the federal system, $49 billion in the states, and $27 billion locally.[7] These costs have been rising due to growing client populations and increasing legal requirements to meet basic standards of humane treatment and constitutional rights. *Source: Kyckelhahn and Martin, Justice Expenditure and Employment Extracts 2010—Preliminary, 2013. Note: Dollar amounts may not add to totals due to BJS calculations that exclude duplicative costs. *Includes civil and criminal law.*

The movement toward mass incarceration has come with equally massive costs. The fiscal costs just mentioned are but one side of the story. Society as a whole pays the social price of mass incarceration. No citizen is immune from the threat of crime. Society's successes or failures in stopping criminal behavior ultimately dictate the state of health of the social environment and the economy. What goes on in prisons and jails spills out into community life. That said, some sectors of society are more directly affected than others.

Influencing Social and Political Factors

Although today's high rates of incarceration suggest that imprisonment is an essential part of corrections, there have been times in U.S. history when it was the exception rather than the norm. Labor was in such short supply in the colonies and young states of the 18th century that lawbreakers were rarely imprisoned—their work was too important to the

Rehabilitation: Restoring or establishing an offender's ability to contribute constructively to his or her individual and community well-being, usually through correctional programming and treatment services targeting the issues that led to his or her criminal behavior

▲ Public spending on mass incarceration has left fewer resources to address other social needs, such as education, healthcare, and jobs.

© Jim West / Alamy

economy. Jail and prison populations typically come from impoverished, (usually) inner-city communities with high unemployment. These communities are further weakened and marginalized by the incarceration of large portions of their residents. This concentrated impact of incarceration is not widely associated with a weakened economy by policymakers and state voters. So the cycles of intergenerational crime and system involvement continue, with only some communities bearing the brunt of the larger society's decisions. Taxpayers all support this expensive system. But marginalized communities suffer the most, with perennial unemployment, low educational achievement, communicable disease, and tense relationships with public service agencies, among other ills.

Many factors influence which individuals are incarcerated, for what crimes, and for how long. Lawmakers, judges, and the voters determine which behaviors constitute a crime and what sentence is appropriate for those crimes. Police strategies and tactics come into play, for instance, on how police focus their resources, on what types of crime, and in what neighborhoods. The police often choose their tactics as a response to public concern—whether or not that concern is based in fact—or to the political crusades that follow in the aftermath of horrendous crimes.

District attorneys (prosecutors) typically have a significant amount of discretion about which cases to pursue and what specific charges to file with the court. These are decisions that have a huge impact on the eventual sentence, especially in this age of determinate sentencing, where the court's discretion is limited and where charging youth in adult court has become commonplace.

Corrections departments play a role in how much of the sentence is served and who returns to custody after release. They influence how probation and parole departments and the courts respond to probation and parole violations—whether to incarcerate or use alternative sanctions—and what services and supports are in place to help system-involved men and women avoid violations in the first place.

Prison administrators influence the incarcerated population, as they decide how to respond to inmate misbehavior. Infractions on an inmate's record can extend his or her time behind bars. Furthermore, inmate behavior is to some extent a function of conditions of confinement, facility services and programming, and the training and expertise of corrections officers. Overcrowded inmate populations become harder to control, leading to more behavior problems and a greater likelihood that inmates will be unprepared for successful reentry. Prison officials also serve on parole boards in many states, and thus make decisions about who is granted parole and who is returned to prison after parole violations.

Violation: An act that violates or breaks the law.

Public health agencies, which are often responsible for correctional health care services, also play a role in this system. Community residents with mental health issues who fall through the cracks of the public health system often end up in corrections. Inmates who receive inadequate treatment are more likely to have longer stays in the system and a harder time reentering.

IN THE COURTS

Introduction to the Courts

This feature—In the Courts—explores a pivotal case that relates to the chapter subject. (The exceptions are Chapter 10, "Law and Corrections," which itself is a survey of many legal cases that have challenged the criminal justice system, and Chapter 14, "Death Row and the Death Penalty," which presents capital punishment through the lens of related legal challenges.) The selected case highlights one aspect of the larger topic; the cases are selected from any number of possibilities, as each chapter subject is a vast territory. Students may find their curiosity sparked and follow up on their own with other relevant cases. In so doing, a student is likely to find that the courts provide a rich venue for exploring the complexities of legal challenges to policies and practice.

In the United States, there are two main adult court systems—federal and state. These are not entirely independent; they interact in some situations. Each state has its own constitution and body of laws that fall under the jurisdiction of the courts of that state. There are also local courts at the municipal or county level. The federal system and each state system are structured as a hierarchy of courts, including the lower trials courts, the courts of appeals, and the Supreme Court. A party dissatisfied with the outcome of one court may appeal to a higher court for judgment. A case that originates in a state trial court may be tested and appealed in higher courts. A few cases go all the way to the U.S. Supreme Court for a final ruling.

The U.S. Supreme Court is the highest federal court, the ultimate word on the cases it hears. Parties from the appellate courts may request that the Supreme Court hear and judge the matter in the case. This is also true with state supreme courts. The Supreme Court is not obligated to hear cases and selects those that affect constitutional rights and those that the justices feel merit the Court's attention.

The federal courts are organized in 12 regional circuits. They handle such issues as U.S. constitutional law, U.S. treaties, disputes between states, military matters, bankruptcy, and other matters governed by federal law. State courts hear most cases having to do with criminal matters, estates, contracts, and family matters. Some cases may be heard in either system, for example, class-action cases or some civil cases that are brought against an individual or organization (defendant) by the government on behalf of society (prosecution). The crime may or may not involve one or more victims. Civil cases involve one party, called the plaintiff, claiming against another, called the defendant, that there was a breach of legal duty that caused personal or financial injury. A guilty verdict in criminal cases results in a sentence, which may involve a penal sanction such as prison or probation, whereas a judgment against the defendant in civil court usually results in a financial penalty, referred to as "damages."

Federal judges are appointed by the president and confirmed by the Senate. State judges may be elected or appointed. Some trials are decided by juries; some are decided by judges (bench trials). Each side in the dispute usually has an attorney or a team of attorneys that represents the defendant or plaintiff. The district attorney is the prosecutor on behalf of the government. The public defender is the government-appointed attorney for defendants who cannot afford private counsel. The courts are staffed with many other personnel including bailiffs, court reporters, and clerks.

Court procedures are governed by complex sets of rules to which all parties, including the judge, must adhere. The civil court process has various stages—pleading (or indictment in criminal court), pretrial, trial, and posttrial. Pretrial activity in civil cases is intended to streamline the court process and increase court efficiency. It includes depositions, sharing of evidence and witness lists, and motions (requests for action) to the courts. In serious criminal cases, a grand jury (up to 23 jurors) may convene to determine whether there is enough evidence to issue an indictment against the defendant and to go to trial. Criminal cases include an arraignment in court, where the defendant hears the charges and submits a plea of guilty or not guilty to the court.

The in-court trial process involves jury selection, opening statements, presentation of evidence, and closing arguments. When the trial is complete, it is followed by the judgment, from either the jury or the judge, and the pronouncement of the sentence or damages. The losing party may decide to file an appeal with a higher court to review the case and determine whether the law was followed properly in the first trial.

And, finally, funding affects everything else. Insufficient funding reduces the number of cases courts can effectively process, reduces the likelihood that services will be in place to help defendants avoid pretrial detention, reduces the identification and treatment of health and mental health issues, reduces the availability and quality of both facility- and community-based programming and services, and generally reduces the ability of correctional agencies to maximize the chances of inmates completing their sentences without incident and successfully reintegrating into their communities.

A Critical View of the System

The nation's corrections systems have always been underresourced and challenged with violence, abusive practices, scandals, and other severe problems, but the sudden and unprecedented growth in incarceration at the end of the last century helped fuel an explosive crisis reflected in prison violence, riots, increasing civil rights violations, and a lack of public confidence. In the early 21st century, more and more commentators began referring to the "rise of mass incarceration" to describe the scale of the national correctional landscape. The obscenely high rates of people of color compared to Whites in the corrections system have resulted in this mass incarceration being dubbed the "New Jim Crow."[8] Dramatic stories of the breakdown in corrections come from all corners, from coast to coast.

In July 2012, the Federal Bureau of Investigation (FBI) was brought into the Los Angeles (LA) jails to investigate the excessive use of force against jail inmates by the county's deputy sheriffs. There had been no internal investigations, despite a score of complaints. Some of these deputies formed a clique, wearing skeleton tattoos and operating as if they were a street gang. Other deputies were accused of having sex with female inmates and participating in drug trafficking inside the jail and in the surrounding community. Although some top managers at the LA County jail have been terminated, there are all too few signs of fundamental reform.[9]

About a year later, in the Baltimore City Detention Center, federal prosecutors handed down criminal indictments of 13 female corrections officers who permitted members of a prison gang, the Black Guerrilla Family, to operate criminal enterprises from the jail, including gun and drug smuggling and prostitution. Several of the indicted officers were having sex with inmates, and four of them became pregnant from these jailhouse liaisons. Some of the corrections officers were taking in more than $15,000 a month selling contraband in the jail. The indicted officers were allegedly retaliating against inmates who refused to participate in these criminal acts.[10] In November, 2013, 14 additional correctional officers were arrested for their participation in the conspiracy, revealing that the scandal was more widespread than the original reports indicated. At that point, nine of the charged officers had pleaded guilty, six current employees were placed on leave without pay, and the rest were charged but had not entered a plea.[11] In both Los Angeles and Baltimore, jail administrators did not dispute the findings of the FBI investigations but claimed that they had been unaware of the gravity and extent of the lawbreaking by jail employees.

Without a doubt, the imprisonment and control of other human beings, especially on this scale, is extremely complicated and fraught with risk; without a doubt, corrections officers and administrators have high-pressure and difficult jobs. Further, for decades the public has been willing to send thousands of people to prison while voting for reduced funding. They have also been willing to cry foul and blame corrections staff when horror stories arise, as they inevitably do. This book takes a hard look at all aspects of the system, with an eye toward areas that can be improved for the good of all—prisoners, probationers, parolees, correctional staff, and the public.

Conditions of confinement: The physical and social environment inside of correctional facilities. Conditions include the overall environment and all of its elements, such as health and safety, food quality, sleeping quarters, rehabilitative services, inmate-to-inmate and inmate-to-guard relations, crowding (as a function of facility design), and the nature of supervision, including use of force and isolation, that impact the safety, health, comfort, and stress level of inmates.

Detention: Holding suspects or defendants as they await court processing prior to trial and a determination of guilt or innocence. More generally, any form of custody or physical control by authorities. In the field of corrections, the term usually refers to pretrial custody, the purpose of which is to ensure the defendant appears in court and does not commit additional offenses.

Civil rights: Personal liberties granted by virtue of an individual's status as a citizen or resident of a country or community. Most commonly, civil rights refers to those guaranteed by the Constitution, such as freedom of speech and freedom from discrimination.

A Keen Eye Toward the Future

There are signs that suggest that the current era of mass incarceration may be abating. The global fiscal crisis that began in 2007 has expanded the national awareness of wasteful spending in all public sectors. Suddenly, we began to see a more pointed scrutiny of public expenditures. In state and federal corrections budgets alike, this scrutiny has resulted in pressure to reduce prison and jail populations. People have begun to recognize that budgets are finite and that incarceration is simply too expensive to use so liberally. The notion is slowly taking hold that incarceration should be reserved for the most serious crimes and the most dangerous individuals. Although driven by economic issues, this change is also supported by research, which shows that the most effective way to reduce recidivism is to concentrate resources on the highest-risk individuals and to address lesser offenders accordingly.[12] This is a refrain that criminologists have been singing for many years. To date, real movement in this area has been limited to a few states. However, after decades of constant growth, the total U.S. correctional population declined in three consecutive years beginning in 2008.[13]

Some states are letting local corrections (versus state systems) manage a larger share of offenders—a strategy referred to as "realignment." Some are modifying their mandatory minimum sentencing schemes and allowing judges far more discretion to reduce sentences to more appropriately fit the crimes. Efforts are also being made to change sentencing practices that have produced stark inequities in sentence lengths for Whites versus people of color who committed similar offenses. These efforts should have the effect of both reducing disparities in the rates of incarceration for people of color and reducing the overall incarcerated population. Many jurisdictions are increasing their use of alternatives to detention, which in turn reduce the number of inmates in jail awaiting trial, and alternatives to incarceration, which allow convicted persons to serve a sort of enhanced probation in the community instead of serving time in jail or prison. Reduced crowding in custody helps allow effective programming to take place. Rehabilitation cannot be accomplished in overcrowded facilities. Agencies are changing their response to probation and parole violators; those who, in the past, would have found themselves behind bars after a violation instead receive increased scrutiny and programming in the community. More broadly, attitudes have been changing about how to respond to those who have committed nonviolent, nonsexual, and nonserious crimes, with the new assumption being that these individuals can be supervised in the community without unduly increasing the risk to public safety.

What is making all of these ventures possible is an underlying sea change that is gathering strength and viability. For the first time since the early 1980s, the posture of tough-on-crime thinking is giving way to smart-on-crime approaches. The political litmus test for candidates running for office has been an adherence to harsh punishment, such as longer sentences for more crimes or maintaining the death penalty. Punishment alone is finally losing its credibility as the most effective penal strategy. Gradually, the simplistic notion that we just need to lock up the troublemakers has been eroded. In its place is a more complex and realistic view that we must have a variety of solutions to deal with a hugely varied set of problems.

Only recently have legislators reached across the aisle to develop bipartisan proposals for reducing incarceration and the related costs. We are now seeing new partnerships between Republican and Democratic leaders; both concede the occurrence of devastating collateral damage—the unintended consequences—of throwing the book at everyone. A growing chorus of elected officials, professionals, and reformers is demanding smarter and more creative correctional practices. Even far-right conservatives, such as members of the think tank Right on Crime, see the fiscal sense in reforming sentencing policy and relying on more targeted correctional approaches such as diversion and treatment.

Dick Durbin (D) of Illinois and Mike Lee (R) of Utah joined forces to create the Smarter Sentencing Act of 2013. This legislation was meant to give judges more discretion to sentence nonviolent criminals below restrictive mandatory minimums. The idea was to reduce mandatory minimums for several drug crimes, thereby lowering costs and cutting down on crowding in a prison system that is estimated to be operating at a national average of 40% more than its capacity.

Attorney General Eric Holder, the nation's highest law enforcement officer, in 2013 revealed his position on corrections issues to be solidly rooted in principles of reform and a more rational, multifaceted strategy for controlling crime and criminals.

Public opinion seems to be broadly shifting to a less punitive direction for drug users and other minor property crimes. Taxpayers have rebelled against an ever-larger share of public funds being consumed by the criminal justice system, especially for things that do not improve behavior or conditions. It makes more and more sense to more and more people to use methods that are based on solid data and research. Many are calling for a renewed national commitment to what works.

On the other hand, in some locations, legislators and the citizenry have called for increasingly harsh penalties for sex offenders. And some commentators maintain that reduced crime rates are a direct consequence of longer prison terms for more crimes. This text explores the political dynamics of correctional practices and whether and where there may be prospects for new alliances on behalf of more rational and effective policy.

There is renewed impetus, and thus a momentous opportunity, to rediscover the potential of rehabilitation and treatment in corrections after several decades in which the conventional

Smart on crime: A buzzword in recent years representing a response to crime that considers such factors as punishments appropriate to offense severity, recidivism reduction, cost-effectiveness, public safety, and equity

Litmus test: A pivotal political issue that demonstrates whether a candidate for office or appointment leans far enough conservative or liberal to please his or her target constituency. It is a metaphor taken from a scientific measure of the relative acidity or alkalinity of a given substance

wisdom said that "nothing works" to reclaim the lives of offenders. Even sociologist Robert Martinson, who famously made such claims, later recanted them.

Although Martinson (1974) is routinely cited as finding rehabilitation ineffective, few policymakers paid attention to other publications in which he suggested that the problem with correctional programs, regardless of their design, is the "life-cycle damage" they cause. The problem with rehabilitative programs is not the construction of any particular program or service offered. Rather, ineffectiveness was a result of disrupting people's lives—usually young people most in need of educational and job skills training—by placing them in prisons for long periods of time. Incarceration, then, potentially creates the very condition it seeks to eliminate—reoffending—by removing people from society and weakening employment and educational opportunities, fostering criminal associations, stifling the growth of social bonds and ties to conventional society, and dehumanizing and stigmatizing offenders. The community corrections field, ironically, is founded on the realization of the potential for life-cycle damage due to institutionalization, as officers individualize supervision and treatment components to most effectively address offender risks and needs. This is a quest to find what, if anything, works, and if something works, whom do such programs work best with?[14]

Of course, much will depend on whether evidence-based reform efforts are implemented with fidelity to their designs and without compromising the original intent and integrity. This book takes a careful look at what is wrong with the corrections system and poses questions about promising reform strategies and directions that can help. Is there a science to reducing recidivism, and what will it take to fully implement best practices?

Dehumanization: Intentional or unintentional treatment of offenders as less than human by ignoring or depriving of them normal human qualities such as respect, compassion, and individuality.

. . . .

SUMMARY

Ultimately, the goal of this text is to instill a sense of critical thinking in its readers. Corrections is not a steadily progressing series of developments marching toward fairer and more humane treatment of offenders, nor is it the case that all corrections workers are heartless individuals who want to exact revenge on the people they control and supervise. A realistic picture of the correctional system—one that allows for a necessary and critical review—must present its particularities and complexities. Only in so doing can there be an effective and thoughtful discussion of what it will take to transform the system to meet the needs of a new age.

DISCUSSION QUESTIONS

1. How does the case of Ebel and Clements point to serious issues facing today's corrections system?

2. What is the public's responsibility to be aware of correctional practice? What is the state's responsibility to maintain transparency?

3. Discuss ways that the law enforcement and corrections systems interact.

4. What are some ways that states have correctional autonomy apart from federal policy?

5. What is the purpose of the corrections system?

6. What are four aspects of that purpose?

7. Discuss ways that our society pays for mass incarceration.

8. What do you think of the U.S. incarceration rate, especially compared to that of other nations?

9. Who has influence over corrections policy?

10. What do you think needs to be done to address the crisis in American corrections?

KEY TERMS

Civil rights, 10

Community supervision, 4

Conditions of confinement, 10

Corrections, 4

Custody, 4

Dehumanization, 13

Detention, 10

Deterrence, 6

Grievance, 3

Incapacitation, 6

Jurisdiction, 5

Litmus test, 12

Prison, 4

Rehabilitation, 7

Smart on crime, 12

Solitary confinement, 3

Violation, 8

NOTES

1. Estes 2013
2. Greene 2013b
3. Greene 2013a
4. International Centre for Prison Studies 2013
5. U.S. Census Bureau 2013
6. Glaze and Parks 2012
7. Kyckelhahn and Martin 2013
8. Alexander 2012
9. *Los Angeles Times* 2012
10. Duncan and Anderson 2013
11. Marimow 2013
12. Lowenkamp, Latessa, and Holsinger 2006
13. Glaze and Parks 2012
14. DeMichele 2007, 25

$SAGE edge™

Sharpen your skills with SAGE edge at edge.sagepub.com/krisberg

SAGE edge for students provides a personalized approach to help you accomplish your coursework goals in an easy-to-use learning environment. This site includes action plans, mobile-friendly eFlashcards and web quizzes as well as web, audio, and video resources and links to SAGE journal articles.

2

A Historical Perspective on Punishment and Social Structure

LEARNING OBJECTIVES

1. To understand some of the early forms of punishment and see how current forms stem from them.

2. To understand how crime control has been rooted in social class and control of the

3. To grasp some of the penal inventions that have supported economic developments, such as colonization of the New World.

4. To be able to discuss how prison labor has supported economic enterprises at various times in

Imprisonment is an extension of other forms of social control, slavery being an extreme example, which set up an inevitable and cyclic escalation of punishment and ever-tighter controls.

Library of Congress, http://www .loc.gov/pictures/item/93507943/

Discerning Historical Constructs

Historian William Appleman Williams wrote, "History offers no answers per se, but it teaches us to use our own minds to make our own history."[1] The historical legacy of American corrections shows us that human beings and social groups make certain choices but that other decisions are possible. This chapter highlights some of the major developments in corrections and illustrates how that legacy affects our thinking and practices today. One is reminded of famous philosopher–baseball player Yogi Berra, who observed, "It is déjà vu all over again." Much of what seems new has happened before, and that prior experience can help us figure out where contemporary trends are likely to lead us.

There are two compelling myths that often underlie conventional treatments of the history of American corrections. The first myth is that there is a steady march of human society toward progress and more enlightened social policy. The second is that corrections history is like a pendulum that swings back and forth, with an invisible, self-balancing logic. Neither of these constructs is an accurate reflection of the story of American corrections. Closer to the truth is the idea that the evolution of punishment is rooted in the social structure and cultures in which it occurs. Ideology, class, race, and gender relationships exert profound influences on all social institutions, especially punishment systems. We can transcend the current status quo only by comprehending this social context and its limitations.

5 To understand the philosophic basis of the Quaker approach to early institutions of confinement in the United States.

a departure from the thinking that preceded them.

7 To grasp how the civil rights movement of the 1960s affected the criminal justice system.

6 To be able to describe the thinking behind the Auburn System and the ideas of Zebulon Brockway and explain why they represented

8 To explain the main influences on the demise of the rehabilitative ideal during the 1970s and 1980s.

Angola Prison was built on a former plantation and then went on to house many African Americans. Angola is still symbolic of the most punitive and racist prison environment

Library of Congress, http://www.loc.gov/pictures/item/2007660073/

In the literature on **penology**, two major works illustrate the linkage of punishment systems with the maintenance of power and privilege in social structures. The first, *Punishment and Social Structure* by historians George Rusche and Otto Kirchheimer (originally published in 1939), is a masterful overview of the evolution of corrections in Europe that illustrates the relationship of evolving punishment systems with transformations in social, political, and economic conditions. The second is J. Thorsten Sellin's *Slavery and the Penal System*, which chronicles how the forms and **jurisprudence** of criminal punishment closely paralleled the transformation of the institution of slavery.[2] Sellin's work covers the period from early Greek civilization up to the post–Civil War period in the United States. His historical analysis encompasses countries in Asia, Africa, Latin America, the United States, and Europe.

Rusche and Kirchheimer sought to expose how **penal systems** are used to suppress whole classes of individuals that are considered threats to the existing social structure. In his introduction to the 1968 reissue of *Punishment and Social Structure*, Sellin argues that all punishments or penal systems are designed to protect society, which should be thought of as systems of social privilege and power. Sellin writes that "the aim of all punishments is the protection of the values that the dominant social group regard as good for society."[3] For Sellin and for Rusche and Kirchheimer, the prime objective of penal systems is to secure obedience, not only from those being controlled but also from the social groups that they represent. The choice of the "best" correctional techniques is derived from a society's traditions, from its level of knowledge, and from its social and economic institutions. This insight into the close ties of penal systems to social relationships is often missing in standard histories of penology, which are frequently devoid of explanations as to why change occurs, assume an inevitable march to greater progress or enlightenment, or connect these changes to the ideas or advocacy of "great men."[4]

Rusche and Kirchheimer criticized the conventional histories of punishment for defending the moral integrity of current practices and attempting to create a story of "progress" and "reform." A more accurate analysis requires a description of how evolving social and

Penology: The study of the punishment of crime and the management of incarceration facilities.

Jurisprudence: The theory or philosophy of law.

Penal systems: Methods, or approaches relating to, used for, or prescribing the punishment of offenders under the legal system.

economic conditions explain the changes in penal systems. They noted that punishment systems are not just the simple consequence of crime. This observation is crucial today as we consider policy debates on whether increases or decreases in the severity of criminal penalties will impact crime rates. For Rusche and Kirchheimer, who were greatly influenced by Marxist thought, the shape and contours of penal systems corresponded to "economic systems of production." For example, sending convicts to penal colonies was congruent with an emerging system of colonialism. Turning prisons into factories was consistent with the growth of industrial manufacturing, and having prisoners work in agriculture made sense if one wanted to suppress the wages of farmworkers and to block unionization. Large-scale prison idleness emerged as the prison population was no longer needed by the economy. Greater use of "alternatives to incarceration" emerged as the fiscal pressures on the state required cheaper forms of punishment and control.[5]

Rusche and Kirchheimer argued that the principal targets of penal systems are the "underprivileged social strata." They wrote, "Penalties must be of such a nature that the latter will fear a further decline in their mode of existence."[6] For Sellin, the paradigm for the ultimate decline in personal control and authority was slavery. But, he also noted that slavery differed over time and was congruent with social developments in the various nations that practiced it.[7]

Examples of the linkage of penal practice and systems of economic production are discussed in more detail below. The European houses of corrections—the precursors to modern prisons—reached their peak in an era of mercantilism (the shifting of wealth to the class dominated by trade and commercial interest). The growth of industrial capitalism and the factory system decreased the economic importance of the 16th-century houses of corrections and created the imperative for new forms of penal practice. The expansion in modern industrial societies minimized the need for convict labor. As convict labor became less important to the economy, fiscal considerations loomed larger. The state needed to balance its need to maintain social order with the costs associated with penal systems.

There have been several important epochs in the evolution of punishment. The dominant methods of the early Middle Ages (from the fall of the Roman Empire until the 10th century A.D.) were fines and public displays of penance, such as the stockade. The

◀ In addition to punishing them, penal colonies used transported convicts to fill the need for cheap labor.

© Bettmann/Corbis

Houses of corrections: Facilities established in the late 16th century as places for the punishment and reform of the poor convicted of petty offenses through hard labor. London contained the first house of correction, Bridewell.

later Middle Ages (roughly from 1200 to 1500 A.D.) witnessed the rise of terrible and cruel systems of corporal and capital punishment. These were gradually replaced in the 17th century by imprisonment as the major mode of punishment. Incarceration was supplemented by transporting prisoners to penal colonies in a number of remote locations including North America, Australia, and Africa. What we think of as the modern era of penology consists of a more complex mix of incarceration, fines, supervised release systems (such as probation and parole), and a growing number of technological control systems including electronic monitoring and global positioning systems (GPS). Following is a brief description of developments in these stages of penology and what links them to changes in social structure.

Penance and Fines

The early Middle Ages in Europe did not have complex systems of state-administered punishments. Existing legal systems were primarily focused on regulating the relationships and interactions among persons who were equals in status and wealth. The legal system was constructed within a society that had sufficient land to support a growing population and maintain a certain standard of living. The colonization of eastern Europe produced a rising demand for agri-

▲ Punishment used to be a public display and disgrace, presumably to discourage crime. Today's methods are characterized more as "out of sight, out of mind."

Library of Congress, http://www .loc.gov/pictures/item/90706209/

cultural labor that allowed peasants to escape pressures from wealthy landowners to produce more food and other products; the peasants were free to escape servitude and move on to better situations. Moreover, the growth in new towns toward the end of this period allowed indentured laborers to obtain their freedom. These economic realities pushed landowners to treat their laborers better. Thus, the social structure of the early Middle Ages rested on the promotion of social cohesion and the resolution of social conflicts.

This world of balanced social dependence—legitimized further by religious ideals—made the formal criminal law unimportant as a means to protect the existing social hierarchy. The criminal law was about the maintenance of public order among persons of comparable social status. This legal system was essentially a private arbitration system that relied almost exclusively on fines as compensation for an offense. An affront to decency, morality, or religion was generally resolved by a body of free men (almost always landowners) who would meet and impose a fine ("wergild") as penance to the victimized party. The goal of the body of free men was to prevent individual disputes from escalating into family blood feuds or open warfare. In this social order, criminal acts were viewed as acts of war. In the absence of strong centralized states, public peace was very fragile. Even the smallest quarrel could erupt into violence. This is not unlike what we see today in certain poor, urban neighborhoods in which petty slights or signs of "disrespect" can quickly turn lethal and where faith in the legal system to resolve conflicts is nonexistent.

Global positioning systems: Technology used to electronically track the whereabouts of persons under supervision, generally probation or parole, and usually in the form of an ankle bracelet.

Class distinctions between victim and offender were reflected in the extent of penance demanded by the aggrieved parties. Over time, this system was transformed into a system of corporal punishment, because the poorer offenders could not pay monetary fines. Penal sanctions emerged in lieu of paying fines, but only for the poor.

The system of private medieval law grew to be an instrument of class domination. Feudal lords used their own penal codes to discipline the economically downtrodden. The only limit on a lord's power to discipline was a jurisdictional claim by another lord. However, the struggle of various kings and princes to consolidate their power and control over land led to a demise of this private system of criminal law. The fines and costs of legal proceedings became a valuable source of revenue for the emerging powerful elites. Confiscation of land and property was part of this system. Rusche and Kirchheimer believed the ability to extract revenue from the administration of justice was a prime factor in transforming the private system of arbitration to a public system of centralized control.

Social Change in the Later Middle Ages

There were significant social changes in Europe in the later Middle Ages. The lives of the poorest citizens continued to deteriorate. Major plagues in the 14th century kept the population from growing, but in the 15th century, urban populations grew rapidly, and the numbers of those who were unemployed, destitute, and without any land increased.[8] Rising population and rudimentary forms of agriculture led to a near exhaustion of the land. Demand for inexpensive foodstuffs rose due to swelling urban populations. Farming became increasingly profitable, and landowners were less predisposed to allow peasants to rent lands for low fees. The price of land rose dramatically.

These economic transformations depressed the wages of landed peasants. The early growth of a capitalist agrarian system, including raising livestock, led to further impoverishment of ordinary people. The increasing poor and angry rural population began to migrate in large numbers into medieval towns. The new immigrants were viewed by existing urban workers and craftsmen as a major economic burden and as a threat to social stability—much as undocumented workers are demonized and feared today. The economy could not absorb the large influx of new workers. This situation led to lower wages.

Many European cities enacted new laws known as Poor Laws to control and regulate the movement of the new immigrants. These laws barred immigrants from becoming citizens and prohibited them from joining the guilds (early unions of skilled workers). Some cities even refused to allow immigrants to legally enter them. The displaced and increasingly desperate rural population was often forced to camp out on the roads outside the city walls, resorting to begging, becoming vagabonds (now we call them "homeless"), or forming criminal gangs to survive.

The medieval world lacked the legal or political structures to cope with this alarming social instability, which came to be defined as a growing "dangerous class." Some of the wayward peasants were recruited as mercenaries by the European warlords. The new mercenaries made the knights dispensable by the ruling elite. Many knights resorted to highway robbery to support themselves. The poor also increased their criminal behavior, robbing other urban dwellers openly.

Faced with the growing "dangerous classes," many cities tried to control the birthrate by prohibiting marriage. But, this policy simply produced more children born out of wedlock and of ambiguous social ties. Also, as the poor became poorer, there was an extraordinary accumulation of wealth among some landowners and urban entrepreneurs. The ever-declining wages produced enormous profits at the top. Other early capitalists became wealthy by extending credit to wage laborers to advance their own economic and political influence. The growing misery of the displaced peasantry and wage laborers led to strikes and boycotts and resulted in harsh reactions by the wealthy. As poverty advanced, so did crime, warfare, and class-based conflicts.

One of the most important consequences of this enlarging social turmoil was the emergence of a brutal criminal law directed against the lower classes. The more privileged wanted to make the system of criminal laws more effective in slowing the rise in crime. Fines and corporal punishment remained in force, but class distinctions in the administration of laws became more obvious. Upper-class offenders were generally treated more leniently, and lower-class "villains" came to be viewed by the legal system as morally inferior. The urban bourgeoisie (the conventional, materialistic middle class) lobbied for tougher crime-control measures. This period witnessed the rise of laws against vagrancy. Punishments became harsher and more brutal, especially physical punishments such as execution, whipping, and mutilation. These alterations emerged gradually over time along with the changing social and economic conditions.[9] During this period, capital punishment became commonplace. Judges used the death penalty for offenders whom they declared to be "threats to society." Rusche and Kirchheimer report that more than 72,000 thieves were executed during the reign of Henry VIII. Queen Elizabeth ordered vagabonds to be hanged in rows—sometimes as many as 300 to 400 at a time. The population of England was only about 3 million at this time. Courts paid little attention to the actual guilt or innocence of the accused. Torture was the norm to coerce confessions and to identify possible accomplices.

There were public debates about how to make the death penalty as painful as possible. Even punishments intended for lesser criminals turned lethal. It was believed that mutilating offenders made them easier to identify and label as recidivists. Convicted criminals often died from these mutilations in an era of primitive medical care. Another popular penalty was exile or banishment, but these punishments had different consequences based on one's social class. For the well-off, exile could mean travel, new business ventures, and even diplomatic service. The wealthy could return from banishment and rejoin their communities. For the lower classes, exile might have meant a temporary escape from death, but they might easily have faced death sentences in the places where they sought to relocate.

This harsh penal system fit with an economy that had large numbers of expendable workers; human life was of little value in this social structure. The penal system was utilized by the elite to destroy perceived threats to the established order.[10] Sellin similarly noted that the emerging European legal system mirrored the treatment of slaves.[11]

A popular myth is that the common people supported these public executions and harsh punishments by showing up en masse and celebrating these brutalities. Evidence suggests that this was not always the case. In a work by E. P. Thompson et al., *Albion's Fatal Tree*,[12] distinguished British historians challenged the idea that the crowds at executions were willing participants in these events. Some attendees were family and friends of the condemned who were there to see that the body was not desecrated and that there would be a proper burial. In addition, it is important to assess the masses at executions in the context of the social conditions of the time.

The common people of the Middle Ages lived amid severe economic hardships and oppression, as well as fear and hatred of "others." Public executions were occasions of bizarre rituals. The mutilations were viewed as ways to appease supernatural forces. The fury and sorrow of the downtrodden were expressed in terms of quasi-religious practices and superstitions. These sentiments were also reflected in the mass violence against Jews, foreigners, and gypsies. The fear and persecution of alleged witches was a parallel social development. These behaviors can be seen as an expression of how ordinary life was becoming increasingly devalued. The reported savagery and sadism of those attending the public spectacles of the criminal law was a reflection of the desperation of the masses. There is little evidence that the public executions were a real deterrent to crime. Crime, as it was defined at the time, continued to increase.

The Discovery of Imprisonment

As the 16th century drew to a close, methods of punishment were changing in gradual but important ways. The exploitation of prisoner labor was introduced as an additional penalty. Eventually, it replaced many existing penal approaches. These changes were motivated not by humanitarian concerns over capital punishment and mutilation, but by the growing value of human capital that was at the disposal of the state. Growing wealth in the larger cities and towns led to a demand for more consumer goods. Expanded trade to Asia and the Mediterranean resulted in new potential to accumulate wealth. Conquest and colonization of foreign territories generated increased prosperity through precious metals and other goods such as coffee, tea, and sugar.

The European population declined as much as 30% to 50% in the 17th century as a result of religious warfare. A declining workforce and rising economic demand caused a spike in wages. Even the Poor Laws that were intended to limit the movement of the poor also contributed to labor scarcities. Once again, workers had an improved bargaining condition. In this socioeconomic context, business owners and the aristocracy appealed to government to fill the labor need and reduce production costs for a wide range of goods and services.

There were efforts to increase the birthrate, and criminals were used in military service. The army came to be viewed as a penal sanction.[13] Countries needing soldiers took criminals from other locations, and military service emerged as an alternative to traditional punishments. Child labor was encouraged; the state provided manufacturers with children from orphanages. Forced labor was an expected part of charity to the destitute, widows, the mentally ill, or the infirm. Traditional Catholic Church doctrines viewed charity as a religious obligation. Giving to the less fortunate was intended to please God. The ideology of the Catholic Church was that its accumulated property ultimately belonged to the poor. But, the emerging business class evolved a very different perspective on social inequality.

Calvinist religious ideas, which formed the foundation for the rise of Protestantism, rested on the concept of "predestination" as the cause of social circumstances. The wealthy would be saved for all eternity, and the poor were less morally worthy. The Calvinists also placed a high value on disciplined work as the road to redemption. Poverty was equated with laziness and moral corruption. This religious ideology fit perfectly with an emerging capitalist economy and the growing need for laborers.

Catholic towns enacted laws punishing vagrants and beggars. The existence of a "plague of beggars" was used to explain the shortage of workers. The concept of the "unworthy poor" emerged—the downtrodden who were to be socially condemned and who did not merit any kind of assistance.

This was the social and historical environment that birthed the early form of the prison in the European houses of corrections. The first English prison was called Bridewell. It was located in London and opened in 1553. Sellin provides the most comprehensive description of the Amsterdam houses of corrections in *Pioneering in Penology*.[14] These early correctional institutions were part poorhouse and part penal institution. The main purpose of the house of corrections was to exploit the labor of unwilling workers; inmates were forced to work in the institution. The explicit philosophy was that the miscreants would gain disciplined work habits and learn vocational skills. Inmates were supposed to enter the labor market after release. Visitors from throughout Europe came to Amsterdam to study this new penological innovation.

Inmates of the houses of corrections were beggars, prostitutes, vagrants, and petty thieves. Later, prisoners with longer sentences were sent to the houses of corrections. Over time, these

▲ The church, state, and economy have been interrelated throughout our history. Religion promised to relieve the presumed unworthiness of the underclass and encouraged hard work as one remedy.

© iStockphoto.com /HakuNellies

▲ The Bridewell was originally established to punish the disorderly poor and to house homeless children. What does this reveal about social class and early prisons?

http://en.wikipedia.org/wiki/File:Prospect_of_Bridewell.jpg

penal facilities accepted delinquent children and dependent youths and emerged as places to house the poor. The French version, called *Hôpitaux généraux*, was opened in Paris in 1656 by the Jesuits and housed widows and orphans.

While some of the houses of corrections ran their own businesses, most contracted out labor to private entrepreneurs. The Amsterdam facility used inmate labor to process hardwood for the Dutch dyeing industry. The Spandau house of corrections in Germany specialized in making textiles. The contractors promised not to treat the inmate laborers so badly as to make them incapable of working, but this vow was often only a false promise. The inmates typically had to work even after their release to repay the cost of their food, board, and education. Those released would often be assigned as apprentices as a condition of their release. Prisoners from the houses of corrections populated the early commercial sailing industry.

Free workers often complained that the houses of corrections created unfair monopolies and depressed their wages. The courts were not sympathetic to these claims. Still, many of the houses of corrections were run by corrupt officials who stole money and diverted profits. Additionally, the productivity of the inmate laborers was never very high. There are reports of enormous profits that were made by the houses of corrections, although these are hard to verify. First and foremost, the houses of corrections ushered in an era in which penal confinement with hard labor became the most frequent punishment. "The institution of the houses of corrections . . . was not the result of brotherly love or an official sense of obligation to the distressed. It was part of the development of capitalism."[15] The emergence of Calvinist religious ideology and the need to promote a disciplined workforce provided the rationale for this precursor to the modern prison.

Galley Slavery, Transportation, and the Emergence of Imprisonment

Galley slavery:
A sentence forcing the convict to work as a rower on a ship. At times, this sentence replaced the death penalty and used to provide a labor pool for military and merchant ships.

Transportation:
A sentence primarily used in the 17th and 18th centuries in which the convict was exiled and transported, usually by ship, to a penal colony.

The linkages between forms of punishment, economic forces, and penal servitude are very clear in the cases of **galley slavery** and **transportation**. The value of human labor increased, and the state found ways to maximize its use of the labor of criminals. Galley slavery was a response to the need for rowers for sailing vessels in the Mediterranean Sea. As European wars drained off the free population, prisoners were drafted into galley slavery. The work was arduous and very dangerous. Sentences to galley slavery were often for 10 to 12 years, and the rulers often pressured the courts to speed up sentencing to fill the growing need for oarsmen. Increasingly, galley slavery replaced the death penalty, not for humanitarian reasons but to exploit forced labor. Galley slavery was characterized by very harsh conditions that often resulted in a slow death. Some criminals would mutilate themselves to avoid this sentence. Galley slavery was an example of the state compelling convicts to do the labor that free workers would never perform, even under the worst financial circumstances.

Even more related to economic developments was the practice of "transportation"— shipping convicts to distant colonies. As the exploitation of material riches from the colonies posed very challenging labor requirements, prisoners became an obvious workforce. Initially, the process of colonization involved trying to enslave the native populations, but these groups often resisted this enslavement and were decimated by colonial warfare. Native peoples were also wiped out by new diseases brought by the colonists; many died due to brutal working conditions. At first, wayward children and the poor were kidnapped and sold into slavery in the colonies, but this practice reduced the domestic workforce. Sending convicts overseas was a temporary solution to the severe labor shortage and the great potential to extract wealth from conquered lands. Prisoners facing death sentences had their penalties commuted to transportation based on the physical condition of the convicts.

In the early 18th century, transportation emerged as the primary penalty for property crimes. Colonial contractors were given modest grants to accept prison laborers, but eventually these contractors "owned" the inmates via a system of indentured servitude. The primary destinations of English convicts were the Americas and, later, Australia. It was anticipated that many of the transported convicts would remain in the colonies or would die during their period of servitude. For example, those sent to Australia faced such horren-

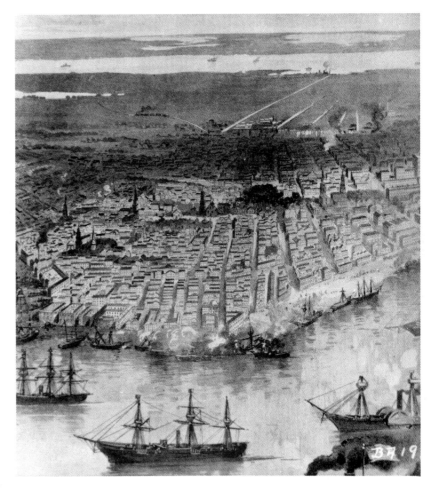

▲ In the early 1700s, trying to boost population in an unpopular location, France transported prisoners to populate New Orleans.

http://en.wikipedia.org/wiki/ File:New_orleans_1862.jpg

dous conditions there that transportation was viewed as akin to a death sentence.[16] Some of the convicts did survive these terrible conditions to become farmers or planters in the colonies.

In North America, the exploitation of African slaves supplanted the use of forced convict labor. Slave labor could be bought and sold and was not limited to a contracted term; these laborers were enslaved for life. The children of slaves expanded the pool of labor. Further, the treatment of African slaves was even crueler than what was imposed on the European convicts. Compared to slavery, the practice of transportation was far less profitable. Moreover, independence movements in the New World expelled the colonizers and abruptly ended this practice in the Americas. Transportation continued to Australia, but the economic value was more limited due to the enormous distance between Australia and England. Other European powers such as France, Belgium, Portugal, and Germany relied most heavily on enslaving local populations or exploiting local peasants by extracting rent from tenant farmers.

The demise of galley slavery and transportation led to the emergence of prisons as a significant component in the penal systems of Europe. Before the 18th century, jails were utilized to hold defendants before trials. Jails also held people briefly who failed to pay fines or were sentenced to corporal punishment. Jailers were paid through fees collected from the inmates. The economic successes of the houses of corrections from the earlier era suggested that the forced labor of inmates could be very profitable. During the 18th century, jails became factories for the manufacture of goods. Jailers would hold good workers as long as they could. It turns out that indeterminate sentences to incarceration had their origin in the value of inmate labor rather than the ideology of rehabilitation. Jail populations continued to grow, and advocates for the penal system emphasized that jails would become self-supporting and even contribute to state fiscal resources. Jails as centers of inmate labor supplanted many jails that only held persons awaiting trial.

SPOTLIGHT

TRANSPORTATION OF PRISONERS TO THE COLONIES

Convict transportation was a primary means of punishing criminals and being rid of prisoners in Britain and Ireland. As early as 1615, merchants would transport convicted criminals—unless their crimes were murder, witchcraft, rape, or burglary—from the British Isles to the plantations of North America and the Caribbean to work as indentured servants. Forty years later, even felons convicted of capital offenses would be pardoned if they accepted the choice of exile and indentured servitude.[1] Because of the harsh conditions aboard ships and in the colonies, by 1720, transportation was a sentence in and of itself. Prior to the American Revolution, 50,000 convicts were transported to the American colonies, mainly to Virginia and Maryland.[2]

When the American Revolution put an end to this practice there, the British government chose their colonies in Australia as the new destination for unwanted criminals. Between 1788 and 1868, 160,000 criminals were shipped to New South Wales, Van Diemen's Land, and Western Australia.[3] Magistrates in these regions could order convicts to be flogged or sent to infamous places of secondary transportation, including Norfolk Island and

Macquarie Harbour. The common law did not provide for the legal rights of felons, and most worked for private masters. Convicts were sentenced to road gangs, which required them to work in leg irons and live in the bush. Women were restricted to female factories as a penal sanction.

By the 1820s, Britain began to construct prisons to accept convicts who would otherwise be transported. The colonies were beginning to protest being the convenient dump for unwanted citizens. In addition, reformers at home were pushing for a national prison system.

QUESTIONS

1 In what ways are today's prisons similar to or different from the colonies to which prisoners were once shipped?

2 What are the more significant moral dilemmas in the shipping of convicts to a penal colony in another land?

Notes

1. Sellin 1976
2. Kercher 2003
3. Ibid.

The Catholic Church operated its own network of prisons that were more focused on the personal reformation of the offender according to church doctrine. A French cleric, Father Jean Mabillon, was one of the first writers to describe the rehabilitative value of prisons. In "Réflexions sur les prisons des ordres religieux,"[17] Mabillon explained that the labor of inmates was central to their moral redemption and urged a system in which penalties were graded in severity and linked to the gravity of the crime. Mabillon urged the adoption of penal measures in which inmates could earn privileges and release based on evidence of their personal reformation. These ideas were later merged with the reality of forced inmate labor to define the origins of the current prison system.

As the 18th century unfolded, Europe witnessed the emergence of a philosophy known as the **Enlightenment**. Perhaps the most influential penal thinker of this era was Cesare Beccaria. His essay *On Crimes and Punishments* advocated for greater fairness and proportionality in the punishment system. Beccaria argued that brutal and arbitrary punishments were counterproductive.[18] Like-minded observers criticized capital punishment, severe corporal penalties, and extremely harsh jail conditions. The concern for procedural fairness and predictability was supported by the interests of an emerging business class that wanted to free itself from the total authority of elites, who based their legitimacy

Enlightenment: Refers to a movement that took place primarily in Europe during the 17th and 18th centuries that impacted the arts, sciences, philosophy, and other intellectual fields. Its participants sought to reform society through reason.

IN THE COURTS

Ruffin v. Commonwealth Supreme Court of Virginia
62 VA 790 (1871)

Woody Ruffin was a convict in a state penitentiary who was put out with other inmates to work on the Chesapeake and Ohio Railway. While in the county of Bath, Mr. Ruffin escaped and killed a guard. He was sent to the city of Richmond and was sentenced to death. The defendant claimed that he should have been sent back to the county of Bath for trial and sentencing. He claimed that his transfer was unlawful under the Virginia Bill of Rights.

The Virginia Supreme Court denied Ruffin's claim and asserted that as a convicted felon he was not a free man and was civilly dead.

The court wrote, "Such men have some rights . . . but not the rights of freemen.

"For the time being and during his term of service in the penitentiary, he is in a state of penal servitude to the State . . . He is for the time being a slave of the State. He is *civiliter mortuus*; and his estate, if he has any, is administered like that of a dead man."

An inmate who committed a misdemeanor offense in prison could be subject to lashing, an iron mask, the gag, or placement in a dungeon. Those inmates who committed felonies did have the privilege of a jury trial, but in any special court that the state determined was appropriate.

The judgment of the Richmond Circuit Court was affirmed, and Mr. Ruffin's death sentence was reinstated.

on hereditary and inherited wealth. The members of the powerful and growing business class wanted a legal system that protected them from unpredictable and capricious state power. For the penal system, the core idea was that "the punishment must fit the crime." Enlightenment philosophers such as Jeremy Bentham published detailed and mathematical formulations linking the seriousness of criminal misconduct and punishments. There was opposition to wide-open discretion by judges. The bourgeoisie wanted legal certainty to protect their property and contract rights.

Writers such as Beccaria expressed concern that the current brutal penal system would lead to juries that would acquit guilty defendants to avoid being part of administering draconian punishments. The Enlightenment writers worried that brutal penal systems might foment social revolts among the underclasses. There were proposals for public jury trials, free choices of lawyers, reduction in the use of torture, and protections against false imprisonment. While the Enlightenment thinkers advocated these reforms for all citizens, the complex legal machinery they sought could only be afforded by the wealthy. Further, the Enlightenment philosophers did not attack the civil rights violations inherent in the Poor Laws and the enforcement of vagrancy laws. These viewpoints gained political influence as the 18th century came to an end.

The Industrial Revolution and Corrections

While a more progressive criminal justice philosophy was gaining some political traction in the 18th century, changing labor conditions led to a decline in existing penal institutions. The demand for inmate labor was drying up, and the conditions in houses of

corrections were deteriorating. Famous English prison reformer John Howard noted, "Neglect, intimidation, and torment of inmates became the rule of the day, and they were given work only for their discomfort or for the profit to be gained."[19]

The general population in Europe was growing, and work became scarce, especially with the productive efficiencies generated by the factory system of production. Rural workers continued to stream into the cities well into the 19th century. Mechanized manufacture replaced the more labor-intensive forms of production. For example, factory-based industry replaced the traditional home-based spinning of textiles. Women and children who were employed in spinning were thrown out of work. So, the poor got poorer as the wealthier citizens increased their assets. The growing business class lobbied for free trade, unlimited competition, freedom of manufacture, and an end to the regulation of working conditions. The ideology of laissez-faire capitalism was the rallying cry of the bourgeoisie.

The poor and the working classes suffered under this new organization of production, because the labor market was saturated. Wages plummeted, and the traditional legal pressures to attract workers were less important. The economic suffering of the lower classes got far worse. Thinkers like Thomas Robert Malthus pointed to a crisis of overpopulation and called for laws and policies to cut the birthrate of the poor. The existing system of relief for the poor collapsed, and death rates from starvation rose sharply. Malthus argued against any programs to help the poor, while others expressed the fear that the plight of the poor would lead to revolutions.

Crime rates rose, and there were calls for a return to the draconian penalties of the late Middle Ages, with advocates calling for more mutilation, corporal punishments, and executions in lieu of imprisonment. Despite these pressures, imprisonment remained the primary form of punishment in the early Industrial Age. Interestingly, the conditions of confinement were better for more privileged inmates. Corrections officials argued that wealthier convicts were "more sensitive to punishments"—an argument that was echoed centuries later by conservative advocate Charles Murray.[20] It was also argued that punishments brought greater hardship to the privileged. Many European countries held upper-class prisoners in separate facilities from those for the poor.

Existing prisons were mostly designed to hold inmates for short periods before their trials, but these jails became increasingly crowded. Existing buildings were renovated to hold more inmates, and funds for prison upkeep were scarce. There were many reports of horrid conditions of confinement, widespread disease, starvation, and death. The population of prisoners was growing rapidly, just as the need for their labor was diminishing. The few advocates for prison reform attributed this dramatic decline of prison conditions to the corruption of corrections administrators. Although this alleged corruption was no doubt true, broader economic forces were driving the deterioration of prison conditions. Ironically, some observers argued that prison conditions were too good, and this led the poor to seek a better life of incarceration.[21] This envy of the prison population illustrated the growing anxiety and declining economic position of the working class.

Few believed that prisoners could actually be made to improve their characters or behavior. It was argued that decent living conditions in prisons reduced the deterrence of incarceration and encouraged people to commit crimes. The consensus view was that prisoners should get the barest minimum and that their living circumstances must be lower than those of the poorest free citizens. Some even argued that allowing prisoners to work permitted them contact to plan criminal conspiracies. The threat of the hardship of prisons was viewed by the more privileged as a way to control free workers.

The industrial era also made forced prison labor appear to reduce the wages and profits of those in the free economy. When there was a labor shortage, the work of inmates was not a big concern, but a labor surplus resulted in criticism of inmate labor. Work disappeared from prisons, or it became another aspect of punishment (breaking rocks and carrying large boulders back and forth) regardless of value to the economy outside of prison. Prison work was reduced to a form of torture. Prisoners were made to walk for many hours on treadmills or to grind stones into sand.

Prison labor and prison industries became less profitable than they once were. The expansion of mechanized manufacture made the manual labor of prisoners all but obsolete. Prison labor no longer provided sufficient money to even pay for the upkeep of inmates. Private control of inmate labor disappeared, and prison managers went bankrupt. The state had to assume a much larger role in running jails. To control costs, many correctional institutions began using retired military men to run them—a cheap and plentiful labor source. The retired military prison staff introduced military discipline to prisons.

Solitary Confinement

The invention of solitary confinement as a penal measure was a development in the 19th century. Solitary confinement is generally attributed to the work of Quakers in Pennsylvania who advocated for this new form of punishment. Although solitary confinement was justified on religious grounds, its evolution was tied to the economic and fiscal forces described above.

Prison conditions in the United States were declining in the same ways as in Europe, albeit slightly later in time. Fiscal considerations loomed large. The Quakers based their penology on the core idea that religion would lead to the moral redemption of offenders. Prisoners were locked in single cells and isolated from other inmates. They never left these cells until their terms expired, they died, or they declined into mental illness. Convicts were not even allowed to work; they were to spend all their time contemplating God. Bibles were the only reading material permitted. The extreme isolation of prisoners was thought to prevent some inmates from negatively influencing others. It was viewed as the only true mode of punishment, but it was (and still is) a penal method that allows a small staff to manage a large number of mostly idle prisoners. Most important, the Quakers reintroduced a religious rationale into penal systems similar to the Catholic prisons of an earlier era, those championed by Father Mabillon.

Despite the forceful lobbying of the Quakers, the system of solitary confinement, or **Pennsylvania System**, was soon abandoned in all the places it had been introduced. As

Pennsylvania System: A 19th-century penal system advocated by some Quakers, in which prisoners were kept in solitary confinement and expected to repent and reform through contemplation of their sins and God. In practice, many prisoners developed mental illnesses.

▲ Opened in 1829, Eastern State Penitentiary was the pinnacle of corrections of the day. The large facility became world famous. Its concept combined solitary confinement with labor.

© iStockphoto.com /OGphoto; http://lcweb2.loc.gov/service/ pnp/ppmsc/00600/00661r.jpg;

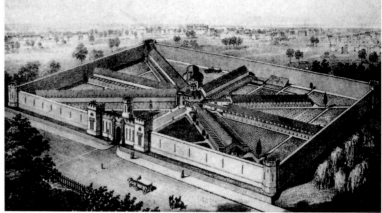

mentioned earlier, there was the serious problem of prisoners' deteriorating mental condition—a problem that persists in penal settings using isolation today, the so-called supermax prisons. However, changing labor conditions in the early- to mid-19th-century United States also contributed to the collapse of the Pennsylvania System. The need for labor, especially in the northeastern states, was growing, and slave labor was being limited through legislative enactments pushed by the abolitionists. Rapid industrial growth created a need for laborers that could not be filled by a new wave of immigration from Ireland and Germany. Workers were needed, and wages were higher than those being paid in Europe.

In this economic environment, the forced idleness of convicts in solitary confinement made no sense. In 1829, Pennsylvania reintroduced work that inmates could perform in their cells, and this generated a new stream of revenue. But, real profits could only be achieved if prison administrators could bring in manufacturing machinery and get convicts to work in factory-like settings. New York State pioneered a very different approach to penal labor known as the Auburn System. The core of this system was solitary confinement at night but collective labor in prison workshops during the day. The convicts were required to labor in total silence to prevent them from communicating with one another, and they wore black hoods to prevent them from recognizing one another. Unlike the European penal institutions in the 19th century, American prisons made profits, and prison work was not viewed as entirely punitive.

Abolitionist: A person who favors the abolition of any law or practice they deem harmful to society: for example, there are abolitionists who are opposed to capital punishment.

Auburn System: A 19th-century penal system in which prisoners would perform silent labor in groups by day, and be placed in solitary confinement by night.

Private entrepreneurs contracted with prison administrators for the fruits of inmate labor, but later the lease system was replaced with businessmen actually running the prison factories themselves. This system was supplanted by prisons selling their goods on a per-piece basis. The American Civil War increased the demand for prison labor as the free workers were conscripted in the army; the war created a huge demand for boots, blankets, and uniforms.

The Auburn System also used privileges for inmates as a method of increasing productivity. Good behavior was measured by the amount of work that a convict completed. In 1817, New York passed a law that awarded up to 25% off of the sentence for those with sentences of more than five years. This emerged as a powerful control over inmate behavior, and time off of sentences replaced payment of convict laborers.

Toward the end of the 19th century, organizations of free laborers expressed opposition to prison labor and to increased immigration—especially from Mexico, the Caribbean, and Asia. These early precursors of the labor movement were often successful in blocking the introduction of modern machinery into prisons, and in some cases actually abolished inmate labor. During this period, states prohibited the sale of inmate-made goods in the free market, restricting their use by government agencies.

In Europe, where surplus labor still existed, solitary confinement was part of the disciplinary system. Though some reformers urged that solitary confinement be utilized as an alternative to corporal punishments, the more frequent use of extreme isolation was to respond to riots, violence, and work stoppages in increasingly harsh prison settings. New prisons were built to allow more solitary confinement, reinforced by the "rule of silence." Interestingly, absolute silence among inmates was the practice in many American prisons well into the 20th century. Even though solitary confinement made convict labor very difficult, this practice expanded in Europe. Social critics such as Charles Dickens condemned such practices, but his advocacy gained no political traction. Solitary confinement emerged as the preferred treatment of rebellious or defiant

Old Prison, New Museum

In connection with a historical celebration, some city officials would like to reopen a very old prison as a museum. The plan is to offer tours of the prison to visitors to the city. Revenue from the tours is to be paid into a welfare fund for the children of current city prisoners. Former inmates will have jobs as tour guides. Proponents of the plan note that Alcatraz prison is one of the most popular tourist destinations in San Francisco.

Historians and criminologists would like people to understand the origins of solitary confinement in the United States. Others would prefer to tear down the old prison and build a shopping mall or industrial park to create jobs for people in the city. It is argued that the old prison is a testimony to historic cruelty and tends to minimize the social harm caused by the huge imprisonment rate of the city's African American population. The revenues and jobs created by new construction would be of enormous benefit to the local economy.

YOU DECIDE: **Do you create the prison museum or bulldoze the old prison?**

inmates. The linkage to moral redemption was lost, and the Quaker ideal was transformed into yet another means to brutalize the poor and other lawbreakers.

Zebulon Brockway and the Rise of the Adult Reformatory

The Auburn penitentiary in New York state emerged as the model for adult corrections in the United States, although a plantation system based on slavery remained strong in the prisons of the southern states. Zebulon Brockway gained an important training experience at Auburn as he pursued a career running workhouses and prisons in various parts of upstate New York. Brockway became a world-renowned penologist, and his ideas had far-reaching influence.

Reducing the costs of penal operations and making prisons self-sustaining was a major Brockway goal. He argued for a reorganization of penal methods that would defray most operational expenditures. He also asserted that the regimen of work would be curative. In his widely read autobiography, Brockway explained that with the "productive employment of prisoners, the public expenditures for prisons should be limited to the cost of providing the plant; the matter of selecting and organizing the prison industries became at first and naturally the central purpose of management at a new county prison."[22]

Emerging as a national figure, Brockway galvanized the support of reformers, correctional managers, lawyers, judges, physicians, and clergy to promote the ideal of an adult reformatory. He also wrote and helped pass the first **indeterminate sentencing** law in 1877, and he became the first superintendent of the Elmira Reformatory where he got to put his

Indeterminate sentencing: The law required a sentencing judge to fix maximum and minimum limits to the offender's confinement, the actual release date to be controlled by a board of parole. The indeterminate sentence allows judges their discretion in consideration of the defendant's behavior, circumstances, and potential for reform.

theories into practice. Brockway was the acknowledged leader of American corrections in the last decades of the 19th century. His writings also had a profound effect on how the public and elected officials viewed criminals.

At its heart, Brockway's penal philosophy rested on the assumption that criminals were the product of physical, moral, and intellectual imperfections; he believed their behavior was not determined by reason and logic. In fact, Brockway emphasized that lawbreakers were incapable of controlling their own conduct either in prisons or in the community. He attributed this basic inferiority to genetic inheritance and to inadequate early family experiences. The mission of the reformatory was to promote conforming behavior among these inferior humans. For example, the Indeterminate Sentence Law required that offenders demonstrate their conformity to the rule of law and to the authority of superiors before they could be released from incarceration. Brockway developed a **classification system** that differentiated criminals into those with arrested development, the truly dangerous, those whose moral compass failed when they were under stress, and those who lack a fully developed moral sense.[23] Brockway personally interviewed hundreds of inmates at Elmira to perfect his ideas.

Brockway held a firm belief in the value of physical punishments, and he was often criticized for harsh corporal punishment by the media and some citizen groups. To him, there was no other method of dealing with habitual offenders. These views and practices caused Brockway to eventually lose his position at Elmira.

As the father of modern American penology, Brockway succeeded in generating large profits from the forced labor of inmates. In 1880, Elmira's 485 prisoners were grossing more than a quarter of a million dollars annually. The net profit was over $60,000.[24] Brockway's aggressive attempts to expand inmate labor created a backlash in which both business and labor groups in New York lobbied to end prison industry. In 1888, New York prohibited all profit-generating labor in its prisons. Faced with the demise of inmate labor, Brockway experimented with the use of military regimens and discipline at Elmira. Starting with a small "officer training" program, Brockway expanded this effort to eight companies. The inmates were taught to drill and to practice battalion movements to the sound of military band music. Convicts wore military-like uniforms complete with insignia of rank, and they marched with dummy rifles.[25] Prison discipline at Elmira was accomplished through mock courts-martial. The sanctions could include reductions in grade, fines, delays in release times, corporal punishment, and solitary confinement. Prison work continued to produce products that could be used by other state agencies. Visitors marveled at the proficiency of

Classification system: The grouping of corrections-involved individuals according to their risk of further behavioral problems, which is meant to allow corrections managers to use the most appropriate and cost-effective level of security and supervision.

Zebulon Brockway's theory of adult reform was that criminal behavior was a sign of moral and genetic inferiority that can only be reversed to harsh punishment and strict conformity. The Elmira Reformatory expressed these ideas.

Library of Congress, http://www.loc.gov/pictures/item/2005680899/

the military marches at Elmira. In the 1990s, Brockway's ideas gained widespread popularity in the expansion of correctional **boot camps**.[26]

Elmira also utilized the "mark system" in which inmates could earn merits or demerits that would be converted into monetary payments or extra time in prison. The mark system is a precursor to later behavior modification systems that were popular in U.S. prisons and juvenile facilities in the 1970s.

Added to this correctional program was an educational program in which inmates would hear lectures at the end of exhausting days of drill and labor. The lectures would explain the "evil of idleness," and there were debates among the students on a number of ethical and moral questions of the day.

Elmira was also famous for a series of medical experiments that Brockway led with Dr. Hamilton Wey. These were efforts to test the reformative qualities of massage, special baths, diets, exercise, and military drill. Although no remarkable results were ever sustained over time, Brockway maintained his interest in perfecting the pseudoscience of rehabilitation.

▲ Immigration fed the economic engine and grew the underclass. How do attitudes toward immigrants impact our national response to crime?

Library of Congress, http://www.loc.gov/pictures/item/89715190/

Corrections and the Progressive Era (1880–1920)

The Progressive Era in the United States was a period of intense change with the advance of industrialism, accelerated migration to urban centers, unprecedented levels of immigration, the expansion of American colonial empires, and intense racial divisions and violence. Americans fought in foreign wars on several continents. This period was also characterized by the growth of a political ideology that advocated for an expanded role of government and serious questioning about the value of laissez-faire capitalism. Women launched campaigns that lasted for years for voting and other basic civil and legal rights.

The nation was still reeling from the Civil War. Many states, especially in the South, enacted **Jim Crow laws** to force permanent segregation and second-class citizenship on African Americans and Latinos. Lynching reached epidemic levels against African Americans. The war against Native Americans resulted in most native peoples being isolated in remote tribal reservations. In this same period, many Native Americans (especially children) were forced to assimilate through participation in boarding schools, such as the Carlisle Indian Industrial School, and those created by the Bureau of Indian Affairs. Such schools indoctrinated Native American youth with Euro-American culture and separated youth from their families, often permanently. Anti-immigrant sentiment led to laws designed to exclude Asian Americans from citizen rights and to ban further immigration.

The Progressive Era witnessed the rise of the modern criminal justice system. The early ideas about professionalized police were introduced. The courts and the prosecution function expanded. States created bar associations to regulate the legal profession. In Massachusetts and California, legal aid and public defense were created. States such as Illinois and Colorado created a special juvenile court, and several other states quickly joined this movement, some establishing special prisons for youthful lawbreakers.

Boot camp: A program for juvenile offenders characterized by strict discipline, hard physical exercise, and community labor.

Jim Crow laws: Laws enacted after the end of the Civil War that enforced complete racial segregation and that helped to maintain the subjugation of former slaves.

SPOTLIGHT

THE CONVICT LEASE SYSTEM

The practice of slavery in the United States may have been made illegal by a stroke of the pen at the end of the Civil War, but the ideas and attitudes that allowed it to happen were not erased in that same motion. Furthermore, in the post-bellum South, there was an entire population of suddenly freed slaves who were still considered an inferior class that had to be "absorbed" somehow into the economy in a new way. A combination of factors led to a version of slavery that was just as bad as what existed before the war and in some ways may have been worse: the convict lease system.[1]

The need for laborers did not diminish after the Civil War. On the contrary, at the end of the war and after the passage of the Thirteenth Amendment, there was a high demand for labor to rebuild the shattered southern economy and infrastructure. The existing penitentiaries were intended for the master class, and the prospect of bringing in revenue in exchange for the labor of the captive underclass was far more appealing to states than spending to build new penitentiaries for them. This new penal servitude turned the surplus labor into profits from private concerns such as railway corporations, mining companies, and plantations.[2]

The vast majority of the prisoners were African Americans incarcerated in the southern states of Alabama, Arkansas, Kentucky, Georgia, Louisiana, Mississippi, the Carolinas, Tennessee, and even Nebraska.

Often convicted for the pettiest of crimes—simple stealing or fighting—prisoners could find themselves in forced work situations for months or years. The bosses had little

---

Ongoing scandals surrounding prisons and jails led to investigations and the creation of state-level review boards, often known as boards of corrections. Also important in the Progressive Era was the rise of early professional associations such as the American Correctional Association (1870) and the National Probation Association (1907), which were organized to build the profession of corrections and to develop and promote national standards.

After the Progressive Era (1920–1960)

The pace of reform in corrections sped up at the end of the Progressive Era. The nation was in deep economic collapse, with 25% of the American workforce unemployed. Poverty and desperation led many Americans to migrate northward and westward. The enactment of Prohibition led to a rise in criminal violence and a growing law enforcement enterprise. In 1929, the federal government created the Federal Bureau of Investigation and a federal prison system, partly in response to the crime surge during Prohibition and in recognition of the increasing importance of interstate criminal law enforcement.

Prisons in the 1930s began to develop early prison classification systems and to professionalize parole release decisions. The language—if not the reality—of rehabilitation was expanded in corrections. While the actual number of treatment programs remained very limited, states such as California, New York, and Illinois experimented with group therapy and other psychological interventions, including shock therapy. Some observers, such as Clear and his associates, have estimated that the prison system spent less than 5% of its budget on rehabilitation programs.[27] Custody and punishment remained the dominant paradigm of prisons.

Most prisoners were still kept busy primarily with producing license plates, furniture, and other manufactured goods for no wages or for minimal pay. The emerging power of the

incentive to treat captive laborers well; the incentives had to do with increased profits from using this undermarket labor source. The conditions under which prisoners had to work were often brutal and inhumane. Laborers lived in camps that became notorious for filthy conditions and treatment as harsh as slavery. They were flogged for failing to meet their daily production quotas, chained together, forced to eat and drink contaminated food and water, and denied even minimal cleanliness. Indeed, 10 years was considered the maximum that a person could survive in the convict labor camp.[3]

Eventually public sympathy for the victims of this new form of slavery eroded the support that allowed it to exist. Prison labor did not stop, but it did transition away from the private leasing of convicts. Prison labor continued to contribute to state projects and public works. The chain gang became the subsequent norm for prison labor.

QUESTIONS

1   What does prison labor produce, if anything, in your state? (Research this question for discussion.)

2   How does the assumption of a group's inferiority still justify racist policies and practices today?

3   What are some similarities and differences between the convict lease system of the late 1800s and current criminal justice policy and practice?

Notes

1.   PBS 2012

2.   Sellin 1976

3.   Douglass 1893

labor movement and the sustained rates of civilian unemployment meant that most prison industry was used by other government agencies. Interstate commerce in prison goods was banned. On the other hand, in agricultural states, prisoners were often used to defeat farmworkers' unions by picking produce during strikes. In the South, prison chain gangs played a major role in building and repairing roads. The use of prisoners to crush unions was a persistent theme through the 1960s.

The Era of Civil Rights and Community Corrections (1960–1970)

Sociologist LaMar Empey suggested that the 1960s ushered in an era in which there were attempts to extend basic constitutional protections to prison and jail inmates.[28] In particular, federal judges increased the scrutiny of prison conditions in southern prisons. The President's Commission on Law Enforcement and Administration of Justice (1967) echoed the growing concern about the state of corrections and urged the expansion of programs designed to divert individuals from custody and to increase community-based sanctions in lieu of incarceration.

The focus on community corrections fit well with the emerging "fiscal crisis of the state," in which governments were trying to reduce costs in response to a slowing economy and declining tax revenues.[29] New Jersey and California were early leaders in community corrections. For example, California enacted the Probation Subsidy Program, which paid localities to keep people on probation. The movement was supported at the national level, and even conservative politicians such as California Governor Ronald Reagan and President Richard Nixon gave verbal and political support for managing more individuals in the community. Massachusetts went so far as to shut down all of its state juvenile prisons in favor of community services.[30] Researchers argued that these efforts were largely

▲ Prison riots, such as the one in Attica in 1971, made headlines and focused attention on the tension, violence, and poor conditions inside prisons.

© Everett Collection/Newscom

motivated by a need to reduce state costs for controlling behavior.[31] Others argued that rehabilitation programs were ineffective and violated basic civil rights.[32] The same arguments were used to downsize state hospitals for the mentally ill and the developmentally disabled. It was argued that better and cheaper care would be provided in the community. Critics of community corrections and other efforts to move troubled and troublesome individuals out of institutions argued that the community alternatives were never funded, moving the mentally ill into the jails or to homelessness.

The Prisons Explode (1970–1980)

There had always been occasional prison riots, but in 1971 the eruption of New York's Attica Correctional Facility turned especially lethal after a dispute between guards and prisoners escalated and the inmates took over the prison and held the custodial staff as hostages. The inmates gained control of sections of the prison, began listing their grievances, and entered into negotiations with state officials. The inmates wanted to negotiate directly with then Governor Nelson Rockefeller, who continued to refuse to do so. New York State corrections officials reacted several days later with a military response. Almost a decade later in 1980, the New Mexico State Penitentiary experienced a deadly riot that took the lives of 38 inmates and guards. An additional hostage died of injuries almost a month later.

This and other major prison riots dramatized how inmates were still abused in prisons and the lack of progress in actualizing the rehabilitative ideal. Prison inmates were becoming influenced by growing community political movements such as the Black Muslims and the Black Panther Party. In California, inmates formed a prisoners' union to assert their human rights.

Powerful street gangs such as the Crips and the Bloods, the Mexican Mafia, Nuestra Familia, and the Blackstone Rangers were also growing in influence in prisons around the country. These developments led to contradictory demands to reform prison conditions or to tighten prison security and treat convicts more harshly.

The Demise of Rehabilitation and the Get-Tough Era (1970–Present)

Growing skepticism about rehabilitation grew through the 1970s and 1990s. An influential study by Robert Martinson asserted that nothing works in terms of reducing rates of recidivism, although he later recanted that view.[33] More conservative voices such as James Q. Wilson and Charles Murray echoed this pessimistic view and urged reliance on harsh punishments to deter crime.[34] John DiIulio warned of the rise of a generation of "superpredators."[35]

There were calls to stiffen sentencing penalties, eliminate plea bargaining, and build more prisons. States passed hundreds of laws designed to lengthen prison terms, make specific sentences mandatory, and make parole release harder to achieve. The epitome of this movement was the enactment of three-strikes laws and the restriction of any time reductions for inmate good behavior.

Even more ominous, conservative politicians argued that inmates were being coddled and that the basic conditions of confinement should be tougher. During the Reagan and (George H. W.) Bush years (when there was a significant decline in the real wages of average Americans), the "soft lives" of inmates became the topic of much resentment. These feelings were translated into penal policies that removed from American prisons many educational and rehabilitative services, such as exercise equipment. In 1995, Congress enacted the Prison Litigation Reform Act (PLRA), which asserted that lawsuits by inmates were out of control and needed to be restricted.

Even probation and parole took on the more punitive ethos of the day. Community supervision was dominated by a philosophy of "surveil them, nail them, and jail them." These developments led to skyrocketing growth in prison populations, severe crowding, and further deterioration of prison conditions. There was some investment in new prison construction, but not nearly enough to accommodate the surging inmate population. The public remained very reluctant to support new taxes for prison expansion.

As the U.S. economy stumbled in the late 1990s and early 2000s, states sought ways to cut their corrections costs. One development was the expansion of private prisons, which were alleged to be cheaper than state-run facilities. As the fiscal crisis deepened, many states began concerted efforts to reduce prison and jail populations and to close empty facilities. After years of growing prison and jail populations, some states were witnessing declining institutional populations. Even prominent conservative leaders organized a lobbying effort known as "Right on Crime" that argued that the get-tough movement had gone too far and that expanding community corrections was warranted. Archconservatives, such as the evangelist Pat Robertson, began to argue against the moral (and fiscal) irresponsibility of overincarceration. The potential success of the new politics of decarceration remains to be seen.

. . . .

SUMMARY

Ideas about crime and punishment are rooted in social structures and culture. Political ideology, economic realities, and class, race, and gender norms all exert a powerful influence on systems of punishment.

By controlling specific individuals, penal systems suppress and control whole classes of people whose obedience is essential to the maintenance of the social and economic order, especially for the benefit of the privileged and empowered classes. Slavery is both an extreme expression of the exertion of power over an oppressed class of people for economic gain and an extreme form of the imposition of punishment. It is also directly linked to the evolution of the American penal system. Eruptions of social turmoil have occurred throughout history and are a consequence of this systematized oppression.

From the fall of the Roman Empire to the early Middle Ages, the principal responses to crime were designed to regulate the relationships among members of a given class—fines for the wealthy and enslaved, hard labor for the poor.

In the Middle Ages, an increasingly destitute rural population began to migrate to cities, adding to poverty and competition. The dominant methods of punishment during this time were acts of brutal physical torture and either agonizing death or (the quicker and more humane) beheading or hanging carried out in the public square for all to see.

Galley slavery and transportation as a form of exile played an important role in the viability of colonialism. These practices later gave way to imprisonment in institutions.

Extracting revenue from the administration of justice was a prime factor in transforming the private system of arbitration to a public system of centralized control. The exploitation of prisoner labor was introduced at the end of the 16th century. The early forms of the prison were the European and English houses of corrections, where inmates were forced to work. This inmate labor source has often been in economic competition with the free and law-abiding pool of workers.

In the United States, the demand for prison labor has increased and decreased with changing economic conditions over time. Prisons provide labor, in both rural and urban settings. But a surplus of labor led to a movement away from prisoners as laborers. Large-scale prison idleness is an issue when prison labor is less in demand. Isolation emerged as a strategy for penitence as well as managing idle prisoners. During the Enlightenment, Cesare Beccaria argued for proportional punishment, humane conditions of confinement, and renouncing brutality.

Harsh corporal punishment, along with military regimentation, reemerged under the influence of Zebulon Brockway, whose ideas were based on the premise that criminals were morally inferior.

The modern criminal and juvenile justice systems arose during the Progressive Era. Prison classification, federal law enforcement, and professionalizing corrections administration were all developed during this time. However, even modern prisons must deal with the tension inherent between the jailers and the jailed. Current policy debates on what are the most effective and cost-conscious ways of addressing crime can be enlightened by an accurate analysis of how penal systems have evolved from social and economic conditions.

DISCUSSION QUESTIONS

1. Choose an era in history and discuss ways in which modes of punishment help support the social order of the day.

2. Discuss the ways in which the modern-day poor are criminalized and the historical traces of that phenomenon.

3. How have prisons supplied labor for industry? Discuss the economic value of prison labor.

4. Discuss the linkages between slavery and prison labor.

5. How did the Enlightenment philosophers contribute to current ideas on punishment?

6. How does solitary confinement allow or thwart the goals of prison labor?

7. How did the ideas of Brockway help or harm the cause of prisoners?

8. How did the Progressive Era contribute to modern corrections?

9. Discuss the growth of prisons and the tension between prison reforms and the needs of prison administrators.

10. Discuss the forces that limit the state's ability to expand the prison system.

KEY TERMS

Abolitionists, 30

Auburn System, 30

Boot camp, 32

Classification system, 33

Enlightenment, 26

Galley slavery, 24

Global positioning systems, 20

Houses of correction, 19

Indeterminate sentencing, 31

Jim Crow laws, 33

Jurisprudence, 18

Penal systems, 18

Penology, 18

Pennsylvania system, 29

Transportation, 24

NOTES

1. Williams 1973, 480
2. Sellin 1976
3. Sellin, in Rusche and Kirchheimer 1968, vi
4. Barnes and Teeters 1945
5. Scull 1977
6. Rusche and Kirchheimer 1968, 6
7. Sellin 1976
8. Rusche and Kirchheimer 1968

9. Rusche and Kirchheimer 1968, 11
10. von Hentig 1973
11. Sellin 1976
12. Thompson et al. 1975
13. Rusche and Kirchheimer 1968
14. Sellin 1944
15. Rusche and Kirchheimer 1968, 50
16. Hughes 1986
17. Mabillon 1724
18. Beccaria [1764] 1963
19. Howard, in Rusche and Kirchheimer 1968, 85
20. Murray 1984
21. Rusche and Kirchheimer 1968
22. Brockway 1912, 64

23. Krisberg 1975
24. Miller 1991
25. Ibid.
26. McKenzie and Armstrong 2004
27. Clear, Reisig, and Cole 2012
28. Empey 1973
29. Liazos 1974; O'Connor 1973
30. Miller 1991
31. Lemert and Dill 1978; Lerman 1973
32. Kittrie 1971; Schur 1973
33. Martinson 1974, 1979
34. Murray and Cox 1979; Wilson 1983
35. DiIiulio 1995

$SAGE edge™

Sharpen your skills with SAGE edge at edge.sagepub.com/krisberg

SAGE edge for students provides a personalized approach to help you accomplish your coursework goals in an easy-to-use learning environment. This site includes action plans, mobile-friendly eFlashcards and web quizzes as well as web, audio, and video resources and links to SAGE journal articles.

© ZUMA Press, Inc. / Alamy

3 The Purpose of Punishment and Sentencing Trends

Sentencing policies and practices exert a huge influence on the corrections system. They determine which individuals are managed through which correctional options. Sentencing and sentencing requirements, which are often dictated by law, affect the length of time that persons remain under correctional supervision and generally set the conditions for correctional social control. This chapter describes how the sentencing process works, reviews the underlying theories and ideologies that guide sentencing, examines how these theories influence practices in the correctional system, and looks at emerging sentencing trends.

How Sentencing Works

After conviction in the criminal justice system, the court makes a determination on the appropriate penal response to the offense and the offender, which is called a sentence. The sentencing decision is determined by state laws and by the recommendations of prosecutors, defense attorneys, and the probation staff that conduct presentence investigations and suggest community supervision options to the court. In many cases, a parole board determines when a person will complete his or her incarceration and the terms of the release. Parole boards also decide whether the released prisoner will return to prison for violating the rules of parole. Incarcerated offenders may sometimes have their initial sentences shortened based on court orders that cap the size of prison or jail populations. Inmates also may earn time off their total sentences based on "good behavior" and participation in certain approved education or treatment programs. So the popular image of the judge rendering a sentence from the bench is partially true, but the sentencing process is highly complex—made even more so by a wave of new laws.

Sentencing laws and practices vary widely among the 50 states and the federal system. In most cases, these laws specify the expected penalty for various crimes. Often they define a wide range of punishments from which the court can select its preferred option. Typically, terms of incarceration are bounded by minimum and maximum limits. The actual term is set by a parole board at some time in the future. These are referred to as systems of indeterminate sentencing.

California, Maine, Washington, and Indiana have determinate sentencing schemes, which define in more exact terms the sentence that should be given to a defendant. There is usually an upper limit, a bottom limit, and a middle sentence. Judges can depart from those determinate sentences by stating certain aggravating or mitigating factors that call for a lessening or an increasing of the sentence, such as whether the defendant was under the domination of another person or whether he or she has an extensive criminal record. Some states and the federal court system have sentencing guidelines that use a variation of these defined sentencing options. In contrast to states in which the defined sentences appear in statutes, those with guidelines rely on a sentencing commission that decides on the range of sentencing options. More than 20 states and the federal government utilize sentencing commissions. The decisions of these commissions must be approved by the

Conviction: When an individual is found by a court of law to be guilty of a criminal offense.

Sentence: The punishment declared by the court to a defendant for being found guilty for a crime, such as a period of incarceration, a period of community supervision, or payment of a fine.

Presentence investigations: An investigation of a person convicted of a crime, which is used to produce a presentence investigation report to the court and to inform the judge and the sentencing outcome.

Parole board: A panel of individuals that decides whether an offender should be released from prison to parole after serving at least a minimum portion of his or her sentence, as prescribed by the sentencing judge.

Determinate sentence: A sentence to confinement for a fixed or minimum period that is specified by statute.

 5 To be able to name and discuss four theories of sentencing.

 7 To be aware of the social factors that influence sentencing policy.

6 To gain an understanding of restorative justice philosophy and practice.

legislature but can be adopted via passive consent—in other words, when the legislature allows the report of the commission to stand.

Sentencing commissions were created in the 1970s to attempt to regulate the presumed disparity of sentences within states by individual judges. They were advocated for by those who argued that sentencing should be developed by experts in penology and reflect the latest research findings. Some states attempted to use guidelines to control their prison and jail populations. In practice, states with guidelines and the federal system are actually mixed models that have legislatively mandated sentences along with commission findings. Structured sentencing states use a grid that looks at the severity of the current offense and the length and content of the defendant's prior criminal record.

As complicated as these sentencing schemes appear, they became even more muddled after a series of U.S. Supreme Court decisions (*U.S. v. Booker*; *U.S. v. Fan Fan*) that required that the facts used in "structured sentencing systems" be proved before a jury or agreed to through a plea agreement.[1] These cases resulted in increased judicial discretion, even within highly structured sentencing schemes.

Most important, sentencing remains an "insider's game," little understood by victims, offenders, other criminal justice actors, the media, or the public at large. Most governors or legislators have only a very limited knowledge as to how the sentencing system functions. Prosecutors exert a huge influence on sentencing policies, because elected officials assume that the prosecutors are experts in the process. The expertise of the defense bar is sometimes dismissed because it is presumed to be a biased advocacy role. The role of corrections officials as experts in sentencing has been diminished over time. Sentencing, like most other aspects of criminal justice policy, has become increasingly politicized.

It is common that after a horrific crime is committed by a formerly convicted person, elected officials will rail against the leniency or unfairness of the sentencing process, which may have been, in fact, carried out to the letter of the law.

Some in the defense bar are now presenting their own informal presentence reports, and retaining experts specifically to prepare these reports. The defense bar assumes that if its reports are more thorough and better presented than the reports submitted by the probation department, the judge might lean toward the defense's sentencing recommendations. This is especially true if the sentencing plan by the defense is very detailed and includes a plan for paying for needed services such as drug treatment. However, there is a significant cost for a privately prepared presentence report; only convicted persons with private attorneys and those who can afford to pay for them are likely to benefit from this strategy. The preparation of a presentence report for the court is central to the sentencing process. Although convicted persons have some ability to challenge the findings and recommendations of these reports, the legal deck is stacked against the convicted person.

Sentencing guidelines: A set of sentencing minimums and maximums for specific crimes. Guidelines were designed to bring more judicial uniformity to sentencing policy.

Sentencing commission: A professional panel charged with determining sentencing options for a given jurisdiction.

Disparity: An imbalance or inconsistency, a great difference. In the context of corrections, we usually speak of a racial imbalance of the effects of correctional policy and practice.

The Presentence Report

Probation staff prepare presentence reports, which organize the pertinent information for the sentencing judge. Probation staff have wide latitude in how these reports are organized, the specific content, the level of detail, and the sentencing recommendations. To begin with, the report examines the severity of the current offense. The probation officer reviews police reports and statements made by the defendant to law enforcement and prosecutors, as well as any prior contacts the defendant has had with the police, the courts, or the corrections system. The presentence report notes any outstanding arrests, court (bench) warrants, or immigration holds for the individual, including those from other jurisdictions.

Another important part of the report has to do with the likelihood that the defendant will reoffend in the future, as measured by a risk assessment instrument (RAI). The RAI helps to evaluate risk level by ranking offense severity and offense history, among other factors. A presentence investigation may rely on "hearsay evidence," and the defendant does not have the right to confront his or her accusers, as he or she would have in criminal court.

Presentence reports cover significant safety factors, such as whether the defendant allegedly used a weapon as part of the crime, and medical reports about the harm caused to victims. Increasingly, presentence reports include statements by the victim or victims about the emotional, physical, and economic impacts of the crime on the victim's life. Typically, the probation officer will conduct an in-depth interview with the defendant to determine whether he or she feels responsibility or remorse for having committed the crime. The presentence report may also determine if the defendant has any insight into the factors that led to the crime and identify the defendant's potential amenability for rehabilitative services.

The probation officer could, but is not always required to, interview the defendant's family members, neighbors, and employers. These interviews may suggest the potential for rehabilitation and help to uncover the sorts of community support available to an individual. For example, an employer might suggest that a probationer is an important and very positive contributor to the workplace—that incarceration of the defendant would create a hardship for the employer. Some have argued that a similar evaluation be made on behalf of the children of a convicted person, as children often suffer due to the absence of their parent. The courts have considered these arguments but have typically not given parental responsibilities the same weight as employment issues.

Presentence reports also explore the significance of the probation client's physical and mental health issues. Alcohol and drug dependency are sometimes presented as mitigating factors in the offense but may also be considered impediments to rehabilitation. Clients may be required to submit to drug testing as part of the postconviction process. Similarly, the presentence report can cover mental health issues, so long as state and federal laws covering medical confidentiality and the doctor–patient relationship are not violated. The client, with advice of counsel, may voluntarily offer up this information. Presentence reports also include information about developmental and physical disabilities.

Another key area addressed in presentence reports is the convicted person's social relationships (both positive and negative). The probation officer must determine whether the client associates with antisocial peers or groups. Here again, the standards for determining these issues and how to interpret them for the court are not well defined in law.

There is a wide range in the quality of presentence investigations, how probation officers use or ignore the body of information that they collect, and how this information is actually used by the court. Presentence reports often contain the judgments of the probation staff on the person's character and personality. There may also be speculation—albeit informed by professional experience—by the probation officer about the motives for the crime. As noted earlier, sentences may be largely determined by the results of plea bargains or by statutes that mandate the penalties for various crimes. This means that, though presentence reports may be used by correctional personnel, these analyses may in the end play a small role in the actual determinate sentencing decision. However, in instances in which judges can exercise their own discretion, the opinions stated in the presentence report will be very important. Research suggests that judges follow the recommendations of the presentence reports in over 90% of the decisions that they make. This high level of agreement between the bench and probation recommendations may also be a reflection of probation officers' anticipation of judicial values and expectations. This suggests that sentencing reform efforts must go beyond judicial training and reach out to those preparing the presentence reports.

Risk assessment instrument: A tool used to examine relevant factors to measure an offender's risk of recidivism or risk of violent behavior.

Plea bargain: An agreement between the prosecutor and defendant whereby the defendant pleads guilty to a (usually lesser) charge in return for some concession from the prosecutor.

What is an appropriate balance between judges and prosecutors in discretion over sentencing?

© iStockphoto.com /Deborah Cheramie

Risk and Needs Assessment

Concerns about the uneven quality of presentence reports and attention to precisely allocating scarce resources where they can have the most positive effect have led to the use of very structured risk and needs assessment tools in the sentencing process. To be reliable, these tools should be validated through empirical studies. Many departments have made a concerted effort to develop tools appropriate for their specific population. The key is to structure the presentence report as a series of factors that are linked by research evidence to the likelihood that the defendant will reoffend. These tools contain a limited set of factors that are given a weighted numerical value. The scores are then related to "presumptive" sentences. These recommendations may not be followed by the probation department or the court, but there is usually a process that requires probation officers to state their reasons to the courts and justify an override.

Risk factors: Individual characteristics and background found by research to be correlated to criminal behavior, especially to reoffending during or after correction-system involvement, such as current offense type and severity, prior offense history and system involvement, and mental health history.

These assessment tools enhance the risk and needs profile more than using professional judgment alone. Advancements will no doubt build on existing models and research from the field, factoring in the particular circumstances and priorities of local jurisdictions.

There are two types of assessments. The first type measures static factors such as age, criminal background, and current offense type. These are usually done fairly quickly and are used as "triage," to conduct the first "sorting" of defendants into broad risk categories. The second type assesses more dynamic factors. These assessments usually involve a much longer set of questions and measure factors that have to do with the defendant's tendency to commit crime. These are referred to as criminogenic needs and focus on changeable factors such as antisocial behavior, personality traits, and associates; family and marital status; substance abuse status; and whether the defendant is employed or in school.

Criminogenic needs: Changeable characteristics and circumstances found in research to be correlated to criminal behavior, especially that place an individual at risk of reoffending during or after correction-systems involvement, such as drug addiction or joblessness

Risk factors are of a largely static nature and are based on the type and severity of the offense leading to the current incarceration, prior offenses and system involvement, and behavioral and mental health history.

Criminogenic needs are also correlated with a likelihood of reoffending, but are generally of a dynamic or changeable nature. They may include antisocial behavior; antisocial personality traits, attitudes, or peers; family and marital dysfunction; substance abuse; low achievement and stability in school and employment; and lack of prosocial leisure activities.[2]

Noncriminogenic needs are related to criminogenic needs but have not been found to directly correlate to reoffending. They include anxiety, vague feelings of emotional distress, and low self-esteem or ambition. Major mental health problems such as schizophrenia and manic depression and a history of victimization are also in this category. Although they may be valuable in understanding how parole officers and other providers may best interact with the parolee, it can be wasteful of time and resources and generally detrimental to devote too much time and resources to discussing and managing these factors. Although these issues may need to be addressed to facilitate other work, reducing criminogenic needs should be the central goal of parole supervision and programming.

The implementation of these more formalized risk and needs screening tools is still relatively new, but their great promise is to reduce arbitrary and capricious decision making in the sentencing process.

Sentencing Theories

The evolution of correctional systems is deeply rooted in social and economic transformations. The explanations or rationales for penal systems have also changed over time. The theories are the cultural supports behind methods of punishment. They are embedded in law and political discourse and reflect powerful cultural and religious doctrines. This is the language through which the changes in corrections are justified. Major penal ideologies should be reviewed and evaluated in light of existing research and criminal justice practices. These theories may play a role in reforms of correctional systems.

It is important to note that penal systems often incorporate multiple ideologies. Although a single theory may dominate a specific historical period, all of these theories of penal systems exert an influence. Further, different parts of the criminal justice system may embrace differing or competing ideologies. Media and political perspectives are not always aligned with ideologies embraced by the public at large. For example, many recent public opinion polls suggest that the public supports approaches to corrections that are grounded in ideals of rehabilitation and treatment, especially for less serious offenders.[3] However, the dominant political rhetoric is still focused on ideologies of deterrence and retributive justice. Though political leaders can help shape the broad outlines of public thinking on corrections, influence can work in the opposite direction. Evolving public views can sometimes be reflected in changes in official policies and practices, or at least the attempt of political leaders to accommodate, or appear to accommodate, altered public viewpoints.

The writings of academics and public intellectuals may also play a role in changing penal philosophies. Most often the work of the research community is very selectively utilized to justify and support various correctional philosophies; political leaders use research results to support their claims to objectivity and fairness. The viewpoints of correctional leaders may also help shape penal theories.

In the past, the writings and speeches of leading correctional administrators were influential in the public conversation on corrections. In addition, professional associations such as the American Correctional Association and the American Probation and Parole Association played very active roles in these debates. Some have observed that this style of correctional leadership has been greatly diminished. For example, noted penologist Allen Breed has argued that contemporary corrections is devoid of real leaders. The often articulate and visionary administrators of the past have generally been replaced by skilled managers who know how to follow the orders of political leaders and who are averse to risk.[4] Professional correctional groups have become far more modest in their efforts to

Noncriminogenic needs: Individual characteristics and circumstances that may be or seem to be related to criminal behavior but which research has not found to be directly correlated to offending or reoffending, such as low self-esteem and depression.

Retributive justice: A theory of justice that sees punishment and exacting just deserts as the best response to crime.

reform correctional systems, relying more on attempts to institute minimal operational standards. Moreover, the professional groups have become heavily dependent on businesses that market their goods and services to correctional agencies. Professional meetings have essentially become "trade shows," relegating discussions about policy and programmatic concerns to little more than window-dressing status. Another important source of correctional philosophy and potential reforms has been nonprofit advocacy groups and "think tanks" such as the Vera Institute of Justice and the National Council on Crime and Delinquency (NCCD). These and other nonprofit groups are financially supported by private philanthropies that wish to advance certain approaches to correctional policy. These groups have generally shaped correctional theories far more than university-based researchers.

In the following sections, we will review the major penal philosophies that have guided the history of sentencing and punishment and continue to form the intellectual legacy of contemporary corrections.

Retributive Justice

"An eye for an eye"—this simple formulation is at the core of many of the world's belief systems. The underlying ideology is that punishment is society's price for the harm done by lawbreakers. Retribution is assumed to be a normal human response to victimization of individuals or social groups. Retributive justice is presumed to satisfy basic human instincts to exact a price from those who offend us or our social group. It assumes that the criminal justice system is in place to punish rather than rehabilitate offenders. Retribution is a powerful communication method that allows social groups to define their core values, teaching all observers about what is valued and what violates basic cultural tenets.

A central issue in the ideology of retributive justice is the proper calibration of penalties. Wildly excessive punishments might be perceived as arbitrary and cruel. Even under slavery, states enacted **slave codes** that attempted to regulate what owners could do to their human chattel. The slave codes recognized that excessive cruelty could lead to rebellion among the slaves. Likewise, penal philosophers, especially writers such as Cesare Beccaria and Jeremy Bentham, advocated for a more nuanced and calibrated penal system that was tied to the severity of the offense. These Enlightenment thinkers also argued

Some people want the issue of punishment to be a simple matter. They often site the Bible's Old Testament to help make the case that simplicity is not only possible but desirable.

© iStockphoto.com /forgiss

Slave codes: U.S. laws under slavery that governed the relationship between slaves and slave owners and that gave slave owners absolute power over slaves.

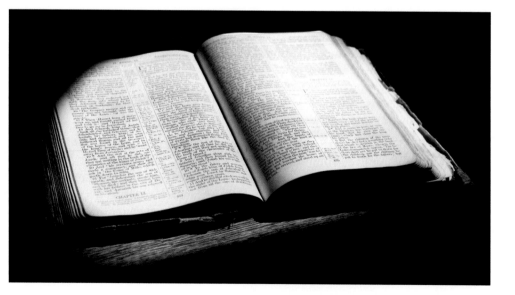

◀ Our court system is based on ideals of fairness and balance, but what constitutes balance, or justice? For example, who should determine whether a punishment fits the crime?

© iStockphoto.com / VladimirCetinski

for a measured penal response, fearing that overly harsh punishments would lead juries to acquit otherwise guilty defendants or would foment social revolutions. Unbounded retributive justice is consistent with a totalitarian political system that is enforced by the military. An unrestrained retributive penal system was not consistent with emerging republican political traditions. For example, the founders of the American political tradition rejected many aspects of the British legal system, which was associated with colonial oppression.

Exacting revenge is a powerful human urge. It resonates with many traditional religious doctrines and is expressed in sacred texts such as the Bible and the Koran. It is still at the core of the rhetoric of modern politicians who try to appeal to the mass of voters by emphasizing harsh penalties. "Do the crime, do the time." Further, retributive justice reflects public attitudes of resentment and fear of serious lawbreakers.

In his influential book *Doing Justice*, British criminologist Andrew Von Hirsch attempted to resurrect the Enlightenment tradition of limiting retributive justice through the concept of "just deserts."[5] He articulated the view that excessive punishment undercuts the legitimacy of the sentencing system. He further argued that other penal philosophies, such as rehabilitation, actually pose serious dangers to human liberty. Von Hirsch imagined a precise, even mathematical calculation of the right penalty based on an objective analysis of the harm caused by the offender to the victim or the community in general. This theory of sentencing received strong acceptance in jurisprudential and criminological circles and was also expressed by others as the philosophic foundation of the movement toward determinate or fixed penalties in sentencing.[6] Just deserts appeared as a potential antidote to unchecked state power that was observed by several criminologists and corrections practitioners.[7] Von Hirsch did concede that a potential problem in his theory of punishment was in actually establishing the "anchor point" to ground a whole system of penalties. Without a sound foundation, the scale of the system of punishment was easily corrupted. As the criminal justice policy developments of the 1980s and 1990s unfolded, this "fatal flaw" in just deserts theory was revealed as policymakers competed to show how tough they could be on crime. Penalties escalated throughout this period, driven by the political rhetoric of retributive justice.

Deterrence

Deterrence is related to retributive justice, but is a very different justification for penal practice. This theory of punishment is perhaps the most widely accepted in Western criminal law systems. It rests on the assumption that the goal of punishment is not reactive but rather preventive. Punishment is intended to head off future criminal behavior. This philosophy assumes that humans are rational creatures who calculate the costs and benefits of criminal misconduct. Deterrence theory rests on the belief in an economic model of how individuals and groups make decisions to obey or break the law.

Deterrence can operate at both an individual and a societal level. Individual deterrence refers to the idea that a specific potential offender will avoid criminal acts because of the odds that he or she will be captured and punished. This idea is prominent in efforts to head off repeat offending, or recidivism. General deterrence refers to a broader message to the community that certain acts will likely result in adverse consequences for anyone committing them. General deterrence is assumed to be the force that stops the average person from breaking the law.

The logic of deterrence consists of a calculation of the necessary penalties to shift the potential offender's cost–benefit ratio in favor of law-abiding behavior. Although it is easy to imagine how the economics of punishment operates in the sphere of financial and business crimes, it is less clear how the logic of deterrence operates in situations that are highly emotional, impetuous, or unpremeditated.

A number of studies have attempted to demonstrate or discredit the deterrent effects of tougher penalties, especially capital punishment. In general, these analyses show little evidence for a strong deterrent effect, except for some white-collar crimes, traffic violations, and crimes committed by middle-class lawbreakers. Research on the deterrent impact on crimes such as domestic violence and drunk driving suggests that lower-class and unemployed defendants show little or no sensitivity to deterrence. As folk singer Bob Dylan wrote, "When you ain't got nothin', you got nothin' to lose."

Research by Zimring and others also suggests that deterrence effects are influenced not just by the severity of penalties but also by the celerity of punishment (how quickly the punishment follows the crime) and the offender's probability of being apprehended.[8] You can't be punished if you don't get caught. Deterrence is further weakened by the offender's mental capacity to link current actions with future consequences. This means that deterrence is generally less effective for youth and for those with mental impairments—those who have difficulty connecting action and consequence. Further, there are nonmonetary rewards for criminal behavior such as prestige in criminal subcultures, friendships among "thieves," and other social and economic pressures to break the law. Chronic offenders, including those in prison, often proclaim that they are too smart to get apprehended, even if their present incarceration proves them wrong. All these forces tend to weaken the argument that tougher penalties deter crime.

Regarding general deterrence, it is not clear that potential offenders are closely tuned in to marginal increases or decreases in penalties. We may intend to send messages to offenders about the increased costs of committing crime, but the messages may not be received. Further, there is ample evidence that marginal reductions in punishment, such as accelerated release of inmates, has not had any measurable negative effect on recidivism or community crime rates.[9] In other words, releasing low-level offenders from prison slightly early does not result in a crime increase.

Still, the logic of deterrence is a core of Anglo-American jurisprudence. Lawmakers believe in deterrence despite evidence of its ineffectiveness. Manipulating penalties to try to

Recidivism: The return to criminal behavior after being supervised for a conviction. In research, recidivism is measured over a given period of time (e.g., 12 months following release from prison) and is defined in various ways, such as arrest, conviction, or incarceration for a new offense.

◀ Most people don't plan to get caught committing a crime. Public awareness of law enforcement practice is a key ingredient of deterrence.

© Associated Press/ Keith R. Stevenson

reduce undesirable behavior is a tactic heavily relied upon in the political arena. Unfortunately, deterrence is overrated as a mechanism for controlling or changing a wide range of human behavior.

Rehabilitation

Although originally grounded in religious ideology, including the Catholic Church or the emerging Protestant denominations such as the Religious Society of Friends (Quakers), the modern secular concept of rehabilitation emerged during the late 19th and early 20th centuries. The core idea was that the corrections system could engage inmates in activities including work, education, religion, counseling, and other therapeutic interventions that could supposedly transform offenders into law-abiding citizens. The new scientific disciplines of medicine, psychology, and psychiatry were harnessed by advocates of offender rehabilitation to accomplish this goal. Practitioners were developing a technology to fix broken souls and to return them to productive lives.

Consistent with the rehabilitative ideal was the concept of indeterminate sentencing. Presumed experts in human behavior would judge when a prisoner's behavior had improved enough to indicate true reform and warranted release. Incarceration was viewed as part of an overall system of graduated sanctions to control offenders that also included community supervision. In the 1920s, some states, Illinois was one, developed predictive tools designed to mathematically compute the odds that a potential parolee would succeed upon release.[10] Prison systems sponsored research on inmates to identify the key elements of effective rehabilitative approaches. The American Correctional Association and most leading corrections practitioners of the day embraced rehabilitation as a major goal of the penal system.

The concept of rehabilitation advanced most rapidly with juvenile offenders, who were thought to be more amenable to reform. The jurisprudence of the juvenile court was based on rehabilitation. In adult corrections, rehabilitation was based more on rhetoric than on actual practices, where only minimal investments were made in education and counseling programs. Inmate labor or enforced idleness still dominated the daily routines of prisons. Parole boards were dominated by political appointees with a strong bias toward law enforcement. Few parole boards included experts in the behavioral sciences or social work. Release decisions were heavily influenced by political considerations or outright bribery by influential inmates or their advocates. The idea of rehabilitation was popular in academic circles, law reform groups, and professional associations.

The fiction that rehabilitation was actually occurring in prisons provided a legal rationale for a hands-off approach by the appellate courts when due process and equal protection issues were raised about sentencing or correctional and parole decision making. It was argued that excessive formality and regulation guided by the U.S. Constitution would interfere with the rehabilitative process.

During the 1960s, there was mounting skepticism from across the political spectrum. Critics of rehabilitation argued that (1) there was scant evidence that rehabilitation actually succeeded very often, (2) rehabilitation actually was an excuse for "coddling criminals," and (3) rehabilitation programs could trample on the rights of convicted felons or were being applied in a racially discriminatory manner. Such views came from very different political and philosophic quarters, and their confluence led to a dramatic decline in the support for rehabilitation as a legitimate goal of sentencing and the corrections systems.

The work of Robert Martinson and his colleagues suggested that there was very little evidence showing the positive value of most rehabilitation programs to reduce reoffending.[11] His influential essay "What Works" fit perfectly with an emerging political consensus that favored deterrence and incapacitation as the dominant rationales for sentencing and corrections systems. Some years later, Martinson recanted these views, although his reversal was not given nearly as much attention in the media or political circles as the first essay.[12] Other critics suggested that rehabilitation programs actually made offenders worse by sticking them with negative labels that could not be overcome.[13] New York University sociologist Edwin Schur even coined the phrase "Radical Non-Intervention," suggesting that the state should intervene (i.e., rehabilitate) as little as possible.[14]

Liberal critics of the justice system decried the lack of due process and equal protection afforded convicted felons under the banner of rehabilitation. The famous U.S. Supreme Court decision *In re Gault* described the treatment approach of the juvenile court as a "kangaroo court."[15] Civil libertarians expressed concerns that prisoners were held for too long and for arbitrary and capricious reasons.

More conservative observers disliked rehabilitation and thought of it as "soft on crime." Their ideology did not include the idea that human beings could be perfected through education and other social interventions. They favored harsh penalties instead.

Beginning in the 1980s, many states revised their penal codes to emphasize punishment as the primary goal of the corrections system, to restrict the discretionary release of prisoners, to lengthen terms of incarceration, and to make prison conditions more unpleasant to offenders. The rehabilitative ideal had lost its political currency.

◄ Cycles of imprisonment, release, reoffending, and reincarceration are sometimes called the revolving door of justice. The question of rehabilitation centers on the dilemma of recidivism, its causes and its remedies.

© iStockphoto.com / dlewis33

The most direct result of the demise of the ideology of rehabilitation was an extraordinary growth in the numbers and rates of people who were in prisons and jails. Prison and jail conditions deteriorated, and education, job training, and counseling programs all but disappeared.

But "what goes in must come out." The growth of incarceration led to a commensurate number of prisoners who were eventually released from custody. All but the very small fraction of inmates who were "lifers" were freed shortly thereafter. Jeremy Travis illustrated the social and community consequences of a vast number of ex-prisoners who were returning home.[16] Many of these returning inmates were worse off after the prison experience, having high rates of substance abuse and mental illnesses and very poor life skills. An emerging focus on reentry has led to some limited federal legislation (the Second Chance Act), signaling a beginning, however limited, to investments in rehabilitation programs for prisoners and for those on parole. Rehabilitation is making a political comeback in terms of voter attitudes and the perspectives of correctional practitioners.[17]

Incapacitation

The incapacitation theory of punishment suggests that the principal goal of the penal system is to separate offenders from the community. It does not assume that punishment makes offenders more or less criminal; rather, it prevents them from victimizing people outside of prison. Crimes occurring inside of prison and jails are not accounted for in this calculation.

Incapacitation rests on the assumption that a small number of offenders commit the vast majority of serious crimes. Isolating them behind bars presumably subtracts those crimes from the overall crime rate. Some observers such as Edwin Zedlewski asserted that the savings produced by the reduction in crime more than made up for the cost of incarceration.[18] Zedlewski's calculations suggested that each year of additional prison time per prisoner saved

YOU DECIDE

Revising an LWOP Sentence Received as a Juvenile

When J. G. was 16 years old, he and two fellow gang members attempted a carjacking that resulted in the murder of a 31-year-old mother of two small children. J. G.'s two codefendants, who were age 18 at the time of the crime, pled guilty to voluntary manslaughter, and each received a 10-year prison sentence. Hoping for leniency because he was not the shooter and did not initiate the carjacking, J. G. chose to go to trial. He was convicted and sentenced to life without the possibility of parole, or LWOP, because "he was a co-conspirator in a felony that resulted in a death." He was too young to receive the death penalty under state law. State juvenile authorities conducted a diagnostic assessment of J. G. and recommended that he be sent to a state juvenile facility rather than an adult prison. The judge ignored this assessment and decided to make an example out of the case to stop gang behavior among youth.

J. G. has already spent 22 years in state maximum-security prisons. While incarcerated, J. G. earned his high school degree and certifications in a number of trades. He has no history of mental health issues, nor has he been involved in prison gang activities. He received only four disciplinary charges over his two decades in high-security prisons, and none of these were for violent crimes or weapons offenses. His file contains several notations by corrections officers suggesting that J. G. is very cooperative and a good worker.

Under a newly enacted law, J. G. is entitled to petition the original sentencing court for a change of his sentence to life with the possibility of parole. If the petition were granted by the court, J. G. would then have to request a review by the parole board for his eventual release.

YOU DECIDE: **Given the recent research on the brain development of adolescents, should the court grant J. G.'s petition and give him an opportunity for release by the parole board?**

the taxpayers $430,000 in averted victim costs and reduced criminal justice expenditures by not having to rearrest, convict, and incarcerate those who had been let out of prisons and jails. Others such as DiIulio and Reynolds presented somewhat lower cost-savings estimates of incapacitation, but asserted that "it was cheaper to keep 'em."[19] According to these observers, even if you didn't believe in deterrent effects or the efficacy of rehabilitation, keeping criminals away from communities was smart public policy. This view was enthusiastically embraced by Presidents Ronald Reagan and George H. W. Bush.

The research and logic of Zedlewski and others has been critiqued and largely discredited by leading criminologists such as Zimring, Hawkins, and Blumstein.[20] Support for incapacitation as a theory of penology declined in influence in academic circles but still has great influence in the political world. There is a certain apparent logic that if people are behind bars, they can't hurt us.

The idea of incapacitation rests on the assumption that there are a very small number of "high rate" offenders. Further, it is clear that even "high-rate" offenders slow down with age and commit fewer crimes. As incarceration rates have increased over the decades, the marginal payoff of incapacitation is less, because we are extending confinement to lower-level offenders.

Researcher Greenwood, from the RAND Corporation, attempted to figure out how to maximize the effect of incapacitation though "selective incapacitation"—doing a better job at identifying the frequent offenders at the peak of their crime-committing years.[21] Despite early claims, ultimately the RAND researchers could not successfully predict who would be the most frequent repeat offenders. Researchers such as Haapanen found that selective incapacitation was an illusion.[22] Eventually, even Greenwood rejected selective incapacitation and has spent most of his later years researching effective rehabilitation programs.

Restorative justice:
An approach to repairing the harm caused by crime through cooperative practices among victims, offenders, and the community.

Theories of Restorative Justice and Reintegrative Shaming

Other theories of punishment such as restorative justice and reintegrative shaming shift the focus onto transforming the harm done to victims and to the community and leaving them more committed and integrated than before. Crime is conceptualized as an injury that

must be repaired. The offender is required to acknowledge his or her accountability to the aggrieved victims, express remorse, and engage in positive activities to mitigate the harm to individual victims and the community at large.[23]

These theories propose that justice is best served when an offender is confronted by community peers and agrees to make restitution and perform a service to the community. Restorative justice is not considered to be "pro-victim" or "pro-offender."

Reintegrative shaming is a version of restorative justice. Originally articulated by Australian criminologist John Braithwaite, reintegrative shaming emphasizes the power of public condemnation to change offender behavior and heal the victim's injury.[24] Braithwaite contends that some sanctions label offenders and others, such as incarceration, isolate the criminal from the community and promote more lawbreaking behavior. A different concept of sanctioning can provide pathways back to acceptance by the community.

Both of these ideologies have commonalities with basic religious concepts about how a transgressor can earn redemption and forgiveness. There is a focus on direct relationships between the criminal and his or her victims. One version of this philosophy, victim–offender reconciliation, asserts that both the offender and the victim cannot resolve the conflict without a personal acknowledgement of remorse by the offender, tangible actions to help the victim, and the victim eventually offering forgiveness.[25]

Advocates of restorative justice often refer to justice traditions in native populations in the Americas and in Australia, referring to ways in which small and rural communities deal with crime problems.

Examples of programs that are consistent with reintegrative shaming are peer courts designed for juvenile offenders; David Kennedy's Operation Ceasefire model, which employs community representatives to verbally condemn the behavior of serious offenders; or community circles where groups of neighbors meet with offenders and negotiate the terms of victim compensation and community service. These programs set clear

▲ The public wants accountability, and justly so. But, in scenarios like plea bargaining and restorative justice, can the public accept the idea that negotiation may lead to concessions by both offender and victims?

© iStockphoto.com / Alina555

Restitution:
A repayment of money or services to the victim or society, which may be mandated as part of an offender's sentence.

Involving the community in implementing justice is one way to help restore wholeness to victims.

© iStockphoto.com / EdStock

boundaries and define the behavior that must stop. The neighborhood circle is equally clear that the community will be available to help the offender with his or her social or educational needs.

These victim-focused penal philosophies implicitly, and sometimes explicitly, reject the notion that incarceration is a useful tool for victims and offenders. Although restorative models are being included in some prisons and jails, it is more typical to see these philosophies implemented in diversion programs, in lieu of criminal justice processing, or as adjuncts to probation.

To date, restorative models and reintegrative shaming have been used with less serious offenders. Some argue that middle-class or more privileged individuals are given access to these alternatives, while the less privileged are not. There is only minimal research evidence so far that these alternative philosophies can reduce offender recidivism or reduce victim suffering. (See Chapter 5.)

Modern Movements in Sentencing Laws and Policies

Most of the modern American sentencing system was established during the first part of the 20th century. This is when most states created laws governing probation and parole. Prisons and jails were built in the 19th century throughout the nation, but after the Civil War, many southern correctional systems were in shambles.

The dominant model that used broad ranges of sentences from judges, with parole boards making the final determination, was in place for almost the entire 20th century. Over time, probation, which began as an informal and voluntary practice, was formalized and operated by state agencies.[26] A separate court system for children evolved in the first decades of the 20th century.

Diversion: Programming designed to enable law violators to avoid incarceration, criminal charges, or a criminal record.

This structure and process of sentencing was largely unchanged for over 75 years. But, beginning in the late 1970s, the winds of change in sentencing grew very strong. First, there was a movement toward more structured sentencing systems such as California's determinate sentencing law, Minnesota's sentencing guidelines, and the federal sentencing guidelines. Many states and the federal government have sentencing guidelines commissions that review and regulate sentencing practices. These groups are supported by research staff and meet regularly to review sentencing practices and propose improvements. Advocates of reducing prison crowding point to the experiences in Virginia, North Carolina, Washington, and Minnesota, where sentencing guidelines have actually increased the time served by violent offenders while they have diverted more minor offenders to probation or have reduced the time served for property offenses, minor drug offenses, and other less serious crimes.

The impetus to rationalize and create fairness in sentencing, however, was quickly frustrated by other legislative actions that mandated increased penalties for specific crimes. Thus, sentencing commissions must try to harmonize the political positions of elected legislative bodies with their own legal definitions of the state penalty structure.

In the 1980s, the political fad was "mandatory" incarceration—a guaranteed sentence to prison. In California, the buzzwords were "Use a Gun, Go to Prison." This warning was soon expanded to a number of laws that required incarceration for residential burglaries, carjacking, assaults, **DUIs**, and an ever-increasing number of drug crimes. The inflammatory rhetoric connected to the **"War on Drugs"** encouraged many legislators to embrace mandatory incarceration for even minor possession of controlled substances, including marijuana. The net effect of this political pressure was to radically restrict the kinds of offenders who could be referred to probation supervision. It was argued that probation was largely ineffective and represented insufficient punishment. Budgets for probation agencies were reduced in many locales. In response, some probation leaders tried to portray their programs as tough penalties, downplaying treatment or rehabilitation services. Many probation agencies permitted officers to carry weapons and wear uniforms that looked like those of police SWAT units. Departments tried to promote the notion that probation officers were just like other cops.

The trend toward mandatory incarceration was coupled with new laws that set mandatory minimum terms for particular crimes. These sentencing reforms fundamentally changed the practice of sentencing in indeterminate sentencing states and altered the

DUI: Driving Under the Influence, also DWI (Driving While Intoxicated), is the crime of operating a motor vehicle with impaired abilities. Measuring blood alcohol level is one way of determining a driver's intoxication status.

War on Drugs: The collective policies, laws, and practices intended to reduce the trade and use of illegal drugs.

Defendants who agree to plea bargains waive their right to a jury trial and their right against self-incrimination and plead guilty to criminal offenses.

© JOHN KUNTZ/The Plain Dealer /Landov

SPOTLIGHT

PLEA BARGAINS AND PROSECUTOR DISCRETION

Most people involved in the U.S. corrections system today have never had their day in court, except perhaps to assure a judge that they indeed were acting voluntarily as they pled guilty to the offenses laid out by the prosecutor. Instead, 90% to 95% of all cases in federal and state criminal court turn on plea bargains.[1]

In a plea bargain, the defendant is offered a difficult choice: risk trial and its uncertain outcome or plead guilty to either a lesser charge than the prosecutor intends to pursue in court or the same charge but with a less severe sentence. Perhaps plea bargains are a necessary part of the cumbersome, congested, and expensive judicial system, but they are, at the same time, complicated and imperfect.

On one hand, a defendant may think that, with a quality defense during a full trial, with a full disclosure of the facts of the case and any contributing circumstances, and with an objective—perhaps even sympathetic—judge and jury, the trial may turn out better than the plea. But maybe not.

The unpredictability of judges, juries, counsel, witnesses, and evidence makes going to trial risky, even for the innocent. Also, a great deal of research has found that those who opt for trial and are convicted suffer harsher outcomes for the same crimes.[2] This could be due to a number of reasons depending on the individual trial. However, some recent research suggests a trial may more often than not be a good option for a defendant, perhaps because some of the unpredictability of the court process has been reduced due to sentencing guidelines, determinant sentencing, and three-strikes laws.[3]

Many factors have been shown to contribute to the likelihood of a defendant being offered and accepting a plea agreement, including the higher seriousness of the charges, having a prior record, and the apparent strength of the evidence. A plea bargain is more likely if the defendant is in jail while awaiting trial or if a public defender is used. Conversely, charges are more likely to be dropped altogether, and a plea bargain is less likely, when the defendant is free in the community awaiting trial or if private counsel is hired. Race is also a factor, with African Americans less likely to receive a reduced charge or reduced sentence through plea bargaining. Geography—that is, in what region the case is being processed—also impacts the likelihood of a plea bargain.

The key element behind many of the factors named above is whether the prosecutor is willing to reduce the charge or sentence and by how much. Prosecutors hold a great deal of discretion in who is offered a plea, the maximum charge and sentence put forward in trial and in the bargaining process, the reduced charge or sentence offered as an alternative, and the other tactics used in the bargaining process.

impact of sentencing commissions. Mandatory minimums curtailed the ability of judges to consider traditional mitigating factors. These laws were touted as having a strong deterrent impact on potential criminals. Proponents also argued that mandatory constraints would limit the power of liberal and activist judges to make their own decisions. Courts were required to punish according to penal code sections, not the circumstances of individuals.

This development greatly increased the power of prosecutors in the sentencing process by allowing them broad authority to decide what charges to press. The plea bargaining process was also a key, as offenders agreed to plead guilty to reduce the charges against them. Defendants who agreed to cooperate with police and who testified against others might get departures from the mandatory sentencing provisions. In practice, both mandatory incarceration and mandatory terms did not necessarily bring certainty and predictability

In a system where the vast majority of defendants accept a plea deal, the process by which the deal is reached and (especially for the defendant) the details of the offer become paramount. One impact of the existing plea bargaining process is variation in how similar cases are resolved. Defendants with the same charge and similar records may have quite different outcomes. That the chief prosecutor—district attorney—is usually in an elected position also adds a political element into the equation. It is true, however, that there is much variation in the outcome of jury trials as well, and judges are also often elected to the bench. In most cases, the prosecutor presumably tries to reach an equitable agreement and makes a good-faith effort to provide a thorough account of the state's case and a realistic estimate of what the defendant should expect if he chooses trial.[4]

What is absent in the process is the elaborate and formal system of checks and balances present in open court. Unlike court proceedings, in which rules and procedures are painstakingly defined and reviewed, with the prospect of appeal to a higher court providing a constant pressure for all parties to follow the rules, the process and outcomes of plea bargains have had little scrutiny from the courts or other branches of government and are very rarely subject to appeal. Judges have discretion to refuse plea bargains, but they rarely do. There have been a few important cases addressing plea issues, especially a 2010 case regarding immigrant status that stressed the right to effective defense counsel.[5] But for the most part, plea bargains still operate in their own sphere.

Finally, pleading guilty does not necessarily equate with being guilty, any more than being innocent guarantees an acquittal in court. Some still argue that defendants would never plead guilty to a crime they did not commit. Indeed, the notion of plea bargaining to a large extent hinges on this assumption, since a system that regularly punishes the innocent is apparently failing to fulfill its mandate. Yet innocent people do sometimes plead guilty. Recent exonerations have shown this definitively.[6] These are often the mentally disabled or youth, which only emphasizes the fact that safeguards need to be in place.

QUESTIONS

1 What are the most significant inherent problems with the plea bargaining system?

2 If you were facing a trial for a crime you did not commit, would you consider pleading guilty to a lesser crime to avoid a trial? What factors would influence your decision?

3 Should plea bargaining be allowed for youth or for the mentally disabled?

Notes

1. Devers 2011
2. Ulmer and Bradley 2006
3. Abrams 2011
4. Yaroshefsky 2008
5. Bibas 2011; *Padilla v. Kentucky* 2010
6. Bibas 2011

to the sentencing process. For example, prosecutors might choose to ignore the presence of a gun during a crime or decrease the amount of drugs found on the offender.

During the 1990s, there was an avalanche of new sentencing laws that were almost all designed to increase penalties for a wide range of crimes. Legislators sometimes referred to each of these as "the crime of the week." After a highly publicized crime, legislators would rush to prove their crime-fighting credentials by sponsoring bills that created mandates either to send offenders to prison or to raise the mandatory minimum terms of incarceration. Interest groups like victim advocates, prison guards' unions, and operators of private prisons joined in these lobbying efforts. These new laws contributed to a rapid growth in the number of convicted persons who were sent to prisons and the length of time that they served. Rarely, if ever, did legislatures attempt to quantify the impact of new laws on the prison population or to project the need for new prison beds. Indeed, during this period of

SPOTLIGHT

THREE-STRIKES LAWS

Among the long-term impacts of the tough-on-crime attitudes of the 1980s and 1990s was a wave of "Three Strikes and You're Out" laws that ratcheted up prison terms for repeat offenders. Meant to close the so-called revolving door of justice that let the convicted back onto the streets only to be rearrested for new crimes, the intent of these laws was incapacitation: Public safety would be protected and taxpayer dollars saved by placing *and keeping* repeat offenders behind bars. It was also argued that the laws deterred reoffending by making it abundantly clear to potential lawbreakers that more crime meant more time, and lots of it.

Riding the wave of media coverage of rare but horrible crimes like the 1993 abduction and murder of 12-year-old Polly Klaas, three-strikes laws were eventually enacted in over half of the U.S. states. They have resulted in a significant number of convictions in several states, including Florida, Georgia, Nevada, North Carolina, Virginia, and Washington. But no state has a more severe or more impactful three-strikes law than California.

California's law, passed by a popular landslide in 1994, is notable for its particularly low threshold for what constitutes a second or third strike, for the length of the resulting prison sentences, and for its extensive (if not consistent) application by prosecutors. Sentences are doubled when those with a prior conviction for a serious or violent felony are convicted of *any* new felony, including nonviolent and nonserious felonies.[1] And, according to the original law, for those with two serious or violent felony prior convictions, a third conviction for *any* new felony automatically receives a minimum sentence of 25 years to life.

Several additional elements add to the severity of the California law and make clear its punitive intent. Multiple new felonies must be served consecutively rather than concurrently so that, if the third strike represents two felony offenses, the minimum term is 50 years to life. Good-time credits, which normally can shorten a sentence substantially for cooperative inmates who participate in programming, can reduce the minimum term by no more than one fifth. Suspension of sentence, probation, and diversion are not allowed. The length of time between convictions cannot be used as a reason to shorten the sentence.

Stories of the law missing its mark began hitting the media almost as soon as the stories that propelled it to passage faded away—the two-time burglar sentenced to 25 to life after stealing a pair of sneakers and another 25-to-lifer whose third strike for possession of crack cocaine came after three decades without a strike. Although the law ensured that those with multiple convictions for the most serious offenses served much if not all of their remaining life in prison, it could also send those convicted of much lesser crimes to prison for the same amount of time. The number of prisoners serving long sentences because of a very low-level third strike was kept in check, in theory, by the use of discretion by judges and prosecutors as to which felonies formally counted as "strikes." But this discretion also led to another concern about the law—inconsistent application.[2]

The three-strikes law has survived several court challenges, including the argument that it was cruel and unusual punishment. The U.S. Supreme Court in that case said the law was constitutional because of the state's interest in incapacitating and deterring recidivists. The

rapid growth in the prison population, voters consistently defeated measures to raise funding for new prisons. The politicians found ways of getting around that obstacle. As in other American wars, they kept the new battle against crime or drugs "off the books," by finding less overt means of expanding corrections. In so doing, elected officials did not need to account to the public for the huge growth in government spending that they were creating.

However, they neglected to foresee the consequences of overcrowding the prisons with people who were getting very little in the way of services; lawsuits on unconstitutional prison conditions began to surface. Many elected officials did not imagine that even

justices added that determining whether "the time fits the crime" was a political rather than a judicial decision but that judges did have the authority to void previous convictions that might otherwise be counted as strikes.[3]

Predictions that three strikes in California and elsewhere would drastically reduce crime did not come true. While a long decline in crime rates started in the 1990s, researchers attribute the decline to other factors, with most studies reporting no significant difference between states with three-strikes legislation and those without.[4] When there does appear to be a correlation between three strikes and lower crime rates, it is small—far less than proponents of the laws claim and not enough to justify the costs of keeping the aging population of three-strikers in prison.[5] Furthermore, the "striker" population in prison does not represent the serious offenders the law was meant to target but rather represents lesser offenders who account for a relatively small proportion of California's convicted felons.[6]

Ongoing efforts to revise or repeal the law into the 2000s made clear that support for the law was not nearly as strong as it was at its passage. Even the family of Polly Klaas, who actively campaigned for passage of three strikes in 1994, supported efforts to reshape the law so that it more accurately targeted very serious repeat offenders. Finally in 2012, voter-approved Proposition 36 modified three strikes so that, in most cases, a serious or violent felony is required to warrant a third strike and the associated sentence of 25 years to life. Still, harsh elements of the original law remain, including 25 to life for many types of third strikes, and double sentences for second strikes and for third strikes that do not receive life sentences.

As Proposition 36 results in some current three-strikers having their sentence reduced and fewer new convictions leading to life sentences, estimates suggest that the state will save up to $90 million annually. (California counties will incur some new costs, estimated as a few million dollars among them; under realignment, they will oversee some of those avoiding life sentences.)[7] However, the three-strikes law continues to impact California's burdened prison system: Strikers represented almost one third of state prisoners in 2012, including 33,251 two-strikers and 8,876 three-strikers.[8]

QUESTIONS

1 What makes California's three-strikes law different than what other states have?

2 Discuss whether three strikes in California should be considered cruel and unusual punishment.

3 What is the crime-reduction theory behind three strikes, and how have crime rates supported or undermined support for the theory?

Notes

1. Certain felonies are legally designated "violent," such as murder, aggravated assault, rape, and robbery, or "serious," such as residential burglary, assault on a police officer, and assault with intent to commit robbery.

2. Chen 2008a

3. Brown and Jolivette 2005

4. Brown and Jolivette 2005; Males 2011

5. California Department of Corrections and Rehabilitation (CDCR) 2010; Chen 2008b

6. Brown and Jolivette 2005; CDCR 2010; Zimring, Kamin, and Hawkins 1999, 73

7. California Budget Project 2012

8. CDCR 2012

greater costs to the taxpayer would result from this litigation on top of the constitutionally required services for prisoners.

In some states, such as California, members of the legislature attempted to derail the new "get tough" sentencing laws by using procedural techniques to prevent votes on the new laws. However, soon the proponents of enhanced punishment packaged their proposals in ballot measures that went to the voters. Most of these punishment enhancements were embraced by the voters, although data on the costs or crime control effects of these laws were rarely discussed in the ballot campaigns. Most politicians ducked these discussions

Legislators are often only partially informed about the real consequences of the laws they vote to enact.

© Thinkstock/ Stockbyte

and sided with the tough-on-crime advocates. There were few examples of any courageous attempt to have an open and public debate on the real effects of the legislation.

Unsatisfied by many new enhanced punishment laws, some pushed for even harsher treatment for repeat offenders. The most dramatic examples borrowed a phrase from baseball and were known popularly as "Three Strikes and You're Out." Although many states already had laws to increase punishment for chronic recidivists, these new three-strikes laws promised life sentences for individuals with multiple convictions. Washington was the first state to enact a three-strikes law; in California, the law was enacted by the voters and has the status of a constitutional amendment. President Bill Clinton supported a three-strikes law for the federal system, and many other states quickly passed their own versions of **three strikes** in the 1990s. Appeals to the U.S. Supreme Court have tried to challenge these laws, but the court has so far been reluctant to intervene in the state legislative process.

Some naïve liberals believed that three-strikes laws would end the trend toward more punishment. These "progressives" assumed that three-strikes laws could be written very narrowly so that that only a small number of convicted persons would be impacted. They also assumed that parole boards could rectify manifest injustices later in the sentencing process. They were very wrong.

Three strikes: Statutes that mandate courts to impose harsher sentences on habitual offenders convicted of three or more serious offenses.

Truth in sentencing: Policy stemming from the belief that convicts should serve the period that they have been sentenced to and not be allowed to earn good-time credit toward a parole release.

In rapid succession, conservative criminal justice advocates seized on the alleged problem that sentences given in open court were not actually served by the individuals because they were given time off their sentences for good behavior. In many states, prisoners could earn a reduction of up to half of their sentences by not engaging in any activities prohibited by prison rules and by participating in education and rehabilitation programs. "Good time" was used as a low-profile way to reduce prison crowding. In addition, the courts imposed capacity limits on prisons and jails, leading corrections officials to accelerate the release of inmates through a variety of ad hoc mechanisms.[27] The response to these practices was a series of laws known under the generic name of **"truth in sentencing."** These laws either eliminated or severely limited the reduction of sentences by any means. They mandated that persons convicted of violent offenses, sex crimes, and some drug offenses serve at least 90% of their originally assigned prison terms. The behavior of inmates while in

IN THE COURTS

Ewing v. California

538 U.S. 11, 2003

Gary Ewing was sentenced under California's three-strikes law to 25 years to life. His third strike was the theft of a set of golf clubs worth $399. He had two prior convictions for theft charges that had occurred more than 12 years before the current offense. Under California law, the theft of the golf clubs, by itself, could have been considered a misdemeanor. In that case, Mr. Ewing might have received probation and a short jail term. However, the judge chose the harshest sentence possible.

Mr. Ewing challenged the state's three-strikes law as cruel and unusual punishment in violation of the Eighth Amendment. The U.S. Supreme Court turned down his appeal on a 5-to-4 decision.

For the majority, Justice Sandra Day O'Connor wrote that legislatures make a "deliberate policy choice" to deter those who have "repeatedly engaged in serious or violent criminal behavior" and to incapacitate them to protect the public safety. Although she acknowledged that California's three-strikes law may have generated some controversy, she went on to state that "we do not sit as a superlegislature to second-guess the policy choices made by particular states . . . It is enough that the State of California has a reasonable basis for believing that dramatically enhanced sentences for habitual felons advances the goals of its criminal justice system in any substantial way."

The justices who dissented (Stevens, Breyer, Souter, and Ginsburg) all referenced the core value of proportionality of punishment as central to the Eighth Amendment.

The *Ewing* case and *Lockyer v. Andrade* (538 U.S. 63, 2003) effectively ended the judicial challenges to California's three-strikes law.

Mr. Ewing will not get a parole hearing until at least 2025. There are currently more than 8,000 inmates in California prisons serving a 25-to-life term under the three-strikes law. Almost half have nonviolent crimes as their third strike. There have been at least two attempts to get the voters to change the law, at least for nonviolent offenders, but none of these have passed so far. In 2012, another ballot measure was designed to allow some nonviolent offenders to avoid the draconian three-strikes law.

prison could no longer impact their release dates. Corrections officials generally opposed these truth-in-sentencing provisions, arguing that they removed incentives for inmates to follow the rules of the institution. Indeed, prisons became even more violent and dangerous. At the national level, President Clinton gave in to political pressure and included truth in sentencing as part of a federal crime bill. States had to promise to make a good-faith effort to study and enact truth in sentencing as a condition to receive federal funding.

During the latter half of the 1990s, many states made it easier to prosecute juveniles in criminal courts, shifting to prosecutors the discretion to file juvenile cases directly into criminal courts, bypassing judicial reviews to determine the appropriateness of removing those cases from the juvenile court system. Many states also enacted laws vastly increasing penalties based on evidence that an individual was a gang member. But the most punitive sentencing laws were specifically targeted toward sex offenders. These laws included increased penalties, lifelong requirements to register with the police department, and mandatory life sentences for some sex crimes, as well as provisions to continue the custody of sex offenders using civil commitment laws—even after these individuals had served their entire criminal court sentences.

Changes also came to parole laws and practices. Ironically, some states that tried to abolish parole in the 1980s later extended parole supervision after prison release. Parole was

SPOTLIGHT

FAIR SENTENCING ACT OF 2010

For approximately 30 years, persons arrested for possession of crack cocaine (or cocaine base) were sentenced far more severely than those who were caught with powder cocaine. Prior to this historic legislation, if a person were arrested for possession of 5 grams of crack cocaine, he or she likely faced a mandatory minimum sentence of five years, according to federal law. It took 500 grams of powder cocaine to mandate that same five-year sentence. The 100:1 sentencing structure that has drawn so much criticism was primarily the result of the Anti-Drug Abuse Act of 1986. This disparity was justified on the basis that crack cocaine was supposedly far more addictive than powder cocaine, was more frequently associated with crime, and was far cheaper—and thus more likely to be consumed in large quantities. This specter of the "crack baby" became a symbol and figured into the fear factor surrounding this drug.

The inherent racial bias of this policy was discussed for over 15 years before the passage of the Fair Sentencing Act of 2010.[1] It was assumed that crack was predominantly used by members of the poor Black community and was associated with a dissolute lifestyle. Powder cocaine, being far pricier, was considered a party drug and was used largely by the affluent.

In fact, in 2003, more than 66% of crack users were White or Hispanic, but the vast majority of federal crack cocaine defendants were African American.[2] Furthermore, the two substances are pharmaceutically identical. The difference in its effect can be attributed to how the user ingests it; smoking crack versus snorting cocaine produces a more intense and faster high.[3]

The Fair Sentencing Act was also meant to increase penalties for drug trafficking as opposed to drug use or possession and to allow judges more discretion in departing from the presumed sentence using mitigating or aggravating factors.

The repeal of the applicable portion of the federal sentencing guidelines was signed into law by President Barack Obama in August 2010. The legislation recognizes the role of this single issue in the vast racial disparity of African Americans behind bars.

QUESTIONS

1 What information should Congress rely on to determine appropriate drug sentencing?

2 Why should drug trafficking be treated differently than drug possession or use?

Notes

1. Fair Sentencing Act of 2010
2. Vagins and McCurdy 2006
3. U.S. Sentencing Commission 1997

changed from its traditional role as an alternative to serving one's term in prison to a system of mandatory postrelease supervision. Parole failure rates rose, and the majority of admissions to prison were for violations of parole conditions, not for new convictions. Laws also defined new conditions of parole that prohibited sex offenders or drug offenders from living near schools or other places defined as risky. These "no live" zones made it nearly impossible for released prisoners to obtain legal housing in urban areas.

Other laws further penalized released prisoners by restricting them from living in public housing or receiving federal welfare, disability benefits, educational scholarships, or loans. And they were barred from many jobs. These new legal barriers made successful community reentry after incarceration very difficult.

As the United States entered the 21st century, it had the highest incarceration rate in the world. Public expenditures for prisons and jails soared, as did recidivism rates. There was growing skepticism among the public that these get-tough approaches were effective in improving public safety and were appropriate for the convicted, especially minor drug offenders.[28] In particular, there was a sense that the War on Drugs was very costly—that it had decimated African American and Latino communities by locking up so many young people and leaving behind a generation of children whose parents were behind bars. Some states actually passed ballot measures to reduce penalties for drug offenders and direct them to treatment programs in the community. In other cases, elected officials rolled back the most draconian penalties for minor drug users—although this process was tentative and limited.

A number of judges had a different response to legislative **decriminalization**. They proposed the establishment of "drug courts" to provide intensive supervision and services to some individuals in lieu of imprisonment. The drug court movement has expanded to include specialized courts for mentally ill offenders, domestic violence, and reentry. These special courts practice what has been called "**therapeutic justice**"—a legal approach that is similar to the traditional ideal of the juvenile court. At its core, therapeutic justice attempts to actualize the principles of rehabilitation theory but has updated these ideas with the emerging theories of restorative justice and reintegrative shaming. This development promises to profoundly change corrections by reducing the reliance on incarceration and transforming traditional probation programs.

Decriminalization:
The process of reducing or abolishing criminal penalties related to a certain action or behavior.

Therapeutic justice:
An approach to justice that considers the therapeutic harm and benefits experienced by people engaging with the system.

SUMMARY

Sentencing is a key function of the justice system, determining what kind and duration of penal sanction will be exacted from which individual defendants. Perhaps more than any other aspect of the justice system, sentencing expresses the prevailing attitudes and values of society as it regards punishment for lawbreaking.

Sentencing is affected primarily by state law, prosecution and defense practices, presentence reporting, and the judiciary. Among the 50 states, there is great variety in the structure of sentencing, but most schemes are either determinate or indeterminate, and most try to strike a balance and address the dilemma between adequate discretion and consistency in decision making.

The main theories of sentencing are retribution, deterrence, incapacitation, and rehabilitation. Most systems combine these goals. The structure and process of sentencing in the United States remained stable for over 75 years before guidelines became more prevalent. There are other approaches as well, including increasing trends of trying youth in adult court, mandatory incarceration, and restorative justice. Sentencing is directly related to rates of incarceration and the resulting associated costs.

DISCUSSION QUESTIONS

1. Research and discuss the sentencing structure in your state.

2. Devise a set of presentence investigation interview questions for family members and friends of defendants. Conduct mock interviews.

3. Describe and discuss the theories of sentencing.

4. What are specific deterrence and general deterrence? What do you think is deterrence that works?

5. If you were a victim of a burglary and could confront the person who victimized you, what would you ask from that person?

6. Discuss the merits of indeterminate sentencing versus determinate sentencing.

KEY TERMS

Conviction, 41

Criminogenic needs: 44

Decriminalization, 63

Determinate sentencing, 41

Disparity, 42

Diversion, 54

DUI, 55

Noncriminogenic needs, 45

Parole board, 41

Plea bargain, 43

Presentence investigations, 41

Recidivism, 48

Restitution, 53

Restorative justice, 52

Retributive justice, 45

Risk assessment instrument, 43

Risk factor, 44

Sentence, 41

Sentencing commissions, 42

Sentencing guidelines, 41

Slave codes, 46

Therapeutic justice, 63

Three strikes, 60

Truth in sentencing, 60

War on Drugs, 55

NOTES

1. *U.S. v. Booker* 2005; *U.S. v. Fan Fan* 2005
2. Bonta and Andrews 2007; Warwick, Dodd, and Neusteter 2012
3. Krisberg and Marchionna 2006
4. Breed, in Krisberg, Baird, and Marchionna 2007
5. Von Hirsch 1976
6. American Friends Service Committee 1971
7. Fogel 1975
8. Zimring 1971
9. Guzman, Krisberg, and Tsukida 2008
10. Burgess 1928
11. Martinson, Lipton, and Wilks 1975
12. Martinson 1979
13. Lemert 1972
14. Schur 1973
15. *In re Gault* 1967
16. Travis 2005
17. California Department of Corrections and Rehabilitation 2007; Krisberg and Marchionna 2006
18. Zedlewski 1987
19. DiIulio 1990; Reynolds 1991
20. Blumstein et al. 1986; Zimring and Hawkins 1988
21. Greenwood 1982
22. Haapanen 1988
23. Bazemore and Maloney 1994
24. Braithwaite 1989
25. Umbreit 1998
26. Krisberg, Baird, and Marchionna 2007
27. Guzman, Krisberg, and Tsukida 2008
28. Hartney and Marchionna 2009

$SAGE edge™

Sharpen your skills with SAGE edge at edge.sagepub.com/krisberg

SAGE edge for students provides a personalized approach to help you accomplish your coursework goals in an easy-to-use learning environment. This site includes action plans, mobile-friendly eFlashcards and web quizzes as well as web, audio, and video resources and links to SAGE journal articles.

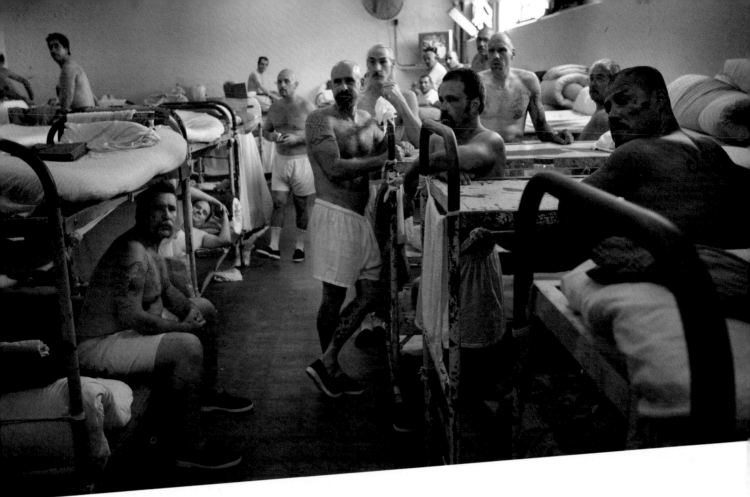

PART

Correctional Practice

© Kevork Djansezian / Getty Im

4 Jails

Most people have never seen the inside of a jail cell except on television. Sensational accounts in the popular media of celebrities in trouble with the law offer a slightly glitzy look into the workings of the justice system. Consider Lindsay Lohan, for instance. Almost 20% of jail inmates nationwide are confined for a drug or alcohol bust, as in the case of Ms. Lohan.[1] Failing a drug test or having a judge send you to treatment may look vaguely romantic in the press. But, most noncelebrities are held, tried, and sentenced with considerably less notice from the media and with considerably less means to rally a defense. In most people's lives, going to jail has a significant and lasting impact.

▲ Most Americans have no idea of how many people are in jail or how many purposes jails fulfill.

© iStockphoto.com / oneword

Even the earliest European settlements in the North American colonies had some place to hold suspects and lawbreakers under lock and key. The local jail was most likely a small holding cell for anyone and everyone in custody. The merely drunk or troublesome might be confined with a recently apprehended murderer. Most jail inmates at this time either were awaiting trial or were debtors. Incarceration was used as rarely as possible, one reason being that local economies could not afford to have potential workers locked away. Although jails have changed over time, they still house a complex variety of people with diverse needs and circumstances. They are still a central part of the criminal justice system at the local level. And they are still used as a means of controlling those suspected or convicted of criminal behavior as they move through the system. A difference today is that confinement in jails has also become a sentence in itself.

The broadly defined functions of jails are to hold and control people, to serve as a form of punishment, and, as some argue, to act as a deterrent to crime—to be a concrete and symbolic reminder of that control and punishment. The nature and purposes of incarceration in jail have similarities to those in prisons, but also many differences, which are discussed in Chapter 6.

The Functions of Jails

The U.S. Department of Justice, in its *Annual Survey of Jails*,[2] defines the specific functions of jails as follows:

5 To be introduced to basic facts about jails—such as their location, size, and design—and how jails are administered.

6 To learn about some of the alternatives to jail.

7 To grasp the challenging realities of everyday life in jail for inmates and staff alike.

SPOTLIGHT

AMERICA'S FIRST JAIL

Historically, jails (or *gaols*) have been the most crowded, chaotic, and filthy penal institutions. In the United States, county jails were used for holding people temporarily—people awaiting trial, under suspicion, serving a short sentence, or needing to appear as witnesses. Every person in those situations, whether old or young; black, brown, or white; male or female; hardened criminal or mistaken misdemeanant, was thrown in with all the others. The jail was not necessarily meant to be a punishment to each person held there, but under the typical conditions, it certainly would have been.

The first jail in colonial Philadelphia was a seven-foot-by-five-foot cage erected in 1682.

In 1718, the Old Stone Jail was built at 3rd and Market Streets in the heart of town. There were separate sections for debtors and criminals. There were no individual cells, no heat, and no food, except what prisoners could buy or have brought to them by charitable individuals. Additionally, the jailed had to pay fees for the privilege of being there, which went to paying the jailer. The sheriff was in the top position and enjoyed a degree of prestige.

Roberts Vaux, a Quaker prison reformer, described the conditions of the jail:

> What a spectacle must this abode of guilt and wretchedness have presented, when in one common herd were kept by day and night prisoners of all ages, colors and sexes! No separation was made of the most flagrant offender and convict, from the prisoner who might, perhaps, be falsely suspected of some trifling

- Receive individuals pending **arraignment** and hold them awaiting trial, conviction, or sentencing.
- Readmit probation, parole, and bail-bond violators and absconders.
- Temporarily detain juveniles pending transfer to juvenile authorities.
- Hold mentally ill persons pending transfer to appropriate mental health facilities.
- Hold individuals for the military, for protective custody, for contempt, and for the courts as witnesses.
- Release inmates to the community upon completion of their sentence.
- Transfer inmates to federal, state, or other authorities.
- House inmates for federal, state, or other authorities because of crowding of their facilities.
- Sometimes operate community-based programs as alternatives to incarceration.

Who Is in Jail?

Arraignment: A court proceeding to read criminal charges in the presence of the defendant and hear his plea of guilty or not guilty.

If we look at who is in jail, we come to understand a bit more about how jails function and about how people get there. To put it simply, *prisons* generally hold convicted felons with sentences longer than 12 months, and *jails* hold everyone else. While prison populations tend to remain more static, there is on average a 60% weekly turnover rate for jails, meaning most of the population comes and goes at a rapid pace.[3] Jails function like an enormous valve to control both intake and release; they are clearinghouses and sorting facilities for the criminal justice system.

misdemeanor; none of the old and hardened culprits from the youthful, trembling novice in crime; none even of the fraudulent swindler from the unfortunate and possibly the most estimable debtor; and when intermingled with all these, in one corrupt and corrupting assemblage were to be found the disgusting object of popular contempt, besmeared with filth from the pillory—the unhappy victim of the lash, streaming with blood from the whipping post—the half-naked vagrant—the loathsome drunkard—the sick, suffering from various bodily pains, and too often the unaneled malefactor, whose precious hours of probation had been numbered by his earthly judge.[1]

These horrid conditions eventually led to the adoption of a policy to build an institution where captive persons would be separated from one another. In 1822, construction began on Philadelphia's Eastern State Penitentiary, which is still open today as a museum. When it was completed in 1836, it was one of the largest structures in the country.[2]

QUESTIONS

1 Why is it important to separate different kinds of jail inmates from one another?

2 Discuss the connection between poverty and imprisonment in early jails. How is this similar to or different from what we see today?

Notes

1. Barnes and Teeters 1943, 844

2. Johnston 2012

A WORD ABOUT JAIL DATA

In part because there is so much movement of individuals in and out of jails, and because jail administration is diffuse rather than centralized (that is, most counties and large cities have their own jails, whereas prisons are run by states or the federal government), consistent and detailed data about jail populations are difficult to come by. However, the basic demographic data that may be collected in jails usually include the gender, age, race and ethnicity, offense category, and conviction status of those detained. More nuanced information, such as mental and physical health status, offense history, education level, and family connections, requires more time-consuming assessments and is thus harder to collect. When these data are available, they are very useful in determining the impact of policy and the effectiveness of programming.

Despite the central role that jails play in the nation's complex criminal justice system, there are no comprehensive or standardized protocols for collecting and maintaining data. Everyone does it differently. For example, one county may collect ethnicity data on every booking; another may not. However, the Bureau of Justice Statistics (BJS) conducts an *Annual Survey of Jails* (ASJ) and, approximately every five years, a more comprehensive *Census of Jail Facilities*. The *Survey of Inmates in Local Jails* offers the most complete picture available of crime-related histories and characteristics of the jail population but is only conducted periodically, the last in 2006.[4]

These surveys are mailed to jurisdictions across the country, and various methods are used to account for nonresponders and inconsistencies in the data. Statistics from these surveys are reported mainly in terms of average daily population, or ADP—an estimate of a constantly fluctuating population. To calculate the ADP, the BJS uses the sum of the population for each day of the year and divides that sum by 365. In addition, there are separate data for specialized facilities, such as detention centers and jails on Native American lands. A detailed methodology is in the survey reports, which are available on the BJS website (www.bjs.gov).

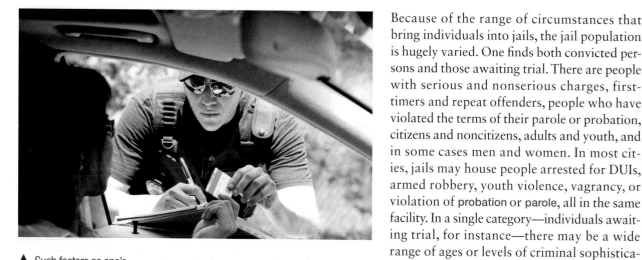

▲ Such factors as one's race or ethnicity, immigration status, criminal background, and socioeconomic class can change the complexion of an otherwise routine traffic stop.

© iStockphoto.com / Pamela Moore

Probation: A court-ordered period of conditional correctional supervision in the community, generally served as an alternative to incarceration.

Parole: The provisional release to community supervision by a parole officer. The parolee agrees to supervision conditions and serves the completion of the sentence out of custody.

Revocation: The formal withdrawal of probation or parole status after a court determines the offender has not met the conditions of release, usually resulting in incarceration.

Pretrial services: Processing, supervising, and providing services to defendants awaiting trial while free in the community, with the purpose of avoiding the unnecessary use of detention while still ensuring the defendant appears in court as required and avoids criminal conduct.

Because of the range of circumstances that bring individuals into jails, the jail population is hugely varied. One finds both convicted persons and those awaiting trial. There are people with serious and nonserious charges, first-timers and repeat offenders, people who have violated the terms of their parole or probation, citizens and noncitizens, adults and youth, and in some cases men and women. In most cities, jails may house people arrested for DUIs, armed robbery, youth violence, vagrancy, or violation of probation or parole, all in the same facility. In a single category—individuals awaiting trial, for instance—there may be a wide range of ages or levels of criminal sophistication. Jails house people on their way in, people who are staying for a while, and people on their way out.

Roughly half of those in jail are people awaiting trial or sentencing. In a nation where one is innocent until proven guilty, that known criminals are held with those still awaiting trial creates a conundrum that is, in practice, largely ignored in today's system. Should these two groups be subjected to the same treatment and conditions? In reality, little consideration is given to this question once the custody decision is made.

How long a person waits for a trial ranges greatly by jurisdiction and depends on many factors, including the seriousness of the charges, the workload of defense attorneys and prosecutors, and courtroom availability. This waiting period can become protracted and turn into many weeks or months. As people wait, others continue to arrive. On the other hand, the jail population turns over at a much faster rate than the prison population.

Individuals that have been tried and convicted may return to jail pending sentencing, which can occur in a separate hearing and take days or weeks after the trial in overburdened systems. They may also then stay in the jail facility awaiting transfer to the setting where they will serve their sentence. If a person's sentence is less than 12 months, he or she will likely serve the sentence in jail. Individuals with such sentences make up the other main category of detainees—jail inmates serving time postconviction.

Over the past several decades, the portion of jail inmates held for less serious crimes, especially drug offenses, has increased. In 2002, the jail population was divided into almost even quarters between public order, drug, property, and violent crimes. As explained above, obtaining extremely reliable data on primary offenses among jail inmates is difficult. However, estimates based on history and context suggest that, among subsequent jail and prison inmates, less than one third have committed a serious or violent crime.[5]

Further, what is considered a crime is a changeable factor as well; laws and policing practices change over time. For example, in the 1920s, suffragettes were thrown into jail (and treated brutally) for demonstrating for the right to vote. Those caught driving while intoxicated may have been escorted home or merely reprimanded, whereas now jail time is mandatory in many states, especially for repeat offenders. Local culture also plays a role in who goes to jail. For example, marijuana possession is tolerated in some communities, and in others it results in jail time.

Jail time is a recurring event in some people's lives. In 2002, about three quarters of jail inmates had at least one sentence of incarceration or probation in their past. Just over half were system involved at the time of their most recent arrest. Most of these were on probation or parole, but some were out on **bail** awaiting trial (for a different arrest) or in a drug or alcohol diversion program or some other alternative.[6]

Just over a quarter were being held for a new offense. This means that most were being held for violations— not meeting the conditions of their release, often a dirty drug test or failure to attend required meetings or treatment services. The repercussions of these violations vary by state and community and are determined by policy, which in turn is affected by the current political climate, budget constraints, and local conventions. Probation or parole officers may instigate a short period of detention—a night or two— both as punishment for the violation and, they hope, as a deterrent to further violations. But in most states, a serious violation is likely to lead (sometimes automatically) to **revocation**, which means an imposition of a custody sentence and additional weeks, months, or years behind bars.[7]

Jail administrators are under constant pressure to manage conditions inside facilities. There are many strategies to controlling jail populations. For example, improving **pretrial services**—which include effectively and safely sorting out who should and should not be detained while awaiting trial—can speed up case processing and help reduce crowding in jails. Similarly, increasing the use of probation and alternatives to incarceration reduces the number of inmates serving sentences in jails.

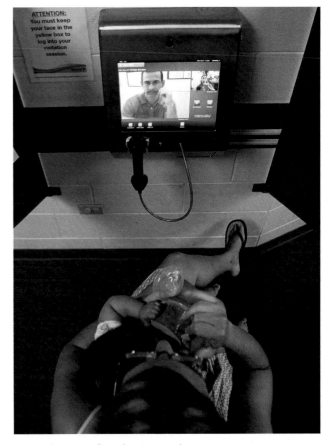

▲ Twin Falls County Jail inmate Michael Bonales, who is deaf, signs with Suzanne Blair while she holds her daughter during a video visitation Monday, August 15, 2011, at the jail in Twin Falls, Idaho. The county is testing a system of webcam technology to provide inmate visitations. Staying in touch with family members is of great significance to the incarcerated.

© Associated Press/Drew Nash

Transfers

Jails are often used as holding facilities for people being transferred from one place to another. For instance, a mentally ill person whose behavior resulted in arrest but who needs mental health screening and treatment may await transfer to a more appropriate facility. A postconviction felon who will serve his or her sentence in state prison starts out in jail. A detained person without U.S. citizenship is often held in jail before being transferred to the custody of the federal immigration authorities. Further, one might find "overflow" from a nearby prison that is over capacity, and those being held for the military, for **contempt of court**, or even for protective custody, as in the case of a threatened witness.

A jail may hold a juvenile awaiting a judge's decision on whether his or her case will proceed through the adult court or the juvenile court. Some youth are eventually processed through the adult system and spend some time in adult facilities. Juveniles make up less than 1% of the jail population (5,400 in 2012).[8] Although this is a small portion of the jail population and federal law mandates that youth be separated by "sight and sound" in such situations, the jail experience is likely to have an even more enormous impact on the life of a young person than on that of an adult.

Mental Illness and Jails

It is estimated that a significant percentage, almost two thirds, of inmates have a serious mental health issue.[9] Sometimes these mental health issues are contributing factors to the individual's criminal behavior, or inability to be stabilized and rehabilitated, especially

Bail: A deposit made to the court in exchange for the release of a defendant from jail and to help ensure his or her appearance at trial. The amount for bail is set by the court.

SPOTLIGHT

VIDEO JAIL VISITATION

Jail administrators are on the lookout for technological solutions to traditional problems, especially if they cost less. Family visits by computer are one such alternative to shatterproof glass and handset visitation booths. This technology was introduced in the 1990s, but has been more widely accepted only recently.

It is estimated that hundreds of jails in almost half of U.S. states have incorporated video technology for visits between jail inmates and their friends and family

members. Some jails are even charging for visits and have fees along the lines of $15 for 30 minutes.

Some of the security advantages, according to proponents, are that inmates can stay in their cells and do not leave the secure area. Smaller facilities may have portable "units" that get wheeled around to cells. Less movement of prisoners means less security risk and fewer demands on jail staff. In addition, the risk of visitors transferring contraband to inmates is decreased. Visits can be monitored in real time and recorded for future review. Some make the point that prisoners have more privacy by staying in their cells. The advantages for visitors may be less time spent waiting in line, less screening and security

---

Contempt of court: A charge of disobeying or disrespecting the court's authority in the context of a trial or hearing.

Booking: The process by which jail staff register charges against a person held for a law violation.

Gender responsive: Attentive, aware, and accommodating of the particular needs of women and girls.

when proper services are not available. The fact remains that mental illness and jail have a rather disturbing partnership; the behavior of the mentally ill is all too often criminalized rather than treated.

For much of American history, the mentally ill were confined in mental institutions. In reality, such facilities were often plagued by horrible conditions. However, their purpose and mission was not to exact punishment. In the 1970s and 1980s, as a result of pressure from advocates and federal legislation intended to ensure that the mentally ill were served in community settings, these facilities were systematically closed. At that time, poor planning and implementation opened an enormous social crack through which the mentally ill have fallen. In 1955, over 500,000 persons were confined in state mental hospitals. By 2002, that number was less than 70,000, one third of whom had been sent to those institutions by the courts following arrest and booking in jail.[10] In the meantime, hundreds of new jails and prisons opened, and, given the continued lack of mental health services, the mentally ill helped to fill them. This shift from mental institutions to incarceration for the mentally ill raises serious moral and ethical questions. (See Chapter 13.)

Women and Jails

Women have historically made up a small fraction of the jail population, but that fraction is growing. Between 2000 and 2012, women went from making up 11% of the jail population to making up 13% of the jail population.[11] Most of that increase was for convicted women versus those who were not yet convicted and were awaiting trial. Women in custody have significantly different backgrounds and treatment needs than men. This has been the case throughout history, yet few jails have a staff trained adequately in gender-responsive approaches most appropriate for incarcerated women. Women may have reproductive health issues—primarily pregnancy and childbirth—or other physical and mental health–related issues specific to their gender. A large majority of incarcerated women have histories of physical, sexual, and emotional abuse. They are more often than men the primary caregivers for young children. Their relationships are critical to

checks, and ease of making an appointment by phone or online.[1]

In some jails, video visitation may be or may become the only option, eliminating in-person visits. Connection to family is well established as a key to maintaining morale and a successful reentry to the community.[2] It remains to be seen if video visits add to that connection or detract from it. In crowded urban jails, video may mean streamlined and more efficient contact, less waiting and no security searches for visitors, and more opportunities for family members as the technology expands to libraries, churches, or even the homes of visitors. However, not being able to see someone in person, in front of you, diminishes the quality of the contact. Assessing and understanding the effect of this use of technology on prisoners opens up a new area of study for researchers.

QUESTIONS

1 Would you want to visit an imprisoned loved one via a video?

2 Discuss the merits and disadvantages of video visitation as compared to face-to-face visits.

Notes

1. District of Columbia Department of Corrections 2012
2. Emmanuel 2012

---

their recovery and successful reentry. Furthermore, women tend to commit less serious crimes than those men commit. (See Chapter 12.)

People of Color and Jails

Jails house people of color and, in particular, African Americans in gross disproportion to their percentage of the nation's total population. In 2012, Whites made up 63% of the general U.S. population, but 46% of the jail population. African Americans were just 13% of the general population, but made up 37% of those in jail. Latinos were 15% of the general population and 15% of those in jail, and Asian, other, and mixed-race persons made up 9% of the general population but 2% of those in jail.[12, 13] The disproportion for African Americans has been high for decades.

Various policies and practices have contributed significantly to the rise of the general rate of incarceration and its disproportionate impact on people of color. Communities of color have born the brunt of the "War on Drugs," three-strikes laws, and sentencing policies such as differential punishment for crack and powder cocaine. (See Chapter 3, "Spotlight" on page 58.)

YOU DECIDE

Mental Health Patients and Jail Administration

Roger is at the Sage County Jail, having been arrested the previous night for a minor offense. He had been booked into the jail several times in the past for minor crimes. He appears dazed, sitting in the back of the holding area and talking to himself.

Roger has a past involving involuntary commitment on mental health issues. He told the jail staff that he commits crime to get sent to jail for a warm place to sleep, for a meal, and to get his meds. He is homeless and has no medical insurance or regular health care provider. Roger occasionally gets into fights with other jail inmates, has threatened suicide, and yells at the custody staff.

Due to the minor nature of the crime, Roger will likely be released in 24 hours. His meds are expensive; it costs the jail officials $200 per day to house him. While at the Sage County Jail, he will receive no counseling or treatment for his mental health issues.

*YOU DECIDE: **As the jail administrator, what do you do about Roger?***

SPOTLIGHT

JAILS AND IMMIGRATION: SECURE COMMUNITIES

Just before the election of 2008, the Bush administration began to pilot a federal program to control immigration called Secure Communities. The program expanded dramatically during the Obama administration. The division of the Department of Homeland Security (DHS) that handles immigration issues is Immigration and Customs Enforcement (ICE). According to its website, ICE "prioritizes the removal of criminal aliens, those who pose a threat to public safety, and repeat immigration violators." In effect, the program allows local police to be trained as immigration officials in their jurisdiction.

The program mandates that local law enforcement agencies forward fingerprint information on everyone they arrest to the DHS, which compares those prints to its fingerprint repository. The database contains information on travelers, applicants for immigration benefits, and those who previously violated immigration laws.

In implementing the Secure Communities program, the federal government's initial position was to allow states and local communities to opt out of participation. However, it reversed this position when it became clear that voluntary participation was below the anticipated levels. The feds began compelling communities to turn over information and persons presumed to be undocumented. The stated goal was to have complete national buy-in by 2013; the website says that the program is on track to meet this goal.[1] Many states and localities (such as New York and Massachusetts) were less than enthusiastic about such participation and have taken measures to resist the mandate, believing that it "does more harm than good."[2]

Native Americans

In 2011, Native Americans were confined in approximately 80 jails in Indian country (reservations, pueblos, and other lands under tribal jurisdiction) as well as in other local jails. According to the Bureau of Justice Statistics, the number of American Indians and Alaska Natives held in jails outside of Indian country (9,400) was four times greater than the number of those held on Indian lands (2,239).

From 2004 to 2011, the number of facilities operating in Indian country increased from a total of 68 to 80. However, this total includes 11 permanent facility closures and new construction of 21 facilities. As with jails outside of Indian territories, jails on Indian lands are subject to overcrowding and its related challenges.[14]

Jails on Indian lands are administered by the tribal authorities and may not be subject to local or state authority, depending on the status of the defendant and the victim. The greatest advantage to that arrangement may be that the Indian jail can devise programming specific to Native culture. For example, in one case, jail officials were building a sweat lodge to promote healing and traditional native religious observation.[15]

Overcrowding

Overcrowding is a serious problem in jails as well as in prisons. Facilities filled to more than their capacity are less safe for everyone. In addition, programming is all the more difficult, due to lack of space and general chaos. The Los Angeles County jail is certainly one of the most extremely overburdened jail systems in the nation. There are some ideas designed to relieve the stress of crowding; however, these are not without controversy. For example, of the 10,000 people in pretrial detention in LA County, about 10% could be safely released on electronic monitoring, according to some.[16] These individuals are being held because they cannot afford to post bail and await trial at home.

Although the program is supposedly intended to apprehend dangerous undocumented criminals, apparently the majority of deportees had minor law violations, including traffic violations. The program also appears to open the door to profiling, cutting it close with civil rights matters, and using local jails to carry out federal policy.

It is important to bear in mind that immigration violations are not criminal in nature; they are violations of the civil code. There are serious questions about due process rights of individuals detained by ICE, the vast majority of whom are from Latin America.

Thus, insofar as they hold persons detained for immigration matters, or, more to the point, suspected immigration matters, the local jails become complicit in the process of immigration enforcement. The problems are that many citizens (one estimate is 3,600) are swept up in this effort; 88,000 families with U.S. citizen members were affected by the program, and Latinos are clearly disproportionately impacted.[3]

QUESTIONS

1 Should local jurisdictions be allowed to opt out of the federal program?

2 How should federal or local authorities distinguish between the criminal and noncriminal violations of undocumented individuals?

Notes

1. U.S. Immigration and Customs Enforcement 2013
2. Clark 2012
3. Kohli, Markowitz, and Chavez 2011

In general, jail crowding prompts discussions about ways to relieve the problem, including whether to build more jail bed space, accelerate release, rely on alternatives, expedite court processing and change sentencing policy.

Facts About Jails

Not only do the individuals who make up the jail population vary, but jail facilities themselves also range greatly with respect to their location, size, age, and design, among other factors.

Location

Most jails are centrally located, close to police headquarters and courthouses. Legal offices and bail bond businesses also locate near jail sites. Local politics dictate where jails are located and the state of their budgets. Jails manifest and must handle whatever social problems exist in their communities. Poverty, lack of education, generational cycles of criminality, violence, racial tension, and gang activity are not held away by the bars of jail cells. Jails are also both products of and influencers of the political structure they help form, and their funding is intimately tied to these dynamics.

Size

In 2006, according to the most recent facility census by the U.S. Department of Justice, there were 3,283 jails of all sizes in the United States. (The number of jails probably grew in the years following the last census; most states continued to see increases in rates of incarceration.) The size of a jail is measured by capacity, which ranges from fewer than 50 inmates to more than 1,000.

▲ The proportion of people of color in the general U.S. population is not reflected inside prisons.

© Michael Rondou/KRT/ Newscom

Most jails were not built to accommodate today's mass incarceration practice and operate on average at over 85% of capacity.[17] Counties have commonly responded to this problem by building larger facilities, mostly for reasons of economy of scale but also because of the general reliance on incarceration as a solution to crime control problems. Neighboring smaller or rural communities often maintain a single, shared jail instead of each building its own, and large urban communities often build a large, centralized jail instead of two or more smaller facilities.

The jail incarceration rate rose steadily through the 2000s. In 1990, the jail incarceration rate was 163 for every 100,000 in the general population.[18] In 2000, the rate was 220. It rose annually, to 259 in 2007. The first year that there was a decrease in the incarceration rate from the previous year was 2008, after which it declined to 237 in 2012.[19] However, the absolute numbers of inmates and beds still grew every year.

The lesson to be learned from the recent past is that if we build more jails, we fill them. This appears to be a dynamic in large part separate from crime rates, which have been on the decline since the mid 1990s.[20] What is important to note is that incarceration rates appear to be more closely related to criminal justice policy and practice than the number or seriousness of the crime being committed. The national rate of reported crime fell drastically in the 1990s and 2000s—violent crime by approximately 50% and property crime by approximately 40%.[21]

Age

Many jails were built decades ago and have not aged well, sometimes leading to deplorable conditions of confinement and hazardous environments for prisoners and guards alike.

This is a situation fraught with contradictions as the pretrial population (more than 50% on average) is "presumed innocent" according to U.S. law. However, decrepit facilities and poor conditions, not to mention harsh treatment by jailers, create a punitive environment. Those jailed individuals who are able to bail out of jail do so. A person whose family or friends are not able to come up with bail is forced to await trial behind bars. This is perhaps one of the starkest examples of the class differential in the application of justice in the United States. The pressures of confinement also play a role in the dynamic of the plea bargain. (See Chapter 3.)

Design

A great deal of planning goes into the design of custody facilities, as a facility's functions—for better or for worse—are directly linked to its design. Jail architecture is guided by professional association standards, politics, budget, and the prevailing supervision philosophy. In the early 1980s, an enormous shift took place in the dominant thinking about the most functional and effective design for jail supervision. Of course, jail design and construction are lengthy and costly businesses. Whatever the merits or flaws of the jail design, staff and inmates have to live with them for a very long time. New ideas take hold only when leaders are well informed and willing to embrace an innovation. For roughly 200 years, jail design remained the same—a linear arrangement of cells that required custodial officers to walk the halls and conduct intermittent surveillance through the windows or bars of the cell doors. Many jails currently in use are built in exactly this way. Some very small jails or those dedicated to minimum security have dormitory-style inmate housing, where dozens of bunk beds fill a large room. These are limited in their usefulness and security, but certainly much less expensive to build. In fact, most of these rooms were originally common areas or recreational spaces until administrators switched their use to ease overcrowding.

The new design idea that took hold in the 1980s and remains prevalent today is one of a radial design that allows a centrally located surveillance post to conduct continual supervision of the surrounding cells and the inmates inside them. This is often referred to as a "pod." Officers have a constant view of inmates, have remote control of the doors to the cells, and are in communication with the facility's main

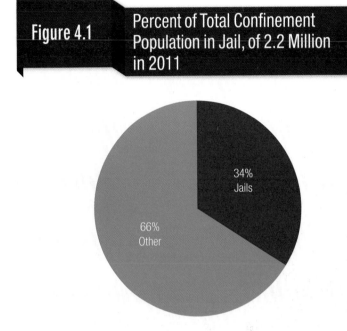

Figure 4.1 — Percent of Total Confinement Population in Jail, of 2.2 Million in 2011

- 34% Jails
- 66% Other

Collectively, U.S. jails held a total of almost 740,000 people in 2011, or one third of the 2.2 million people confined in the United States (including state and federal facilities) and 11% of the almost 7 million individuals who were under some form of correctional control (including probation and parole). *Source: Glaze and Parks 2012.*

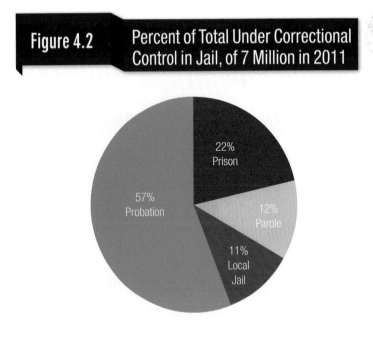

Figure 4.2 — Percent of Total Under Correctional Control in Jail, of 7 Million in 2011

- 22% Prison
- 12% Parole
- 11% Local Jail
- 57% Probation

Among all forms of correctional control in 2011, jails accounted for the smallest proportion (11%), about half as much as prisons (22%) and far less than probation (57%). (Due to rounding, numbers do not add up to 100.) *Source: Glaze and Parks 2012.*

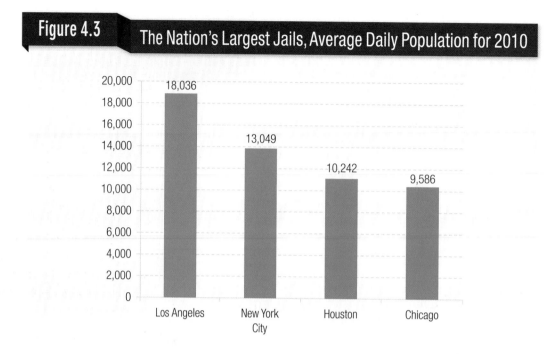

Figure 4.3   The Nation's Largest Jails, Average Daily Population for 2010

In 2010, the largest jail jurisdictions (measured by the combined ADP in all county facilities) were Los Angeles County at 18,036; New York City at 13,049; Harris County (Houston), Texas, at 10,242; and Cook County (Chicago), Illinois, at 9,586. Out of the 50 largest jail jurisdictions in the United States, 9 were in California, 5 were in Texas, and 8 were in Florida. Eight of the states with the largest jail jurisdictions had at least one with more jail inmates than the facilities were meant to hold. *Source: Minton 2011.*

control center. Security cameras operate as an additional surveillance measure. The officer station may be open to the day room where inmates congregate during times they are allowed outside of their cells or enclosed in a secure room. This radial design is most appropriate for minimum- and medium-security classifications. With its constant supervision, it is considered to be much safer than the outdated linear design with its intermittent observation. The American Correctional Association publishes standards for jail facilities that cover areas such as occupancy and space requirements, light and noise levels, accommodations for handicapped inmates, and air quality.[22]

Jail Administration

As previously mentioned, even though they must adhere to all applicable federal or state laws, jails are administered locally, with few exceptions. Prisons, by contrast, are run either at the state level or by the federal government. Texas, for example, has state-run jails, and several states have combined jail and prison systems, including Connecticut, Delaware, Hawaii, Rhode Island, Vermont, and Alaska.

Sheriff's departments operate the vast majority of jails, usually at the county level. Sheriffs are either elected by the public or appointed by county authorities—such as a county commissioner or the board of supervisors. In some cases, jails are administered by the chief of police—an arrangement common in large cities, which have their own corrections departments, such as Los Angeles and New York. These larger jurisdictions may have facilities specialized for women, juveniles, or pretrial detainees.

IN THE COURTS

Albert W. Florence, Petitioner v. Board of Chosen Freeholders of the County of Burlington et al.

No. 10–945. Argued 12, 2011—Decided April 2, 2012

In a 5-to-4 decision in *Florence v. Board of Chosen Freeholders of Burlington and Essex Counties*, the U.S. Supreme Court held that jail administrators could require all inmates in the general population to submit to visual strip searches without any reasonable suspicion that the inmate might commit some serious rule infraction or crime. Such a search occurred in two New Jersey jails. An African American man, Albert Florence, was stopped by police while driving with his family to dinner. He was taken into custody for an alleged warrant for unpaid fines. Mr. Florence had been stopped previously by the police for alleged traffic incidents. He had no prior arrest record and possessed a letter indicating that he had no outstanding fines or warrants. However, he was taken into custody and asked to strip, shower with a delousing agent, open his mouth, lift his tongue, hold out his arms, and lift his genitals.[1]

The majority of justices ruled that some people held in jails could be quite dangerous and cited the case of domestic terrorist Timothy McVeigh. Furthermore, Justice Kennedy argued that jails were very dangerous places that are subject to gang violence, contagious diseases, and drug smuggling. These uncertainties of jail safety led the majority to consider the interests of security in jail to outweigh the support for a ban on the searching of every inmate. In a dissenting opinion, Justice Breyer denounced such routine strip searches as a "serious affront to human dignity and to individual privacy. In my view, such a search of an individual arrested for a minor offense that does not involve drugs or violence . . . is an unreasonable search forbidden by the Fourth Amendment."[2]

Most professional groups such as the American Correctional Association, the National Institute of Corrections, and the National Sheriffs' Association supported a ban on suspicionless strip searches and filed an *amicus* brief on behalf of Mr. Florence.

Ten states and the Federal Bureau of Prisons do not permit random strip searches.

Notes

1. Liptak 2012
2. Supreme Court of the United States 2011–2012

Whoever is in charge, essential concerns are levels of education, training, professional integrity, and competency among the staff. The staff-to-inmate ratio is also a major factor in facility safety and program implementation; it takes staff to properly supervise the jail and staff to run treatment and education programs. Even if a jail has an adequate number of staff persons, conscientious administrators are nonetheless constantly concerned with policies that incorporate best practices, proper training, appropriate skill levels, and staff morale. These affect every aspect of jail functioning. Unfortunately, when jails are understaffed, life in jail is harder for everyone concerned.

Jail facilities operated by sheriff's departments are often staffed by deputies who are assigned to jail duty. Sheriff's department staff are more often trained in police work, as opposed to corrections. Although the two jobs certainly require overlapping skill sets, jail work emphasizes surveillance, prevention, conflict resolution, and client care versus the intervention and enforcement emphasis in police work. Many of these may consider the jail assignment a temporary delay before a more preferable reassignment, such as active patrol duty. A staff trained deliberately for a career in corrections, and not police work, can contribute to staff being comfortable with and suited to the role, which in turn can lead to improved facility operations.

Strip search: The search of a person's body for weapons or contraband that requires removal of clothing. Performing such a search requires legal authority.

SPOTLIGHT

MINISTRY IN JAILS

One kind of assistance for prisoners in both jails and prisons is religious ministry. Considered a form of godly service, reaching "behind the walls" and ministering to people in captivity satisfies the giver's need to be of service and the captive's need for contact, counsel, and solace.[1] Many religious organizations sponsor jail ministries and use a variety of means to achieve them.[2] Their mission may be to follow holy teachings and remember those in prison as if they were imprisoned with them. Seeds of Hope is a Christian jail ministry in southwest Kansas that reminds its parishioners that "today's inmates will be tomorrow's neighbors."[3]

The minister in jail has a special status in the view of many prisoners, separate from the administrators of incarceration. It is easier to for a prisoner to build a trusting relationship with a holy person, whose teachings come from the larger spiritual world than that of policy and earthly law.[4] Many prisoners find their path to personal growth and prosocial behavior through religious teaching. As a group of Muslim followers phrase it, a jail can be "a tomb or a womb."[5]

Some of the ways ministries assist prisoners involve establishing a relationship with a prisoner through visits or writing letters. They may concentrate on a prisoner's family members. They may also establish agreements with prison

Jail administrators govern a wide variety of functions in their facilities including security, supervision, records, discipline, physical and mental health care, education, religious services, recreation, food services, sanitation, inmate communication and visitation, admission and release of inmates, personnel recruitment and training, and fiscal management. They are responsible for the welfare of inmates in custody as well as the staff whom they employ. They must also answer to the agency's governing authority and maintain good public relations with the community.

Although it is a controversial practice, some jurisdictions house jail inmates in private facilities. The count of inmates in privately run jails is not well documented, but the U.S. Department of Justice's *Census of Jail Facilities, 2006* reported that 2% of the total jail inmates in the United States were held in facilities run by either private contractors or other nonjail public agencies.[23] Some contend that jail services (such as meals and medical care), jail operation, and jail construction can often be accomplished at a lower cost in private facilities. Research on this question is mixed. Regardless, the question of whether the private sector *should* fill these roles is debatable. Certainly, the profit motive could easily be at odds with the interests of justice and fair sentencing practices. There is a hugely problematic dynamic inherent in private companies being paid per prisoner—as is often the case—and thus having an incentive for keeping beds full through more sentences of incarceration, longer sentences, and inmates serving their maximum sentence. Prison companies spend millions of dollars each year to sway the opinions of policymakers and the public on these issues. Legislators and governors often turn to private incarceration facilities in hopes of balancing budgets, reducing overcrowding without new public facility construction, and maintaining a politically expedient "tough on crime" reputation. Each jurisdiction must wrestle with the appropriate equation of public versus private services for jail operation and maintenance. (See Chapter 15.)

administrators to minister inside facilities, distribute literature, hold religious study sessions, conduct services, run education programs, and even become partners in prerelease and reentry strategies.

Of course, prisoners practice and adhere to many different religious traditions. One of the challenges for Christian ministers is to recognize and deal with a variety of denominations and faiths other than Christianity. Ministers need to negotiate the tendency to proselytize or handle confrontation and even cult mentality. There are organizations specific to other religions that have established programs of outreach to prisoners of those faiths—for example, Judaism, Islam, and Buddhism.

QUESTIONS

1   Discuss ways that religious ministry may be of service to prisoners and their families.

2   How much access should prisoners have to religious services, and how much should jail administrators be expected to provide?

Notes

1.   Evans 2012
2.   Prison Mindfulness Institute n.d.
3.   Seeds of Hope Jail Ministry n.d.
4.   Hope Aglow Ministries n.d.
5.   Renaissance Islam 2009
6.   Aleph Institute n.d.

Jail Procedures

Most of those who are arrested are processed through a jail or another detention facility. An arrestee may first be brought to a police station, be held there and put through some of the steps of processing, and then be transferred to the city or county jail. There may be a central booking location where all city or county arrestees are processed, which may or may not be located at one or more jail facilities in the jurisdiction. There also may be designated detention settings for certain populations, such as women or juveniles, and for those requiring hospitalization for mental illness, injury, or other immediate health needs.

Booking (or processing) into jail is so called because traditionally each person entering the jail was recorded in the "book." Booking is usually handled through an electronic system now. It generally includes an interview, at which time the arrestee's personal information is recorded. It often includes a mug shot and fingerprinting, either through the traditional ink blotter method or via a digitized pad. Jail officials conduct criminal background checks on those they arrest. They also confiscate personal items and save them in a property room.

Once processed, detainees are given limited telephone access for the purpose of contacting family, an attorney, or a bail bondsman (these days usually using an access code that allows them to make collect calls to certain telephone numbers). In addition to any bodily search conducted at the time of arrest, there will likely be another search at booking and a thorough search before final admittance to the jail.

Before a judge is involved, a decision may be made to release the arrestee without filing charges, to release with a ticket or a summons to appear in court, or to release to a diversion program. Depending on the jurisdiction, several people may influence this decision, including agents of the police, prosecutor, public defender, probation department, and

Mug shot: An official photograph taken for an individual's police record, usually when that individual is booked into jail.

pretrial service agency. Those held until they can be seen by a judge are booked into jail and locked up to await arraignment, usually within two business days.

Arrestees are often subjected to a number of assessments that evaluate risk to self, risk to other inmates and guards, sobriety, immediate and long-term health needs (including drug dependency, communicable disease, and pharmaceutical prescriptions), background and criminal history, and accessibility needs (hearing impairment or limited mobility). These assessments can allow inmates to access services or special needs, although in most facilities, these are limited in availability and only the most immediate and serious needs are addressed. Besides identifying those who may need to be held in specialized settings, such as the hospital or the mental health ward, assessments allow jail administrators to classify inmates according to their likelihood of victimization of or by other inmates and to place them accordingly— again, to the extent the facility has the capacity, procedure, and staffing necessary.

Jails are often overcrowded, which increases their unpredictability and the risk of conflict or violence. Jail conditions, especially in older facilities, are utilitarian and tend to be harsh and noisy, with hard benches and bunks, concrete walls, and metal bars. The cells or dorms tend to be crowded spaces, with anywhere from one or two individuals up to dozens of detainees. The more crowded the space, the more difficult it is for corrections officials to maintain safety and calm. Many jails keep their cells at low temperatures to limit the spread of airborne germs, to mollify the occupants somewhat, and, no doubt, to save on heating bills.

Prosecutor: The legal party responsible for presenting the case in a criminal trial on behalf of the public against an individual accused of breaking criminal law.

Remand: When a case is sent back from a higher court to a lower court for further action or when an offender is returned to custody.

Following arraignment, at which charges are read before the court and the defendant's plea is heard, a pretrial detention decision is made by the judge, usually after consulting with the **prosecutor**, defense attorney, and, perhaps, representatives of other agencies. There are three main options. The judge may release the defendant on his or her own recognizance, require that the defendant post a specified amount of bail in addition to or instead of meeting other requirements of release (such as maintaining employment, staying sober, or completing a diversion program), or **remand** the defendant to jail custody to await trial.

Strictly speaking, the purpose of pretrial detention (that is, being held in jail while awaiting your day in court) is twofold: to ensure that defendants show up to their court appearances and to protect the community—that is, to limit the likelihood of defendants

▲ Getting booked into jail can be a humiliating experience. Whom would you call if you found yourself in jail and were in need of being bailed out?

© Lynn Ischay/The Plain Dealer /Landov

The courts and the jails work in tandem. A jail inmate may enter court directly from the jail holding cell.

© David R. Frazier Photolibrary, Inc. / Alamy

committing new offenses before trial. Pretrial detention may also be meant as a deterrent to crime or, for that matter, a punishment—even though these detainees have not yet been convicted of wrongdoing.

In addition to poor conditions, risk of victimization, and exposure to crime culture, there are detrimental impacts of pretrial detention on case outcomes, including a higher likelihood of conviction and more severe sentencing. As previously mentioned, those with few resources and little social support may not be able to arrange bail and thus will be subject to jail, not because society thinks they are dangerous or likely to abscond, but because they are poor or marginalized. Because they have fewer options to bail out of the early stages, the disadvantages for the poor and for people of color tend to accumulate.[24]

If the defendant is eligible, the judge may also release the arrestee to alternatives to pretrial detention—home arrest, electronic monitoring, day or evening reporting programs—or to diversion programs. Diversion programs are a sentencing option typically reserved for certain types of usually first-time or low-level offenders, such as simple drug possession or DUI. These programs may or may not require an admission of guilt, usually (but not always) involve the court, and usually allow the arrestee to avoid formal prosecution and a criminal record by completing the program and avoiding further system involvement.

In-Custody Programs

It is a relatively modern concept to provide rehabilitative treatment for people in jail for the conditions that helped land them there, as is taking steps to prepare them for a return to society. Incarcerated individuals often have needs for substance abuse treatment, physical and mental health treatment, education, and vocation and job training, among others. The controversy rages about what prisoners deserve. And the argument that jails should detain and punish and nothing more is sometimes countered with the argument that once released from jail without having received any preparation for a return to society, prisoners pose more of a threat—not less—than before they served their time. In addition, primary language issues, facility space, service provider shortages, and a perpetual shortage of funds are obstacles to providing services in jail, perhaps even more so than in prisons. Regardless of where one may stand on the issue of rehabilitation, it is a fact that constant turnover in jail populations,

Abscond: To fail to appear in court on an appointed day or to fail to report to one's probation or parole officer or to make them aware of a change of residence.

▲ Delivery of jail programming and services is a difficult issue to manage for jail administrators and inmates alike.

© Reuters/Lucy Nicholson

combined with the jail environment itself, make education and treatment difficult to provide. Programs need to be structured as short-term, ongoing, or suited for "drop in" attendance.

Some of the programs currently offered in jail require the inmate to pay a fee to attend. Although it is understandable that jail administrators must balance budgets, such fees reinforce class pressures and contribute to a continuing disadvantage for the poor.

One example of an evidence-based program currently in use, in both jails and prisons, is the Transition Accountability Plan (TAP). The concept of the program is to begin planning for a prisoner's release as soon as he or she begins a stay in custody. By mapping out specific needs, goals, tasks, and activities, the plan helps supervision staff more accurately monitor and manage an inmate's progress and gives the inmate more motivation to stay on track.

Another promising approach to inmate programming is called Moral Reconation Therapy (MRT), which uses cognitive-behavioral principles intended to help adult inmates increase their ability to examine ego, social behavior, and positive growth, with the larger goal of increasing moral reasoning. Using group sessions and exercises, this program contains a set of goals that include confronting beliefs, attitudes, and behaviors; assessing current relationships; developing tolerance for frustration; reinforcing positive habits; and forming positive identity.[25]

Occasionally, jail personnel find a way to implement an enlightened or innovative jail program that represents a significant shift in culture. One example of this is San Francisco's RSVP (Resolve to Stop the Violence Project). Compelled by high recidivism rates and an awareness of principles of restorative justice, Sunny Schwartz and her colleagues, including then Sheriff Michael Hennessey, instituted RSVP, which was designed for men with violent histories to help one another analyze and understand their crimes and hold one another accountable for changing their behavior.[26] In her book, *Dreams from the Monster Factory,* Schwartz relates a compelling story of a challenging, but effective, approach to dealing with a difficult population.

The challenge of implementing programming in jail is a complex one, given the range of prisoner needs, including high rates of communicable diseases, joblessness, gang affiliations, and various forms of disconnect from society.

Alternatives to Incarceration

Net-widening: Applying sanctions to individuals who would otherwise have been warned or released had those sanctions not existed. This can be an unintended consequence of expanding the range of correctional options.

For both pretrial defendants and sentenced offenders, most counties maintain forms of control that the judge may order in lieu of time in locked facilities. These alternatives include the more traditional parole and probation and the more innovative electronic monitoring, reporting centers, and specialized courts. These options usually have eligibility criteria designed to ensure that they are applied to the individuals with whom they will be most effective. The eligibility is based on such factors as offense, risk level, criminal background, and treatment needs.

Again, controversy. Some argue that alternatives contribute to "net-widening"—that is, used too often for persons whose low-level crimes would not otherwise result in a jail sentence, and so are not truly alternatives to jail and, therefore, do not help overcrowding issues inside of jail and do not address high incarceration rates. On the contrary, these critics argue, these measures simply increase the reach—widen the net—of the justice system and control even greater numbers of individuals. Others believe that, when implemented properly, alternative measures are entirely appropriate for low-level drug and property crimes and can function to keep prison and jail space reserved for the most dangerous criminals. (See Chapter 5.)

. . . .

SUMMARY

Jails are distinct from prisons and function as the centers of confinement for people entering into the larger criminal justice system, exiting that system, or awaiting transfer to another institution. Jails hold people who are at many different points in processing through the system, and there is constant flux and turnover in the jail population. Jails are operated and administered at the city or county level, while prisons are state-level institutions. Since jails are run by local jurisdictions, they are subject to local political and budgetary pressures. Jail conditions are often substandard and made worse by overcrowded facilities.

The jail incarceration rate and the number of people in jail have increased greatly during the last few decades. The portion of women in jails is increasing, and there is a disproportionate number of people of color held in jails and prisons. Almost half of those in jail have not yet been tried or convicted. The poorest among them cannot afford bail and must await trial behind bars. Prisoners, tried or not, exhibit and magnify the city's social ills. Treatment programs to prepare jail inmates for release constitute a politically volatile issue and are difficult to accomplish in the jail environment. There are some alternatives to jail, including specialized courts and electronic monitoring. More research needs to be done to adequately evaluate the effectiveness of these intermediate sanctions.

DISCUSSION QUESTIONS

1. How are jails different than prisons?

2. What are the main functions of jails?

3. What are some of the alternatives to jail? What are the disadvantages or advantages of these for the arrested person? For jail administrators?

4. What are the challenges for jail administrators dealing with a wide range of detainees?

5. If you were in charge of innovating a strategy for handling pretrial detainees outside of jail, what would you recommend?

6. Discuss ways that a jail may include or reflect the problems of the community in which it is located.

7. What are some of the ways that cities and counties may respond to prison overcrowding? What are the pros and cons of each option?

8. Why is it challenging to administer quality programming in jail? What could help solve these problems?

KEY TERMS

Abscond, 83

Arraignment, 68

Bail, 71

Booking, 72

Contempt of court, 71

Gender responsive, 72

Mug shot, 81

Net-widening, 84

Parole, 70

NOTES

1. Winton and Blankstein 2010
2. Bureau of Justice Statistics 2012
3. Minton 2013
4. Stephan and Walsh 2011
5. James 2004
6. Ibid.
7. Ibid.
8. Minton 2013
9. James and Glaze 2006
10. The Sentencing Project 2002
11. Minton 2013
12. Minton 2013; U.S. Census Bureau 2013b
13. Population percentages sum to over 100% because Hispanics may also be represented in racial categories.
14. Minton 2012
15. Knochel 2013
16. *Los Angeles Times* 2013
17. Beck and Gilliard 1997
18. Minton 2013
19. Ibid.
20. Disaster Center 2013
21. Federal Bureau of Investigation 2012
22. American Correctional Association 1991, 32 (Standard 3-ALDF-2B-03); Beck 2006; Kimme, Bowker, and Deichman 2011
23. Stephan and Walsh 2011
24. Hartney and Vuong 2009; National Council on Crime and Delinquency 2007
25. Little et al. 2010
26. Schwartz 2009

$SAGE edge™

Sharpen your skills with SAGE edge at edge.sagepub.com/krisberg

SAGE edge for students provides a personalized approach to help you accomplish your coursework goals in an easy-to-use learning environment. This site includes action plans, mobile-friendly eFlashcards and web quizzes as well as web, audio, and video resources and links to SAGE journal articles.

5 Probation and Alternatives to Incarceration

 1 To be able to define probation, community corrections, and alternatives to incarceration.

2 To learn to explain the goals of probation and its role in the criminal justice system.

3 To understand the origins of intensive probation as well as its complexity.

4 To grasp the tension between law enforcement and rehabilitative approaches to probation and what leeway probation officers have to combine them.

Probation has been an integral part of U.S. corrections for over a century. Today, probation is the most utilized correctional option, with more individuals on probation in the community than in prison, in jail, and on parole, combined. Probation and alternatives to detention are meant to satisfy the purpose of the public and the government in prosecuting crime in a way that avoids the harsh, costly, and in many ways counterproductive option of incarceration.

Although views of the usefulness of probation have evolved over the years, the basic purposes remain the same: to sanction lawbreakers through restrictions placed on their freedoms, to protect public safety by supervising probationers and responding to their violations or new offenses, and to help the probationer avoid more illegal activity through treatment, education, and other services.

The question of whether probation "works" is related to these purposes and several other issues. To measure the effectiveness of probation as a means of crime control, one can track recidivism rates and crime rates. Then there is the issue of whether probation satisfies the public's need for accountability on the part of the offender and whether the consequence is appropriate to the offense. Public opinion and political agendas both influence and are influenced by how justice is carried out. The public has its ideas about what is fitting punishment. Politicians often exploit and inflame the public sentiment for political purposes. At present, probation tends to be viewed as a lenient outcome, and the public at times questions whether the system is meeting its mandate. At the same time, people generally understand that not all offenders can or should be put behind bars. It currently appears that a large portion of the public currently supports probation, especially for low-level cases.

With the right practices and resources, probation can, in fact, fulfill the public's desire for a punitive response to crime and protect public safety. The recent trend toward

 5 To gain a sense of what probation officers do to investigate and supervise their clients.

 7 To be able to discuss different alternatives to incarceration and how effective they might be in increasing public safety.

6 To understand the interactions between the court, the probation officer, and the probationer.

"evidence-based practice" (EBP—practices that have been rigorously evaluated and found effective) has helped departments implement strategies that have the greatest potential for positive impact. Through EBP research, progressive ideas that have long been met with skepticism are now being validated and are becoming more accepted. The effectiveness of probation is connected to adequate funding, training, implementation of policies, and caseload size. Underfunded probation departments often demand that officers handle caseloads in the hundreds. These case burdens, among other factors, impact the quality of supervision that the probation officer (PO) is able to deliver.

What Is Probation?

The justice system encompasses a range of sanctions for criminal behavior, with degrees of severity and control. Prison and jail emphasize isolation, incapacitation, and punishment. Probation in its most progressive form emphasizes community involvement, rehabilitation, and a proportional response to crime. Depending on the severity of the offense and the risk the defendant poses to public safety, probation can be supplemented with tools and programs, referred to as alternatives to incarceration. These alternatives, such as electronic monitoring or specialized courts, can address the individual's risk factors.

Probation and alternatives to incarceration are forms of community supervision. They allow the defendant to maintain ties to family, community, and employment while being under correctional supervision. Community supervision restricts a defendant's liberties and monitors his or her activities. The court may determine that the probationer must fulfill additional conditions of probation, such as attending community-based treatment or other programs focused on the individual's needs and circumstances that contributed to the offense. These programs may include mental health counseling, substance abuse treatment, occupational training, or family therapy. The court may also put restrictions on the offender to protect public safety and to reduce the chances of recidivism, such as prohibiting the client from visiting certain neighborhoods or associating with known criminals or victims of the individual's crimes.

The threat of incarceration underpins this arrangement. A sentence of probation usually includes the suspension of a custody sentence. As part of monitoring behavior under probation supervision, the PO has regular contacts with the client, in the office and in the field. The officer visits the probationer's home and workplace, and speaks with family, friends, coworkers, and service providers. Should the probationer violate the court's conditions, he or she is subject to a probation revocation and custody.

A judge may impose a sentence of probation before or after the judgment of guilt or innocence in court, which is called adjudication. Sentencing a person to probation before trial is less common and allows the defendant awaiting trial to avoid a record of conviction. The defendant is released pending trial; however, if he or she fails to meet the conditions of release, he or she may be remanded to detention in jail until trial. Most commonly, the judge sentences a defendant after conviction.

Who Is on Probation?

At the end of 2012, there were almost 4 million American men and women on probation—1 out of every 61 adults in the United States. The average length of stay on probation in 2012 was 23 months.[1]

Evidence-based practice: Practices that have been proven to be effective through rigorous and quantitative analysis.

Conditions of probation: The terms or requirements that an offender must meet to maintain his or her probation status and avoid incarceration. Conditions typically require the offender to keep in contact with a probation officer, maintain employment, avoid criminal behavior, and participate in any court-ordered programming.

Adjudication: A court's decision regarding the guilt or innocence of a defendant.

Historically, probation was reserved mainly for very low-level offenses—infractions and misdemeanors—but since the 1980s, the percentage of probationers with felony convictions, including those with serious crime histories, has risen.[2]

After rising every year since 1980—the year that the federal Bureau of Justice Statistics (BJS) began collecting these data—the total U.S. probation population started a decline in 2008, which continued through 2012. In that year, the total was just under 4 million (3,942,800)—about equal to 2001 levels (3,934,713). The probation *rate* (per 100,000 U.S. adult residents) also declined in this period, from 1,878 in 2007 to 1,633 in 2012.

Between 2011 and 2012, 31 states, the District of Columbia, and the federal system each reported a decline in probationers, while 19 states reported increases. Thus, despite a national decline, some states were moving in the opposite direction. It is often a few states that account for most of these changes. For instance, most of the recent decline in the national probation population was accounted for by just a handful of states, including California, Florida, Georgia, Michigan, New York, North Carolina, and Texas.[3] In several states that reported lower probation counts, state budgetary issues led lawmakers to intentionally reduce the number of low-level, nonviolent clients on their probation roles. These changes highlight several characteristics of probation in the 21st century. The very nature of probation has changed, as resources are usually insufficient to serve the low-level cases for which probation was originally designed. Probation rates are lower in part due to lower crime rates, increased use of pretrial diversion programs, shorter terms of probation (although the national average has remained consistent throughout this period of decline), and an easing of tough-on-crime attitudes.

Efforts to decrease the number of people under state correctional supervision, including **early release** programs, have generally not resulted in a related rise in crime rates, suggesting that a careful reduction in the use of incarceration can protect public safety.[4] The effectiveness of probation is discussed later in this chapter.

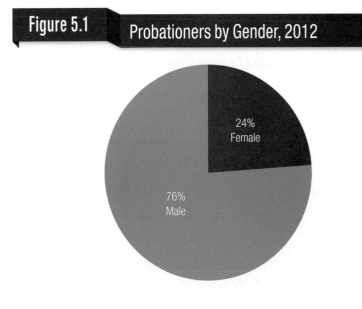

Figure 5.1 — Probationers by Gender, 2012

Source: Maruschak and Bonczar 2013.

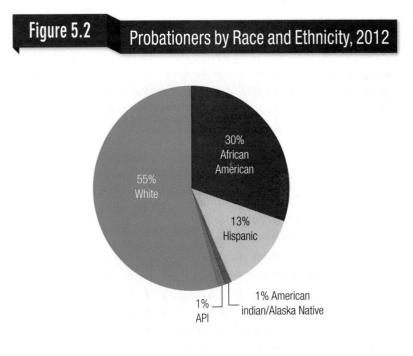

Figure 5.2 — Probationers by Race and Ethnicity, 2012

Figures 5.1 and 5.2 show that three quarters of those on probation in 2012 were male, and just under half were White (55%). *Source: Maruschak and Bonczar 2013.*
Note: API = Asia-Pacific Islander.

Early release: Release from custody or supervision prior to completion of original sentence, often due to good behavior or to relieve facility overcrowding.

Figure 5.3   Probationers by Offense Level, 2012

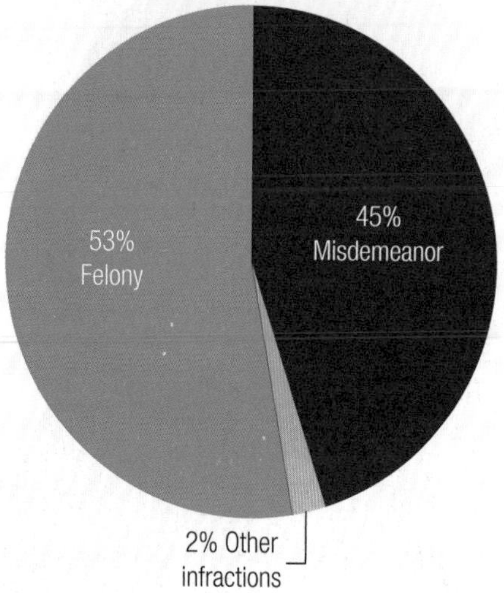

45% Misdemeanor

53% Felony

2% Other infractions

Source: Maruschak and Bonczar 2013.

Figure 5.4   Probationers by Most Serious Offense, 2012

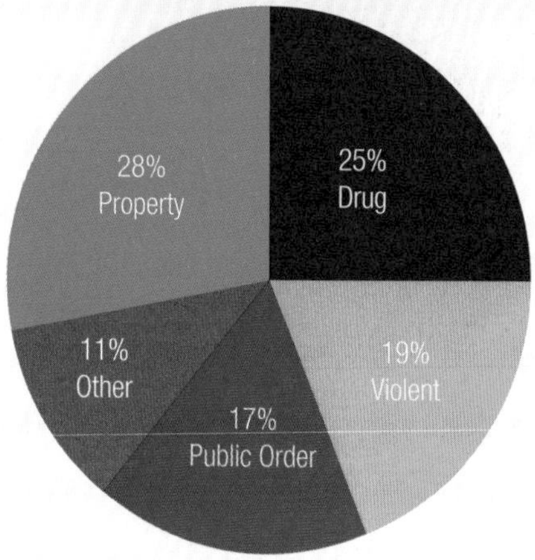

28% Property

25% Drug

11% Other

19% Violent

17% Public Order

Figures 5.3 and 5.4 show that probation cases in 2012 were of all types, with almost one fifth violent, and just over half felonies. *Source: Maruschak and Bonczar 2013.*

Judicial reprieve: An early form of probation where, at the discretion of a judge, lawbreakers could avoid time behind bars if they avoided further criminal behavior.

A Brief History of Probation

Many of the elements of today's probation stem from its 19th-century roots. In the Western world, its roots go back centuries, perhaps to England of the 1200s, when lawbreakers might have received the "benefit of clergy" by reciting a psalm in front of a judge. This was often little more than a way for the educated and connected (to the church, in particular) to avoid the plight of commoners. Still, the practice continued into the 1800s. A practice called judicial reprieve—popular in England and then in the United States of the 1800s—was a more formalized process by which judges could use their discretion to suspend incarceration or not impose it at all, as long as the offender continued to toe the line. The U.S. Supreme Court eventually decided that judicial reprieve inappropriately took the power to respond to crime away from the legislative and executive branches, mainly because there were no requirements for judges to set an end point to the probation period.

Some judges continued to look for ways they could use their discretion to mitigate punishments they felt to be unduly harsh. Releasing offenders on recognizance was one such method developed in the 1800s. Similar to today's practice of releasing those accused of crimes on bail until their court date, recognizance is also the basic concept underlying today's probation. It allowed judges to release convicted persons if they promised to meet some condition, such as commit no more crimes or pay a debt. Usually this included a payment—a precursor to today's bail—to the court that would be returned only if the individuals held up their end of the bargain. If they did not, they forfeited the money and typically went to jail. Thus, by the mid-1800s, there was precedent for the court to use discretion in administering the penal code and to maintain jurisdiction over persons released to the community.

In 1841, a cobbler named John Augustus convinced a Boston court to put a man charged with public drunkenness in his charge instead of in jail. He promised the court he would help the offender stay straight or else the court could reinstate the sentence. Over the next 18 years, Augustus helped hundreds of would-be inmates and established the underpinnings of modern probation. Augustus not only gave probation its name (from the Latin *probatio* for testing or showing to be fit or worthy), but his philosophy and the methods he developed still guide the practice of probation today. Still an integral part of the modern job, Augustus's methods included building rapport with his clients, connecting with their families and communities, and identifying and providing assistance for individual needs. In screening his clients, Augustus felt it important to get to know the individual and the circumstances that precipitated the offense; he established what is now called the presentence investigation. His approaches to case supervision and revocation are also the roots for today's practices. Thirty years after Augustus, juvenile probation was formally established in Massachusetts, and in 1901, adult probation was established in New York. Although the U.S. Supreme Court ruled in 1916 that courts did not necessarily have the authority to impose probation, the practice continued to spread as state legislators enacted laws to the same effect. By 1956, probation was legally established in all U.S. states and the federal government.[5]

Two Key Perspectives on Probation

Early in the process of institutionalizing probation, two perspectives on its purpose and administration arose that probation departments still try to balance. The Augustus-inspired social worker approach emphasizes the needs of the offender and support and rehabilitative services. The law enforcement perspective emphasizes surveillance, the enforcement of rules and conditions of probation, and detecting and responding to violations by intensifying sanctions or revoking probation.

▲ John Augustus is considered the father of probation.

AFE, http://www.mass.gov/ courts/docs/probation/fact-sheet.pdf

In the 1960s and 1970s, approaches to community supervision were primarily guided by the theories of rehabilitation and reintegration. This view assumes that personal issues and circumstances that led to criminal behavior can be "fixed" or ameliorated, and that law-breakers can be guided toward a **prosocial** lifestyle. However, behind bars, prisoners do not face the real-life circumstances and challenges in the community that influence their inappropriate behavior. The reintegrative theory of corrections takes the rehabilitative perspective to the next step. Rehabilitation tends to work best in the client's home community, where new relationships with service providers and newly positive relationships with other community members can help the probationer stay on track. In the best case, the probationer is reintegrated as a healthier and more productive member of the community, and the community itself is renewed and strengthened.

By the 1980s, and increasingly in the 1990s, probation in the United States began to move toward a law enforcement perspective. For reasons that are still being debated by historians and crime experts, there was an upswing in violent crime between 1960 and the mid 1990s. Additionally, social movements, such as civil rights, seemed to threaten the established social and political order. Advocates for a harsher criminal justice system used these changes to incite and exploit public unease and push for harsher sentencing and punishment. The public began to demand that corrections, including probation, change its course

Prosocial: Actions and behaviors that are beneficial to the larger society.

away from rehabilitation. This tough-on-crime movement resulted in a rapid rise in incarceration rates, serious facility overcrowding, and ballooning corrections costs.

The law enforcement perspective is still prevalent today. The primary purpose of probation is most often to mete out punishment (retribution) and safeguard public safety—that is, to reduce crime during the offender's sentence (incapacitation) and deter future crime. Nevertheless, rehabilitative services can be part of the state's effort to reach these ends, and Augustus's caseworker perspective is still an important part of community corrections. In fact, the dominance of the law enforcement perspective may well be giving way once again to rehabilitative objectives as EBP demonstrates the benefits of engagement and empathy, backed by certain and swift sanctions that are more finely graduated and that keep the probationer in the community.

Probation Administration

Probation is administered at various levels of government—at the state, county, or city level, or a combination of state and local. Administrative responsibilities are usually handled by state departments of corrections, but the courts and the executive branch may also play a role. There are more than 2,000 probation agencies in the United States. Probation philosophy and approaches are partially shaped by the values and demands of the local public and political leaders. The local agencies that translate the philosophy into policies and procedures are the courts, the probation department, the police department, service providers, and other local groups. The individuals who function in these entities are judges and court administrators, prosecutors and defense attorneys, probation officers and supervisors (and, in some jurisdictions, pretrial services officers), police officers and brass, and front-line service professionals, among others. Supervision decisions fall mostly to judges, probation officers, and their supervisors.

The Role of Probation Officers

The role of probation officers (POs) is broadly divided into two areas—investigation and supervision. Although the supervision function is the one most commonly associated with probation officers, investigation takes a large percentage of an officer's time. Especially in larger agencies, officers may specialize in one area or the other. In larger systems, including the federal probation system, "pretrial services officers" investigate and supervise defendants awaiting trial, and "probation officers" investigate and supervise individuals after conviction. Pretrial services may be its own department, distinct from regular probation. Within these roles, officers may specialize in certain groups, such as gang members, domestic violence cases, or sex offenders.

Probation agencies vary a great deal in how they manage probation officers. Their recruitment strategies, the type and amount of training officers receive, the size of caseloads, the level of officer autonomy, the institutional support officers receive, and many other factors vary from one agency to another.

Caseload: The total body of client cases under a probation or parole officer's care. Also, a probation or parole specialty, such as intensive supervision or domestic violence.

Probation agencies also differ in their approach to supervision, depending on whether their perspective leans toward the rehabilitative approach or punitive law enforcement. In reality, probation officers serve both these functions. But an officer's personal opinion about the appropriate balance between the two roles can have a marked impact on how he or she approaches the work. A department's leaders also exert a great deal of influence over the culture of the organization and the values it expresses. One way that departments are focusing on reducing recidivism is to consciously alter their recruiting and hiring practices and select candidates who are more likely to succeed using a rehabilitative approach.

Probation officers rely on their own creativity as well as collaboration with other public sector professionals to do the best job possible and to individually case manage their clients.

© Boston Globe / Getty Images

Depending on the jurisdiction, the PO will have the support of a number of other professionals including supervisors and administrators; representatives of other governmental agencies such as the court, police, public health, and child protective services; and service and programming providers in the community. This support may be more or less formalized. For instance, some jurisdictions assemble teams of professionals from a variety of governmental and nongovernmental groups that formally meet to discuss and make recommendations about a particular probationer. Some jurisdictions may allow or require members of the probationer's family and community to be included. Other jurisdictions have similar teams but only on an informal or as-needed basis, and still others collaborate infrequently with other agencies and stakeholders. In all of these variations, the probation officer plays a central role.

Today's probation departments often use risk assessment instruments and **case management systems**. These can assist probation officers in making sentencing recommendations, deciding on what approach or tactics will work best with each probationer, and tracking a probationer's progress in meeting conditions. These tools can also assist with balancing workload, ensuring quality, collecting system statistics, using resources efficiently, identifying gaps in services, and managing staffing and training. Well-designed systems can ensure that probation officers have adequate guidance and institutional support for the myriad decisions they have to make.

A probation officer's caseload can vary widely depending on the size and resources of the department, the officer's experience, the types of probationers being supervised, and the level of supervision that each requires. More experienced POs can handle larger numbers of more complex cases. Some cases involve hardened, system-savvy career criminals, others involve first-time DUIs. Probation officers that supervise high-risk probationers will have lower caseloads, perhaps 20 to 30, while those that supervise low-level probationers may have caseloads as high as 145 or more.[6] Principles of EBP direct higher levels of resources to the probation clients most at risk for additional consequential criminal behavior. Officers with specialized caseloads—such as violent offenders, sex offenders, clients on electronic monitoring, and the seriously mentally ill—see their clients often, spend more time with them, and work harder to help them change their problem behavior. However, budget constraints tend to increase officer caseload size.

Case management system: Computer programs that assist caseworkers with many aspects of their work, such as recording and tracking client data (e.g., contact information, background, court orders, risk assessment scores, drug test results, GPS monitoring, progress toward meeting conditions, etc.); recording daily work flow notes (i.e., how officer spent his or her day); integrating client data with information from the court, law enforcement, and other agencies; receiving automated recommendations regarding how best to approach each case; assistance in meeting agency policies, and reporting requirements.

Face-to-face interviews provide valuable information. A PO needs to know when *not* to speak to an employer, who may be unaware of the employee's probation status.

© iStockphoto.com / Christa Brunt

Many officers have reported feeling their caseload was too high for them to provide adequate supervision to all of their clients.[7] A large and diverse probationer caseload certainly makes the probation officer's job more difficult, and the media and public are quick to criticize when an overburdened department fails to prevent a serious new offense by a probationer. However, research has shown that the number of cases alone does not determine the quality of the supervision or the rate of recidivism.[8] Other factors are germane, such as departmental support, the nature of the supervision over the PO, the quality of the PO's training, and the seriousness of the specific cases. It is important that efforts to reduce caseloads be coupled with training in best practices.[9]

Probation officers usually have the authority to arrest and detain clients suspected of violations of probation or new offenses. This authority may be used rarely and only for the PO's own cases. Probation officers may also work closely with law enforcement and participate in raids and arrests when probationers are likely to be present. Some POs are trained and certified to carry weapons (such as firearms or pepper spray), and some wear uniforms while on duty. Most wear street clothes and do not carry guns or other weapons.

Sentencing and Investigation

A sentence of probation is not as straightforward as a sentence of incarceration. For incarceration, a judge mainly decides only the length of the sentence, parole eligibility, and the security level of the facility. When sentencing a person to probation, the judge must specify parameters including the duration of the sentence, terms of early release, type and intensity of supervision, and programs and service requirements. Each of these areas may entail fairly complex choices for the bench.

The role of the probation agency begins before sentencing, when a PO completes a presentence investigation and report (PSI). The PSI is presented to the court and used to assist in the sentencing decision. It is closely linked to the process of risk classifications for behavioral problems and new offenses and to assign programming and services. (See Chapter 3.)

The PSI includes sentencing recommendations, which the judge usually relies on in determining what sentence to choose after a conviction, or as part of a plea bargain. From initial sentencing decisions to termination of probation, the PO's recommendations are strongly considered. Most research finds that judges follow the PO's sentencing recommendations in the majority of cases.[10]

A judge may also hear the recommendations of the prosecutor and defense attorneys or other professionals such as psychologists. The PO's recommendations tend to have the most influence, because they are presumably based on the officer's objective research into the defendant and the circumstances of the offense as well as the officer's knowledge of the programming and services available and how those might serve a specific defendant.

A probation client may not serve any time in secure custody, apart from time in detention, at arrest or awaiting trial. The judge may also impose a combination of secure custody and probation. A split sentence is a period in custody, often six months, followed by a period on probation. An intermittent sentence is a term of probation interspersed with time in custody—each night or each weekend.

Supervision

Each probationer sentenced to probation is assigned a probation officer who will oversee his or her supervision. After sentencing, the officer and probationer meet to discuss the particulars as to how the individual will meet the court's orders, such as how and when they will stay in contact, the methods of supervision and surveillance, behavioral expectations for both of them, and in what community services the probationer will participate.

With the important exception of the power to investigate crime and make arrests, in most states, the probation officer holds little formal authority over the probationer; the judge makes the major decisions about sentencing and revocations. The PO typically does not

Probation officers must constantly weigh the client's needs, the client's behavior, and the protection of public safety.

© Reuters/Lucy Nicholson

SPOTLIGHT

STATE EFFORTS TO REDUCE PROBATION REVOCATIONS

In the face of perpetually crowded facilities, and given that upwards of half of probation revocations stem from technical violations rather than new crimes, some states have implemented laws and policies to limit the use of probation revocation. The National Conference of State Legislatures and the Pew Charitable Trusts produced a summary of state efforts to limit the impact of revocations on prison and jail crowding and to increase the options that courts and probation departments have in responding to violations.[1]

Some statutes dictate when probationers can be returned to custody and for how long. Georgia, for example, limits prison time to two years for revocations, even when the probation term would have been longer. Vermont does not allow incarceration for revocations except when public safety is clearly threatened or the client will receive treatment available only in a custodial setting. A Pennsylvania law says that, except for the most serious cases, those returned to custody for revocation must be allowed to leave the facility for court-approved activities like work, school, or medical care. Iowa and Wyoming allow judges to remand probation violators to jail for short periods without a formal revocation, making their time on probation a mixed sentence of jail and community supervision.

Some states, including Louisiana, Maine, Nevada, Tennessee, and Texas, have established custodial facilities as alternative forms of incarceration for probation violations. These are often community-based options that place greater emphasis on rehabilitation than jails and prisons.

have the authority to substantively change the conditions of probation independently, but he or she can request changes of the court—to step up conditions for a client doing poorly (such as increase the frequency of drug testing) or to step down conditions for a client doing well (such as reduced community service hours). Similarly, the probation officer cannot remand a client independently. Rather, the officer can instigate a hearing, by which the court decides on the matter. If and when the court determines that all conditions have been met, the judge could terminate the probation.

Despite the lack of formal authority, the probation officer in large part dictates the tone and content of the probation experience. The PO is the client's primary link to the system. He or she is a sort of gatekeeper to other system representatives, such as the court, the police, or service providers. When the client begins to stray, commits a violation, or is rearrested, the probation officer has discretion to decide how to proceed. The PO may ramp up the punishment and restrictions through a request of the court for modification or a formal revocation of probation.

Instead of these formal proceedings, the probation officer will often use discretion to handle issues "in house" rather than involving the court, leveraging minor transgressions to encourage greater cooperation and build trust. The PO has significant leeway to more or less strictly apply court orders; that is, he or she can make probation seem more or less restrictive and burdensome to the probationer. On the other hand, the officer might adjust expectations or logistics to give the probationer a better chance of success, for instance, by rescheduling appointments so that the client does not have to miss work or to better meet public transit schedules.

Perhaps most significantly, there are a number of states—including Delaware, Georgia, Maine, Minnesota, Montana, and Oregon—that have granted greater autonomy to probation departments to alter the conditions of probation without court involvement, in some cases even to remand violators to custody. Typically, the state provides a set of "intermediate sanctions"—and a process for applying them—that the agency can employ, also without a revocation hearing. These are meant to address the nature of the violation and allow the probationer continued contact with his or her community. They may include electronic monitoring, intensive probation, day reporting, stepped-up drug testing, fines, community service, and new or additional programming like drug treatment, education, or restorative justice. Some states use short-term stays in jail, often referred to as "flash incarceration." Although mainly intended as a means to clear busy court calendars, reduce revocations, and save expensive bed space for the most serious cases, this authority also gives POs extra tools to use in their efforts to motivate clients and sends a clear message to probationers that violations will be dealt with quickly and decisively.

QUESTIONS

1 What is the main objective of reducing prison revocation for probation violations?

2 What are some of the strategies used by corrections departments to reduce revocations to prison or jail?

3 Under what circumstances do you think a short-term jail sentence is a good response to a probation violation?

Note

1. Lawrence 2008

Some jurisdictions give the probation department more discretion to modify the conditions of probation, which can give the PO more tools to encourage cooperation and buy-in from the probationer and can save the time and costs associated with going to court. This approach is an example of EBP and has proven effective in reducing overall recidivism.

Probation and law enforcement officers are vested with the authority to investigate, detect, and prosecute offenses perpetrated by probationers. Importantly, probationers can be searched based on a lower legal threshold—reasonable suspicion rather than **probable cause**—which in practice means that probationers are subject to search of their person and property at almost any time. This facilitates one of the key objectives of the probation officer's job—supervision to ensure that court orders are followed and to promote public safety. This is another example of the way the officer plays a pervasive and decisive role in the life of his or her clients.

Probable cause: Sufficient reason based upon known facts to believe a crime has been committed or that certain property is connected with a crime.

Technical violations: A breach of those conditions of probation (or parole) that on their own would not be considered criminal or would not lead to criminal proceedings, such as failing to hold down a job or failing a drug test.

Violation, Revocation, and Termination

Technical violations are instances of the probationer not complying with conditions of supervision, although such incidents may not necessarily represent major behavior issues or law violations. Technical violations include such behaviors as failing to keep appointments with the probation officer, not attending services mandated by the court, or moving residences without informing the probation officer. Failing a periodic drug test, neglecting to pay court-ordered restitution or fines, skipping class, or missing work can also be violations.

▲ Time in jail and in court often brings celebrities down to earth. Perhaps it shouldn't, but status may bring special treatment to the well-connected.

© iStockphoto.com / EdStock

Law violations, or new offenses, can lead to a revocation hearing. Probationers have **due process rights** in the revocation proceeding that are similar to those of new offenders. They have the right to a preliminary hearing when the facts of the new case are presented and probable cause of a violation is shown. They then have the right to a hearing before a judge in which written notice of the charges is presented and evidence and witnesses for both sides are heard and confronted. Except in certain cases, probationers have the right to representation by an attorney during hearings and sentencing. The probationer may be held in custody during revocation proceedings.

If a revocation hearing results in a determination that a violation has occurred, the judge may lift the suspended sentence and remand the probationer to custody, continue probation but with a longer term or with heightened levels of supervision and requirements, or censure the probationer but otherwise make no changes. A revocation hearing is a major step that the officer may often try to forestall as long as possible. Probation officers may choose to not pursue incarceration for technical violations unless they become chronic or might lead to more serious illegal behavior. Still, technical violations account for a large proportion of revocations—many experts estimating about 50%.[11]

There is inconsistency in how probation and the courts handle technical violations and new offenses. Relatively minor violations sometimes result in incarceration, while some serious new offenses may not. Although discretion on the part of POs and judges is sometimes necessary to consider changes in circumstances and context, this inconsistency has prompted criticism that probation may be unfair or ineffective.

The number of revocations stemming solely from technical violations, as opposed to those stemming from new offenses or a combination, is difficult to ascertain, because probationers who are thought to have committed a new offense are sometimes revoked on a technical violation. This is done to speed the process and ease the caseload in criminal courts. However, this practice denies the probationer a thorough defense, as revocation hearings are typically not as thorough as regular court. In some cases, a probationer may have a more favorable outcome in court fighting the new charges.

Courts and probation agencies have learned that it is important to make probation conditions reasonable, achievable, and meaningful. It is also important to provide the right level of supervision and conditions. If probation is too lenient, the individual may not take it seriously, and the public's demand for accountability may not be met. On the other hand, too many requirements can lead to frustration and a sense of futility in the probationer, which can, in turn, lead to violations and probation failures. Probation officers are in the best position to gauge this balance, and with adequate training and resources, they can help their clients succeed.

Does Probation Work? Probation Research

It is important for probation agencies to ascertain which approaches are the most effective for a given context. Research can help agencies choose the most appropriate strategies to address specific factors, such as limited resources or a particular sort of client. The typical outcome measures used to study the effectiveness of probation are violations or new offenses during the probation period, successful completion of probation, or recidivism in the months and years following a probation period.

BJS reports that, of those leaving probation in 2012, 68% had successfully completed their terms or had early terminations, while 15% were incarcerated and 13% had some other unsatisfactory result that did not include incarceration. Among the 68%, it is not clear how many had violations before completion.[12] Various studies indicate that the percentage of probationers who violate the terms of their probation either through a technical violation or a new offense ranges from 12% to 55%. The wide variation may be due to multiple factors and the various ways probation is practiced in different jurisdictions. These factors may include probationer characteristics, jurisdiction, community, department, and the probation officer. Probationer characteristics include offense history, crime triggers, and criminogenic needs. Each probation department will have protocols for when to use probation for more serious cases; this is

YOU DECIDE

Absconding Probationers

Roughly 20% of probationers never appear at their appointments with probation officers. This is called absconding. There is no evidence that these probation clients are being arrested for new crimes, but no one knows this for sure. However, one absconder killed his mother-in-law. The incident received extensive media attention.

The local jail is crowded, and the county cannot afford to spend more than it already does tracking down, arresting, and incarcerating absconding probationers. The county has tried requiring electronic monitors for high-risk probationers, but these same individuals just disconnect the monitors. Some jurisdictions have proposed using very short jail stays ("flash incarceration")—up to 24 hours—to deter absconding. Other observers argue that the probation department should improve its service and treatment offerings and provide alternatives to incarceration for probation violators.

YOU DECIDE: **How should the probation department respond to probationers who are "in the wind"?**

partly driven by the political climate. In addition, each has its own method of distributing cases and level of support for its officers. Rural departments have different cultures than urban ones, and varying socioeconomic and treatment options. Each officer has his or her own skills, experience, and approach to supervision. Despite a variety of evaluation methods, there are no definitive or established measures of violations that indicate whether probation "works."

Most studies of probation focus on persons convicted of felonies, even though probation is used about as often for less serious convictions. When the results of studies include misdemeanants and felons, the recidivism rates drop substantially. Misdemeanants often require and receive few services and little supervision compared to felons, but it is important to note that probation is particularly effective for these lower-level individuals, with up to 75% successfully completing their sentences.[13]

The effectiveness of probation and alternatives to incarceration must be considered in light of the apparent ineffectiveness of prison and jail as a method of deterring future crime. Over half of those behind bars have been there before, usually not long before their most recent system involvement. It is difficult to design research that compares the behavior of those held in secure custody—where there is 24/7 surveillance and strict behavioral restrictions—to the behavior of those who are largely free in their communities. However, one study was able to account for this challenge by matching study participants on offense type and history and several other variables. It found that offenders subject to short-term incarceration had significantly higher recidivism rates than those sentenced to community service instead of imprisonment.[14] Another study found that traditional probation was more effective than jail and as effective as alternatives to incarceration at reducing new arrests.[15]

Due process rights: Broadly, an entitlement or legally binding guarantee that established principles and procedures are applied uniformly to each case. Specifically, due process may mean different things in different proceedings, but usually every defendant gets an advance notice of hearings and an opportunity to be present, to be heard, and to defend himself or herself. It also typically includes the rights to legal counsel, to confront and cross examine the witnesses, to not have to testify against yourself, and to have an offense proven beyond a reasonable doubt.

SPOTLIGHT

PERCEPTIONS OF PROBATION AND ALTERNATIVES: PUNITIVE ENOUGH?

Most members of the public seem to feel that incarceration does not help reduce recidivism, and many believe that time behind bars actually makes it more likely that persons will reoffend after release. Research is difficult to carry out on this topic, but carefully conducted studies have found no reduced recidivism and sometimes increases in recidivism after time behind bars.[1]

Members of the public certainly have an interest in not releasing persons who are highly likely to reoffend, but most support a role for community-based supervision, especially when it is coupled with rehabilitative programming.[2] However, the public does not always consider probation as punitive enough—that is, as holding law-breakers sufficiently accountable for their actions.

Alternatives to incarceration and probation should not be considered necessarily more lenient than time served in prisons or jails.

Regardless of how the public views it, probationers perceive probation as punishment. They say they find the supervision by a probation officer and meeting the terms of their probation a strongly negative experience—burdensome and stigmatizing.[3] In particular, the threat of time behind bars that hangs over the probation sentence can be a stressful (and motivating) factor, especially for those interested in successfully moving past their

Probation and, in particular, alternatives to incarceration were partly founded on the idea that rehabilitative programming, such as anger management or drug treatment, has a greater likelihood of success when administered in a community setting rather than in prison. A study of drug offenders found probation more effective than prison at reducing new arrests and convictions.[16] It is also true that certain treatment services may yield their best results when associated with a probation sentence rather than when offered freely in the community. Linking drug treatment to a probation sentence increases the likelihood of successful treatment, because drug users tend to stay in treatment longer when it is linked to success or failure in probation (and possible time behind bars) than if there are no consequences for quitting. Additionally, the longer a client remains in treatment, the greater the reduction in criminality. Given that drug offenders account for a quarter of all probation sentences, this finding has ramifications for probation and alternatives to incarceration.

There is good reason to broaden the study of probation. Beyond punishment, incapacitation, and rehabilitation, probation is often meant to meet one or more other valuable goals, such as more appropriately matching the severity of the crime to the severity of the societal response, conserving public resources, and minimizing the negative impact of incarceration on individuals, families, and communities.

Alternatives to Incarceration

Alternatives to incarceration, also known as intermediate sanctions, are types of special probation that combine treatment with a higher level of surveillance and more restrictive conditions than traditional probation. With enhanced supervision, alternatives to incarceration are designed for more serious cases at higher risk for reoffending. They are designed for those who would not be eligible for traditional probation due to the seriousness of their behavior or other factors. Alternative sentences typically entail at least conviction. "Surveys of offenders in Minnesota, Arizona, New Jersey, Oregon, and Texas reveal that when offenders are asked to equate criminal sentences, they judge certain types of community punishments [especially special probation and alternatives] as more severe than prison."[4] In fact, when given the choice, some opt for time behind bars instead of probation.[5] Note that this is not only due to the hardships associated with probation. Prison time has grown to be less scary, especially for repeat offenders who have learned the system, and less stigmatizing in some communities, especially for those whose family members and peers have served time themselves. Nevertheless, the terms of probation can be daunting: regular probation meetings; drug testing; curfews; attending substance abuse treatment, school, vocational, and life skills training; paying restitution; doing community service; and holding down a job.

QUESTIONS

1 Why might time spent in lockup increase recidivism?

2 Discuss the ways that probation is rehabilitative and how it is punitive.

3 What would you find most burdensome about being on probation?

Notes

1. Nagin, Cullen, and Jonson 2009; Smith, Goggin, and Gendreau 2002

2. Hart 2002; Hartney and Marchionna 2009; Krisberg and Marchionna 2006

3. Petersilia and Deschenes 1994; Wood and Grasmick 1995

4. Petersilia 1997, 45

5. Williams, May, and Wood 2008

one rehabilitation component. Failure to successfully complete an alternative could mean return to regular court proceedings or reinstatement of a suspended prison or jail sentence, as with revocation of probation.

By 1989, alternatives to incarceration such as intensive supervision probation, electronic monitoring, or house arrest were being used in 48 states, and today, they are used to some degree in every U.S. state.[17] States are using alternatives to incarceration for probation as well as other stages in the corrections system such as pretrial detention, parole, and early release programs designed to ease overcrowding.

As with probation, alternatives to incarceration allow people to maintain a connection with their families and communities and to hold down a job, hopefully so they can transition into a noncriminal lifestyle. In contrast, incarceration can reinforce negative interactions in prison and jail, weaken ties to society, and often increase the likelihood of reoffending.[18] To maximize the likelihood of success, the various types of alternatives to incarceration are targeted for offenders with particular characteristics and circumstances.

Intensive Supervision Probation

Intensive supervision probation (ISP, also referred to as intensive probation supervision) was one of the first alternatives to incarceration and was already in use in the early 1980s. ISP can take various forms, but typically emphasizes ramped-up surveillance and control strategies compared to traditional probation. These strategies include a higher restriction on movement, often a curfew, more meetings and check-ins with officers, tighter scrutiny of participation in treatment services, and strong responses to violations. Probationers on ISP may have additional rules to follow—such as refraining from substance use or association with antisocial peers—and will typically have other intermediate sanctions imposed as well—such as fines or community service. Probation officers supervising those on ISP often have smaller caseloads to facilitate the heightened surveillance and interaction.

Electronic Monitoring

Electronic monitoring is a type of surveillance used widely across the United States in several situations, including pretrial, postconviction probation, and postincarceration parole. It is typically not a sanction or alternative to incarceration in its own right, but is used to monitor the movements of persons on other forms of supervision. Electronic monitoring may or may not be coupled with home confinement or house arrest, in which the supervised person needs to follow a strict curfew, often having to remain at home at all times except for employment, school, court-mandated programming or community service, or religious services.

Generally, electronic monitoring devices are either active or passive. Active devices use a global positioning system (GPS) and continuously track the client via an ankle bracelet that transmits his or her whereabouts to the supervising officer in real time. The device automatically and immediately detects any deviation from an established schedule or route. Passive devices, such as voice verification systems, require the client to call a specific number to check in or to answer the phone at home. Active systems are generally more commonly used and more cost-effective.[19] Electronic monitoring has also become commonly used with Driving Under the Influence or Driving While Intoxicated (DUI/DWI) offenders, combined with technology that requires drivers to take a breathalyzer test before they can start their cars. States are also using ATM-style kiosks, which use biometric identification.[20] Using this technology, persons on supervision can remotely check in, deposit money toward payment of fines, and leave messages for their PO. Alerts automatically go to the probation officer if the check-in raises any red flags that need a response, such as the probationer reporting a change of address or a new arrest. These systems are often maintained and monitored by private agencies that contract with the probation department.

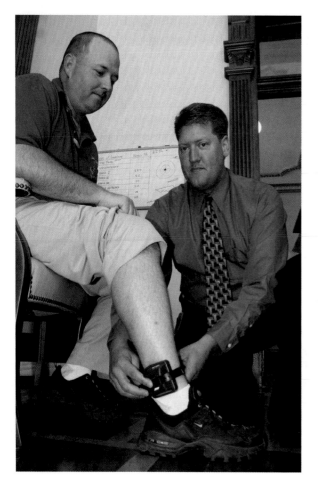

▲ A PO demonstrates a new ankle bracelet, which can detect the use of alcohol through the wearer's sweat. Such devices are being used with increasing frequency by courts and probation offices around the state on offenders whose freedom requires them to refrain from drinking.

© Associated Press/ Bill Garlow

Electronic monitoring can be a significant hindrance to additional criminal activity. Studies have found that it is most effective when used in conjunction with a major treatment component.[21] Even when used without specific rehabilitative programming requirements, electronic monitoring provides the potential for rehabilitation within the community.

Reporting Programs

Day reporting centers and work release programs are sanctions that serve both punitive and rehabilitative purposes by allowing defendants to return to or remain in their communities under strict guidelines. Day reporting centers are highly structured, nonresidential programs that provide treatment and close supervision. Participants usually have to report daily to the center, which typically resembles a probation office. They discuss their schedule for the day, steps they will take to fulfill conditions of probation, such as finding a job and attending treatment services, and they may be drug tested. They are allowed to return home in the evenings but are required to maintain a strict, closely monitored schedule. Programs vary in duration and specific components. Although most offer a range of services, some programs focus on drug treatment. Others focus on vocational training or are primarily check-in centers. The flexibility and wide range of programs and services makes them adaptable to different groups of offenders. The National

IN THE COURTS

Gagnon, Warden v. Scarpelli, 1973
No. 71–1225 Supreme Court of the United States

411 U.S. 778; 93 S. Ct. 1756; 36 L. Ed. 2d 656; 1973 U.S. LEXIS 70; 71 Ohio Op. 2d 279

In the state of Wisconsin, Mr. Gerald Scarpelli pleaded guilty to felony burglary and was sentenced to 7 years of probation in lieu of incarceration for 15 years. He was permitted to live in Illinois and was supervised by the Cook County Adult Probation Department under the Interstate Compact law. One of the conditions of probation was that Mr. Scarpelli "make a sincere effort to avoid all acts forbidden by law." The consequences of violating this agreement would lead to the imposition of the original sentence of 15 years. Subsequently, Mr. Scarpelli was found by the police while he was in the course of a household burglary. His probation was revoked based on his association with known criminals and his arrest for burglary. Mr. Scarpelli was committed to prison to serve his original sentence. At no time did he receive a hearing of any kind.

Mr. Scarpelli later challenged his probation revocation. The case eventually went to the Supreme Court, which held that Mr. Scarpelli was entitled to a preliminary and a final hearing with a formal transcript and a right to hear the evidence against him. Moreover, the court also ordered that he should be afforded the right to representation by counsel, if indigent. Although this right to legal representation was to be determined on a case-by-case basis, deference should be given to the discretion of the probation officer who is acting as an agent of rehabilitation. Still, the court recognized that the revocation process must adhere to basic principles of due process and put into place protection of the rights of persons in violation of probation or parole.

Institute of Justice (NIJ) recognizes the use of day reporting centers to reduce prison and jail overcrowding and details two essential elements: enhanced surveillance for people who have problems under traditional probation and the provision of or referral to treatment services.[22]

Work release programs are residential programs that allow clients to work during the day but require them to return to a locked facility each evening. These programs limit the individual's movement in the community and reduce his or her opportunities for reoffending.

Drug Treatment

Drug treatment programs for substance abusers include outpatient, short-term residential, and long-term residential placements. Many programs serve first-time offenders exclusively, few accept violent offenders, and all are selective regarding the mentally ill population. Despite a growing number of programs, the number of persons served over the past decade represents a small portion of those who meet eligibility criteria for treatment.

Evaluations of individual programs tend to show similar results. Recidivism rates are significantly lower for those who complete their programs. However, most drug treatment programs have a 40% to 60% completion rate. Those who drop out or are terminated early tend to have similar recidivism rates as nonparticipants, highlighting the importance of correctly matching a probationer's needs to the proper programming option and actively supporting and encouraging completion.[23] Completion rates depend in part on how relapse is addressed by the program. Although practitioners believe that relapse is an inevitable part of therapy, many programs terminate participants after a single relapse incident.

SPOTLIGHT

FOR THE BENEFIT OF THE DEFENDANT? THE RISK OF NET-WIDENING

One strength of alternatives to incarceration is that they broaden the menu of options for sentencing judges. Appropriate implementation of alternatives requires care to limit the use of alternatives to only those who would have been subject to incarceration. "Net-widening" can occur when an individual comes to the attention of law enforcement or the court through behavior that would

not otherwise lead to an arrest or formal processing such as an infraction, mental health–related acting out, or minor drug use. Instead of responding with a citation or referring the case to public health services, the police officer may decide to arrest the person and bring him or her into the system, knowing that he or she would likely end up in an alternative that provides substance abuse treatment or mental health care that may be appropriate, such as therapy or anger management. In doing this, the officer may be acting out of genuine regard for the individual's well-being, or may be thinking more punitively, to "teach a lesson." Either way, the person may end up in the system when, had the option for alternatives not

Drug Courts

The drug court model originated in Dade County, Florida, in 1989, when prison over-crowding coincided with a severe funding crisis. The panel that was appointed to address the issue found that a large proportion of inmates had drug-related offenses and had been repeatedly incarcerated. Drug courts create a nonadversarial environment that combines long-term treatment with the structure and accountability of the justice system. Most combine at least one year of drug treatment with intensive supervision and may include rehabilitative programming apart from substance abuse treatment. These programs include routine drug testing, regular court appearances, and a system of rewards and sanctions. Participants are generally selected by the district attorney's office and can agree to participate or not. Successful completion of the program most often results in dropped charges, while failure to complete it can result in regular court proceedings or immediate activation of the custody sentence. Today, drug courts are one of many kinds of collaborative courts; others deal with the mentally ill population, the homeless, and domestic violence cases.

In 2010, there were more than 2,300 drug courts across the nation and in every U.S. state, with many more in the planning stages. The level of success in each depends on available resources and the coordinated strategy and collaboration of stakeholders such as courts, attorneys, and community agencies. Drug courts serve different populations and vary in cost. Cost differences are tied to the scale of the program, the level of treatment, the degree of participation on the part of agencies, and the services available to participants.

Restorative Justice

Restorative justice seeks to enhance public safety by involving all stakeholders and repairing harmful actions caused by criminal behavior. Restorative practices and programs reflect several important values that outline the roles of stakeholders: positive encounters between victims, offenders, and community members; amends for the harm; reintegration of both victims and offenders into society; and inclusion of all stakeholders in the resolution of the crime and the broken relationships it caused. Restorative justice practices include victim–offender mediation sessions, restorative justice conferences, peacemaking

been there, there would never have been an arrest in the first place.[1]

A key piece of the probation equation is the recognition that overly punitive sanctions are not neutral; they entail risks to the public.[2] There are individuals who get in trouble but are unlikely to recidivate or become more serious or chronic offenders. For these, short of purely retributive punishment, any sentence beyond light probation would serve little purpose. Overcriminalizing low-level offenses can alienate defendants, further marginalize them economically and socially, and raise their likelihood of reoffending.

QUESTIONS

1 Describe a situation that might fit the definition of net-widening.

2 Do you think that net-widening is always a negative thing?

Notes

1. Weissman 2009
2. Bowers and Pierce 1980; Potter 1997

circles, victim impact panels, and restorative boards. In 2010, the states most actively utilizing restorative justice approaches were Minnesota, Vermont, Wisconsin, Maine, New Mexico, Pennsylvania, and Montana.

Restorative justice began as a response to youth justice and as a means to address minor offenses. However, as the United States and other nations struggle to reduce imprisonment and improve public safety and community bonds, restorative justice practices have expanded to address serious crimes and offenses committed by adults. As research continues to confirm its success, restorative justice may become an increasingly common response to crime.

Restorative justice can be implemented in a variety of ways prior to and throughout the criminal justice process. For example, some schools have turned to restorative justice programs as an alternative to formal processing for bullying and other issues, and some jurisdictions offer restorative justice–based "diversion" programs that channel certain youth away from criminal prosecution.[24] When offenders are sentenced to community supervision, this may include restorative justice–inspired conditions such as community service, or reparations to victims.[25] There are also programs within prisons that make repairing harm done to victims a centerpiece of prisoners' rehabilitation and reintegration plans.

Studies of the participants of restorative justice practices show that perpetrators are more likely to find their treatment fair and to apologize to the victim(s), whereas victims tend to find greater satisfaction than what they had expected and are more likely to forgive the offender than if they were in a regular court proceeding. In addition, victims and offenders appreciate being able to explain their sides of the story.[26]

Some evidence also shows that restorative justice programs lead to greater compliance with reparation and victim compensation. In comparison with control groups with diversionary or other court sentences, restitution compliance rates range from 75% to 100%. Last, another claim for the effectiveness of restorative justice practices is a reduction in recidivism rates. In a 2003 meta-analysis, victim–offender mediation participants were one third less likely to reoffend during the subsequent six months than were those who had not participated in these sessions.[27] However, many challenges still remain in assessing the effectiveness of restorative justice programs, due to the difficulty of conducting controlled experiments for different treatment conditions. There is also a great deal of variety in the purposes, structures, and functioning of restorative justice programs, as well as in the political, social, and cultural contexts in which they are employed.

Community Service and Restitution

Performing community service and paying monetary recompense for offenses are two common elements of a sentence of alternatives to incarceration. Fines and community service are meant as punishment in their own right. Another monetary recompense is victim restitution, where the offender pays the victim to account for physical harm and medical expenses, property damage or loss, and the less tangible emotional impacts of the victimization.

Fines, victim restitution, and community service are all aspects of restorative justice, as they facilitate the offender giving back, ameliorating the impact of crime, and rebuilding relationships in the community.

Fines compensate the system for the costs incurred in arrest, court processing, detention, and administration of probation. Tariff fines are based on the offense. For instance, all those convicted of a DUI may incur a $500 fine. Other fines, sometimes called "day fines," are adjusted according to the client's ability to pay—based on his or her income or other resources.[28] Day fines attempt to equalize the impact of the fine, so that low-income probationers will not be unduly burdened, and wealthier individuals will still have to pay a meaningful fine.

Community service involves unpaid work in the community, usually for a set number of hours or until the completion of a particular project. The number of hours assigned, and assurance of satisfactory completion on the part of the probation officer, will typically be more stringent for community service associated with an alternative to incarceration than with traditional probation. The type of assignment can be linked to the person's crime or to his or her skills and occupation. For instance, those convicted of vehicular manslaughter may perform community service in a trauma center, and a construction contractor convicted of fraud may help build homes for the poor.

Community service may conjure images of prison work crews and raise the complex issue of prisoner labor. However, with probation clients, it is largely seen as a constructive way for probationers to pay back the community while retaining relative freedom.

http://www.bop.gov/resources/ news/20140227_paving_ project.jsp

Evaluating Alternatives to Incarceration

As alternatives to incarceration were first being introduced in the late 1980s, they were often implemented before probation departments had the capacity to appropriately administer them and before community services were sufficiently available to ensure that offenders received mandated treatment.[29] Even so, those programs that provided appropriate levels of supervision and made sure their clients received the treatment services they required were shown to reduce recidivism.[30] Research has continued to show that programs that combine treatment services with strong supervision can be rehabilitative without sacrificing public safety.[31]

Intensive supervision probation has not had a very good track record with regard to reducing recidivism, possibly because of variations in the way the model is implemented. Studies do show that when it is administered in a client-focused manner that emphasizes rehabilitation over deterrence, recidivism outcomes improve.[32]

Critics complain that electronic monitoring is too controlling, violates an individual's privacy, and is often used instead of rehabilitation. Others say it unduly risks public safety, because supervisors can't always respond quickly enough when the person strays.[33] However, in a small study of 49 individuals who served one third of their sentence on electronic monitoring, these complaints were not reported. Instead, an overwhelming majority said it was an effective supervision tool, and most said they would not have considered trying to evade the surveillance.[34]

A preliminary study of programs in Wisconsin showed that day reporting participants had fewer incidents of rearrest and a lower severity of offense than those in a comparison group.[35] A Utah study showed that 22% of participants were rearrested after one year.[36]

Work release programs in Texas are currently geared toward parole and probation violators and are used in place of return to prison.[37] A 2007 study found that Florida's work release program significantly improved an early release offender's postprison employment outcomes but that there were not enough beds for the individuals who qualify. There were 3,000 beds available, but another 1,000 prisoners were on the waiting list.[38]

Work release programs, though not as heavily centered on treatment as day reporting, allow individuals to earn a living and acquire positive living habits.[39] A meta-analysis of existing research found that such programs reduce recidivism and improve the job readiness skills.[40] An evaluation of programs in Ohio that serve moderate- and high-risk offenders at the end of their terms reveals significantly decreased recidivism rates up to 34% lower than those in the comparison group.[41] A Washington state report finds that early release persons who participate in work release programs have lower rates of recidivism (6%–15%) than non–work release participants (22%).[42]

Evaluations of drug courts reveal promising results. A national review by the Government Accountability Office of 27 evaluations representing 39 programs showed that drug court participation reduced recidivism levels both during the program and after completion; program completion further reduced recidivism. This conclusion is supported by a growing body of research.[43] A study conducted by the Urban Institute found that drug courts, though effective, target only a very small population. Approximately 80% of drug courts exclude defendants with any prior conviction or those charged with sales (regardless of the defendant's dependency issues). A number of drug courts reject those whose problems are too severe, while others reject those whose problems are not severe enough. Many programs must reject clients for lack of capacity. The Urban Institute estimates that, of the millions arrested yearly on drug charges, only 30,000 are accepted into drug courts.[44]

Cost Savings

Considering the cost savings that can be achieved using probation instead of incarceration, probation certainly has an important place in the modern corrections system. It is estimated that federal, state, and local governments spent $68 billion on corrections in 2008, approximately 90% of which was for prisons and jails, the remainder going to community corrections. Probation costs about $1,200 per year per person; prison costs at least $28,000 annually.[45] Even though the cost of community supervision varies widely among jurisdictions, it can be administered at a fraction of the cost of jail or prison. When conditions of probation or alternatives to incarceration include monetary fines, governmental costs can be further reduced. For instance, some alternative programs require participants to pay for their court-ordered treatment services. Alternatives to incarceration, especially when coupled with high-quality treatment services, generally cost more than traditional probation, but still far less than secure custody.[46] A cost–benefit analysis that factors in the reduced costs to law enforcement, the courts, corrections, and other public agencies shows a more favorable cost–benefit equation for quality community corrections programming. For instance, a cost–benefit study tracked recidivism for 2 to 4 years following participation in a selection of California's 200 drug court programs. The study found that 17% of drug court graduates were rearrested, compared to 41% of nonparticipants. Participants who did not complete the program still received some benefit; they were rearrested at a rate of 29%. The nine sites studied saved the state $90 million per year in costs associated with law enforcement and corrections.[47] Alternatives are generally strategies that can be successful with large numbers of offenders as long as they are implemented carefully, with appropriate system supports and community resources. Representatives of the courts, district attorney's offices, public defenders, and the community need to be made aware of the nature and effectiveness of alternatives, which would increase support for them and expand their use. It is estimated that billions of dollars could be saved if the use of alternatives to incarceration were even slightly expanded.[48]

· ·

SUMMARY

Probation has a long history and is the most widely used correctional sanction in the United States today. Probation is a form of community supervision that can be imposed by the court either before or after conviction. The probationer must answer to a probation officer and the court and adhere to the conditions of supervision to avoid a revocation of probation and the imposition of a harsher punishment—usually a jail or prison sentence.

The probation officer plays a key role in this intermediate sanction, investigating the defendant's background and needs, preparing a report to inform the court, and maintaining a supervisory relationship that works on both trust and discipline.

Probation departments use risk assessment and case management tools to allocate resources. Departments are typically underfunded, however, despite costing a

fraction of what incarceration costs. Probation officers often have to handle huge caseloads.

Probation and alternatives to incarceration sit at the intersection of some of the most difficult and often conflicting purposes of the corrections system: balancing punishment with fairness, protecting public safety but reasonably limiting the use of expensive incarceration, and helping lawbreakers avoid future system involvement.

Alternatives to incarceration provide a range of options and help judges "customize" the consequences for individuals. They include ISP, electronic monitoring, day reporting centers, work release programs, drug courts, and drug treatment.

Society's response to crime is still dominated by either the threat of or actual imprisonment, the harshest and most punitive measure. Despite the vastly higher costs for secure custody facilities, when budgets need to be cut, it is easier to reduce alternative programs than prisons and jails. This may be partly because alternatives have not fully taken hold in the system. The term itself—*alternatives*—suggests they are optional or peripheral. There is growing support, although not yet sufficiently strong individual leadership, from state and federal agencies mandating the expansion of alternative programs. The clout of prison guard unions, lobbyists, and the political strength of the private prison industry all are factors in the slow growth of alternatives, as is the continued belief in tough-on-crime approaches. The effectiveness of probation and alternatives to incarceration is the subject of much inquiry. Probation and alternatives to incarceration have never received the wholehearted support and funding they need to fully test them. Evaluation is difficult, due to the complexity of administering these sanctions. At the very least, a serious exploration of alternatives, including shifts of resources away from traditional custody, could give new strategies and programs a greater chance of success.

DISCUSSION QUESTIONS

1. What are the two major perspectives on the purpose of probation? What theories, assumptions, and goals underlie each approach? Which perspective makes the most sense to you, and why?

2. Discuss how and why probation and alternatives are more complex penal sanctions than a term in prison or jail.

3. Discuss ways that the court and probation officer encourage the probationer to remain in compliance with the terms of supervision.

4. Should probation officers be given more authority to change the terms of probation and to remand their clients to custody? Why or why not?

5. Discuss the various kinds of alternatives to incarceration and their advantages and disadvantages. Think of a more apt term for them than *alternatives*.

6. Are alternatives to incarceration too lenient? Costs aside, under what circumstances, and for whom, might incarceration be necessary or effective?

KEY TERMS

Adjudication, 90

Caseload, 94

Case management system, 95

Conditions of probation, 90

Due process rights, 100

Early release, 91

Evidence-based practice, 90

Judicial reprieve, 92

Probable cause, 99

Prosocial, 93

Technical violations, 99

NOTES

1. Maruschak and Bonczar 2013
2. May, Williams, and Wood 2008
3. Maruschak and Bonczar 2013
4. Guzman, Krisberg, and Tsukida 2008
5. American Probation and Parole Association 2012
6. Vale 2011
7. DeMichele 2007
8. Burrell 2006; Worrall et al. 2004
9. Jalbert et al. 2011
10. Freiburger and Hilinsky 2011; Leiber, Reitzel, and Mack 2011
11. Burke, Gelb, and Horowitz 2007
12. Maruschak and Bonczar 2013
13. Petersilia 1997
14. Wermink et al. 2010
15. Savolainen 2003
16. Spohn and Holleran 2002
17. General Accounting Office 1990

18. Courtright, Berg, and Mutchnick 2000

19. National Law Enforcement and Corrections Technology Center 1999; Harkness and Walker-Fraser 2009

20. Biometric identification uses intrinsic physiological identifiers including fingerprints, palm prints, face recognition, and iris recognition.

21. Courtright, Berg, and Mutchnick 2000; Gable 2007; Payne and Gainey 2004

22. Parent et al. 1995

23. Inciardi, Martin, and Butzin 2004; Jolin and Stipak 1992; McMurran 2007; Warner and Kramer 2009

24. Brown 2013

25. Karp and Clear 2002

26. Menkel-Meadow 2007

27. Nugent, Williams, and Umbreit 2004; Sherman and Strang 2007

28. Zedlewski 2010

29. Petersilia 1997

30. Lowenkamp et al. 2010

31. Savolainen 2003; Porter, Lee, and Lutz 2002

32. Lowenkamp et al. 2010

33. Gable 2007

34. Payne and Gainey 2004

35. Craddock 2000

36. Van Vleet, Hickert, and Becker 2006

37. Levin 2008

38. Berk 2007

39. Aos, Miller, and Drake 2006; Aos et al. 2001

40. Seiter and Kadela 2003

41. Lowenkamp and Latessa 2002

42. Sommers, Mauldin, and Levin 2000

43. Barnoski and Aos 2003; Wilson, Mitchell, and MacKenzie 2006

44. Bhati, Roman, and Chalfin 2008

45. Pew Center on the States 2009

46. Federal probation officers are directed to consider such cost savings as part of their presentence investigation.

47. Byrne et al. 2006

48. Vuong et al. 2010

$SAGE edge™

Sharpen your skills with SAGE edge at edge.sagepub.com/krisberg

SAGE edge for students provides a personalized approach to help you accomplish your coursework goals in an easy-to-use learning environment. This site includes action plans, mobile-friendly eFlashcards and web quizzes as well as web, audio, and video resources and links to SAGE journal articles.

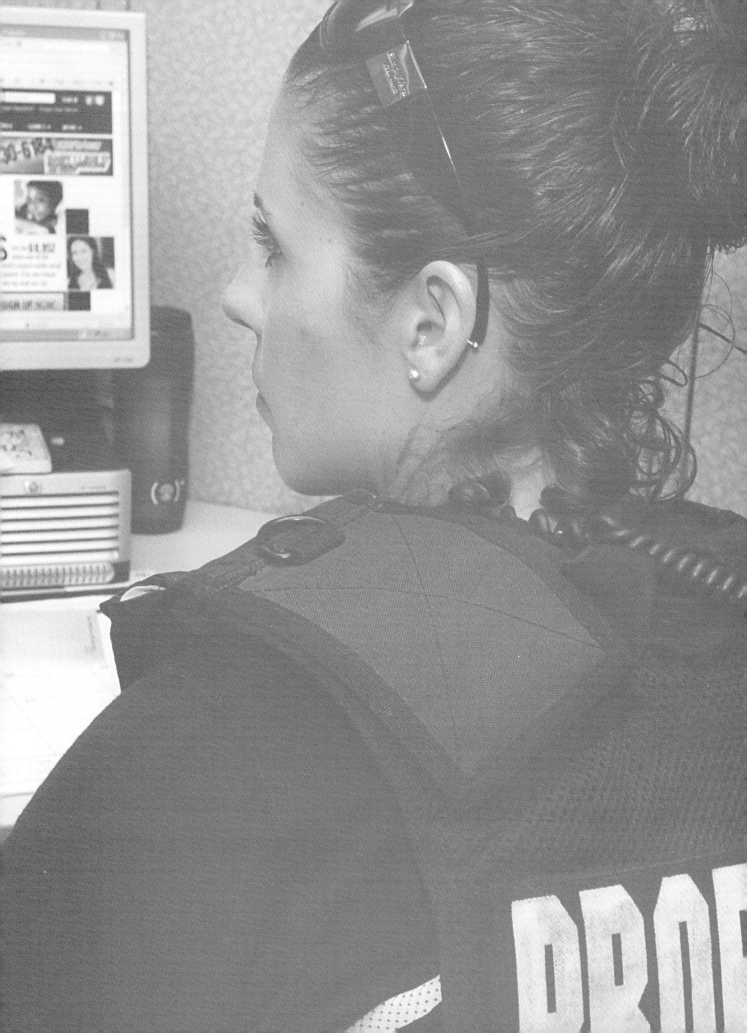

© Kevin Moloney/KRT/News

Prisons

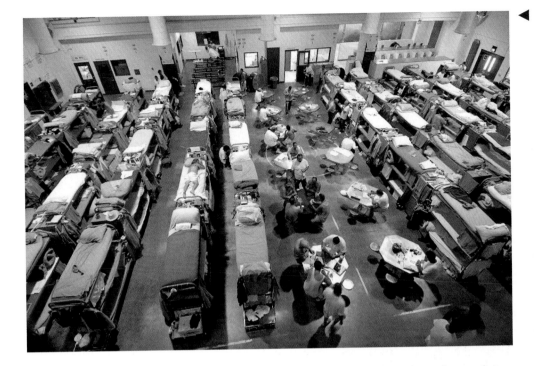

The crowded living quarters of San Quentin Prison in California, in January 2006. As a result of overcrowding in the California state prison system, the United States Supreme Court ordered California to reduce its prison population (the second largest in the nation, after Texas).

California Department of Corrections

Prisons are the most iconic of all correctional institutions; they have been featured time and again in film and fiction, almost as characters in their own right, certainly as settings for riveting drama. But, in reality, prison and prison life are not all that romantic. The prison environment is harsh, and life in prison is full of stress and tedium, conditions made worse in situations where overcrowding is a major issue. In 2011, the U.S. Supreme Court ruled, in an unprecedented decision, that chronic overcrowding in California's prisons amounted to **cruel and unusual** punishment. According to the narrow majority of the court, the California Department of Corrections and Rehabilitation was in violation of the U.S. Constitution. To meet the court's requirement to substantially reduce overcrowding within two years, the state's beleaguered prison system set about planning for the release of 33,000 nonviolent, low-level prisoners to the counties for supervision at the local level or transfer out of state. (See "In the Courts" on page 121.)

The new mandate to reduce overcrowding sparked debates over its implementation and consequences in California and across the country. Some believed that instead of releasing prisoners the prison system should be expanded further and that high rates of incarceration—fueled by tough sentencing laws and practices—were the key to lowering crime rates. But it would take many years to build enough beds to house the number of prisoners over capacity, too much time for California to meet the two-year timetable ordered by the court. Fiscal constraints and a desire for change drove others to support new reforms, including many observers who previously argued for expansion. The public and the body politic are finally having to admit that it is simply too expensive to keep locking everyone up.

Cruel and unusual: The Eighth Amendment of the U.S. Constitution protects Americans against cruel and unusual punishments—those that are unacceptable because they subject a person to undue pain, suffering, or humiliation.

5 To understand prison classification systems and risk levels.

6 To grasp some of the extremes in the system such as crowding, the supermax, and isolation.

7 To know about basic types of prisoner services and understand some of the challenges involved in delivering them.

8 To gain a basic sense of the prison environment.

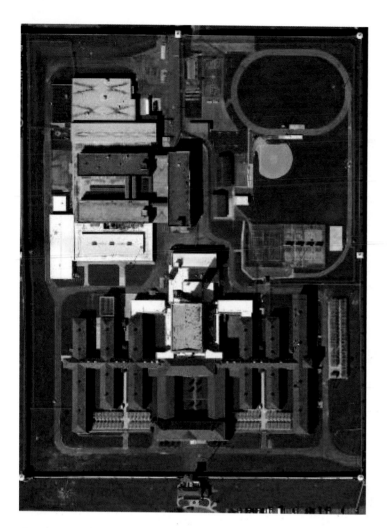

▲ From the air, one might think this is a typical rural high school, but it is the U.S. Penitentiary at Lewisburg, Pennsylvania.

©Jelson25

Lockdown: Confining inmates to their cells to regain or maintain facility security in response to a fight, riot, escape, or other serious disturbance. During a lockdown, which could last minutes, hours, or days, inmate movement about the facility for meals, recreation, classes, or programming is prohibited.

The Means to an End

As discussed in Chapter 3, prisons have several ostensible functions—punishment, deterrence, retribution, and incapacitation. Whether prison accomplishes these goals—whether it falls short or, for that matter, goes too far—is the subject of much debate. For example, some criminologists contend that the certainty of punishment and the swiftness of its delivery contribute more to deterrence than the length of the sentence. And there is a long-standing debate about whether the death penalty truly serves to deter homicide.[1] Debate also continues about whether rehabilitation is or should be a core function of prisons. Incarceration serves other societal functions as well. Many would argue that prisons function as a means of social control and a political weapon used against entire communities. The fact that U.S. prisons are filled disproportionately with people of color points to a thorny and persistent problem. (See Chapter 11.)

There are more specific goals within institutions, such as providing services or maintaining a healthy, safe environment. However, security is the predominant concern inside a prison. The goal of control always trumps other considerations, especially in an emergency situation. For example, in the event of a prison riot, the prison would go on total **lockdown**, which interrupts rehabilitative education and counseling.

Although the goals of prison may include retribution and punishment, it is not generally accepted that prison should lead to the deterioration of a prisoner's physical and mental health. The punishment is meant to be the denial of liberty. The *ideal* modern prison institution is safe, clean, and orderly, and maybe even productive and cost-effective. However, this ideal is difficult to achieve for many reasons, beginning with the tensions inherent in the very concept of locking people up. There are few if any prisons that always meet all legal and ethical standards, and many breach the most basic standards of humane practice.

Prisons are different than jails. They are federally or state-run institutions meant for those convicted and sentenced to more than a year of incarceration; jails detain people in many short-term custody situations. Consequently, the jail population turns over far more often than the prison population. According to the National Institute of Corrections (NIC), on average, a 1,000-bed jail turns over completely 36 times a year (36,000 individuals), whereas a 1,000-bed prison may turn over 750 inmates in a year.[2] (See Chapter 4.) Prisons vary widely in their design, size, and security level, among other factors. However, common structural elements typically include barbed wire, concrete, high perimeter walls, armed guard towers, external and internal patrols, surveillance cameras, geographic barriers (cliffs, forests, water), systematic dehumanization, and psychological domination. They are often located away from urban centers in more remote locations— far also from the public's view.

Design of Prisons

The architecture of prisons in large part defines the human interactions that occur within them. Various correctional goals have given rise to some of the forms described in this section. A prison's design expresses and facilitates the intended level of security and surveillance. Prison architects consider what kinds of prisoners and what kind of prison life the walls will contain. They plan for maintaining control over prisoner movement, watching and counting inmates, housing styles, meals, laundry, exercise, treatment, medical care, religious service, education, visiting, and administrative functions. All of these considerations must be combined with location and climate and, of course, cost.

The most common designs are variations on either a linear theme or a radial one. Maximum-security facilities are often laid out with branches set at right angles. Cells are lined up along a straight central corridor and stacked several levels up. These may allow for easy movement, but require regular surveillance by guards who must walk past a cell to see inside it. Radial designs have a central control room where guards can see into a number of cells at once. There are also courtyard designs and clusters, or pods, of multiple radial units, which allow for more direct supervision and interaction between guards and prisoners.

A precursor to the current radial design was the panopticon, meaning "all-seeing," a creation of an English social theorist from the late 18th century named Jeremy Bentham.

◀ Pelican Bay State Prison, California. Prison architecture is a professional specialty— form and function bent to a sociopolitical purpose.

http://commons.wikimedia.org/ wiki/File:Aerial_shot_of_ Pelican_Bay_State_Prison,_ taken_27-July-2009.jpg

▲ Some might call Bentham's "all-seeing" design for prisons ingenious, others diabolical.

http://en.wikipedia.org/wiki/File:Jeremy_Bentham_by_Henry_William_Pickersgill_detail.jpg

Bentham lobbied for many years to see his idea built in reality, but it never was built in the United States. The concept was a wheel-like structure with a central tower from which guards could see into every cell. However, because the tower's design would shield the guards, the occupants of the cells would not be able to tell when they were or were not being watched. Bentham thought one of the strong selling points of his idea was how little it would cost to staff the structure.

What the Numbers Say

At the end of 2012, the national prison population was more than 1.57 million prisoners, or approximately one out of every 200 individuals living in the United States. Prisoners included almost 220,000 held in the federal system and 1.35 million held by the states.[3] These numbers do not include the jail population or the millions on parole or probation.

The Growth of U.S. Prisons

The phenomenal growth of the U.S. prison complex is a subject worthy of its own volume. In brief, the U.S. prison population remained relatively stable for most of the last century, dipping during wartimes—the 1940s and the 1960s. Beginning in the late 1970s, the number of incarcerated Americans took a sharp turn upward and continued at an accelerated pace until 2010.

Both the federal and state systems grew consistently in this period. However, the total state prison population declined slightly in the three years beginning with 2009, the first downward trend since 1977. Time will tell if these trends will continue. Regardless, they represent significant changes from the extreme curve upward of the previous 30 years. The federal prison system has continued to grow during this period of decline in the state system.

The "roundhouse" at Illinois State Penitentiary at Stateville was built in the 1920s using a panopticon-inspired design. ▶

http://prisonphotography.org/2010/08/21/stateville-prison-joliet-il-art-object/

Figure 6.1 — National Rate of Imprisonment, 1925 to 2012

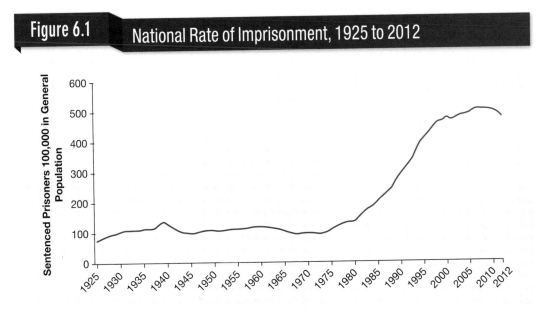

Figure 6.1 shows that, throughout most of the last century, the imprisonment rate was stable, only rising above 130 per 100,000 for a couple of years just prior to World War II. However, in the late 1970s, it started a sharp rise that showed signs of ending in 2009. The imprisonment rate per 100,000 was 96 in 1970, 139 in 1980, 297 in 1990, 478 in 2000, and 500 in 2010. The high point was 506 in 2008, at which point a slight decline began, down to 480 in 2012. *Source: http://www.albany.edu/sourcebook/tost_6.html#6_bf.*

The surge upward cannot be explained by general population growth. The rate of imprisonment—the number of inmates for every 100,000 U.S. residents—would have remained relatively constant. Instead, the rate rose drastically during this period.

State and Regional Differences

The U.S. states vary widely in many ways that impact state incarceration rates, from size, region, climate, topography, and demographics, to culture, political climate, legislation, law enforcement policy, characteristics of the judiciary, and reform efforts. Consequently, prison population sizes and rates have an enormous range among the states. In addition, some state rates may be falling, while in other states they are rising.

Gender, Race, and Ethnicity

A closer look at overall incarceration rates reveals an even greater range depending on gender and race. To illustrate, the 2011 incarceration rate for sentenced men was 932 and for sentenced women was 65. For White women, the rate was 51, for Hispanic women 71, and for African American women 129. For White men, the rate was 478, for Hispanic men 1,238, and for African American men 3,023. Note the enormous disparity in rates of incarceration for different groups.

Length of Stay in Custody

Along with new admissions, length of stay is a primary factor in prison population counts. If, over time, the number of individuals who are beginning a prison sentence stays the same but their time served decreases, then overall prison population counts will also decrease. Even a small reduction in sentence length can have an impact on the prison population, and sentencing reform is certainly an avenue toward relieving pressure on overburdened systems.

Table 6.1	Prison Population and Rate of Imprisonment for Prisoners* in Federal and State Systems, 2012

Jurisdiction	Total	Rate**	Jurisdiction	Total	Rate**
Total in U.S	1,512,391	480	Missouri	31,244	518
Federal Total	196,574	62	Montana	3,609	358
State Total	1,315,817	418	Nebraska	4,594	247
Alabama	31,437	650	Nevada***	12,639	461
Alaska	2,940	401	New Hampshire	2,790	211
Arizona	38,402	583	New Jersey	23,225	261
Arkansas	14,615	494	New Mexico	6,574	315
California	134,211	351	New York	54,073	276
Colorado	20,462	392	North Carolina	34,983	357
Connecticut	11,961	333	North Dakota	1,512	213
Delaware	4,129	448	Ohio	50,876	440
Florida	101,930	524	Oklahoma	24,830	648
Georgia	53,990	542	Oregon	14,801	378
Hawaii	3,819	273	Pennsylvania	50,918	398
Idaho	7,985	499	Rhode Island	1,999	190
Illinois***	48,427	376	South Carolina	21,725	458
Indiana	28,822	440	South Dakota	3,644	434
Iowa	8,686	282	Tennessee	28,411	438
Kansas	9,398	325	Texas	157,900	601
Kentucky	21,466	489	Utah	6,960	242
Louisiana	41,246	893	Vermont	1,516	242
Maine	1,932	145	Virginia	37,044	451
Maryland	21,281	360	Washington***	17,808	260
Massachusetts	9,999	199	West Virginia	7,027	378
Michigan	43,594	441	Wisconsin	20,474	357
Minnesota	9,938	184	Wyoming	2,204	379
Mississippi	21,426	717			

The overall rate of imprisonment in the United States in 2012 was 480 for every 100,000 in the general population. State rates ranged from under 200 for Maine, Minnesota, Massachusetts, and Rhode Island to rates of more than 600 for Texas, Alabama, Oklahoma, Mississippi, and Louisiana. The federal rate in 2012 was 62. The federal rate is always low compared to the states' rates, because most criminal law is under state jurisdiction. * Sentenced to one year or more.

** Rate of imprisonment per 100,000 in general population, all ages.

*** 2012 data not available for Illinois, Nevada, Washington; 2011 data reported.

Source: Carson and Golinelli 2013.

IN THE COURTS

Brown, Governor of California, et al. v. Plata et al

Appeal from the U.S. District Courts for the Eastern and Northern Districts of California No. 09–1233.

Argued November 30, 2010—Decided May 23, 2011

In 2011, the total design capacity for California prisons was about 80,000 inmates, but the population had grown to over 170,000. This crowding contributed to a fundamental breakdown in safety, security, health services, and suicide prevention and to making the prisons very dangerous for staff and inmates alike. The governor declared that California's prisons were in a state of emergency. A series of class-action judgments attempted to remedy these problems without much success. Plaintiffs utilized the federal Prison Litigation Reform Act to argue that only immediate reductions in the inmate population could solve the breakdown of fundamental Eighth Amendment protections.

The U.S. Supreme Court upheld the plaintiff's claims and sustained the order of a federal three-judge panel to reduce the California prison population to 137% of its design capacity in two years. Writing for the Court, Justice Kennedy found:

> As a consequence of their own actions, prisoners may be deprived of rights that are fundamental to liberty. Yet the law and the Constitution demand recognition of certain other rights. Prisoners retain the essence of human dignity inherent in all persons. Respect for that dignity animates the Eighth Amendment prohibition against cruel and unusual punishment. "The basic concept underlying the Eighth Amendment is nothing less than the dignity of man."[1]

To incarcerate, society takes from prisoners the means to provide for their own needs. Prisoners are dependent on the State for food, clothing, and necessary medical care. A prison's failure to provide sustenance for inmates "may actually produce physical 'torture or a lingering death.'"[2] Just as a prisoner may starve if not fed, he or she may suffer or die if not provided adequate medical care. A prison that deprives prisoners of basic sustenance, including adequate medical care, is incompatible with the concept of human dignity and has no place in civilized society.[3]

This case was an unprecedented occasion of the U.S. Supreme Court ordering a state to release inmates. If government fails to fulfill this obligation, the courts have a responsibility to remedy the resulting Eighth Amendment violation. California was still working on the problem in 2013, with the governor trying to negotiate with the federal judges about viable solutions.

Notes

1. *Atkins v. Virginia*, 536 U.S. 304, 311 2002 (quoting *Trop v. Dulles*, 356 U.S. 86, 100 1958 (plurality opinion).
2. *Estelle v. Gamble*, 429 U.S. 97, 103 1976 (quoting *In re Kemmler*, 136 U.S. 436, 447 1890 see generally Alan Elsner, *Gates of Injustice: The Crisis in America's Prisons* (Upper Saddle River, NJ: Pearson Education, 2004).
3. See also *Hutto v. Finney*, 437 U.S. 678, 687, n. 9 (1978).

Facilities

In 2005, there were 1,719 state and 106 federal prison facilities dispersed across the country, 135 more than in 2000.[4] (More recent counts are not available, although new prison construction, both private and public, continued after the release of the last national census.) These facilities ranged in size from **halfway houses** that hold just a few low-risk inmates to sprawling complexes that house thousands of prisoners of all types.[5]

State facilities included 1,190 secure confinement facilities and 529 community-based facilities. Confinement facilities (prisons, farms, camps) are typically larger and more remotely located than community-based facilities (halfway houses, restitution centers, prerelease centers, work release centers, and study centers). All or most of those held in community-based facilities are regularly allowed to leave on their own for work or

Halfway house: A house usually located in a residential neighborhood where newly released prisoners can live and gradually reintegrate into the community while still benefiting from support and supervision.

In America, a person's race and ethnicity have a strong correlation to one's likelihood of incarceration.

© iStockphoto.com / simonmcconico

Secure confinement:
Custody or detention that involves locked spaces that are controlled by agency authorities.

Consent decree:
A binding agreement between parties in a lawsuit for the withdrawal of a criminal charge or civil litigation. The decree acknowledges the voluntary cessation of the lawbreaking behavior relevant in the case.

Figure 6.2 — Offense Types of Sentenced Prisoners* in State Prisons, 2011

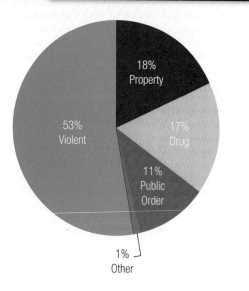

- 53% Violent
- 18% Property
- 17% Drug
- 11% Public Order
- 1% Other

* *Serving a sentence of at least one year. Most serious conviction offense is reported.*

Violent offenses include murder, nonnegligent manslaughter, manslaughter, rape, other sexual assault, robbery, assault, and other.

Property offenses include burglary, larceny, motor vehicle theft, fraud, and other.

Drug offenses include trafficking, possession, and other.

Public order offenses include weapons, drunk driving, court offenses, commercialized vice, morals and decency offenses, liquor law violations, and other.

Other includes juvenile offenses and other unspecified offense categories.

Source: Carson and Sabol 2012.

study, while those in confinement facilities generally do not have this liberty. Community-based settings cost less than prisons and allow inmates to retain or reestablish connections with their families and communities, employment, education, rehabilitative programming, and other services. These settings can be used as alternatives to traditional **secure confinement** or as a transition between prison and the community.

Although representing just 4% (54,233) of the total state and federal prison population, between 1995 and 2005, the number serving time in community-based facilities rose at almost twice the rate of those serving time in secure facilities.

Facility Capacity

As one would expect, the 30-year growth in prison populations described above was accompanied by similar increases in the number of prison facilities. Issues with crowding and conditions of confinement also grew. All but 12 U.S. states had at least one prison under court order (**consent decree**) either to reduce overcrowding or for specific issues with conditions of confinement in 2000 or 2005. At the end of 2010, 25 states held more inmates than their facilities were designed to hold.[6]

Prison Costs

Burgeoning prison systems have exerted increasing strain on government budgets. As state revenues have decreased, housing, feeding, and providing medical care for growing numbers of low-risk prisoners has emerged as an extravagant use of scarce taxpayer dollars—ever more difficult to justify as other vital services suffer, such as education, health care, and transportation. Interestingly, these fiscal constraints are prompting lawmakers to cut corrections expenses. Just as policy decisions have driven growth, they also drive cuts. Some states are looking at lower-cost measures that emphasize such strategies as treatment in the community, collaboration among relevant agencies, and keeping families together.

According to a review by the Pew Center on the States, the collective total for state corrections expenditures for 1987 was $12 billion.[7] In 2009, that figure was $52.3 billion. Of that, $9.5 billion was spent in California, representing 7.2% of the state's general fund.[8] The portion of the budget dedicated to corrections varies widely among states—from a staggering 22.9% in Michigan (the next highest was 12.6% in Oregon) to 2.7% in Minnesota. State corrections budgets are supplemented in some measure by federal funding, other state sources, and bonds (approximately 5% combined). However, the total expense figures are conservative in most cases; in many states, they do not include such additional expenses as juvenile facilities, juvenile counseling, drug rehab centers, or pensions and health benefits for staff.

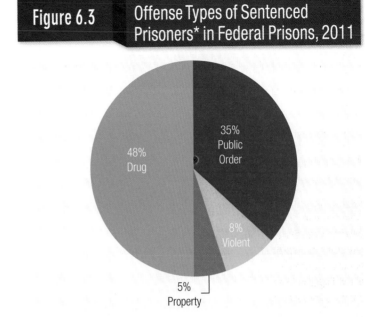

Figure 6.3   Offense Types of Sentenced Prisoners* in Federal Prisons, 2011

- 35% Public Order
- 48% Drug
- 8% Violent
- 5% Property

In 2011, violent offenders made up just over half (53%) of state prisoners, property offenders 18%, drug offenders 17%, and public order offenders 11%. (See Figure 6.2.) In the same year, violent offenders made up just 8% of federal prisoners, property offenders 5%, drug offenders 48%, and public order offenders 35%. * *Serving a sentence of at least one year. Most serious conviction offense is reported.*

Violent offenses include murder, nonnegligent manslaughter, manslaughter, rape, other sexual assault, robbery, assault, and other.

Property offenses include burglary, larceny, motor vehicle theft, fraud, and other.

Drug offenses include trafficking, possession, and other.

Public order offenses include weapons, drunk driving, court offenses, commercialized vice, morals and decency offenses, liquor law violations, and other.

Source: Carson and Sabol 2012.

The level of expense per prisoner varies widely from one state to another as well, especially given the range in the cost of living among states. However, the average in 2005 was roughly $24,000 (ranging from $44,000 in Rhode Island to $13,000 in Louisiana). One of the main contributors to prison costs besides staff is health care for prisoners. The average annual cost for an older prisoner was $70,000, almost three times the general average.[9] As prison populations get older, and individual prisoners get sicker, states have an increasing burden to cover prisoners' medical expenses, even though medical care for prisoners is of a quality that is both variable and problematic.

The Federal System

Federal prisoners are those convicted of or charged with breaking a federal law such as drug trafficking across state borders, bank robbery, tax evasion, white-collar crimes that involve interstate commerce, mail fraud, crimes that occur on federal property, or immigration law violations. However, the federal penal code covers a vast range of areas—for example, commerce, federal elections, food and drugs, customs, and income tax issues.

Table 6.2 Length of Stay (in months) of Sentenced State Prisoners

Offense category	2000	2008
Total	24.8	23.5
Violent	45.8	43.7
Property	17.1	15.1
Drug	17.1	15.2
Public order	14.3	14.9
Other/unspecified	19.6	34.9

Between 2000 and 2010, the average length of stay for state prisoners remained relatively constant at about two years. Table 6.2 shows that there was a small shift toward shorter stays in prison for the broadest offense categories—violent, property, and drug.[10] Source: West, Sabol, and Greenman 2010.

Those convicted of felonies in the District of Columbia and on Indian lands also fall under federal jurisdiction. A former student who was convicted of hacking Sarah Palin's e-mail was sentenced to a year and a day in federal prison.[11]

The Federal Bureau of Prisons (BOP) operates institutions of five different security levels. It also operates prison camps and a number of administrative facilities that have special missions, including detaining pretrial defendants or treating prisoners with serious medical conditions. There is one federal super-maximum-security prison called the U.S. Penitentiary Administrative Maximum Facility, or ADMAX, in Florence, Colorado, which has the capacity for 490 prisoners and 800 staff. The federal system operates one low-security prison for women and three others that house both women and men. It operated Alcatraz in San Francisco Bay until its closure as a prison in 1963. Alcatraz is one of the most frequently visited of the national parks.

History and Growth of Federal Prisons

The first federal prison was authorized in 1891 and took more than 10 years to build. Prior to that, the few federal prisoners that there were stayed in military facilities such as what existed in Leavenworth, Kansas. The federal government gradually added more specialized prisons for women and juveniles to the system.

President Herbert Hoover signed the bill to create the Bureau of Prisons in 1930. The BOP was intended to bring about a more centralized and standardized system that had higher professional standards and exercised more humane care of prisoners than those that existed at the time.

Over the decades, the major increases in prisoner population were driven mainly by changes in federal legislation and sentencing policy. The Volstead Act of 1919 (Prohibition, or the Eighteenth Amendment) resulted in laws criminalizing alcohol and therefore created thousands of new prisoners. The Sentencing Reform Act of 1984 abolished federal parole and ushered in determinate sentencing and mandatory minimums. This was a move away from judicial discretion and earned good-time credit. The resulting lengthening of sentences helped fuel the rapid growth of the federal prison population.

Immigration and Federal Prisons

Tensions run high over issues surrounding immigration—especially in the border states. Increases in illegal immigration and the related policies and practices of law enforcement have altered the federal prison population's racial and ethnic composition. Racial disparity is a chronic problem in all parts of America's criminal justice system. Clear-cut evidence that policy drives the disproportion is perhaps nowhere more evident than in federal prisons. (See Chapter 11.)

Good-time credits: Time reduction of a sentence length based on the prisoner's problem-free behavior in custody. The number of days taken off the sentence is usually calculated using a specific formula determined by law, such as one day of credit for every two days of "good time."

| Figure 6.4 | Federal Prison Population Growth |

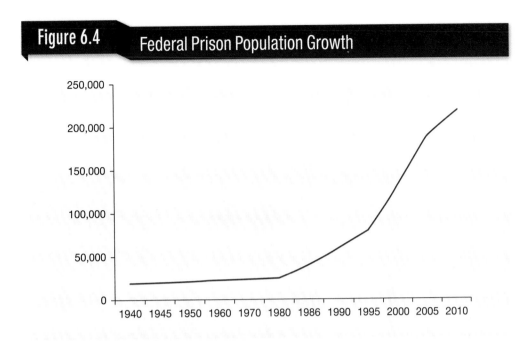

In 1940, the population of the federal prison system was approximately 20,000. By 1980, that population had only grown by 5,000. However, it increased to 40,000 in 1986 and had doubled again to 80,000 by 1995. A mere 10 years later in 2005, the federal prison population had exploded to 187,000. In that same year, an additional 20,000 prisoners under federal jurisdiction were held in private facilities, and 11,000 were handled through community corrections field offices. As of 2005, federal prisons held 12% of incarcerated persons in the nation. Still dwarfed in number by the state system, this nevertheless represents an explosion of prison expansion. In 2012, the federal system had jurisdiction over 219,000 prisoners, 14% of the total prison population in the United States.[12] *Source: Federal Bureau of Prisons 2011.*

State Prisons

State prisons are the "workhorses" of corrections in the United States. In 2012, they held 86% of the nation's 1.57 million prisoners (again, not counting jail inmates). Five states accounted for 38% of state prisoners—Texas, California, Florida, Georgia, and New York.[13] State corrections systems are administered by the executive branch of state government, whereas jails are usually administered at the county or city level, and probation is often under the authority of the judicial branch.

Not surprisingly, states vary significantly in the locations of their facilities, how many there are, how many prisoners they hold, what types of security levels they maintain, and whether they adhere to a more centralized or decentralized model. Rural prisons are a boon to local economies. Building a prison near a small town is often viewed as a way out of economic depression. Besides prison construction and operation, there are many private and influential producers of supporting services and goods that make prison a mainstay of the economy. However, a community that has such a focused industry also runs the risk of subsequent economic hardship should the prison shut down.

Military Prisons and the War on Terror

In the 2000s, the prisons that were most commonly making news were those run by the U.S. military and associated with the War on Terror, especially Abu Ghraib in Iraq (now under sole Iraqi control) and Guantánamo in Cuba. These most resemble maximum-security

Illegal immigrants line up against a U.S. Department of Homeland Security bus in El Paso, Texas, so they can be unshackled and led across the border to Juarez, Mexico, by Immigration and Customs Enforcement agents, 2009.

© Alex Garcia/MCT/Newscom

Habeas corpus: A court summons that demands that the custodian present to the prisoner or a representative of the prisoner proof of lawful authority to detain the prisoner. Habeas corpus is intended to prevent the state from detaining individuals capriciously or arbitrarily.

Disciplinary segregation: Placing an inmate in a separate cell for the purposes of punishment and discipline following an incident, a rule infraction, or other disruption.

Protective custody: Placing an individual in a secure location for the purpose of maintaining that person's physical protection.

prisons in the United States for their heavily fortified settings and stark conditions of confinement, but they are not considered part of the U.S. corrections system as defined in this text. They hold mainly foreign inmates suspected of terrorist acts who are not afforded basic U.S. constitutional protections such as **habeas corpus** and legal representation. The facilities are, for the most part, not subject to the same laws, regulations, and processes as state and federal prisons and mainstream prisons and jails. However, largely because of their separate legal realm, military prisons offer cautionary tales that apply to mainstream corrections. These facilities have documented and egregious histories of abuse by prison guards and military personnel and demonstrate the risk of a harshly punitive culture among staff that is exacerbated by policies that are at best unclear and culturally insensitive and at worst inhumane.

Classification Systems

By the middle of the 19th century, prisoners were routinely separated—men from women, children from adults, and the healthy from the unwell. However, reformers began to demand that prisons separate groups of individuals by their degree of criminality. Over time, a logical means of sorting prisoners grew in importance. Today, the general prison population is classified by risk level into units, some of which are for special populations such as **disciplinary segregation, protective custody,** mental health, or medical units. Systems of classification are based on the premise that individuals with varying offense profiles, levels of risk, and methods of supervision require different security levels in custody.

The first prison classification screening tools were based on psychological and personality tests that were used on men entering the armed services during World War I. Up until the Progressive Era, when the concept of rehabilitation began to take hold, prisoners were separated simply according to their age, gender, and number of offenses; first-timers were kept away from repeat offenders, when possible. Beginning in the 1970s, the growing prison population led to a series of riots and allegations of prisoner abuse. Charges of arbitrariness and unfair placements helped solidify the classification system as an essential part of

Figure 6.5   Number of Sentenced Federal Offenders, 1991–2007

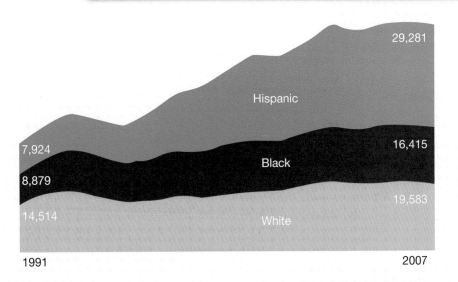

Immigration violations fall under federal jurisdiction. In 2007, a full 40% of all federally sentenced offenders were Latino. Almost half of all federal court sentences for Latinos were for immigration offenses in that same year; another 37% were for drug offenses. And 75% of these immigration offenses were for entering or residing in the United States illegally; another 19% were for smuggling or harboring an illegal alien. Of all Latino federal prisoners, 29% were non-U.S. citizens, compared to their White (8%) or African American (6%) counterparts.[14] Some convicted noncitizens can be deported before they serve their sentence, but most, especially serious or violent offenders, are deported only after serving time in the United States. *Source: Lopez 2009.*

a well-run institution. Institutions shifted toward objective classification based on more reliable and valid criteria. This more diagnostic approach led to a medical-style model of identifying problems and prescribing treatments. However, there was no standardization, and decisions were still made according to subjective and often arbitrary criteria.[15]

Narrow schemes based on a single variable have given way to a more modern approach that uses tools based on predictive data—tools that have been validated by an accepted method of evaluation. California and the Federal Bureau of Prisons were the first to develop such systems to improve consistency and the accuracy of predictions of risk.

Prison administrators have their choice of many classification tools. These tools create a profile for each prisoner using tested predictors of behavior. The NIC has developed a system called the Custody Determination Model. According to the NIC, the essential components of classification cover goals and planning, thorough implementation, the use of valid instruments, a formal and centralized housing plan, appropriate override factors, data collection and monitoring, and evaluation of the system's process and impact.

Sophisticated systems designed to classify prisoners are intended as a strategic tool to manage prisons and a safeguard to treat prisoners fairly and safely. For many years, the standard has been to assign the least restrictive classification necessary to protect safety at all levels, to assess the needs of prisoners, and to promote positive change among prisoners through incentives rather than relying on the experience of prison officials to "know" how to place prisoners, or any other subjective method of decision making. Rules about how to place inmates were meant to ensure proper decision making, orderliness, and appropriate conditions for prisoners.

SPOTLIGHT

ARIZONA'S IMMIGRATION LAWS

Controversy rages over immigration policies at the state level as well as on the national stage. Immigration laws present a host of thorny issues, among them the intersection of legislation, prison industry lobbyists, and persons entering the country illegally. Arizona passed a hotly debated law (SB 1070) that opponents see as racial profiling and supporters see as a bold step toward addressing illegal immigration from Mexico. Arizona's highly charged policy of requiring the police to stop anyone who the officer has "reasonable suspicion" is in the country illegally and to detain anyone who is not in possession of proof of legal entry is certain to increase the number of persons detained by the state. National Public Radio aired a story several months after the legislation passed about the interests of the private prison corporations that helped pass the legislation.[1] Viewed from a business perspective, new detainees equate to a new market; from this perspective, the law opens the door to for-profit prison industry "opportunities." This clearly raises a new set of moral questions related to immigration. Political pressure promptly resulted in some modifications of the law, but critics no doubt will pursue challenges to the bill's constitutionality. It may eventually be up to the courts to decide where to draw the line in what appears to be a serious ethical conflict, which is embodied in companies contracting for building prison space and lobbying the government to pass the laws that would ensure those prisons stay filled and profitable.[2] Besides the profit-motive issue, the law has been challenged on several civil rights and constitutional grounds. In its first ruling on the law in 2012, the U.S. Supreme Court upheld police investigations of the immigration status of suspects, but struck down other parts of the law, including its criminalization of the failure to apply for and carry a registration card indicating one's legal status.

QUESTIONS

1   Should each state decide its own policies related to immigration?

2   Discuss what would be an appropriate definition of "reasonable suspicion."

3   Discuss the problem inherent in private prisons lobbying for punitive sentencing.

Notes

1.   Sullivan 2010

2.   *Arizona v. United States* 2012

The basic parameters of interest are the prisoner's conviction offense, age, gender (although almost all classification systems are designed for men), custody level, gang affiliation, general motivation level, and history of institutional "adjustment." Assessment tools collect and measure further details on mental and physical health status, substance abuse issues, academic and vocational education, work experience, relationships, history of trauma or victimization, and life skills needs. In a more qualitative vein, instruments assess personality traits, especially those related to prison life, such as attitude toward authority, level of motivation, expression of predatory tendencies, ability to form friendships, aggressiveness, passivity, fearfulness, and level of remorse.

Prisoners are assessed for classification when they enter the prison system, either state or federal; when they are admitted to the specific facility where they will serve their sentence; upon assignment to a specific housing unit; and any time they are transferred. Reassessments might be scheduled according to a person's security level, or could occur for a variety of other reasons determined by prison administrators, such as significant changes in an individual's behavior. Classification systems can also help with developing the right kind and the right number of treatment programs based on the needs of the prisoner population, identification of good candidates for **therapeutic communities**, establishing appropriate work opportunities, monitoring the gang population, and reducing racial disparities. Prison administrators must balance the assessment results with practical considerations, such as bed space; they must also revalidate their classification systems and instruments to make sure they are working as intended for the current prison population.

Security Levels

The security level of a facility is defined by a combination of architecture, rules, technology, and regimentation. Security levels are based on the level of control deemed necessary to accomplish the goals of incarceration, and to prevent escape, violence to staff or other inmates, and other in-custody criminal or disruptive behavior. Both the state and federal prison systems have at least minimum-, medium-, and high-security (maximum) institutions. Each level of prison is subject to its own challenges in controlling behavior and in monitoring abuses of power. The physical and staffing differences in facilities related to security level include gun towers, external security barriers, cameras, razor wire, staff-to-inmate ratios, external patrols, and frequency of head counts.

▲ Rigorous research and careful implementation can increase the precision and reliability of assessment and classification tools.

© iStockphoto.com / GiorgioMagini

Minimum Security

These are the least restrictive facilities and have a range of forms, such as ranches, farms, or cottages. They are for prisoners who pose very little physical security risk—first-timers, white-collar criminals, or nonviolent prisoners with short sentences. Minimum-security facilities are the least oppressive and imposing. Minimum-security prisoners often wear their own clothing, but there is still regulation and regimentation. The less restrictive atmosphere is not necessarily the most predictable or easiest to manage. Minimum-security facilities have their disadvantages; more interaction and less surveillance can open up opportunities for violence or abuse among prisoners and between prisoners and staff.

Medium Security

These facilities are more restrictive, designed typically with razor wire perimeters. They may have gun towers and guards on foot or in vehicles. They often have dormitory-style housing and fewer rules than maximum-security facilities. Prisoners wear institutional clothing but may have more freedom of movement within the facility, which is allowed for a population at lower risk for violence or escape. Medium-security facilities are often sectors of entire prison complexes, adjoining higher-security units or campuses. Administrators can easily transfer prisoners as they change classification levels. The possibility of transfer to a higher security level with stricter, more oppressive conditions serves as leverage that prison administrators can hold over inmates as a means of control.

Therapeutic community: A participative, group approach to rehabilitation or treatment services, which may be residential or nonresidential.

Negotiating With Protesting Prisoners

In response to complaints by some inmates about their deprivation of rights by being placed in administrative segregated housing units, a large number of prisoners go on a hunger strike. Spokespersons for the inmates say that many inmates are willing to sacrifice their health and safety to stop the harsh segregation policies. Dozens of inmates refuse to eat prison food and will not perform their work assignments. Some refuse to come out of their cells for daily exercise. The hunger strikers appear to represent inmates from diverse racial groups and gangs.

Prison officials claim that the hunger strike is a ploy by powerful prison gangs to increase their influence behind the walls. They claim that inmates are still eating food bought in the prison commissary and no one is at great risk. The corrections staff claim that current segregation policies are necessary to protect the safety of inmates and staff. They argue that to give in to inmates' demands for change will undermine the authority of correctional officers and could lead to more violence. Prison officials ask the courts to allow them to engage in force-feeding of convicts who are facing imminent threat of death or serious health problems.

Families of inmates are protesting outside the prison gates, and they tell of dire health challenges faced by those refusing food. Many prominent celebrities, editorial writers, and politicians have rallied on behalf of the inmates' cause, demanding that prison officials negotiate a resolution with the hunger strikers.

YOU DECIDE: **As director of corrections, do you negotiate with the striking inmates or their spokespersons to resolve the protest?**

Maximum Security

Maximum-security facilities operate with a focus mostly on custody and control and less on treatment and rehabilitation. These facilities often impose 22 to 24 hours of lockup every day. They are the highest security level in most prison complexes. Because movement is so highly controlled and prisoners are more isolated from one another, these facilities may tend to have a lower incidence of violence and abuse than what is found in lower-security settings. However, orderliness is not necessarily a sign of effectiveness in achieving any kind of lasting behavior change.

The Supermax

The super maximum-security prison—or **supermax**—is the most extremely fortified form of incarceration in the United States, ostensibly reserved for the "worst of the worst." Supermax facilities are intended for the most violent, escape-prone, and rebellious prisoners and gangsters who pose the greatest threat to the institution, to society, or to other prisoners. However, supermax prisoners are not all lifers; most of those held in the supermax are eventually released.

Separate facilities or adjunct units in prison complexes, supermaxes, and specialty housing units referred to as "SHUs," hold prisoners in extreme isolation, confined to their typically six-foot-by-eight-foot cells for 22 to 24 hours a day; any other hours might be spent on exercise in a separate solitary enclosure. Conditions vary from one to another of more than 55 such facilities in approximately 40 states, with a total capacity of 25,000 prisoners.[16] However, some of the commonalities consist of heavily reinforced concrete walls, floors, ceilings, doors, and windows; lights left on 24 hours a day; constant video surveillance; meals served through an opening in the door (the "bean slot"); and highly limited visits, mail, phone calls, and human contact. In addition, the administrators of these facilities have wide leeway to use their judgment in determining who goes to isolation and for what, how long prisoners must stay in isolation, and how to manage and discipline those prisoners, without a great deal of review from outside the facility and without a regular prisoner grievance procedure.

According to one theory of corrections, the supermax concentrates troublesome inmates and cliques into one high-security environment—instead of dispersing them throughout the system—for a uniform scheme of supervision.

Supermax: "super maximum security prisons," which are the most extremely fortified form of incarceration in the United States and are intended to house individuals convicted of serious crimes.

A 1999 NIC study revealed that there is no single agreed-upon definition about what a supermax is and who should be housed in one. Specifics vary widely on the criteria for admission or release, the maximum length of stay, the transition out of isolation, the inclusion or exclusion of the mentally ill, the amount and type of programming (in many cases, there is none), and the degree to which human contact is allowed.

The NIC finally adopted this definition:

> A highly restrictive, high-custody housing unit within a secure facility, or an entire secure facility that isolates inmates from the general prison population and from each other due to grievous crimes, repetitive assault, or violent institutional behavior, the threat of escape or actual escape from high custody facility(s), or inciting or threatening to incite disturbances in a correctional institution.[17]

Cruel and Usual?

Proponents of supermax isolation include prison officials and politicians who claim that it is a necessary means of control for those it houses and a deterrent to other prisoners. They say there are few alternatives for those prisoners who present a clear and imminent danger. However, even during the period of expansion, when states were planning and constructing new supermax prisons, controversy swirled around them.

It is now widely accepted among penologists and researchers, and even some correctional officers and wardens, that the extreme conditions of the supermax exact a human cost in terms of cognitive and emotional health that is well beyond the goals of incarceration

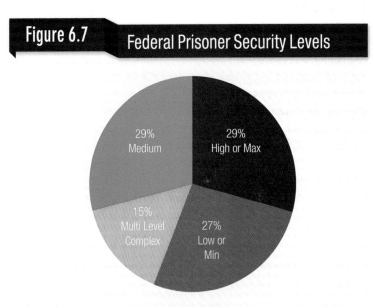

Figure 6.6   State Prisoner Security Levels

- 25% Medium
- 54% Low
- 21% High

Source: Stephan 2008.

Figure 6.7   Federal Prisoner Security Levels

- 29% Medium
- 29% High or Max
- 15% Multi Level Complex
- 27% Low or Min

Overall, more than half (54%) of U.S. state prisons are low security, a quarter are medium security, and just under a quarter are high security. Federal prison facilities are 27% low or minimum security, 29% medium, and 29% high or maximum; about 15% are multilevel complexes.[20] *Source: Stephan 2008.*

and may cross the border into "pointless suffering."[18] Indeed, esteemed criminologist Norval Morris stated that supermaxes "raise the level of punishment close to that of psychological torture."[19]

The deleterious impact of extreme and prolonged isolation is now known to be significant not only for inmates, but also for staff. Professor Craig Haney argues that the supermax environment reaches perverse extremes and negatively influences staff, who are also subjected to the dehumanizing architecture, degrading rituals, and emotional tensions. These conditions lead to a higher probability of maltreatment of prisoners ranging from indifference to brutality.[21]

SPOTLIGHT

ISOLATION AND THE SUPERMAX

Alcatraz, in the center of San Francisco Bay, is the fore-runner of the modern supermax. In the nearly 30 years "The Rock" was in operation, the nation's most notorious and hard-core prisoners lived there. Similarly, the likes of the Unabomber, Zacarias Moussaoui, and Juan Matta-Ballesteros are serving life sentences in the U.S. Penitentiary Administrative Maximum Facility (ADMAX) near Florence, Colorado. Their crimes are notorious, but many other unknown prisoners occupy the 550 under-ground beds of the only supermax operated by the Federal Bureau of Prisons.[1]

Isolation as a tactic for control of prisoners is not a new concept, nor is the use of solitary confinement (the "hole") new as a prison within a prison. These measures have been used for decades to break the spirit and make an example out of certain prisoners for certain behavior. In 1829, the Quakers who established the Eastern State Penitentiary believed that isolation with a Bible would lead a prisoner to recognize and repent for his failings.[2] Within decades, isolation had shown little appreciable effectiveness in accomplishing this goal and was largely abandoned for being an inhumane strategy.

The idea of the supermax came much later. In two sepa-rate incidents in 1983, two officers and one inmate were killed in the U.S. penitentiary at Marion, Illinois, which led to indefinite lockdown of the entire facility.[3] This peniten-tiary housed the most violent and rebellious prisoners and hard-core gangsters who manipulated their empires from inside prison. Later, in 1994, the federal government opened ADMAX, the first of many such super-secure-custody prisons. A majority of, but not all, states operate one or more supermax facilities.

QUESTIONS

1 Should isolation be used as a behavior-control strat-egy? Who should be subject to it?

2 Research accounts by former prisoners who have spent time in extreme isolation. Discuss their experi-ences.

3 Discuss how you think you would be affected by spending time in isolation.

Notes
1. Collins 2004
2. Eastern State Penitentiary n.d.
3. Federal Bureau of Prisons n.d.-b

Although the supermax is supposed to be used only for the extremely dangerous, there are many instances of its use for punitive sanctions for lower-level prisoners or as "protective" isolation for HIV-positive or mentally ill inmates. The NIC suggests that prison administra-tors should conservatively and clearly define the population for the SHU. Other prisoners should be housed in less extreme conditions, including the mentally ill, the "incorrigible" who need frequent segregation, those who need protection, those who need administrative confinement for separation but not control, and those in need of observation. "These facili-ties are inappropriate for the nuisance inmate."[22]

Due process is meant to govern any placement in the SHU. The criteria for release (deter-minate time, behavior change) must also be defined. SHU inmates are sometimes released directly to the streets, creating a public safety risk of unknown proportions. It has been shown that mental states can deteriorate rapidly inside these units, sometimes within days. Few prisons have a well-organized, stepped-down release plan for inmates who spend time in the SHU or the supermax.

Challenges in court (*Ruiz v. Johnson*, *Wilkinson v. Austin*) have contested the standards for the operation of a supermax facility. In the 1995 case of *Madrid v. Gomez*, a federal judge found that conditions at the now notorious Pelican Bay prison in California "may well hover on the edge of what is humanly tolerable."

Besides their human toll, supermax facilities cost significantly more to build because of the heavily reinforced structure, perimeters, doors, locks, and electronic surveillance equipment. Operations cost more as well; the staff-to-prisoner ratio is as high as two to one.

Programs and Services

There is a range of programs and services in prisons; the prison population has multiple needs that programs are intended to address. Structuring time and engaging prisoners in productive activity is widely seen as a key method of maintaining a safe and well-functioning facility. Punishment alone is not effective in reforming prisoners. Rehabilitative programs in prison, like those for probation and parole, are based on criminogenic factors—the risk factors that contribute to criminal behavior such as antisocial values and peers, certain personality traits, low self-control, and family dysfunction. They are designed to address education, employment, substance abuse treatment, behavior and counseling, medical services, and recreation. However, the main function of prison is behavior control, and when officials are faced with a choice between the two, it is always security that trumps the delivery of services.

▲ ADX Federal Prison, the Federal Bureau of Prison's Administrative Maximum Security facility in Florence, Colorado, holds about 400 very high-risk inmates including Terry Nichols and Ted Kaczynski.

© Lizzie Himmel/Sygma/Corbis

Criminogenic: Tending to give rise to crime or criminality. The factors that generate an individual or group's tendency to commit crime.

Disenfranchisement: Preventing an individual from having the right to vote. More generally this refers to obstacles to full participation in civic life.

Prisoners typically present with significantly higher rates of substance abuse, history of victimization, undiagnosed or untreated mental health problems, illiteracy, poverty, and underemployment and other forms of disenfranchisement than the general population. Thus, the treatment they do or do not get in prison can have a significant impact on subsequent successes and failures.

Attitudes about how to handle inmate needs fluctuate over time. Treatment as viewed from a medical model fell from favor during the 1970s, when the view that "nothing works" in rehabilitation took hold, and programs were greatly reduced nationwide. Representatives from both sides of the political aisle became suspicious of rehabilitation. Liberals criticized behavior change as mind control, and conservatives characterized addressing prisoner needs as pampering. Many of these attitudes persist, but the United States appears to be reawakening to the idea that smart correctional policy includes well-designed and tested methods for dealing with the risk factors that are known to correlate with crime.

Still, much of the public, lawmakers, and correctional professionals alike are skeptical about the value of treatment and services for prisoners. The public often resents prisoners when the perception is that they have more opportunities than what is available to many in the community. It is understandable that prisoner access to medical care, for example, seems unfair to many law-abiding people who cannot afford it themselves. Despite the inequities, the solution surely can't be to deny health care to the sick and elderly in prison.

Once the site of harsh punishment and strict isolation—while tantalizingly close to freedom—Alcatraz is now one of the most visited of the U.S. national parks.

© iStockphoto. comfranckreporter

Prisons enlist a gamut of providers, including teachers, counselors, case managers, social workers, psychologists, psychiatrists, doctors, nurses, and chaplains. Their working conditions are often more challenging and their compensation is often lower than what they would earn for the same work in the private sector. Whereas the role of prison custodial staff calls upon their powers of control and intimidation, program and treatment providers offer benefits to the prisoner and relationships that are defined more by trust.

Service providers in prison, including teachers, encounter many obstacles to continuity and consistency. One of the major challenges in the delivery of effective programming is overcrowding. Not only is it impossible to conduct classes when classrooms have been retooled as dormitories, but a more pressurized atmosphere also leads to more frequent disruption and chaos, making scheduling, concentration, and learning or treatment even more difficult.

Program effectiveness is extremely variable and highly dependent upon the way programs are conceived and implemented. All prison programs are by no means created equal. Evaluating them is an ongoing task of the research community and departments of corrections. The findings of research inquiry have the potential to inform and improve the delivery of effective programming. Moving toward more effective treatment in prison hinges in large part on the ability of leadership to enlist the buy-in of its line staff, whose day-to-day interactions and practical application of policy are crucial to the definition of the social order behind bars.

Federal Programming

The federal system runs educational programs such as literacy, English as a second language, and GED courses. Completion of the GED is a requirement to obtain an inmate job in federal prison. In 2005, there were 24,000 inmates enrolled in GED programs; 6,000

In some prisons, especially women's facilities, inmates take part in service dog training, which has many emotional benefits for the participants.

BOP.gov; US Department of Corrections

of them graduated. The system also administers hundreds of occupational programs, plus courses offered by other entities, including the Department of Labor. All federal facilities have some level of psychological and psychiatric counseling, substance abuse treatment being one focus of counseling. Federal prisons are under a mandate to provide drug treatment to every eligible inmate.[23]

Education

Education has for decades been the cornerstone of rehabilitation philosophy. Support for prison education has grown and waned over the years. But research gives credence to the concept that education is a sound, long-term investment in public safety. To paraphrase one reporter, not only does an education make it much easier for a parolee to find and hold a decent job, but—unlike drug users—there are no relapses for those who escape illiteracy.[24]

A person's education level may be one of the more reliable predictors of criminal behavior. According to the Bureau of Justice Statistics (BJS), roughly two thirds of prisoners have less than a high school education, and many have learning disabilities. High numbers of prisoners need remedial education and basic literacy skills. Education is one type of prison program that is more understandable for its direct link to participation in the economy (and avoiding crime) and, therefore, more acceptable to the public.

The capacity of prison educational programs is inadequate compared to the need. Even though 85% of all state and federal prisons have some kind of education programs, there are long waiting lists for enrollment, especially for GEDs.[25] In the federal system, having a GED is a prerequisite to eligibility for the higher-paying prison jobs.

Vocational training is also offered in 52% of prisons. However, vocational training in prison too rarely teaches skills that are truly marketable, especially in a rapidly changing marketplace. In addition, ex-prisoners, even if they do have skills, face public stigma and legal restrictions from assuming employment in a broad range of jobs.

Some studies have begun to evaluate the link between prison education and recidivism. A Texas study found that educational programs might be most effective in reducing recidivism, especially for the most educationally disadvantaged.[26] Brewster and Sharp concluded that a GED, whether it was mandatory or voluntary, was strongly associated with being less likely to reoffend, especially for women.[27] Although education is clearly a way to increase the skills and self-respect of prisoners, researchers have yet to fully evaluate the power of education to keep prisoners from committing new crime.

▲ Inmates training to become commercial underwater divers receive classroom instruction on diving history, science, and techniques at the Marine Technology Training Center, part of the California Prison Industry Authority (CALPIA), of the state prison in Chino, California.

© Bloomberg / Getty Images

The recommendations from the California Legislative Analyst's Office points to the difficulties in funding, participation, and program interruptions, among others:

- Fund programs based on actual attendance, not enrollment.
- Develop incentives for inmate participation and achievement.
- Fill teacher vacancies.
- Limit the negative impact of lockdowns on programs.
- Develop a case management system that assigns inmates to the most appropriate programs based on risk and needs.
- Base decisions for funding education on ongoing assessments of programs.[28]

Drug Treatment

According to a report from the Center on Addiction and Substance Abuse (CASA) at Columbia University, the prevalence of drug and alcohol abuse among the prison population rose 43% from 1996 to 2006. The CASA research concludes that 65% of prisoners meet the medical criteria for substance abuse, and another 15% to 20% were substance involved and under the influence at the time of their crimes.[29] These are, as expected, higher rates of use and abuse than among the general prison population.

Clearly, the need for treatment is immense. But there is a great deal of discrepancy between that need and how many prisoners are actually receiving related services. There were drug and alcohol dependency programs in 74% of state and federal prisons in 2005.[30] Other sources claim that only 17% of programs are effective, and only 12% of prisoners are enrolled in substance abuse treatment.[31] Furthermore, in many ways, the prison environment is antithetical to treatment, which relies on trust, honesty, and a certain willingness to be receptive or vulnerable.

Physical and Mental Health Care

Prisoners have high rates of infectious diseases, such as HIV/AIDS, hepatitis C, and STDs. Many of these conditions are associated with a high-risk way of life. These health conditions, especially HIV/AIDS, present challenges for prison administrators. Whether to test all entering prisoners as well as standing populations of inmates is highly controversial. Administrators may want to identify prisoners who test positive for the virus to segregate them and protect the others. However, such segregation stigmatizes prisoners and does nothing to promote education and appropriate protection for everyone in the system.

Prisoners also have high rates of chronic diseases, such as cancer, hypertension, diabetes, and heart conditions. Of the 3,353 inmates who died in state prison in 2011 (not including death penalty cases), the leading causes of death were cancer (31%), heart disease (25%), liver disease (10%), respiratory disease (6%), and AIDS-related causes (2%). Suicide accounted for 6% of the deaths, and homicides and drug or alcohol overdoses 2% each.[32]

There are high rates of mental health problems among prisoners, especially women. According to a special report from the BJS, 56% of state prisoners in 2005 had a history of mental health problems.[33] Many argue that mental health has been criminalized in U.S. society, resulting in the incarceration of people with mental health problems. Further, prisons and jails are not well equipped, and corrections personnel are not well-trained staff, to deal effectively and humanely with the mentally ill. Mental health treatment is sorely inadequate in prison and mostly consists of the dispensing of behavior-modifying medication. Prison itself is considered to be a risk factor for mental health conditions.

Recreation

Recreation programs for prisoners are generally considered to be part of a healthy rehabilitation plan. It is not hard to imagine that recreational activities are closely tied to prison morale. Some of the activities offered in prisons may include exercise courses, team sports, woodworking, musical activities, open gym time, weightlifting, and an outdoor yard. These activities may be supervised by a specialist in recreation or a general correctional officer. Participation in some recreational programs may be contingent on good behavior; participants may have to be free of any behavior problems or rule infractions for a certain period to be eligible for recreation. Some programs may entail a fee.

There is some controversy about the subject of recreation for prisoners. Most prison administrators recognize the value in maintaining some normal and healthy activity among the prison population. Recreation certainly contributes to that. On the other hand, media images of prisoners participating in recreation tend to convey the idea that prisoners have an easy and comfortable life. The public seems easily swayed into thinking that prisoners are not being punished enough if they have time to play baseball. In addition, images of prisoners lifting weights and getting stronger and more muscular seem to raise anxiety among the public, and perhaps even among prison administrators and guards.

In fact, weightlifting was highlighted as the symbol of prisoner leniency during the get-tough 1990s. During the Clinton administration, Richard Zimmer, a Republican member of the House of Representatives from New Jersey, introduced legislation called the No Frills Prison Act: Amendment to Prevent Luxurious Conditions in Prisons. It was this legislation that helped to spur a debate on prisoner privilege in general, and weightlifting in particular. In the wake of the federal legislation, some states enacted similar laws, which also eliminate or limit cable television, computers, legal research materials, and many other amenities. Another side of this debate was well articulated by a group called the National Correctional Recreation Association (NCRA), which was founded by custody officers in the mid-1960s. The NCRA defends recreation, including weightlifting,

SPOTLIGHT

PERSONALITY AND PRISON LEADERSHIP

Prisons have been run with a certain effectiveness by the force of personality of a single administrator or warden. Dr. George Beto, who ran Texas prisons from 1962 to 1972, had such a personality. He imposed a paramilitary model of control that was highly effective in maintaining order and accomplishing his personal goals for the prison. He enlisted the "natural" prison leaders to help run or "tend" the prison and rewarded them for doing so. His method placed a nonnegotiable value on work and learning to read. Discipline was unwaveringly strict—with swift and certain consequences for stepping outside the lines; Beto literally had inmates walk between painted lines on the floor. He reinforced the behavior he wanted with a system of rewards as well. One problem with these methods is that it is almost impossible to pass them on to a successor. The personality itself becomes the method and is central to its effectiveness. Also problematic is the tricky balance between control as a means to instilling order and discipline taken to an inhumane extreme:

A great problem in American prisons is finding something constructive for the inmates to do. In many prisons, especially in the north and east, they warehouse convicts—they keep them in cells and permit them to lie around all day long. Every able man in our department works. And he works hard . . . If we don't do anything else in the Department of Corrections we at least teach them the dignity of work and the necessity of work.[1]

They've got this place so regulated that there's no chance to screw up. Here, every decision, even the tiniest one, is made for you . . . It's like running a poultry farm. There's good feed, the cages are clean, they wash down the animals, but it's all mechanical. Honor, integrity, decency—these are the human things that there is no attempt to instill. It's the antithesis of the outside world, where you have to take some measure of responsibility for yourself. They turn out great prisoners here—but broken people.[2]

QUESTIONS

1 What are the most important qualities for a prison warden to have? Why?

2 Should a warden institutionalize his or her personal methods? Discuss ways a warden might accomplish this.

Notes

1. George Beto, from *Manpower, Motivation, and Management: The Key to Our Future*, as cited in Chase 2009, 111

2. Frank Leahy, Texas inmate, 1978, as cited in Chase 2009, 111

as building self-esteem and self-discipline, counteracting idleness, creating incentives, and relieving stress.

The American Bar Association (ABA) developed and adopted standards for the treatment of prisoners. These standards address recreation and leisure activities and call for minimizing time in cells and daily opportunities to maintain physical health—in the open air, if possible.

Work and Inmate Labor

Of all public state and federal facilities, 95% have work programs. Inmates earn very little; wages are usually under $1 per hour. In some states, prisoners earn nothing for their work.

Exploiting captive labor and labor as punishment and as a way to accomplish large-scale public works projects is not a new idea. Slaves in Egypt built the pyramids, according to some theorists. Prisoners housed on a ship in San Francisco Bay built their own prison at San Quentin. One of the most potent images of captivity is the prison chain gang at work in the fields or on the roads in the southern states. Prison labor has been used and exploited in various schemes and with varying degrees of attention to the welfare and civil rights of the prisoners.

There is a legitimate claim to valuing work as a productive use of time and as an opportunity to learn responsibility, self-discipline, and marketable skills. Structured time can increase the safety of the prison environment. Work as a rehabilitative strategy is also a legitimate value. However, there is great potential to abuse and exploit prisoner labor.

Controversy still surrounds prison labor, and objections come from different camps. Labor unions complain that cheap prisoner labor undercuts them, and they object to unfair competition. Prisoners' work often supports the very institution that confines them, but these jobs (from laundry to making license plates) rarely prepare inmates for work on the outside. Contracting prisoner labor out to local industry creates a conflict of interest for wardens and sets up an unseemly motivation to maintain a prison population of a profitable size and fitness. These problematic interests have led to laws restricting the use, movement, or sale of prison labor and goods produced by prisoners.

The Prison Environment

Prisons are large and complex organizations with several levels of administrative hierarchy. The prison warden is at the top of the chain of command and has ultimate responsibility for the facility. Leadership sets a tone and communicates a level of confidence and competence. Low confidence can destabilize the institution, which then becomes a more dangerous place. A power vacuum is always filled in prison. If prison administrators lose power, the strongest among the prisoners stand to gain it.[34]

Wardens are accountable to commissioners or the head of the state's department of corrections. Deputies oversee subdepartments, such as custody, programs, and industries. Line staff work directly with the prisoners performing such custody duties as searches, movements of prisoners, and head counts. Other staff support the functions of the prison, such as office personnel, accounting, purchasing, food services, and training. Providers of professional services are separate from the regular prison employees and are often under the direction of the department of corrections. However, prisoners do much of the daily work of running the facility.

The prison environment is one in which all aspects of the prisoner's life are regimented and overseen. Individuality is systematically reduced through uniform clothing, removal

▲ A Southern chain gang circa 1903 and a modern prison work crew. How are they similar? How are they different?

http://en.wikipedia.org/wiki/ File:A_Southern_chain_gang_ c1903-restore.jpg; © Jay Janner/KRT/Newscom

SPOTLIGHT

PRISON SEX CULTURE

The National Institute of Corrections (NIC) was assigned the responsibility of assisting the corrections field in addressing the problem of prison sexual violence as part of the Prison Rape Elimination Act of 2003. One element in that effort was a series of focus groups and interviews with staff from 12 facilities across the nation to increase knowledge about the realities of sexual culture in prisons and jails from the perspective of those who work closely with inmates.

The NIC conducted these interviews and produced three volumes of results from the research in partnership with the Moss Group, a Washington, D.C.–based consulting firm. The first volume focused on preventing and responding to sexual assaults in adult prisons and jails; the second, on investigating sexual assault; and the third, on sexual violence in women's prisons and jails. These three documents provide a unique and in-depth look at the staff point of view on the subject of sexual behavior among prisoners and between staff and prisoners.[1]

According to the reports, the majority of staff recognize the gravity of the issue of sexual misconduct and abuse; they believe that preventing it is an important part of their

job. Staff generally believed that incidents were infrequent, although they conceded that they are difficult to count. Even without having direct or firsthand knowledge, and even if the victim doesn't come forward, staff had a sense of when "something was wrong." Staff develop a sense of who in the institution is likely to be vulnerable or likely to be predatory; they contend that smaller, younger, or more effeminate individuals are more likely to be victimized. Staff recognize what is referred to as the "grooming process" (cultivating a sexual relationship) or "protective pairing" (seeking shelter from a stronger, more experienced inmate as a benefit of a sexual relationship). Because of the deprivations of prison and jail, both women and men may engage in "situational" same-sex behavior. Others of their fellow prisoners may be offended by same-sex physical contact.

One of the main challenges cited by staff was being able to distinguish coerced sex from consensual sex. Though sexual relationships among prisoners are against the rules, they may not constitute a law violation. The difficulty in getting to the truth about an incident has to do with a number of factors, including inmates being reluctant to tell because of the risk of retaliation for "snitching," stories changing from one period of questioning to the next, or a lack of evidence. Also, falsely accusing a person of sexual misconduct or worse—whether it is alleged against a staff member or another inmate—can

of personal belongings, and assignment of numbers, among other measures. Prisoners get up, dress, eat, shower, exercise, and sleep according to the prison schedule.

The relationship between officers and prisoners is more complex and nuanced than one might assume. They are more dependent on one another than may be evident on the surface, and they are together for months or years on end. Except for the highest-security facilities, inmates and guards are in close physical proximity to one another for much of the day. Prison guards have the backing of the state and the institution—they have the weapons and the resources—but prisoners have many idle hours, devise creative solutions to problems, and outnumber the guards. It is in the interest of guards to engage in subtle negotiations of the more minor rules to gain cooperation with the more important rules that have to do with safety.

Prisons are social systems as well as penal institutions, with hierarchies, enterprise, and alliances—subtle and not so subtle politics and agendas—it's what people do. However, prison relationships are fundamentally coercive. Inmate social systems are guided by a code that solidifies prisoner unity against officials, even though there are other social

be used as a strategic weapon by individuals who have very little power otherwise. Almost all staff agreed that all reports of sexual abuse or violence must be taken seriously and investigated appropriately, regardless of who the alleged perpetrator might be. They also agreed that there can be no consensual relationship between a staff member and an inmate; such an alliance is by definition coercive and wrong—morally, ethically, and legally.[2]

In responding to victimization, it is difficult for staff to balance their desire to be compassionate toward inmates and not wanting to open themselves up to being manipulated or accused of wrongdoing. As an example, staff opinion varied about whether and when it was appropriate to give a prisoner a hug.

Particularly in women's facilities, sexual violence may tend to be less common than it is in men's facilities, and incarcerated women focus more on relationships than men do. Staff observed that many conflicts or physical violence among women prisoners stemmed ultimately from personal intimate relationships. Many incarcerated women have histories of abuse and unhealthy ideas about what constitutes a relationship. Some women don't even know that they have a right to say no. There may be a great deal of confusion or misunderstanding of intentions, both among inmates and between them and the staff members. And intimacy—especially inappropriate intimacy—tends to exacerbate vulnerabilities and create drama.[3]

In general, staff admit to having inadequate training in detecting problem situations, responding to them in a professional manner, and preventing them from happening in the future. Some forward-thinking administrators are making a concerted effort to thoughtfully change facility and agency culture and to foster an environment that is safe for staff and prisoners alike.

QUESTIONS

1 Discuss ways that custody staff might be able to balance compassion and professional distance.

2 Why might a prisoner not want to report an incident of sexual misconduct or abuse?

3 Should staff try to intervene in prisoner relationships when they feel someone might be vulnerable to victimization? How should they do so?

Notes

1. National Institute of Corrections and the Moss Group 2006, 2007, 2009
2. National Institute of Corrections and the Moss Group 2006
3. National Institute of Corrections and the Moss Group 2009

---

divisions as well. Numerous subgroups within the inmate population and the staff often divide along lines of race, age, gang affiliation, or language, and loyalties within and between these groups vary to a wide degree. Nevertheless, corrections officers, as police (and, to some extent, most employee groups), tend to live by a code of silence—a value of never revealing damaging information about a colleague.

Correctional officers view their work role as everything from human service provider to brutal custodian. Their training is in many ways similar to basic military training, with emphasis on physical conditioning, disciplined behavior, and a component of classroom learning. Prison guards have the same daily environment as the prisoners. Their responsibilities do indeed include both the custodial and the rehabilitative, roles that can be challenging to balance. Because prison is a stressful and dangerous environment, there tends to be high turnover and rates of burnout. Personnel issues make management of the prison even more difficult. Where the ethnic makeup of the staff is distinctly different from that of the prisoners, significant cultural barriers between officers and prisoners often exist, including language barriers. Some officer training may include learning Spanish, for instance, in places where the prisoner population includes many Spanish speakers. Staff training is often an ongoing effort, especially in light of constantly changing legal requirements, such as proper handling of prison sexual safety and accommodations for disabled prisoners. (See Chapter 9.)

Discipline

Prison discipline encompasses several levels of hierarchy. Prison administrators control prisoner behavior—a basic function of incarceration. Doing so presents the basic administrative challenge of keeping order and safety inside a facility. There is also the balance between control of a prisoner and ease of abusing the power differential between captors and captives. Because of the "slippery slope" of total authority, prisons themselves must also be subject to oversight to monitor performance in carrying out the goals of incarceration and protecting the civil rights of prisoners. What happens when prisoners break the rules inside, and what happens when prison officials do?

The California Department of Corrections and Rehabilitation introduces prisoner discipline as follows in its *Operations Manual*:

> The Department provides a graduated system of inmate discipline designed to be administered commensurate with the seriousness of the offense. Discipline shall be so administered as to maintain control, conserve human values and individual dignity and promote socially desirable changes in attitude and behavior.[35]

People in prison (presumably) have already broken society's laws and are not necessarily compelled to submit to authority. In prison, they are governed by an even more stringent set of rules and regulations than what exists on the outside. Despite all the means of control inside a facility, people break the rules all the time, both prisoners and staff. Serious and violent crime as well as minor disorder occurs inside of prison. The warden is ultimately responsible for disciplining prison staff as well as prisoners.

Prisons have formal and informal schemes of consequences for breaking the rules, usually based on the granting or removal of privileges and comforts and presumably proportional to the seriousness of the behavior. Prisons have many rules, so rule breaking can range from relatively minor issues (petty theft or vandalism, misuse of telephone privileges, use of vulgar language) to more serious matters (possession of **contraband**, assault, or homicide). Privileges include mail, visits, phone calls, and recreation. Prisoners can be issued "tickets" for misconduct, whether minor or more serious. Typically, a disciplinary committee reviews prisoner complaints and charges against prisoners, conducts hearings, and makes determinations of guilt and punishment. Of course, a great deal of the daily negotiation for control goes on all the time in informal ways that are dictated by the relationships and culture inside the institution.

Especially for very serious behaviors, every prison must have a procedure that incorporates due process elements similar to what exists on the outside—in effect, a justice system within a justice system. Prisoners have a right to receive a complaint, have a fair hearing, confront witnesses, have help to prepare for the hearing, have the decision in writing, and appeal the decision. The right to counsel was granted by the court at first, then was taken away after two years.

Contraband: Any item that is prohibited. In prison, this could include cell phones or cigarettes as well as drugs or weapons.

The issue of prisoner discipline and prison oversight tests one of the stickier tensions inside prison. Espousing a more hands-off approach, John DiIulio stated that "prison officials oversee prisoners, and the courts oversee the prison officials. Courts have increased bureaucratization—more reliance on 'bulky training manuals' than the 'integrity, personalize, keen wit' and discretion of the line staff."[36]

Until the 1960s, prisoners were generally thought to have no rights, and the courts took a hands-off approach to corrections. The civil rights era helped to create a climate of change that affected prisoners as well. The Supreme Court case of *Cooper v. Pate* recognized prisoners as persons whose rights are protected by the Constitution.[37] As such, they are allowed to sue prison officials for such issues as brutality, deprivation of medical care, or denial of other basic rights. They can also challenge the legality of their confinement through a writ of habeas corpus. Predictably, prisoner litigation skyrocketed after the *Cooper* decision. The next obstacle for prisoners was gaining access to legal counsel and the courts. It was not always the case, but now, most prisons have law libraries, and prisoners are supposed to have access to legal counsel. Many prisoners have pressed charges and succeeded in testing their rights in court, prompting judges to take more of an interest in prison oversight and influence reform measures. Despite the protections of the court, prisoners are still at a disadvantage to exert their rights and may fear retaliation by prison officials.

One of the difficulties with prisoner discipline is its potential for being applied in a capricious or unjust manner. Some wardens may make no apology for this. Others have instituted a more structured matrix for applying specific punishments for specific behaviors. In addition, a department should have prescribed methods for disciplining prisoners, procedures for investigation, and requirements for detailed documentation of incidents and their consequences.

SUMMARY

Prisons are intended to be the means by which society carries out its objectives of punishment, deterrence, incapacitation, and rehabilitation. Although there are other ways to achieve these goals of society, the United States relies heavily on prisons as a correctional sanction.

Correctional facilities run by the federal government are for people who break federal laws such as those governing immigration and drug trafficking across state borders. Each state operates its own prison system as well, and over 85% of prisoners are in state prisons. There are many regional differences among state prisons and state criminal law. Many of these are problematic differences, with some states criminalizing the same actions that are legal in other states—crossing borders, marijuana possession, gay marriages, and abortion, to name a few. Rates of incarceration serve as the best method of comparison. There are striking differences in rates for minorities compared to Whites, for the wealthy compared to the poor, and for women compared to men.

Prisoners are usually classified into risk levels depending on their histories, their current offense, and other factors. Their classification level helps administrators separate prisoners into groups according to the degree of supervision needed to control behavior and administer services.

Prisons are architecturally varied, but are typified by fortified structures, armed guards, razor wire, regimentation, controlled connections with the outside, and harsh conditions inside. Prisons are designed to accommodate a number of security levels—minimum being the least fortified for those prisoners who pose the lowest threat to public safety and safety within the facility. Medium security is more restrictive, and maximum is even more so. The supermax exerts the most control and isolation over prisoners. Its use is fraught with controversy. There are ongoing tensions and legal challenges between the administration of prisons and the rights of those confined inside.

Prison is used in the United States more than in any other nation, and the consequent financial and social costs are extremely high. Prisons are expensive to build and to operate. Addressing the basic needs of prisoners costs the taxpayers. Addressing the underlying issues that contribute to criminal offending is also expensive but may be considered an investment in the future safety of the community, as healthier, better educated, less drug-dependent, more employable former prisoners have a better chance of staying out of prison.

Conditions inside of prisons affect the prisoners and the prison staff as well. Discipline and maintaining order involve a complex balance of objectives for prison administrators. Research can help identify the ways in which prisons can operate more efficiently and with better success in rehabilitation.

DISCUSSION QUESTIONS

1. What are the main objectives and functions of incarceration?

2. Discuss the U.S. reliance on prison as the main means of correctional control. What might be viable alternatives?

3. How do state correctional systems compare to the federal system?

4. Discuss comparative rates of incarceration for males and females and for different ethnicities and races.

5. How does prison crowding affect administrators, guards, and prisoners?

6. How do immigration laws interact with prison privatization?

7. Discuss a plausible "step-down" strategy for releasing inmates from supermax facilities.

8. Describe the main intent behind prisoner classification systems and discuss the problems administrators face in implementing them.

9. What kind of services should prisons provide to prisoners, and why?

10. How are prisoners and guards dependent on one another?

KEY TERMS

Consent decree, 122

Contraband, 142

Criminogenic, 133

Cruel and unusual, 115

Disciplinary segregation, 126

Disenfranchisement, 133

Good-time credits, 124

Habeas corpus, 126

Halfway house, 121

Lockdown, 116

Protective custody, 126

Secure confinement, 122

Supermax, 130

Therapeutic community, 129

NOTES

1. Death Penalty Focus 2013b; Radelet and LaCock 2009
2. Hall n.d.
3. Carson and Golinelli 2013; U.S. Census Bureau 2013. All data, except where noted, are from Carson and Golinelli 2013.
4. Stephan 2008
5. Federal prisons are managed by the Bureau of Prisons and generally hold individuals awaiting trial, awaiting sentencing, or serving sentences for violations of federal law. These facilities also hold some individuals awaiting trial or sentencing by Immigration and Customs Enforcement (ICE) or the U.S. Marshals Service. Sentenced felons from the District of Columbia also serve their sentences in federal prisons.
6. West, Sabol, and Greenman 2010
7. Warren 2008

8. National Association of State Budget Officers 2010
9. Warren 2008
10. West, Sabol, and Greenman 2010
11. Protalinski 2011
12. Carson and Golinelli 2013; Federal Bureau of Prisons n.d.a
13. Carson and Golinelli 2013
14. Lopez 2009
15. Austin and Hardyman 2004
16. Mears 2005
17. Riveland 1999, 6
18. Human Rights Watch 2000
19. Stephan 2008
20. Morris 2000, 98

21. Haney 2008; Lovell 2008

22. Riveland 1999, 7

23. Federal Bureau of Prisons n.d.

24. Sterngold 2006

25. Stephan 2008

26. Adams et al. 1994

27. Brewster and Sharp 2002

28. Legislative Analyst's Office 2008

29. CASA 2010

30. Stephan 2008

31. CASA 2010

32. Mumola 2007; Noonan and Ginder 2013

33. Bureau of Justice Statistics 2006

34. Ross and Richards 2002

35. California Department of Corrections and Rehabilitation 2014

36. DiIulio 1987, 73

37. *Cooper v. Pate* 1964

Sharpen your skills with SAGE edge at edge.sagepub.com/krisberg

SAGE edge for students provides a personalized approach to help you accomplish your coursework goals in an easy-to-use learning environment. This site includes action plans, mobile-friendly eFlashcards and web quizzes as well as web, audio, and video resources and links to SAGE journal articles.

7 Coming Home

Reentry and Parole

LEARNING OBJECTIVES

1 To grasp the origins of parole and how parole has evolved.

2 To understand the basic function of parole and its role in the corrections system.

3 To be able to name and describe the different types of parole release.

4 To grasp how a parole board is constituted and what its functions are.

So far, this text has presented many facts about incarceration in the United States: the huge numbers of prisoners being held for long periods of time, the harsh physical and social prison environment, the health and safety risks of incarceration, and inadequate in-custody rehabilitative programming. These must be considered along with another simple fact: Around 95% of prisoners are eventually released back into American society. With the general exception of those on death row, prisoners serving sentences of life without parole (LWOP), and those who die in prison, all others return home. Each year, well over a half million men and women leave prison and reenter society. Most return to the communities where they were living when they committed their offenses.

Most ex-prisoners will reenter society worse off than when they were arrested and jailed, wiser in the ways of criminal culture and further alienated from mainstream American life. They will be older but often no more educated or prepared for employment. They will be ineligible for many jobs and unlikely to be hired in many others, due to the stigma of incarceration. Depending on their offense history and the state in which they reside, they will be less able to participate in civil society (unable to vote or hold political office) and ineligible for many forms of public assistance such as welfare and public housing. They might be estranged from their families and prosocial relationships, and more likely to lose custody of their children. Although most will remain under some level of community-based supervision for a period time, release means an end to the strict structure and constant surveillance of prison and a return to the unpredictability of life in the outside world. Perhaps not surprisingly, approximately half of former inmates return to prison within three years of release.[1]

This chapter is mostly concerned with the two thirds of released prisoners who remain under supervision of state or federal corrections, which is generally called parole. These individuals are released "conditionally," which means that misconduct or a failure to meet a list of conditions may result in a return to custody.

This chapter also discusses those released "unconditionally," usually because their sentence has fully expired. These ex-prisoners have all the risks and needs of those released to parole—sometimes more, because they tend to have committed more serious crimes or to have behavioral or mental health issues—but they are no longer under any type of correctional monitoring. Each scheme of community supervision after incarceration has its strengths and weaknesses, and its advantages and disadvantages, for authorities and prisoners alike.

Parole as a Form of Community Corrections

Generally speaking, parole is a period of conditional community-based correctional supervision following incarceration. Like prison, parole is most often administered by the state. (By contrast, jail and probation are typically administered locally.) Parole is most

(5) To gain a sense of the tension between a law enforcement and a social work approach to parole supervision.

(6) To understand what parole officers do and how they do it.

(7) To understand the differences and similarities between probation and parole.

(8) To grasp how evidence-based practice relates to parole and how parole success is measured.

(9) To be able to describe common obstacles to successful reentry for parolees.

often granted to ex-prisoners after they serve a sentence in state or federal prison or local jail. Parole is a type of community corrections, along with alternatives to (pretrial) detention, probation, and alternatives to incarceration. These have many shared elements, and indeed, some of the processes involved and much of the supervision techniques and the programming and services offered are very similar. Some jurisdictions will have separate agencies and separate officers for each, while others combine probation and parole.

Many of the difficulties faced by those sentenced to each type of community corrections are also similar. However, persons facing parole are typically among the most serious offenders in the corrections system; thus, they are likely to have the most pronounced needs once released to their community.

Each type of community corrections applies to a specific point in the criminal justice process. Alternatives to detention apply before the trial in cases where the defendant may be jailed until the trial date. Probation applies after the trial and is a sentence for community supervision instead of incarceration for those cases that do not warrant time behind bars (for instance, if the offense was not serious enough). Alternatives to incarceration are also used as a sentence instead of incarceration. They apply to cases where jail or prison time *is* warranted, but where public safety protection and the other goals of incarceration can be met without its harsh and expensive terms.

Parole comes at the last stage of the system—after release from prison. Parolees have time remaining on their sentences that they are allowed or, in some cases, ordered to serve while under supervision in the community. At this point, the goals of incarceration are deemed largely completed, and a crime-free and productive transition back to life in society is the core goal.

The Early History of Parole

Captain Alexander Maconochie, the superintendent of an English penal colony on Norfolk Island in 1840, developed and put into practice the notion of the indeterminate sentence, where release was based on prisoner achievement instead of a fixed length of time.[2] Maconochie believed that prisoners who had some sense of control over their destinies and a direct impact on their sentence length would behave better while in custody and would do what it took to get out. He believed that a system characterized by brutality, hard labor, and no rehabilitative programming did not work and was immoral. He instituted indefinite prison terms, which considered a person's work, achievements, study, and behavior. He established a system whereby prisoners could gain freedom by progressing from traditional prison to furloughs to release. Marks were awarded for good behavior and achievements, and they were removed for bad behavior. Maconochie was, in effect, putting into practice the rehabilitative theory of corrections. He was among the first to recognize that a well-behaved and rehabilitated prisoner is a good thing for both the prisoner and society.

Sir Walter Crofton used some of Maconochie's ideas while administering the Irish penal system in the 1850s. Both men recognized some nuances of rehabilitation that have been verified by contemporary social science research. For instance, they recognized that a prisoner's readiness for a full return to free life in society could not be ascertained while in the confines and unusual environment of prison, so a period of further supervision in the community was needed—a limited freedom with close oversight. In the current world, treatment providers recognize that program success behind bars, for instance in drug treatment, does not necessarily translate to success avoiding drug abuse once a person is back on the street. Crofton developed this postrelease supervision concept to include elements still used in parole today, such as regular reporting to a police inspector, who also helped with job placement and other needs.

These ideas of rehabilitation, indeterminate sentencing, and supervised release were further developed through the second half of the 1800s by a penologist named Zebulon Brockway. Brockway made them an integral part of the first-of-its-kind Elmira Reformatory in New York State when it opened in 1876. By 1907, New York had the first statewide parole system, and by 1943, every state and the federal government had developed one as well. Various forms of parole have evolved over the years, but the basic notion remains the same. Even the word itself—*parole*—refers to a person's good word to maintain acceptable behavior.[3]

Parole Basics

Each state has its own statutes, policies, processes, and practices regarding release from incarceration. There is also a federal system that oversees release from federal prison and Washington, D.C. Many states have moved away from traditional parole and now use different approaches to release and postprison supervision. Still, there are basic elements and processes inherent to these approaches that look largely the same, regardless of jurisdiction or release mechanism. An important thing to note is that parolees are still serving their sentences. Parole is not a relief from conviction or a pardon of any kind. The repercussions for not meeting the terms of release can include increased supervision, more stringent terms of parole, or reincarceration.

Conditions of Parole

In modern corrections, parolees are assigned to different supervision categories depending on their estimated risk of additional criminal behavior and the likely seriousness of this behavior, which is a way of determining their risk to public safety. Risk is usually estimated through a risk assessment, a standardized evaluation of factors believed to be correlated with continued criminal behavior. The different supervision categories represent different types and extents of parole requirements and the general intensity of supervision. Put another way, released prisoners deemed to have lower risk will have less demanding parole requirements and experience less intense scrutiny in the community than those with higher risk. A parolee's particular needs that relate to dynamic factors—substance abuse treatment, mental health treatment, occupational training—will also be elements of parole requirements.

Standard conditions of parole are required of each parolee. Special conditions are based on the specific criminal history, circumstances, and needs of the parolee. Standard conditions typically include avoiding all criminal behavior; informing the parole officer of new jobs, plans to move, plans to travel, or any new arrest; and following the parole officer's instructions. Conditions will also typically include finding appropriate housing and finding and maintaining employment or pursuing an education. Conditions may also include random drug testing, participating in health and behavioral programming, and abstaining from alcohol. There may be travel restrictions, a curfew, and the requirement to avoid other parolees, former criminal associates, and weapons of all sorts. Fines, fees for supervision services, and victim restitution may also be required, as well as community service. Parolees must acknowledge that they are subject to search by law enforcement or corrections officers at any time, with or without a court warrant and, for the most part, without a reason.

The terms of supervision can include a range of reporting requirements, from frequent, in-person meetings with the supervising officer to monthly phone or kiosk check-ins. Most terms and conditions of parole combine office meetings, meetings in the community (sometimes unannounced), and phone meetings. A parolee may earn a reduction in reporting requirements or other aspects of parole if he or she is consistently in compliance, demonstrates good behavior, and has stable housing and employment.

An important aspect of supervision is surveillance—the various ways parole officers keep tabs on their clients. In addition to both scheduled and unscheduled meetings and check-ins between the officer and the client, surveillance may include drug testing, electronic or global positioning system (GPS) monitoring, and unannounced home visits. Surveillance will likely include the officer interviewing the client's family members, employers, teachers, service providers, law enforcement officers, religious figures, and other community representatives. A goal of surveillance is to identify any possible violations or criminal behavior, but also to garner support for the client's continued success and to gain information that will help the parole officer help the client to succeed. When the client is doing well, the regularity and intensity of the surveillance may ease, whereas if there are minor violations or indications of potential failure, the surveillance might intensify. Escalating surveillance is meant to ensure public safety and remind the client to stay on track. Surveillance is another form of leverage that the parole officer can use to gain cooperation from the client.

Violations and Revocations

Failing to meet conditions of parole constitutes a parole violation. Although the additional scrutiny applied to a parolee (as compared to a regular citizen) can provide support and motivation to succeed on parole, it can also mean that violations and new offenses are more likely to be identified and acted upon by corrections and law enforcement. Parole agents use discretion in their responses to violations. For example, a parole officer may decide to overlook some violations of parole, even those that technically constitute lawbreaking—such as use of illegal drugs—in light of the parolee's particular progress toward meeting goals, likelihood of the offense repeating, and other factors. Similar to probation, violations can provide the parole officer leverage to promote better cooperation on the parolee's part.

If a parole officer chooses to act upon a violation of parole, he or she can file a petition with the parole authority for a hearing. It is the parole officer's responsibility to investigate the offense and present his or her findings to the court. Although the hearings related to a violation are not as strict and structured as regular criminal court, the legal rights of due process still apply to parole (and probation). A case that went to the Supreme Court in 1972 (*Morrissey v. Brewer*) extended the due process rights of parolees in regard to hearings.[4] The court must advise a defendant that a violation has been alleged, that the parolee can seek legal counsel, and that a preliminary hearing will be held (unless the parolee waives this right) to establish probable cause for continued proceedings. An earlier case (*Mempa v. Rhay*) established a probationer's right to counsel in hearings before the imposition of a deferred prison sentence.[5]

The court may decide to hold the parolee in custody pending the revocation hearing or release the parolee, with or without bail. Related to revocation, the parolee has the right to be present at the *Morrissey* hearing (as it is often called), the right to counsel, the right to review the evidence the government is relying on, the right to bring witnesses and testimony and to question the government's witnesses, and the right to receive a written explanation of the proceedings and findings. If the court finds the violation did occur, it may do nothing, it may modify the terms of parole, it may revoke parole but immediately reinstate it (perhaps with new, harsher terms), or it may revoke parole and return the parolee to prison, usually for no longer than the original sentence length. To avoid returns to prison, some states use intermediate sanctions that may mean a period in a community-based correctional facility or a residential treatment facility, locked or unlocked.

A criminal offense committed while on parole is both a violation of parole and a new criminal act in its own right. If a parolee is arrested for a new offense, the parole agency and district attorney have several options. They may use the new offense as grounds for a revocation hearing and potential return to prison under the original sentence. This is an

DEPARTMENT OF DEFENSE
CERTIFICATE OF SUPERVISED RELEASE

1.a. PROBATION/PAROLE OFFICER NAME *(Last, First, Middle)*		b. TELEPHONE NUMBER *(Include area code)*	
c. AGENCY ADDRESS	d. CITY	e. STATE	f. ZIP CODE

2. SUPERVISED RELEASE DESTINATION *(Limitation of travel is designated by Parole Officer)*

3. CONDITIONS

This Certificate of Supervised Release shall become operative when the prisoner has been notified in writing of the following conditions:

a. When released, the supervisee will go without delay to the supervision destination as specified above.

b. Within three working days of release, supervisees will report in person to their probation officer, unless directed otherwise by their probation officer. They will follow their probation officer's reporting instructions and report as directed. After reporting, the supervisee will complete the Notification of Arrival letter and forward it to

Supervisee's Facility Address *(Facility Name/State/ZIP Code)*

c. Supervisees will remain within the limits prescribed by their probation officer, and, if they have justifiable cause to leave these limits temporarily, they will first obtain permission from their probation officer.

d. Supervisees will not change the residence and employment approved in their supervised release plan without first receiving permission from their probation officer. In the event their residence or employment is involuntarily terminated, they will report these events to their probation officer within one working day of being notified of such termination.

e. Failure to maintain contact with their probation officer constitutes absconding.

f. Supervisees will promptly and truthfully answer all inquiries directed to them by their respective branch of service, their commander, their probation officer, or other persons acting in an official capacity.

g. Supervisees will not associate with persons of bad or questionable reputation, nor enter or frequent places where controlled substances are sold, used, distributed or administered.

h. Supervisees will in all respects conduct themselves in an honorable manner, work diligently at a lawful occupation, support those dependent on them, meet other family and financial responsibilities to the best of their ability, and avoid unnecessary or excessive debt.

i. Supervisees will live and remain at liberty without violating the law. Supervisees shall consider themselves convicted felons and understand that all laws regulating convicted felons may apply; should they have questions they will seek guidance from their probation officer or Service Clemency and Parole Board.

j. Supervisees will refrain from the excessive use of alcohol and will not purchase, possess, use, distribute or administer any narcotic or other controlled substance or any paraphernalia related to such substances, except as prescribed by a physician.

k. Supervisees will notify their probation officer within 24 hours of being arrested, detained, or questioned by a law enforcement officer.

l. Supervisees will not enter into any agreement to act as an informer or special agent of a law enforcement agency without the permission of their Service Clemency and Parole Board.

m. Supervisees also understand and agree that if they violate any of the conditions of their supervised release, they may be apprehended or returned to military control, and be held liable to serve the remainder of their sentence to confinement and forfeit their time served on supervised release, as well as previously earned good conduct time and other abatements.

n. If accepting parole, supervisees waive all good conduct time and abatement earned up to their release date (not applicable to Mandatory Supervised Release).

o. Supervisees will not possess a firearm, ammunition, or other dangerous weapon.

p. Supervisees will comply with additional conditions of their Supervised Release. *(Listed on subsequent pages)*

◀ Sample Conditions of Release contract

Source: Department of Defense, http://www.dtic.mil/whs/ directives/infomgt/forms/eforms/ dd2716-1.pdf

option whether or not the new offense would typically lead to prison time were the offender not on parole. A second option is to file the new charges and prosecute the offense as a new case. If the defendant is found guilty (through trial or plea bargain), a new sentence may then be added on to the original sentence. The new charges can also be used as leverage to convince the parolee to accept a revocation in lieu of a new trial (and potentially longer overall sentence). Another option is for the parole agency to defer the new charges and hold them over the parolee as a sort of strong-armed incentive to get back on track or else have the charges reinstated.

Parole is terminated and the ex-prisoner is no longer subject to correctional supervision when the original sentence is complete and the parole authority—usually a parole board, the parole agency, or the court—formally affirms that the conditions of parole have been met.

As with all aspects of U.S. corrections, there are variations in most parts of the parole process according to state or local jurisdiction. Occasionally, parole is terminated prior to the end of the original sentence, usually because the parolee has met terms of parole (fines, community service, victim compensation), good behavior, and strong job performance. However, a parole release decision could also be to reduce caseloads and costs for the agency. In some cases, parole is terminated before certain terms are satisfied, most commonly fines. The ex-parolee is encouraged to pay the fine, but failure to do so is not grounds for further action by the parole agency or courts. Further, there is a range of how much support a new parolee may receive for finding housing or a job after release; sometimes release is denied pending establishment of housing or employment. A parolee may be released to a halfway house or other residential facility until finding a more permanent place to live. Finally, certain types of parolees are subject to a continuation of correctional control after the original sentence expires, even if they avoid parole violations or new offenses. Depending on the state, these may include sex offenders, the mentally ill, or very serious and violent offenders.

Release Mechanisms

In practice, parole has two linked parts. First is the process of deciding if and when to release and setting the conditions of release. This process has come to be known as the release mechanism, described here. The second part of parole is what happens in the community as the former prisoner attempts to reestablish his or her life while under the watchful and, ideally, helpful eye of the parole officer.

The decision to grant release is the first and most crucial step in the process. Traditionally, across the United States, a parole board would decide each case on its own merits. Changes in parole policies during the last few decades have been mostly driven by the prevailing tough-on-crime sentiment. However, more often than not this "decision" is now actually determined at the time of sentencing and is largely prescribed by policymakers and voters. Each state chooses its own mechanism and most often will use more than one, depending on the offense type and details of each case.

Discretionary parole requires the approval of a parole board or other paroling authority. A certain portion of the full sentence must be served. Various statutes may further define eligibility, such as maintaining good behavior for a given period of time or earning a GED. If those requirements are met, the parole board reviews the inmate's profile. The board considers offense history and custody record, the comments of stakeholders such as facility personnel or victims, the inmate's readiness to return to society, whether housing and employment are in place, and any treatment plans. If the board determines the prisoner is ready to leave, it grants parole.

Mandatory parole is a nondiscretionary release mechanism whereby a parole release date is set during sentencing. Additionally, inmates receive "good-time credit" for each day they avoid misconduct while in custody. A typical arrangement would be one day of credit for every two days served. Thus, the inmate would be eligible for parole and released after serving two thirds of the full sentence. A parole board or corrections department may impose terms of parole but cannot refuse release if the inmate has earned the good time.

Terms of supervised release are used most often in the federal corrections system but also in several states.* A term of supervised release, also called probation release, is a nondiscretionary form of parole. Like other types of parole, it entails a period of correctional supervision in the community following a period of incarceration. The key difference is that the community supervision is not in lieu of finishing a sentence in custody but is an additional sentence. Thus these individuals are sentenced to two predetermined and consecutive terms

Discretionary parole: A term of parole determined by a parole board or other paroling authority. A certain portion of the court's sentence must be served prior to the granting of parole.

Mandatory parole: A nondiscretionary release mechanism whereby a parole release date is set during sentencing.

Terms of supervised release: A sentence of a period of correctional supervision in the community following, as part of the same sentence, a period of incarceration. Violating the terms of supervised release may lead to a new sentence of incarceration and additional supervised release.

---

* The federal parole board, the U.S. Parole Commission, does not oversee this type of parole. Rather, federal district courts oversee the process, and federal probation officers supervise the parolees.

of supervision, the first in prison and the second in the community. In this case, spending more time in prison does not reduce the length of the term of supervision. A term of supervised release is more like mandatory parole than discretionary parole, in that the release to the community is not subject to the decision of a parole board. Revocation due to a violation typically results in the sentence of community supervision being changed into a term of incarceration, often followed by another term of supervised release.[6] A similar practice, called a split sentence, was until recently used mainly for jail inmates, where a term of jail time is coupled with a term of probation. Some states now use split sentences for more serious felonies that couple time in state prison facilities or in local facilities (as in California) with a term of supervision under the local probation department.

Other types of parole or conditional release involve drug transition programs, medical or mental health releases, and work furloughs. These usually address special circumstances or needs of the prisoner, or circumstances of the facility, such as overcrowding; they may or may not be subject to the review of a parole board. Medical parole, sometimes called compassionate release, occurs when a prisoner is medically incapacitated or terminally ill; these individuals are granted parole, subject to revocation if their medical status changes.

Unconditional release or "maxing out" refers to inmates serving out their entire sentence in prison. Unconditional releases often represent the most serious and violent of all previous inmates. When they are released, they have completed their entire obligation to the state and are not subject to any further correctional supervision. They still face all of the difficulties that other parolees face, but without state-sponsored support.

Parole Authorities

Parole Agencies

In 2006, there were 2,287 individual parole offices around the country with 65,000 full-time workers and 2,900 part-time. An estimated 14,000 of these workers directly supervised an average caseload of 38. Almost three quarters of parole agencies were part of their state's department of corrections. Two thirds of state parole agencies also supervised convicted

◄ Parole officers need to build a rapport with their clients while also maintaining authority and respect.

© Frank Couch/AL.COM /Landov

Unconditional release: Exit from prison after full sentence completion, so there is no further obligation to the state. These individuals are not subject to any further correctional supervision.

SPOTLIGHT

FINDING A HOME AFTER PRISON

Parolees face a host of problems when they are released from custody, including employment, education, family responsibilities, substance abuse issues, mental health problems, and physical illnesses or disabilities. However, housing may be the most critical of these.

Parole officers say that finding appropriate long-term housing for newly released prisoners is one of the toughest but most important parts of their job.[1] In fact, housing may be the single most important factor in successful reentry because, besides satisfying the basic need for shelter, it provides a stable base or "platform" for other core needs and conditions of parole such as education, employment, abstinence from substance abuse, reconnection with family and prosocial relationships, and participation in prosocial activities such as sports, church, or community groups. A permanent address for a new driver's license or bank account can help give a reentering prisoner a sense that he or she is on track and truly belongs back in the community.[2]

Housing is also the most immediate need. The very first nights out of prison can be crucial for many parolees, especially those with mental health or substance abuse issues. For most parolees, not having housing for an extended period or moving from place to place heightens the risk of parole failure.[3] Further, it is estimated that 10% to 50% of parolees are homeless,[4] and homelessness after release is strongly correlated with parole failures and returns to prison.[5]

Parole boards may deny release for prisoners who have not yet arranged housing, not as punishment but for the good of the parolee and his or her likelihood of success. However, this is not a factor in mandatory parole and terms of supervised release, which account for the majority of paroles today. Parole agencies, especially in determinate sentencing jurisdictions, do not consistently provide housing support to parolees. Only a few state parole agencies have formal relationships with housing assistance groups[6]; parole officers who do get involved usually depend on their own connections and methods.

It is common for new parolees to spend their first nights in the extra bedroom or on the couch of family members or friends; many find themselves still living in similar "temporary" housing months later. Although living with family may be preferable in some cases, it is often true that the parolee—if he or she is jobless, unable to contribute to rent, and largely idle—becomes a burden. Similarly, negative issues in the host family often can make a living situation detrimental. At least one study found parolees who live alone fare better than those who live with family or friends.[7]

Housing is difficult to secure, even with the help of the parole officer or community-based housing assistance. Federal public housing laws ban certain sex offenders and certain drug offenders from living in public housing or receiving housing subsidies. Moreover, each public housing authority usually restricts benefits further.[8] Also, since the early 1990s, there has been a shortage of affordable housing across the United States, with almost 11 million

offenders on probation, and seven also supervised juveniles on probation or parole.[7] Some elements of parole, such as electronic monitoring or drug testing, may be administered by a private (usually for-profit) company. Some states looking for ways to reduce prison populations are expanding privatization to include parole violation centers—short-term detention centers that hold and provide services to parole violators—allowing parolees to avoid a return to regular prison if they successfully complete the programming.

Parole Officers

The American Probation and Parole Association (APPA) puts it simply: "Probation and parole officers are unique in that they are neither police officers nor social workers, yet they are regularly called upon to fill each of these roles."[8]

needy households but only half that many affordable rental units, including public housing.[9] Parolees typically cannot afford private housing even after they have a regular paycheck. Additionally, areas where landlords are less likely to discriminate against ex-felons are those more likely to have housing shortages and to be unfavorable for successful parole. A large percentage of parolees return home to a relatively small number of communities and neighborhoods, creating a competitive market for the few affordable homes and apartments available.[10]

Sex offenders and violent offenders, especially those whose crimes involved children, typically have restricted housing zones around parks and schools, which can often leave whole swaths of a community off limits to parolees. Most of the 71% of women in prison who report having children under the age of 18 say they intend to live with their children after their release.[11, 12] The prospects for attaining appropriate housing are even lower for them than for other parolees.

The past decade has seen an increase of interest and activity in these issues as federal and state corrections systems try to address housing for reentering prisoners. For instance, more parole agencies are planning for housing as a key element of case management and release plans. States are trying to reduce the policy obstacles to obtaining public housing. The federal and state parole agencies are increasingly making use of halfway houses and other types of transitional and permanent housing. Corrections authorities have come to recognize the connection between the availability of appropriate housing for ex-prisoners, lower corrections costs, and lower recidivism rates.[13]

QUESTIONS

1 Why is housing such an important element of successful prisoner reentry?

2 Should reentering prisoners have a right to public housing?

3 Should prison terms be extended pending suitable housing arrangements for reentering prisoners?

4 What are possible policy solutions regarding the community's desire to prohibit sex offenders from living near places children congregate and these individuals' need to find a place to live and work after completing their sentence?

Notes

1. Petersilia 2003
2. Fontaine and Biess 2012
3. Travis, Solomon, and Waul 2001
4. Travis and Roman 2004
5. Metraux and Culhane 2004
6. Bonczar 2008
7. Yahner and Visher 2008
8. Federal Interagency Reentry Council 2012
9. Institute for Children, Poverty and Homelessness 2012
10. Travis and Roman 2004
11. Greenfeld and Snell 1999
12. Hairston 2002
13. Burke, Giguere, and Gilligan 2011

Parole officers (also known as community supervision officers or community corrections officers) have daily opportunities to positively influence another human being's life—to help an individual navigate the corrections bureaucracy, apply for a job, pursue education, or stick with treatment. On the other hand, they have the authority to make a parolee's life even harder, and they can instigate a return to prison for violations or new offenses. Parole officers must have plenty of heart but be thick-skinned so they can handle the interpersonal relationships with clients and community members, even in potentially volatile situations. They must also be aware that their mistakes can make headlines. They must understand complicated law and policy and how to interact with the courts, health providers, and others. At the same time, their success often depends on being able to talk "street" and convince some tough and distrusting clients and community members to respect and trust them, and that

▲ A San Bernardino County probation officer arrests a parolee who had been out of custody after 9 prison stints and 15 swings through county jail, mostly on parole violations.

© Damian Dovarganes/ /AP/ Corbis

they have the parolee's and community's interests in mind. Parole officers also regularly face stressful circumstances, such as resistant clients, emotional tension, violence or the threat of violence, high caseloads, burdensome paperwork, the changing expectations of the parole agency and the public, relatively low pay, and limited opportunities for career advancement.

Most states require prospective parole officers to have at least a bachelor's degree in a related field such as social work, criminology, sociology, or psychology. Parole officers typically need to submit to a background check and must successfully complete training and examinations. Then they begin a trial period of employment, which usually lasts about 12 months and includes extensive on-the-job training.

A major part of a parole officer's job is getting to know the parolees. This is partially done through in-office visits, telephone calls, in-person field visits, and other activities that build rapport and establish normative behavior so that potential problems can be more easily identified. The instincts and experience of the parole officer play a role along with formalized practice. Parole officers also help formulate a plan for each parolee, preferably prior to release from custody.

Parole officers also have investigation duties to ensure client compliance with conditions of parole. These may include interviewing witnesses and family members; searching homes, cars, and work areas; drug testing; and collaborating with law enforcement. As described above, parole agents can report potential violations to the courts or parole board for formal processing and potential revocation, or they may use the violation as a motivational tool for the client.

Eighty-five percent of states allow parole officers to carry a firearm; in 14 states, carrying a firearm is a job requirement. In approximately two thirds of states, parole officers have the authority to arrest and detain parolees they suspect of criminal behavior.[9]

Caseloads may be as low as 30 clients for officers specializing in certain types of crimes or programs, such as sex offenders or intensive supervision, or as high as 150 or more. In urban areas, parole agents may be assigned to a certain neighborhood to reduce travel time and to more thoroughly know—and be known in—the community. But in more rural areas, an officer may have to travel miles between clients. There is no standard caseload size; it varies based on the risk and needs level of parolees, departmental expectations and support, parole officer training and experience, geography, and funding.[10]

The practice of parole has been influenced by the development of new approaches to probation and alternatives to incarceration. Many of the same tools probation officers use are also regular tools for parole officers, including intensive supervision and electronic monitoring. Specialized courts such as drug courts are also used for parolees, and reentry courts have opened as a new development in this area.

Parole Boards

Parole boards historically have been the gatekeepers of the indeterminate, discretionary sentencing system. For persons found guilty of an offense punishable by imprisonment, courts determined a range of time the individual should serve—from the minimum sentence length that society thinks appropriate and necessary to answer for the crimes committed, to the maximum sentence. After this important step, the courts largely stepped aside. With discretionary parole, and to some extent even with nondiscretionary mechanisms, it was left to a parole authority to decide the proper balance of those two requirements, based on an evaluation of each case. In this sense, parole boards are at the heart of the rehabilitative model of corrections and parole, which holds that every individual deserves an opportunity to show readiness to reenter society. It also assumes that even persons who commit similar crimes have substantial differences that require individualized consideration. Each state devises its process for releasing prisoners from incarceration; those states that have traditional parole decide on the makeup of the board, the authority it has, and the decision-making process it follows in awarding or denying parole.

Parole boards are meant to represent and act independently of the various stakeholders impacted by a release from prison. The stakeholders are the criminal justice system (law enforcement, corrections, the courts), other elements of the government (elected officials and lawmakers, other agencies, and, by extension, voters), the victims of crime, the community where the offense took place, the family of the offender, and the parolee.

Parole board membership may include government representatives, local business owners, educators, or church leaders. Usually appointed by the governor, individual parole board

◀ A parolee, far right, at his parole board hearing, where he learned that he would not be released. His next chance would be four years later. He was sentenced in 1987 for his role in a robbery and killing.

© Brent Wojahn/The Oregonian / Landov

members may or may not have expertise in corrections or criminal justice. In some states, the board is part of the corrections department and is thus more intimately aware of the prison experience and of administrative issues like prison crowding. In other states, the board is purposely kept separate from corrections. Some states with discretionary parole do not use parole boards per se, but employ another decision-making body. Whether an independent parole board or an element of the correctional agency or courts, or some combination thereof, similar considerations and processes take place.

Determining the right time to release a prisoner requires balancing the various goals of the correctional system. On one hand, the length of sentence has to meet demands for retribution, deterrence, and incapacitation. On the other hand, to avoid unduly harsh or expensive terms of incarceration and to facilitate rehabilitation, the individual needs to be returned to the community as soon as appropriate.

Parole boards consider the seriousness of the offense leading to incarceration, prior criminal activity, efforts to rehabilitate during custody, and plans for the future. Health status and age may also be factors. Parole boards may also consider the impact of the offense on victims, any efforts by the parolee to restore the victim's losses, and the extent to which victims and the community may be at further risk if the person is released. Victims and community members may be invited to attend parole hearings and submit written or in-person testimony.

In response to concerns that parole boards lack objectivity, many states have developed guidelines for increasing their consistency, such as formalized process checklists, validated risk assessments, and other tools. But in the end, the parole board still has the final say in discretionary releases, except in states where paroles need to be approved by the governor. In states that switched to nondiscretionary release mechanisms, the parole boards still make release decisions for inmates who committed their crime prior to the change in policy. Parole boards may use measures of an individual's readiness for release that are significantly different from the factors that the court considers in sentencing. The parole board may be more interested in factors that are heavily weighted at sentencing such as current behavior and age. In effect, the parole board reassesses the prisoners who come before it.

In addition to the basic parole decision, parole boards hold revocation hearings if the inmate violates parole terms and decide whether parole should be reinstated after any additional incarceration. In some states, the board is responsible for granting clemency and commuting sentences. These responsibilities largely remain in place for parole boards in jurisdictions that have adopted nondiscretionary release mechanisms. In these nondiscretionary states, the parole board often still oversees release decisions.

The Challenges of Reentry

Commuting: The reduction in the length or severity of a sentence (for example, the reduction of the death penalty to life in prison), usually by the discretion of a chief executive (governor or U.S. president) or a parole board.

Reentry: The process through which incarcerated individuals return to society after serving their sentence.

Reentry is a challenging time for ex-prisoners. Housing is, of course, an immediate and crucial concern for released prisoners. Yet affordable and appropriate housing is hard to find in most communities. Those looking for housing in the private market, as most are forced to do, are subject to discrimination due to the stigma of incarceration, expensive deposits and high rent, and geographic limitations (too far from employment or school and too close to the neighborhoods they are supposed to avoid). Housing issues are exacerbated for those with mental illness, who require not only housing but, often, training in independent living. Some programs do exist—community-based correctional housing, halfway and transitional housing, homeless assistance supportive housing—but these usually have waiting lists or have restrictions for ex-prisoners. As many as three quarters of returning prisoners live with family members or an intimate partner, but this is often a temporary situation; up to half of ex-prisoners change residences, or plan to, in the months after release.[11]

Those leaving jail may have lost their job even after a short sentence, while those leaving prison have been out of the job market for at least a year, possibly much more. Although finding and maintaining a job is a common condition of parole—and successful employment is associated with parole success—ex-prisoners have less education than the general population and lack work experience and vocational skills. The latest federal data reported 41% of incarcerated persons lacked a high school diploma or GED, compared to 18% of the general population.[12] Each state bars those convicted of felonies from some jobs, typically law, medicine, education, and realty. A few states disallow public employment of felons, while in others it depends on whether the offense is related to the job tasks. Those employers (and landlords) willing to take on the perceived risk are likely to have already hired other ex-prisoners, given that a large proportion of prisoners come home to just a few overburdened communities.[13] Practical considerations are also factors in maintaining full-time employment, like distance of work from home residence and finding consistent transportation to and from work. Consequently, finding work is difficult. One study reported 55% of parolees were still unemployed eight months after release.[14] The same study reported that finding work is hardest for non-White ex-prisoners, or those with a mental health or chronic medical condition (which upwards of 40% have), those over 30 years old, and drug users. On the other hand, characteristics that made finding employment less difficult were having a good work record before prison, reconnecting with a previous employer, and having a healthy family life.[15] Other factors have been shown to be a benefit to ex-prisoners seeking employment, including participating in work release while in prison and having a good relationship with their parole officer.

Although society asks that ex-prisoners work to become contributing members of society, at the same time, restrictions are placed on their ability to do so. Voting rights are

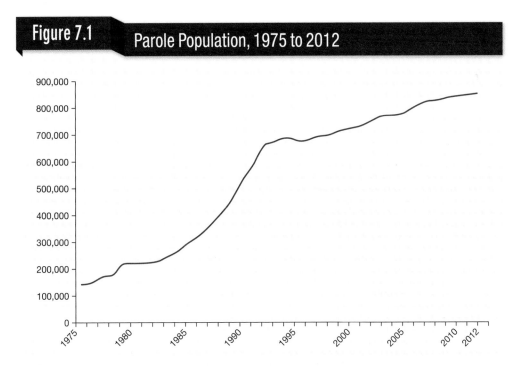

Figure 7.1 Parole Population, 1975 to 2012

Figure 7.1 shows a striking increase in the numbers of individuals on parole in the United States between 1975 and 2012. There was from 1975 to 1992 a steep, 360% increase and from 1992 to 2011 a more moderate increase, with the number of parolees rising another 30%. The most recent year reported, 2012, showed one of only three drops in the parole population in almost four decades (1982, 1995). Since the prison population has also decreased recently, it is likely that the 2012 parole decline is the start of a trend, although it is not clear how long it will last.[16] *Source: Maruschak, Glaze, and Bonczar 2013.*

permanently denied in 14 states, while in most others voting is curtailed at least during correctional supervision. Thirty-two states permanently restrict jury service for felons; gun ownership is restricted in 31.[17]

Reestablishing family and social relationships is also difficult. Some ex-prisoners are interested in their "street cred"; others suffer from the stigmatization of their status and experience a loss of social standing and support, alienation from prior friends and colleagues, and difficulty finding housing and employment.[18] Long-term intimate relationships are prone to difficulty and dissolution during and after imprisonment, and the likelihood of losing custody of children is raised for those in custody or after release.[19]

The logistics of release alone can be daunting—how to get to meetings with parole officers or service providers, where and how to restore Medicaid health coverage and other public assistance, where to get a prescription renewed and refilled, and setting up a bank account. Avoiding the people and places that facilitated risky behavior before incarceration is the biggest difficulty for many reentering prisoners. Yet these may be the only neighborhoods they know, the only places they are comfortable, and often where their prosocial contacts reside as well.

Fourteen percent or more of corrections-involved individuals overall have serious diagnosed mental illness like depression, schizophrenia, or posttraumatic stress disorder; many more have less severe but still debilitating conditions including periods of depression or anxiety, anger management issues, and low self-esteem.[20] Rates of mental health issues are almost twice as high among male parolees as other men. Those on parole are also almost half as likely to receive appropriate care for their mental health issue. Illicit drug use and alcoholism are twice as prevalent among male parolees (38%) than nonparolees (17%).[21] More than half of women on parole experience mental health problems, and almost a third have a serious disorder. These figures are twice and three times the rate of the general population, respectively.[22] Fifty-three percent of state prisoners and 46% of federal prisoners had drug abuse or dependency issues in 2004. Women were somewhat more likely to have issues than men (60% vs. 53% in state prison).[23]

Parolees with mental health disorders are twice as likely to return to prison within a year; similar individuals released from jail have even higher recidivism. Scholars and researchers attribute much of the cycle of incarceration and release for this population to the **criminalization** of behavior associated with mental disorders and the inability of public systems—including public health and corrections—to properly address the issue.[24]

The stress and uncertainty of reentry can exacerbate existing physical and mental health issues, making a vulnerable population—a large portion of the overall population of ex-prisoners—still more at risk of victimization, reverting to old habits, and returning to prison. Worse, during reentry, ex-prisoners typically experience gaps in medical and mental health services upon leaving custody, so medications and therapeutic care may not be available at the time they need it most. Parole officers are not always helpful in this regard. In at least one study, ex-prisoners who reported health issues were no more likely than those who reported themselves to be in good health to receive referrals to providers after their release.[25]

Several studies have found that the majority of parolees regard their parole officer as distant, too busy to help, not genuinely interested in their success or failure, and generally not a reliable resource.[26] In a study that found that parolees had positive impressions of their parole officers, parolees still did not give much credit to their parole officers for providing substantive help in their reentry. Many of these parolees reported that their parole officer gave encouragement, communicated well, and was understanding, and that this positive reinforcement was helpful in avoiding criminality and meeting conditions of parole. However, just 3% said their parole officer had helped in finding a drug program and 2% in finding housing. Thirteen percent said their officer had helped them look for a job, but only 1% said they had found a job through their parole officer.[27]

Criminalization:
De facto or formal (by law) designation of particular behavior or characteristics as illegal and punishable. Also, a widening of the scope of the types of behavior that are considered criminal or delinquent, including behaviors that the "offender" cannot control, such as acting out on the part of the mentally ill.

Those returning home from jail face similar difficulties as ex-prisoners, although there are important distinctions. Many of those exiting jail are subject to community supervision for a period of time; this is most often through the probation department rather than parole. Jail inmates tend to be confined close to their home communities, so they face less of the lost contact and alienation experienced by prisoners returning from long prison terms far from home. Those returning from jail tend to have committed less serious crimes and to have been in custody for substantially less time, so their needs and challenges tend to be fewer. Exceptions include those with housing and health needs, as many who cycle through the jail system have histories of chronic homelessness and mental health problems. Also, across the United States, jails are more often than ever used for more serious felony sentences. This is especially true under California's realignment policy. (See Chapter 16.)

Reentry Data

According to the most recent available data, there were 851,158 men and women on some form of parole at the end of 2012. This number represented a slight (less than 1%) decrease between 2011 and 2012. California, which is seeing a prison population decline as well as the redirection of parolees to county probation, accounted for almost three quarters of the overall national decline; in fact, the national parole population would have grown were California removed from the totals. Twenty-five states and the federal system experienced parole population growth.[28]

There are several factors that drive the number of parolees under supervision each year. The number of prison inmates certainly does. But so do laws and policies related to the time served in prison and on parole, releases from prison, conditions of parole, parolee behavior, and the system's response to misconduct, both in prison and in the community, including the number of parole revocations for parole violations or prosecutions for new crimes.

The average length of stay in state parole in 2012 was 20.6 months, although this term varies by offense type and other factors.[29] In comparison, the average length of stay on parole was 23 months[30] in 1990 and 26 months in 1999.[31] Parole violators made up 17% of new admissions to prison in 1990, 32% in 2000, and 31% in 2011.[32] Sentence lengths for federal parole (usually called terms of supervised release) typically range from 1 to 5 years, with an average across all cases of 41 months.[33]

Perspectives on the Current Purpose and Practice of Parole

Parole is partly punitive in that it is a continuation of the punishment of prison time. The supervision and, in particular, the surveillance that are part of typical conditions of parole—curfews, electronic monitoring, check-ins and meetings with the parole officer, restrictions on movement and social interaction—are burdensome and are meant to incapacitate and deter. However, the parolee moves about more or less freely; can earn money, study, and recreate; and is reunited with most family and

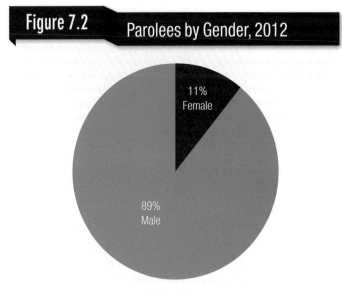

Figure 7.2   Parolees by Gender, 2012

11% Female

89% Male

Source: Maruschak and Bonczar 2013.

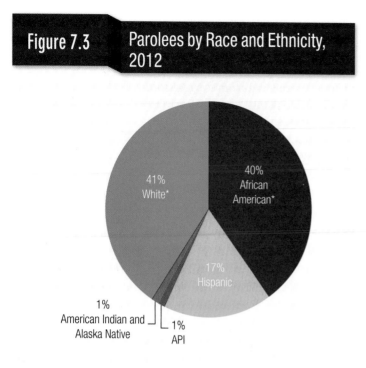

Figure 7.3 — Parolees by Race and Ethnicity, 2012

40%
African
American*

41%
White*

17%
Hispanic

1%
American Indian and
Alaska Native

1%
API

Figure 7.2 shows almost 90% of parolees were male in 2012. Figure 7.3 shows Whites and African Americans made up nearly equal parts of the parole population (41% and 40%, respectively), while Hispanics represented 17%. *Source: Maruschak and Bonczar 2013. * Non-Hispanic. Note: API = Asian-Pacific Islander.*

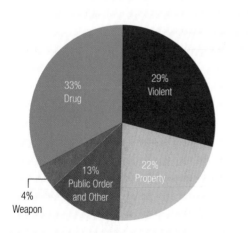

Figure 7.4 — Parolees by Most Serious Offense, 2012

29%
Violent

33%
Drug

13%
Public Order
and Other

22%
Property

4%
Weapon

Figure 7.4 shows that parolees in 2012 were more likely to have been convicted of drug-related crimes than of violent or property offenses. Because parole is rarely used in misdemeanor cases, these offenses represent felony cases usually (95%) with sentences of at least one year.[37] *Source: Maruschak and Bonczar 2013.*

friends. Further, the same elements of supervision that can be seen as punitive are also meant to facilitate rehabilitation. The goal of rehabilitation is or should be at the forefront in parole. Parole can provide a transitional period to restore an individual's life outside of prison. Parole was built on this notion, and the rehabilitative model prevailed into the last quarter of the 20th century.

The Change From Discretionary to Mandatory Parole

A combination of factors came together in the 1970s that led to skepticism that parole was serving its intended purpose. Studies exposed problems with the practice of parole—disparate lengths of stay in prison, inconsistencies in the manner parole was granted, poor parole success rates, and other issues.[34] At the same time, research began to suggest that the rehabilitative model had significant flaws. According to studies released at the time, correctional programming provided little or no benefit to offenders.[35] This meant, by extension, that the only effective role corrections could play in society's response to crime was to punish, incapacitate, and deter other crime. Parole, as both a theory of corrections and a practice, was failing. State and federal policymakers responded by moving away from traditional discretionary parole and toward mandatory parole. This movement to abolish discretionary parole led to 16 states switching to mandatory release mechanisms by 1990, and many others using a combination of mechanisms, often depending on the offense and criminal history.[36] By a vote in Congress, federal discretionary parole was ended for federal crimes committed after November 1, 1987; traditional parole was replaced by terms of supervised release. In an effort to distance themselves from the reputation of parole as ineffective and coddling, states began using other language to refer to release, such as extended supervision, control release, community control, community custody, and postrelease probation supervision. States that retained discretionary mechanisms put structures in place to increase the consistency and objectivity of parole decision making.

It is important to note that states that abolished discretionary parole did not abolish postrelease supervision. From the late 1970s into the 2000s, the emphasis in parole supervision was on

enforcement. This was at least in part by necessity; it has been simply too expensive and resource intensive to provide comprehensive services to every parolee. Parole agencies have had to direct their efforts to the most basic demands of public safety in the immediate sense of surveillance, identifying violations, and instigating revocations. This approach fits well with tough-on-crime attitudes. Ironically, parole officers may find themselves working to maximize violations and revocations, when those exact events are considered failures of the system.

To illustrate further, the enforcement emphasis in parole supervision is part of a complicated cycle. Tough-on-crime laws put more offenders in prison for longer periods of time. Incarcerating so many felons results in spending corrections dollars on more beds and more guards, not on in-custody or community-based programming and services and not on parole agencies. Eventually, the prisoners are released, having received little or no programming, with less hope of turning their lives around and avoiding a criminal lifestyle. They often return with little to offer to communities that are already absorbing significant numbers of new parolees and probationers. There, they come under the control of parole agencies focused not on rehabilitation but on the enforcement of ever more stringent conditions of parole. When the parole officer plays the role of the parolee's own personal and vigilant law enforcement officer, high levels of failure and returns to custody are hardly surprising.

In response to high rates of returns to already crowded prisons, states have more recently begun to reevaluate policies and practices concerning what constitutes a parole violation, how to respond to violations, and how reincarceration can be avoided without risking public safety or reducing the punitive impact of parole.

Since the initial wave of states abolished parole, several subsequently reinstated most of the elements of discretionary parole. Just as research had shown that rehabilitation programs were ineffective, new studies showed that a tough-on-crime surveillance approach to supervision was also untenable.[38] Early research comparing discretionary and mandatory parole

▲ Being released from prison may be the end of incarceration, but it is the beginning of many other challenges that face reentering individuals.

© Andrew Lichtenstein

Table 7.1 Parole Exits by Reason, 1990, 2001, 2012

Reason for Exit	1990	2001	2012
Completion	50%	46%	58%
Return to Incarceration	46%	40%	25%
With new sentence	17%	9%	8%
With revocation or violation	29%	30%	17%
Absconder	1%	9%	11%
Other unsatisfactory*	1%	2%	2%
Transfer out of state	1%	1%	1%
Death	1%	1%	1%
Other	—	1%	3%
Total exits	274,697	464,500	496,100

Table 7.1 shows the reasons for leaving parole for all of those who did so in 2012, 2001, and 1990. Trends across this 22-year period show a decrease in the percentage returning to prison and an increase in successful completion. In 2012, 58% successfully completed their parole, while 25% were returned to prison. Comparable numbers from 2001 and 1990 show 46% and 50%, respectively, had successfully completed parole, while 40% and 46%, respectively, had returned to prison.* Combining returns to incarceration, absconding (refusing to participate, not reporting to the parole officer, or moving without informing the PO), and other unsatisfactory exits, 38% of those exiting had failed parole in 2012, 44% in 2001, and 48% in 1990. *Sources: Hughes, Wilson, and Beck 2001; Jankowski 1991; Maruschak and Bonczar 2013. *Includes discharges that did not meet all conditions, such as when parole is revoked but then reinstated without incarceration, or early termination or expiration of sentence with some conditions pending.*

found that inmates released under discretionary parole had actually served longer sentences. Discretionary parolees were also more likely to successfully complete parole.[39] The rehabilitative model began gaining popularity once again, as long as it was appropriately targeted and was part of a cost-saving and prison population–reducing approach to corrections.

Discretionary Versus Nondiscretionary Parole Decisions

Broadly speaking, public attitudes about what are the most important functions of parole fluctuate based on statistical trends and perceptions of criminal behavior and public safety. The public is concerned about the effectiveness of current correctional practice and how much it costs.

The rise of a more determinate approach to both sentencing and parole reflects a conflict between two sometimes opposing goals of corrections—punishment and rehabilitation. As we have seen, mandatory parole removes the discretion of the parole board or other paroling authority. It attempts to make sure that, within a jurisdiction (usually the state), inmates who committed similar crimes will actually serve similar sentences. However, much of the impetus to behave and seek rehabilitation provided by the hope of early parole is removed, as is the ability of the parole board to differentiate based on the individual circumstances of inmates.

---

* Another way of tracking success (or failure) in the parole system is the rate of return to incarceration for those at risk for such a return. Unlike the figures in Table 7.1, this measures the average number of parolees per day who are returned to custody from among all parolees under supervision. In 2011, this rate was 20%. On any given day, 20 out of every 100 individuals on parole were revoked and returned to custody.

A parolee listens to the judge at his revocation hearing. There is a great deal of discretion involved on the part of parole officers and judges in deciding whether a violation of parole should result in a return to incarceration.

© ZUMA Press, Inc. / Alamy

The move toward determinate sentencing and mandatory parole has weakened the role of parole boards as gatekeepers in the sense that they no longer make the parole decisions for the majority of felony cases. However, discontinuing discretionary parole has not generally meant disbanding parole boards: their importance is still enormous. They still dictate who receives parole in many states—almost 150,000 parolees in 2011—and, even in most mandatory parole states, they still have ongoing roles deciding the terms of parole, overseeing revocation hearings, and overseeing parole reinstatements. These activities have a huge influence on the numbers of parolees on the streets as well the numbers behind bars.

Prisoners who know they will be subject to the assessment of a board before being granted parole have an incentive for good behavior while in custody. Even if an inmate seeks out "good time" credits purely for the sake of being paroled and not because of a desire for self-improvement, part of the effect is the same—fewer behavior problems, at least some benefit from program participation, and a safer prison environment for other inmates and staff.

In states where traditional discretionary parole is still the standard, parole boards or other paroling authorities review a large number of cases. Although the intention is to consider each case individually, the sheer number of cases, coupled with scrutiny about consistency and objectivity, forces paroling authorities to categorize cases and prioritize the factors they consider in each. The most salient factors often are offense type and severity and criminal history.[40] This reduces the importance in the parole decision of factors an inmate can actually affect, such as in-custody behavior, rehabilitation efforts, and prerelease preparations. In effect, this blurs the difference between discretionary and nondiscretionary mechanisms. Standardized assessments that consider not only criminal history but in-custody behavior and other changeable factors help ameliorate this issue.

Taking away the discretion of the parole board to make parole decisions, coupled with mandatory minimums at sentencing, increases the influence of district attorneys (typically elected positions), politicians, and voters over these complicated decisions. The latest public perceptions of public safety, the latest horrifying crime reported in the media, or the latest political rant can sway votes in the ballot box or legislative hall, leading to changes in

YOU DECIDE

Not in My Backyard

Research strongly indicates that transitional housing reduces the recidivism rates of parolees. Housing for many released inmates is very difficult to obtain for a variety of reasons, including prohibitions against people with drug convictions living in federally subsidized public housing.

The state department of corrections has decided to rent a multiple-dwelling unit in a low-income area and to allow 200 inmates to live there for six months following their release from prison. Neighbors complain that this parole housing unit will increase crime in an already troubled area, will endanger local children, and will place an undue burden on local police and social services. The department of corrections claims that many of the reentering prisoners would live in this same neighborhood anyway and that the dedicated housing helps stabilize their situations. The department promises to pay for private security as a measure to reduce drug dealing and crime in the parole housing.

YOU DECIDE: **Do you open the parole transitional housing unit or comply with the wishes of local residents?**

law that are difficult to reverse and have a huge and lasting impact on hundreds of thousands of inmates and parolees. Parole boards are certainly not immune to outside influence, hence the efforts in states with discretionary release mechanisms to standardize and monitor parole decision making.

None of the more dynamic factors plays a role under mandatory release. It can be argued that knowing that nobody can stand in the way of a definite release date or the frustration of being denied parole allows inmates to serve their time without the stress of uncertainty, which can be associated with better behavior. Reentering prisoners can even prepare—let their loved ones know, give an employer a reliable start date.

Another important factor in reentry decisions is victims. Victims have the legal right to testify at parole board hearings and to request that protective orders or other restrictions be part of the terms of parole.[41] Their voice is not heard when release is mandatory.

One or another type of release mechanism may be more successful depending on the circumstances, such as the offense type and the risk and needs of the parolee. An Urban Institute analysis of 1994 federal release data found that, within two years of release, "maxed out" unconditional releases and those released to mandatory parole were rearrested at a statistically equal rate (62% vs. 61%) while those released through discretionary parole were rearrested at a rate of 54%. There may be a need for both discretionary and mandatory supervised release, and in fact, many states use both. Nondiscretionary release mechanisms may have a role to play in achieving fairness and consistency in sentencing and time served. Discretionary mechanisms and the strengthening of a rehabilitative model for corrections are also important considerations.

Choosing to "Max Out" With Unconditional Release

In 2001, 203,000 prisoners were released unconditionally nationwide. Although some of these are less serious offenders who do not require supervision, it is more common that unconditional releases are among the most serious offenders. They are some of those most at-risk for new crime or parole violations, yet they reenter their community with no correctional oversight whatsoever. They may have "maxed out," because (1) the severity of their offense or their behavior while in custody did not qualify them for early release, (2) a parole board or some other paroling authority was not convinced they were ready for release, or (3) they chose to remain in prison to avoid the burden of correctional supervision on the outside. A study in New Jersey found that 40% of prisoners who "maxed out" in 2006 did so by their own choice. This represented 15% of the total number released.[42] Opting out of early release may be desirable to inmates who consider prison time less of a burden than supervision in the community. They may have no intention of ending their criminal behavior and thus prefer to avoid the additional scrutiny and surveillance of postrelease supervision. While in prison, inmates can continue to receive good-time credits, which reduce the overall length of the sentence. In this way, staying behind bars hastens their final release from all forms of correctional control.

Although courts and parole authorities want the option to maximize the time some prisoners stay in prison, it is not necessarily their intention to then set high-risk offenders free in the community without the added surveillance and treatment that supervision brings. Parolees are free to seek out the same types of programming and services available to prisoners released unconditionally—and often do—but the state cannot compel them to participate.[43] In response to the growing number of these inmates, states find ways to ensure that they receive at least some supervision after release. Terms of supervised release provide a mechanism for states to take opting-out off the table—that is, to require high-risk offenders to serve out their full sentence in prison as mandated by the courts *and* serve a separate term of postrelease supervision. New Jersey passed a law mandating that prisoners who were eligible for discretionary parole spend at least the last six months of their sentence in community-based supervision.

▲ Reentering prisoners face a great deal of uncertainty. They often wonder if they will be able to make it on the outside. Planning for reentry can begin on the date of sentencing, but more often is hardly considered at all.

© Thinkstock/Stockbyte

What Works in Parole

Perhaps recidivism cannot be eliminated, but research shows that it can certainly be reduced. It matters how society handles each parolee. Research shows that, when the type of parole and the intensity of supervision are appropriate, recidivism can be reduced by as much as 30%.[44] Even though that estimate may not seem very high, if even half of these numbers were consistently achieved, approximately 40,000 fewer men and women would be returned to prison each year.[45]

The Role of Research

Although empirical study has always played a role in parole theory, policy, and practice, formal research became an integral part of correctional policy and decision making in recent decades. Evidence-based practice (EBP) is backed by rigorous research, and programs based in EBP have been found successful at achieving desired outcomes such as reduced recidivism, measured as parole violations and revocations, as well as arrests, prosecutions, or commitments for new offenses. Other outcomes may include success in some other aspect of parole such as finding a job, graduating high school or vocational school, fulfilling restitution, staying off drugs, and attendance and successful completion of such services as drug treatment or anger management. They may also include institutional factors, like organizational fit and cost-effectiveness, and impacts on other stakeholders, such as families, communities, schools, other agencies, or public sentiment. Also, recidivism as defined in these studies may extend beyond the period of parole—studies typically track new arrests, convictions, and commitments for one to three years after release.

When parolees commit crimes worthy of headlines, it is a significant benefit to parole agencies and officers to be able to justify their practices as based in evidence. However, given the complexity of reentry, it is challenging to duplicate in one place an approach that is working in another. Agencies also weigh practical considerations, such as whether

IN THE COURTS

Pennsylvania Board of Probation and Parole v. Scott
524 U.S. 357 (1998)

After serving 11 years in prison for third-degree murder in Pennsylvania, Keith M. Scott was released on parole. As with most parole cases, one of the conditions of Mr. Scott's parole was that he not possess weapons. He also gave standing consent to searches of his person, property, or residence for any items that may constitute a violation of parole, with the understanding that any items found could be seized and used as evidence in a parole revocation hearing. Five months later, Mr. Scott was arrested for various parole violations, after which parole officers searched the home where he had been living, without his or the homeowner's consent, and found guns and a bow and arrows. These were used in evidence against Scott at a revocation hearing, and his parole was revoked. On appeal, the search was found to have violated Mr. Scott's Fourth Amendment rights against unreasonable search and seizure. It was found that his consent at the time of parole did not cover the type of search conducted and that the weapons should have been excluded from the revocation hearing.

The U.S. Supreme Court eventually overturned this decision and ruled that Fourth Amendment rights, which clearly do apply in regular criminal court, did not apply in a parole revocation hearing. Part of the court's reasoning was based on the deterrent effect of the exclusionary rule of the Fourth Amendment, which says that law enforcement officers will avoid illegal searches if they know evidence found this way will be excluded from consideration in court. The Supreme Court decided the deterrent effect in this case (and, by precedence, all revocation hearings) did not outweigh the risk to society if known parole violators are allowed to remain free. The court also found that the exclusionary rule did not fit with the less formal nature of parole revocation hearings with regard to criminal trials.

This ruling gave parole officers a great amount of leeway in their approach to surveillance and detection of violations by parolees—practices that have contributed to high rates of parole revocations across the United States.

the approach fits with the organization, whether it has political support, and whether it is cost-effective.* It must also withstand the test of capricious funding streams and public opinion.

There are many reasons for replication failure that may have nothing to do with inadequacies in the objectives and design of the program itself. Program fidelity (how closely a program adheres to its theory and design while it is put into practice) may be low, despite best intentions and efforts. Every jurisdiction is unique in important ways with respect to general conditions such as corrections culture, the management styles and personal commitment of agency leadership, available resources, or program support from law enforcement or the courts.

Funding can dry up as federal or state grant programs lose political support. Promised in-kind support from stakeholder groups, like probation departments or local providers, may end because of external circumstances such as an economic crisis. Public opinion may

---

* Cost-effectiveness can also be evaluated through research. After showing that intensive supervision programs focused solely on surveillance did not decrease recidivism and that similar programs that incorporated a strong rehabilitative element did reduce recidivism, the Washington State Institute for Public Policy then did cost–benefit analyses and produced a strong argument for why corrections systems should seriously consider adopting the intensive supervision probation (ISP) *with treatment* model. The analysis found that, despite ISP with treatment being relatively expensive to administer compared to other approaches, jurisdictions could expect to avoid more than $11,000 in victim and taxpayer costs per participating offender. Conversely, the ISP approach without the treatment component represented an overall *loss* of over $3,000 per offender (Aos, Miller, and Drake 2006b).

shift, creating an emphasis on one part of a new program over another. This was the case in the 1980s, as intensive supervision in probation and parole (ISP) gradually de-emphasized the social services approach to casework that was part of the original design, because it was expensive and did not fit with a growing tough-on-crime attitude among politicians and the public. ISP came to represent intensive surveillance, strict enforcement of terms of probation, and prevalent revocations and returns to custody. Researchers accounted for this loss of program fidelity and indeed found a reduction in positive outcomes associated with this new form of ISP.

Recidivism

Rates of returns to prison after release vary according to the time period studied, jurisdictional differences, and research methods. However, it is clear that return rates are generally high. According to a federal study for prisoners released in 1994, within three years, 52% had been reincarcerated, either for a new offense or for a parole violation, and 68% had been rearrested.[46] Using different methods, the Pew Center on the States found that 45% of releases in 1999 and 43% of releases in 2004 led to reincarceration within three years.[47] National statistics need always be read with an understanding that correctional laws, policies, practices, and other factors vary immensely by state. When California data were removed from the above findings, the rate of return to prison was about 40% in all three analyses.

A few studies have compared recidivism and other outcomes among conditional, supervised releases and unconditional, "maxed out" releases. A key difficulty is that supervision by a parole officer leads to a higher likelihood that authorities will become aware of any inappropriate behavior, and, depending on revocation policies, such behavior may be more likely to lead to arrest, prosecution, and reincarceration. The research literature reports a mix of results, but it usually finds that ex-prisoners who are placed under supervision after release fare somewhat better than those who are not.[48]

A study of releases in Illinois, Ohio, and Texas found ex-prisoners that received postrelease supervision had more positive outcomes with regard to employment and avoiding substance abuse than those released with no supervision.[49] Those supervised were not more likely to be arrested than those who were not supervised, but, as has been found in other research, those under supervision were more likely to be reincarcerated. This higher reincarceration rate was due to technical violations of parole—stricter requirements coupled with added scrutiny—rather than new offenses, which were statistically equal for both types of release. A study in New Jersey found mixed results, but three years after release, maxed-out offenders had been reincarcerated slightly more often and generally had higher recidivism.[50]

In any case, research findings that indicate a lack of efficacy for postsupervision release do not mean it is unsuccessful in every jurisdiction or that no forms or elements of parole can be effective. Effectiveness of parole can be heightened when best practices are consistently applied at each step of the process, including assigning the appropriate level of supervision and surveillance and targeting programming and services to each parolee.

Evidence-Based Practice and Parole

The National Institute of Corrections and other groups have identified the key elements of an evidence-based approach to postrelease supervision designed to save money while increasing positive outcomes with regard to public safety and the successful reintegration of ex-prisoners into their home communities. These best practices are summarized in this section.[51]

SPOTLIGHT

EFFECTIVE COMMUNITY-BASED PROGRAMS FOR PAROLEES

Contrary to the claims of critics that nothing worked in correctional rehabilitation in the 1970s,[1] and others more recently,[2] there *are* programs that work to help former prisoners reenter society and get their lives on track. In measuring success, it is important to keep in mind that, when talking about the hundreds of thousands of impacted ex-prisoners, even a small reduction of negative outcomes such as violations, new offenses, and recommitments to prison can mean that tens of thousands of individuals—and millions of taxpayer dollars—can be moved from the loss column to the win column.

Areas of need that are common among parolees can be addressed effectively with targeted programming and services, as reported by the Washington State Institute for Public Policy in Olympia.[3] This report summarizes the average reduction in recidivism for parolees who participate in these special programs as compared to those who receive regular parole (or time in prison) without special programming.

PROGRAMS FOR PAROLE AND PRISON

Cognitive-behavioral treatment programs, whether delivered in prison or in the community, reduce recidivism by 8%. Intensive supervision with an emphasis on treatment rather than surveillance reduces recidivism by almost 22%. Conversely, intensive supervision and other approaches to supervision that *lack* a strong treatment element, including adult boot camps and electronic monitoring, have been shown in multiple studies to have no impact on recidivism.

Employment training and job assistance programs in the community also consistently reduce recidivism by an average of almost 5%. Several prison programs have consistently been shown to reduce recidivism, including vocational education (13% reduction), basic adult education (5% reduction), and correctional industries (8% reduction).

SUBSTANCE ABUSE

In 2009, over 26% of male parolees reported a substance abuse issue, and a third reported having received substance abuse treatment in the past year.[4] Formerly incarcerated women have similar rates of substance abuse issues.[5] Community-based drug treatment and adult drug courts are shown to be effective at producing reductions in recidivism of more than 10% and 12%, respectively.

Assess Risk and Needs

The first step of a successful parole process is an assessment of the risk of recidivism and criminogenic needs of each exiting prisoner. Using validated actuarial tools, parole agencies develop risk and needs profiles to customize individual parole plans. At least 33 states use actuarial tools to guide the parole process.[52] (See Chapter 3.)

The needs identified by the assessments can be addressed through services and programming and improve the effectiveness of risk reduction.[53] In some jurisdictions, risk assessments are given at the beginning of an inmate's stay in prison and again halfway through his or her sentence. The parole decision can then consider (in some states it is required) whether the inmate's risk level has decreased.

In addition to standardized assessments used for all potential parolees, specialized instruments need to be used for subpopulations of prisoners, including women, youth, the mentally ill, and sex offenders.

Drug therapies delivered in the prison environment were also found to be helpful, although with about half as much future reduction in recidivism.

SEX OFFENDERS

Sex offenders represented 9% of the parole population in 2011.[6] Recidivism in sex offender cases is most often of a nonsexual nature, so sex offenders need to receive programming that addresses risk and criminogenic needs that are common to the general parole population as well as those specific to sex offenders.[7] Cognitive-behavioral programming for sex offenders consistently reduces recidivism rates by up to 31%. However, psychotherapy and behavioral therapy for sex offenders have been found to have no impact on recidivism.

Several other sex offender programs that focus on community-based care have not been studied enough to know their efficacy, including intensive supervision, mixed treatment, and medical treatment of sex offenders. However, one of these, a faith-based supervision program called Circles of Support and Accountability (COSA), was shown in a single study to reduce recidivism by about 31%.

DOMESTIC VIOLENCE

A common and well-studied type of domestic violence program that combines education and cognitive-behavioral treatment has not been found to impact recidivism rates, even in multiple studies. Domestic violence courts have not yet been studied enough to determine their efficacy.

QUESTIONS

1 What are other ways of defining "success" for a program besides its ability to reduce recidivism?

2 What would be options for policy and practice if no programs helped reduce recidivism in domestic violence offenders?

3 To what extent should (or should not) the results of academic research override the opinion and instincts of professionals in the field?

Notes

1. Martinson 1974
2. Farabee 2005
3. Aos, Miller, and Drake 2006
4. Feucht and Gfroerer 2011
5. James and Glaze 2006; Women in prison reported similar substance abuse issues as men.
6. Maruschak and Parks 2012
7. Burke, Giguere, and Gilligan 2011

The Risk Principle

The risk principle says that recidivism is reduced the most when parolees with a high risk of reoffending (as identified through the assessment process) receive a high level of intervention—meaning tighter surveillance as well as more intense and longer-term programming and services. Parolees with a moderate risk of recidivism respond best to a relatively moderate level of intervention. Low-risk parolees require low-level intervention and may in fact have an increased risk of recidivism if supervision is too intense.[54]

The Need Principle

The need principle says that recidivism will be reduced the most if identified criminogenic needs are targeted for programming and, conversely, if criminogenic needs *not* relevant to a particular parolee, as well as noncriminogenic needs, are *not* targeted. Targeting the wrong needs misdirects attention and resources and may become a stumbling block to success in the areas most likely to produce positive outcomes.[55]

A related notion of evidence-based parole is that every interaction the parolee has with the parole officer, other corrections representatives, and providers should keep things moving toward success and not be redundant or unnecessary. Parole officers and providers need to build rapport with their clients, but too much time spent discussing noncriminogenic needs or focusing on secondary or irrelevant issues is just that, time spent not working on factors of importance.

This sample demonstrates the types of questions and scoring that may be found on a risk assessment instrument. Specifically, this sample is designed to estimate risk of continued criminal behavior and failure in parole. Items and scoring should be targeted for specific gender, age, and purpose (e.g., custody, probation, parole, or reassessment after revocation).

▶

Sample Risk Assessment: Adult Males Entering Community Supervision

Client Name: Date of Assessment:

DOC #:   Release Date:

Reassessment: Yes/No   Assessed by:

	Responses	Weight
STATIC CRIMINAL HISTORY (Compiled from criminal record)		
1. Age at First Arrest	25 or older	0
	16 to 24	1
	15 or younger	2
2. Most Serious Arrest Under Age 18	None	0
	Misdemeanor	1
	Felony	2
3. Current Offense Drug Related	No	0
	Yes	1
4. Number of Prior Adult Felony Convictions	None	0
	One	1
	Two or more	2
5. Number of Prior Adult Commitments	None	0
	One	1
	Two or more	2
6. Ever Received Infraction for Violence While Incarcerated	No	0
	Yes	1
7. Total Number of Prior Probation or Parole Violations	None or one	0
	Two or more	1
CONDITIONS, BEHAVIOR, AND ATTITUDES (Compiled from self-report and interviews with appropriate correctional officers/program provider)		
8. Employed or enrolled in school at time of arrest	No	0
	Yes	1
9. Marital Status at time of arrest	Married or cohabitating	0
	Single, Separated, Divorced	1
10. Substance Abuse	Never assessed as alcohol/drug dependent, or was assessed as dependent, but successfully completed treatment and is not currently using drugs	0
	Previously assessed as dependent, and did not successfully complete treatment or is currently using drugs	2
11. Response to Supervision (in custody or in community)	Consistently adhered to supervision requirements and actively participated in programming	-1
	Sometimes violated supervision requirements and/or inconsistently participated in programming	1
	Consistently violated supervision requirements and/or refused to participate in programming	3

ATTITUDES AND CRIMINALITY (Compiled from self-report and interviews with appropriate correctional officers/program provider)		
12. Pride in Past Criminal Behavior	No pride Some pride A lot of pride	0 1 2
13. Able to Solve Problems Without Aggression	Consistently Sometimes Rarely	-1 1 2
14. Shows Concern or Empathy For Other's	Consistently Sometimes Rarely	-1 1 2
SCORING		
Scored Risk Level (ranges determined by research and policy)	-3 to 2 3 to 5 6 to 8 9-10	Low Medium High Very High
Discretionary Override (according to policy, raise or lower risk level due to documented reasons): If yes, reason (e.g., mental illness, low intelligence, history of abuse/neglect, etc.):		Yes / No

The Responsivity Principle

Programs and services that have been shown in robust studies to fulfill their intended purpose should be chosen over those that have not shown similarly promising results. It is not always possible to find programs that have been fully studied, but the list of "what works" is growing every year. It is important that parole agencies assess the availability and appropriateness of local programming and services, with efforts made to fill gaps in capacity.

Additionally, EBP calls for a good fit between the specific program and the parolee. This is called the responsivity principle. For instance, cognitive-behavioral programs that teach new ways of thinking about and responding to difficult situations have been found to benefit more serious, high-risk offenders. However, the same programs may be unnecessarily intense for lower-level offenders. The right programming for a particular parolee will also be a good fit with his or her individual traits and personality—that is, gender, culture, race, age, most effective learning style, intellectual abilities, and strengths. Not all substance-abusing ex-prisoners will respond to 12-step programs, so other options should be available and used. Also, programming offered in a comfortable and realistic environment works best, as opposed to, for example, the overly structured and insular prison setting or parole agency offices.

EBP prescribes a single comprehensive case plan established during incarceration and continuing into the community for each inmate. All involved agencies and service providers need to follow this plan. Ideally, an assessment is performed long before release, and the information it provides is used to begin service delivery during incarceration and continue through the parolee's transition into the community. When possible, the parole officer meets with the client before release to build rapport, review the conditions of release, and discuss what needs to happen immediately upon release.[56] Targeted treatment plans focused on higher-risk levels both conserve system resources and give help where it is most likely to have a positive impact.[57]

Appropriate Level of Supervision and Response to Misconduct

Approaches that rely most heavily on enforcement have not been shown to decrease recidivism or increase public safety. Modern surveillance techniques, including electronic monitoring, GPS, and intensive supervision, on their own do not lower recidivism levels.[58] Rather, these techniques need to be balanced with appropriate programming.

A parolee smiles before graduating from his drug rehabilitation program at Folsom Prison in California. For many inmates, graduations like this are their first such experience.

© Brian Baer/MCT /Landov

When parolees make mistakes, it is important that the correctional response be quick, consistent, and proportional to the misconduct. Graduated sanctions, which are responses matched in intensity to the seriousness of the behavior, formalize something that experienced and effective parole officers do already. They allow the response to become stronger as misconduct repeats or worsens, and help ensure that initial responses are not unnecessarily strong and do not run counter to fairness and proportion.

Ownership of the plan should extend to all parties, including the reentering prisoner.[59] For example, alcohol should obviously be off limits for a known alcoholic, but for a parolee without substance abuse issues, use of alcohol in moderation should not constitute a violation of parole. A laundry list of generic requirements can be overly burdensome to the parolee, the parole officer, and the system and can promote failure.

These evidence-based practices have been shown to reduce recidivism and produce other desirable outcomes for parolees. Almost universally, they also allow for the most efficient management of parole agency resources.

Specialty courts are a recently developed response to high rates of failure in parole and probation. These courts focus on a single kind of offense; the judge plays the role of intensive supervisor and collaborates with social service agencies to carry out case management and address underlying issues. The judge leads this interdisciplinary team, which provides a sort of intensive but flexible oversight of parolees' progress, using a wider range of sanctions before resorting to reincarceration. The reentry court incorporates many evidence-based practices and moves the responsibility for supervision away from the parole authorities. In 2012, there were reentry courts established in approximately 10 locations across the country.[60] Some courts target high-risk offenders, while in others, eligibility includes any parolee who violates parole conditions.[61]

Residential reentry centers (RRCs, community or "halfway houses") are designed to be a structured and supportive residential environment to help reentering individuals transition back to society. RRCs involve some supervision and accountability on the part of the parolee. While offering immediate and stabilizing housing, RRCs also provide assistance with critical matters such as employment, health services, legal services, family reunification, and various kinds of counseling, including substance use. The Federal Bureau of Prisons contracts for 190 such facilities, which have a bed capacity ranging from under 10 to more than

Graduated sanctions: A set of responses to parole violations that range in severity and are applied to match the severity of the problem behavior.

Specialty courts: Courts that focus on a single kind of offense such as drug offenses. The judge plays the role of intensive supervisor and collaborates with social service agencies to carry out case management and to address underlying issues.

150; some of these house women as well as men.[62] Planning for reentry to an RRC begins at least a year before the release date. Parolees are screened in consideration of several factors, including the resources of the facility, the nature and circumstances of the offense, the history and characteristics of the reentering prisoner, and any court recommendations. State departments of corrections also contract with halfway houses for reentering state prisoners.

SUMMARY

Most prisoners are eventually released back into society. Two thirds of these are released on some form of postrelease community supervision. Others are released without such conditions.

The decision to release a prisoner—the release mechanism—varies from one state to another. Release mechanisms are of two broad types—discretionary and nondiscretionary. Parole boards make decisions in discretionary systems; they must balance the demands of public safety, the law, and the objective of readmitting prisoners into society. With nondiscretionary release, the release date is set at the time of sentencing. However, while in custody, prisoners can usually earn an earlier release with credits for "good behavior." Each type of release system has strengths and weaknesses.

As they attempt to fit back into their families, jobs, and communities, reentering prisoners are often burdened by a host of challenges such as housing, employment, education, family responsibilities, substance abuse issues, mental health problems, and physical illnesses or disabilities. Prison rarely improves these problems. Parole officers have the dual responsibility of supporting the reentering prisoner to establish and maintain a crime-free life and surveillance and enforcing sanctions, including reincarceration, when necessary. POs serve as both law enforcement officers and social workers.

To the extent that prisons and parole agencies can establish a plan to connect the reentering prisoner to the means of overcoming these challenges, that individual has a greater chance of success, and the institution and the community have a reduced burden of recidivism and increased pubic safety.

Although perceptions of justice and fairness, relative lenience or severity, and other factors are relevant in evaluating the merits of the various aspects of parole, from a research perspective, the core method for measuring the quality or "success" of parole is recidivism. Evidence-based practices are those shown by vigorous research to be effective. Although it is difficult and expensive for every promising program to undergo this sort of evaluation, the enormous costs of administering parole and providing programming and services for hundreds of thousands of parolees make it crucial that approaches most likely to work receive sufficient funding and approaches not likely to work are either revised or discontinued. Determining which programs are and which are not subject to intensive evaluation is often less a function of merit and equity than of available resources or gaining the interest of a well-funded research university. There is a movement to label programs as "promising" if they have been shown to be effective in less strict research. This can reduce the likelihood that a truly beneficial program is overlooked or cancelled before it has a chance at full evaluation.

Despite the ever-fluctuating notion of what works for parole, over time, much has been learned about which system elements and characteristics do the most to maximize the ability of parole to protect public safety and facilitate successful reintegration for reentering prisoners.

DISCUSSION QUESTIONS

1. What are the main differences between probation and parole?

2. Where did the name *parole* come from? Discuss the concept the word implies.

3. What are some of the factors that impact the numbers of individuals on parole in a given year?

4. What are the four main mechanisms for being released from prison?

5. What are the key differences between discretionary and mandatory parole?

6. What is the role of a parole board? What are the arguments for and against parole boards having discretion over parole decisions?

7. What are the benefits and potential pitfalls of evidence-based practices from the perspective of parole agency policymaking and management?

8. What are the various ways parole "success" can be defined and measured? What are the factors impeding success? Consider this from various perspectives, including the parolee, the parole officer, and society.

9. How does prison time impact parole time? Consider this from various perspectives, including the parolee, the parole officer, and society.

10. Why should the government care about prisoner rehabilitation?

KEY TERMS

Commuting, 158

Criminalization, 160

Discretionary parole, 152

Graduated sanctions, 174

Mandatory parole, 152

Reentry, 158

Specialty courts, 174

Terms of supervised release, 152

Unconditional release, 153

NOTES

1. Langan and Levin 2002
2. Petersilia 2003
3. Petersilia 2000
4. *Morrissey v. Brewer*, 408 U.S. 471, 1972
5. *Mempa v. Rhay*, 389 U.S. 128, 1967
6. U.S. Sentencing Commission 2010
7. Bonczar 2008
8. APPA 1994
9. APPA 2006a
10. APPA 2006b
11. Solomon et al. 2006
12. Harlow 2003
13. Solomon et al. 2006
14. Visher, Debus-Sherrill, and Yahner 2010
15. Ibid.
16. Marushak, Glaze, and Bonczar 2013
17. Petersilia 2003
18. Gunnison and Helfgott 2010
19. Lopoo and Western 2005
20. Fazel and Danesh 2002
21. Feucht and Gfroerer 2011
22. Substance Abuse and Mental Health Services Administration 2012
23. Mumola and Karberg 2006
24. Ringhoff, Rapp, and Robst 2012
25. Solomon et al. 2006
26. Gunnison and Helfgott 2010
27. Helfgott 2007
28. Maruschak and Bonczar 2013
29. Ibid.
30. Ibid.
31. Ibid.
32. Hughes, Wilson, and Beck 2001
33. Carson and Sabol 2012
34. U.S. Sentencing Commission 2010
35. Glaser 1969; Petersilia 2003
36. Martinson 1974
37. Hughes, Wilson, and Beck 2001
38. Petersilia 2000
39. Ireland and Prause 2005
40. Yahner, Visher, and Solomon 2008
41. Petersilia 2003
42. Ostermann 2011
43. Yahner, Visher, and Solomon 2008
44. Solomon, Kachnowski, and Bhati 2005
45. Carter 2011
46. Langan and Levin 2002
47. Pew Center on the States 2011
48. Hughes, Wilson, and Beck 2001; Rosenfeld et al. 2005
49. Yahner, Visher, and Solomon 2008
50. Schlager and Robbins 2008
51. Carter 2011; Gendreau, French, and Taylor 2002
52. Caplan and Kinnevy 2010

53. Andrews, Bonta, and Wormith 2006; Bonta and Andrews 2007

54. Lowenkamp et al. 2006

55. Bonta and Andrews 2007

56. Warwick, Dodd, and Neusteter 2012

57. Lowenkamp, Latessa, and Holsinger 2006; Lowenkamp, Pealer, et al. 2006

58. Aos, Miller, and Drake 2006a

59. Warwick, Dodd, and Neusteter 2012

60. Administrative Office of the Courts 2012a

61. Administrative Office of the Courts 2012b

62. Federal Bureau of Prisons 2014

§SAGE edge™

Sharpen your skills with SAGE edge at edge.sagepub.com/krisberg

SAGE edge for students provides a personalized approach to help you accomplish your coursework goals in an easy-to-use learning environment. This site includes action plans, mobile-friendly eFlashcards and web quizzes as well as web, audio, and video resources and links to SAGE journal articles.

© iStockphoto.com / Bob In...

8 Juvenile Corrections

Until the start of the 20th century, young lawbreakers were generally treated no differently than adults. They were subject to the same penalties for misbehavior and incarcerated in the same cells as adult offenders. Early efforts to separate youth from adults in lockup began with the first reform schools in New York. These and subsequent efforts to improve society's response to youth crime were largely driven by fear, social control, paternalism, retribution, and the desire for cheap labor. What followed through the 1900s and into the current century were cycles of reform and scandal, each against a backdrop of shifting public attitudes about crime in general and youth crime in particular.

Today's juvenile justice systems—different in each state and each locality—continue to evolve. Some best practices are emerging; for instance, smaller facilities seem to work best. But youth in today's juvenile facilities still too often face poor conditions and abuse, and once released, system-involved youth still too often end up back in trouble.

A Brief History

The first corrections facility dedicated to juveniles was the New York **House of Refuge**, established in 1825. The facility was opened by the Society for the Prevention of Juvenile Delinquency, made up mostly of religious leaders concerned about the prevalence of wayward young people.[1] In part, the mission of the House of Refuge was to remove children from adult jails and workhouses. These early reformers believed that locking up juveniles with adult criminals would make the young people more likely to continue lawbreaking behavior. There was also concern about the growing number of children who were living in abject poverty on the streets of America's cities. However, the creation of the Refuge was motivated not so much by humanitarian or child welfare concerns; it was designed to respond to fears that a growing number of poor and immigrant youth could be recruited by corrupt local politicians as their henchmen and might even lead a class-based revolt in the United States. The popular movie *Gangs of New York* is a vivid portrayal of this period of U.S. urban history. There was growing fear among well-heeled citizens that informal social control was breaking down and that more restrictive institutions were needed.[2]

The founders of the House of Refuge would send out their agents to pick up street children and bring them to the Refuge. There was virtually no judicial process to regulate this practice. When parents of the youth complained that Refuge staff were sweeping the streets and depriving the parents of their "private property," the courts were usually unsympathetic to these mostly poor, immigrant families. The methods of the House of Refuge sprang from the core ideas of religious indoctrination, forced work, and rigid discipline. The Refuge was meant to serve as both school and prison. Upon release, the wards of the Refuge would be placed in apprenticeships, often on ships in the emerging merchant marine. The Refuge movement spread rapidly to most major East Coast cities during the first half of the 19th century. Similar institutions were soon opened in Boston, Philadelphia, Chicago, and over 20 other locations.[3]

House of Refuge: A type of early prison for juvenile delinquents begun in New York, similar to adult houses of correction.

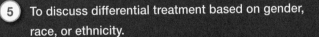

(5) To discuss differential treatment based on gender, race, or ethnicity.

(6) To name several important ways that juvenile and adult facilities are different.

(7) To grasp the basics of the measurement of youth program effectiveness.

(8) To be able to discuss programs such as boot camps and how their effectiveness should be determined.

The House of Refuge stood as if a monument to a noble and benevolent ideal of reform. Their young charges undoubtedly had more negative reports of the reality.

Rochester Public Library; © 2001 George Eastman House, Rochester, NY

WESTERN HOUSE OF REFUGE,
ROCHESTER, N.Y.

From the outset, these new juvenile facilities were plagued with major problems. There were riots, violence, and fires. One observer estimated that almost 40% of the youth ran away from the Refuges.[4] The Catholic Church also expressed concerns that its youth were being forcibly converted to Protestantism.

The Refuges supported themselves in part by selling the labor of their inmates to private manufacturing businesses. There were allegations of poor working conditions and that the

Joseph Hoffman, 13, was sent to the House of Refuge for hitting his mother on the head with a shovel. Other children ended up there for simply being homeless.

Image by Lewis Hine, 1895

Refuge managers often reaped substantial personal income from these deals. Early trade unionists asserted that the labor of the Refuge inmates was being used to suppress wages for free laborers. The newspapers regularly reported abusive practices toward the youth and corruption by the Refuge managers.

One response to the growing criticism of the privately run Refuges was inspections and oversight of these facilities by state agencies. These developments led to the creation in 1847 of the first statewide juvenile correctional facility in Massachusetts, the Theodore Lyman School.

There were many voices in the early 19th century arguing that the large-scale congregate facilities were doomed to failure. "Child savers" such as Charles Loring Brace advocated for a different approach for delinquent and wayward children that involved "placing" urban youngsters with farm families in the Midwest. Brace and his followers created a powerful image of the healthful and reformative nature of rural life. The advocates of placing youth on farms would also kidnap poor youth from the streets and transport them on trains to these rural communities. This practice is vividly described in the book and documentary, *Orphan Trains*.[5] Families were split apart by these practices, and often siblings spent years trying to locate their lost brothers and sisters. These youth were apprenticed to farmers for as long as seven years and provided free labor in exchange for minimal food, clothing, and housing. There were many reports that the children transported to farm families were abused as badly as the Refuge inmates and that many of the "orphans" ran away from their placements.

The proponents of juvenile correctional facilities and their critics debated each other for years. Again, the discussion was not really about what was best for the children, but about which approach was more effective in managing urban poverty and youth crime. Ultimately the juvenile facility lobby tried to accommodate some of the critics of their operations by relocating the juvenile training schools in rural areas, calling the custodial staff "house parents," and calling the residential units "cottages." Despite these cosmetic changes, these were a continuation of the training school model that was first developed in the Houses of Refuge.

Tragically, the legacy of abuse and corruption continued to plague large juvenile correctional facilities. For example, Florida's oldest juvenile corrections facility, the Dozier

Training school: A detention home that offers vocational training to juvenile offenders.

Shipping children out of the city to work on farms seems impossible by today's standards.

Photo courtesy National Orphan Train Complex

School for Boys, had a well-documented history of young residents being brutally beaten by the guards. Youth at Dozier were kept in extreme isolation and hog-tied as punishment. Hundreds of former inmates at Dozier from the 1950s and 1960s eventually sued the state of Florida for their maltreatment as children.[6]

The severe problems of juvenile corrections stood in stark contrast to its benign rhetoric. Yet it was only in the late 1950s and 1960s that states including New Jersey and California engaged in limited experimentation with alternative custody arrangements for juveniles. Few serious legal challenges to conditions of confinement in these facilities arose until the 1970s.

In the meantime, several ethnographic accounts of juvenile corrections documented the violence and coercive practices of these facilities. Howard Polsky in his classic book *Cottage Six* described how the weaker inmates were exploited by the stronger ones.[7] Several of the victimized youth were so traumatized that they ended up in mental hospitals. Research by Fisher and Street, Vinter, and Perrow told of similar occurrences.[8] An extraordinary journalistic account by ABC reporter Kenneth Wooden, *Weeping in the Playtime of Others*, revealed more of the corrosive and destructive nature of juvenile corrections and ignited a national discussion about the need for major reforms.[9]

Not long after, the political roof caved in on juvenile corrections. A series of well-publicized scandals and investigations by federal agencies in the late 1960s led the state of Massachusetts to recruit Dr. Jerome Miller to run its youth corrections system. Miller was a professor of social work at Ohio State University and former Air Force mental health clinician. He came to Massachusetts with the goal of introducing therapeutic communities into state training schools. However, Miller ran into fierce opposition from state workers for even the most modest reforms, such as letting youth wear normal clothing instead of jail inmate uniforms or not shaving their heads. The guards resisted any restrictions on the

IN THE COURTS

In re Gault

387 U.S. 1, 27 (1967)

The landmark U.S. Supreme Court decision, *In re Gault*, changed the legal contours of juvenile corrections, exerting a profound impact on juvenile corrections policy and practice. It ushered in a new era of extending due legal protections to youth in the juvenile court and in juvenile corrections. The case involved a 15-year-old who was confined in an Arizona youth corrections facility for nine years for allegedly making an obscene phone call. There was no direct witness to this offense. It was argued that the benign, treatment-oriented philosophy of the juvenile justice system permitted states to engage in more flexible procedures that were consistent with rehabilitation, the goals of which require an unfettered flexibility.

Chief Justice Abe Fortas observed that the benign rhetoric of the juvenile court sometimes clashed with its reality. The court wrote as follows:

> The boy is committed to an institution where he may be restrained of liberty for years. . . . His world becomes a building with whitewashed walls, regimented routine and institutional hours. Instead of mother and father and sisters and brothers and friends and classmates, his world is populated by guards, custodians, state employees and "delinquents" confined with him for anything from waywardness to rape and homicide.

Justice Fortas also observed that "the status of being a boy, doesn't not justify a kangaroo court."

The *Gault* decision held that juveniles are entitled to most of the due process and equal protection guarantees that were available to adults.

Gault became the basis of a series of legal challenges regarding the treatment of juveniles in correctional facilities. The next two decades saw a growing number of major federal lawsuits that challenged the abuse and neglect that were occurring in state juvenile corrections facilities in Texas, North Carolina, Florida, Tennessee, Mississippi, Missouri, Utah, Louisiana, Georgia, and the District of Columbia. California introduced a plan to subsidize localities to divert youth from state facilities.

---

use of force or on solitary confinement. Miller concluded that reforms were impossible and decided to close down the entire Massachusetts training school system.[10]

By 1972, Miller closed all of the state training schools in Massachusetts, moving almost 1,000 wards to a diverse network of very small, secure facilities, each with fewer than 15 beds and a range of community-based placements and programs. Research by Harvard Law School and by the National Council on Crime and Delinquency (NCCD) suggested that the reforms were largely successful in improving the quality of care and in reducing recidivism rates.[11] Symbolically, the first Massachusetts training school that Jerome Miller closed was the nation's oldest one—the Theodore Lyman School.

Miller later served as the director of juvenile corrections in Pennsylvania and in Illinois. Although the reforms in those states were not as far reaching as in Massachusetts, Miller made substantial progress in reducing the population of state youth prisons in favor of expanding smaller, community-based residential and nonresidential correctional options.

Finally, propelled by a growing wave of litigation that challenged the constitutionality of conditions of confinement in juvenile correctional facilities, many other states moved toward the Massachusetts approach to juvenile corrections: Utah, Vermont, Missouri, Texas, Florida, Maryland, Indiana, Colorado, Oregon, New Jersey, and Arizona joined in

▲ What went on inside of reform schools was kept largely behind closed doors. It took litigation to reveal the problematic truth.

http://en.wikipedia.org/wiki/ File:Lyman-hall-old.jpg; http:// freepages.history.rootsweb. ancestry.com/~history/grafton/ LymanSchool.html

the movement to reduce the number of youth in large-scale congregate training schools. In 1974, Congress passed what many say is the most important piece of federal legislation to set standards for juvenile justice across the nation. The Juvenile Justice and Delinquency Prevention Act established the federal Office of Juvenile Justice and Delinquency Prevention (OJJDP). The OJJDP promoted the Massachusetts approach as part of its overall strategy on what it then called serious, violent, and chronic juvenile offenders.[12]

The Past 30 Years: More Cycles of Scandal and Reform

This reform movement appeared to usher in a "new normal" in juvenile corrections. But in the mid 1990s, a national hysteria fanned by the media and by some criminologists, such as James Q. Wilson, John DiIulio, Richard Herrnstein, and Charles Murray, warned Americans about an impending wave of "superpredators" among the growing youth population.[13] Also, a very conservative philosophy dominated the national discussion on crime policy, through the two Bush administrations and the presidency of Bill Clinton. This period was characterized by a more punitive response to juvenile offenses, with state criminal codes and policies governing juvenile justice incorporating more crimes, longer sentences, and fewer protections based on juvenile status.[14] One specific result of this politically powerful rhetoric about cracking down on criminals was the enactment in 1995 of the Prison Litigation Reform Act, which made class-action lawsuits against corrections systems much more difficult. (See Chapter 10.)

The number of youth held in residential placement rose in the late 1980s and 1990s, leading to deteriorating conditions in many facilities. These facilities became increasingly crowded, and resources for treatment and education declined. A resurgence of unlawful practices and more laissez-faire regulation of state juvenile institutions led to dramatic examples of abuse that plagued many states, especially California, Florida, Texas, Oklahoma, Maryland, and New York.

Chemical and mechanical force: The use of chemical agents, such as pepper spray, or mechanical restraints, such as handcuffs, straightjackets, or shackles, to control behavior or exact punishment.

In California, a comprehensive investigation requested by the state attorney general found youth receiving their education and recreation in cages.[15] The levels of fear and violence in California facilities were very high; racial and gang conflicts and riots were regular occurrences. Many youth were subjected to solitary confinement, spending an average of 21 hours a day in their cells. There was virtually daily use of chemical and mechanical force to control the youth. Some facilities used guard dogs to maintain order. Sexual assaults occurred in this horrific atmosphere. Four youth committed suicide in just two years. In addition, investigations found that California state institutions were in violation of a wide range of federal and state laws covering education, health care, and mental health services. In 2004, California entered into a complex and far-reaching consent decree to remedy these harsh conditions.

In 2007, the nation became aware of widespread sexual abuse of youth in a West Texas juvenile facility at Pyote. An independent investigation revealed that high-level staff at Pyote were among the abusers.[16] Officials at the Texas Youth Commission (TYC) denied knowledge of these problems, even though caseworkers reported that they had tried on multiple occasions to bring the issues to light. Even the U.S. Department of Justice failed to take action, despite knowing about staff abuses for over four years. An assistant superintendent and a former school principal allegedly engaged in repeated sexual activity with youth residents using various enticements or threats of punishment—such as added time—for youth who refused their sexual advances. Eventually, over 750 TYC youth came forward with allegations of sexual misconduct by staff. As many as 2,000 offenses by staff between 2003 and 2006 were confirmed. As the scope of the scandal came to light, the state legislature ordered the overhaul of TYC; the top managers were replaced, and the governor appointed a conservator to run the agency.[17]

Florida experienced its own version of the national juvenile corrections nightmare. There were 2,285 allegations of abuse of youth in Florida juvenile corrections facilities from 2000 to 2001, almost double the number of these allegations from just three years

▲ Do you think it's true that if you treat someone like an animal, that person is more likely to behave like one?

SPOTLIGHT

THE MYTH OF THE SUPERPREDATOR

In the mid-1990s, Princeton professor John Dilulio made an alarming prediction of an impending wave of violent crime perpetrated by a new breed of "superpredator" that would last for two decades. The professor's estimates of 270,000 new and dangerous youth were based on population growth figures and involved fairly simple mathematics; by his calculations, 6% of young males "turn out to be" career criminals. And it wasn't just the numbers; he also stated with confidence that these natural-born killers were of an entirely different nature than anything seen before. Furthermore, he stated that "each succeeding generation of young male criminals commits about three times as much serious crime as the one before it. The occasional fatal knife fight of 1950s street gangs has given way to the frequent drive-by shootings of 1990s gangs."[1]

Although the description of the early generation evokes images of *West Side Story*, the image of the alleged threat was considerably more sinister and lethal. Dilulio portrayed a group of killers that are truly the "other." He was unapologetic for making claims that clearly implicated young African American males. However, he pooh-poohed any allegation of racial bias in the justice system, mentioned studies without citations, and blankly stated, "If blacks are overrepresented in the ranks of the imprisoned, it is because blacks are overrepresented in the criminal ranks."[2]

Critics of Dilulio maintained that he had just "invented" the threat and that there was no true factual basis for his inflated predictions, that crime rates (even measured by arrest) had increased across the board to the mid 1990s, that Dilulio's claims were based on a self-justified racial bias, and that, in any case, crime rates are affected by a complex of factors and not merely population growth. During this second half of the 1990s, crime in all categories began a rather steep and sustained decline.[3]

---

earlier.[18] Abusive practices at a maximum-security facility for girls (the Florida Institute for Girls) led to its closure in 2005. But, even as the facility was being closed down, a longtime corrections officer was arrested for sexually assaulting a 15-year-old female resident. At another facility, Sawmill Academy, a supervisor was charged with eight felony counts involving sexual contact with the resident girls.

Florida's boys' programs were equally mired in scandal and abuses. In 2003, the death of Omar Paisley in the Dade County juvenile detention center became a national symbol of the failings of the Florida juvenile justice system. The boy died of a ruptured appendix because the staff refused him medical attention, despite his complaints of severe pain and distress. In 2006, another high-profile case emerged in a Florida juvenile facility. At a juvenile boot camp operated by the Bay County Sheriff's Office, 14-year-old Martin Lee Anderson was beaten to the point of passing out by seven guards and suffocated when staff used ammonia capsules in a futile attempt to revive him.

Since 2004, Florida has had to close 56 programs for boys and 25 programs for girls, due to complaints about abusive practices by staff, including giving drugs to youth, falsifying logbooks, and failing to provide pregnant teens with basic prenatal care. Inexplicably, both Texas and Florida had stopped doing criminal background checks on applicants for staff positions. Administrators of juvenile facilities in those states hired staff who were later found to be convicted sex offenders.

In Indianapolis, Indiana, a number of staff were indicted for engaging in inappropriate sexual contact with female youth residents. The Los Angeles County juvenile facilities

However, at the time, the reaction in the media went "viral." The idea struck a fearful nerve and caught on rapidly. Sensational news reports of youth violence were far more frequent than the proportion of actual incidents involving the so-called superpredators would indicate.[4] These stories helped to legitimize the theory and to convince the public to accept it as truth. The media attention, in turn, helped instigate a wave of criminalization of youth and more punitive federal legislation such as trying more youth in adult court, lowering the age at which those youth could be so tried, tying federal law enforcement block grants to adoption of stricter sanctions, and relaxing standards for separating youth from adults inside facilities.[5]

As we all know now, the wave of superpredators never materialized. Even DiIulio eventually backed off his assertions and stressed that he felt the church should play a role in addressing gang violence. The public needs a framework for understanding crime problems and is willing to accept an idea that seems plausible, even though the reasoning for it may be obscure.

QUESTIONS

1 What are some of the flaws in the thinking behind the superpredator idea?

2 Research news articles from the era; can you find opposing points of view?

3 Discuss other historical events that were inflamed by fears of crime.

Notes

1. DiIulio 1996
2. Ibid.
3. Bilchik 2000
4. Templeton 1998
5. Ibid.

were cited by the U.S. Department of Justice for excessive use of isolation, inadequate mental health, and a culture of violence. Federal officials have also alleged that New York State juvenile facilities are characterized by excessive use of force against youth and very poor mental health services. In 2010, New York State entered into an agreement with the U.S. Department of Justice to remedy these problems.

These scandals, in turn, led to several legislative inquiries and threats of further investigations and additional lawsuits by the U.S. Department of Justice Civil Rights Division. In particular, the Special Litigation Section has initiated dozens of investigations and filed civil rights complaints against many youth corrections systems, in particular for violations of the 1980 Civil Rights of Institutionalized Persons Act that was passed during President Carter's administration. Resolving these legal challenges has led to a significant increase in the costs of operating juvenile corrections facilities.

Findings from recently instituted national surveys of youth in residential placement show that unacceptable conditions of confinement for these youth persist. Over 9% of youth in residential placement in 2012 reported sexual victimization while in custody, usually involving staff.[19] In 2003, 29% of surveyed youth reported being physically assaulted or threatened, often multiple times, with 29% of these suffering injury. Ten percent suffered face-to-face robberies by threat or force, often by staff. Youth also reported theft was a common occurrence, with 46% having property stolen on at least one occasion. Almost half of youth in placement in 2003 reported being subjected to the widespread use of group punishment, and about one quarter reported solitary confinement, forced physical exercise, and room confinement. They expressed basic concerns about sanitation and safety in case of fires or other emergencies. They also generally reported that correctional programs were not very useful to them.[20]

During the 1990s, the overall number of youth sent to state and local corrections facilities increased by 36%, but it then declined by 14% from 1999 to 2006. In California, the population of youth prisons declined by more than 33% between 1997 and 2006. During this same period, juveniles in custody dropped by 49% in Louisiana, by 40% in Georgia, by 38% in Washington, and by 38% in Tennessee.[21] Juvenile arrest rates also dropped by 28% as the juvenile custody population declined. However, while juvenile incarceration was dropping, the populations in adult prisons and jails continued to climb.

This population decline was influenced by the media attention on continued abuse in juvenile facilities and the exploding costs to maintain these systems. There was also heightened awareness of the shortcomings of even well-run correctional facilities and an emphasis on reserving time behind bars for all but the most challenging youth offenders. States began to reconsider their youth incarceration practices and renew reform efforts. For example, reforms developed in Missouri were instituted in other jurisdictions. Also, the Annie E. Casey Foundation launched a major reform effort designed to reduce the number of youth in local juvenile pretrial detention facilities. By 2013, the Juvenile Detention Alternatives Initiative (JDAI) was operating in over 200 cities and instituting significant improvements in how youth are processed through the court system and increasing the use of noncustody alternatives, with plans to use similar approaches to reduce posttrial placements.[22]

Almost 200 years after the founding of the New York House of Refuge, the future of juvenile corrections is uncertain. The current political climate is not supportive of expanding the use of juvenile corrections facilities, but it is hard to predict if this current policy direction will be trumped by the politics of fear that derailed the trend away from the use of institutions during the 1970s and 1980s.

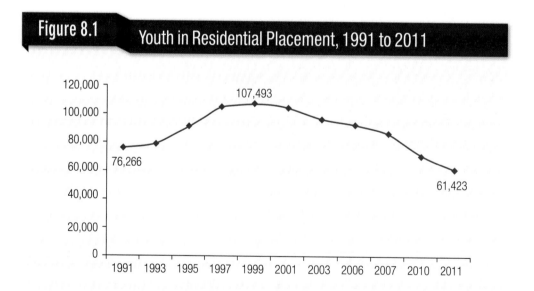

Figure 8.1   Youth in Residential Placement, 1991 to 2011

Figure 8.1 shows that the number of youth in residential placement across the United States rose from 76,266 in 1991 to a high of over 107,000 in 1999. It then fell each year, to 61,423 in 2011. (These data are from the Census of Juveniles in Residential Placement, a one-day count performed biannually by the Bureau of the Census on behalf of the U.S. Department of Justice OJJDP.)[23] *Source: Sickmund et al. 2013.*

The Structure of the Juvenile Justice System

Today's juvenile system consists of a broad range of small facilities with just a few institutions that are larger than 300 beds.

Juvenile facilities range from maximum-security institutions with razor wire perimeters, locked rooms, and uniformed correctional staff to boot camps, environmental conservation camps, open facilities, temporary shelters, runaway shelters, halfway houses, and supervised independent living programs for youth about to be released from court jurisdiction. There are even juvenile corrections programs on sailing ships. However, the vast majority of youth (83% in 2011) reside in facilities that are locked and have secure perimeters.[24] Detention centers, long-term secure facilities, and boot camps are almost always

Table 8.1 Status of Juveniles in Residential Placement, 2011

Type of Custody	Percentage of Detained Youth
Detention	31%
Awaiting adjudication	17%
Awaiting disposition	6%
Awaiting placement	6%
Awaiting adult court processing	2%
Commitment	68%
Reception/diagnostic	2%
Group home	30%
Secure facility	27%
Boot camp	1%
Camp	4%
Adult commitment	1%
Diversion	1%

Juveniles in custody are referred to as "youth in residential placement" and most often are either detained (31% in 2011) or committed (68%). Detained youth are those in short-term placement—usually in a juvenile hall or a detention center—as they await trial or await long-term placement after trial. Committed youth are those serving sentences after trial (postadjudication), most often in a community-based group home or a secure facility. Other committed youth may be in a short-term reception or diagnostic center, where they are assessed and classified for long-term placement, a military-style boot camp, or a ranch or wilderness camp. Some juveniles are also held as part of a diversion program (1%), which allows them to avoid a formal adjudication for delinquency. A small number (about 3%) of youth are held in juvenile facilities while being processed for trial in adult court or serving an adult sentence.[25] *Source: Sickmund et al. (2013).*

SPOTLIGHT

JUVENILE VERSUS ADULT COURT

In addition to the adult courts, there is a separate system of courts for juveniles. The juvenile court system was established during the Progressive Era. In 1899, Illinois was the first state to initiate separate delinquency, neglect, and dependency trials for youth. The idea caught on quickly for the time, and by 1925, all but two states had established a separate court for children.[1] Currently, every state has a juvenile court that is separate from the adult court.

The basic concept is that children are fundamentally different than adults and must be held to age-appropriate standards of culpability. Therefore, a different set of legal responses and standards is necessary for juveniles. The role of the juvenile court, due process, and the level of formality in juvenile proceedings have been the subject of much debate. Critics of the youth court claim that it has too much discretion and that it tramples the rights of youth instead of protecting them. Several of these arguments have made it as far as the Supreme Court.

Different language applies in the juvenile court as well. Proceedings in juvenile court are considered civil matters. The juvenile court is often less adversarial than adult court. A youth is not indicted; the district attorney files a petition with the court. A youth is not convicted; he or she has a petition sustained or not sustained. And a youth is not sentenced; the matter is adjudicated.

It is no simple matter to determine at what age and for what crimes a minor is prosecuted through the adult court instead of the juvenile delinquency court. Though many are working to reverse the trend, prosecution in the adult system has increased, and punishments for youth have become harsher and have been applied to ever younger children.

The age of jurisdiction—that is, the maximum age at which a youth is automatically tried in adult court—varies

locked, while about one third of group homes and wilderness camps are not locked. Camps, ranches, and group homes, including halfway houses and independent living programs, provide the most freedom of movement for youth, with residents often spending some of their time in the community, attending school or work, receiving services, and seeing family.

Youth facilities are about equally as likely (approximately one third each) to be run by state, local, or private groups. In 2011, 34% of youth in placement lived in facilities operated by state agencies; another 36% were in facilities run by local county, city, or municipal government; and 31% of youth were in private juvenile corrections facilities. Each type of setting might be run by the state, locally, or privately. Long-term secure facilities are most often run by the state; detention centers are most often locally operated; and group homes are most often private. Many youth facilities were built over three decades ago. In general, governments have been more willing to invest in new adult prisons than in juvenile facilities.

Some states such as Colorado, Georgia, and Florida operate all their juvenile corrections programs through state agencies. In other states such as California, Ohio, and Pennsylvania, juvenile corrections is a shared state–local responsibility. Increasingly, states such as Maryland, Utah, Florida, Rhode Island, New York, and Massachusetts depend on private for-profit or nonprofit agencies under contract with the state to operate juvenile corrections facilities. Adding further complexity to these organizational structures, some states send youth to other states for placements in long-term secure, mental health, special education, or foster care facilities. Judges determine the place and the length of stay in juvenile

by state. For most states in 2012, that age was 17, for 10 states it was 16, and in New York and North Carolina it was 15.[2] All states have statutes allowing for or requiring prosecution in the adult system of youth below the age of jurisdiction for certain crimes.[3] National data are not available on youth held in adult prison, but this is a common occurrence as well, with an estimated 100,000 youth under 18 years of age sentenced to time in adult facilities each year.[4] For those convicted in adult court, states sometimes hold the youth in juvenile facilities until they age out of the juvenile system. This maximum age varies considerably by state. For example, in New York and North Carolina, juvenile corrections facilities typically hold youth only up to age 16 before releasing them or transferring them to an adult facility. In California, a youth might stay until age 25.

The focus and goals of juvenile court have changed with the times. It remains to be seen, as the lines between juvenile and adult court processes become blurred, what the role of the juvenile court will be in the future.

QUESTIONS

1 For what crimes and at what age should youth be prosecuted in adult court?

2 Should juveniles have a right to a trial by jury? Who should be on the jury?

3 How should court proceedings differ if a youth in court is delinquent, dependent, or the victim of neglect?

Notes

1. Krisberg and Austin 1993
2. Office of Juvenile Justice and Delinquency Prevention 2013
3. Griffin et al. 2011
4. Daugherty 2013

| Figure 8.2 | Percentage of Youth in Residential Placement by Facility Size, 2011 |

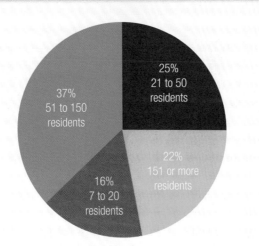

Figure 8.2 shows most youth are placed in smaller facilities, with only 22% in the largest prisonlike facilities in 2011. Also in that year, 16% of youth in placement lived in a facility with 20 or fewer residents, 25% with 21 to 50 residents, 37% with 51 to 150 residents, and 22% with over 150 residents.[26]

Source: Sickmund et al. 2013.

SPOTLIGHT

JJDPA REAUTHORIZATION

The Juvenile Justice and Delinquency Prevention Act (JJDPA) originally passed in 1974—then and now a pivotal piece of federal legislation that established standards for the treatment of delinquent youth in state and local juvenile systems. The act also set up funding vehicles for training, research, technical assistance, and evaluation.

The JJDPA has four core protections:

1. **Deinstitutionalization** of Status Offenders: Status offenders (runaways, truants, minors in possession of alcohol, etc.) should not be held in detention, but should instead receive community- and home-based services.[1]

2. Jail Removal: Juveniles may not be held in adult facilities, except while awaiting transport and within time limits— 6 hours in urban areas, 24 hours in rural areas.

3. Sight and Sound Separation: Even during temporary custody in adult facilities, youth must have no contact, visual or auditory, with adults.

4. Disproportionate Minority Contact (DMC): States must assess and address DMC at key decision points in the juvenile justice process.[2]

The act has had to go through periodic reauthorizations, each of which has resurfaced tensions, for both practical and philosophical motives, between those who advocate for even stronger protections and those who would relax and release administrators and judges from the constraints of the legislation. Proponents of the reauthorization wish to

facilities in some states, whereas state juvenile corrections agencies and parole boards make these decisions in other states. Practices vary tremendously among the states in which youth actually go to juvenile corrections facilities and how community-based probation services are used. The nature of aftercare or reentry services for youth varies widely as well.

Unlike adult facilities, juvenile correctional institutions are required by law to provide education and special education services. Few facilities are in compliance with these

A teenager convicted as an adult serves out his decades-long prison sentence in the Clemens Unit prison, an adult facility run by the Texas Department of Criminal Justice.

© Andrew Lichtenstein/Corbis

Deinstitutionalization: The systematic release or removal of offenders from an institution, especially secure residential facilities, for placement and care in the community.

limit the "valid court order" allowance, which put in place a loophole for detaining status offenses on a judicial discretionary basis. Youth advocates are also in favor of improving the second and third safeguards, citing the increased risk for youth in adult facilities for recidivism, suicide, and assault. In addition, they would strengthen and clarify the DMC requirements, which to date have been relatively vague and difficult to enforce.[3]

Despite the opposition to the JJDPA, all but one of the 56 eligible states and territories participate, and a large majority of them are in compliance with the current requirements. The legislation introduced by Senator Patrick Leahy (D-VT) had bipartisan support. If there is one lesson in this, it may be that as long as there is contention over how best to design a system for juveniles, any gains should never be taken for granted.

QUESTIONS

1 Why do you think federal legislation is necessary to set standards for the response to juvenile delinquency?

2 Discuss the four core protections. Which do you think is the most important, and why?

3 Do additional research on the statistics for suicide, assault, or recidivism for youth in adult facilities.

Notes

1. Hornberger 2010

2. Library of Congress 2009

3. Center for Children's Law and Policy n.d.

---

laws, however, and there are increasing legal challenges for the failure to provide adequate education, mental health, and special services for youth with disabilities. Juvenile facilities generally have higher ratios of staff to residents than adult facilities. As a consequence, the operating costs of juvenile facilities are much higher on a per capita basis than adult facilities. In 2007, the national average annualized cost for a juvenile in residential placement was $88,000 while the cost for an adult in state prison was approximately $28,000.[27] Further, these costs vary due to differences in economies, demographics, incarceration practices, and the needs of the youth. In California in 2010, the cost was $240,000 per year for the most serious youthful offenders held by the Division of Juvenile Justice.[28] In an era of fiscal insolvency for many states and localities, these enormous expenditures are prompting further diversion of youth to community-based programming.

Characteristics of Juveniles in Custody

Similar to the adult system, the majority of juvenile inmates are males and members of racial and ethnic minority groups. In 2011, only 32% of the incarcerated youth were White, and 86% were male. The typical ages of these youth were 15 to 17, but 5% were age 13 or younger, 9% were 14, and 14% were over age 18. Stays in juvenile facilities tend to be shorter than in adult corrections. In 2011, 95% of detained youth and 71% of committed youth had been in the facility for less than six months. It also true that young people are often incarcerated for relatively minor crimes. In 2011, only about one third of the youth in juvenile corrections were there for a violent offense; most were charged with property crimes, crimes of public order, or technical violations of the conditions of their probation. Roughly 4% of the youth in confinement were charged with juvenile status offenses such as truancy, curfew violations, running away, or being

Status offenses: An action that is prohibited only to minors (in this instance). Status offenses may include consumption of alcohol, tobacco smoking, truancy, and running away from home. These acts may be illegal for minors but are legal for all others.

incorrigible.[29] The more violent and dangerous juvenile offenders are often sentenced to serve their time in adult institutions or, as in California, in separate state-run youth prisons.

Overrepresentation of Youth of Color

Youth of color, especially African American and Latino youth, predominate in juvenile correctional facilities. Indeed in some urban jurisdictions, it is rare to find any White youth in confinement. Rates of incarceration for youth of color are also much higher than for White youth. For example, in 2006, African American youth were held in pretrial detention centers at a rate 5.3 times that of Whites. Latino and Native American rates of detention were 2.4 and 3.5 times that of Whites. For juvenile residential facilities, African American youth were confined at a rate 4.5 times that of Whites; Latino youth and Native American youth had rates 1.9 and 3.2 times that of White youth.[30]

One factor that contributes to this disproportion is that sentencing practices for youth of color are stricter than for White youth. For example, studies have found that, even after correcting for such factors as offense severity and prior records, youth of color are more likely to be formally processed in court, less likely to be sentenced to probation instead of incarceration, and likely to be held in confinement longer than White youth.[31] Youth of color are also more likely than White youth to be locked up in substandard and crowded juvenile corrections facilities.[32]

There are numerous theories that attempt to account for the racial and ethnic disparities discussed above. Some have argued that youth of color face harsher attitudes toward their misconduct and that they lack adequate legal representation. Others have suggested that there are fewer community-based alternatives available for youth of color. Almost certainly, the poisonous and false rhetoric about "superpredators" and "crack babies" has supported the harsher treatment of minority youth in the juvenile justice system.

| Figure 8.3 | Youth in Residential Placement by Race and Ethnicity, 2011 |

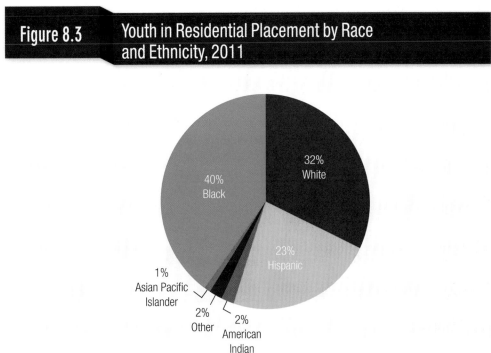

Figure 8.3 shows that, in 2011 African American youth made up the largest segment of youth in residential placement (40%), with Whites (32%) and Latinos/Hispanics (23%) the next largest groups.
Source: Sickmund et al. 2013.

Young Women and Juvenile Corrections

In general, girls comprise about 15% of all the residents of juvenile corrections facilities, but in some states, females make up almost a third of juveniles in custody. Despite the widespread decline in the number of males in juvenile correctional facilities from 1997 to 2006, in 14 states the incarceration rate of young women grew by almost 30% in that period. Between 2006 and 2011, the population of both genders declined in all states but one.[33]

Criminologist and law professor Paul Tappan first pointed out that young women were often locked up for less serious crimes than young men.[34] Tappan suggested that girls were institutionalized due to societal biases that young women must be "protected" from their emerging sexuality and their potential exploitation by older males. Boys are much less often arrested or incarcerated for their adolescent sexual activities, unless their partners are very young girls. Girls are more likely than boys to be incarcerated for juvenile status offenses such as running away, truancy, curfew violations, and incorrigibility. Young women are also likely to be placed in residential settings for probation violations. Minor misconduct is used as a pretext to lock up girls who are already on probation—a practice known as "bootstrapping."[35] Research by Bishop and Frazier, and Chesney-Lind and Shelden, documented this double standard for females.[36] A study in Maryland showed that even for those girls who were incarcerated for assaultive behavior, the vast majority of these crimes involved family disputes with parents or siblings.[37]

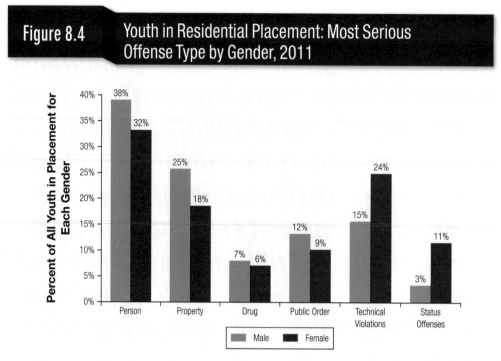

Figure 8.4 Youth in Residential Placement: Most Serious Offense Type by Gender, 2011

Figure 8.4 shows the most serious offense leading to residential placement for all youth in 2011. The figure shows the percentage of males and the percentage of females who had committed each type of offense. The most common offenses for both genders were person (violent), property, and technical violations of probation. Males were more likely to be placed for person, property, and public-order offenses than females. Females were much more likely to be placed for technical violations and status offenses. (Youth may be adjudicated for more than one offense; only the most serious offense is represented here as is common in most correctional data reporting.) *Source: Sickmund et al. 2013.*

The dominance of boys in the juvenile corrections population has often resulted in lower investments in programming for girls. Girls in juvenile corrections have fewer educational, recreational, and vocational opportunities. Staff are rarely given training in the unique needs of adolescent young women.

Traditional sexist stereotypes dominate the content of juvenile corrections programs for girls. For example, girls in many jurisdictions are required to participate in "tea parties," and proper selection of future mates is a key focus of education and therapy sessions. These activities are rarely seen in boys' programs. Vocational programming for girls tends to emphasize traditional female occupations such as cosmetology, dog grooming, or child care, with few opportunities for girls to learn trades that pay high wages. Many locales simply do not have residential programs for girls, and so they are often sent to residential programs in other states. Girls' programs rarely provide for gender-responsive health care or mental health services.

As troubled as juvenile corrections facilities for boys are, it may be that girls suffer even worse maltreatment. Several observers have noted that there are high levels of harm to young women in juvenile corrections. Rose Giallombardo was one of the first social scientists to document the sexual and physical victimization of incarcerated young women.[38] More recently, Acoca and Dedel reported on degrading and excessively punitive treatment of confined young women in California.[39] Krisberg wrote about the exploitation and cruelty in juvenile corrections for girls in California, Florida, and Indiana.[40] A recent national survey conducted by the federal Bureau of Justice Statistics found much higher rates of sexual abuse for incarcerated girls compared to boys.[41]

Young women on a bus near Phoenix, Arizona. Despite girls and young women having very different needs than boys, the concept of gender-responsive practice is relatively new.

© Scott Houston / Alamy

National attention is just now being paid to the failings of juvenile corrections for girls. Until very recently, litigation and advocacy in support of incarcerated young women has been very limited. As a beginning step, the Jessie Ball duPont Fund created a national Center for Girls and Young Women in 2008 to help disseminate ideas on how to fix these dire circumstances. The OJJDP and the Robert Wood Johnson Foundation also provided seed funding for the Center for Girls and Young Women.

Recidivism Rates and Juvenile Corrections

As noted earlier, the debate over whether confinement in juvenile corrections facilities reduces or increases the likelihood of future criminal conduct goes back to the 19th century and the founders of the juvenile court. Defenders of juvenile corrections such as Charles Murray asserted that incarceration, even in terrible facilities, is justified because it exerts a deterrent effect on young offenders.[42] Others such as Edward Rhine have emphasized the positive effects of institutional treatment programs.[43] This policy discussion has rarely been illuminated by sound research data.

Neither the federal government nor most states track the recidivism rates of juveniles routinely or systematically. A pilot study conducted by the NCCD that was designed to begin regular collection of these juvenile data was de-funded by the OJJDP in the 1990s. It is true that tracking recidivism for juveniles is a more complex process than for adults. Young people eventually "age out" of the juvenile corrections system, so data on recidivism for juveniles must include information on any subsequent adult system involvement. This linking of data across multiple systems is difficult. Some data are protected by the confidentiality requirements of the juvenile court. Further, there is no consensus on how to define and measure the success or failure of youth corrections programs, and the wide variety of settings and policies in juvenile systems across the country make it a challenging task to compare jurisdictions. Still, given the great public interest in reducing youth crime and the large investments of tax dollars in juvenile programs, it is discouraging that even minimally

YOU DECIDE

Juvenile Corrections or Child Welfare?

A. M. killed his father after a fight. He was 10 years old at the time. The father had a history of battering A. M., A. M.'s mother, and a younger sibling. The mother had already left the family and moved to another state. A. M. had been living with the father, who was a notorious leader of the American Nazi Party and had allegedly shot migrant farmworkers who ventured onto his property. A diagnostic assessment revealed that A. M. has minor mental health issues and significant learning disabilities. The youth was home schooled and spent little time with children his own age. While in custody, A. M. has been disciplined for threats against other inmates and for not cooperating with staff. There are no other living relatives besides A. M.'s mother. Although she has substance abuse issues, when authorities contacted her, she said that A. M. could live with her.

The prosecutor wants A. M. to be sentenced to a commitment to a state juvenile facility for up to 13 years. The prosecutor alleges that the state juvenile corrections facility can provide appropriate treatment and education services. If he were to go there, A. M. would be the youngest resident of the state juvenile facility.

Lawyers for A. M. would prefer that he be placed in a specialized mental health or child welfare group home and receive intensive educational and counseling services. A. M.'s lawyers argue that placement in the state correctional facility is unsafe, due to gang activities and the older and more criminally sophisticated juveniles housed there, and that services there are inconsistent. A specialized placement would be very expensive for county officials, while a state juvenile facility would be paid for by the state.

YOU DECIDE: **What disposition would you order for A. M.?**

reliable national and state data on the outcomes of juvenile corrections are not regularly collected.

Fortunately, a few interesting studies have looked at postrelease results from a variety of jurisdictions. Each of these studies suffers from some research design limitations, but in total, they indicate the current performance of juvenile corrections systems.

The NCCD pilot study mentioned above covered 40 states and found that, by the most conservative measure of continued misconduct, as many as 27% of youth released in 1993 were returned to state juvenile custody within one year.[44] However, this figure was an underestimate, as the study did not have access to data on youth who were incarcerated again in local detention programs or in adult prisons and jails.

A Florida study by Tollett tracked almost 1,700 youth released from a range of state juvenile corrections programs.[45] He found that 44% of these youth were arrested for a new juvenile or adult charge within one year of their release, and 30% were incarcerated in that period. Tollett found that youth with the most prior confinement experiences and those who were in the most secure facilities had the highest failure rates. Of course, these youth may have possessed other personal characteristics that could explain these results.

A Pennsylvania study of 10 residential programs revealed that 48% of the youth were arrested within 12 months, and 55% were rearrested within 18 months of their release.[46] Similar to the Florida study, those Pennsylvania youth who had experienced incarceration at earlier ages and those who had been in juvenile correctional programs repeatedly had the highest recidivism rates.

A study of the Massachusetts training schools that were subsequently closed by Jerome Miller revealed a failure rate of nearly 66% based on the last cohort of youth released from those facilities.[47] A study by NCCD of youth released from Utah training schools reported a one-year rearrest rate of 79%.[48] An analysis of a random sample of young people exiting the California Youth Authority (CYA) showed a 70% rate of being arrested within one year of release. Haapanen documented that 96% of CYA youth were later arrested as adults.[49] A later study of youth released from California youth facilities in 2004 revealed very similar high rates of recidivism.

There is some research indicating that youth who were incarcerated in smaller facilities that were less prisonlike had lower rates of postrelease failure. States such as Missouri and

Random sample: A sample in which every element has an equal chance of being selected; a small part of something intended as representative of the whole.

THE MISSOURI MODEL[1]

The "Missouri Model" has become synonymous with the most humane and effective practice in the United States for addressing youth crime and delinquency. It arose in part as a reaction against the typical American training school that has unsafe, unhealthy, and sometimes unconstitutional conditions; is costly and ineffective; and is too often plagued by abuse.

Missouri closed its training schools in the early 1980s. After doing so, the state adopted an approach that emphasizes small-scale units, a homelike environment, normal clothing, and supervision by teams of trained youth counselors rather than by guards. The youth are treated with respect and dignity, and the environment is a therapeutic one. The goal is for the youth to make changes in their behavior that are truly positive and that last.

Most important, the method of ensuring safety and security emphasizes "eyes on" supervision, not isolation or physical hardware restraints.

Detractors may claim that Missouri's youth are different from youth in the rest of the country, that the system only treats the "lightweights," and that it only serves younger juveniles and the rest go to adult facilities. These claims are refuted by the model's proponents.

Evaluations of the model consistently return positive results in terms of youth outcomes. Furthermore, it costs less than large-scale institutions. The Missouri Model continues to gain praise as the best treatment for youth who break the law, but surprisingly few places have adopted it and replicated it.

QUESTIONS

1 View the images (follow the reference link[2]) of the kind of facilities that Missouri is known for. How do they compare to your idea of youth detention facilities? Why might the differences matter?

2 Why do you think the Missouri Model might not be readily adopted in other states, despite its track record?

Notes

1. Mendel 2010

2. http://www.aecf.org/~/media/Pubs/Initiatives/Juvenile%20Detention%20Alternatives%20Initiative/MOModel/MO_Fullreport_webfinal.pdf

---

Massachusetts have reported better recidivism data than more traditional juvenile corrections systems.[50] Other summaries of a large number of different evaluations of juvenile corrections programs by Steve Aos, Peter Greenwood et al., and Mark Lipsey have consistently found far better results in programs that emphasize intensive home- or community-based services compared with the outcomes of locked programs.[51]

There is scant evidence that secure residential programs produce positive results in terms of reducing recidivism. A recent study by Canadian researchers showed that the more a youth penetrates the correctional system, especially in secure programs, the worse the long-term outcomes in terms of continued lawbreaking.[52] The Canadian authors speculate that the experience of juvenile confinement encourages vulnerable youth to take on a negative self-image and that the daily pressures of group residential living promote criminal behavior. As an emerging body of research, these studies suggest that juvenile corrections programs are not producing positive results commensurate with their substantial cost. Further, the consistent finding that youth who were locked up younger and who spent more time in juvenile corrections had the worst recidivism rates supports diversion and alternatives to incarceration for all but the most serious offenders.

Juvenile Corrections Fads

A century after New York's Elmira Reformatory pioneered military drill as a reformative technique, the idea reemerged in the late 1980s that correctional boot camps were a panacea for youth crime. The U.S. Congress and many other elected officials were captivated by the idea of boot camps and allocated tens of millions of dollars for juvenile and adult correctional camps. Some advocates argued that these programs would save money because they would require shorter lengths of stay in confinement than traditional training schools. Some thought that boot camps delivering harsh punishment would deter youthful offenders, and some thought that the tough discipline and physical exercise held the key to rehabilitation. Many other juvenile correctional leaders advocated instead for a counseling and education model.

Government-run boot camps were followed by the growth of privately run boot camps. Some of the private camps marketed their presumed reformative results to worried parents whose teens were rebellious, sexually promiscuous, abusing substances, or failing in schools. The boot camps made a compelling story that the media hyped and helped sell to a naïve public.

The problem was that these programs produced very few positive results. Most boot camps had no data on outcomes, and those that received independent review did not show impressive results in youth outcomes or cost-savings. A major analysis of delinquency programs conducted by the University of Maryland concluded that boot camps were largely ineffective in reducing recidivism.[53] Another study of "model boot camp" programs funded by the OJJDP showed that camps produced results no different than traditional juvenile correctional programs. Worse, the OJJDP research concluded that boot camps were often used for youth who otherwise would have received probation or less expensive sanctions.[54]

Far worse, boot camps seemed prone to tragedies. Although boot camps did not systematically collect data, deaths in boot camps occurred in Florida, Texas, South Dakota, and

At a New York correctional facility, a corrections officer checks an inmate's beard growth, which is strictly regulated.

© Mike Groll / Associated Press

Delinquency: An offense or misdeed, especially one committed by a minor. Habitual misconduct by a minor.

Nevada. Many reports surfaced of juvenile boot camps using excessive physical force and denying youth emergency medical attention. In Maryland, state boot camp employees broke the arms of a recalcitrant youth. Untrained boot camp staff, lacking clinical skills, attributed the behavior of mentally ill or medically infirm inmates to "malingering or playing possum."[55] Also, states sometimes sent youthful offenders to boot camps across state lines, without any effective regulation or oversight of those programs.

As we entered the 21st century, the boot camp fad began to lose some of its political support, and the federal government reduced funding for these programs. Boot camps still exist in many states, but they held less than 1% of youth in residential placement in 2011.[56] Lawsuits against public boot camps for injuries and wrongful deaths made juvenile courts more reluctant to utilize them in sentencing. For example, after the 2006 beating death of 14-year-old Martin Lee Anderson by staff in a Florida boot camp, the state stopped funding these programs. The case became a national news story because the assault was captured on videotape. A state coroner attempted to say that Anderson died of complications from sickle cell anemia, but a valid autopsy proved that Martin Anderson died from his beating. Later, an all-White jury acquitted all the staff involved in the attack.

Research continued to document the poor results of boot camps in stopping youthful lawbreaking. These primitive attempts to "scare" youth were endangering the lives of very vulnerable young people.[57]

Malinger: To fake an illness or other type of incapacitation to avoid work or school.

Wrongful death: A death that results from a wrongful act or from negligence. In the criminal justice system, the execution of an innocent person is a wrongful death.

▲ Aversion programs such as "Scared Straight" (though they may intuitively seem effective) are actually of dubious value.

© zuma/americasnine/Newscom

Related to the trend of expanding juvenile corrections boot camps were programs known as "Tough Love" and "Scared Straight." The logic of Tough Love was that placing juveniles in adult jails exerted rehabilitative effects. The proponents of the concept even argued that parents should encourage the incarceration of wayward youth. There was no research supporting these claims, but this theory dominated TV talk shows, as well as debates in legislative forums.

Scared Straight was a program that asserted that exposing low-level juvenile offenders to a prison visit would deter them from future criminality. Youth visited prisons in many states where they were taunted and threatened by hardened prisoners. The youth were told that if they came to prison, they would be raped and beaten by the older inmates. One version of Scared Straight at Rahway State Prison (now East Jersey State Prison) in New Jersey was made into an award-winning documentary, claiming dramatic crime reduction results. More careful social science research showed no positive results from Scared Straight and suggested that youth in these programs became even more delinquent.[58]

SUMMARY

The first juvenile facilities were founded by religious leaders and were meant to separate young people from adults, keeping them out of workhouses and jails. However, there was no judicial process put into place, and these first juvenile facilities were plagued with problems such as forced labor, abuse, and deplorable conditions. Government gradually became more involved in overseeing these troubled facilities. The model of the training school developed in Massachusetts and persisted into the late 1900s. After the revelation of scandals led to a series of reforms in Massachusetts by Dr. Jerome Miller, the movement for reducing youth prison populations in favor of smaller, community-based corrections approaches began to take hold.

However, a conservative political climate in the 1990s led to the weakening of reforms. Abuse, harsh conditions, and the resulting lawsuits plagued many states. Several states such as Florida, California, Texas, and Illinois turned the administration of state juvenile facilities over to prison officials—often with disastrous results. Litigation against juvenile justice agencies over the conditions and treatment of youth has become more frequent. There has also been an increase in lawsuits alleging that juvenile corrections systems are not providing adequate educational and mental health services to incarcerated children. These lawsuits have resulted in some limited improvements as well as higher costs, at least in the short term.

Current juvenile sanctions range widely across jurisdictions, as do juvenile correctional facilities in terms of their size, their type, and who runs them. Nonetheless, youth of color are disproportionately represented in juvenile corrections. The debate goes on over whether confinement of youth in juvenile facilities reduces or increases the likelihood of future criminal conduct. Recidivism rates among juveniles are difficult to measure and complex to interpret. However, research indicates high recidivism among youth. Youth advocates would like to see the Office of Juvenile Justice and Delinquency Prevention play a larger role in improving the conditions of juvenile corrections in terms of training in evidence-based practices, exposing dangerous conditions in juvenile corrections facilities, and routinely collecting data on recidivism and other juvenile justice outcomes.

DISCUSSION QUESTIONS

1. What are the similarities and differences between the early Houses of Refuge and current juvenile corrections practice?

2. Discuss the role of the federal government in regulating juvenile corrections.

3. What is the "superpredator" idea, and how has it shaped national and local policy?

4. Discuss what are, or might be, innovative approaches to juvenile delinquency prevention and intervention.

5. How should juvenile correctional policy and practice be different for girls and boys?

6. Discuss how juvenile corrections agencies could improve data collection.

7. Come up with five ideas for research studies that could help advance understanding of youth in custody.

8. Discuss a design for an alternative to detention that is likely to be effective.

KEY TERMS

Chemical and mechanical force, 184

Deinstitutionalization, 192

Delinquency, 200

House of Refuge, 179

Malinger, 201

Random sample, 198

Status offenses, 193

Training school, 181

Wrongful death, 201

NOTES

1. Mennel 1973; Pickett 1969
2. Friedman 1993; Rothman 1971
3. Center on Juvenile and Criminal Justice 2013
4. Mennel 1973
5. O'Connor 2001
6. Montgomery and Moore 2009
7. Polsky 1962
8. Bartollas and Miller 1997; Fisher 1961; Street, Vinter, and Perrow 1966
9. Wooden 1976
10. Miller 1998
11. Coates, Miller, and Ohlin 1978; Krisberg, Austin, and Steele 1991
12. Howell 1995
13. DiIulio 1995; Herrnstein and Murray 1994; Wilson 1992
14. Bilchik 1999
15. Krisberg 2003
16. Swanson 2007a
17. Swanson 2007b
18. Hurtibise 2002
19. Beck et al. 2013
20. Sedlack and McPherson 2010
21. Davis et al. 2008
22. Annie E. Casey Foundation 2013
23. Sickmund et al. 2013
24. Ibid.
25. Ibid.
26. Ibid.
27. Kyckelhahn 2012; Petteruti, Walsh, and Velázquez 2009
28. California Department of Corrections and Rehabilitation 2011
29. Sickmund et al. 2013
30. Hartney and Vuong 2009
31. Krisberg et al. 1995; National Council on Crime and Delinquency 2007
32. Krisberg 1993
33. Sickmund et al. 2013
34. Tappan 1948
35. Chesney-Lind 1997
36. Bishop and Frazier 1992; Chesney-Lind and Shelden 1992
37. Mayer 1994
38. Giallombardo 1974
39. Acoca and Dedel 1998
40. Krisberg 2009
41. Beck, Guerino, and Harrison 2010
42. Murray and Cox 1979
43. Rhine 1996
44. Austin et al. 1995
45. Tollett 1987
46. Goodstein and Sontheimer 1987
47. Krisberg et al. 1991
48. Austin et al. 1998
49. Haapanen 1988
50. Howell 1997; Krisberg 2005
51. Aos 2004; Greenwood et al. 1996; Lipsey 1992
52. Gatti, Tremblay, and Vitaro 2009

53. Sherman et al. 1997
54. Peters, Thomas, and Zamberlan 1997
55. Carlton 2007

56. Sickmund et al. 2013
57. Aos et al. 1999; Sherman et al. 1997
58. Finckenauer et al. 1999

$SAGE edge™

Sharpen your skills with SAGE edge at edge.sagepub.com/krisberg

SAGE edge for students provides a personalized approach to help you accomplish your coursework goals in an easy-to-use learning environment. This site includes action plans, mobile-friendly eFlashcards and web quizzes as well as web, audio, and video resources and links to SAGE journal articles.

The Corrections Workforce

1 To gain a sense of the scope of the kinds of jobs and roles included in the corrections workforce.

2 To be able to discuss how prisoners and staff alike must deal with some of the same kinds of pressures generated by the custody environment.

3 To grasp some of the important differences between working in custody situations and working in community corrections.

4 To become familiar with the demands of community corrections work from a surveillance perspective and from a rehabilitation perspective.

Corrections is a large industry in the United States and employs hundreds of thousands of individual workers. The work of corrections encompasses a wide array of roles, levels of responsibility, and job descriptions, depending on the specific context. Equally varied are the personality traits and skills sought in the hiring process as well as the reasons individuals pursue work in the corrections field.

This chapter focuses on the part of the corrections workforce that has the most direct contact with prisoners and correctional clients on probation or parole—corrections officers (guards), probation and parole officers, and the administrators who supervise them. These are the roles that are most distinctively related to the corrections field and make up the majority of correctional workers. There are, of course, many other jobs in corrections, including those that encompass treatment, programming, and other support services. Many of these jobs are covered by agencies outside of corrections departments. They nonetheless interact closely with staff and clients and have great importance to leadership. (See Chapters 4–7.)

One main subsector of the corrections workforce deals with prisoners in custody situations such as prisons, jails, camps, and other secure facilities. The other main subsector is composed of those who work in community corrections. Within each subsector, the "line staff" directly supervise inmates or clients, while others serve as administrators and top leadership.

Federal, state, and local agencies employ different personnel depending on such factors as agency size, facility location (urban or rural), racial diversity, and the location's socioeconomic profile.

Corrections work is difficult work. There are many challenges for all ranks and roles in the corrections arena. Recruiting and maintaining a high-quality workforce is a major challenge for administrators, particularly in the face of many social changes—more women and minorities in the workforce, constrained budgets, and union interests. Entry-level ranks have a steep learning curve as they try to orient to a job with many stresses, high expectations, and the potential for a variety of rewards. And service providers work under the challenges of secure environments, with people who are trying to deal with a multitude of personal and legal obstacles.

Corrections Work

Community Corrections

The workforce in community corrections—primarily probation and parole—varies in many significant ways from that in custody settings. A key distinction is that probation and parole are generally 9-to-5 operations. There may be occasional nighttime and weekend work, but community corrections work does not involve 24/7 surveillance and care.

 To gain an insight into the career paths, training, and requirements for employment that are typical in the corrections field.

 To understand the nature of the pressures on leadership to recruit and maintain a skilled and high-performing workforce, while fulfilling the agency mission and maintaining safety.

 To be able to discuss other stresses faced by correctional workers, such as gender or racial bias.

Community corrections is not responsible for directly clothing, feeding, educating, and providing for physical and mental health care, although all of these basic needs are important concerns for community supervision.

Probation. A probation department typically employs probation officers, unit supervisors, division directors, deputies, and a chief. In addition, larger departments have more staff for clerical, information technology, personnel, training, and other supporting duties. The larger departments have specialized supervision units for probationers, such as those convicted of gang offenses, domestic violence, sex offenses, DUIs, or drug offenses. Client caseloads may be distributed according to the risk level of the probationers. In any case, the more senior and experienced staff usually supervise the higher-risk, violent, or repeat offenders—those who pose the greatest threat to public safety.

Probation work is generally divided into investigation, which mainly occurs prior to sentencing, and supervision, which occurs after sentencing. The investigating probation officer compiles background information about the defendant prior to court for the benefit of the judge. This is called the presentence investigation (PSI). The PSI contains information about the defendant's criminal record, drug dependencies, physical and mental health status, employment and education status, and family situation, among other things. (See Chapter 5.)

EXAMPLE CONTENTS OF A PSI

Legal Information

- Juvenile record
- Adult record
- Probation/parole history
- Official version of offense
- Plea bargain
- Custody status
- Pending cases

Other social and personal Information

- Acceptance of responsibility
- Gang affiliation
- Background and ties to the community

- Substance abuse history
- Physical health
- Mental and emotional health
- Financial circumstances, ability to pay
- Employment history
- Education, vocational, and skill history
- Home investigation
- Victim-impact statement
- Marital history
- Military record
- Evaluative needs summary
- Defense summary
- Probation officer recommendations

After an individual is granted probation, the supervising probation officer works directly with the probationer during regular office and home visits, conducts risk assessments and reassessments, devises treatment plans, refers clients to services and tracks progress, logs interactions with clients, administers drug testing, and writes reports for the probation agency and the court. The probation officer also performs surveillance on clients, investigates potential violations of conditions of supervision, and appears in court to report on client successes and to address violations or new arrests.

Every department must strike its own balance between the supervisorial duties that a probation officer must perform and the support an officer can lend to help the probationer overcome his or her obstacles to a law-abiding life. Some departments stress a harder-line, law enforcement approach, and others put a greater emphasis on reducing recidivism and focusing on treatment and changing client behavior. A department's specific approach has a major impact on the work environment for the staff. However, individual temperament and outlook also affect the way a department's values are expressed within each officer–client relationship.

The approach that emphasizes social work over law enforcement involves a complex set of skills and work duties. It is challenging to understand the needs and strengths of probationers, to stay abreast of the programs and services available and choose the right ones for each client, and to take steps to work with clients in overcoming difficulties *before* recommending a return to custody.

Parole. Parole work is similar in many ways to probation; however, it differs in several significant ways. To begin with, parole officers generally handle higher-risk offenders who have spent time in prison. Because of the greater risk to public safety, parole officers usually have smaller caseloads, more frequent **contact standards**, and more stringent supervision goals. That said, many probation caseloads now involve higher-risk individuals as well and thus require the smaller caseloads and more frequent contact that is more common to parole.

As with probation, there is a balance between the law enforcement aspect of community supervision and providing treatment and programming to help clients change their lives. The emphasis of the department may be dictated to some extent by state policy. (See Chapter 5.)

Standards are changing in favor of a more rehabilitative or behavior-based model. In part due to budget constraints and the desire to move to a "smart on crime" approach, some parole departments require their officers to document the measures they have taken to assist and work with the client before resorting to a return to custody.[1]

Custody

Custody is a round-the-clock operation. It takes three shifts each day to staff all hours and all jobs. Routine duties, both daily and otherwise, are described in detail in the

◀ Probation and parole officers conducting a home visit for a parolee who had been incarcerated for domestic violence. The degree of trust between the officer and the client has a significant impact on the level of safety for officers in the field.

© Torsten Kjellstrand/The Oregonian /Landov

Contact standards: The prescribed frequency, location, purpose, and processes for meetings between probation or parole officers and their clients.

SPOTLIGHT

THE STANFORD EXPERIMENT

A 1971 experiment of human behavior that focused on captors and captives has become an infamous classic. The experiment took place at Stanford University, initiated by a professor named Philip Zimbardo, who characterized his hypothesis by asking, "What happens when you put good people in an evil place?"[1]

To illuminate the psychology of prison life, Zimbardo recruited a group of 24 average, healthy male undergraduates to participate in a simulation of a prison environment. The students were randomly divided into the roles of prisoners and guards. The "prisoners" were subjected to a surprise arrest, strip search, shackles, prisoner garb, and prisoner numbers—measures designed to dehumanize the subjects. They were dressed in hospital-like gowns with no underwear and had to wear stockings on their heads to simulate their heads being shaved.

The guard group was given only minimal instruction to do whatever was necessary to maintain control and order. These students wore khaki uniforms and mirrored sunglasses and carried whistles and billy clubs. Regular roll calls helped to familiarize each of the groups with how to behave in their new roles. As the days passed, the members of the two groups increasingly identified with their roles and took the potential danger as a more serious and realistic threat.

On the second day of the experiment, which originally was to run for two weeks, the prisoners mounted a revolt against the guards, who then took measures—which Zimbardo himself called "sadistic"—to regain control and stifle the rebellion. The guards turned fire extinguishers on the prisoners, took their clothes and beds away, and began to harass and intimidate them. They instigated these tactics, which they devised themselves, to confuse the prisoners and foment mistrust among them, effectively deflecting the aggression from themselves.

Even a group of visitors who came to see the "prisoners" in this simulated prison environment became unwitting partners in the experiment, complying with the arbitrary rules with which the guards confronted them.

To break the solidarity of the prisoner group, the guards allowed special privileges to some, restoring their previous

department's policies and procedures. Daily routines can be very regimented. The role that first comes to mind for most people when thinking of jail or prison is the guard. Historically, there have been numerous names for "guards" or "correctional officers." Researchers say that they refer to themselves in both ways.[2] Terms such as *watchman*, *keeper* (*keeper of the keys*, *brother's keeper*), and *guard* stress the custodial role. More recently, as the field has become more professionalized, the terms *prison official*, *correctional officer*, and *correctional worker* are used more commonly.

Jail. The typical duties of a correctional officer in a jail are primarily based on the safety and security of the public, inmates, and staff. During the day, jail staff are responsible for seeing to the basic needs of the inmates such as clothing, meals, exercise, and physical and mental health care. Officers must escort inmates to the mess hall, the canteen or commissary, medical appointments, family visits, phone calls, legal visits, and court appearances.

Night duties differ from daytime responsibilities. Night-shift duties place more emphasis on counting and surveillance. Officers walk the tier at night doing well-being checks on a regular basis, sometimes every hour or two. Mail, both personal and legal, is often distributed at night.

Some newer facilities are designed radially or with extensive video surveillance, allowing correctional officers to observe multiple cells and locations from one vantage point. This

comforts. The situation began to take a very real toll. After only three days, one of the prisoners began to show signs of severe emotional distress, with disorganized thinking, uncontrollable crying, and rage. Nevertheless, the guards escalated their intimidation tactics.

The lines between reality and experiment blurred to a dramatic point. Stressed prisoners forgot that they could decide to leave the experiment. The "prison" took on a life of its own, and the effect was startling to the experimenters. Guards increased their abuse at night when they thought that they were not being observed. Only one outside observer expressed a sense of moral outrage that, up to that point, nobody else had. Everyone directly involved felt powerless to intervene.

After only six days, Zimbardo was compelled to shut the experiment down. The conclusion was that, given the power differential between the two groups, even though it may be a sanctioned one, people tend to devolve into a base kind of behavior. A certain kind of corruption sets in and exerts an influence on otherwise law-abiding and self-respecting individuals.

Zimbardo was later quoted in a news story in response to the abuse of Iraqi prisoners: "It's not that we put bad apples in a good barrel. We put good apples in a bad barrel. The barrel corrupts anything that it touches."[2]

QUESTIONS

1   What does this experiment seem to say about human nature?

2   This experiment was noted when the news of the Abu Ghraib scandal surfaced. Discuss how these two situations are alike or different.

3   Discuss the implications for the potential for reform given the relative secrecy under which prisons operate and within which the correctional officer is responsible for maintaining ethical behavior.

Notes

1.   Zimbardo n.d.

2.   Schwartz 2004

---

arrangement translates into a significantly different means of keeping watch over prisoners, and therefore different job duties.

The officer's main responsibility is to maintain facility safety and security. At all times, officers are the first responders to situations that arise, such as inmate disputes, illnesses and injuries, fights, or other problems. Attempting to resolve conflicts between inmates before they become violent is a regular responsibility.

Jail staff also must contend with an important factor that is not present in prisons: Half or more of jail inmates are being held as they await trial. These inmates have not been convicted of the crime that put them behind bars; they are innocent until proven guilty. Although some of these defendants have previous records or were determined to be too dangerous to release, many are in custody because they cannot afford bail or failed to appear in court. Yet they may be housed with serious offenders and those already convicted and serving sentences. Others are in jail for noncriminal violations of probation conditions. The range of backgrounds and risk levels of jail inmates adds to the challenges that jail staff face.

As departments evolve and become more complex, so too do the duties of jail staff. Responsibilities have changed over time; many jail workers now spend more of their time than in the past writing reports, interpreting rules and policies, conducting investigations, and participating in inmate rehabilitation programming.

Prison. A large prison is almost like a small city—a microcosm of the larger society. A large prison has its own security force, food service, laundry, business office, health care facility, communications system, education department, and fire department. Some of these services may be contracted through local organizations, and some, like fire and emergency service, may be shared with the local government. Each of these functions employs specifically assigned staff. The roles are often so varied that many different unions may be represented within one prison environment.

Even the basic work in custody situations encompasses a wide variety of job responsibilities and roles, including yard officers, perimeter surveillance officers, work detail supervisors, school officers, and "block" officers (living quarters supervision). Each environment has its own challenges and demands of the correctional staff responsible for supervision.

Each job is associated with a different work environment, and each environment is characterized by a variety of factors. Perhaps the single most salient factor related to job description is the degree of contact the staff member has with prisoners. A yard officer works in close proximity to inmates, while a tower guard is in a relatively removed position. Generally, administrative positions entail much less direct contact with prisoners. In fact, those working in administrative positions may have more contact with family members of prisoners and the public than with the prisoners themselves.

Each role also entails a certain amount of structured activity. Such duties as work and school supervision have a fair amount of structure; the prisoners have specific behaviors to fulfill, as opposed to the relatively unstructured behavior of the prison yard.

▲ How much contact with inmates would you prefer if you were working as a correctional officer in a prison?

© Jim West imageBROKER/Newscom

The cellblock job assignment may be a very demanding one with tasks that include making rounds or monitoring inmate behavior, human services, and housekeeping duties.

> In the block my job is to keep the block running orderly and on schedule. Special things to do during the school week and others on weekends. Let them in and out on time, making regular accounts. Let those in coming from work. Give out medication. Lock them in and count again. Then let them out into the yard. All the while I have to handle all kinds of problems, personal, plumbing or electrical. I hand out newspapers and mail. I make check rounds to make sure there's no two in the cell. Let some in at seven o'clock and after eight o'clock let those in from the yard. Then I make the final count. There's call-outs and everything else in between. Anything can happen and always does.[3]

Service Providers and Treatment in Custody

There are numerous job opportunities for health care and treatment providers in the corrections system. Prisoners require the services of physicians, nurses, dentists, psychologists, psychiatrists, substance abuse specialists, and therapists skilled in approaches known to be effective in correctional settings, among others. When implemented as designed, approaches such as Multisystemic Therapy, Moral Reconation Therapy, and the Residential Drug Abuse Program appear to be highly reliable. Larger prison systems may employ their own treatment providers, while others may contract with existing community providers. In either case, maintaining healthy relationships and partnerships between administrators and staff is important to the quality and effectiveness of prisoner services and to the effectiveness and safety of the facility as a whole.

Often the goals of treatment and the goals of custody supervision seem to be at odds. It is not uncommon for custodial staff and treatment staff to view themselves in opposition with one another.

For example, if violence erupts in a facility, it usually goes on lockdown, which means that treatment and classes may be suspended. Such interruptions prove frustrating to the providers who are trying to make headway with prisoners. In addition, some contend that the custody environment is itself an obstacle to effective treatment. Providing treatment services in custody situations is indeed problematic; some even say that it cannot be accomplished at all in the prison environment due to an unavoidable element of coercion. However, on a daily basis, whether the dynamics between custodial and treatment staff constitute significant barriers to the agency mission depends in large part on the ability of leadership to promote a cooperative culture among all staff. One thing is certain: The need for services in custody and in community corrections is greater by far than the capacity of existing providers to meet them. There are many reasons for these limitations. Agencies are limited certainly by funding, but also by space and other practical considerations. In addition, attracting and keeping competent providers is a constant challenge.

Why Corrections Work?

Why do people choose corrections work as a profession? There are many reasons, of course. Among those reasons are job security, pay, benefits, and opportunities for advancement. Some people enter corrections work for less tangible benefits related to job satisfaction such as a desire to help people, to hold a position of authority, or to handle real responsibilities.

As in other sectors of the economy, skill and responsibility levels are usually directly linked to the level of pay and benefits. One of the appeals of entry-level corrections work is that, in many

Graduating corrections officers take their oath of office during a ceremony at the Alabama Department of Corrections Criminal Justice Training Center Auditorium in Selma. As in other professions, the oath is meant to be a solemn promise to uphold standards.

Source: ©Tamika Moore/AL. COM/Landov.

jurisdictions, it does not require more than a high school education, and the pay, job stability, and benefits can be more attractive than in other jobs with similar background requirements.

The educational requirements for corrections jobs may be in part spelled out in union contracts. In California, for example, the California Correctional Peace Officers Association (CCPOA) has played a significant role in determining hiring requirements, in some cases relaxing standards and making it easier for prison professionals and job candidates to meet those requirements.[4]

However, wages for corrections work vary widely. In some states and localities, the comparably low wage may be a distinct disadvantage, especially when a remote location, an onerous schedule, and stressful duties are added in. Other government agencies as well as other areas of criminal justice, such as law enforcement and the legal system, can appear more attractive to the prospective worker.

In addition, within the range of jobs available in corrections work, specific aspects may be attractive to some people and not to others, depending on personal preference. Workers and candidates alike weigh the degree of autonomy a job may entail, the amount and nature of contact with prisoners or clients, the level of risk involved, the degree of regimentation or tedium, and how the schedule fits with the individual's life outside of work.

Characteristics of the Corrections Workforce*

According to the 2010 U.S. Census, there were a total of 780,960 federal, state, or local correctional employees nationwide, including correctional officers (guards), probation and parole officers, administrators, and various treatment and support staff.[5]

---

*The payroll statistics in this section include all levels of full-time employees, including top administrators. For corrections and law enforcement, these statistics are not limited to sworn officers (e.g., prison guards) but include administrators, clerical and maintenance workers, some service and programming providers, and others. Thus these salaries do not precisely indicate what the average corrections officer earns, but can be used to roughly compare corrections workers salaries to salaries of other government workers and to broadly assess the relative importance policymakers place on corrections workers (as indicated by their pay rate) compared to other sectors.

State and Local Employees

Across all state and local governments in 2010, corrections employees represented approximately 4% of almost 20 million public employees. Average monthly earnings for full-time state or local corrections workers were $4,105, putting these employees at the lower end of the pay spectrum, below law enforcement ($5,297).[6]

The number of correctional employees relative to the state population gives us an idea of the emphasis each state places on correctional issues. The average rate across all states in 2010 was 24 corrections workers for every 10,000 state residents. The states with the lowest rates were Massachusetts (9), Maine and New Hampshire (14 each), Iowa and Rhode Island (15 each), and Hawaii, Illinois, Kentucky, Minnesota, North Dakota, and Vermont (17 each). The states with the highest rates were Wyoming (36), Delaware (32), Georgia and New Mexico (31 each), Louisiana and New York (30 each), Texas (29), and Alaska, Maryland, North Carolina, and Virginia (28 each).[7]

Federal Employees

In 2010, a very small proportion—approximately 1%—of federal government employees were corrections workers, 37,589 out of 3,007,938 (not including most military personnel).[8] Federal corrections workers earned an average of $5,755 per month, almost $1,000 less per month than federal law enforcement ($6,684).[9]

Total federal annual payroll costs for corrections in 2010 were approximately $2.6 billion. In comparison, the postal service accounted for $43.8 billion, law enforcement $14.6 billion, and parks and recreation $1.7 billion.[10]

Demographics. Up-to-date workforce demographic data are not generally available, but the profile of the typical correctional employee inside institutions in the mid 2000s was similar to that of other government or law enforcement agencies—namely, White,

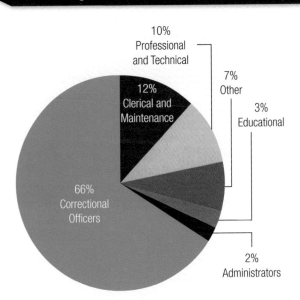

Figure 9.1   Percentage of Prison Employees by Occupation, 2005

10%
Professional
and Technical

7%
Other

3%
Educational

12%
Clerical and
Maintenance

66%
Correctional
Officers

2%
Administrators

Figure 9.1 shows that in 2005, two thirds (66%) of all (federal and state, public and private) prison employees were correctional officers, 12% were support staff, 10% were professional or technical workers, 3% provided educational services to inmates, and 2% were administrators.[11] *Source: Stephan 2000.*

SPOTLIGHT

THE CALIFORNIA CORRECTIONAL PEACE OFFICERS ASSOCIATION

In many states, correctional work is unionized, at either the local or state level, or both. Unions typically collectively bargain for wages, schedules, working conditions, vacations, and other benefits. In general, unions for workers in penal systems are similar to those in other sectors of the economy. However, in some states, the unions go farther in influencing correctional policy, which raises some interesting ethical questions.

The California Correctional Peace Officers Association (CCPOA) is widely recognized as one of the most influential and powerful prison guards unions in the nation. It offers a case study about the political strategy used to achieve this status and the ramifications of its unprecedented power.

Starting in the 1940s and for the following decades, the mission of California's prisons was to rehabilitate and reform prisoners and not just warehouse them. It was in this context that a new professional standard arose.

Instead of *prison*, the term *correctional institution* came into use, as did the term *treatment professional*.

Indeterminate sentencing was a key to the state's approach, which relied on the parole board to assess the progress toward rehabilitation in the case of each prisoner. When sentencing changed to a determinate model and removed discretion from the judges and parole board, the basis of rehabilitation was undermined, and the state began its long-term swing to becoming one of the most punitive systems in the nation, reliant primarily on incarceration as the dominant response to crime. Both conservatives and liberals were in favor of the determinate sentence, although for different reasons. Conservatives wanted the certainty of punishment as just deserts; liberals wanted insurance against the vagaries of judicial discretion. Truth in sentencing and three-strikes laws have underlined the tough-on-crime approach. According to observers, California's institutions became more "stark, depressing, and punitive."

This reliance on incarceration led to a prison building boom and a steep rise in the prison population, which grew from 25,000 to 260,000 between 1980 and 2000. This growth in the number of prisoners was good for the union. The CCPOA membership tripled in size from 1982 to 1992 (5,000–15,000) and then doubled in the next 10

---

non-Hispanic, mid-30s, high school graduate—according to an assessment from the American Correctional Association (ACA).[12]

Of the total number of people employed in state and federal correctional facilities in 2005, fully one third were women. However, among correctional officers and custody staff, who work directly with inmates, men outnumbered women three to one.[13]

It is important to note that the demographics of the nation are dynamic; the proportion of ethnic minorities is increasing relative to Whites. And women continue to participate in the workforce in increasing numbers. At the same time, the rate of participation in the workforce for White, non-Hispanic men is declining. Projections of the workforce by the Department of Labor estimate that, by 2016, only 15% of new workforce participants will be White, non-Hispanic men, and the rest will be women, ethnic minorities, and immigrants.[14]

In addition, the workforce is approaching retirement age, and a great deal of institutional knowledge could be at risk. On the other hand, a younger, more diverse workforce may help to usher in some much-needed innovation.

Along with the composition of the workforce, attitudes about job assignments and promotions are also changing. Assessments of the newer members of the workforce characterize their larger cultural values and suggest they are more likely to change jobs

years (to 30,000 in 2002). Consequently, the cost of the correctional system rose steeply as well.[1]

As part of its strategy to gain influence, the union became politically active by contributing to electoral campaigns—promoting the political players that shared their views and opposing those who did not. Over the years, the agency became progressively more astute and successful in its efforts to sway policy. As a result, the union gained direct access to the governor and, at times, was able to bypass the legislative process entirely.

Another rather brilliant political strategy of the union was to align itself with victims' groups—sympathetic partners that also came to have a powerful political voice. Together they have influenced policy of the corrections department and its personnel, at times to the detriment of institutions.[2]

For example, the union fought for and won more relaxed educational standards for officers and lucrative overtime policies. One could argue that the union's favoring of punitive segregation and prison growth is self-serving, antithetical to public safety, and unethical.

To the extent that its activities directly or indirectly contributed to the growth of California's prisons, the union has helped to create severely overcrowded facilities. The system attracted the attention of the U.S. Supreme Court, which declared its conditions "cruel and unusual," in violation of the Eighth Amendment. The court found that health services were impossible to deliver adequately, and one prisoner every week was dying unnecessarily. The crowding of the prisons has, at the same time, made the needed reforms nearly impossible.

QUESTIONS

1 Discuss the conflict of interest for prison guards being involved—through their union—in maintaining high incarceration rates.

2 Should a union be able to negotiate lower education requirements for employment in the department?

3 What is the appropriate way for prison unions to participate in electoral politics?

Notes

1. Page 2011
2. Ibid.

---

frequently, more resistant to authoritative management styles, and less likely to focus on work for their identity.[15] The willingness of workers to apply for promotions and to hold generally optimistic views on their chances for career advancement is considered to be an indicator of whether an agency has a healthy and open environment.

Correctional Staffing

Nationwide censuses of correctional agencies in the mid 2000s provide the most detailed portrait of federal and state workforce statistics available. In prison facilities under the jurisdiction of the states or the federal government in 2005, an estimated 445,055 prison employees served 1.4 million inmates in 1,821 facilities; 93% of these were employed by states, and 7% (31,289) were federal employees. Private prison companies employed 6% (26,911) of all prison employees. Males represented 66% (296,852) of all prison employees and 75% (295,261) of all corrections officers.[16]

The last nationwide jail census provides jail workforce statistics for 2006, with comparison numbers from 1999. In the US in 2006, approximately 234,000 full- and part-time jail employees served 762,003 inmates in 3,283 jail facilities.[17] As expected, most employees in the field of corrections are correctional officers.

The last national census of state parole agencies, from 2006, estimated that there were 67,900 parole employees, including 14,000 front-line parole officers, working in more than 2,200 individual offices or facilities. The majority (35) of the 52 state parole agencies responding to the 2006 survey were responsible for both parolees and probationers; their clients included a total of 661,000 parolees and 1.2 million probationers. Average caseload was 38, although individual caseloads could range from 20 to 150 or more.[18]

There were roughly 4,500 federal parole and probation officers in 2008.[19] That year there were approximately 23,000 individuals on federal probation and 91,000 on various types of federal parole.[20]

Inmate-to-Staff Ratios

The question of whether staffing levels are adequate for the job to be done is challenging for prison administrators. Adequate staffing levels are key to fulfilling the mission of correctional agencies and maintaining safe facilities.

Although there is no precise standard or "best" balance of inmates and facility staff in jails and prisons, inmate-to-staff ratios can illuminate how resources are distributed across job types within prison systems and give an idea of how relatively secure and safe the facility environment is for officers and inmates.

Inmate-to-staff ratios—and other workforce factors such as employee training, salaries, facility culture, and job stress—vary according to available resources, the security level of the facility, the risk level of its inmates, and the design of the facility—that is, whether facility planning incorporates current best practices and uses modern technologies. So, although privately run prisons have a higher inmate-to-staff ratio than public facilities, private facilities also tend to be more modern and to house inmates with the lowest security

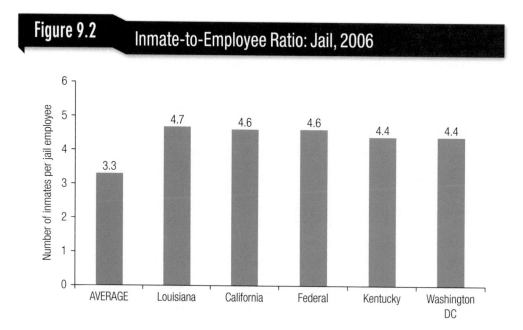

Figure 9.2 shows the number of inmates for each jail employee (not only correctional officers or guards) across the United States in 2006. The national average was 3.3, but the ratio was higher in several states and the District of Columbia. *Source: Stephan and Walsh 2011.*

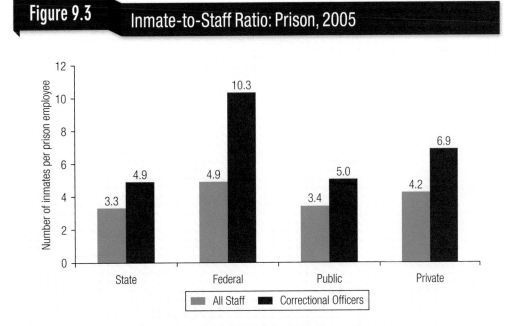

Figure 9.3   Inmate-to-Staff Ratio: Prison, 2005

Figure 9.3 shows two types of ratios for prisons in 2005—the number of inmates per prison employee (of all types) and the number of inmates per correctional officer. The ratio of inmates to correctional officers was highest for federal prisons (10.3) and privately operated prisons (6.9). *Source: Stephan 2008.*

level, factors that may make it feasible to run a facility with fewer staff members. However, federal prisons have the fewest employees per inmate but tend to hold more medium- and high-level inmates than public facilities.*

Education and Training

There are many pathways into careers in the corrections field. Some people have corrections as a career goal from early on. Those individuals may seek out a specific education at one of the many criminal justice programs that exist at the college level throughout the country. Other people find their way into corrections through another profession or a specialty that they have developed in a different segment of the economy; for instance, some who work in corrections began their careers in the military. Still others come into the corrections field by way of an entry-level position and work their way up the ranks.

Wendy Still, the chief adult probation officer of San Francisco, described her indirect path to her position. Although Chief Still had a long career in corrections, she began her professional life as a business specialist. Her expertise in fiscal matters and budgeting led her to work in a prison in need of that particular acumen. There she was impressed by the possibilities and knew she had found the arena where she wanted to devote her professional life.[21]

The specific kinds of skills required in corrections work vary a great deal depending on the role and the location. Required skills are determined by the jurisdiction and depend

---

*No obvious explanation for this finding lies in the prison census data, although facilities do tend to be more modern in the federal system than in the states. It is also likely that immigration detention facilities may influence these data, since such facilities, which are typically privately operated, account for a high proportion of federal inmates as well as a high proportion of facilities with conditions of confinement issues.

▲ John Jay College of Criminal Justice is one of the more renowned academic institutions in the field.

© Christian Science Monitor/ Getty Images

on the standards set by the administration of the agency or facility. As previously mentioned, specific background requirements for prospective staff must be balanced with the characteristics of the local workforce and the interests of the union, if there is one. Some departments require only a bachelor's degree or even a high school education or GED. Those tend to be in areas where more highly educated workers are harder to attract and harder to keep.

In some areas, the qualifications for probation work are high for the pay. In New York's probation department, for example, where rehabilitation is the overarching value, the preferred qualification for a trainee is a master's degree in social work plus relevant experience. The pay for such a job is relatively low for those requirements—approximately $40,000 per year.

Prisons, jails, and probation and parole departments located in the larger urban centers tend to draw more educated staff—and more progressive ideas about preventing recidivism and promoting rehabilitation.[22]

College Programs

Every state as well as the District of Columbia has schools that offer training in the field of criminal justice. Colleges, universities, or vocational programs offer certificates or undergraduate or graduate degrees in areas such as homeland security, private security, investigation, law enforcement administration, and **forensics**, among other subjects. In addition to working toward becoming a correctional officer or a probation or parole officer, students may be interested in these programs if they are studying law, law enforcement, **paralegal** work, private investigation, social work, advocacy, politics, or research.

Forensics: The use of science and technology to investigate and establish facts in criminal or civil courts of law.

Paralegal: A person trained to undertake and assist with legal work but not specifically qualified as an attorney.

The New York State Department of Corrections and Community Supervision Training Academy, as an example, is the state's primary institution for preparing workers for its correctional system. It offers a 12-month training program for entering recruits, ongoing training for current employees, and specialized training in areas such as firearms, chemical agents, and unarmed defensive tactics. Instruction consists of classroom time as well as on-the-job training.

On-the-Job Training

Regardless of the stated job descriptions and standards for qualifications and performance, corrections agencies are often struggling with leadership and budget constraints that impact the staff. In actuality, despite efforts to professionalize the role, corrections officers may be relatively poorly trained custodians.[23]

For entering recruits, the subjects covered in the primary training include facility functions, inmate behavior, and legal mandates. In particular, the following subjects are key training components:

- Practicing appropriate search and seizure techniques for contraband.
- Mastering techniques for armed (baton, chemical agent, etc.) and unarmed control of prisoners.
- Implementing inmate disciplinary protocol and due process.
- Completing accurate inmate counts.
- Following emergency and accident procedures.
- Using communications systems.
- Following grievance procedures.
- Receiving, classifying, transporting, and orienting inmates.
- Using restraint equipment appropriately.
- Handling keys, tools, equipment, and supplies.

In addition, custodial staff should learn about criminal law procedures, human relations, cultural sensitivity, special populations, physical education, and report writing.

Although conducted many years ago, research by Lucien Lombardo revealed that correctional staff have varied reactions to their training.[24] Some thought their training was valuable, while others considered it useless or even farcical. Some found regimentation to be an exercise designed to help new officers relate to the inmates they would supervise, while others considered the instruction a manipulative stress test. Some felt an increased sense of professionalism, while others found a disconnect between the stated goals and practices of the administrators of the training program.

Federal prison staff undergo 200 hours of on-the-job training. The Federal Bureau of Prisons sends its employees to the Federal Law Enforcement Training Center (FLETC) in Glynn County, Georgia, where they receive training in such subjects as control techniques, ethics, report writing, use of firearms, and self-defense.

The Correctional Hierarchy

Corrections departments and institutions are typically organized hierarchically. This hierarchy is usually referred to as "the chain of command" and in some cases clearly borrows from military structure and terminology. In both jails and prisons, the levels of personnel may be named officer, sergeant, lieutenant, captain, and commander.

SPOTLIGHT

PERFORMANCE-BASED STANDARDS

One problem in corrections administration is promotions that are driven by cronyism instead of performance. Using performance as the basis for staffing assumes a transparent approach to running an agency or a facility. These standards represent a way of identifying talented staff for promotion and a way out of the "good old boys" system.

Performance-based standards (PbS) provide a more equal playing field by using basic measurements that are applied to all staff performance and relied on for evaluations and promotions, and for assessing the general health of a department or facility. A performance-based approach allows for rational accountability and greater transparency.

In evaluating whole institutions, one key measure of performance quality is the number of assaults on staff. Others are revocation rates; the number of paroles, days of program closures, lockdowns, inmate appeals, employees on sick leave, workers' compensation claims, employee grievances, and assaults among inmates; and the leadership's capacity to enlist and utilize volunteers.

Jeanne Woodford served the California Department of Corrections and Rehabilitation (CDCR) from 2004 to 2006, both as director and as undersecretary. She had previously served for five years as warden of San Quentin, where she had worked for a total of 25 years. In her time at the CDCR, she attempted to adjust internal structures to increase equity for all employees. She organized the subdepartments by mission rather than region—for example, high-security facilities, women's facilities, and parole. Each subdepartment had its own policies and procedures.

This kind of organization helped to ensure that issues were addressed across the board and that no single subdepartment's issues dominated all of the conversations. This dynamic style of leadership calls on a management team whose meetings include budget, program, plant staff, attorneys, and labor so that each has a voice and a presence at the table.

QUESTIONS

1   Why should evaluation of facilities and those who work in them be based on performance?

2   What kind of indicators would you use to measure an individual officer's performance?

The higher levels in the chain of command have the least direct contact with the individual subjects of department supervision, be it jail inmates, prisoners, or probation clients. Leaders operate in an advisory capacity to the staff members they oversee. A part of the leader's job is to ensure that officers below them are qualified and trained to make the difficult everyday decisions that affect the lives of their charges while adhering to the department's policies and procedures. It is also the job of the leadership to ensure that facilities and agencies are succeeding in their mission and that both staff and clients are safe.

Drawing on the knowledge and skills of staff members, an administrator must make the best use of the collective abilities of personnel. Administrators who understand the issue of "fit" between job duties and the members of their workforce no doubt have better-functioning institutions. The best leaders generally attempt to build a workforce with a diversity of experience levels, gender, and race or ethnicity.

The warden or department chief and his or her deputies, based on applicable laws and the mandates of elected officials and the public, make the larger policy decisions, establish a direction for the department, set a tone for the kind of supervision the department will carry out, and decide how to allocate department resources. They handle issues with collaborating agencies, unions, the courts, elected officials, the media, and the public and hold all of the staff accountable for meeting the department's goals and challenges.

The correctional officer or prison guard is positioned hierarchically between the prison administration, which dictates the rules, and the prisoners, for whom the guards must enforce those rules. Policies and rules are directed from above, and guards must carry them out. Poorly communicated policy and procedure tend to cause confusion and stress for the in-between guards.

Sustaining a Workforce

Corrections administrators face many complex challenges in the management of their staff members. Attracting skilled and talented personnel, and keeping them and using them well, requires astute leadership. Some experts have predicted labor shortages in fields such as health care; corrections made the list as well.[25] In fact, many fields related to social science are thought to be competing for fewer highly qualified and motivated workers.

Recruiting

The current American economy is a dynamic marketplace, especially when it comes to the workforce. Leaders in every sector have a need to attract the most talented and reliable people possible to hire on as staff. In some local economies, corrections work may seem to be one of the more stable sectors; there seems to be no foreseeable end to the nation's reliance on incarceration, probation, and parole, even though some jurisdictions are actively seeking ways to rely less on incarceration and are adopting a "smart on crime" approach.

The top administrators of corrections agencies often describe difficulties—sometimes extreme ones—with respect to recruiting and retaining qualified staff members. A survey for the American Correctional Association revealed that more than 80% of the

◀ Specialized training in handling use-of-force incidents can decrease the likelihood of serious injury or death. The more officers know and feel confident about defusing dangerous situations safely, the better it is for officers and clients alike.

© Brendan Fitterer/ZUMApress/Newscom

SPOTLIGHT

CODE OF SILENCE

A long accepted cardinal rule among prison guards is that you stay quiet about fellow officers, even if it means withholding knowledge of brutality or corruption.

On one hand, this may seem a necessary "fraternal bond." On the other hand, it opens the door for abuse and cover-up. Whistle-blowers have tried to shed light on what is commonly known but never publicly admitted.[1] The deeply ingrained practice of staying silent makes it extremely hard for people who want to tell the truth about trouble in institutions; they are often subjected to retaliation.[2]

Euphemisms such as "The Green Wall" (which refers to a gang of officers at a California prison) indicate the behind-the-scenes awareness of a power block among the guards.

Good leadership attempts to prevent cliques from forming, knowing that this can lead to what is sometimes referred to as "stinkin' thinkin'"—a loss of perspective or ethical behavior due to peer pressure or groupthink. At its worst, this groupthink can lead to unethical or even criminal behavior, which is covered up and excused. The code of silence is a real phenomenon in prison work.

The *Madrid v. Gomez* case in California broke open the code of silence that allowed the perpetration of abuses in the now infamous Pelican Bay State Prison. One of the results of *Madrid* was that employee discipline became much more determinate, less capricious, and guided by a detailed matrix of behaviors and consequences to instill a higher level of consistency and fairness in curtailing inappropriate or even illegal behavior of correctional staff in the state system.[3]

QUESTIONS

1 What are the advantages and disadvantages of custody officers having a code of silence?

2 How should administrators of custody facilities guide officers with respect to the code of silence?

3 If you were a prison guard and you witnessed abuse, would you stay silent?

Notes

1. Arax 2004

2. Leonard and Faturechi 2011

3. *Madrid v. Gomez* 1995; Jeanne Woodford, personal communication, March 30, 2012

---

correctional administrators who responded felt challenged by this issue, with 25% of them describing recruiting as "extremely difficult."[26]

Shifting values and culture is prompting commensurate shifts in recruiting, hiring, and promoting practices in some departments. Some probation departments, for example, are changing their approach and training probation officers to see themselves as agents of behavior change more than surveillance. This shift in values requires recruiting practices that seek out individuals with not only education or experience, but the appropriate innate qualities and interpersonal skills, such as a greater capacity for warmth and empathy. During hiring, the interview process may emphasize identifying a job candidate's default reaction to a challenging situation, which might be assessed through role-playing scenarios. This approach to staff selection distinguishes a potential employee's innate abilities from those that can be learned.[27]

Staffing and Promotions

As mentioned above, the candidates for corrections in urban areas tend to have more years of college and postgraduate education. However, a degree, which also has high costs associated with it, is not necessarily tied to better performance. In poorly functioning departments, where rewards do not necessarily go to those who are most competent, a degree might be a hindrance; the reality is that leaders may not particularly like hiring others with more education than they have themselves. One of the ways of perpetuating the "good old boys" club is through promoting the status quo candidates rather than promoting according to talent and ability. It is also still the case that some leaders resist promoting women or people of color into positions of authority.[28]

A broad challenge of correctional leaders is to tap the strengths of the members of their staff in a way that supports the mission of the department. As in other industries, maintaining high morale among the staff is closely related to opportunities for increased responsibility and skill, along with better pay and benefits.

Job Assignments

Assigning jobs can be a complex matter. It has to do with skills, personality, employee preference, union regulations, seniority, and other considerations.

Again, the degree of contact with prisoners is an important factor in job assignment. For example, an officer who has a great deal of contact with prisoners will hear about and have to deal with many of the complaints or conflicts among the prisoners. This is a population that has big problems. For the person who is interested in being of assistance, who can balance the necessary empathy with a firm grasp of boundaries, this might be the preferable assignment. For others who might be more interested in the broader challenge of maintaining order and security, the perimeter patrol or guard tower duty might be the best position.

Another factor involved in job assignments is whether the workers are unionized or not unionized. Where unions function, job assignments are mostly made according to the seniority protocols laid out in the union contract. But where workers are not unionized, there may be more discretion on the part of management about which employee works which job.

Diversity

Managing more women and minorities in the correctional workforce is a challenge for the leaders who may not be familiar with their needs, behaviors, and culture. The future of corrections depends on the capacity of managers to engage workers of all kinds, regardless of age, gender, race, or ethnicity.

A key strategy in managing a diverse workforce is to promote the desired diversity at every level of the administrative hierarchy. Women leaders can better understand the concerns and culture of women in the ranks as well as the clients they serve. In addition, women and minorities in leadership positions can be role models for the rest of the staff. Training and promotion opportunities that address gender differences and cultural differences can only broaden the talent pool and enhance managerial capacity. This type of expansion can help support the structure of the whole agency. Conversely, a lack of managerial skill and adaptability can perpetuate the typical system failures: high rates of incidents and grievances, lack of efficiency and effectiveness, and high recidivism rates.

Women on Staff

Within the entire criminal justice system, the corrections arena has perhaps been the last and most resistant to welcoming women into the workforce. In general, women have been and still are concentrated largely in segments of the workforce that have lower pay, less authority, and fewer opportunities for advancement. Women have typically been subjected to gender bias in the form of less desirable work assignments, gender segregation, and sexual harassment.[29] In addition, the informal but highly important avenues for networking are often closed to women.

In 1972, the Civil Rights Act of 1964 was expanded to include Title VII, which covered equal employment opportunity. One result of these changes was that more women entered the corrections workforce. During the 1970s, 16 states allowed women to work in maximum-security prisons. Until that time, maximum security was seen as an exclusively male domain. By 1991, 45 states that responded to a National Institute of Corrections (NIC) survey about women employed in maximum security reported that women worked in at least one such facility. In half of those, women were eligible for all posts.[30]

The reality of women in the corrections workforce has been the topic of much discussion, and researchers have written a great deal on the subject. According to Cheeseman, Mullings, and Marquart, women in corrections tend to have particular strengths that lend themselves to the objectives of behavior change versus behavior control.[31] Women are more often communicative, collaborative, inclusive, empathetic, patient, willing to listen, able to multitask, and interested in relationships.[32]

Strategies that focus on rehabilitation, reentry success, and reducing recidivism rely to a greater degree on staff engaging with prisoners. Women often have more highly developed interpersonal skills, which are an asset in this context. For example, researchers found that prisoners are more likely to confide sensitive issues to a female staff member than to a male staff member.[33]

In addition, compared to men, women tend to offer a different style of leadership—one more focused on collaboration and empathy—that can help support a policy shift toward rehabilitation.[34]

If correctional practice is to evolve, the professional field needs to understand the issues specific to women in corrections jobs. As the number of women in the corrections workforce continues to grow, future research in this area will no doubt help advance the policies and practices of correctional agencies as they relate to women on staff.

Job Stress

Corrections workers share the same environment as the prisoners they keep. Prison and jail guards have the following wry adage: "We're all doing time, only guards do it eight hours at a shot."

▲ As in other traditionally male-dominated professions, women often have to outperform their male counterparts to be considered equals.

(C) Justin Merriman

IN THE COURTS

Martha Berndt et al. v. California Department of Corrections and Rehabilitation

C 03-3174 PJH1

A group of female prison guards filed this suit against the California Department of Corrections and Rehabilitation (CDCR), alleging that the agency failed to do anything to stop sexually harassing behavior on the part of inmates. The women claim that "inmate exhibitionist behavior including inmate indecent exposure, masturbation, and ejaculation" has occurred for years.[2] Not only has the department failed to intervene to curb the behavior, but it has acted in a retaliatory fashion to the women who have complained.

Marta Hastings said that officials at Pelican Bay State Prison not only ignored her complaints but also responded to them by transferring additional known exhibitionists into her unit. The chief deputy that ordered the transfer was a woman.

Sophia Curry was attacked in a Sacramento unit. An inmate threw her down some stairs, got her into a headlock, and tried to cut her with the top of a tin can. A subsequent search of the inmate's cell revealed sexually explicit drawings of Curry.

Another Sacramento guard who runs a treatment group alleged that inmates "constantly expose their genitals, and masturbate and ejaculate during such groups," despite the regulation that the inmates wear exposure-control jumpsuits. In all of these cases, the female guards alleged that prison administrators did nothing to address their concerns.[3]

These women, along with eight others, have attempted to press a class-action lawsuit; however, a class must pass legal certification standards by meeting specific criteria before the suit can go forward with the class as the plaintiff. In the case of the 11 women filing the suit against the CDCR, the judge ruled in March 2012 that the plaintiffs' differing claims failed to meet that standard. U.S. District Judge Phyllis Hamilton found that the plaintiffs had not exhausted administrative remedies and that there were problems with procedure, timing, and commonality. The trial could proceed only as an action brought by the individually named plaintiffs.[4]

Regardless of whether the women constitute a class for legal purposes, the core issue centers on whether female guards in a male prison should expect stricter behavior codes among the inmates and more support from the administration to hold inmates accountable for their behavior. Previously, a suit brought by a single guard who was fired from Pelican Bay after repeated complaints about sexually harassing inmate behavior (exposure and masturbation) ended in an award of $600,000. In 2008, the federal court upheld damages of $500,000 for lost wages and $100,000 for emotional distress. The court also maintained that a recent U.S. Supreme Court ruling that limited government employees' protection for criticizing conditions in the workplace did not apply in this case. The defendant, Deanna Freitag, complained repeatedly during the 1990s, when she was a guard at Pelican Bay State Prison, that prison officials did little or nothing to ensure prisoner discipline. According to news reports, Freitag lost her house after being fired.[5]

Notes

1. *Berndt et al. v. California Department of Corrections et al.* 2013
2. Dotinga 2012
3. Sherbert 2012
4. Dotinga 2012; Sherbert 2012
5. Egelko 2008

Overcrowding and Poor Conditions

Two related factors that can drastically increase the difficulty, stress, and danger involved in prison employment—not to mention imprisonment—are facility overcrowding and poor conditions of confinement for the inmates. In 2006, 8.8% of 2,860 jail jurisdictions were under a court order or consent decree to reduce overcrowding or to improve conditions of confinement. The conditions under scrutiny included staffing, health services, inmate programming, food service, exercise, and religious practice.[35]

Modern prison life is not just electronically controlled doors and video surveillance. It is real guns and, sometimes, hard labor.

© Don B. Stevenson / Alamy

In 2010, the prison systems in 19 states and the federal system were over capacity. The worst overcrowding was in Alabama (196% of capacity), Illinois (144%), Massachusetts (139%), the federal system (136%), North Dakota (136%), and Iowa (131%).[36]

In the same year, 9 of the 50 largest jail jurisdictions in the United States held more inmates than their facilities were designed to hold, with the highest overcrowding in Polk County, Florida (123%), Jacksonville City, Florida (122%), and Bernalillo County, New Mexico (121%).[37]

The Personal Toll

The risks associated with corrections work can have many negative effects on worker health. Stress constitutes one of these risks. Left untended, the effects of stress can have a significant impact on an individual's health, relationships, mental states, relationship to the job, and job performance. Though many experience these detrimental effects, the rank and file as well as management may be ill equipped to identify them and to reverse their negative impact.

In response to this problem, behavioral scientist Kevin Gilmartin analyzed an extremely common but often-unarticulated syndrome.[38] He also brought to light that the occupational hazards of corrections work can be mitigated.

Gilmartin's material has been well received across the nation and has no doubt helped hundreds, if not thousands, of police and corrections professionals reclaim control over their work and personal relationships and reinforce or reestablish a commitment to a high standard of professional conduct. He explains what is an all-too-common scenario among correctional workers. The unpredictable dangers of corrections (and police) work require a heightened awareness, which engages a basic instinct that psychology calls the "fight or flight" response. The exhaustion one feels from maintaining this state of alertness can leave an officer drained and unresponsive at the end of the shift, a condition that tends to worsen over time.

Correctional workers suffering this syndrome often become more alienated from their support system of family and friends. In the process, they may become overidentified with the job and the professional role. Having less and less connection to life outside of work can in turn lead to a resistance to any kind of change in work conditions (such as scheduling and assignments), resentment of management, a sense of entitlement, situational ethics, and unethical or even (worst-case scenario) illegal behavior.

Gilmartin contends that a key to finding one's way out of these woods is to cultivate life outside of the job, to attend to family relationships, hobbies, sports, and time with friends—normal areas of life that often come to be neglected in the life of the average correctional officer.

Progressive Developments in Leadership

Besides the major managerial issues discussed above, there are many others that challenge leadership. Whenever there is a high-profile case, leaders must deal with the media, do damage control, and safeguard the reputation of their agency. They must negotiate with union leaders and coordinate fiscal and personnel issues. They must also answer to the authorizing body, such as the state legislature. Discipline is a constant balancing act; administrators have to control the behavior of their staff as well as the behavior of the incarcerated. Staff performance and motivation may be one of the more psychologically demanding requirements of correctional leadership.

YOU DECIDE

Cross-Gender Staffing

The state prison does not permit women to be corrections officers in state facilities that hold male prisoners. Many male inmates claim that the women staff make them feel uncomfortable and compromise their privacy. They cite federal data about female staff in state prisons being responsible for sexually abusing male inmates. Corrections officers assert that women staff lack the strength and agility to manage larger male inmates and may be assaulted themselves. A female staff member was murdered by an inmate in a male facility before the state corrections department's gender policy was enacted.

Women staff claim that the policy limits their employment opportunities and promotions, because the number of positions in male facilities is far greater than in female facilities. They point out that women play major roles in policing and in the military. The female staff argue that, with proper staffing and training, women can be very effective in a correctional setting. They also argue that the policy violates state and federal laws against gender discrimination.

YOU DECIDE: **Do you overturn the policy of barring women from direct supervision of male inmates?**

Some of the most progressive leaders in correctional agencies are beginning to look at new ways to go beyond just managing their staff. Just as they want to encourage staff to look beyond the mere caretaking of prisoners or those under supervision in the community, leaders who are interested in promoting and improving the field realize that they have the position, authority, and opportunity to improve personnel policy and practice, institute more effective and humane ways of operating facilities, develop safer and healthier cultures, and create a more positive sense of morale among the staff as well as those in custody. The best leaders are the ones who see a higher purpose to their work and want to instill that aspiration in their entire staff. One corrections commissioner from Massachusetts expressed this value simply by saying, "Corrections staff should be the very best people prisoners encounter."[39]

Many of these changes are driven by fiscal considerations. The more progressive and effectiveness-minded leaders in jails, prisons, probation, and parole understand the necessity of becoming more efficient and making a tax dollar go farther. They also realize that approaches that maximize public safety and positive client outcomes are often far more cost-effective than traditional punitive strategies. Many departments are looking toward

reducing recidivism as their primary objective. Thus, in large part, the goal is to have fewer prisoners, defendants, and clients recycling through the system. A focus on reentry is the natural outgrowth of this shift in the corrections world. One could say that reentry has been the weak spot of the entire system—its "Achilles' heel." (See Chapter 7.)

There are other approaches that are intended to have a constructive effect on all parties. For example, restorative justice has the potential to transform the experience of incarceration for prisoners and guards alike. In her book *Dreams From the Monster Factory*, Sunny Schwartz describes implementing a program in the San Francisco jail called the Resolve to Stop the Violence Project or RSVP.[40] The program was designed for the most serious and violent offenders in jail. It focuses on the individuals accepting full responsibility for their actions and learning to confront the true feelings that lie behind their violence. The transformation that the RSVP program helped to bring about affected all of the people working in the jail as well as the prisoners themselves. Accepting responsibility gave the prisoners power to control their own behavior. The principles of restorative justice have the potential to bring about a transformation in the way corrections work is carried out and in the way the correctional workers relate to their jobs and the kind of satisfaction they derive from their work.

At the administrative level, leaders are increasingly interested in organizational culture change. There is a wealth of literature about assessing culture, engaging in self-reflection on strengths and weaknesses, motivating staff to improve performance, effectively communicating with all stakeholders, building effective teams, and using data to evaluate progress toward strategic goals. Much of this literature is being adapted for use in correctional agencies. The National Institute of Corrections has an in-depth and extensive series of tools and documents called the APEX Guidebook Series (Achieving Performance Excellence). This series is designed to help agencies negotiate the complex process of managing change.[41]

Again, some of these developments have to do with fiscal or legislative pressures. Whole agencies are under pressure to comply with Prison Rape Elimination Act (PREA) standards, for example. Achieving sexual safety in institutions is a complex undertaking, which requires nothing less than a change in the fundamental culture of the institution.

SUMMARY

Nationwide, the corrections workforce represents a significant portion of local, state, and federal workers, and includes the private sector. Among this workforce, there is a wide variety of roles and responsibilities. An important distinction is whether people work inside institutions, such as jails and prisons, or outside, in the community. Another key factor is the degree of direct contact a person may have with system-involved individuals. There are many reasons that people find corrections work attractive, such as job security and benefits, having a strong identity, and being of service. There are many stresses related to the job as well, such as physical danger, onerous bureaucracy, and monotony. Corrections administrators face many challenges in running agencies and in recruiting and maintaining a quality workforce, especially in times of budget constraints and with the changing demographics and culture of the national workforce. The more progressive leaders are finding ways to adapt and embrace organizational culture change, workforce diversity, and innovative approaches to rehabilitation.

DISCUSSION QUESTIONS

1. What is your view of the desirability of work as a correctional officer in a custody situation?

2. Discuss the issues that might be associated with inmate-to-staff ratios.

3. How much training and education should a probation officer have?

4. Describe how you would characterize high-quality prison leadership. Why would you describe it this way?

5. Do you think that corrections jobs are seen more favorably at a time when other traditional sectors of the economy are diminishing?

6. What do you think are the reasons for the difficulty of recruiting minority staff in rural areas?

7. Discuss the benefits or pitfalls for staff of emotional involvement with prisoners in custody or clients on a caseload.

8. Discuss the intersection of diversity, performance evaluation, and promotion.

9. What would you do to ensure a progressive environment if you were a prison warden? How would you involve and protect female staff? How would you protect the mental health of all staff?

KEY TERMS

Contact standards, 209 Forensics, 220 Paralegal, 220

NOTES

1. Jeanne Woodford, personal communication, March 30, 2012
2. Lombardo 1981
3. Quote of an interview with a guard, from Lombardo 1981, 39
4. Jeanne Woodford, personal communication, March 30, 2012
5. U.S. Census Bureau 2012a
6. Ibid.
7. Kyckelhahn and Martin 2013
8. Ibid.
9. U.S. Census Bureau 2012b
10. Ibid.
11. Workforce Associates 2004
12. Stephan 2008
13. Workforce Associates 2004
14. Ibid.
15. Stephan 2008
16. Stephan and Walsh 2011
17. Stephan 2008
18. Bonczar 2008

19. Reaves 2012

20. Glaze and Bonczar 2009

21. Wendy Still, personal communication, October 15, 2012

22. Jeanne Woodford, personal communication, March 30, 2012

23. Ibid.

24. Lombardo 1981

25. Workforce Associates 2004

26. Stinchcomb, McCampbell, and Layman 2006; Workforce Associates 2004

27. Woodford, Marchionna, and Delgado 2013

28. Jeanne Woodford, personal communication, March 30, 2012

29. Martin and Jurik 1996

30. NIC 1991

31. Cheeseman, Mullings, and Marquart 2001

32. Nink 2008

33. Cheeseman, Mullings, and Marquart 2001

34. Holland 2008

35. Stephan and Walsh 2011

36. Guerino, Harrison, and Sabol 2011

37. Minton 2011

38. Gilmartin 2002

39. Dennehy, as quoted in Vera Institute of Justice 2006, v

40. Schwartz 2009

41. NIC 2010 -2013

$SAGE edge™

Sharpen your skills with SAGE edge at edge.sagepub.com/krisberg

SAGE edge for students provides a personalized approach to help you accomplish your coursework goals in an easy-to-use learning environment. This site includes action plans, mobile-friendly eFlashcards and web quizzes as well as web, audio, and video resources and links to SAGE journal articles.

Critical Issues
and Policy
Questions

© REUTERS/ Eduardo Mun

10 Law and Corrections

LEARNING OBJECTIVES

1 To grasp the reasons that the corrections system must be held accountable and some of the obstacles to realizing that goal.

2 To be able to list and describe the main mechanisms for holding corrections accountable.

3 To understand the dilemma involved in establishing standards and accrediting institutions.

4 To gain an insight into how the courts work relative to corrections reforms and prisoner rights.

Noted corrections reformer Jerome Miller often observed that the history of corrections is a cycle of abuse and scandal, limited reform efforts, and then a return to abusive practices. The legacy of scandal and abuse in corrections systems has led to many efforts to regulate or control serious problems. These approaches include (1) appointing regulatory boards and commissions, (2) adopting professional standards, (3) litigating, and (4) passing legislation. In this chapter, we will review many of these efforts and discuss their limited successes.

Fundamentally, our jurisprudence on corrections is still rooted in the idea of the prisoner as "a slave of the state." Public opinion has never been very sympathetic to the plight of those who break the law and spend time behind bars. Furthermore, some academics and politicians have argued that harsh prison conditions serve to deter future criminal behavior among current or potential prisoners. Prisoners generally have little or no political power; an extremely small number of their grievances ever make it to a hearing in legislatures, the executive branch, or the courts. As long as the general public does not really know what goes on behind prison walls, it is difficult to build pressure for reform. These cases often go on for years, and the financial resources needed to successfully litigate cases in corrections law are substantial. Further, the courts have been very reluctant to overturn legislative or executive branch decisions, or to interfere in the operations of prisons and parole processes. Remedies can take years and even decades to be implemented.

In 2006, the Vera Institute of Justice released a report of findings from the Commission on Safety and Abuse in America's Prisons. The commission's purpose was to open up discussion of this clandestine and stigmatized corner of our society. In so doing, the hope was to promote a more enlightened and enlightening discussion and, ultimately, arrive at a healthier system for everyone. The commission made a compelling case for the reasons to pursue this goal:

> For all of the hard work and achievements of corrections professionals—most of which the public does not hear about—there is still too much violence in America's prisons and jails, too many facilities that are crowded to the breaking point, two little medical and mental health care, unnecessary use of solitary confinement and other forms of segregation, a desperate need for the kinds of productive activities that discourage violence and make rehabilitation possible, and a culture in many prisons and jails that pits staff against prisoners and management against staff. There is too little help and hope for the individuals we incarcerate and too little respect and support for the men and women who work in our prisons and jails.[1]

State Regulatory Bodies

During the Progressive Era, from the 1890s to the 1920s, a number of states created boards or commissions to examine correctional practices and to report serious problems to the governor and the legislature. Generally, these bodies consisted of the heads

 5 To be able to discuss some of the major relevant issues that have come before the courts.

6 To be able to list and describe some of the major pieces of federal legislation that pertain

to prisoners or individuals under community supervision in the past several decades.

of corrections departments and parole boards, other criminal justice professionals, and, in some instances, citizen advocates. There were efforts to align the terms of commission members to those of elected officials, to establish groups that were "above politics." This goal was rarely achieved in practice. Further, these oversight bodies had few resources for conducting independent inquiries and were almost always staffed by employees of corrections departments.

Although state regulatory bodies had a range of powers, most were advisory groups with limited legal authority. In some states, the board of corrections was given responsibility for selecting wardens and the director of the department of corrections. Usually, the prime activity of such oversight boards was to conduct periodic facility visits and to issue reports. In reality, they existed primarily to "rubber stamp" the operations of corrections officials.

Oversight boards still exist in many states, but most of these regulatory groups have lost influence. In other states, boards were deliberately eliminated or stripped of much of their authority. As lawsuits and judicial oversight became more common as a means of holding correctional systems accountable for their practices, regulatory boards became less relevant and further diminished in influence.

Professional Standards

Established in 1870, the National Prison Association was the first professional association in the field of corrections. The first head of the organization was former U.S. president Rutherford B. Hayes. By 1954, the name of the group had been changed to the American Correctional Association (ACA). The ACA adopted a set of values and principles designed to legitimize and raise standards for the profession of corrections. In 1907, the National Probation Association (later renamed the National Council on Crime and Delinquency) was established to promote the emerging professions of probation and parole. Both groups drafted model legislation and lobbied to enact higher standards for the education and training of correctional workers. Each group held annual meetings to disseminate information on best practices and the major challenges facing correctional systems.[2]

In the 1970s, the ACA launched a special program to accredit correctional agencies. The ACA established a series of standards and then offered itself as an organization that state and local governments could hire to conduct independent assessments of how well correctional institutions and programs were performing. Although the accreditation label was coveted, it was largely a voluntary system. The underlying logic of the accreditation process is to enhance professional practices through voluntary compliance and peer evaluation. Although professional standards lack the force of law, they often serve as benchmarks for regulating corrections. Further, the ACA standards are often cited in lawsuits that challenge existing correctional practices, and accreditation is often used by corrections departments defending themselves in court as justification of their practices. Other professions such as accounting, law, medicine, and financial services have used similar approaches—with very mixed results.

Critics of the ACA standards suggest that the accreditation process sometimes becomes too political. Prominent members of the ACA have attempted to soften the standards to allow their jurisdictions to pass accreditation. For example, the traditional ACA standards proposed the prohibition of placing minors in adult prisons and jails. As laws changed and more young people were sent to adult facilities, the ACA weakened its standards and defined circumstances under which it would be acceptable to hold children in adult facilities. Other segments of the correctional field complained that the ACA standards were too focused on prisons and that the accreditation process was less useful in evaluating juvenile

Accreditation: A formal process to certify competency, authority, or credibility.

facilities or community corrections programs. Further, because the ACA standards were designed to apply across the nation, their minimum salary and education requirements did not consider regional cost-of-living differences and allegedly disadvantaged the poorer states and rural facilities.

The ACA accreditation process became a major source of revenue for the organization. There were more allegations of conflicts of interest; critics claimed that accreditation was influenced by the amount of dues paid by certain ACA members. The ACA attempted to build a firewall between accreditation and the organization's financial health by establishing a separate entity to conduct accreditation audits.

Another concern has been that ACA standards are not based on neutral research on best practices. Many have observed that the ACA standards are primarily based on policies and procedures already in place in various areas.

Some argue that accreditation should rely more on performance as a measure of operational behavior and outcomes. In this way, the issue would not be limited to whether correctional systems *have written* policies on such issues as seclusion and isolation, but would include whether those policies are applied properly and whether the method and frequency of these practices fall within acceptable limits and standards. Performance-based Standards (PbS) attempt to measure *actual behaviors* in the correctional system and reduce complaints that ACA accreditation amounts to little more than a "paper audit." The adult corrections system has resisted the application of performance-based measures. However, because of funding and leadership from the federal Office of Juvenile Justice and Delinquency Prevention, a growing number of juvenile facilities are adopting performance measures that were developed by the Council of Juvenile Correctional Administrators. The standards outline a high level of functioning in the following areas of facility management: safety, security, order, health and mental health, programming, reintegration, and justice.[3]

A fundamental purpose of most professional standards is to codify contemporary practices. However, the accreditation process is not the most effective means of advancing humane, fair, and cost-effective policies and practices. Facilities that have been found in violation of various state or federal laws, including constitutional provisions of the Eighth Amendment against cruel and unusual punishment, have still been fully accredited by the ACA.

▲ Even though they are often developed and applied imprecisely, coherent standards must guide criminal justice policy and practice.

© iStockphoto.com/ belterz

Litigating in the Courts to Stop Abusive Practices

A great deal of effort on behalf of prisoners, parolees, and state agencies has played out in state and federal courtrooms across the nation. Although some of these efforts have led to significant and meaningful changes, the judicial arena has proven to be largely a limited and uncertain route to corrections reform. Some of the most relevant cases offer a look into the social challenge of delineating the responsibilities of prisons and the rights of prisoners.

Eighth Amendment: Excessive bail shall not be required, nor excessive fines imposed, nor cruel and unusual punishments inflicted.

YOU DECIDE

Opting Out of Federal Legislation

Congress has passed a law intended to reduce sexual misconduct and assaults on inmates. The Prison Rape Elimination Act (PREA) was enacted with broad bipartisan support. Corrections officials do not defend sexual abuse of inmates, but they claim that the problems are being exaggerated and that a new set of stringent federal rules will greatly increase the costs of incarceration. Some in corrections argue that most sexual conduct in prisons is consensual and that corrections officials should not get involved. Correctional officers argue that the new law implicates them in sexual misconduct and harms their professional reputations.

There are also specific requirements under PREA covering the protection and treatment of lesbian, gay, bisexual, transgender, and questioning (LGBTQ) inmates. Failure to meet the federal guidelines could result in the loss of grant funding and potential litigation by inmates. In at least four states, corrections officers have faced criminal indictments for alleged sexual abuse of inmates.

The governor wants to "opt out" of PREA and to refuse any federal funding that might require the state to change its policies and procedures related to transgender or LGBTQ convicts. Public opinion polls suggest that state voters are not sympathetic to inmates who claim to be victims of sexual misconduct by other inmates.

YOU DECIDE: **As a legislator, do you support the governor or vote to comply with the federal law?**

Starting with the rise of the civil rights movement of the 1950s and 1960s, prisoners began using the courts more frequently to find relief from their grievances. This marked rise in litigation led to a great deal of attention. Some found this surge of legal activity to be alarming. They attributed it to prisoners having a strong sense of entitlement and therefore too much power. They claimed that prisoners were trying to retry their cases, that they were filing frivolous lawsuits and clogging up the courts, and that these actions undermined the justice system. However, these judgments were not a result of careful evaluation. The counterarguments were that the number of prisoners eligible to file petitions rose in part as a result of the rise of the sheer number of prisoners. These discussions also failed to consider the variations in the types of suits filed, the motivations of the prisoners filing the suits, and state law.[4]

After decades of appeals, many of which reached the U.S. Supreme Court, and many of which failed in the eyes of prisoners and their advocates, other means of seeking justice for prisoners became more prominent. Parties on both sides of these arguments have used federal legislation to bring their version of balance to the situation. Prisoner advocates seek to expand civil rights for persons under supervision, and their opponents push federal law to limit those rights.

The Imprisoned as a Slave

Consider the Thirteenth Amendment to the U.S. Constitution, which ended slavery—in theory. Section 1 of the 1864 amendment reads, "Neither slavery or involuntary servitude except as punishment for crime whereof the party shall have been duly convicted shall exist in the United States nor any place subject to their jurisdiction."[5] On the other hand, other amendments do not specifically exclude convicted felons. The Eighth Amendment outlaws, for all citizens, "cruel and unusual punishments." This ambiguity of constitutional protection has played out in a series of judicial decisions that sometimes advance correctional reforms and other times oppose more rights for inmates. Two early cases exemplify this pattern.

Typical of the more restrictive approach was *Ruffin v. Commonwealth*, which was decided by the Virginia Supreme Court.[6] This case involved an inmate who was contracted out by a private company to do railroad construction work. The prisoner murdered an employee of the Chesapeake and Ohio Railway who was acting as a guard. The inmate petitioned to be tried in the county in which the crime had occurred, but the state of Virginia wanted him tried in the state capitol. The court held that the Virginia Bill of Rights was applicable to "the society of freemen" and not to convicted felons. The court pronounced that the convicted criminal had not only lost his liberty but was, during the term of imprisonment, a "slave of the State" and was subject to whatever laws applied to the

Petition: A formal application made to a court in writing that requests action on a certain matter.

status of penal servitude. The prisoner's legal status was defined as civil death, and his estate was to be administered as that of a dead man.[7]

Habeas Corpus

It was not until 70 years later in 1941 that the U.S. Supreme Court in *Ex Parte Hull* ruled that prisoners could not be prevented from filing writs of habeas corpus before the federal courts.[8] The right to file a writ of habeas corpus prohibits the confinement of persons without any cause. This had been a core tenet of legal rights in British law since the Magna Carta in 1215. However, prior to the *Hull* case, the state of Michigan allowed wardens of its prisons wide latitude to deny inmates the right to file petitions. In *Hull*, a prisoner challenged a prison regulation that gave prison officials discretion over whether a prisoner could file a writ of habeas corpus. The prisoner petitioned the court after prison officials refused to allow him to file such a writ. The U.S. Supreme Court invalidated the prison regulation that required inmates to submit petitions to the institutional welfare office and to the legal investigator of the parole board, finding that "the state and its officers may not abridge or impair petitioner's right to apply to a federal court for a writ of habeas corpus."[9] However, the court did not agree to the temporary release of the inmate subject to the resolution of the writ, nor did it agree that prisoners had a right to legal representation. The core finding was that only the courts could decide on the appropriateness of the petition and that corrections officials could not preempt the authority of the federal courts.

Writ: A court order.

Magna Carta: A document that set out a series of laws establishing the rights of the English nobility and limiting the authority of the throne, signed in 1215.

Cruel and Unusual Punishment

In later cases, the U.S. Supreme Court continued to expand rights to inmates on a very limited basis.

Cases challenging the Eighth Amendment have considered the treatment of prisoners and conditions of their confinement. In 1981, the Supreme Court found in *Rhodes v. Chapman* that "double celling" inmates was not per se cruel and unusual punishment.[10] The Southern Ohio Correctional Facility, a maximum-security prison, had been operating at 38% over its design capacity, and in some cases two inmates shared a 6-foot-by-10-foot cell. Inmates spent most of their day in these cells, and this living condition was not a temporary situation. The federal district court held that these conditions constituted cruel and unusual punishment in violation of the Eighth Amendment, but the Supreme Court disagreed, finding that the double celling of inmates did not violate the Constitution's ban on cruel and unusual punishment. The Supreme Court held that there must be "unnecessary and wanton infliction of pain," including those practices that were "totally without penological justification" or "grossly disproportionate to the severity of crimes that produced the imprisonment."[11]

▲ Few cases make it as far as the Supreme Court, which continues to define the limits of constitutionality.

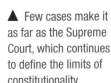

© iStockphoto.com/ nashvilledino2

In other cases, such as *Estelle v. Gamble* and *Hutto v. Finney*, the court found that deliberate indifference to the provision of medical care or "minimum civilized measures of life's necessities" might singly or in combination violate the Eighth Amendment.[12]

SPOTLIGHT

CONSTITUTIONAL AMENDMENTS

THE BILL OF RIGHTS

There are 27 amendments to the U.S. Constitution; they pertain to citizens' rights, the structure of government, the federal courts, and the powers of the states. The original intent of the Bill of Rights, which comprises the first 10 constitutional amendments, was to prevent Congress from abusing its authority.

The First Amendment protects the freedoms of religion, press, speech, assembly, and petition to the government.

The Second Amendment guarantees the people's right to bear arms and form a militia.

The Third Amendment prevents the housing of military troops in civilian homes without consent.

The Fourth Amendment guards against illegal searches and seizures.

The Fifth Amendment protects the rights of the accused and establishes a prohibition on self-incrimination.

The Sixth Amendment guarantees a speedy criminal trial, legal counsel, and witnesses in court.

The Miranda advisement was the result of a 1966 Supreme Court ruling. Miranda is well known from popular culture. It pertains to the Fifth and Sixth Amendment rights: remaining silent and the right to an attorney.

In *Estelle v. Gamble*, a Texas prisoner filed a civil rights complaint against several prison officials, claiming that the officials failed to provide adequate medical care after he was injured while performing a prison work assignment. In the majority opinion, Justice Marshall held that deliberate indifference to a prisoner's medical problems could be enough to constitute cruel and unusual punishment in violation of the Eighth Amendment. The prisoner's case was remanded, however, because the court found that he had been seen and treated by prison medical staff 17 times within three months, which did not establish a case of action against the physician.

In *Hutto v. Finney*, the court heard claims by Arkansas prison inmates that prison conditions violated the Eighth Amendment's prohibition against cruel and unusual punishment. The district court had characterized the typical conditions present in a prison in Arkansas as "a dark and evil world completely alien to the free world," including intense physical labor, fear of prison rape, and punishments that included electrical shocks.[13] The Supreme Court upheld the district court's decision to include a 30-day limit on isolation sentences to correct constitutional violations. The court held that lower courts may consider the severity of violations in assessing the constitutionality of conditions in isolation cells. The standard required a consideration of the totality of circumstances before court intervention was justified. In *Rhodes v. Chapman*, the court also warned against the judiciary imposing its own standards rather than adhering to the constitutional definition of cruel and unusual punishment.[14]

In a case involving a transsexual inmate awaiting gender-altering surgery, the court in *Farmer v. Brennan, Warden et al.* found that, for practices to be considered violations of the Eighth Amendment, it had to be shown that corrections officials possessed specific knowledge that the inmate faced substantial risk of serious harm and that the officials disregarded the risk.[15] The prisoner, who was being transferred to a maximum-security

The Seventh Amendment guarantees a trial by jury in civil cases.

The Eighth Amendment protects against cruel and unusual punishment or excessive bail.

The Ninth Amendment clarifies that rights should be protected, even if they are not specified by the previous amendments.

The Tenth Amendment establishes that the states or the people reserve those powers not granted to the federal government nor prohibited to the state.

RECONSTRUCTION AMENDMENTS

These three amendments were adopted after the end of the Civil War. The concepts of protection encompassed by the Bill of Rights had to be adjusted after the abolition of slavery to codify the nation's basic rights for the newly freed population.

The Thirteenth Amendment is the first of the three; it abolishes slavery.

The Fourteenth Amendment was adopted in 1868. The amendment has a citizenship clause, a due process clause, and an equal protection clause. The first clause affirms that citizenship is based on birth or naturalization and that the states cannot abridge the rights of citizenship. This clause overruled the U.S. Supreme Court *Dred Scott* decision of 1857 that Black people were not and could not be citizens of the United States.

The Fifteenth Amendment is the third reconstruction amendment and prohibits the states from denying a citizen the right to vote based on "race, color, or previous condition of servitude."

facility, accused prison officials of being deliberately indifferent about his safety by putting him into the general prison population. The prisoner argued that officials violated the Eighth Amendment by failing to protect him from being harmed by other prisoners, even though the officials knew that the facility had a history of inmate assaults and that the prisoner's transgender status made him particularly vulnerable. In an opinion by Justice Souter, the court found that prison officials could be held liable if they knew an inmate faced a substantial risk of serious harm and failed to take reasonable steps to protect the inmate by acting with "deliberate indifference" to inmate health or safety.[16]

Extending Due Process Rights

Other cases weighed the potential violations of the Fourth, Fifth, and Fourteenth Amendments. In *Wolff v. McDonnell*, the court held that prisoners were entitled to limited due process protections in prison disciplinary practices.[17] The suit stemmed from a civil rights challenge by prisoners held in the Nebraska Penal and Correctional Complex in Lincoln. The court found that inmates were entitled to written charges, a notice of the hearing, and the right to present witnesses and evidence before an impartial body. These protections stopped short of extending the right to cross-examine witnesses or to be represented by a lawyer. Prisoners were required to be given a written description of the outcome of the hearing. In *Wolff v. McDonnell*, the court made clear that the law required an accommodation of these due process protections, with respect to the reasonable needs of correctional administration, and did not require a specific standard of evidence to support the fact finder's decision.

Two important cases related to individuals under community supervision are *Morrissey v. Brewer* and *Gagnon v. Scarpelli*.[18] These cases extended limited due process rights to parolees who were facing revocation of their parole and potential imprisonment. These

Fourteenth Amendment: Section 1: "All persons born or naturalized in the United States, and subject to the jurisdiction thereof, are citizens of the United States and of the state wherein they reside. No state shall make or enforce any law which shall abridge the privileges or immunities of citizens of the United States; nor shall any state deprive any person of life, liberty, or property, without due process of law; nor deny to any person within its jurisdiction the equal protection of the laws."

Fact finder: In a trial of a lawsuit or criminal prosecution, the jury or judge (if there is no jury) decides if facts have been proven. Also called a finder of fact.

▲ Prisoners typically have few possessions and little room for them. The court must frequently decide the limit between appropriate punishment and what constitutes cruel and unusual.

© Spaces Images / Alamy

cases provided for some prior notice of hearings, a written statement of the charges, the right to confront evidence against oneself, and the right to be present and (in *Gagnon*) to be represented by counsel. However, the court was clear that these were minimal standards that were not intended to disrupt the "flexible" nature of the revocation process. Further, the court made clear that it did not want to rewrite the parole laws of the states and intended to give deference to local parole processes.

Extending due process protections to convicts has not been a priority of the U.S. Supreme Court. In *Hudson v. Palmer*, the court held that the Fourth Amendment protections against unreasonable search and seizure stopped at the prison wall.[19] In *Hudson v. Palmer*, an inmate at a Virginia prison filed suit against a prison officer, accusing that the officer performed an unreasonable search of the inmate's cell. The inmate alleged that the officer violated the inmate's Fourteenth Amendment right not to be deprived of property without due process of law. The court held that the prisoner had no reasonable expectation of privacy in his prison cell. It justified its decision by examining the objectives of prison, finding that "it would be impossible to accomplish the prison objectives of preventing the introduction of weapons, drugs, and other contraband into the premises if inmates retained a right of privacy in their cells."[20] The court also concluded that "prison officials must be free to seize from cells any articles which, in their view, disserve legitimate institutional interests."[21]

In another case involving the extent to which due process protections applied to prison disciplinary hearings, the court held that there needed to be "some evidence," although the threshold of sufficient evidence could be very meager. In *Superintendent v. Hill*, inmates filed suit, claiming that evidence used against them at prison parole hearings did not rise to the constitutional standard supported by the Fourth Amendment.[22] Two prisoners in Massachusetts filed suit after a prison disciplinary board revoked good-time credits based on testimony and a written report of a correctional officer. The prisoners argued that the board's decision—based only on scant evidence—violated due process. The court found that when there is a protected liberty interest, a decision to take away liberty must be supported by some evidence. However, the court also held that an examination of the "some evidence" standard in a case required only a limited review.[23] For example, a court is not required to review the entire record, to independently assess the credibility of a witness, or to weigh the evidence, concluding that the "revocation of good time credits is not comparable to a criminal conviction."[24]

In *Greenholtz v. Nebraska Penal Inmates*, the court said the state provision for the possibility of parole is not a guarantee of a fair parole hearing.[25] In this case, the suit was against the parole board. Chief Justice Burger made clear that the court was not inclined to second-guess parole board decisions. This decision rests, in part, on a traditional notion that parole is part of a rehabilitation process and therefore should not be overly structured by due process considerations. It is, at least, arguable that parole has never been primarily part of a treatment philosophy in prisons. Parole boards have often been seen as making very politicized decisions in individual cases. Parole has more recently evolved in several states as mandatory postrelease surveillance with little or no reentry services; the rationale of the court in this case is thus even more tenuous. (See Chapter 7.)

A prison official shows a collection of confiscated knives, spears, and points. Inmate and staff safety is a significant concern in every facility.

© John Burgess/ZUMA Press/ Newscom

Conditions of Confinement

Litigation in California in the 1990s illustrated the genuine limits of the judiciary to fix horrid prison conditions. In *Madrid v. Gomez*, the district court was made aware via inmate letters of horrendous examples of abuse of inmates by corrections officers—especially extreme isolation and lack of basic mental health services at a supermax prison at Pelican Bay.[26] The district court decision described a "conspiracy of silence" among the officers. The district court, however, treads carefully on regulating prison operations and in this case did not limit the use of the extreme segregation unit except for mentally ill inmates.

In other California cases involving the provision of health care, mental health services, and accommodations for disabled inmates, the District Court attempted to achieve compliance with its orders or with consent decrees, with limited results. In cases such as *Plata, Coleman v. Wilson, Armstrong v. Wilson*, and *Clark v. California*, federal judges have wrestled with a range of strategies to hold the California Department of Corrections and Rehabilitation (CDCR) accountable to constitutional and statutory standards.[27] These efforts have included the appointment of special masters and designated court experts, threats of contempt orders, and, in the case of medical care, placing the health care system of the CDCR under the absolute authority of a court-appointed receiver. None of these enforcement strategies has produced more than modest reforms.

These and other cases reveal a pattern; the U.S. Supreme Court has been very reluctant to apply constitutional protections in the prison setting. Even in cases in which modest rights *were* advanced, the court almost always deferred to the judgment of prison officials. In sum, the judicial avenue to prison reform and accountability has proven to be a narrow and precarious roadway.

Legislating Reforms

During recent decades, several correctional reform efforts have coalesced into the passage of federal legislation. As with court battles, some of this legislation expands the civil rights of prisoners, and some of it curtails those rights. (See Chapter 13.)

Special master: A representative of the court appointed to hear a case involving difficult or specialized issues; an expert whose expertise assists the court or who may help administer a claim.

Receiver: A person or entity authorized as a custodian for an agency (or business) when that agency fails to meet its mandated or financial obligations—considered a remedy of last resort.

An interior courtyard at Pelican Bay prison in Crescent City, California. The prison is used to house the most dangerous inmates in the state and has been the subject of close scrutiny by a federal judge for more than a decade.

© REUTERS/ STR New

The Civil Rights of Institutionalized Persons Act

In 1980, the U.S. Congress passed and signed into law the Civil Rights of Institutionalized Persons Act (CRIPA).[28] This law gave power to the U.S. Department of Justice (USDOJ) Civil Rights Division to bring actions against state or local governments for violating the civil rights of persons housed in publicly operated facilities including prisons and jails, juvenile facilities, mental health institutions, and facilities for the disabled or the elderly. CRIPA does not authorize enforcement on behalf of individuals, but it empowers the USDOJ to remedy systemic violations of rights. CRIPA did not create any new rights but instructed the U.S. attorney general to litigate based on previously established constitutional or statutory rights of confined persons. To carry out this mandate, the USDOJ relies on information from parents of inmates, news reports, community advocates, facility employees, and letters from prisoners. The Civil Rights Division determines if the facility is a public institution and then reviews all allegations or complaints to decide whether to go further. The next step is to initiate an investigation that usually includes a tour of the facility and interviews with impacted youth or adults. If the Civil Rights Division determines that there is a pattern or practice of civil rights violations, it will issue a "findings letter." The findings letter details the violations, provides the supporting evidence for the USDOJ conclusions, and specifies the minimum steps required to rectify the civil rights violations. Next, state and local officials meet to discuss the best resolution of the problems. CRIPA establishes a period of time for negotiation and the opportunity for the unit of state or local government to resolve the violations in a voluntary manner. It also explicitly attempts to avoid undue involvement of the federal judiciary.

To meet the CRIPA standards for action, the violations must be deemed (1) egregious or flagrant violations that harm the institutionalized persons and (2) a pattern or practice of civil rights violations.

The largest number of CRIPA interventions are resolved via settlements and consent decrees that are court-endorsed agreements among the parties. Once this happens, the Civil Rights Division monitors compliance with the agreement through onsite inspections and regular status reports. If the desired level of compliance is not achieved, the USDOJ will return to court to seek further legal relief or enforcement of the agreement or consent decree.

Since the passage of CRIPA, hundreds of facilities have been subject to CRIPA investigations in 39 states, the District of Columbia, and U.S. territories, affecting tens of thousands of residents. Some of the findings revealed life-threatening conditions. Specific areas of investigation include abuse and neglect, sexual victimization, inadequate education, and unmet mental health needs.

CRIPA investigations have been especially helpful in stopping abusive practices in juvenile facilities, reducing harm to institutionalized women, and protecting disabled adults and children. As we will see below, other federal legislation has made class-action litigation on behalf of institutionalized persons much more difficult. Thus, CRIPA and the USDOJ Civil Rights Division have played a vital role in holding corrections systems accountable to minimum standards of decency.

Prison Litigation Reform Act of 1995

Despite the very limited judicial role in remedying prison abuses, the perception nonetheless persists that federal courts micromanage prisons and that judges "coddle" criminals. In a few states, including Texas, Alabama, Arkansas, and Louisiana, federal judges did respond to inmate requests to be protected from Eighth Amendment violations. Conservative politicians seized on one of their favorite themes that "activist judges" were usurping the right of the people to demand punishments that fit the crimes. These politicians also promoted the myth that hundreds of inmates were filing frivolous lawsuits against their captors. For example, Senate Republican leader Robert Dole announced during an early debate on the Prison Litigation Reform Act (PLRA), "This amendment will help put an end to inmate litigation fun and games."[29]

It is critical that lawmakers be adequately and accurately informed to make appropriate decisions in Washington.

Sample "Findings Letter."

Source: U.S. Department of Justice, http://www.justice.gov/crt/about/spl/documents/pdoc_finding_2-24-14.pdf

▶

The following are excerpts from a Letter of Findings from the U.S. Department of Justice Civil Rights Division issued in February, 2014. The letter was addressed to the Governor of Pennsylvania and signed by the Acting Assistant Attorney General, United States Department of Justice, and the United States Attorney, Western District of Pennsylvania. The letter provided detailed findings supporting the following conclusions.

The Civil Rights Division has completed its investigation of the Pennsylvania Department of Corrections ("PDOC") use of solitary confinement on prisoners with serious mental illness ("SMI") and intellectual disabilities ("ID"). The investigation was conducted pursuant to the Civil Rights of Institutionalized Persons Act ("CRIPA"), [which] authorizes the Department of Justice to seek equitable relief where conditions in state correctional facilities violate the rights of prisoners protected by the Constitution or laws of the United States. The manner in which PDOC subjects prisoners with SMI to prolonged periods of solitary confinement involves conditions that are often unjustifiably harsh and in which these prisoners routinely have difficulty obtaining adequate medical care.

PDOC has begun reforming the way in which it uses solitary confinement on prisoners with SMI/ID. . . . While the Commonwealth has made important improvements, much more work needs to be done to ensure sustained compliance with the mandates of the Constitution and the ADA [(Americans with Disabilities Act)]. Below we summarize our factual determinations and our ongoing concerns:

- The manner in which PDOC uses solitary confinement on prisoners with SMI results in serious harm.
- Numerous system deficiencies contribute to PDOC's extensive use of solitary confinement on prisoners with SMI.
- The manner in which PDOC uses solitary confinement also harms prisoners with ID.
- The manner in which PDOC uses solitary confinement often discriminates against prisoners with SMI/ID.

PDOC's solitary confinement practices violate the Eighth Amendment's prohibition against "cruel and unusual punishments."

The practices described in this letter also violates ADA, [which] generally obligates prisons to provide qualified prisoners with disabilities the opportunity to participate in and benefit from prison services, programs, and activities, and, absent legitimate justification, to do so in the most integrated setting appropriate to individual prisoners with disabilities.

Like other state correctional systems, PDOC increasingly has been called upon to take on the task of serving as the state's primary caregiver for those with SMI. Many of these prisoners also have significant intellectual disabilities. However, PDOC's unenviable burden of having take care of these prisoners cannot excuse its all too routine practice of using a harsh form of solitary confinement to control those with SMI and/or ID instead of providing them with the mental health care treatment they need.

Now is the time to put a stop to these harmful solitary confinement practices and to meaningfully improve the mental health services PDOC provides. We look forward to working collaboratively with [Pennsylvania Department of Corrections] Secretary Wetzel and his staff to address the violations of law we have identified in the context of settlement discussions.

The PLRA was enacted as an amendment to a very large federal appropriations bill.[30] The goal was to discourage access to courts by inmates seeking to address constitutional violations in correctional facilities. There were no hearings on the act and scant consideration of its implications. It was part of a political deal agreed to by the Congress and by President Clinton to placate the Republican Party. The Democrats had "bigger fish to fry," and prisoners were not a powerful political constituency.

Some of the major new restrictions required by the PLRA included the onus on inmates to exhaust all existing complaint and grievance systems in prison or jail, complying with all deadlines and procedures in those systems. This is an especially great burden on incarcerated youth and their guardians. (See also Chapter 8.)

Prisoners were barred from seeking compensation for mental or emotional suffering unless there was a prior indication of physical injury. Some inmates who were raped or intentionally abused by staff were denied remedies under this provision. Human Rights Watch argued that inmates who were treated in ways similar to the tortures in Iraq's Abu Ghraib prisons should be compensated under the PLRA, which they were not.[31]

There are also significant restrictions on the powers of federal judges to make or enforce orders that limit crowding or to fix other unlawful prison conditions. Attorney's fees are limited by the PLRA, even in those cases in which prisoners win lawsuits that establish rights violations.

The impact of the PLRA manifested rapidly. Between 1995 and 1997, federal civil rights lawsuits dropped by one third, even as the prison and jail population continued to grow. By 2006, federal court filings by inmates per 1,000 prisoners were 60% below the 1995 rate.[32] Moreover, the PLRA not only reduced the number of filings but also made it tougher for inmates to win these cases by requiring them to adhere strictly to all grievance procedures and deadlines, increasing the burden of proof for physical injury, reducing the power of the federal court to act on unlawful conditions, and limiting attorney's fees, which just makes it harder for inmates to find quality legal representation in these expensive cases.

▲ Federal policy sets the tone for the nation, but the majority of correctional law and practice is set by individual states.

© Harry E. Walker/MCT/Newscom

Sample grievance form. ▶

Source: Federal Bureau of Prisons, http://www.bop.gov/policy/forms/BP_A0176.pdf

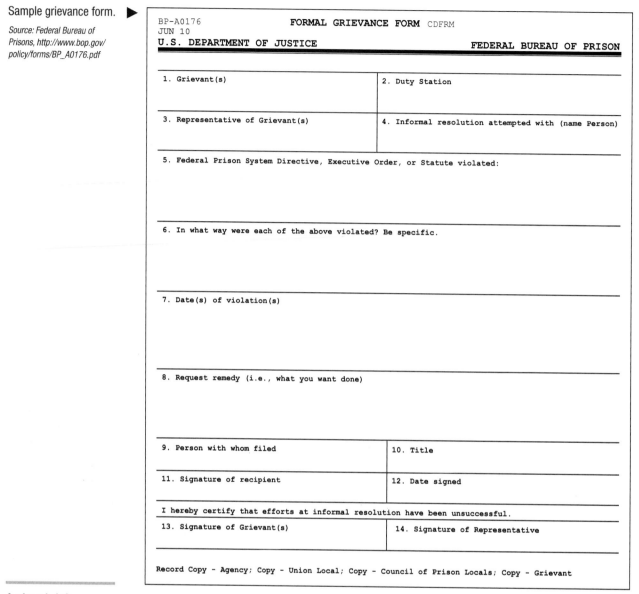

Amicus brief:
Arguments presented by "friends" of the court on points of law relevant to the subject of the case, often one of broad public interest.

Federalism: The principle of government that defines the relationship between the national government and the states. Power and authority are allocated such that each state owns an exclusive sphere of power and authority, while other powers must be shared.

More recently, the U.S. Supreme Court has heard litigation under the PLRA about prison overcrowding, testing the boundaries of the statute. In the fall of 2010, the court heard arguments in *Schwarzenegger v. Plata* (later *Brown v. Plata*) about overcrowding in California's prison system.[33] In 2009, a federal three-judge panel ruled that, to comply with constitutional standards for medical and mental health care, the state had to substantially reduce overcrowding in three years. The three-judge panel determined that the state could limit the number of people in the prison population by reducing sentences, changing the state's parole system, allowing good behavior credits for inmates that would lead to early release, and sending nonviolent felons to county-level programs. The judges affirmed in the case that the state could save between $803 million and $906 million per year by reducing the number of inmates in state prisons. Advocates heralded the three-judge panel's decision as an important victory for inmates, particularly in light of the PLRA's limitations on litigation. On appeal to the Supreme Court, California argued that the three judges violated the PLRA, because the judges could have found less drastic alternatives to solve the prison system's problems, and that the judges exceeded their role by addressing prison overcrowding. Many states filed an amicus brief urging that the court reject the decision of the three-judge panel, arguing for the critical value of federalism to limit the exercise of the supremacy of the federal courts to enforce the Constitution. However, the court upheld the authority of the three-judge panel and its decisions.

Prison Rape Elimination Act of 2003

In 2003, Congress passed the Prison Rape Elimination Act (PREA), affirming the duty of the government to protect incarcerated adults and juveniles from sexual abuse, which has plagued prisoners to an unacceptable extent and been tolerated by prison officials and the public alike as an inevitability of life behind bars. As Assistant Attorney General Karol Mason was quoted as saying, "We believe that sexual abuse is a crime, and should not be the punishment for a crime."[34] PREA is the most significant formalized step to date on the part of the government in recognizing this pervasive and insidious problem and taking steps to rectify it. The act created the National Prison Rape Elimination Commission, which is charged with studying the causes of abuse, providing education about its consequences, and setting standards for its elimination. Besides state and federal prisons, jails, detention centers, and community-based facilities for both adults and juveniles, PREA covers detention facilities for undocumented immigrants and short-term lockups operated by law enforcement agencies.

PREA legislation was supported by a broad bipartisan coalition of advocates and lobbyists, including human rights groups, religious organizations, civil rights organizations, and criminal justice professional organizations. The bipartisan support for PREA was remarkable.

▲ The treatment of prisoners at Guantánamo Bay in Cuba has given rise to some national discourse on legal and civil rights issues such as due process and torture.

© Shane T. McCoy/MCT/Newscom

SPOTLIGHT

NATIONAL PRISON RAPE ELIMINATION COMMISSION

As a formal recognition that rape should not be part of the penalty a person pays for a crime, the National Prison Rape Elimination Commission affirms that

> rape is violent, destructive, and a crime—no less so when the victim is incarcerated. Until recently, however, the public viewed sexual abuse as an inevitable feature of confinement. Even as courts and human rights standards increasingly confirmed that prisoners have the same fundamental rights to safety, dignity, and justice as individuals living at liberty in the community, vulnerable men, women, and children continued to be sexually victimized by other prisoners and corrections staff. Tolerance of sexual abuse of prisoners in the government's custody is totally incompatible with American values.[1]

The objectives of the commission are to investigate the causes of sexual abuse, what circumstances allow it to happen, and how best to protect people from it. Some corrections departments now train their officers routinely on the issue or have established sexual assault response teams (SARTs). However, the problem is a persistent and challenging one that undermines the goals of prisons and makes them more dangerous and destructive. Some argue that PREA standards do not go far enough to protect the incarcerated from sexual abuse and harassment.

The commission's report outlined nine findings about the problem, recommendations for solutions, and how government officials inside and outside of corrections systems can support the work of PREA.

FINDINGS OF THE COMMISSION

- Eliminating rape is a challenge in environments that are supposed to be secure.

As early as 1998, Rep. John Conyers (D-MI) had attempted to include reduction of prison rape in the reauthorization of the Violence Against Women Act, but there was little congressional support for it at that time. Central to quick passage of PREA in 2003 was the strong support of the religious community, especially Christian evangelical groups and conservative think tanks, such as the Hudson Institute.

The first Senate sponsor was Sen. Jeff Sessions (R-AL), one of the most conservative members of Congress at the time. Another sponsor was Rep. Bobby Scott (D-VA), who was then regarded as one of the most liberal members of the House of Representatives. The House version of PREA had 32 cosponsors. Powerful senators such as Dianne Feinstein (D-CA), Edward Kennedy (D-MA), Dick Durbin (D-IL), and Mike Devine (R-OH) also cosponsored the bill. The bill passed both houses of Congress by unanimous consent. It was signed into law by President George W. Bush, although he expressed reservations that the new law might hinder the prerogatives of the executive branch of the federal government. In his signing statement, Bush prohibited full access to information relevant to PREA cases in which "disclosure might impair the deliberative processes of the Executive or the Executive's constitutional duties." This concern now seems very important in light of sexual abuses of prisoners at Guantánamo Bay and other holding facilities for prisoners of the "War on Terror."

PREA envisioned curbing prison rape through a zero-tolerance approach and encouraged the funding of research, auditing, and data collection. The law calls for new standards to

- Leaders need to create cultures that support safety rather than tolerate abuse.

- Vulnerable individuals should be identified and protected.

- Reducing sexual abuse in facilities depends on internal monitoring and external oversight.

- Reporting and investigation must be improved to build confidence and protect individuals from retaliation.

- Perpetrators must be held responsible for their actions and be subject to appropriate sanctions.

- Victims must have immediate and ongoing access to medical and mental health services.

- Sexual abuse prevention, investigation, and treatment must be especially designed for the needs of youth in juvenile facilities; youth are especially vulnerable to sexual abuse.

- Individuals under community supervision are also vulnerable to abuse and should be considered equally deserving of protection as those in locked facilities.

- Incarcerated immigrants are also at special risk for abuse, which calls for special interventions.

QUESTIONS

1 Do the PREA standards go far enough to eliminate sexual abuse in lockup facilities?

2 Discuss the ways that sexual safety should be evaluated; consider leadership, facility security, culture, and staff training.

Note

1. National Prison Rape Elimination Commission 2009, 1

uncover, measure, and address prison sexual violence, making prison officials more accountable for sexual abuse and harassment occurring in their facilities.

PREA empowered a national commission to conduct a comprehensive study of sexual violence in prisons and jails. The commission also held a series of public hearings. Several units in the Department of Justice were authorized to collect statistics, fund research, and offer training and technical assistance on prison rape. Besides the work of the national commission, the attorney general was required under PREA to produce an annual report to Congress on its efforts to reduce prison rape.

Given the history of halting and limited state and federal action to protect the civil rights of prisoners, the enactment of PREA seems an anomaly. It is worth noting that there was no widespread public discussion of the issues. The passage of PREA was very much a "within the Beltway" movement. Although prison sexual violence has had a distinct presence in American popular culture and is often the topic of jokes by comedians, there were few data available on the issue. Juvenile delinquency programs such as "Scared Straight" even tried to use the fear of prison rape to persuade young offenders to abide by the law. Further, many correctional groups expressed the opinion that the extent of the problem was exaggerated—especially the sexual abuse of prisoners by corrections officers.

Though there is little question that PREA catalyzed a national discussion on prison sexual violence, it is too soon to tell what the results will be. Studies have suggested that the phenomenon of prison rape is very rare; however, these have been criticized for inadequate methods. Stanford Law Professor Robert Weisberg and his colleague David Mills wrote in the October 2003 issue of *Slate* that the PREA has accomplished little beyond data collection.[35] Still other prison reformers, such as Mike Farrell, argue that PREA is barely more than a commission that meets regularly to study the topic of prison rape.[36] Recently, PREA has developed some preliminary training materials on prison rape for correctional agencies. There is a new wave of evaluation regarding sexual safety; this movement is still in its early stages. Several groups are working diligently in many states to conduct detailed assessments of PREA compliance in facilities and recommend reforms where they are needed.[37] Despite these ongoing efforts, there are still large gaps in baseline data on the frequency of prison rape, the nature of victims and offenders, or how to overcome an entrenched culture of denial.

SUMMARY

What goes on in prisons and jails occurs largely out of the view of outside observers, and certainly the general public. The nature of custody makes oversight of the institutions responsible for it problematic. The various methods for regulating corrections via external oversight bodies, professional standards, litigating through the courts, civil rights legislation, and other federal laws have had only limited success in bringing about reforms. In general, the reforms that do pass tend to be cyclic. It tends to be extremely difficult to move the reform agenda forward using any of these methods and to make sure that correctional agencies stay true to their missions and are accountable when they fail to do so.

Boards designed to examine agency and facility practice and report on and remedy serious problems have been dogged by politics. Their authority has been weak at times, and their influence has waxed and waned during the 20th century. Professional organizations have attempted to establish standards for excellence in correctional practice. Compliance with these standards has been largely voluntary. The ACA accreditation process has been plagued with questions about its integrity, applicability, and relevance.

The courts—including the U.S. Supreme Court—have been a significant forum for hashing out some of the prisoners' most blatant or essential grievances. Despite the legal precedent for considering prisoners "slaves of the state," they and their advocates have brought before the bench questions of legal due process, cruel and unusual punishment, habeas corpus, and conditions of confinement. Last, prisoner advocates as well as "law and order" conservatives have pushed for new laws to bring about what they view as needed reforms. Some of these laws are CRIPA, PLRA, and PREA. To successfully pass and implement such legislation requires that lawmakers reach across the political aisle and build bipartisan support.

DISCUSSION QUESTIONS

1. What makes oversight of corrections systems so challenging?

2. Describe some of the dilemmas inherent in agencies establishing standards for correctional practice.

3. Discuss the conflicting ideas regarding protection of prisoners embedded in the U.S. Constitution.

4. Discuss the Eighth Amendment and what you think should constitute cruel and unusual punishment.

5. What are ways that prisoners might be protected from retaliation against them after they submit grievances?

6. Research CRIPA cases in your state or region. Choose sides, study the arguments, and debate the issues in the case.

7. What do you think is more effective at controlling corrections systems and holding them accountable, legislation or litigation? Why?

KEY TERMS

Accreditation, 236

Amicus brief, 248

Eighth Amendment, 237

Fact finder, 241

Federalism, 248

Fourteenth Amendment, 241

Magna Carta, 239

Petition, 238

Receiver, 243

Special master, 243

Writ, 239

NOTES

1. Vera Institute of Justice 2006
2. American Correctional Association n.d.
3. Council of Juvenile Correctional Administrators 2013
4. Thomas et al. 1985
5. Ourdocuments.gov n.d.
6. *Ruffin v. Commonwealth* 1871
7. Ibid.
8. *Ex Parte Hull* 1941
9. Ibid.
10. *Rhodes v. Chapman* 1981
11. Ibid.
12. *Estelle v. Gamble* 1976; *Hutto v. Finney* 1978
13. *Hutto v. Finney* 1978.
14. *Rhodes v. Chapman* 1981
15. *Farmer v. Brennan, Warden et al.* 1994
16. Ibid.
17. *Wolff v. McDonnell* 1974
18. *Gagnon v. Scarpelli* 1973; *Morrissey v. Brewer* 1972
19. *Hudson v. Palmer* 1984
20. Ibid.
21. Ibid.
22. *Superintendent v. Hill* 1985
23. Ibid.
24. Ibid.
25. *Greenholtz v. Nebraska Penal Inmates* 1979
26. *Madrid v. Gomez* 1995
27. *Armstrong v. Wilson* 1997; *Clark v. California* 1997; *Plata, Coleman v. Wilson* 1995
28. Civil Rights of Institutionalized Persons Act, U.S. Code Sec. 1997
29. Human Rights Watch 2009
30. Prison Litigation Reform Act, 42 U.S. Code Sec. 1997(e)
31. Human Rights Watch 2009
32. Ibid.
33. *Schwarzenegger v. Plata* (09-1233)
34. Reilly 2014
35. Weisberg and Mills 2003
36. Farrell 2008
37. For example, the Moss Group in Washington, DC (www.mossgroup.us)

⑤SAGE edge™

Sharpen your skills with SAGE edge at edge.sagepub.com/krisberg

SAGE edge for students provides a personalized approach to help you accomplish your coursework goals in an easy-to-use learning environment. This site includes action plans, mobile-friendly eFlashcards and web quizzes as well as web, audio, and video resources and links to SAGE journal articles.

11 Corrections and the Color Line

LEARNING OBJECTIVES

1 To grasp the nature and extent of racial disparity in the criminal and juvenile justice systems.

2 To understand some of the historical roots of that disparity.

3 To be able to name several ways that race intersects with other key social factors.

4 To be able to explain the issue of disproportionate minority contact (DMC) in terms of relative incarceration rates.

5 To grasp the concept of accumulation of disproportion throughout the justice system process.

Sociologist Gunnar Myrdal[1] wrote about the American dilemma—the extraordinary impact of race on American history and on all of our social institutions. In 1903, W. E. B. Du Bois suggested that the color line would be the greatest problem of the 20th century.[2] In the new millennium, it is still the pivotal moral challenge facing our nation. The issue of race is central to understanding the corrections system, past and future. As was discussed in Chapter 2, the social institutions of punishment in the United States are derived from colonial practice and slavery. For example, the Thirteenth and Fourteenth Amendments to the U.S. Constitution extended citizenship rights to former slaves and abolished forced servitude. However, the amendments contain an exemption for persons convicted of crimes.

People of color are vastly overrepresented on probation, on parole, in prisons, and in jails. The U.S. rate of incarceration—the highest in the entire world—is mostly a function of how frequently we incarcerate people of color, especially African Americans. Most states have incarceration rates for Whites that are similar to those in nations that use prisons and jails very sparingly.[3] It is estimated that over 30% of African American males will be imprisoned at some point during their lifetime.[4] In some urban areas, the incarceration and jailing of African American males approaches 80%.[5] Pettit and Western estimated that in the 1990s, African American men in their 30s who were not in college were almost twice as likely to have a prison record than a bachelor's degree and more than twice as likely to be former inmates than to have served in the military.[6]

These extreme rates of incarceration of people of color are often correlated with intersecting social factors, including gender, economic class, and immigration status. This "intersectionality" (as it is sometimes called) represents a compounding of disadvantages that can exert devastating effects on individuals and communities. For young people, even the likelihood of incarceration casts a shadow over their lives. The reality of incarceration can permanently disable them from ever successfully participating in normal social life. These adverse effects impact high numbers of children who have parents in prison and jail. They include poor health and mental health outcomes, diminished probability of marriage, and radically reduced income levels.[7] Legal scholar Michelle Alexander has named this crisis the "New Jim Crow." She notes that more African Americans are under some form of correctional supervision today than were slaves prior to the Civil War. There are more men of color behind bars than enrolled in four-year colleges. Further, the legal barriers imposed on former convicts—disqualification from voting, prohibition from employment, exclusion from student loan programs, denial of access to public housing and other public benefits, and diminished civil rights—are as onerous as the worst historic legal oppression of African Americans, Latinos, and Native Americans throughout our nation's history.[8]

These extreme racial disparities are socially unsustainable. The American Dilemma undermines faith in the justice system, and the collateral damage on children and other loved

 6 To understand some of the issues of race specific to African Americans, Asian Americans and Pacific Islanders, Native Americans, and Latinos in the justice system.

7 To be capable of discussing the intersection of race, immigration, and the criminal justice system.

8 To begin to understand the social context in which racial disproportion and mass incarceration have arisen.

9 To grasp how issues of race in society permeate the boundaries of custody facilities and how they manifest in such facilities.

▲ Slaves, like prisoners, were under constant surveillance, had strictly limited movement, were subject to ill treatment by captors, and had high illiteracy rates.

© Thinkstock/Jupiterimages/ Stockbyte

ones of the incarcerated creates a host of difficult and divisive social policy debates.[9] High rates of racial disproportion worsen ethnic tensions, promote fear and suspicion, and tear at the social fabric of communities.

It is incumbent upon society to examine the magnitude of the disparate incarceration of racial minorities and the explanations that have been offered for this extreme disparity—in particular, the impact of the War on Drugs. This chapter also explores the challenges that racial tensions create within the corrections system and potential remedies for these issues.

Measuring the Extent of the Problem

Data on race, ethnicity, and incarceration can be obtained from a variety of federal and state sources. The accuracy and consistency of the data are problematic due to a variety of definitions for race and ethnicity and a basic misunderstanding of the difference between the two.

For example, Latinos are referred to as Hispanics, which is an ethnic category that can overlap with any racial group. Confusion about categories often results in imprecise counting from the start. Further, Native Americans are often merged with Pacific Islanders, Alaska Natives, Native Hawaiians, and other groups. The Asian American category contains a very wide range of ethnic groups, each of which may have a very low or very high rate of incarceration. The existing information on race and ethnicity cannot be analyzed alongside data on income level and social class. Plus, current data categories fail to consider the incarceration rates of persons of mixed racial ancestry. The data presented below are the best that we have, but must be viewed as incomplete and partially inaccurate (see "A Note About Race and Ethnicity" in the Preface).

THE RELATIVE RATE INDEX

At present, the best method of assessing racial or ethnic disparity is a statistic known as the Relative Rate Index (RRI). This statistic compares the rate of criminal justice involvement of one group to a baseline rate—usually that for Whites—and creates a ratio. For instance, an RRI of 1.0 means that a given group has the same incarceration rate as Whites; an RRI of 0.5 means that the group is incarcerated at half the rate of that for Whites, and an RRI of 3.0 denotes that the group is confined at three times the rate of that for Whites. This ratio allows more meaningful comparisons that take into account the relative size of each racial and ethnic group in the general population.

Let's start the analysis by looking at racial disparity at the point of arrest.[10] Whites accounted for 10.5 million arrests in 2006. Rates of arrest for African Americans were 2.5 times higher than those for Whites. Native Americans were arrested at 1.5 times the White

Figure 11.1   Graph of Comparative Arrest Rates

National Rates of Arrest for Each Race, 1980–2011

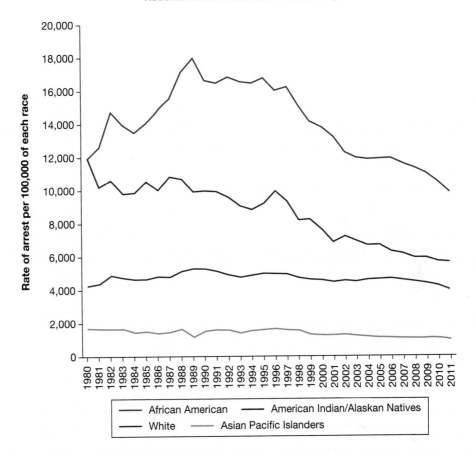

This graph shows adult rates of arrest for all racial groups from 1980 to 2011. The rate of arrest for a particular group may rise and fall according to a number of factors, such as the number of offenses committed by individuals within that group, law enforcement policies and practices, and changing definitions of what constitutes an arrestable offense. During this period, African Americans had the highest rates of arrest, followed by Native Americans, Whites, and Asian Pacific Islanders. After rising rapidly through the 1980s to a high in 1989 of just over 18,000, African American rates fell most years since. Native Americans had the second highest rates, with rates generally falling since 1980. Whites and Asian Pacific Islander rates stayed relatively level through this period, althought both had an overall drop. Note: This is Federal Bureau of Investigation (FBI) data compiled by the Bureau of Justice Statistics. Ethnicity was not distinguished in the FBI data; each racial group includes some hispanics. Also, multiracial individuals were assigned one racial category by the BJS compilers. An arrest could have been for any reason or offense. *Source: Snyder, Howard N. and Joseph Mulako-Wangota. "Arrest Rates of Adults for All Offenses by Race." Washington, DC: Bureau of Justice Statistics. Generated using the Arrest Data Analysis Tool at www.bjs.gov, June 4, 2014.*

rate; Asian Americans, 0.3 times. Unfortunately, the Federal Bureau of Investigation (FBI) does not report data on arrests for Hispanics. For a few states that report data on arrests by ethnicity, such as Arizona, California, Oregon, Pennsylvania, and Texas, Hispanics (versus non-Hispanics) had a higher arrest rate than Whites but a lower one than African Americans.[11] African Americans had a higher arrest rate than Whites for violent offenses and drug offenses.

Turning to data on felony convictions, it appears that Whites are convicted for violent crimes at a rate comparable to African Americans[12] (17% versus 18% comparing the most serious conviction offense). Whites had higher conviction rates for property crimes, and African Americans were much more likely than Whites to be convicted of drug crimes (41% compared to 30%).

Race and Ethnicity Behind the Walls

Historically, most American prisons were segregated by race; African Americans were assigned to completely separate facilities or to separate living units within larger prisons. Continuing the legacy of slavery, southern states assigned African American inmates to chain gangs or work crews. Latino inmates were often assigned to farm labor in western states. All prison programs were segregated by race, and the few available education and treatment programs were assigned to Whites. Until the 1960s and afterward, almost all of the corrections line staff, wardens, and parole agents were White. Despite the images of prison life portrayed in Hollywood movies such as *The Shawshank Redemption*, most inmates did not interact across racial lines.

Prisons were (and still are) most often located in rural areas; however, the vast majority of inmates of color were from urban areas. Staff recruited from these rural communities tended to harbor not only the general social prejudice and hatred of people of color but an enhanced hatred of racial minorities prevalent in rural communities. In the South, it was not uncommon for a White prison guard to be a member of the Ku Klux Klan and to participate in lynching of his Black neighbors.

Despite institutionalized racial division, conflict and tension based on race were part of the prison reality. Violence among the races often broke out in exercise yards, open dorm living units, and other common areas. This situation worsened in the 1960s and 1970s as political activism engendered greater race conflicts and rioting in the community at large. Groups such as the Nation of Islam, the Young Lords, and the Black Panther Party were active in prisons and recruited inmates to their causes. These groups conflicted sharply with White corrections officials over the right to practice their own religions, the content of approved reading materials, the right to hold meetings, the right to accept visitors, and the right to disseminate newsletters. These developments mirrored conflicts outside the prison walls between Whites and people of color—race riots in the community and the brutal suppression by law enforcement agencies of demands for basic civil rights.

Gangs that formed inside prisons exploited the rhetoric of racial conflict as a way of organizing prisoners for the advancement of the gang agenda, such as the illegal prison marketplace in drugs, weapons, and other forbidden commodities. The most potent gangs among White inmates were persons who identified as neo-Nazis or the members of criminal motorcycle societies—groups whose fundamentally militant and overtly racist motives helped to push racial conflicts to explosive and lethal levels. Violent incidents were most often interpreted by prisoners and administrators alike in racial or ethnic terms. Attacks led to counterattacks and retaliations in a devolving cycle of racial hatred and recrimination. The inmates accurately perceived that prison officials were relatively powerless to maintain safety in prisons or to end the violence. The racially or ethnically organized prison gangs seemed like the only practical way to gain protection. Inmates joined gangs for self-preservation. The correctional staff understood that they exerted a very tenuous hold on prison order, especially in a situation where one or two corrections officers were assigned to police a prison yard with hundreds of convicts. The prison staff all too often made bargains with inmate gangs to maintain control, or the illusion of control. In some states, this literally meant turning over prison security to inmates (the "barn boss system"), with minimal oversight and accountability. This accommodation to the power of the prison gangs helped matters of race deteriorate even further.

Increasingly crowded prisons forced administrators to house many inmates in cells designed for single inmates. Inmates housed in double and triple bunks in rooms that were formerly gymnasiums, dining halls, or day rooms intensified racial pressures. The ability to avert racial or ethnic conflicts was minimal in these settings. In addition, budget cutbacks led to a decline in education and counseling programs and more idleness, an additional stressor for prisoners.

Ku Klux Klan: The Ku Klux Klan (KKK) is a White supremacist group founded in 1866. The secret fraternal organization is notorious for acts of terrorism—including murder, lynching, arson, rape, and bombing—to oppose civil rights or any other civic gains for African Americans.

Members of the "Texas Syndicate'" prison gang show off their gang tattoos in the administrative segregation wing of Hughes Prison. As confirmed gang members, they are locked inside their cells for 23 hours a day and are only allowed a brief recreation period with members of their gang.

© Andrew Lichtenstein/Corbis

Prison officials responded to this extremely volatile situation by expanded use of nonlethal and lethal weapons to quell riots and daily violence. They extensively used isolation, solitary confinement, and denial of basic privileges to attempt to maintain control. Prison bureaus designed and opened "supermax" facilities, intended to be "jails within jails." (See Chapter 6.) Heightened tensions also led corrections officers to engage in torture of recalcitrant inmates and a "code of silence" among prison guards to cover up these horrible practices.[13]

Racial and ethnic conflicts were treated as a problem of criminal prison gangs. Corrections officials responded to this definition by using techniques such as undercover intelligence, using prison snitches to gain information, gang identification as a method of assigning housing, warrantless searches for gang income and weapons, and tough punishments for alleged gang behavior. None of these strategies have made prisons safer, and many may have intensified racial and ethnic tensions and violence.[14]

Most dramatically, prison officials reintroduced racial segregation as a formal policy in prison management. These practices were challenged before the U.S. Supreme Court in *Johnson v. California*.

African American Disproportion in the Criminal Justice System

Although disproportionate minority contact (DMC) affects most ethnic groups, it is only African Americans whose discrimination is rooted in the legacy of centuries of slavery, followed by Jim Crow laws, and the formation of urban ghettos. The incarceration rates for African Americans, both men and women, are dramatically higher, in general, than those for any other racial or ethnic group. An analysis by scholar Loïc Wacquant attests to the dual purpose of these social controls as the extraction of labor and the ostracization of the underclass.[15] Wacquant contends that mass incarceration of African Americans is itself less than 30 years old but is the descendent of the other three devices.

IN THE COURTS

Johnson v. California et al.

543 U.S. 03–636 (2005)

Garrison S. Johnson, an inmate in the California Department of Corrections and Rehabilitation (CDCR), challenged the unwritten policy of the CDCR to segregate inmates by race in double cell assignments in its Reception Centers. Besides dividing prisoners by broad racial categories, the CDCR makes cell assignments within these groups so that Southern California Hispanics are not housed with Northern California Hispanics, Chinese are separated from Korean or Southeast Asian inmates, and so on.

The CDCR argued that this policy was necessary to avoid prison violence and that Reception Centers were especially dangerous, as they hold recently arrived inmates about whom little is initially known, such as their gang affiliations or propensity to attack other inmates. The CDCR maintained that all of its other living units were not intentionally segregated, although inmate requests to be housed with one group and not another were often honored in the classification process. The CDCR cited many examples of violence in its facilities that appeared to be motivated by racial or ethnic hostilities.

Mr. Johnson brought this action on his own behalf, without benefit of legal representation, and despite numerous appeals by the CDCR, prevailed in the U.S. Supreme Court. Johnson had been admitted to the CDCR on several occasions either by the courts or as a parole violator. He argued that the practice of assigning him to racially segregated cells was insulting and diminished his self-worth as an individual. The practice was in blatant violation of federal civil rights laws and long settled law in *Brown v. Board of Education.*[1]

The CDCR countered that most inmates requested to be housed in racially separated settings. Furthermore, CDCR representatives argued that this segregation reduced prison violence. Johnson presented studies suggesting that racial segregation actually fueled inmate anger and generated more violence instead of preventing it.

The U.S. Supreme Court held that the CDCR practice of segregation was unconstitutional and not justified by a valid penological purpose. The court referred the matter back to the district court to enforce a remedy and warned the CDCR not to use surrogate criteria to mask the practice of racial segregation.

The attempts of the CDCR to comply with this order tested the limits of the concept of "all deliberate speed." Five years after the *Johnson* decision, only one CDCR reception center allowed double celling for inmates of different racial or ethnic groups.

In 2011, the Prison Law Office and Bingham McCutchen LLP filed a class-action lawsuit alleging that the CDCR was utilizing racially discriminatory lockdowns. This means that whole categories of inmates are subject to lockdowns (mandatory confinement to their cells) not due to their individual behavior but because of their race or ethnicity. This action was brought on behalf of an African American inmate at Folsom State Prison, Robert Mitchell, who complained that he was locked down for more than a year, based solely on his race. Other inmates have joined Mitchell in this legal action. The plaintiffs argue that these racial lockdowns violate their Eighth and Fourteenth Amendment rights and make prisons more dangerous rather than less.

The CDCR acknowledged that it has an official policy to manage inmate populations by ethnicity and by race. When officials believe any incident to involve a racial or ethnic group, all of the inmates of that group are locked in their cells for an indefinite period of time.

The CDCR reported more than 350 race-based lockdowns of an average duration of 60 days or longer. The affected inmates are confined in their cells for 24 hours a day. These inmates are not allowed visits, phone contacts with their family members, outdoor recreation, or access to religious services. During these racial lockdowns, inmates from other groups receive their normal programming.

Note

1. *Brown v. Board of Education* 1954

Analysis of sentencing data from the National Judicial Reporting Program in 2004 reveals that African Americans were more likely than Whites to be sentenced to prison or jail—as opposed to probation—for the same crimes (71% versus 66%).[16] This racial difference in sentencing was also true for those convicted of violent crimes (80% versus 75%) and for drug crimes (70% versus 63%). In addition, these data show that African Americans got longer prison and jail sentences, especially for violent crimes. The more limited data on Hispanic felony defendants show that they were twice as likely to be convicted compared to Whites and 2.4 times more likely to be incarcerated after sentencing.[17] Criminologist Margaret Zatz found that, at both the adult and juvenile levels, poor people and people of color are the most likely to be detained pending trial, and pretrial detention correlates with harsher sentencing outcomes.[18]

The cumulative result of these trends in criminal justice processing is that African Americans were 5.7 times more likely than Whites to be admitted to state and federal prisons. The RRI for prison admissions in 2003 was 1.9 for Hispanics and 4.3 for Native Americans and other Native peoples.[19] Rates of imprisonment were even more disparate for people of color in states such as Wisconsin (16.7), Minnesota (12.5), New Jersey (13.8), New York (10.5), and Pennsylvania (10.7). For Hispanics, the RRI for prison admissions was highest in Pennsylvania (8.2), New York (5.7), New Hampshire (4.9), North Dakota (3.9), and Wisconsin (3.7).[20]

African Americans and Hispanics are more likely than Whites to be sent to prison not only via court commitments but also for probation and parole violations. These racial and ethnic disparities in prison admissions hold true even when one controls for the most serious conviction charge.[21]

▲ There is intense debate about how old is old enough to be charged and processed through the adult criminal justice system. Youth of color are processed through the adult system at higher rates than their White counterparts.

© Joe Cavaretta/MCT /Landov

On any given day, African Americans are disproportionately represented in probation caseloads and on parole. They are 4 times more likely to be under some form of correctional supervision than Whites. Hispanics are 1.4 times more likely than Whites to be under some type of correctional control. This disparity also extends to those inmates under a sentence of death. In 2007, there were 1,352 African Americans under a death sentence, representing 42% of those awaiting execution.[22]

Another indicator of the influence of race on corrections are the data on the recidivism rates for released prisoners. It is important to recall that these statistics are a function of ex-inmate behavior and the policy decisions of corrections officials. For example, a U.S. Department of Justice study that tracked released inmates from 15 states found that African Americans were more likely to be rearrested than Whites (73% versus 63%) and more likely to be returned to prison (54% versus 50%). The rates for rearrest and remand to prison for Hispanic inmates were lower than for non-Hispanics (who might be African American or White). Another analysis conducted by the National Council on Crime and Delinquency (NCCD) reported very similar results.[23]

Racial and ethnic disproportionality are likewise endemic to the juvenile corrections system. African American youth had an RRI of 4.5 for long-term residential placement; Hispanic youth, 1.9; and Native American youth, 3.2. States with the highest racial disparity for youth were Connecticut, Minnesota, New Hampshire, New Jersey, and Pennsylvania.[24]

SPOTLIGHT

THE RACIAL JUSTICE ACT

The South has long been the epicenter of racial tension in the United States, where the terror of lynching and entrenched racial bigotry and hatred was most concentrated. Despite these facts, or perhaps because of them, North Carolina is the only state in the union to have passed legislation that attempts to correct what many feel is an all-too-apparent inequity in the criminal justice system based on race. Racial disparities in the application of the death penalty have compelled efforts to enact legal protections against them. In 2009, North Carolina passed the Racial Justice Act (House Bill 472, Senate Bill 461), which was intended to prevent any person being put to death because of racial bias. The law allows death row defendants to appeal their cases using statistical or other evidence on the grounds that racism had an impact on their sentences. The impetus of the legislation came about in part due to the exoneration (after decades of incarceration) of several African American death row inmates in whose cases there was shown to be such irregularities as withheld evidence, ineffective counsel, prosecutorial misconduct, and perjury by a lead investigator.[1] And, in the case of Edward Chapman, the cause of the victim's death was found to be a drug overdose and not a homicide.[2]

The Racial Justice Act is highly contested in the state, with repeals of the act passing the General Assembly and the governor vetoing the repeal twice.[3] The second time, there were enough legislative votes to overturn the veto. All but one of the state's district attorneys have claimed that appeals clog the system, that dangerous criminals would be released, and that it is unnecessarily costly. These are allegations that can easily be refuted, however. Only two cases had been heard as of 2012, and those proceedings have cost less than a single execution. The result of a successful appeal would mean commuting of the sentence to life in prison without parole; it would not result in release.

QUESTIONS

1   Discuss the fact that North Carolina was the first state to pass a version of the Racial Justice Act.

2   What sorts of facts might you consider if you were a judge in a capital case involving an African American defendant?

3   Why do you think it's so difficult to pass the Racial Justice Act?

Notes

1.   North Carolina Coalition for a Moratorium 2010

2.   YouTube 2009

3.   Bufkin 2011

The most severe response for juvenile offenders is to prosecute them in the adult criminal courts—rather than juvenile courts—and sentence them to adult prison. Among states that reported data on this practice, African American youth were 7.2 times more likely than White youth to be sent to prisons; Native American youth, 2.5 times. Youth identified as Hispanic are 1.4 times as likely as White youth to be sent to prison.[25] This finding is especially tragic, because youth sent to prisons are more likely to be raped by older inmates, to commit suicide, and to spend their incarceration in solitary confinement.[26]

Perjury: Lying in court after vowing to "tell the truth, the whole truth, and nothing but the truth"; to render (oneself) guilty of swearing falsely or of willfully making a false statement under oath or solemn affirmation

Asian Americans and Pacific Islanders and the Corrections System

Although the RRI of Asian Americans appears low relative to other ethnic groups, this is not to say that some members of this group are not subject to racial discrimination and unfair treatment in the corrections system. From 1977 to 1997, overall arrests for Asian American and Pacific Islanders (APIs) grew by 726%, compared to a 30% decline in arrests for African Americans.[27] This growth in arrests for APIs was twice as large as the increase of this group in the general population during the same period. Although the existing national criminal justice data do not separate specific ethnic groups within the larger category of API individuals, limited data suggest that refugee families from Cambodia, Laos, and Vietnam are over-represented in the corrections system. For example, San Francisco data show that Samoans have some of the highest rates of incarceration in both the juvenile and adult systems. In Hawaii, Native Hawaiians have rates of incarceration that are higher than that of any other group; Filipinos constitute another large percentage of the confined population. Data from at least two California counties reveal that Vietnamese youth are arrested and processed in the juvenile and adult systems at levels disproportionate to their percentage of the general population.[28]

Statewide data in California showed a steady increase of API youth in the Division of Juvenile Justice; the number of API youth in state youth prisons almost doubled during the 1990s. These youth were more likely than other ethnic groups to be committed to adult facilities for homicide. API youth in adult and juvenile prisons were likely to be sentenced from the most rural communities.[29]

These findings are at odds with the media image of Asian Americans as the "model minority." There is a false assumption that all Asian Americans have achieved high levels of education and professional status. This "model" is held up to other minorities as a group that has succeeded, despite a history of racial discrimination. The apparent success of Asian Americans has been used by some to discredit the value of affirmative action programs, welfare, and the alleged decline in "family values" in other ethnic groups.

Although the achievements of some segments of the API community are laudable, especially among the long-standing immigrant groups, there are important segments within the API population that are not doing as well.[30] For example, Laotian, Hmong, and

◀ A defendant listens to his attorney after the guilty verdict was read at the Sacramento Courthouse in 2010. He was 16 at the time of the shooting of a Sacramento gang detective and faced life in prison without parole.

© ZUMA Press, Inc. / Alamy

Cambodian Americans had poverty rates that were much higher than those of the general U.S. population.[31]

API youth and adults confront many unique challenges relative to corrections. To begin with, very few APIs work in the corrections system. There is very limited programming to assist API inmates with reentry issues, including language barriers, English language literacy, job training, or drug and psychological counseling. **Culturally competent** programming for API inmates is virtually nonexistent.

API inmates are subjected to a range of racial stereotypes from many justice system officials. For instance, training programs for corrections staff tend to focus on the dangers of evil Chinese gangs that have international ties to criminal syndicates in Hong Kong, Taiwan, and China. These derive from racist stereotypes from the late 19th and early 20th centuries that portrayed Asian women as prostitutes or Asian men as sinister foes who lured White women into forced sexual slavery in opium dens. Corrections officials have sometimes described API inmates who are doing their time quietly as "treacherous."[32]

API inmates do not naturally fit into the racial and ethnic structure of most corrections facilities. API inmates band together for self-protection and may engage in prison violence to establish their credibility in the rough social environments of prisons and jails. A recent collection of essays and poems provides a compelling view of the plight of the API corrections population.[33]

Native Americans and the Corrections System

As with Latinos and APIs, reliable data on Native Americans in the criminal justice system are hard to find. Further complicating the matter is that the information on Native Americans who are arrested and incarcerated in **tribal territories** is incomplete and likely to be inaccurate.[34] Data from tribal territories are collected by each tribal group individually, and there is no consistency among tribes for data collection. Other federal data on crime and justice in tribal territories are collected by the Bureau of Indian Affairs and by U.S. Attorneys.

Native Americans might be confined or supervised by tribal police agencies, federal authorities, or state corrections agencies. Which agency has authority might be determined by the location of the crime or by one of a range of informal agreements among these agencies. Moreover, Native Americans committed to the Federal Bureau of Prisons might be housed in state facilities operated by private prison companies or in state correctional institutions. There is virtually no effective oversight or accountability for facilities operating on tribal lands.

Native Americans face historic prejudice and discrimination in Anglo correctional facilities. As with other racial and ethnic minorities, staff and programs that can respond to Native Americans in a culturally appropriate manner are sorely lacking. Native Americans confront great challenges in terms of alcohol and drug dependency. Tribal territories are havens for illegal activities due to limited law enforcement resources; thus, drug dealing, sex trafficking, and other illegal activities are enormous challenges. However, without a culturally competent approach, programs are ineffective at best and often exacerbate these problems.

Native Americans are often incarcerated hundreds or even thousands of miles from their homes. They have minimal legal resources, and reentry programs are almost nonexistent. They also suffer from the highest rates of violent victimization of any racial or ethnic category, even though that rate declined between 2003 and 2012.[35]

Cultural competence: An ability to interact effectively with people of different cultural backgrounds. This requires self-awareness of culture, knowledge of the other culture, and an open attitude.

Tribal territories: Also referred to as Indian reservations, these are areas of land managed by the federal government and dedicated to native peoples.

▲ Comanche County Law Enforcement Center offers a unique service to its inmates, allowing the inmates to practice their religion through a sweat lodge ritual. Once a month they perform this ceremony to cleanse and reorganize their souls.

© Hillery Smith Garrison/KRT/Newscom

As noted above, the disparity in Native American incarceration is higher than for any other group except African Americans.[36]

Latinos and the Corrections System

Accurate information is scant on the growing number of Latinos behind bars and under community supervision. Many jurisdictions do not even assemble data on Latinos as a separate category. Similar to APIs, the Latino category encompasses a large number of distinct ethnic communities including longtime American citizens as well as immigrants from Cuba, Puerto Rico, Mexico, other parts of the Caribbean, and Central and South America. Very little reliable information is available about the treatment needs of these defendants. Most current correctional assessment tools were developed and normed based on White or African American offenders; the reliability and validity of these classification tools for other groups is unknown.

A prejudicial burden for Latinos in the corrections system is the stereotype that they are all entrenched gang members who are tied to international drug trafficking cartels. Many prisons and jails, particularly in California, are unduly focused on gathering intelligence about alleged inmate affiliations with Latino prison and street gangs such as MS-13, the Mexican Mafia, and Nuestra Familia. This information is used to manage inmates and results in intensive monitoring and surveillance of Latino inmates and their family members.

Corrections agencies rarely, if ever, offer bilingual staff to assist inmates who speak Spanish or other languages and do not speak English. There are virtually no programs that are culturally attuned to Latino communities. In addition, opportunities to access educational programs are extremely limited, because most corrections agencies hold to an "English only" policy. There is no solid evidence that even those correctional programs that research shows to be effective for other groups are at all helpful to Latinos. As will be discussed later in this chapter, it is routine for prisons and jails to segregate Latino inmates from other inmates and to punish all inmates of a certain group for the misbehavior of a few.

SPOTLIGHT

THE TRIBAL LAW AND ORDER ACT OF 2010

The federal government plays an important but limited role in law enforcement, exercising governance over laws that apply to all U.S. citizens. Local governments handle all of the rest. Ironically, on tribal lands, local authority was usurped when the reservation system was imposed on Native peoples. One impact of this system is that tribal lands are notoriously more dangerous, on average, than other American communities. In an attempt to raise the level of justice and public safety, Congress passed the Tribal Law and Order Act of 2010, which established the Indian Law and Order Commission.[1]

The commission's mandate was to study the problems on tribal lands and recommend solutions. The comprehensive

commission report, released in November 2013, encompasses a wide array of public safety recommendations, including restoring authority over justice matters to the local tribal level, reducing the chaotic complexity of jurisdiction (who's in charge of this?); reducing the waste of resources, human and economic; intensifying efforts to protect women and other victims; and increased accountability from federal law enforcement.

Tribal citizens tend to regard federal and state law as having distant origins; to Indians, these laws seem foreign and irrelevant and not rooted in the culture they consider their own. The price of this disconnect is high—delayed and inadequate prosecution, trials in distant locations, and an ultimate degradation of justice. Current chaotic questions about jurisdiction have to do with whether the crime was committed on tribal land, whether the person who committed the crime was a Native or a non-Native, and whether the victim was a Native or a non-Native.

Latino and API inmates and probationers are also enmeshed in the immigration system and may be subject to custody holds and deportation based on the policies of U.S. immigration officials.

Issues of race and ethnicity, crowding, and a culture of violence tends to permeate many custody situations.

© REUTERS/ Lucy Nicholson

Inadequate attention from the federal government has resulted in crimes not being prosecuted properly and criminals exploiting that fact. The increased lawlessness endangers the tribal people; for example, there are extremely high rates of domestic violence on tribal lands. Also according to the commission, the federal government's role in tribal justice must be reconsidered and reformed.

After two years of effort in conjunction with the Bureau of Indian Affairs, the commission released its report. Some of its recommendations are as follows:

- Tribes may opt out of federal or state jurisdiction, except for federal laws that apply to all Americans.
- Establish a new federal circuit court to hear relevant cases arising in Indian country.
- Affirm the jurisdiction of Alaska Native tribal governments.
- Improve the accuracy of data collection and the crime reports generated from those data.

- Improve rehabilitative programming for tribal people.
- Establish sustainable funding for criminal justice programs.[2]

QUESTIONS

1. Why should Native peoples have their own system of criminal justice?

2. Discuss the ways that the geography of Native lands can have an effect on criminal justice matters.

3. Should protections for women follow federal or tribal law?

Notes

1. U.S. Department of Justice 2013

2. Indian Law and Order Commission 2013

Immigration and Incarceration

In addition to the people of color who are confined in state prisons and local jails, a large number are confined in federal detention centers operated by Immigration and Customs Enforcement (ICE). ICE enforces immigration laws under the authority of the federal Department of Homeland Security, a main strategy of which for controlling illegal immigration is mass detention. Immigration and law enforcement overlap significantly due to the move toward policies that many refer to as the "war on immigrants"—increased criminalization of undocumented status, more militarized control of immigrant communities, and a codified system of immigrant detention and deportation (itself a "boom" industry).

This system overlap is nowhere more significant than in the border state of Arizona, where "minutemen" patrol the border. Despite the critical economic contribution of immigrant labor, immigrants themselves are increasingly demonized. Joe Arpaio, the bombastic and controversial sheriff of Maricopa County, embodies some of the most extreme positions on the treatment of undocumented immigrants. Arpaio has proudly proclaimed his "toughness" and unapologetically applied tactics that his critics call racist, an abuse of power, and unconstitutional. (See Chapter 6.)

Programs such as Secure Communities—which operates in almost every state, uses local law enforcement authorities to carry out detentions and relies on federal databases for identifying alleged suspects—are very blunt instruments for an enormously complex issue. ICE raids sweep up U.S. citizens, which result in lengthy detentions, prevent adequate legal representation, and affect tens of thousands of families that *include* U.S. citizens. Of the individuals identified for deportation by Secure Communities, 93% are from Latin American countries, 2% are from Asia, and 1% are from Europe and Canada.[37]

In 2009, almost 370,000 persons were detained by ICE—double the number of a decade earlier. As many as 20% of detainees were moved from one location to another; some were housed in facilities directly under ICE management, others in facilities operated under contract with private prison companies, and some in state prisons and jails. On a given day, over 33,400 persons were confined in more than 1,500 separate facilities. Reliable data on the ethnic composition of these detainees are difficult to obtain, but most of them come from Mexico and South America. Thus, though documentation is not clear, the reality is that the ICE detention system further aggravates the disparity in incarceration for Latinos that already exists in prisons, jails, and juvenile facilities.[38]

Though the flow of immigration is often linked with issues of terrorism and homeland security, it is worth noting that a very minor proportion of ICE detainees are accused of acts of terrorism. Persons taken into custody for terrorism are usually held in facilities operated by the Department of Defense or U.S. intelligence agencies. In 2009 and 2010, half of the immigrant ICE detainees had no criminal history at all; 20% had a history of traffic offenses.[39]

Alterations of U.S. immigration policies have led to more federal prosecutions in addition to deportation. In 2007, there were more than 19,000 federal inmates whose most serious crime was a violation of immigration laws. This has vastly increased the Latino inmate population in the Federal Bureau of Prisons. Whereas Latinos accounted for roughly 13% of the U.S. adult population, they comprised about 40% of all federal prisoners, almost half of whom were charged with violations of immigration laws.[40]

The Obama administration is touting immigration reform as a top priority. And, although a vigorous immigrants' rights movement is growing in momentum, there is dissention between the more mainstream, Democratic Party branch and the more grassroots advocates. The more established advocates feel that current attempts to reform immigration policy (involving guest worker programs, border security, identity verification, and pathways to citizenship) are the best possible solutions for now. Others vehemently disagree

Arizona border agents detained this group after chasing down a suspicious pickup truck. Those found to be illegal immigrants will be fingerprinted and photographed at a detention center, then sent back to Mexico unless a record check shows they are wanted for a crime.

© Patrick Schneider/KRT/ Newscom

and say that the proposed solutions in their current form do not go nearly far enough to protect immigrant workers from such things as workplace exploitation, inhuman working conditions, and the threat of deportation.[41]

Understanding the Causes of Racial Disparity in Corrections

There is an extensive literature of commentary that documents the efforts of researchers seeking to comprehend the huge presence of people of color in the corrections system. Some observers are satisfied with a simplistic explanation—that the disparity is simply a result of people of color being responsible for more crime. Disparity is clearly a very complex social process that encompasses the nature and location of the crimes committed, offender attributes, impoverished communities, the policies and practices of criminal agencies from police through prosecution, access to criminal defender resources, the courts, and corrections agencies themselves. Researchers have used the concept of "accumulated disadvantage" to explain the existence of racial disparity in corrections. This means that small differences in the ways people are treated at each stage of the criminal justice process are compounded along the way.[42] Community variables and racial tensions are involved in the complex mélange of factors that ultimately produce vast levels of racial disparity.

Prison Segregation

Inmate C. J. complains that he is housed in a racially segregated living unit and that he must spend all of his days with convicts of his racial group.

Besides housing, the department of corrections uses race as a criteria for program assignments and even for access to religious services. If there is a mass disturbance in the prison, all inmates of a given racial group are locked down, whether they participated in the disturbance or not. C. J. argues that, since the days of *Brown v. Board of Education*, federal civil rights prohibit these practices.

Prison administrators assert that most prison violence is related to racial hatred and that they enforce the segregation to protect inmates and staff. The officers believe that prison ought to be an exception to blanket desegregation policies. These are not public schools. They claim that inmates do not lose any privilege or services due to these policies.

YOU DECIDE: **Do you eliminate racial and ethnic management policies and risk potential danger and violence in the prison to protect civil rights?**

The nature of sentencing laws and penalties plays a major role. For example, a public policy debate continues about drug laws, especially penalties for possession of crack cocaine many times greater than those for possession of powered cocaine or other dangerous chemicals including methamphetamine. The current crackdown on undocumented immigrants, especially from Mexico, stems in large part from the political focus of law enforcement agencies and official policy and has led to a large increase in Latino inmates in state and federal prisons.

Numerous studies have documented racial bias—both conscious and unconscious—in how probation officials assess the culpability of offenders and the level of threat they may pose to public safety. Other factors such as income, education, and the defendant's demeanor interact and influence these decisions. Grattet, Petersilia, and Lin have shown how race affects the decision to revoke the parole of recently released prisoners for technical violations of their conditions of supervision.[43] There has been extensive research on the impact of race on who is sentenced to death.

Research suggests that public perceptions of dangerousness and trustworthiness are impacted by race and ethnicity. So long as the vast majority of decision makers in the criminal justice system are middle-class Whites who have relatively little contact with people of

SPOTLIGHT

PHILANTHROPIC EFFORTS TO REDUCE DISPROPORTIONATE MINORITY CONTACT FOR YOUTH

There are myriad efforts[1] to address the disproportion in the justice system in terms of contact and confinement of young people. One such effort is titled Models for Change, which is a long-term investment on the part of the MacArthur Foundation. Reducing racial disparity is one of three core reform issues. The initiative is operating in 16 states, the first of which was Pennsylvania.[2]

The Annie E. Casey Foundation also has a long-standing effort to improve justice for youth titled the Juvenile Detention Alternatives Initiative, a core principle of which is to help reduce disparate treatment of youth that arises out of racial bias. The initiative stresses that the rise in youth detention is largely driven by increased rates of detention for youth of color.

A staple of disproportionate minority contact (DMC) reform efforts is to refine the methods and systems of data collection. The assumption is that, unless you can honestly assess levels of disparity, you cannot address the apparent inequities. Therefore, thoughtful and accurate data collection is the foundation for effective policy reform. In an attempt to bring about decision making based on the facts of the case and the needs of the individual youth, reforms also focus on structured assessment tools, tracking of decisions throughout the justice process, training for system practitioners, culturally competent interventions, and recruitment and inclusion of people of color in decision-making positions.

QUESTIONS

1   Discuss the ways that youth detention might have an effect on DMC.

2   Why does data collection matter? Does it matter more than usual in issues that involve DMC?

3   Do philanthropic efforts such as these reduce the responsibility of the government to address issues of racial disparity?

Notes

1.   Hoytt et al. 2001

2.   Models for Change 2014, n.d.

---

color and poor people, these biased perceptions will persist. Allegations of gang membership and immigration status and assumptions about intellectual abilities or "inherent" violent tendencies make targets out of people of color and propel them into prisons and jails.

Unpacking the causes of racial and ethnic bias in corrections is complicated; however, it is hard to deny the bottom-line results that are reflected in the statistics presented here. There are two important concepts to keep in mind. First, race and ethnicity are not scientific facts but are social constructs and thus are tangled up with a host of other social factors. Second, race and ethnicity exert huge effects on all aspects of life such as where you live, what schools you attend, what churches you belong to, the food and music that you enjoy, your employment prospects, and even your life expectancy. It would be naïve to assume that race and ethnicity have only a minimal impact on who is incarcerated. Confronting the forces that fill up our prisons and jails with people of color must be a top priority for corrections reformers, policymakers, and professionals.

In the juvenile arena, the federal Juvenile Justice and Delinquency Prevention Act (JJDPA) was amended in 1980 to require that all states receiving funding under the JJDPA conduct an annual analysis of the extent of DMC in the juvenile justice system and to submit a "good-faith plan" to remedy known and acknowledged disparities. When the act was reauthorized in 2002, Congress recognized that disparities were prevalent at every stage of the system and expanded the core requirements to address arrest, referrals to court, and diversions, in addition to secure confinement and prosecution in the adult court (also referred to as "waiver"). DMC now stands for *disproportionate minority contact* instead of *disproportionate minority confinement*, in recognition of the broader problem.[44] Some states such as Wisconsin and Connecticut have enacted even stronger local mandates to reduce the high rates of confinement for young people of color. North Carolina passed a law extending this analysis to adult inmates and those on death row. A proposal before the U.S. Congress to require a racial and ethnic analysis—with possible solutions—was presented by Rep. Steve Cohen of Memphis, Tennessee, as the "Racial Justice Act," but this proposed law failed to pass the House of Representatives.

Racial Profiling

The presumption of innocence is a fundamental pillar of American democracy. Racial profiling is an affront to that principle. It is the use of physical characteristics instead of behavior as grounds for exercising law enforcement practices such as arrest, investigation, or detention. Racial profiling can be informal or institutionalized. It is not a new problem; profiling is as old as discrimination. But it has taken some interesting forms in recent years.

Debates rage in many corners of the nation over specific law enforcement policies and whether they run contrary to our constitutional guarantees of equal protection. The profiling of Arabs and Muslims increased dramatically after the attacks on the World Trade Center in 2001. Intense reactions of fear and loathing made this practice seem reasonable to some. Profiling Latinos for suspected immigration violations in Arizona is codified into a highly controversial law there (SB 1070). The bill's original version *required* the police

Waiver: A transfer of a juvenile case to the adult criminal court, by the prosecutor, the judge, or according to statute.

Racial profiling: Consideration of race, ethnicity, or national origin by an officer of the law in deciding when and how to intervene in an enforcement capacity. The selection by authorities of certain types of persons they think are more likely to commit crime.

◄ The controversy over New York City's stop and frisk policy focuses on racial profiling in violation of civil rights.

© John Marshall Mantel/ ZUMAPRESS/Newscom

to stop, question, and demand documents from anyone they suspected of being in the country illegally. To its authors, this type of profiling is considered a legitimate and large-scale strategy to create an atmosphere in which undocumented immigrants (mostly from Mexico, clearly) will "self-deport." In Florida, the police in Miami Gardens were embroiled in a profiling controversy that surfaced after a year's worth of convenience store videotape revealed a pattern of wanton police harassment in the predominantly African American neighborhood business. Storeowners and customers filed a lawsuit, and the police chief resigned.[45]

In a glaring example, New York City has had a policy of "stop and frisk" for over a decade—a key component of the city's crime-fighting strategy. Police officers may stop and search anyone they suspect of criminal behavior. Given the looseness of the criteria, officers have extremely wide latitude in deciding what "suspicious" means. Those who defend stop and frisk claim that it is largely responsible for the crime decline in New York, and therefore necessary. Opponents argue that it is an unconstitutional violation of basic civil rights of innocent people going about their daily lives, undermining the trust of the community in the police without making anyone safer. Officers speaking under the protection of anonymity have revealed the pressure they are under from top-level administrators to reach certain quotas. And private citizens have documented their experiences and lodged complaints about the harassment they experience on the street.

The practice has prompted strenuous objection and several lawsuits, one of which ended with the release of department data. These data showed that in 2002, the department logged almost 100,000 stop and frisk incidents. By 2011, this number had climbed to over 685,000. In 90% of those stops, the police found no criminal activity; only 10% resulted in an arrest or a court summons. In over 80% of those stops, African Americans and Latinos were the targets.[46] Beyond the question of civil rights, these numbers beg the question of whether the policy is an effective and efficient use of law enforcement resources. Although the practice has spread to several other states, political winds are blowing from the direction of reform; stop and frisk in New York may be in for a change.

SUMMARY

Race has had an extraordinary impact on American history, including the history of crime and punishment, which has left a legacy of enormous disproportion of people of color in the criminal and juvenile justice systems. This disproportion is in large part responsible for the record high rates of American incarceration, which has had devastating effects on individuals and communities alike. Although data are imperfect, all indicators point to a striking and accumulated disadvantage in corrections for members of minority groups. Stereotypes and ingrained prejudices form a burden for African Americans, Native Americans, Latinos, and sectors of the API population, among others. The cultural differences in these groups and the language barriers they face are rarely addressed or accommodated in correctional facilities, where staff diversity is lacking as is culturally competent programming. Immigrants tend to suffer additional consequences merely because of their immigration status. Native Americans are subject to maltreatment and are incarcerated in facilities that are outside official scrutiny and accountability. Segregation policies within prison walls tend to exacerbate racial tensions and gang activities. Racial disparity is a complex issue with many causes that stem from issues of race in U.S. society. A great deal more needs to be done to acknowledge and address the nature and scope of racial problems in corrections.

DISCUSSION QUESTIONS

1. Discuss ways in which you experience or witness or are aware of racial bias in your community.

2. What do you think are the implications of the fact that more African Americans are under criminal justice supervision than were slaves prior to the Civil War?

3. What are some of the disadvantages or problems with collecting criminal justice data on race and ethnicity?

4. Explore through discussion how the effects of disproportionality might compound as people become more entrenched in the system.

5. How should data about Hispanic ethnicity be collected and analyzed?

6. What do you think of the idea of the "model minority"? What facts might challenge this idea?

7. Discuss the plight of undocumented immigrants and the implications of and response to incarcerating them.

8. What are the advantages and disadvantages of Native Americans having a separate system of justice on Native lands?

9. Should prisons be segregated by race? Why or why not?

KEY TERMS

Cultural competence, 264

Ku Klux Klan, 258

Perjury, 262

Racial profiling, 271

Tribal territories, 264

Waiver, 271

NOTES

1. Myrdal 1944
2. Du Bois 1903
3. Hartney and Vuong 2009
4. Blumstein 1982
5. Miller 1994
6. Pettit and Western 2004
7. JFA Institute 2007
8. Alexander 2010
9. Human Rights Watch 2008
10. It is worth noting the data on how much crime is actually committed by each racial or ethnic group. The only relevant sources of these data are self-reported crime activities or the accounts of victims, neither of which is very reliable. Moreover, arrest data are also an unreliable gauge of offenses by race or ethnicity, because the race of the alleged offender is unknown until an arrest is made, but who gets arrested (and who does not) may be intentionally or unintentionally correlated with race.
11. Hartney and Vuong 2009
12. In these analyses, Hispanics might be included in either group.
13. *Madrid v. Gomez* 1995
14. *Johnson v. California et al.* 2005
15. Wacquant 2002
16. National Judicial Reporting Program 2004
17. Hartney and Vuong 2009
18. Zatz 2000
19. National Corrections Reporting Program 2003
20. Ibid.
21. Ibid.
22. Hartney and Vuong 2009
23. Ibid.
24. NCCD 2007
25. National Corrections Reporting Program 2003. These data do not distinguish Hispanic from non-Hispanic youth.
26. Campaign for Youth Justice 2014; Deitch et al. 2009
27. FBI 1997
28. Le et al. 2001
29. Ibid.
30. Takagi 1989
31. President's Advisory Commission on Asian Americans and Pacific Islanders 2001
32. Krisberg 2007
33. Zheng and Zia 2007
34. Maguire and Pastore 2000
35. Truman, Langton, and Planty 2013

36. NCCD 2007

37. Kohli, Markowitz, and Chavez 2011; Tan 2011

38. Tan 2011

39. National Immigration Forum 2011

40. Lopez and Light 2009

41. Robinson 2013

42. Bushway and Piehl 2007

43. Grattet, Petersilia, and Lin 2009

44. Office of Juvenile Justice and Delinquency Prevention 2009

45. J. Brown 2013

46. Ibid.

$SAGE edge™

Sharpen your skills with SAGE edge at edge.sagepub.com/krisberg

SAGE edge for students provides a personalized approach to help you accomplish your coursework goals in an easy-to-use learning environment. This site includes action plans, mobile-friendly eFlashcards and web quizzes as well as web, audio, and video resources and links to SAGE journal articles.

12 Women in the Corrections System

LEARNING OBJECTIVES

1 To understand the ways in which the corrections system does or does not address the needs of women.

3 To be able to discuss at least five ways that girls and women have different experiences than men as regards the juvenile and criminal justice systems.

2 To gain a sense of the growth of incarceration of women in the United States.

4 To grasp the levels of physical and mental health problems prevalent among incarcerated women and girls.

The "Pink Syndrome"

If one were able to design and construct a truly just and effective system of corrections for women, including women of color, it would be different in almost every way from what exists currently—from policing, arrest policies, and court procedures to facility designs, programming, and the cultural competence of staff. Although the current system is far from ideal for either gender, and despite some recent improvements related to gender issues, it is one conceived by and for men. Women and their needs are underappreciated in the operation and programming of prisons, detention facilities, and community corrections. In fact, women's prisons are often referred to as men's prisons "painted pink."

We use ideas about gender as a filter through which to perceive and understand behavior. As with men, assumptions about women are used to predict behavior as well as judge it after the fact. If those assumptions are based on misunderstandings, responses to behavior will also miss this mark. Some correctional leaders have recognized that the goals of criminal justice are thwarted by attempting to apply to women rules and programming that were designed for men. According to such leaders, this strategy simply doesn't work, and opportunities to help women make lasting change are lost.

Women and men have different avenues into the justice system, different patterns of crime behavior, different responses to being institutionalized, and different motivations to change. Women also face a more complex mix of difficulties under correctional supervision than do their male counterparts.

According to some of our society's gender norms, women are meant to be obedient and concerned for the welfare of others. When a woman commits a crime of any severity, she breaks not only the law, but social taboo as well, and is considered doubly deviant.

Women and girls in the justice system have risks and needs in greater proportions, certainly compared to women in the general population but also compared to their incarcerated male counterparts. Imprisoned women have a very high prevalence of physical, emotional, and sexual abuse in their backgrounds; they have more strained economic circumstances; they have greater responsibility to and dependence on family; they have a higher incidence of physical health concerns, including chronic and serious diseases; they have more mental health problems; and they suffer a greater societal stigma for being under correctional control.[1]

Women of color have even more challenges, both in custody and in society in general. Compared to White women, for example, African American women are more often heads of household and more often of lower economic status.[2] Despite being the largest demographic group of incarcerated women and having the highest rates of female incarceration, African American women may be the most invisible and disregarded of all prisoners.

 5 To understand how corrections-involved women's unmet needs tend to compound and contribute to lawbreaking behavior.

6 To comprehend the ways that children, family, and relationships are significant to women under correctional control.

7 To gain a sense of what gender-responsive treatment is.

8 To see how additional research on women and girls would enhance our understanding and improve correctional treatment for women and girls.

IN THE COURTS

The Defense of Women Accused of Murdering Their Abusive Partners

For centuries, society has condoned domestic violence. Indeed, even in some current cultures, brutality toward women is expected, if not encouraged. In the United States, a woman is battered every nine seconds of every day. It is estimated that 80% to 85% of women in prison are incarcerated for crimes that directly result from their relationship with an abusing partner.[1] Many of these women had no previous trouble with the law and in general pose very little threat to public safety. Also, in many cases, there are children involved.

Court procedure and legislation continue to evolve with regard to the defense of women accused of murdering their abusing partners. In the past 25 years, an advocacy movement has taken shape around this compelling human and legal dilemma. A coalition of advocates called the Habeas Project formed following the 2002 passage of legislation in California that permitted women serving time for killing their abusers the right to file a writ of habeas corpus with new evidence about how the battering contributed to their actions—evidence that was not admissible at the time of their trials.[2] California was the first state to pass such legislation. Expert testimony had been allowed since 1991, but only affected trials after that date. In 2005, the law was extended to women convicted of other serious felonies related to domestic violence.

The project's efforts are based on the principle that women who were convicted without the benefit of expert testimony may be unjustly incarcerated. Ultimately, constitutional rights must be protected, and that protection requires information. Through the Habeas Project, dozens of women eligible for appealing their cases with new expert testimony have been able to secure their freedom or have their sentences reduced.

Domestic violence is by nature hidden from view; indeed, one of the coping strategies of women in such situations is to keep their abuse as hidden as possible. As a result of pervasive secrecy, many assumptions about these troubled relationships have been incomplete and erroneous. Jurors often have no frame of reference to understand the dynamics of an abusive relationship. Society in general is resistant to changing its notions about violence toward women in a durable way. Therefore, educating juries through expert testimony must be ongoing.

Advocates have argued that the defense has a right to raise a reasonable doubt about the specific intent to commit a crime and that a defendant's experience of years of victimization is relevant to her defense. The defendant is up against the characterization of her defense as a "sob story" or a copout.[3]

Until relatively recently, an argument from the defense that the defendant's behavior was rooted in self-preservation and stemmed from a pattern of degradation, humiliation, and domination by her abusing partner lacked the status of "expert testimony." And lay testimony was inadequate to establish a credible and complete context in which to understand the actions of the accused woman.[4]

The disparities in the treatment of African American women compared to White women in the justice system, from searches and arrest to sentencing and harsh handling inside facilities, have roots in the history of slavery.[3] African Americans were considered to be "naturally criminal" and were subjected to harsh punishments for minor, noncriminal behaviors, even impolite gestures or name-calling. This long-standing and often unquestioned premise has left its traces in our society, including on the police, the bar, the courts, and correctional personnel.[4]

Although research on this subject is relatively recent, it has revealed a great deal of illuminating and important information about the strategies for avoiding violence, the psychological responses to battering, and the cumulative effects of long-term abuse.

The 1970s saw the advent of the "battered women's defense." At the time, it represented the most advanced thinking on the subject. It was put forth to convince juries that women faced a mortal danger in abusive relationships. This defense had some serious shortcomings. It described reactions that individuals have to victimization as a sort of "learned helplessness" in a cycle of abuse. However, the notion of women as pathologically impaired defined a need for a diagnosis. If a woman did not exhibit a specific set of traits, she failed to qualify as a "battered woman." With the benefit of time and additional research, those ideas have become stereotypical and outdated.[5]

Not all battered women conform to a single profile. A woman who does not fit the stereotype—one who has fought back (despite the dangers of doing so) or tried to leave or whose act appears as an isolated or minor incident—is still less likely to overcome bias on the part of the jury. In addition, the battered woman stereotype is significantly biased against women of color, especially if they are assertive or appear to the jury as insufficiently remorseful or too uncontrollable to be dominated, and therefore not credible. It also fails to encompass men or transgender individuals who may also suffer similar circumstances.

With regard to both the general dynamics of abusive relationships and the particulars of a case, expert testimony can shed light in court on the impact of that abuse on a person's behavior—how victims attempt to protect themselves by being obedient to their abusers, and how their behavior may be driven by trying to keep peace with someone upon whom they may be wholly dependent and who routinely attacks them.

One of the most common questions people have about abusive partnerships is "Why doesn't she just leave?" The solution may seem simple to the observer, but in reality, it is extremely complex. It is just this complexity that expert testimony can enlighten. The nature of domination in these cases ensures a woman's dependency and isolation, making it extremely difficult for her to "just leave." And, as previously mentioned, there are often children involved, complicating the issue even further. In real life, women who are being abused and threatened with abuse are actually many times more likely to be killed or seriously injured when they attempt to leave their partner.[6]

Notes

1. Moore 2003
2. Legal Services for Prisoners With Children n.d.
3. California Partnership to End Domestic Violence 2011
4. Adams 2005
5. California Partnership to End Domestic Violence 2011
6. Moore 2003

Incarcerated women of all ethnicities have high levels of drug addiction and dependence. Drug-related arrests account for a significant portion of arrests for women. Besides drugs, women are arrested and charged more often than not with minor domestic violence, public-order, and property crimes. However, the women who do commit violent crimes—even murder—more often than men act out to defend themselves or their children against an abuser or an attacker. The vast majority of the time, such an abuser is someone known to the woman.[5]

Despite all of these needs, services and programming for corrections-involved women are strikingly inadequate in quantity and quality, especially gender-specific services designed to effectively address the realities that women face. Women and girls in the system are often "disconnected" from the health care, mental health, educational, and employment services that are widely accepted as means to reduce recidivism.

In this chapter, we explore more fully the reasons for increased incarceration of women, what constitutes crime, the various needs women have, and how policies can have far-reaching and sometimes unintended consequences.

The Rising Tide of Incarcerated Women—What the Numbers Say

The historical pattern of incarceration for women in the United States roughly follows the same trend as that for men. That is, despite some dips and bumps, rates of incarceration remained relatively stable during the majority of the 20th century, until the 1970s. From that period onward, rates of incarceration, as well as the consequent numbers of imprisoned persons and costs to government, began a steep and steady rise.

The United States now locks up more women than ever before. Women represented only 17% of the criminal justice population in 2000, but the acceleration of their incarceration rate is far outpacing that of men. Between 1990 and 2000, there was an 81% increase in the female population, compared to a 45% increase in the male population during the same period.[6]

The fact that large numbers of women are imprisoned in the United States has far-reaching effects in nearly every aspect of society. What may be most obvious to the larger society are the direct economic costs of locking up people of either gender—that is, costs of incarceration paid by taxpayers and lost income for both the individual and her family and community. Beyond that are the somewhat less obvious costs of the deteriorating physical and mental health of incarcerated women, the separation of children from their mothers at crucial developmental stages, the generational cycles of incarceration and poverty, and the dissolution of families and communities.

Besides those women in prisons and jails, there are hundreds of thousands more under some other form of correctional control, such as probation and alternatives to incarceration such as house arrest, intensive supervision, electronic monitoring, or day or evening reporting.[7] Among adults involved in the justice system, women are more likely than men to be the primary provider for young children, to be the primary breadwinner for their household, and to have a high number of health needs.[8] A range of sanctions is better than using imprisonment as a single response to crime, as they allow some women to remain in the community, closer to family and employment opportunities. Despite the existing range of responses, there is still a need for a greater variety and expanded use of alternatives to incarceration that focus on family integrity, employment, family housing, and women's and children's mental and physical health.

Drastic Increases in Overall Correctional Control

There were 1.3 million women under some form of correctional control in the United States in 2009—15% in state or federal prison or local jail and 85% on probation or parole. In contrast, a greater percentage (35%) of the just under 6 million men under correctional control were in prison or jail.

Figures 12.1 and 12.2 show that, although the numbers of system-involved adults generally grew for several decades leading up to 2009, the story is not identical for women and

Figure 12.1   Number of Men Under Correctional Control, 1990–2009

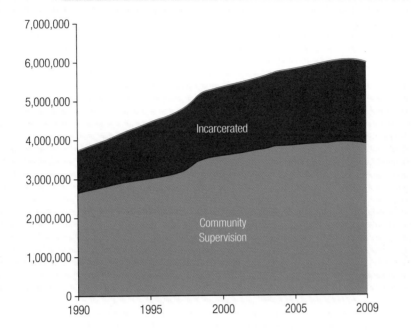

Figure 12.2   Number of Women Under Correctional Control, 1990–2009

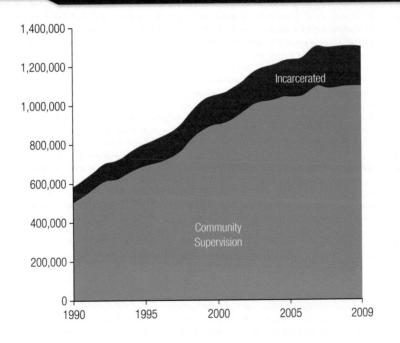

Figures 12.1 and 12.2 show the number of men and women, respectively, under correctional control (prison, jail, probation, or parole) from 1990 to 2009. The population of both genders under correctional control grew in this time period, but the upward slope of the purple area shows the increase was substantially more rapid for women. Still, fewer women are under correctional control, just under 1.1 million women versus almost 4 million men in 2009. *Source: Reproduced from Glaze 2010.*

men. The long period of increase was much more dramatic for women. The overall number of women under correctional control in 2006 (the historic peak year) was 2.2 times the number in 1990—a 120% increase in 16 years.[9] The increase in female prison inmates is particularly striking, a rise of over 700% in three decades (13,000 in 1980 to over than 113,000 in 2009).[10]

Along with the raw numbers, the proportion of women in the system compared to men also grew. Women represented 18% of the total number of persons under correctional control in 2009, compared to 14% in 1990.[11] After years of steep increases, the growth rate of the correctional population for both genders slowed in the 2000s and may have leveled off at the end of the decade.[12] Nevertheless, their sheer numbers, and the evidence that the system could not adapt quickly enough to their rising proportions compared to men, make it crucial that more attention be paid to corrections-involved women.

Gender and Incarceration Rates

As with other groups, rates of incarceration for women vary widely according to the type of incarceration, geography, and race or ethnicity. The most striking contrast is the incarceration rate for women compared to that for men. In state and federal prison in 2009, 67 women were incarcerated versus 949 men (per 100,000 in the general U.S. population).[13] This may be a reflection of different offending behavior between the genders and, to a lesser extent, different justice-system responses to that offending behavior.

Looking at state rates shows an enormous variation in rates of incarceration for women. They range from 12 in Massachusetts to 135 in Oklahoma (in 2009). There are similarly wide variations of incarceration rates for men.[14]

A closer look at incarceration rates by gender and race or ethnicity reveals a striking disproportion for women of color. In 2009, African American women were approximately three times more likely to be incarcerated as White women (a rate of 142 compared to 50). Hispanic women were one and a half times more likely (74 compared to 50) to be incarcerated.[15]

Figure 12.3   Offenses for Women in State Prison, 2006

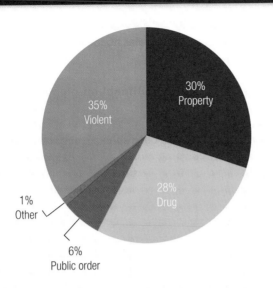

30% Property

35% Violent

1% Other

28% Drug

6% Public order

Figure 12.4   Offenses for Men in State Prison, 2006

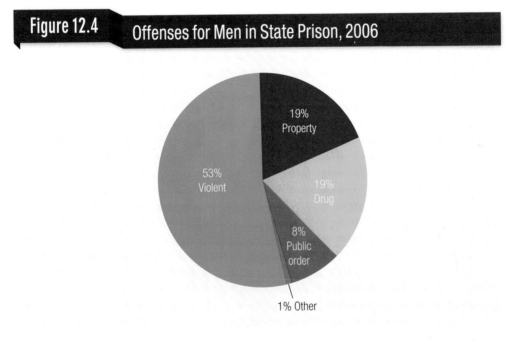

19% Property

53% Violent

19% Drug

8% Public order

1% Other

In general, women are incarcerated for less serious crimes than men. Figures 12.3 and 12.4 show the most serious offense type for sentenced inmates under state jurisdiction in 2006.

Incarcerated women were imprisoned in 2006 more often for drug and property offenses and less often for violent offenses than men.[16] Women were more likely than men to be sent to prison for possession or other drug offenses (23% vs. 16%) but are nearly equal on trafficking (14% vs. 13.5%).[17]   *Source: West, Sabol, and Greenman 2010.*

Girls and the System

An understanding of women and corrections begins with a look at the experience of girls and young women. Society imposes a double standard, locking up more young women than young men for less serious crimes, for "their own protection," and for status offenses, such as truancy, running away, and incorrigibility—behaviors classified as crimes only for youth younger than 18 years old. There is a long-standing pattern of policing girls' sexuality, of characterizing normal growing-up behavior as "disobedience" or "immorality" and trying to control it through law enforcement.[18]

Some forms of youth behavior undeniably require a swift and certain response from law enforcement to protect public safety and hold youth accountable. However, objectively and regularly reviewing policy and practice for the purpose of evaluating gender discrepancies could advance the cause of justice for young girls and boys alike.

A prevailing theme in the media, which tends to have a capricious, anecdotal approach to crime reporting rather than a scientific one, is that young women are becoming more violent over time. The media are reporting more violence by girls and use examples of sensational stories of brutality on the part of certain girls as if to indicate a trend of increasing criminality. Similar incidents on the part of boys fail to bend the gender stereotype.[19]

In addition, changes in policy rather than actual changes in behavior can often dictate rates of arrest. Violent arrest rates and self-report of violence by juveniles—both male and female—indicate a consistent and significant decline since the mid 1990s. One departure from the trend is arrests for violent assault. Researchers have examined these trends in some detail. The Girls Study Group used a combination of data sources to analyze the increase of arrests for girls. The group suggests a number of factors that must be considered if the data are to be understood, including gender-based parental expectations of obedience and the apparent tendency of girls to act out inside the home rather than in public

▲ Who should be in a position to decide whether a young woman needs protection from herself?

Table 12.1 Most Serious Crime Leading to Youth Residential Placement, 2011*

Crime	Girls	Boys
Violent	42%	45%
Criminal homicide	1%	2%
Sexual assault	1%	9%
Robbery	4%	12%
Aggravated assault	12%	10%
Simple assault	19%	9%
Other person	5%	4%
Property	23%	29%
Burglary	5%	14%
Theft	9%	6%
Auto theft	3%	3%
Arson	1%	1%
Other property	5%	5%
Drug	8%	8%
Drug trafficking	1%	2%
Other drug	7%	7%
Public Order	12%	14%
Weapons	2%	6%
Other public order	10%	9%
Status Offenses	14%	3%

In general, girls are arrested and incarcerated for much less serious charges than boys are. In 2011, status offenses as the most serious offense leading to residential placement were over four times more prevalent for girls as they were for boys (14% vs. 3%). The most common offenses for girls were property (23%), simple assault (19%), status, and drug or public-order offenses (20%). Boys were most often arrested and detained for property (29%), drug or public-order offenses (22%), robbery (12%), and murder or sexual assault (11%).[20] *Source: Sickmund et al. 2013. * Percentages may not add to 100% due to rounding; technical violations not included.*

or at school.[21] Others assert that arrest rates for assault have to do mostly with redefining incidents of domestic violence and law enforcement policy.[22]

A wave of state legislation has mandated a police response to domestic incidents. Originally intended to increase protections for the victims of domestic conflicts, this legislation has had a number of unintended consequences. A frustrated or frightened parent may call the police for assistance. The incident results in an arrest that would have previously been handled informally. Multiply this scenario many times, and a new set of statistics emerges. The term coined for this trend is *up-criming*, another form of "net-widening" or catching

SPOTLIGHT

BABIES IN CHAINS

The criminalization of girls has at times taken on misguided extremes. In Florida, two separate but similar incidents stand out—one in St. Petersburg involving a 5-year-old, and another in Avon Park involving a 6-year-old. In both cases, school officials called in the police, and it took several officers to handcuff, arrest, and take the child to jail for having a tantrum and being "uncontrollable" in the classroom. In both cases, the girls were African American.[1] Both were cuffed around the biceps (because their wrists were too small), taken to jail, fingerprinted, and photographed for mug shots. The 6-year-old from Avon Park was charged with felony assault and two misdemeanors, resisting arrest, and causing a disruption.[2] The chiefs of police responsible in both of the incidents maintained a calm and rational explanation of their need to apprehend these children. To reach out to the police for additional help with a child's challenging (but arguably normal) behavior is a disturbing commentary on how

accustomed some caretakers of children have become to using law enforcement to intervene in conflict they might have handled themselves. Equally disturbing, if not more so, is the defensiveness of law enforcement officials.

QUESTIONS

1   How would you develop a school policy to address acting-out behavior?

2   What resources should be available to schoolteachers for dealing with problem students, short of calling the police?

3   Discuss how these incidents may be part of a continuum of biased responses toward African American young women.

Notes

1.   CBSNews.com 2005; WFTV.com 2007

2.   WFTV.com 2007

---

more youth into the system, not because of any change in typical behavior but through policy and practice. "Zero tolerance" policies at schools—calling the police for every incidence of bad behavior—are another example of net-widening that have led to more girls being arrested.

The results of such a response to domestic violence can be observed in changes in arrest data for assaults. Between 1999 and 2008, arrests for aggravated assault among young men dropped 22%. Among young women, the drop was only 2.5%. In the case of simple assault, arrests for young men dropped 6%. However, for young women, arrests in this category *increased* 16%.[23] Furthermore, young women who are arrested for violent or person offenses are more likely than their male counterparts to know their victims personally or to be related to them (82% of young women vs. 67% of young men).[24]

Girls in Custody

Young women in placement have profiles similar to those of their adult counterparts. They have high rates of mental health and substance abuse issues, histories of physical abuse (almost twice as much as young men—42% vs. 22%), sexual abuse (more than four times as much—35% vs. 8%), and suicide attempts (44% vs. 19%).[25]

Young women in residential placement report greater use of drugs than young men (91% vs. 87%), including more frequent drug use and experimenting with a wider variety of drugs. They also report having a higher incidence of drug-related problems, such as failure to meet responsibilities or blacking out from alcohol consumption. Despite the prevalence

Zero tolerance:
A policy, usually in schools, of punishing every instance of rule-breaking, regardless of any extenuating circumstances such as accidental infractions, not knowing the behavior was not allowed, or first-time offenses. Zero-tolerance policies are often applied to specific infractions, such as fighting or possession of drugs or weapons.

of these problems, young women have less access than young men do to substance abuse treatment while in placement.

Young women also have greater health care needs in general—for illness, dental and hearing conditions, and prescribed medication. A high percentage of young women in placement (59%) take prescribed medication to treat emotional or mental problems.

Although young women in placement aged 10 to 20 have a high prevalence of learning disabilities (30% vs. 5% in the general population), they demonstrate an aspiration to earn advanced education degrees more often than their male counterparts. More often than boys, they enter custody from situations where there is no parent or from foster care.[26]

Women's Pathways Into Crime

Women typically get into trouble with the law for significantly different reasons than men. What motivates women to commit crime has to do more with survival, providing for children, coping with early trauma, or dependence on men who are more often persistent lawbreakers and who involve their female partners or relatives in minor roles in their operations. Women are usually not career criminals but accomplices, and they have less to bargain with in the plea-bargaining process. Women relate differently to the factors that typically influence whether a person commits crime—the taste for risk, likelihood of shame, level of self-control, and assessment of costs and benefits of crime. Additionally, women more often than men have the responsibility for building and maintaining relationships and for nurturing families, which can exert a profound set of emotional pressures.[27]

Prior to their incarceration, many women live lives on the margins of society, sometimes literally, in homelessness. As mentioned, poverty and cycles of victimization—often coupled with substance abuse—combine to form a critical disenfranchisement where a simple mistake or a terrible one can prove to be disastrous.

In addition, changes in policy can change a narrow pathway to the criminal justice system into a freeway. The sharp increase in the incarceration of women is certainly the result of a complex of factors. However, changes in drug and sentencing policy are widely perceived

◀ It took many years for the discrepancy between sentencing practices for powder and crack cocaine to surface in the public discourse.

© iStockphoto.com/ Mercè Bellera

SPOTLIGHT

WAR ON DRUGS

President Richard Nixon declared a "War on Drugs" in 1971, calling drugs the nation's "Public Enemy #1." In 1973, he created the Drug Enforcement Administration to coordinate the work of all other agencies dedicated to reducing the drug economy. The climate of fear over drug use and drug dealing helped to pass state-level legislation.

New York is the fifth most populous state in the nation. Policy changes in these larger states offer a glimpse at the dynamics at work in corrections in the broader arena; precedent and influence affect the smaller states.[1] A sharp increase in the women's prison population in New York can be traced to the War on Drugs. In 1973, New York instituted the Rockefeller drug laws—named for then Governor Nelson Rockefeller—which constituted the nation's harshest scheme for punishing drug crimes.

These statutes increased the penalties for possession and trafficking of narcotics and were notorious for their stringent application. As with other legislation, there is often unintended and unforeseen collateral damage. The original intent may have been to catch major dealers, but in reality, scores of low-level, nonviolent drug users, many with first-time offenses, were caught in a severely punitive web of incarceration.

Much of what happened to women as a result of these laws was likely both unintended and unforeseen, and extremely damaging to the communities most affected. The penalties for selling 56 grams (2 ounces) of heroin, cocaine, morphine, opium, or cannabis or possessing 4 ounces of the same substances were mandatory sentences of 15 to 25 years to life. The portion of the law pertaining to marijuana was repealed during the democratic administration of Governor Hugh Carey in 1979.

The Rockefeller drug laws are still considered to be synonymous with draconian and racially biased policy,

to be one of the most significant ones.[28] According to the Bureau of Justice Statistics (BJS), between 1986 and 1996, there was an increase of almost 1,000% for women drug offenders.[29]

A Complex Mix of Risk Factors

The "typical" woman in prison or jail is between 20 and 30 years old, African American, the mother of young children, undereducated, underemployed, and dependent on substances, and she has a history of physical or sexual victimization. These multiple factors often form a complex mix of problems for incarcerated women.[30]

Incarcerated women have low levels of violence but high rates of disciplinary infractions compared to those found in men's prisons. Women have a profound need for closeness, and the search for connection drives much of their behavior. They are more likely than men to act out of self-preservation. They may act out for psychological or emotional reasons such as low self-esteem, guilt for abandoning children, or searching for an outside rescue.[31]

Cycles of Victimization

One of the most significant differences between men and women involved in the criminal justice system is their rates of physical, mental, and sexual victimization and the nature of

reviled by liberals and conservatives alike. By many measures, they proved a social, fiscal, and political fiasco, putting punishments for drug law violations on a par with those for murder and failing to lead to any significant reduction in drug use or violent crime.

Efforts to reform the Rockefeller laws have been long-standing and persistent. In 2004, the threshold amounts were increased, the sentencing scheme was changed to determinate, and life sentences were eliminated.

In his first State of the State address in January 2009, then New York Governor David Paterson was critical of the Rockefeller drug laws, stating, "Few public safety initiatives have failed as badly and for as long as the Rockefeller Drug Laws. These laws did not work when I was elected Senator in 1985, and they do not work today."[2]

QUESTIONS

1 Discuss the so-called War on Drugs and how to develop a rational federal position on drug control.

2 Should lawmakers compare the punishments for all crimes before devising or altering sentencing schemes for one part of the penal code?

3 What is the sentencing range for marijuana in your state?

Notes

1. Michigan adopted an even more severe version of the law in 1978; the state's "650 lifer law" required life without possibility of parole for anyone convicted of the sale, manufacture, or possession of 650 grams (1.4 pounds) of cocaine or scheduled opiates. This law was reformed slightly in 1998.

2. Syracuse.com 2009

that victimization. Large segments of system-involved women on probation, in local jails, and in prison report histories of abuse and victimization.[32] There is copious research concluding that delinquent girls and adult women in the system have disproportionately high rates of physical and sexual abuse compared to women in the general population and compared to men in the system.[33]

One 2004 study of women in jail by Green and colleagues reported that 71% were exposed to domestic violence, 90% reported at least one interpersonal trauma, and nearly all (98%) had been exposed to some kind of a traumatic event.[34]

Invisibility

Whether in reference to women in prison or women in the general population, it has taken generations for the realities of women's victimization to come to light. It has taken even longer for society to accept that women's victimization is highly correlated with risk for criminal behavior. Physical abuse by a stranger toward a woman (or a girl) has long been recognized as a crime; it took longer for rape by an acquaintance, however, to be recognized as a crime. And more recently than one might expect, it was assumed that a woman could not be raped by her husband—that a man had proprietary rights to every aspect of his wife's person, making rape impossible by definition. The marriage contract was interpreted as a woman's consent to all of her husband's sexual advances. According to Belknap, even taking into account that women often redefine (in a minimizing way) what they experience, marital rape occurs with "alarming frequency."[35]

SPOTLIGHT

VIOLENCE AGAINST WOMEN

The term *violence against women* (VAW) refers to crimes such as rape and domestic violence, where the vast majority of victims are women. For most of U.S. history, sexualized violence and other forms of violence against women were considered matters that should be handled privately and not involve law enforcement. In the 1970s, the feminist movement brought the issue to the forefront and compelled a national discussion. Grassroots, female-run groups and organizations created the first resources to support rape victims, including shelters for victims of domestic violence and rape crisis centers to help rape survivors navigate the usually hostile and confusing criminal justice system. After decades of pressure to take VAW seriously, Congress passed the Violence Against Women Act (VAWA) in 1994, and President Clinton signed it into law. The act's first reauthorization in 2000 established the

Office on Violence Against Women, which provides national leadership on reducing violence against women. The office oversees and funds research and programs on rape, incest, domestic violence, sexual assault, and stalking. All victims, regardless of gender, are to be protected by this legislation and office. After a drawn-out battle in Congress—sparked in part by the extension of VAWA protections for lesbian, gay, bisexual, transgender, and questioning (LGBTQ), Native American, and undocumented individuals—the act was reauthorized in 2013.

Still, there is significant work that needs to be done in the area of VAW. Nearly 1 in 5 women in the United States has been sexually assaulted. More than 1 in 3 women (35.6%) in the United States has experienced rape, physical violence, or stalking by an intimate partner in her lifetime.[1] Estimates are that, between 2008 and 2012, approximately 60% of rape victims did not report to the police. This is in part a reflection of how inhospitable the criminal justice system is to survivors of VAW.[2] Factoring

Legal justification of women as property took on an extreme form in the relations between African American women under slavery and the sexual liberties assumed by their captors. Women of color are still the most invisible segment of the prison population. Their voices are all but absent from public discussion and public policy.[36]

Awareness of the prevalence and nature of crimes against women is growing. However, the types of crimes that women are often exposed to and victimized by, such as battering and sexual assault, are fear inducing, humiliating, and violent. More often than men, women endure a debilitating sense of betrayal, because much of the physical and sexual abuse that they experience is perpetrated by not only someone they know but an intimate partner or a family member.[37]

These crimes are also among the most underreported. This is evidenced, in part, by the discrepancy in the data collected by, for example, the Uniform Crime Reports (UCR) of the Federal Bureau of Investigation (FBI) and the National Crime Victimization Survey (NCVS).[38] Although there are differences in definitions and method, NCVS reports more than 200,000 sexual victimizations, and the UCR reports fewer than 100,000 forcible rapes.[39] Underreporting contributes to a failure by society and legislators to grasp the extent and severity of the reality facing women in the corrections system (and in society), which creates a barrier to effective responses.

Societal expectations set up a variety of problematic dynamics. Passivity in women encourages gender stereotyping. At the same time, personality traits perceived as aggressive are all too often considered a reason for a woman's predicament. Women are often blamed for attracting negative attention and for playing a part in their own victimization, even within the criminal justice system.

in these unreported rapes, only about 3% of rapists serve a single day in prison. The failure of government agencies and the criminal justice system to respond adequately to violence against women has a significant impact on incarcerated women.

The majority of incarcerated women and girls have experienced some form of sexual violence. Women are often further victimized while they are incarcerated. Limited access to resources to help them heal decreases their chances of rehabilitation. In some states, women convicted of a felony cannot access victim's compensation while they serve their sentence. This may mean that a woman who is raped while on felony probation, for example, may not have the funds to move to a safe home or cover the cost of medical bills or therapy. Experiencing VAW can also be a contributing factor to women's criminal behavior. For example, women may find themselves involved in crime as a means of support after escaping abusive relationships.

QUESTIONS

1 What would be an argument for failing to reauthorize the VAWA? Find out your local legislator's position on this issue.

2 How do system failures to address VAW make things harder for incarcerated women?

3 How do you think law enforcement does treat or should treat a woman who is reporting a rape?

Notes

1. Centers for Disease Control and Prevention 2014
2. Bureau of Justice Statistics 2013

Another reason that women do not report victimization and abuse is the fear of retaliation from their attackers. Too often, economic dependence contributes to a woman feeling trapped in an abusive situation. She may judge the danger of reporting the crime to be worse than the crime itself, ongoing though it may be.

Many women have been blamed for their attacks and have had little support from the police or the legal system. This victim blaming can be far-reaching and severely damaging. To a significant degree, our culture accepts male violence as normal and at times even a logical reaction to common provocation by the women in their lives. Too often, women internalize this as guilt, and too often they blame themselves, ensuring their silence.

Childhood Trauma

Often, the victimization of women has roots stemming from childhood. This early, formative experience puts women at risk for later involvement in the justice system.[40]

Covington has done groundbreaking research on the topic of trauma and risk. Her research reveals compelling evidence that incarcerated women and girls have histories of extensive early trauma and that these early life events have a direct impact on risky behaviors, mental and physical health problems, and related lawbreaking behavior—prostitution, drugs, and violence toward themselves or others.[41]

She elaborates further on childhood traumatic events, or CTEs, drawing a direct correlation to gynecological problems, STDs, prostitution, eating disorders, the use of psychotropic medication, alcohol abuse, suicide attempts, and other mental health issues.[42]

▲ A woman's vulnerability to involvement in the criminal justice system often has its roots in early childhood trauma.

© iStockphoto.com/ Christopher Futcher

Physical Health

Women's health issues differ from those of men in many ways. Women enter the system with higher rates of chronic health problems (asthma, diabetes, STDs, hypertension), poor nutrition, poverty, drug dependence, and mental health disorders such as depression, anxiety, eating dysfunction, and posttraumatic stress disorder (PTSD). Prison tends to worsen these conditions. Women in prison have often learned to distrust authority figures, including health care providers, and have little health education.[43]

Incarcerated women have high rates of drug dependence. Their drug use, in turn, refracts into a spectrum of additional physical problems. Drug-dependent women in prison are more likely than their male counterparts to have tuberculosis, hepatitis, toxemia, anemia, hypertension, obesity, and diabetes. They also have a higher incidence of STDs and HIV/AIDS due to higher rates of prostitution and a greater prevalence of sexual abuse. Inadequate or nonexistent treatment for STDs can contribute to cervical cancer, secondary infections, infertility, and birth defects.[44]

Obviously, women and men in the criminal justice system have vastly different reproductive health needs. In 2007, on average, 5% of women entering state prison and 6% of those entering jails were pregnant. The Rebecca Project and the National Women's Law Center conducted a review and graded the differences among states with regard to several family health measures specific to women—prenatal care, shackling during delivery and transport, family-based alternatives to incarceration, and prison nurseries. Only Pennsylvania received an overall grade of A, and only seven other states got a B. Twenty-one states received failing grades.[45]

Staying healthy during incarceration is difficult at best, and even more of a challenge during pregnancy, when all health factors, such as nutrition, stress levels, and sleep, can have a significant impact on the health of the baby. But the special needs of a pregnant woman in prison can provoke hostility and resentment from staff members who may have to break their routine to accommodate them. Even a seemingly simple matter of maternity clothes can present a problem.

Accessing quality medical services can be a struggle for incarcerated women for a variety of reasons. Stories of serious health conditions being ignored are not uncommon. There are reported instances of a staff member assuming a prisoner is faking a need for attention and ignoring her request for medical attention for a condition that tragically proves to be fatal.[46] Prison medical providers are actually trained to be aloof, not to touch inmates unless absolutely necessary, to regard prisoner politeness as suspicious, and not to use first names.[47]

Mental Health

Rates of mental health disorders are extremely high for incarcerated women. In 2005, 73% of women in state prisons had mental health problems, compared to 12% of women in the general public and 55% of men in state prisons.[48]

The most common mental health problems for women found by researchers are substance use, PTSD, and depression.[49] Women prisoners also have a high prevalence of schizophrenia, psychosexual dysfunction, antisocial personality disorders, and homelessness.[50] In 2005, approximately 75% of the women with a mental health problem also had a substance problem. Women with mental health issues, like their male counterparts, tend to self-medicate with illicit drugs. (They are also more likely to have been homeless, to have a history of physical or sexual abuse, to have had a parent who abused alcohol or drugs, and to have broken institutional rules.)[51]

◀ The prevalence of abuse and victimization in the backgrounds of system-involved women make it crucial that those with physical or mental health issues receive gender-responsive, trauma-informed care.

©Bill Gentile/CORBIS

Without treatment and subjected to the stresses of incarceration, mental health among incarcerated women tends to deteriorate, which sets up a cyclic dynamic between problem behavior and increased punishment.

Incarcerated Women as Mothers

As mentioned, family relationships are of critical importance for women in prison. Their children, especially, are one of the greatest concerns for women in prison. Of all incarcerated women, 66,000 were mothers to children under age 18 in 2007. An estimated 147,000 U.S. children had an incarcerated mother. From 1991 to 2007, that number grew by 131%.[52]

Women have caregiving responsibilities that they obviously cannot fulfill while in prison. Many incarcerated women speak with frustration, sadness, and anger at being separated from their children. Children suffer from this separation as well; in effect, the children are punished along with their mothers, despite their innocence. Women suffer intense guilt and frustration in this regard, and they are often highly sensitive to the risk of adding more days to their time.

Coping

Many factors affect a woman's ability to cope with the severe stresses of prison life—age, offense background, temperament, socioeconomic class, length of sentence, and physical and mental constitution, among others. Separation from family—especially children—is one of the main stressors for incarcerated women, in addition to inadequate medical care, vulnerability to abuse, and other hardships. On the other hand, the desire of reuniting with their children and families is a significantly motivating factor for women. Some of the ways that women cope are through religion, forming social groups, mentoring and being mentored, "reinterpreting" their situation, or disassociating from their reality.[53]

Both women and men create social structures and hierarchies in prison. However, women tend to form their social groups to mimic the family structure, sometimes with specifically assigned roles, and they tend to treat one another with more tolerance and support than one sees in men's prisons, even across racial and ethnic lines. Social structures within prisons reflect women's need for relationships and intimate bonds. In women's prisons, administrators may be suspicious of women forming bonds of an intimate nature. Partially for this reason, common prison policies require frequent changes of work assignments and roommates.[54]

YOU DECIDE

Petitions to Have Children Live In With Mothers

J. L. entered custody already pregnant and gave birth to a daughter after five months of her incarceration. The new mother was able to spend only a few hours with her infant. Nurses came and took the baby away, despite J. L.'s objections. Months later, J. L. wants to reunite with her baby.

The child development literature suggests that mother and child bonding is critical to the healthy development of all children. Advocates for incarcerated women argue that occasional prison visits are not sufficient to create this bond. The prison administrators respond that prisons are not designed to house babies, and they have concerns that the child could be subject to abuse. They also contend that children raised in prison will be stigmatized in the outside community. The alternative for J. L.'s daughter is foster care or adoption. J. L. and her advocates propose creating a nursery in the prison with appropriate medical and social service staff.

YOU DECIDE: **Should the children of new mothers be allowed to live in the prison? Should prison administrators accommodate mothers and children in this way?**

Women find common ground in their role as mothers. According to Owen, women bond over their common need to speak of their children, their need to acknowledge their guilt about their absence from their children's lives, and their rejection of other inmates who have harmed children.[55]

Some means of coping are destructive rather than productive, such as substance abuse, self-injury, or suicide. Unfortunately, there is very little research in this area. What does exist points to enormous and poorly understood needs of women prisoners and highly inadequate treatment to address those needs. Given the dominance–dependence dynamic in correctional settings, complaining about anything in prison is problematic. Women fear retaliation for having complained, and that fear is sometimes well justified.

Programs and Services

In general, we see that the women's prison population is largely low risk for violence or serious behavior problems but high needs for all of the reasons stated above. Even though the number of women under all forms of correctional control is significant and growing, the proportion of women to men in the total prison population is still relatively small—and their sentences are generally shorter. These facts may be used to justify less attention to women's facilities and programming. Both conditions of confinement and treatment for women tend to be of an even lower standard than what exists for men. Ross and Fabiano

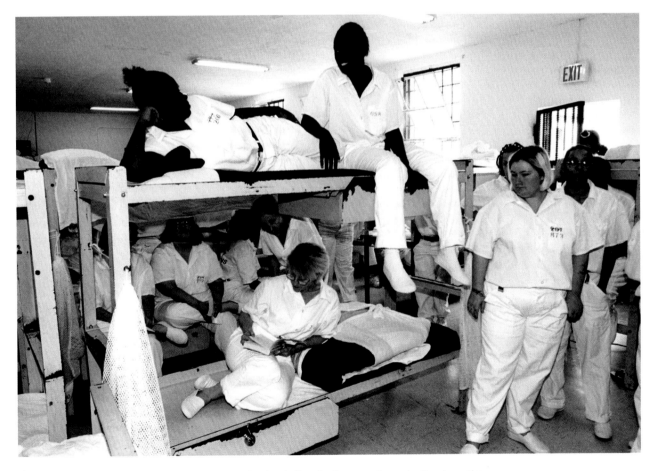

▲ Individualized service and treatment programming is a hallmark of progressive correctional practice.

© Robin Nelson/ZUMA Press/Corbis

SPOTLIGHT

DELIVERY FROM SHACKLES

One of the most disturbing images from prisons is that of a pregnant woman going through labor and delivery shackled to a bed—a highly controversial institutional practice specific to women. Prisoner advocates describe it as barbaric and contend that it constitutes cruel and unusual punishment. The American Medical Association, the American Civil Liberties Union, Amnesty International, and the United Nations have all condemned the practice, which is legal in 36 states. Even the American Correctional Association has a clear standard prohibiting shackling. In 2008, the Federal Bureau of Prisons ended the practice of shackling women in federal prisons.[1] California prohibits the use of shackles for transporting pregnant women or for women prisoners who are in labor, childbirth, or recovery after delivery unless there are specific security concerns that would justify the use of shackles.

The reasons for shackling from a control perspective are to prevent escape and assault. Opponents to the practice brush off these concerns as irrelevant, given that labor and delivery make such events highly unlikely, women are always under guard, and other measures that pose less risk to mother and baby are completely effective. Shackles for transportation purposes impede a woman's ability to walk and move and increase the risk of falling. Shackling a woman's limbs or abdomen to her labor bed makes it difficult to change positions and impedes the progress of the delivery. Precious time can be lost if a C-section becomes necessary. And shackling forces women to endure an additional stigma at this crucial and vulnerable moment.

Public exposure and lawsuits by women who were injured or whose babies' health was impacted by these practices are affecting legislation in many states; 16 states have introduced legislation to ban shackling. Still, much of the public remains unaware of the practice, and the laws

---

state that "in general, treatment and training programs for female offenders are distinctively poorer in quantity, quality, and variety, and considerably different in nature from those for male offenders."[56] Programs and services for women are not only fewer in number, but there is less variety as well than those for men. These inadequacies tend to reinforce the state of dependency that plague system-involved women.

Substance abuse and mental health counseling are key components to treatment that is most likely to relate to the causes of women's lawbreaking behavior, yet these services are often too scarce, a situation exaggerated even more by the explosive growth in the number of women in prison. Education and job training programs are valued among incarcerated women; however, there are not nearly enough of such programs. Recreational facilities are far poorer for women than men, possibly due to an assumption that women have less of a need for physical activity. Similarly, conjugal visits are rare in women's prisons.[57]

Operational Issues in Custody

It is difficult for corrections administrators to manage a population that they do not understand well. Many correctional staff (especially male staff) find it difficult to work with girls and women. There are complex issues surrounding sexual safety in women's facilities—staffing issues about gender, legitimate security concerns, and the protection of inmate safety and privacy. Some leaders are trying to improve institutional practice and training so that staff can appropriately recognize and handle the behavior of women in

that restrict it can be difficult to enforce. Corrections authorities tend to resist having their control choices limited or dictated by statute.

A 2009 case helped to advance the cause for banning restraints on pregnant women. *Nelson v. Correctional Medical Services* resulted in a federal court decision that shackling during childbirth is unconstitutional.[2]

Perhaps the movement in general toward rehabilitation will continue to promote the concept of the profound life events of pregnancy, delivery, and new motherhood as an opportunity for women to make positive changes in their lives.

QUESTIONS

1 How should prison officials deal with women delivering babies?

2 What other health-related situations specific to women might need special consideration during incarceration?

3 Should prisons be compelled to make their health care policies public?

Notes

1. National Women's Law Center and the Rebecca Project for Human Rights 2010

2. *Nelson v. Correctional Medical Services* 2009

custody, help improve their outcomes, and reduce recidivism. Administrators also have to manage a delicate balance between addressing the particular needs of women and complying with laws that guarantee equal protection.

Poorly trained staff may fail to notice cues such as expressions of hopelessness or worthlessness and may not understand what triggers problem behavior in women. Instead of being able to take a proactive approach and intervene, unskilled staff are more likely to react to behavior in ways that make it worse. This dynamic can quickly devolve, leading to cycles of more frustration, more problem behavior, and more disciplinary actions.

There are a number of privacy concerns for women in custody. They have a greater need for physical privacy and private space, they are extremely sensitive to protection of personal property, and they have a strong need to maintain the privacy of personal or medical information. These concerns can present challenges for facility administrators.

Women tend to seek medical help sooner than men, placing a burden on medical resources in prison. Again, by seeking help frequently, women are often seen as malingering or faking. Even the more mundane aspects of prison life—such as clothing and diet specific to women rather than to men—have repercussions for inmates and staff alike.

Some leaders are recognizing that well-trained staff (whether female or male) can offer help and support, can take a proactive position in modeling problem-solving techniques, and can better de-escalate tense situations. More enlightened leaders are finding that programming for incarcerated women that stresses self-efficacy, resilience, and meaningful work is a key to smoother facility operations.[58]

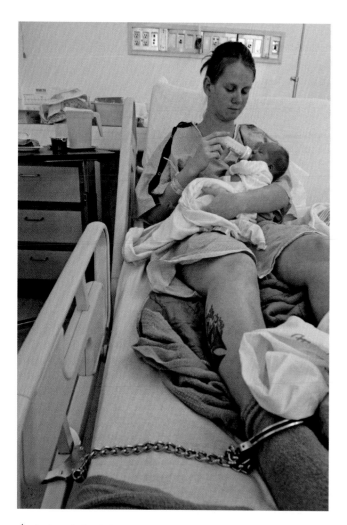

▲ An inmate feeds her newborn baby for the last time before being returned to prison. The average stay in hospital for a pregnant prisoner delivering her baby is 48 to 72 hours, during which time the mother is allowed to visit with her child. The hospital acts as a broker to distribute the newborn infants to their temporary or permanent guardians.

© Mark Allen Johnson/ ZUMAPRESS/Newscom

Conditions of Confinement

The deprivations of prison are stressful and harsh, and the punishment of prison is far more than just the denial of liberty. The effects of the experience can only be hinted at with statistics about mental health and family needs. In general, the conditions in women's facilities are poorer than in those for men. Conditions of confinement are often the basis for sex discrimination litigation brought by women.[59]

In her exhaustive 2007 work on women in the criminal justice system, *The Invisible Woman*, Joanne Belknap states,

> the conditions of women's prisons are worse than the deplorable conditions of men's prisons. Whether we measure this as proximity to family and loved ones or access to health care, recreation, education; or disproportionate rates of people of color and HIV-positive status; or distribution of psychotropic drugs; or likelihood of being raped by a guard, women in prison appear to be far worse off than most men in prison. The only way that women appear to be better off—and it is a significant one—is that incarcerated women appear to be far less likely than their male counterparts to be raped by fellow prisoners.[60]

Research suggests that conditions for women in local jails are even worse than those in prison. That said, however, though it may be dismal and inadequate, health care and other services in prison and jail may be better than what was available on the outside.

Research on Women and the Justice System

Perhaps because women have historically made up a small portion of the criminal justice population, research on women may be considered less interesting or less important than research on men. Women have typically been excluded from criminology research, being unspecified and undifferentiated in the collection and analysis of data. The BJS collects a vast amount of data each year (much of it used here), but very little of its reporting specifies women and men as distinct groups. Even less of it breaks the gender categories down further by other variables, such as race, ethnicity, or socioeconomic class.

Women's criminal behavior is not well understood; only recently has it become more often the subject of serious study. Some research has led to interesting conclusions. The "liberation theory," for example, asserts that the women's movement of the 1960s, which stressed equality with men in new arenas, resulted in increased crime commission by women—an idea that has largely been discredited.[61]

Predictions that women's crime behavior would become more like that of men as women took on more roles in society like those of men have not been realized. More apparent is that women who are trapped in traditional gender roles and trapped in persistent patterns of economic disadvantage are at higher risk for becoming engaged in crime.[62]

Research has progressed to some extent on the gender differences in what motivates criminal behavior. For instance, we know that women are more likely than men to be engaged in supporting their partners' criminal activity than initiating it; that they are more often couriers of drugs rather than high-level drug dealers; that they often use drugs to self-medicate; and that theft by women is often driven by the need to survive poverty, homelessness, and drug addiction.[63]

Moving Forward With Research on Women

More fully understanding the facts of the lives of women and girls (not to mention the marginalization of groups based on race, ethnicity, class, and so on) that contribute to their criminal activity can illuminate the entire field. For example, delinquent boys and adult male prisoners also suffer from abuse and neglect, which is not addressed adequately in rehabilitative programming, in terms of both quality and quantity, and which has come to light as researchers have probed the backgrounds of incarcerated women.

As social science progresses, some researchers have determined that studies are more useful if they disaggregate data by race and gender. Better than simple racial comparisons are those between women from different races and men and women from the same race. Comparing multiple variables can lead to a more nuanced, complex, realistic, and therefore useful view of the justice system.

To be effective, risk assessment instruments, classification systems, and rehabilitation programs should all be gender specific and informed by a careful analysis of data. As the field advances, existing work may contribute to the design of ever more insightful research questions.

Prospects for Gender-Responsive Programming

What is the future for programming and treatment for women in correctional facilities? Once again, if we could design a system that was effective and just, we would look to programming and treatment backed by scientific evidence of efficacy. There is more push than ever before to use data to guide practice. Knowing exactly what kind of data to collect has yet to be adequately defined.

To conceive and implement effective responses to women's criminal behavior, those responses must recognize women's needs and realities. Gender-responsive programming is becoming more widely recognized for its appropriateness and effectiveness. It is becoming more widely accepted that treatment for women must recognize the pervasiveness of victimization and the occurrence of multiple risk factors.

To begin with, gender-responsive principles require that assessment and classification tools be validated for use with women; these tools must evaluate the factors most relevant to justice-involved women. As we have seen, these tend to be such concerns as children, family, substance abuse, and prior victimization. Many jails and prisons have inadequate risk and needs screening tools and procedures for detecting conditions relevant to appropriate planning and treatment, including childhood trauma and sexual victimization.

Risk assessment: The process for determining the level of security and supervision corrections-involved individuals require. Risk assessment usually uses a written checklist of weighted criteria (e.g., an assessment instrument or screening tool) that is used to estimate the likelihood that an individual will have disciplinary issues while in custody or will commit offenses after release.

▲ There is already a great deal of information about what is most effective in restoring women to law-abiding lifestyles.

© iStockphoto.com/Justin Horrocks

Essential for women is treatment of co-occurring disorders, for example, substance abuse and mental health issues—two areas that have historically been separate realms of treatment. A woman who has an alcohol abuse condition and a bipolar condition needs an integrated, rather than a compartmentalized, mode of treatment. Until recent experiments with such integration, many substance abuse practitioners were afraid of uncovering trauma and delaying sobriety. Most mental health programs do not accept a person who is actively using substances. These factors often specifically relate to each other. Underlying mental health issues are often related to lapses in sobriety. Recent programming is moving toward an integrated, trauma-informed approach.[64]

There is a body of new work exploring the best ways to work with women in prison and jail. The following are some of the most important principles of gender-responsive practice:

- Use gender-appropriate screening and assessment tools.
- Take the trauma into account.
- Avoid triggering trauma reactions and/or retraumatizing the individual.
- Promptly follow up to intake when abuse is detected.
- Adjust the behavior of counselors, other staff, and the organization to support the individual's coping capacity.
- Allow survivors to manage their trauma symptoms successfully so that they are able to access, retain, and benefit from these services.
- Ensure continuity of treatment and services upon release from custody, which is a key to successful reentry and low recidivism.[65]

The more advanced or complex correctional approaches—such as restorative justice—delve into repairing harm. A key to this approach is to understand the motives and forces that drive and shape the individual's behavior.

Forward-thinking correctional officials who are interested in truly rehabilitative programs are looking toward gender-responsive practices. Such policies are part of an emerging strategy to be "smart on crime."

SUMMARY

More women than ever before are locked up in prisons and jails and are under various forms of correctional control. Rates of incarceration have risen faster for women than for men during the last 20 years. The proportion of women out of the total incarcerated population has also grown. Women are generally incarcerated more often for less serious offenses, such as drug and property crimes; theirs are more often crimes of survival. For the most part, incarcerated women are low risk and high needs. The so-called War on Drugs resulted in skyrocketing numbers of women—mostly from poor communities—in prison for drug offenses. Women are more likely to be drawn into crime by their male partners' influence than the other way around.

Corrections-involved women are significantly different than their male counterparts in myriad ways. Women more often have histories of abuse, they have pathways into the justice system that are distinctly different than those for men, they have more family responsibilities, and they are more stigmatized by prison. Their risks for offending are fundamentally different and are driven by a different set of problems and needs. Women of color have even greater challenges than White women. Women's criminal behavior is poorly understood and only recently has become the subject of serious study.

Prison tends to worsen chronic physical and mental health problems. Incarcerated women have much higher rates of victimization and trauma than do men. High rates of early trauma are coming to light as research in this area advances. Such trauma has a direct impact on later risky behavior and related lawbreaking.

Gender differences with respect to the law are already apparent in the youth population. Just as adult women, adolescent girls in custody have higher rates of serious physical and mental health issues than their male counterparts. Children, families, and other relationships are often powerful motivators for incarcerated women. A large segment of women in the justice system are mothers of dependent children. The children of incarcerated mothers suffer losses that affect their own risk taking and outcomes later in life. An integrated, holistic, and gender-responsive approach to problem solving that accounts for early trauma and victimization is a promising area for further study, policy development, and legislation.

DISCUSSION QUESTIONS

1. How do societal gender stereotypes affect crime control for women?

2. How are the needs of incarcerated women of color different or the same as those of White women?

3. Discuss some of the most prevalent ways that women become involved in the justice system.

4. Write a news article that would counter typical gender stereotypes rather than reinforce them; your subject is a nonviolent criminal incident involving a woman perpetrator.

5. Imagine an incident from your adolescence that could have landed you in jail if the police had been present. Discuss how this incident could have affected your future.

6. Explore the FBI Uniform Crime Reports online. Use data that relate to arrests for women and write a one-page brief based on your findings.

7. Discuss how various physical and mental health conditions may influence women's lawbreaking behavior.

8. What would be the key components of a fair drug policy for women?

9. How should jail and prison administrators address women's rehabilitation, given the prevalence of histories of trauma and victimization among women prisoners?

10. What are ways that women cope with their time in prison?

11. Discuss how research can or should affect the development of policy questions related to women and the justice system.

KEY TERMS

Risk assessment, 299   Zero tolerance, 286

NOTES

1. Bloom and Covington 2008
2. Bresler and Lewis 1983
3. Bosworth 2010
4. Rafter 1997
5. Covington 2007
6. Bloom and Owen 2002
7. Glaze 2010
8. Greenfeld and Snell 1999
9. Glaze 2010
10. General Accounting Office 1999; West, Sabol, and Greenman 2010
11. Glaze 2010
12. Ibid.
13. West, Sabol, and Greenman 2010
14. Ibid.
15. Ibid.
16. Bonczar 2010
17. West, Sabol, and Greenman 2010
18. Colomy and Kretzmann 1997
19. Chesney-Lind 2004
20. Sickmund et al. 2013
21. Zahn et al. 2008
22. Chesney-Lind 2004
23. Federal Bureau of Investigation 2011
24. Sedlak and Bruce 2010
25. Ibid.
26. Ibid.
27. Schwartz and Steffensmeier 2007
28. Schwartz, Steffensmeier, and Feldmeyer 2009
29. BJS 2001; Gillard and Beck 1998; Snell 1994
30. Bloom and Owen 2002
31. Bush et al. 2013
32. Greenfeld and Snell 1999
33. Eliason, Taylor, and Williams 2004
34. Green et al. 2005
35. Belknap 2007, 291
36. Ibid.
37. Ibid.
38. Federal Bureau of Investigation 2004
39. Blackburn, Mullings, and Marquart 2008
40. Messina and Grella 2006
41. Covington 2007
42. Ibid.
43. Bloom and Covington 2008
44. Messina and Grella 2006
45. National Women's Law Center 2010
46. Acoca 1998; Amnesty International 1999
47. Eliason, Taylor, and Williams 2004
48. James and Glaze 2006
49. Bloom and Covington 2008
50. Ross, Glaser, and Stiasny 1998
51. James and Glaze 2006
52. Glaze and Maruschak 2008
53. Partyka 2001; Roscher 2005
54. Rathbone 2005
55. Owen 1998
56. Ross and Fabiano 1986
57. Ibid.
58. Bush et al. 2013
59. Rafter 1989
60. Belknap 2007, 225
61. Chesney-Lind 1986; Weis 1976
62. Schwartz and Steffensmeier 2007
63. Ibid.
64. Covington 2007
65. Harris and Fallot 2001

$SAGE edge™

Sharpen your skills with SAGE edge at edge.sagepub.com/krisberg

SAGE edge for students provides a personalized approach to help you accomplish your coursework goals in an easy-to-use learning environment. This site includes action plans, mobile-friendly eFlashcards and web quizzes as well as web, audio, and video resources and links to SAGE journal articles.

© REUTERS/ Robert Galbrait

13 Challenging and Vulnerable Populations

Along with the general population of inmates in U.S. prisons and jails, the already overstressed corrections system must confront the daily challenges of inmates with special needs. These include persons with severe medical and mental health issues as well as inmates with physical and cognitive disabilities. In addition, U.S. sentencing policies in the past several decades—with both longer sentences and reduced opportunities for parole—have increased the aging population in correctional facilities. There are also inmates whose gender identities and sexual orientations put them at particular risk behind bars. Lesbian, gay, bisexual, transgender, and questioning (LGBTQ) inmates frequently face hostile attitudes and violence from other inmates and staff.

The basic nature of confinement—rules, rigid structure, strict discipline—run counter to the needs of many inmates. From a purely practical perspective, the custody environment creates challenges for prisoners, staff, and administrators alike. Intense regimentation could be exactly what triggers problem behavior in mentally ill inmates, for example, setting up a no-win situation that leads to more time and stricter confinement or isolation. In addition, unaddressed problems in custody spill over and remain problems, sometimes worse ones, after reentry into the community.

Even probation and parole can entail requirements that many supervised individuals find impossible to meet. Regular, in-office meetings with a probation officer are far more difficult for someone in a wheelchair to manage than for a person with normal mobility.

Administrators must balance a host of factors including legal mandates, budget constraints, physical facility limitations, due process and welfare of prisoners, and training staff in the skills necessary to handle those with special needs. Staff must be able to recognize the warning signs of mental illness and victimization and react appropriately to a range of inmate behaviors. Prisoners with special needs have to face obstacles such as proper food and medication, mobility, vulnerability to assault and harassment, deteriorating mental states, and dying.

This chapter describes the nature and extent of issues involving special corrections populations, the increasing legal scrutiny of their treatment, and strategies for appropriate and safe treatment.

Prisons and Jails as Community Health Providers

The corrections system has been forced to respond to problems created outside jail and prison walls. Prisoners typically come from impoverished backgrounds and have generally received inadequate medical, mental health, and dental services for most of their lives. Cutbacks in government health care funding have eroded care in the community;

5 To grasp some of the challenges for staff and administrators with segregated vulnerable prisoners.

6 To gain a sense of the problems faced by LGBTQ individuals in highly gender-segregated institutions.

7 To be able to discuss the dilemma of prisoners receiving health care that they may not have received

in their own community and that may rival what staff can afford.

8 Understand how custody can be an opportunity to address prisoner vulnerability before release to the community.

Corrections officers swarm a maximum-security cell block in Turner Guilford Knight Correctional Center after an inmate was attacked and hurled himself off the second tier. The episode came after a security gaffe caused all the doors to open at once.

incarceration is sometimes the first opportunity many inmates have had to receive treatment for chronic health issues. Diminishing mental health services in the community and the reduction of acute mental health beds in public hospitals often result in severely ill persons ending up in prisons and jails, which are not geared to deal with mental health treatment, suicide attempts, and other difficult behavior. In fact, it is broadly argued that decisions to close state mental hospitals and community clinics have made the corrections system the largest de facto delivery system for mental health services. Yet prisons are rarely, if ever, therapeutic settings for effective and positive interventions.

Inmates typically have several health issues. Pernicious high levels of drug and alcohol use are health issues in themselves and worsen other medical problems of inmates. The large number of prisoners who are intravenous drug users contributes to vastly increased rates of hepatitis, pneumonia, tuberculosis, and HIV/AIDS.[1] High levels of tobacco use contribute to high rates of cancer, emphysema, strokes, diabetes, rheumatoid arthritis, and heart disease. These and other unhealthy behaviors and absence of adequate community medical care also lead to premature aging. It is estimated that many inmates experience the health challenges of persons who are much older. These age-related maladies include loss of hearing and sight, severe physical mobility problems, Alzheimer's disease, and dementia.

Prisons and jails were never intended or designed to provide regular care to chronically sick persons. The few exceptions are very expensive and low-capacity correctional medical facilities or locked wards of public hospitals. Few corrections facilities are properly equipped to manage inmates with infectious diseases. A lack of trained medical staff and the rural location of many corrections facilities make attracting qualified medical personnel, particularly specialists, very hard to accomplish. Correctional facilities rarely have automated health records. Pharmacy control is a major challenge; medications for inmates are often diverted into the illegal marketplace that exists in almost all prisons and jails.

Further, frontline correctional workers receive little or no training in identifying or responding to severe physical or mental health problems. Staff may view inmates who demand medical attention as "malingerers" or manipulators trying to gain special privileges. It is difficult enough to just move large numbers of inmates through daily activities; illness among inmates complicates these tasks. Corrections staff are trained to be law enforcement officers, not health care providers. The staff may resent the fact that inmates get free health care that, in some facilities, may be better than what the prison workers can purchase for their own families.

A Wide Range of Medical Problems

The most recent Bureau of Justice Statistics (BJS) surveys (conducted for jails in 2002[2] and prisons in 2004[3]) found that approximately 40% of inmates in jails, state prisons, and federal facilities had a serious chronic medical condition, such as asthma, arthritis, STDs, hypertension, hepatitis, cancer, or HIV/AIDS. The most frequent conditions were diabetes, heart problems, and asthma.

For most of these chronic conditions, the rates among inmates were significantly higher than for the general U.S. population, even when sociodemographic and other factors like alcohol consumption were equalized. This was true for asthma, arthritis, cancer, hepatitis, and high blood pressure. Differences between the incarcerated and the general public were most pronounced for non-Hispanic Whites.[4]

Not surprisingly, the prevalence of medical and dental issues increased among the older inmates. Almost two thirds of all inmates over the age of 45 had a current medical problem, versus less than a quarter of those under 25. Women inmates were more likely than men to report two or more medical problems. Three to five percent of female inmates were pregnant when they were admitted to custody. A related jail study found female inmates

▼ Prisoners and jail inmates have a wide variety of medical needs. Attracting and maintaining high-quality practitioners to meet those needs is also an institutional challenge.

© REUTERS/ Robert Galbraith

Vulnerable prisoners can become targets of violence. A hospital photograph shows the bruising on an inmate's face that he alleged was inflicted by correctional officers at the Roxbury Correctional Institution near Hagerstown, Maryland. More than twenty correctional officers were fired and criminally charged in the resulting investigation.

© Washington County Hospital/ ASSOCIATED PRESS

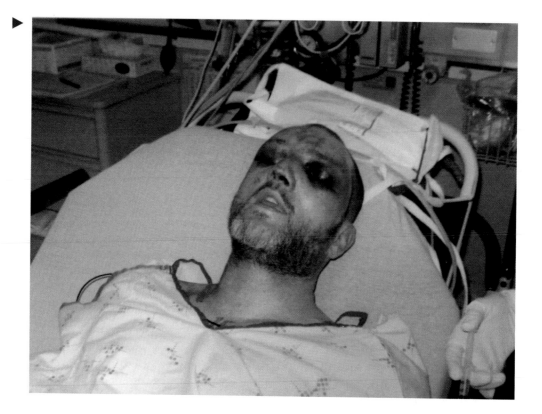

were more likely than male inmates to have chronic conditions, especially cancer, hypertension, diabetes, arthritis, asthma, hepatitis, and cirrhosis.[5]

Inmates who reported the greatest frequency of medical problems were more likely than other inmates to be intravenous drug users, homeless, unemployed, or receiving government financial assistance prior to incarceration.

Apart from medical conditions, about a third of all inmates reported having at least one functional impairment related to learning, hearing, vision, mobility, or mental function. Eight to fifteen percent of inmates had multiple impairments. Male inmates were more likely than female inmates to report a learning impairment, while female inmates were about twice as likely to suffer from mental impairments as were their male counterparts.

About 13% of jail inmates and one third of prisoners suffered injuries while in custody. Males were somewhat more likely to report injuries in jail or prison compared to females but were twice as likely as females to report that their injury stemmed from a fight. Younger inmates and those incarcerated for violent crimes reported the highest number of injuries from fighting. Jail inmates with impairments, especially mental impairments, were twice as likely as those without these problems to be injured in fights. Inmates with the longest jail stays had the highest likelihood of injuries due to fighting.

Health Care Services

Many inmates do not receive proper care for their problems, especially while incarcerated. For those with a persistent medical issue, 68% of jail inmates, 20% of state prisoners, and 14% of federal inmates had *not* been examined by medical personnel. For those with a medical issue requiring regular prescription drug treatment, 37% of jail inmates, 24% of state prisoners, and 21% of federal inmates had discontinued that treatment after incarceration.

Overall, most of those requiring regular blood tests had received at least one such test, but 60% of jail inmates, 6% of state prisoners, and 4% of federal inmates had not.[6]

For those seriously injured while in custody (for instance, knife or gun wounds, broken bones, or being knocked unconscious), 25% of jail inmates, 12% of state prisoners, and 8% of federal inmates did not receive medical treatment for the injury.[7] (Broken skin not properly treated is one of the reasons that infectious diseases spread more rapidly in prison or jail than in other settings.)

On the other hand, given the lower socioeconomic status of most prisoners, the medical care that some receive in custody may be better than what they receive in the community. Most state and federal inmates (approximately 90%) were at least verbally screened for health issues at admission, and most (70% of state prisoners and 76% of federal prisoners) reported seeing a medical professional while in confinement. More than 80% of inmates reported getting a blood test, and 95% were tested for tuberculosis (TB).

Of female state prison inmates who reported being pregnant at admission, 94% reported receiving an obstetric exam, and 54% reported receiving prenatal care such as special diet, medication, or instructions on child care. For pregnant jail inmates, 48% had received an exam, and 35% had received prenatal care.

For various reasons, jail health care is harder to administer and less consistently available than what prisons provide. Of those jail inmates who reported a serious health problem, less than half saw a medical professional while in custody, and only 40% had a medical exam. Two thirds of jail inmates were tested for TB, but only about one fifth were screened for HIV.

The prevalence of these medical problems in jails is especially challenging, because jails generally have fewer on-staff medical personnel and much lower budgets for health care than state prison systems. Jails often must draw on the medical resources of local public hospitals

◄ Many prisoners' mental health problems are exacerbated by the conditions inside of prison. How would you remedy this problem?

© Christian Schmidt/Corbis

SPOTLIGHT

THE AMERICANS WITH DISABILITIES ACT

Although many of the specifics will need to be interpreted by the courts for years to come, the basic principle of protecting the rights of people with disabilities, even in prison, were acknowledged by the passage of the Americans With Disabilities Act (ADA) in 1990. Regardless of whether a person with a disability is confined in a state, 1 local, or federal facility, and whether that facility is public or private, reasonable accommodations must be made for an inmate's physical and mental limitations. Legislation is meant to rectify unjust circumstances in which people with disabilities suffer unduly in prison.

The most common bases for litigation is that individuals are not receiving needed services or are being discriminated against. In denying appropriate medical care, for example, prison administrators may be in violation of the Eighth Amendment's protection against cruel and unusual punishment.[1]

The main goals of the ADA are to prevent discrimination, integrate people with disabilities into the mainstream, and provide strong and consistent enforceable standards to address disability discrimination.

The ADA defines broad categories of discrimination such as denying a person the opportunity to participate in or benefit from a program or service solely because of a disability. A prison cannot deny a person access to a program simply because he or she has a disability. And any special programs for such persons must be of at least equal quality.

Disability is defined by the ADA as a physical or mental impairment that substantially limits one or more of a

or free health care clinics to attend to inmate health needs. The "inmate exception" in federal Medicaid funding excludes counties from receiving reimbursements for providing care to inmates, and most jail health care must be paid out of local budgets. Very few jail inmates have even minimal medical insurance to cover the cost of expensive health care services.

Most jail inmates have much shorter stays in custody than state prisoners; the shorter-term nature of jail time further complicates the delivery of even minimal health care services. Shorter stays also make comparison of jail and prison health service delivery difficult, because there is less time for symptoms to be identified and for care to be provided.

Mental Illness in Prisons and Jails

More than half the inmates in prisons and jails reported having had some kind of mental health problem within 12 months prior to their incarceration, according to a 2005 national survey conducted by the BJS. This amounted to almost 800,000 federal and state prisoners and almost 480,000 residents of local jails. Over one third of all federal inmates had major depression or another kind of serious mental disorder.[8] Almost 13% of inmates had attempted suicide in the 12 months prior to the survey. Between 30% and 50% reported prolonged insomnia, loss of appetite, persistent anger or irritability, diminished capacity to think, persistent sadness, a numb or empty mood, psychomotor agitation or retardation, or feelings of worthlessness or guilt.[9]

Jail inmates had the highest rate of mental health disorders and serious symptoms. Almost two thirds of jail inmates had major depressive disorders, and one fourth had a psychotic

person's major life activities, a record of such impairment, or being regarded as having such an impairment. Major life activities include caring for oneself, performing manual tasks, seeing, hearing, eating, sleeping, walking, standing, lifting, bending, speaking, concentrating, thinking, communicating, and working.

In general, whether an accommodation is "reasonable" depends on the circumstances. A reasonable modification may be something simple, for example, allowing a person with diabetes an exception to the rule of not being able to keep food in the cell so that person can maintain his or her blood sugar levels. Other accommodations are more complex and may involve modifications to custody facility structures, which obviously have a fiscal impact. The courts attempt to balance the needs of the prisoners with the concerns of the prison and consider whether modification will "fundamentally alter" a program or activity, the costs of the modification, the burden on the administration of the prison, and other penological concerns such as safety.[2]

QUESTIONS

1   Discuss what it might be like to be blind and in prison or jail.

2   What are reasonable accommodations that a prison might make for a person in a wheelchair?

3   Should persons with mental or developmental disabilities be housed separately or in the mainstream in prisons and jails?

Notes

1.   Columbia Human Rights Law Review 2011

2.   Evans 2006

▲ Group counseling can address some of the needs of some prisoners. However, individualized therapy is often necessary for the most difficult cases.

© David Woo/KRT/Newscom

disorder in the 12 months prior to incarceration. Twelve percent of state prisoners and 18% of jail inmates reported delusions; 8% of prisoners and 14% of jail inmates experienced hallucinations. These very high rates of mental health issues compare with a prevalence of mental illness in the general adult population of about 10%. These findings reflect the role of jails as short-term holding facilities housing many people who have just been arrested and may be transferred to other community health care or mental health facilities. As noted earlier, jails are less likely than state prisons to have mental health staff available for crisis care. Most jails were not designed to separate inmates with severe mental health issues from other inmates, and jail personnel are generally ill equipped to respond appropriately to behaviors that stem from these mental conditions.

According to the BJS survey, White, Asian Pacific Islander, and Native American inmates had higher rates of mental illness than African American and Hispanic inmates in both prisons and jails. It must be noted that these data may reflect cultural differences in willingness to admit to mental health problems. There is often a serious cultural **stigma** associated with such problems.

Mental health issues often correlate with other factors that cause challenges and special needs for inmates and facility administrators. Women prisoners, prisoners who had recently been homeless or on public assistance, prisoners who had been in foster care, and those who had been physically or sexually abused had higher rates of mental illness. Inmates with mental health problems also had higher rates of substance dependence or abuse than those without mental illness. Almost half of jail inmates and about 40% of prison inmates were suffering from co-occurring mental health problems *and* serious substance abuse issues.[10]

▲ Lucille Keppen's badge identifies her as an inmate in Minnesota. She celebrated her 92nd birthday in jail and is the state's oldest female inmate. She was 88 when she shot and seriously wounded a man she once considered her adopted son.

© Darlene Prois/ZUMA Press/ Newscom

Stigma: A social stain on a person's reputation, often suffered unfairly due to the prejudice of others.

Violent criminal records are slightly more prevalent among inmates who have mental health issues. However, this does not mean that there is a causal relationship between mental illness and violent crime. Higher rates of violent criminal records can be attributable to any of the other factors that correlate highly with mental health issues. For example, drug abuse can contribute to more violent crime, and more mentally ill inmates have reportedly been using drugs at the time of their offense than inmates who were not mentally ill.

More than half of those inmates with mental illness who were surveyed by the BJS were scheduled to be released within six months, which underscores the potential public safety benefit of providing care to the mentally ill while they are in custody.

Approximately one third of prisoners and one fifth of jail inmates received some mental health services after their most recent incarceration. This rate of care was 50% higher than the rate of care in the community that the individual received during the 12 months prior to incarceration. In general, prison inmates were more likely to receive medical and mental health care than jail inmates. Between 1997 and 2004, there was only a slight increase in the proportion of inmates receiving mental health services, including medications.

IN THE COURTS

Clark v. California
U.S. District Court N.D. California

No. C96–1496-FMS Oct. 1, 1996

Derrick Clark, on behalf of all disabled inmates in California prisons, filed for injunctive relief under the Rehabilitation Act, the Americans With Disabilities Act, and the Eighth Amendment. The inmates claimed that prison officials were not providing the protection, accommodation, and special services warranted by their disabilities. They alleged that they were denied access to work, education, and reading programs due to their disability.

The *Clark* plaintiffs also alleged that developmentally disabled inmates were less able to comply with prison rules and procedures and were forced into isolation or segregation or lost good-time credits.

This claim was upheld by the California Supreme Court, which was subsequently appealed in federal courts up to the Supreme Court. The Supreme Court held that prior federal and state court decisions were appropriate.

This case required the state of California and other jurisdictions to provide necessary services and adopt policies to protect developmentally disabled inmates and provide for their fair access to all prison programs and services.

California began complying with the requirements of *Clark* over the next decade, and substantial improvements could be seen for developmentally disabled inmates. But in 2010, the California Department of Corrections and Rehabilitation (CDCR) filed a motion under the Prison Litigation Reform Act to terminate the injunction, arguing that the CDCR had done what was needed and that the civil rights violations were in the past. The federal courts ordered an investigation of this assertion and found that there were still many challenges faced by developmentally disabled inmates. The court mandated that the injunctive relief continued and required regular monitoring of conditions in CDCR facilities for developmentally disabled inmates. The court's decision establishes a virtual "bill of rights" for inmates who face severe cognitive challenges.

Inmates with mental health issues pose difficult problems for prison management. These inmates are more likely to commit serious disciplinary infractions, to physically and verbally assault others, or to be injured in fights with other inmates. They are also more likely to be exploited and victimized by other inmates.

The Increasing Elderly Prison Population

Mass incarceration policies have produced a huge increase in the number of prisoners growing old behind bars.[11] In fact, elderly prisoners are the fastest-growing segment of the prison population. There were an estimated 41,586 prisoners age 50 or older in 1992, 113,358 in 2001, and 239,837 in 2011—more than double each decade. This age group represented less than 6% of the prison population in 1992[12] but 16% in 2011.[13]

As previously mentioned, stress, substance abuse, and related health problems of prisoners, including such factors as poverty and untreated health issues prior to incarceration, cause them to experience the symptoms of aging sooner than those in the general population.[14] Partly for this reason, states define *elderly* or *geriatric* for correctional purposes, such as medical parole, variously as older than 65 to as young as 45,[15] while researchers usually use an age of 50 or 55.

SPOTLIGHT

THE COFFIN MAKERS

Prisoners started making coffins at the Louisiana State Penitentiary at Angola when the warden wanted a more dignified send-off than a thin plywood box for the prisoners he had to bury. Warden Burl Cain tapped the skills of an inmate at the time, Eugene Redwine. The warden wanted coffins for the prisoners he would have to bury. Mr. Redwine showed he could build coffins of a high quality for a lower cost.

At Angola, most of the prisoners are lifers, the average sentence is 93 years, and 97% die in prison. But as prisoners age all across the nation, more of them will die in prison and need a burial. And many of these prisoners will have lost touch with their family and friends and have no one to attend their funerals but their fellow inmates. This is an issue that prisons have to address. Warden Cain thought that Louisiana sentencing laws were too harsh and believed that prison space should be reserved for the younger, more aggressive prisoners rather than aging or dying men.

The question arises as to whether, in death—the great equalizer—an individual should pass with some dignity, despite what he may have done in his life. At Angola, the prisoners express their acceptance of this value by holding elaborate funerals with a horse-drawn hearse, every detail of which they take care of themselves.

They opened up a new burial ground at Angola, because it became too common to dig up human remains in unmarked graves at the old burial site.

Redwine eventually chose an apprentice, Richard Leggett, to mentor and to carry on his craft. Leggett eventually became a skilled carpenter and coffin maker. But the only funeral he attended himself was that of his mentor, Redwine. Leggett also figured that he'd be making his own coffin.[1]

In recent years, Angola has undergone something of a transformation credited in part to Christian ministries. Cain insists on moral rehabilitation; and he himself credits "the work of God" as the source of the good the prison's ministries accomplish. These include restoring wheelchairs for children and adults with disabilities, a hospice program, and the inmate funerals. Billy Graham intends to be buried in a coffin made at Angola; his wife was already buried in one.[2]

QUESTIONS

1   Discuss the issue of prisoner dignity. Should all prisoners receive a dignified burial? Only some? Where would you draw the line?

2   What value might there be in allowing prisoners to organize funerals and burials for their fellow inmates?

3   Do you think prisoners should be given the opportunity to develop high-level skills?

Notes

1.   Fields 2005
2.   Nothstine 2012

The rise in elderly prisoners is a function of several factors. First, the overall U.S. population is aging; second, longer mandatory sentences, more life sentences, and stricter paroling practices mean that inmates remain in prison for longer periods of time and, third, advances in medical science along with inmate access to health care (although it is inconsistent, what exists is often mandated by the court) are keeping some elderly prisoners alive longer.

We have already discussed that older inmates are the most likely to experience health and disability problems in prisons and jails. Further, other attributes of aging, including loss of mental acuity, dementia, and Alzheimer's disease, are increasingly common in the elderly prison population.

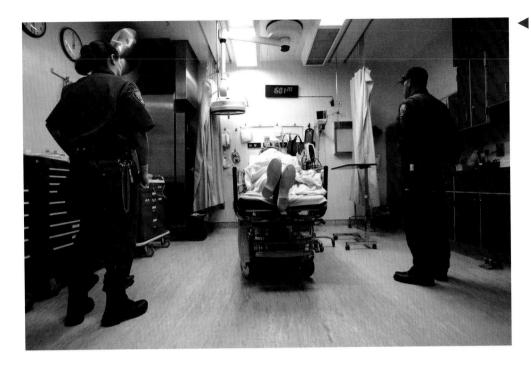

Prisoners that need to be transported to outside facilities must have an escort. Personnel costs are part of the overall increase in prison health care budgets.

© Rich Pedroncelli/Associated Press

The costs of providing medical care for the aging prison population are escalating at a dramatic rate. It appears that the cost of providing care to elderly inmates is more than three times the amount needed for younger inmates ($67,000 vs. $22,000 per year).[16]

Prisoners with long-standing and chronic health problems such as diabetes, hepatitis, and emphysema experience declines in their health status over time, requiring liver transplants, dialysis, bone marrow transplants, chemotherapy, and open-heart surgery. Prisons now must gear up to treat the illnesses of the elderly, which include cancer, heart disease, stroke, and other terminal diseases. The care of prisoners with these illnesses requires costly procedures, such as CAT scans, MRIs, and surgery. The medical costs of "end of life" care are very expensive and require specialized health facilities and geriatric health care professionals. Prisons are beginning to offer hospice care for dying inmates.

Corrections must confront a range of other issues as elderly inmates experience declines in their hearing, sight, and physical mobility. Older prisoners need hearing aids, glasses, and dentures. It is very common in large prison yards to see inmates with canes, walkers, wheelchairs, and scooters. Yet prisons and jails were not designed with elderly prisoners in mind. There are few ramps, and virtually no elevators or moving pathways. Cells are cramped, and toilet facilities and showers are not easy for elderly inmates to maneuver. There are almost no counseling services, special dietary services, or health care programs for the elderly.

Common conditions among the elderly, such as loss of mental acuity and dementia, present major challenges for prison officials. Aging inmates are vulnerable to physical attacks, exploitation, and extortion by other—usually younger—inmates.

Some corrections staff are sympathetic to the needs of older inmates, but the overall culture of most correctional facilities is characterized by following rules and exacting punishment. The aging inmate population requires more effort on the part of corrections officers to help them get needed medical attention or to assist disabled inmates to move through the daily correctional routine. There is inadequate physical and mental health care to begin with, and these additional challenges of the aging inmate population go mostly unmet.

SPOTLIGHT

COMPASSIONATE RELEASE

On the surface, it may seem obvious that a terminally ill prisoner poses little public safety threat and could be safely released. However, if the motivation is one of compassion, releasing a terminally ill prisoner may or may not be the most compassionate thing to do. Many factors come into play about how that person will be cared for and who will pay for the care. In some cases, prisons establish their own hospice arrangements, for those who have a prognosis of six months or less, for example. End-of-life care often entails scheduled medication, medical equipment, and special nursing. In addition, there are considerations of religious counseling, legal matters, and funeral arrangements.

However, beyond all practical matters is the question of whether an individual should have the right to die outside prison walls and with a measure of dignity, despite what he or she may have done in the past. Law and order conservatives maintain opposition against modifying sentences in the case of elderly or dying inmates regardless of the fiscal benefits there may be to the state, partly due to a lack of confidence that those making the decision to release have appropriate motivation.[1]

Compassionate release is also referred to as medical release, medical furlough, medical parole, or humanitarian parole. In federal prisons, an individual inmate may request such a special release when there are "particularly

extraordinary or compelling circumstances which could not reasonably have been foreseen by the court at the time of sentencing." Clearly, how one interprets "extraordinary or compelling" is significant. In 2009, the U.S. Sentencing Commission approved expanded grounds for such reductions of sentences to include persons suffering from permanent or deteriorating conditions that prevent them from caring for themselves and the death or incapacitation of the defendant's only family member who can care for the prisoner's minor child.[2] This is particularly important in the federal system, which has not had parole since 1984; compassionate release remains one of the few ways a federal sentence can be reduced.[3]

QUESTIONS

1. Discuss the challenge facing a hospice worker who is asked to provide compassionate care for a dying prisoner who committed murder.

2. Who should pay for the care of the dying inmate outside of prison?

3. How would you decide when a person no longer posed a threat to society because of old age or illness?

Notes

1. Murphy 2012
2. Families Against Mandatory Minimums 2013
3. Berry 2012

U.S. Sentencing Commission: A federal agency created in 1984 to establish guidelines for appropriate sentencing policy and practice in U.S. federal courts and to assist other branches of government in establishing effective crime policy.

A few states have set aside separate housing units for elderly prisoners with special needs or those who need hospice care. For example, the Minnesota Correctional Facility at Faribault operates a special unit for older inmates with chronic health problems. It employs practical nurses for 16 hours a day and 24-hour care in the prison medical clinic. The Pennsylvania State Correctional Institution at Laurel Highlands offers the correctional version of long-term care and assisted living.

There is a small but growing number of advocates that are trying to focus public attention on the plight of the elderly inmate. The Project for Older Prisoners at George Washington Law School is conducting research on these issues, promoting legislative reforms, and providing direct help to a number of elderly inmates across the nation.[17] Human Rights Watch and the Vera Institute of Justice have promoted the idea of "compassionate release" for geriatric inmates who can no longer function in the prison setting. These programs would be primarily for those inmates who are approaching death. There are other proposals that might allow older, nonviolent inmates to serve the balance of their sentences in smaller community facilities. Some have called for specialized reentry programs for aged convicts.

Although it might not be hard to make a moral case for these nonprison settings for older inmates, there are very complex issues of how to pay for these programs. Most long-term inmates have virtually no savings, Social Security benefits, health insurance, or means to support themselves outside the prison walls. The concern has been expressed that these release programs will pass many of the health care costs to the inmate's family—who often can ill afford to pay—or to other public agencies and community providers. Research has not yet been conducted to assess the impact of the Patient Protection and Affordable Care Act of 2010 on access to medical and mental health services in impoverished communities and those entering or exiting correctional custody.

Lesbian, Gay, Bisexual, Transgender, and Questioning Inmates

No one knows for sure how many LGBTQ persons are locked in the nation's prisons and jails. What seems increasingly clear is that these inmates face a host of problems behind prison and jail walls. Perhaps the most dramatic of these challenges is the large number of LGBTQ people who have been assaulted and raped in prisons and jails. The presence of LGBTQ inmates has been a reality but until recently was, rarely if ever, acknowledged as requiring specific policies and procedures. Some individuals attempt to keep their sexual identities secret for fear that corrections staff or other inmates will punish or victimize them in some way. Part of the challenge is that LGBTQ individuals (and effeminate men and "masculine" women) who are perceived as outside traditional

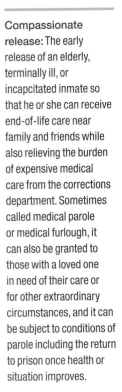

Compassionate release: The early release of an elderly, terminally ill, or incapcitated inmate so that he or she can receive end-of-life care near family and friends while also relieving the burden of expensive medical care from the corrections department. Sometimes called medical parole or medical furlough, it can also be granted to those with a loved one in need of their care or for other extraordinary circumstances, and it can be subject to conditions of parole including the return to prison once health or situation improves.

◀ Phillip "Sabrina" Trujillo, a transgender inmate at Sterling Correctional Facility in Colorado, asked the state to pay for a sex-change operation.

© Denver Post via Getty Images

SPOTLIGHT

NEW PREA REGULATIONS

In May 2012, the U.S. Department of Justice (DOJ) released a ruling on the Prison Rape Elimination Act (PREA). The 2003 act is intended to prevent, detect, and respond to all forms of sexual abuse inside of facilities, in both adult and juvenile prisons, jails, lockups, and community confinement centers. The 2012 rule is the first federal effort to set protection standards for federal, state, and local facilities.[1]

The rule shows a significant recognition on the part of the DOJ of how devastating and far reaching the effects of in-custody sexual abuse can be and the state's responsibility for protecting the rights of the incarcerated.

The ruling also addressed the costs of full implementation of the standards. A thorough analysis of that implementation resulted in an estimated cost to the correctional community nationwide of $468 million per year. Compared to the total expenditures of approximately $80 billion, the additional costs to implement the PREA were deemed insignificant by the DOJ, especially in light of how many people are affected. Although arriving at them is challenging, the estimates for 2008 alone are that more than 209,000 incarcerated individuals were victims of sexual abuse—more than 10,000 of these were juveniles.[2] Many of these individuals had been victimized multiple times.

The ruling enumerated specific standards of compliance in the three major areas. These are to be audited every three years. One consequence of noncompliance would be a reduction or withholding of federal funds. This final rule reflects the consideration given by the designated task force of more than 1,300 comments from the public. The DOJ established the National PREA Resource Center to assist agencies in their efforts.[3]

PREVENTION

- Follow a zero-tolerance policy toward sexual abuse.
- Employ a PREA compliance coordinator.
- Screen prisoners for risk.
- Maintain adequate levels of staffing.
- Train staff.

---

gender definitions cannot really hide their identities. Fear of harm and retaliation for reporting appear to be well founded.[18] Such fear creates even more stress and additional obstacles to solving problems.

Advocates for LGBTQ inmates have documented a wide range of problems. The most significant harms include violent victimization by other inmates and staff and neglect of needed medical and mental health services. Prison rape of members of this population is commonplace and often goes unreported.[19] LGBTQ inmates are subject to verbal as well as physical abuse by staff and other inmates. Staff often dismiss or devalue the complaints coming from LGBTQ inmates. LGTBQ inmates are often exploited by staff and other inmates.

Although by no means the sole victims of prison sexual violence, LGBTQ inmates have gained national attention as part of federal and state efforts to reduce the incidence of prison rape. Based on the self-reports of inmates, the BJS found that inmate-on-inmate sexual victimization rates were much higher for LGBTQ people.[20] A 2009 research report cited findings that transgender prisoners experienced sexual victimization at a rate 13 times higher than a random sampling of offenders in the same facility.[21]

The challenges facing LGBTQ inmates are often related to limited resources despite sincere concern on the part of prison and jail staff for the safety of these inmates. However, discrimination, bias, and ignorance on the part of staff are also commonplace and are a

- Conduct background checks for staff.

- Separate juveniles from adults.

- Impose a ban on cross-gender searches.

- Institute same-sex supervision during showering and personal care.

- Restrict solitary confinement for protection.

- Require compliance from contracted entities.

DETECTION

- Increase inmate awareness of policies and reporting protocols.

- Provide multiple reporting channels.

- Provide a method for staff reporting.

- Prevent and detect retaliation.

- Ensure proper communication with inmates with disabilities and limited English proficiency.

RESPONSE

- Ensure timely and appropriate mental and medical health care.

- Allow access to victim advocates.

- Preserve evidence.

- Investigate all allegations of abuse.

- Discipline culpable staff.

- Allow inmates to file grievances.

- Maintain records of incidents.

QUESTIONS

1 Do these new regulations go far enough or too far in protecting prisoners against in-custody sexual abuse?

2 How much consideration should be given to the costs of implementing these rules?

3 How would you approach data collection about prison sexual abuse to adequately reflect the problem and measure the effect of proposed solutions?

Notes

1. U.S. Department of Justice 2012a

2. National PREA Resource Center, U.S. Department of Justice 2012b

3. National PREA Resource Center 2014

serious threat to the well-being of this population. LGBTQ inmates report high rates of verbal abuse from staff. There are instances in which correctional chaplains have denied access to religious services to LGBTQ inmates. A Protestant clergy in California declared that "they are going to hell anyway, so why let them attend religious services."[22] Federal law on access to religion in correctional institutions forbids acting on this view. In other cases, LGBTQ inmates have been denied work assignments or privileges allowed to other inmates. Some corrections officials cite fear of HIV transmission as a justification to limit the movements and program participation of LGBTQ inmates, even though other inmates, especially those with histories of intravenous drug use, may be more likely to have HIV.

There are also particular issues regarding medical services for transgender prisoners. Special counseling, health care, and other services for LGTBQ inmates are very rare in prisons and jails. Some transgender inmates have been denied hormone therapy regardless of whether they have received this medical care in the recent past, and even though interrupting hormonal therapy for these inmates may have catastrophic results. Several recent cases have centered on determining if hormone therapy and sex reassignment surgeries must be provided to transgender inmates. For example, in 2012, a federal court ordered Massachusetts to pay for sex change surgery for a prisoner, but this decision was being considered by an appeals court.[23] A Canadian court ordered a similar treatment for transgender inmates in 2003.[24]

Compassionate Release

K. P. was sentenced when she was 15 years old to life without the possibility of parole (LWOP) for the murder of her elderly aunt. At trial, evidence was introduced that the aunt was physically abusing the youth. K. P. has already served almost 19 years in prison and has been free of major disciplinary problems.

K. P. is now 33 years old and has Stage IV breast cancer. Her case is before the parole board, which must decide whether to grant her a compassionate release. The initial medical diagnosis estimated that she had six months to live, but since receiving hormonal therapy, K. P. may survive for a longer time. K. P.'s lawyers and family would like her paroled to community-based care so that she can die outside of prison with her family nearby.

*YOU DECIDE: **Should the parole board grant compassionate release to K. P., despite the severity of her crime?***

There currently is no consistent method for managing LGBTQ inmates. It has been a challenge for many facilities to find ways to safely house vulnerable inmates without compromising their right to equal access to services or neglecting their sense of identity. Some facilities place LGBTQ persons in solitary confinement and call it protective custody.[25] These housing assignments may limit access to exercise yards, day rooms, school and counseling sessions, or work assignments. Prolonged isolation from others may, itself, lead to the onset of mental health issues and other medical problems. Other facilities, such as the Los Angeles County Men's Central Jail, have established separate units for "vulnerable" prisoners. This approach has been criticized for using stereotypes about LGBTQ people as the subjective basis of determining placement. Some of these stereotypes make it harder for people of color, or others who do not fit into the facility staff's understanding of how LGBTQ individuals present themselves, to be placed in these units.[26] Some corrections institutions place transgender

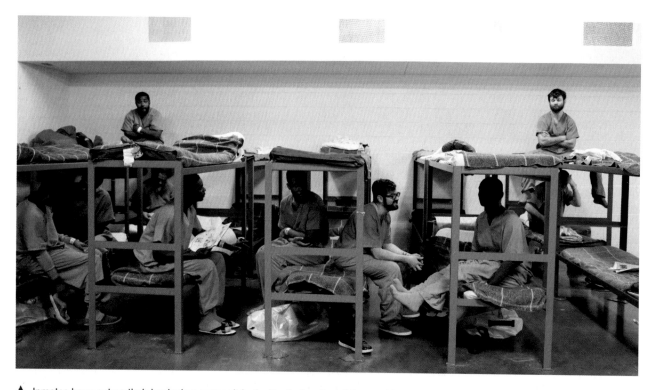

▲ Inmates hang out on their bunks in a new unit in the Harris County Jail for gay, bisexual, and transgender inmates in Houston, Texas. Harris County is one of many around the country changing the way it treats its LGBTQ population.

inmates with either male or female inmates based on staff perceptions of where the transgender person will be easiest to manage. Other facilities make housing assignments without regard to the inmate's sexual and gender identity.

In general, advocates for LGBTQ inmates emphasize the importance of allowing LGBTQ individuals to self-identify, and laws and regulations have begun to mirror this approach. The Prison Rape Elimination Act (PREA) regulations discourage the automatic use of solitary confinement for LGBTQ inmates, and some federal courts have held that involuntary solitary confinement of youth for protective custody violates the U.S. Constitution.[27] The legal principles governing these practices emphasize that the utilization of protective custody should be as "a last resort" and must be considered on a case-by-case basis. Another major issue for transgender and gender-variant inmates involved strip searches by opposite-sex staff. PREA regulations bar cross-gender body searches for juveniles and suggest that all transgender inmates be permitted to select the gender of the staff person who performs these strip searches; several correctional facilities have already adopted these policies.

Best Practices for Managing LGBTQ inmates

The written policies of the Denver Sheriff Department (DSD) illustrate what a corrections agency can do to protect and provide fair treatment to transgender and gender-variant inmates. The policy states that the DSD intends to eliminate discrimination, provide appropriate treatment, and provide for the safety, security, and medical needs of "transgender and gender-variant inmates." The policy acknowledges that gender covers a wide range of social identities, psychological states, and human behaviors. The DSD seeks to respect the person's own internal sense of identity, regardless of the identity that was apparent in the person at birth.

With respect to classification, the DSD takes into consideration whether the inmate's appearance or behavior fits conventional markers, but recommends that the staff rely on the inmate's self-report and that supervisory personnel are to be consulted if the situation is ambiguous.

If they are necessary, **pat searches** are to be conducted by an officer of the same sex, defined by the inmate. Staff who are assigned to transporting inmates are also alerted in these instances. Strip searches are never to be performed as punitive measures but are to be conducted where there is a legitimate custody or security issue.

The DSD requires that transgender or gender-variant inmates sign a "Statement of Preference Form" that includes their preferred name and the preferred pronoun with which to refer to them. The DSD has established a Transgender Review Board to oversee and make recommendations on housing assignments and medical and mental health needs. The DSD policy limits the temporary segregation of LGBTQ inmates to 72 hours with immediate review by medical personnel. Longer-term housing assignments are to be the least restrictive possible.

When possible, the inmate's request for housing with similar inmates will be honored as are requests for private showers and single cells. DSD staff are clearly informed that they may not discriminate against LBGTQ inmates or abuse them in any way. Violations of these rules are subject to personnel disciplinary actions. The DSD training department is required to ensure that all existing curriculum is compliant with the principles and specifics of this order.

The DSD regularly consults with members of the LGBTQ community for advice on handling specific issues and allows advocates or representatives from the LGBTQ community to accompany inmates when they appear before the Transgender Review Board.

Pat searches: Also called a frisk or pat down, a pat search is a search of a person's body for weapons or contraband by running the hands over the subject's clothing.

SUMMARY

As the corrections population grows, correctional systems will be required to safely care for inmates with a range of specialized needs including prisoners with serious physical or mental illnesses and disabilities, aging prisoners, and those with a variety of sexual and gender identities.

All of these individuals require physical and mental health care, protection from abusive staff and inmates, and attention to their civil rights. Not only do their needs typically go unmet in the majority of facilities, but their special status also makes them more vulnerable to the harsh conditions and cultures in prisons and jails. The prisoners who fall into several of these special categories simultaneously face even greater challenges. The stress of prison tends to worsen conditions such as chronic disease, mental illness, Alzheimer's, and victimization.

Caring for these individuals puts added burdens on already stretched correctional systems. The costs of managing these special populations are much higher than those for more mainstream correctional residents. Providing appropriate care often requires an empathetic or compassionate culture among staff and other inmates, which is currently rare in prisons and jails, and to some extent in probation and parole. But, the corrections system has little choice in these matters; federal and state laws governing persons with disabilities, a range of civil rights laws, and a growing number of court decisions have held that the Eighth and Fourteenth Amendments require a clear standard for handling these special inmate populations.

As poor as care inside of prisons may be, many inmates have had little to no care in the community. For the poorest inmates, being released from prison hardly solves their problems. Appropriate treatment of the elderly in prison is also elusive, inside or outside. Especially if an elderly person has served an extremely long sentence, he or she is likely to have few resources or even family members outside of prison who can tend to their medical or death expenses.

A number of advocacy groups are trying to address the legal, ethical, and practical considerations in dealing with special populations behind bars.

DISCUSSION QUESTIONS

1. What obligations do or should prison administrators have for ensuring the safety of vulnerable populations?

2. Is it reasonable to expect prisons to respond to the needs of special populations?

3. What kind of staff training for special needs inmates would you institute if you were a prison warden?

4. How should accommodations for special populations be different in jails than in prisons?

5. Should isolation be used to protect individual prisoners?

6. Who should conduct strip searches for the LGBTQ population?

7. What factors would you consider in making a decision about whether to release an elderly or terminally ill prisoner?

KEY TERMS

Compassionate release, 316   Stigma, 312   U.S. Sentencing Commission, 316

Pat searches, 321

NOTES

1. Maruschak 2006
2. Ibid.
3. Maruschak 2008
4. Binswanger, Krueger, and Steiner 2009
5. Ibid.
6. Wilper et al. 2009
7. Ibid.
8. Note that those determined by the court to be mentally incompetent to stand trial or not guilty by reason of insanity are not included in these statistics.
9. James and Glaze 2006
10. Ibid.
11. Abner 2006
12. Anno et al. 2004
13. Carson and Sabol 2012
14. Williams and Abraldes 2007
15. Chui 2010
16. Ibid.
17. http://www.law.gwu.edu/Academics/EL/clinics/Pages/POPS.aspx
18. Beck and Johnson 2012
19. Lee 2010
20. National Prison Rape Elimination Commission 2012
21. Sexton, Jenness, and Sumner 2010
22. Personal interaction in the course of investigation into the California Youth Authority (Krisberg 2003a)
23. Palazzolo 2012
24. Lifesitenews.com 2003
25. Irvine 2010
26. Robinson 2011
27. *R.G. v. Koller* 2006

$SAGE edge™

Sharpen your skills with SAGE edge at edge.sagepub.com/krisberg

SAGE edge for students provides a personalized approach to help you accomplish your coursework goals in an easy-to-use learning environment. This site includes action plans, mobile-friendly eFlashcards and web quizzes as well as web, audio, and video resources and links to SAGE journal articles.

© Kim Naylor/Nordicphotos

14 Death Row and the Death Penalty

LEARNING OBJECTIVES

1 To understand the basic controversies related to the death penalty.

2 To grasp the decline in the use of the death penalty compared to the death row population.

3 To be able to argue either side of the debate about the death penalty as a deterrent and as just deserts.

4 To grasp the issue of racial disparity and capital punishment.

5 To be able to describe the significance of at least three of the most important legal challenges to the death penalty that have come through the U.S. Supreme Court.

The Controversial Moral Imperative

Troy Davis's sister fought tirelessly to win a stay of execution in the state of Georgia on the basis of "too much doubt" in her brother's case. There was no physical evidence linking Davis to the 1989 murder of an off-duty police officer. Seven witnesses recanted their testimonies, claiming they were coerced. The U.S. Supreme Court denied him a stay of execution, and the state of Georgia executed Troy Davis on September 21, 2011. The Davis case became a widely publicized cause, at home and abroad, not because it was so unusual but, perhaps, because it is far too common. For those who were already disillusioned with the criminal justice system, Davis's case was one too many.

The death penalty[*] is considered the most extreme punishment that the state can hand out as a formal sentence and is intended for the most extreme crimes. Its very nature, however, invites a controversy over morality and religious or spiritual belief. Advocates both for and against capital punishment claim equal measures of moral righteousness in their arguments.

▲ What would be the advantages of making modern executions viewable by the public?

© iStockphoto.com/ raw206

The corrections system must house and care for inmates awaiting execution, usually for many years. This drawn-out process exacts untold emotional costs from the families of victims and convicted alike. Additionally, it is specially assigned correctional staff who actually administer this extreme sanction that is pressed for by prosecutors and ordered by judges. We have little understanding of the emotional and psychic toll that this exacts on them.

Proponents of capital punishment consider it a just consequence for the most tragically barbaric crimes. This "eye for an eye" Old Testament philosophy holds up the notion of a commensurate form of justice, especially for murder. If you take a life, you must give yours in return. According to this way of thinking, whether the execution methods we use are humane is entirely secondary. In addition, many in this camp think that the death penalty is a deterrent to crime—punishment so extreme that, if murderers considered their options rationally, they would avoid the criminal act.

---

[*]The death penalty is also referred to as *capital punishment*. The term comes from the Latin *capitalis*, which means "of the head." Early on, the death penalty was carried out by decapitation.

 6 To be able to name the states that use the death penalty the most and at least two states that have rejected it most recently.

 8 To gain an insight into the dilemma surrounding methods of execution.

7 To learn about the comparative costs of death row.

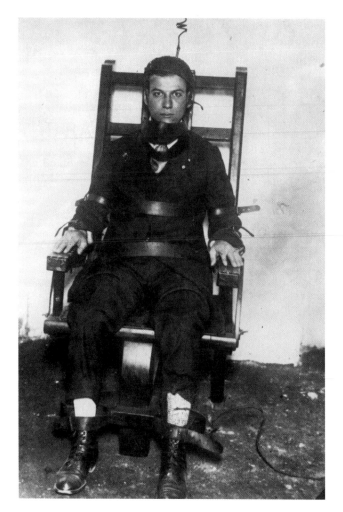

▲ The electric chair was designed by Thomas Edison, the inventor of the electric lightbulb. This is the electric chair in New York's Sing Sing penitentiary, circa 1925.

© akg-images/Newscom

Ultimately, those who favor capital punishment argue that there is a moral imperative to kill heinous murderers, no matter the costs. The great American death penalty abolitionist Sister Helen Prejean observed that people may deserve to die but pointed out the key moral question of whether we deserve to kill them.[1] The great American criminologist Marvin Wolfgang, who observed an execution in Pennsylvania, wrote, "I wish only to report that death in wartime combat, as ugly as it is, has no parallel to the state's premeditated, highly organized, calculated death of a human being, however heinous his crimes."[2]

Much of the public sees the death penalty as an economic issue as well and feels indignant about "supporting" a murderer for the remainder of his or her life in prison. They wish to be rid of the financial burden as well as the perceived threat of possible harm, should the murderer find a way to freedom. Death penalty supporters also argue that capital punishment brings "closure" to the victim's family members and helps them to "move on" with their lives.

Each of these points has compelling opposing arguments. Regarding perhaps the most subjective point, the basic moral question of whether anyone has the right to take the life of another is fundamental. That the inherent paradox of punishing murder with a state-sanctioned version of the same crime is an insurmountable conflict seems self-evident to opponents of capital punishment.

Death penalty opponents refer to the work of researchers who study the subject, the majority of whom maintain that the threat of execution does not deter crime in any way that has ever been measurable. Differences of opinion about research methods exist on this point. However, 88% of criminologists are of the opinion that capital punishment does not reduce homicide rates, while the remaining 5% think it does.[3]

Opponents of capital punishment hold that the death penalty actually costs more than putting people away for life. Maintaining a death row and the detailed court processes involved in appealing capital cases is actually many times more expensive than the annual costs of regular housing for a prisoner in most states. In California, it is estimated that each capital case costs the state $300 million (California has spent $4 billion on capital punishment, resulting in 13 executions). Life without the possibility of parole (LWOP) for adults is the logical alternative to a death sentence. Many consider LWOP the "new death penalty." A 2012 ballot measure in California (Proposition 34) called for the abolition of capital punishment based in part on this fiscal argument and was favored by almost half of voters.

An extremely troubling controversy about the death penalty is the evidence that there may be no such thing as a "painless" execution, at least among the currently used methods. The appearance of painlessness of lethal injection stems from the preliminary drugs administered during a lethal injection execution, which paralyze the prisoner, making it impossible for others to detect an outward reaction to the body's internal process or sensation. Medical experts argue vehemently over this point. The other methods of execution that have been used by states, though in much smaller numbers, are electrocution, the gas chamber, hanging, and firing squad.

Another thorny issue is that the death penalty is handed out unequally with respect to race and socioeconomic class. There are few rich people on death row. It has been shown in multiple rigorous studies that the race of the victim in capital crimes translates into a stark disproportion of death sentences. According to Amnesty International, the number of White and African American homicide victims since 1977 is roughly the same. However, 80% of death sentences occur in cases where the victim was White. Anti–death penalty activists usually handle this point with care, lest the opposition suggest addressing the problem by increasing the frequency of death sentences to reduce this disparity.[4]

The international perspective on the death penalty raises once again the image of the United States as an outlier on the global stage. As previously mentioned, the U.S. has an incarceration rate higher by far than the nations to which it is most closely linked by other cultural, social, and economic measures—the industrialized world. In addition, none of these other nations allows the death penalty. Indeed, European Union member states are expressly committed to the abolition of the death penalty. Some of the other countries that allow the death penalty are China, Iraq, Iran, Saudi Arabia, and Pakistan.

A factor that continues to haunt the debate on the death penalty is the lingering doubt about whether all death row prisoners are truly guilty of the crimes for which they are awaiting execution. Since 1973, 138 persons have been exonerated from death row.[5] If not for technology such as DNA testing, and a careful review of cases, these facts may have never been established, and innocent people would have been put to death. There is no logical reason to think that all such mistakes were recognized in time. And DNA evidence is only available and applicable in a small percentage of cases.

Underscoring the principle that wrongful execution is unacceptably onerous from an ethical standpoint, Illinois governor George Ryan released 156 state inmates from death row, commuting all of their death sentences, in 2003. This was a move considered to be one in a series of recent events weakening capital punishment in the United States. Some of the most serious and common reasons for wrongful conviction are inadequate legal representation, police and prosecutorial misconduct, perjured testimony, mistaken eyewitnesses, and racial prejudice.[6] These problems no doubt played a role in Ryan's impassioned decision. The governor announced his decision by stating, "I cannot support a system which, in its administration, has proven so fraught with error and has come so close to the ultimate nightmare, the state's taking of innocent life. . . . Until I can be sure that everyone sentenced to death in Illinois is truly guilty, until I can be sure with moral certainty that no innocent man or woman is facing a lethal injection, no one will meet that fate."[7]

Ever fewer states allow the death penalty. In 2012, a wide range of concerns over the imposition of death sentences led Connecticut officials to eliminate the state's death penalty. There had been two executions in Connecticut in the prior 50 years.

In early 2013, Maryland was poised to outlaw the state's death penalty. There has not been an execution in Maryland since 2005. A state moratorium has been in effect due to the controversies around lethal injection. During this time, Governor Martin O'Malley pushed legislation to abolish the death penalty altogether. It appears there is enough support among the state's lawmakers for doing so.[8]

As perspectives change and knowledge accumulates, society presumably evolves. We may one day view any form of capital punishment with the same revulsion we reserve for the centuries-old practice of drawing and quartering in the public square. It appears that we are still a long way from a general consensus on that point.

The State of Capital Punishment

At the end of 2012, 35 states and the Federal Bureau of Prisons (BOP) housed a total of 3,033 prisoners awaiting execution. After growing each year from 1976 to 2000, the death row population has been on the decline. During 2012, 111 inmates were removed from death rows, while 79 new capital cases arrived. Of those removed, 43 inmates were executed, 17 died due to reasons other than execution, and another 51 had their convictions or sentences overturned or commuted.[9]

The 79 admissions were the lowest number of new cases since 1976, when capital punishment was reinstated by the U.S. Supreme Court. More than 60% of these were admitted to prisons in four states: Florida (20), California (13), Texas (9), and Pennsylvania (6). These same four states also housed more than half of all inmates on death row in 2012: California (712), Florida (403), Texas (290), and Pennsylvania (200). There were 56 BOP inmates awaiting execution that year.[10]

Characteristics of Death Row Inmates

The vast majority of death row inmates are male—98% in 2012. Also in 2012, slightly more than half were White (56%), and 42% were African American. Another 2% were from other races, mostly Native Americans and Asians or Pacific Islanders. Latinos (of any race) composed 14% of the death row population.

Death row inmates have a wide range of ages—in 2012, 5% were under the age of 30, 58% were between the ages of 30 and 49 years, and 37% were 50 years or older. Just under half (48%) had never graduated from high school or gained a GED, including 13% with an eighth-grade education or less. Forty-three percent did have a high school diploma or equivalent, and 9% had some college credits.

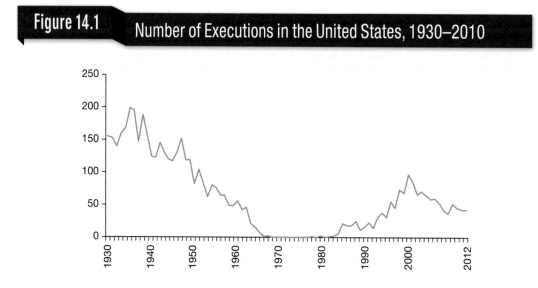

Figure 14.1   Number of Executions in the United States, 1930–2010

Figure 14.1 illustrates the dramatic drop in persons put to death between 1930 and 2010. There were approximately 200 executions in 1940—the peak year. Executions declined steadily until the practice was suspended by the U.S. Supreme Court. In the 1976 case of *Gregg v. Georgia*, the court allowed states to rewrite their capital laws and restart executions. The frequency of executions rose to 100 in 2000 but has been generally declining ever since. In 2011, there were 43 inmates put to death in 13 states, with the largest numbers killed in Texas (13), Alabama (6), and Ohio (3). *Source: Snell 2014.*

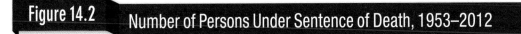

Figure 14.2   Number of Persons Under Sentence of Death, 1953–2012

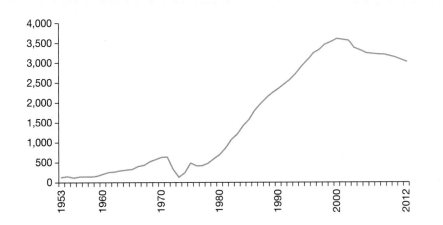

Although the number of executions has declined, the population of prisoners awaiting execution has grown dramatically, largely due to the lengthy legal process required to review convictions and death sentences that most states and the federal courts have required. For example, 7,879 persons received a death sentence between 1977 and 2010. Of these, 16% were put to death, another 6% died due to other reasons, and 39% had their convictions or sentences overturned or commuted. The inmates executed in 2012 had spent on average almost 16 years on death row before their execution.[11] *Source: Snell 2014.*

More than half of the death row residents had never married (55%), 22% were married, and 24% were divorced, separated, or widowed.

Two thirds of death row inmates had prior felony convictions before their current capital offense (67%), including 9% with a previous homicide conviction. Forty percent

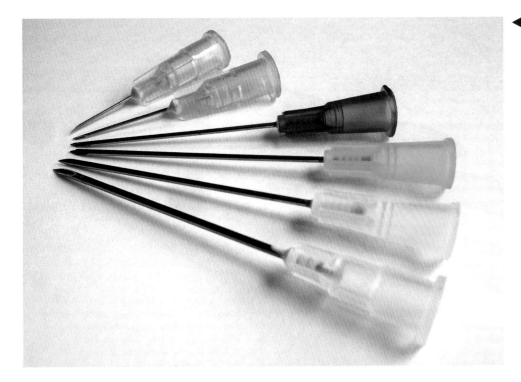

◀ Whether lethal injection is actually the most humane method of execution is open to considerable debate.

© Zephyris

Table 14.1 States With and Without the Death Penalty

States With the Death Penalty as of 2013		
Alabama	Louisiana	Pennsylvania
Arizona		South Carolina
Arkansas	Mississippi	South Dakota
California	Missouri	Tennessee
Colorado	Montana	Texas
Delaware	Nebraska	Utah
Florida	Nevada	Virginia
Georgia	New Hampshire	Washington
Idaho	North Carolina	Wyoming
Indiana	Ohio	
Kansas	Oklahoma	ALSO
Kentucky	Oregon	U.S. Government
		U.S. Military
States Without the Death Penalty and the Year of Abolishment		
Alaska (1957)	Minnesota (1911)	West Virginia (1965)
Connecticut* (2012)	New Jersey (2007)	Wisconsin (1853)
Hawaii (1957)	New Mexico* (2009)	
Illinois (2011)	New York (2007)#	ALSO
Iowa (1965)	North Dakota (1973)	District of Columbia (1981)
Maine (1887)	Rhode Island (1984) ^	
Maryland (2013)	Vermont (1964)	
Massachusetts (1984)		
Michigan (1846)		

All 35 states that had inmates on death row in 2013 authorized the use of lethal injections. Nine states also permitted electrocutions, three states allowed lethal gas, and three states permitted hangings. There are two states (Ohio and Utah) that still authorize the use of firing squads. Oklahoma permitted the use of a firing squad, but only if electrocution or lethal injections are declared unconstitutional. In 2010, the state of Utah employed a five-person firing squad to kill Ronnie Lee Gardner, who was seated and wore a hood over his head. The rifle of one of the five shooters was loaded with a nonlethal wax bullet, a traditional way to make it impossible to determine who fired the fatal bullet. It was the first execution by firing squad in the United States in 14 years.[12]

*When Connecticut, Maryland, and New Mexico abolished the death penalty, the repeals were not retroactive, leaving 11, 5, and 2 (respectively) inmates on death row.

^ In 1979, the Supreme Court of Rhode Island held that a statute making a death sentence mandatory for someone who killed a fellow prisoner was unconstitutional. The legislature removed the statute in 1984.

In 2004, the New York Court of Appeals held that a portion of the state's death penalty law was unconstitutional. In 2007, they ruled that their prior holding applied to the last remaining person on the state's death row. The legislature has voted down attempts to restore the statute.

Source: Death Penalty Information Center. "States With and Without the Death Penalty," 2014. http://www.deathpenaltyinfo.org/states-and-without-death-penalty, accessed June 2, 2014.

had been system involved when they committed the crime for which they were sentenced to death, including 3% in prison and 28% on probation or parole.[13]

Legal Challenges to the Death Penalty

Because of the finality and importance of the death penalty, several key U.S. Supreme Court decisions weighed the constitutionality of this sanction. Challenges to capital punishment have also stemmed from statutory and regulatory reviews. These legal decisions illustrate the complex social, legal, and humanitarian concerns that surface around the death penalty. For example, in *Louisiana ex rel. Francis v. Resweber* (1947), the court held that it was neither double jeopardy nor cruel and unusual punishment to subject inmates who had not died during an electrocution to a second method of execution.

One of the most important court decisions on capital punishment was *Furman v. Georgia* (1972), in which the court held that capital punishment was itself constitutional but that the methods of its use violate the Eighth Amendment prohibitions against cruel and unusual punishment.[14]

▲ Ronnie Lee Gardner listens to proceedings during his commutation hearing in Draper, Utah. In June 2010, Gardner died by gunfire as Utah carried out its first firing squad execution in 14 years.

© POOL The Salt Lake Tribune/ Associated Press

There were three related cases in which the defendant was sentenced to death—one homicide and two rape cases. The 1972 Supreme Court found that capital punishment was applied in an arbitrary, capricious, and discriminatory manner in which race, gender, socioeconomic status, quality of legal representation, and victim characteristics unfairly affected the outcome of the case. Only Justices Brennan and Marshall argued that the death penalty was per se cruel and unusual punishment. Justices Douglas, Stewart, and White were persuaded by the large amount of evidence on racial bias in selecting offenders for the death penalty. However, Justices Rehnquist, Burger, Blackmun, and Powell refused to overturn the death penalty completely. The majority called for states to revisit their capital punishment statutes and to rewrite them to remove the legal deficiencies in *Furman*.

The *Furman* case suspended the imposition of death sentences in the United States for several years. Virtually every state with capital punishment rewrote its laws. The *Furman* case invalidated laws governing capital punishment in 30 states and the District of Columbia. New state laws generally replaced previous methods of execution with lethal injection, a method thought at that time to be less cruel.

The Supreme Court reviewed the redrafted death penalty laws in *Gregg v. Georgia* (1976), and by a 7-to-2 vote permitted most states to resume executions.[15] The only two dissenting judges were Justices Brennan and Marshall. One of the most important components of the *Gregg* case was the requirement that there must be a separate hearing by a judge or a jury covering the finding of guilt or innocence and then a later hearing in which aggravating and mitigating circumstances were considered before the death sentence could be imposed.

Double jeopardy: The subjecting of a person to a second trial or punishment for the same offense for which the person has already been tried or punished.

SPOTLIGHT

WOMEN AND THE DEATH PENALTY

The reasons that women have been executed in the United States have changed over time. Historically, women were executed for "crimes" such as witchcraft and heresy; in the modern era, women are sentenced to death and executed for murder. Of the 12 women executed for homicide in the United States since 1976, all but two of them murdered a family member or someone else with whom they had a personal relationship.[1] Of those same women, 2 were executed by electrocution, and 10 were executed by lethal injection.[2]

There have been 174 death sentences imposed on women since 1973. More than half of these occurred in five states: North Carolina, Florida, California, Ohio, and Texas. The average number of death sentences for women is 2.1% of the total number of death sentences.

Unlike men on death row, women on death row are predominantly White. Of the women on death row at the end of 2012, 62% were White, 21% were Black, 14% were Latina, 2% were Asian, and 2% were Native American. Of the 12 women executed since 1976, 10 were White, and 2 were African American.[3]

Modern society seems to have a long-standing bias against executing women.[4] The rate of the imposition of the death sentence and actual executions is very low for women compared to men.

On the other hand, when it does occur, the execution of a woman tends to draw inordinate attention. Karla Faye Tucker was executed in Texas in 1998—the first woman to be executed since 1984. Her execution occurred amidst a media furor. By all accounts, she had completely transformed and appeared to pose no threat to society. However, then Governor George Bush was facing reelection in Texas and was a contender for the Republican nomination for the 2000 presidential race. Politics may have played a significant role in Bush's

Table 14.2   Women Under the Sentence of Death, Top 5 States, 1973–2012

State	White	Black	Latina	Native American	Total
California	12	3	6	1	22
Florida	13	5	3	0	21
Texas	12	7	1	0	20
North Carolina	10	4	0	2	16
Ohio	6	6	0	0	12
Total	53	25	10	3	91

Source: Death Penalty Information Center 2013a.

The most significant challenge to capital punishment following its reinstatement was *McCleskey v. Kemp* in 1987. This case looked at whether the death penalty was applied in a racially discriminatory manner. When capital punishment was restored by the Supreme Court in 1976, more than 35% of all the inmates on death row were African American. The proportion of African Americans in the general population was 12.9% at that time—so, on the surface, there appeared to be compelling evidence that capital punishment most heavily impacted Black defendants.[16]

Warren McCleskey was African American and was sentenced to death for homicide in Georgia. Mr. McCleskey claimed that Georgia administered capital punishment in a racially disparate manner, which violated the Eighth and Fourteenth Amendments of the

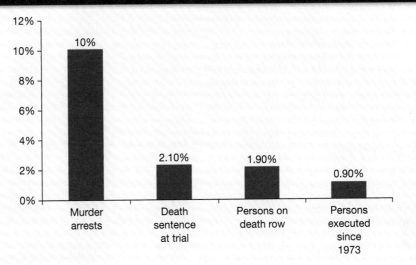

Figure 14.3   Percentage of Women and Stages of the Death Penalty, 1973–2010

Source: Streib 2010.

decision. During the 1928 execution of Ruth Brown Snyder in New York's electric chair, a journalist snapped an unauthorized photo that was printed as front-page news the following day.[5]

Two award-winning actresses played condemned women in feature films: Susan Hayward portrayed Barbara Graham, executed in 1955, in the film titled *I Want to Live*. Charlize Theron played Aileen Wuornos, who was executed in Florida in 2002, in the film *Monster*.

QUESTIONS

1 Are there justifications for women being sentenced to death far less often than men for the same crimes?

2 If the death penalty had a deterrent effect, would this be different for women than for men?

3 Discuss reasons that the racial breakdown on death row might be significantly different for women than for men.

Notes

1. Death Penalty Information Center 2013c
2. Ibid.
3. Ibid.
4. Streib 2010
5. Rapaport 2000; Streib 2005

U.S. Constitution. The plaintiff's argument rested on a comprehensive and exhaustive study of the death penalty in Georgia that was conducted by a respected law professor and social scientist at the University of Iowa, David Baldus.

The Baldus study analyzed a statistically valid sample of almost 2,500 murder cases in Georgia that occurred in the decade after the *Gregg* decision.[17] The researchers examined more than 36 legal, personal, and situational variables that might explain the differences between African American and White homicides that actually resulted in a death sentence. The most salient factor was the relationship between the race of the victim and the race of the offender. Georgia prosecutors asked for capital punishment in 71% of cases involving an African American defendant and a White victim. By contrast, capital punishment was

▲ Bishop Ray W. Chamberlin, Jr., speaks during a rally against the death penalty on the 30th anniversary of *Gregg v. Georgia*, in which the Supreme Court upheld laws written to reinstate the death penalty, in front of the Supreme Court.

© Roger L. Wollenberg/UPI / Landov

sought in only 32% of cases in which both the victim and the offender were White. In the case of African American victims, the death penalty was the sentence for 19% of Whites who killed African Americans and 15% of the cases in which both the victim and the offender were African American.[18] More recent research by Paternoster and Brame continues to support the finding that African American defendants who kill White victims are more likely to receive the death penalty than other types of offenders.[19]

The U.S. Supreme Court decided, however, to discount the powerful statistical evidence in *McCleskey v. Kemp*, the majority arguing that the plaintiff failed to show that racial discrimination actually occurred in his case. The slim majority of justices (5 to 4) argued that state legislatures were better suited to hear and resolve the evidence that was presented in the Baldus study. Four years later, the state of Georgia put Mr. McCleskey to death.

Juveniles and the Death Penalty

The U.S. Supreme Court has considered and ruled on many aspects of the death penalty as they relate to youth. By a dramatic, narrow decision (5 to 4) in 2005, the U.S. Supreme Court limited the use of capital punishment even further by banning its use for persons who committed their crimes before the age of 18—*Roper v. Simmons*.[20] Justice Kennedy, writing for the majority, argued that capital punishment for crimes committed before the age of 18 violated both the Eighth and Fourteenth Amendments of the Constitution. In his decision, Justice Kennedy referred to international standards that banned the death penalty for juveniles, an evolving sense that putting minors to death was exceedingly rare, and the emerging findings of neuroscience that held that persons under 18 are generally incapable of understanding the future consequences of their actions and should not be held to the same standard of accountability as adults.

Extending the protections allowed by *Roper*, the court ruled in 2010 (*Graham v. Florida*) that LWOP could not be imposed on youth for crimes that were not homicides; in 2012, the court ruled that LWOP also violates Eighth Amendment protections for youth convicted of homicide (*Jackson v. Hobbs*).

The Death Sentence and Mental Competence

Another pivotal challenge to capital punishment was *Atkins v. Virginia* (2002), in which the U.S. Supreme Court found that putting the developmentally disabled to death constituted cruel and unusual punishment and is thus prohibited by the Eighth Amendment.* The case was decided by a 6-to-3 majority that included Justices Stevens, O'Connor, Souter, Ginsburg, Breyer, and Kennedy. Dissenting justices were Scalia, Thomas, and Rehnquist. Justice Stevens wrote the majority opinion and found that the number of states that had banned the execution of developmentally disabled defendants had increased significantly from 2 states in 1989 to 18 states in 2002. Justice Stevens observed that developmentally disabled defendants had multiple disadvantages at trial including their ability to identify witnesses, to testify with credibility, and to properly consult with their defense counsel.

The question of executing the mentally ill is still unresolved by the U.S. Supreme Court. This controversy dates back over a quarter century to 1974, when Alvin Ford committed a murder and was sentenced to death in Florida. By 1982, Mr. Ford was still awaiting his execution, but he manifested symptoms of a severe mental disorder. A psychiatrist examined the defendant and concluded that Mr. Ford could not comprehend the relationship between his crime and the fact of his death sentence. Lawyers for Ford requested that the governor appoint a panel of three psychiatrists to determine if Ford had "the mental capacity to understand the nature of the death penalty and the reasons why it was imposed upon him." The panel of mental health professionals could not agree on Ford's diagnosis, but all agreed that he was sane under the Florida statutory definition. Then Governor Bob Graham of Florida ordered Ford's death warrant to be carried out. Subsequent appeals in the federal district court of the court of appeals brought no change in Mr. Ford's legal status.

In 1986, the U.S. Supreme Court agreed to hear the case to determine whether executing an insane defendant violates the Eighth Amendment and whether the district court should have heard Ford's claim, focused on the denial of procedural safeguards, and ordered a new evidentiary hearing. The court also held that executing a person who was insane was a violation of the Eighth Amendment. In a very close decision, Justices Marshall, Brennan, Blackmun, Powell, and Stevens concluded that an insane person must not be executed. Justice Marshall wrote that historical principles of English and American common law dictated that acts that were "intolerable and savage" and lacked any valid penological purpose violated an evolving standard of decency. In *Ford v. Wainwright* (1986), Justices Rehnquist, Burger, White, and O'Connor dissented and argued that executing an insane person was not necessarily inhumane; however, Justices White and O'Connor agreed that Mr. Ford was not given adequate due process in his hearings before federal courts. Mr. Ford was then transferred to a Florida state hospital for a psychiatric reevaluation.

This decision hardly settled the matter. In Texas, in 2007, Scott Panetti defended himself in his capital case. Unlike the *Ford* case, Panetti said that he understood that the state of

Evidentiary hearing: A preliminary hearing, after a criminal complaint has been filed by the prosecutor, to determine whether there is enough evidence to require a trial. In the United States, the judge must find it probable that a crime was committed.

---

* The court actually used the term retarded, *which is more narrowly defined. The term* developmentally disabled *is open to wider interpretation, which is the source of legal contention in related cases.*

▲ An inmate goes through a psychological evaluation, in this case for dementia caused by HIV.

© Andy Scott/KRT/Newscom

Texas intended to put him to death for the murder of his in-laws, but Panetti also asserted that Texas was following Satan's instructions to kill him and prevent him from preaching the Gospel. He fired his lawyers, because he thought they were colluding with the police. The judge allowed Panetti to represent himself. Panetti showed up in court wearing a cowboy suit. He doodled on his legal documents. Panetti was found guilty and sentenced to death. Numerous appeals followed. In 2007, the U.S. Supreme Court ruled in favor of Panetti and blocked his scheduled execution. However, the case returned to the federal district court, which concluded that Mr. Panetti was suffering from schizophrenia but was competent to be executed. At issue is his competence to rationally understand the connection between his deeds and the execution. Clinicians have determined that his mental state has deteriorated during the years of his incarceration. As of May 2014, Mr. Panetti was still on death row in Texas.

Although exact data are difficult to obtain, many death row inmates have been diagnosed with schizophrenia, bipolar disorder, delusions, and other severe mental health problems. Some of these inmates were already suffering from these illnesses before they were placed on death row, but others deteriorated due to spending long periods in harsh settings awaiting execution, or the stress of not knowing when the execution might be carried out. Some inmates are delusional. For example, Florida executed Thomas Provenzano in 2000. Mr. Provenzano claimed that he was Jesus Christ and was being executed by people who hated Jesus.[21] In 2002, Texas imposed a sentence of death on Monty Delk, who exhibited gross delusions and incoherent speech and smeared himself with his own feces. Charles Singleton believed that his victim was still alive and that he shared his cell with demons. Mr. Singleton was forcibly medicated and was put to death in Arkansas in 2004.

Professional organizations such as the American Bar Association, the American Psychiatric Association, the American Psychological Association, and the National Alliance on Mental Illness have promulgated statements condemning current practices involving capital punishment and the mentally ill. These groups argue that defendants must be competent to participate in their own defense and to competently decide if further appeals are warranted. Defendants must have the ability to appreciate the consequences of their death sentences and to comprehend the purpose of their death sentence and the connection of capital punishment to their own cases.

In the states that allow the death penalty, federal and state courts have yet to embrace these professional standards. Mental health professionals who are involved in such cases face significant ethical challenges. In 2012, the Supreme Court declined to hear a petition from an Oklahoma inmate who argued that he had a constitutional right to a competency examination.

The nation's death rows house significant numbers of the mentally ill, and yet the American legal system remains undecided on the boundaries of justice in this area—one among many tragic dimensions of the death penalty in the United States.

> **YOU DECIDE**
>
> ### Mentally Ill Death Row Inmates
>
> Robert has been sentenced to death and is awaiting execution. He has been on death row for 10 years. His mental condition has deteriorated, and he will no longer eat prison food, does not clean himself, and refuses to leave his cell for exercise, showering, or health services. He regularly assaults staff who attempt to give him the medications he needs. Robert has attempted suicide several times.
>
> His lawyers object to the use of tear gas and Tasers to remove Robert from his cell. They argue that he should get intensive psychiatric care and be moved to an acute mental health unit. Prison officials argue that the costs of this care would be prohibitive and that, since Robert is awaiting execution, his current situation is not "cruel and unusual punishment."
>
> *YOU DECIDE*: **What level of care should Robert get? Should prison staff continue efforts to keep him alive?**

Innocence and Those Awaiting Executions

The ultimate nightmare surrounding capital punishment is the potential for a truly innocent person being put to death. The actual numbers are shocking. According to the Death Penalty Information Center, 142 persons have been released from death row since 1973. No one knows how many innocent persons were put to death in the United States before that or even since. One exoneration case involved Damon Thibodeaux, whose charges were all dropped in 2012 after he had spent 15 years awaiting execution in Louisiana.[22]

To be considered innocent in this context, defendants must have been convicted, sentenced to death, and then had their conviction overturned. The overturned conviction is most often a result of acquittal at retrial, dropped charges, or the grant of an absolute pardon by the governor based on new evidence of innocence. The average time that exonerated inmates spent in prison before their release is almost 10 years. Peter Limone was on death row in Massachusetts for 33 years; the charges against him were dropped. Laurence Adams spent 30 years awaiting execution in Massachusetts until his charges were dismissed. Timothy Howard and Gary Lamar Jones each spent 26 years on Ohio's death row until they were exonerated. Nathan Fields was on death row in Illinois and was exonerated 23 years after his sentencing. And Paul House was on Tennessee's death row for

Exoneration: To clear, as of an accusation; to free from guilt or blame.

22 years before the capital charges against him were dismissed. There are dozens of other tragic stories of people who can never have that time restored—can never be compensated for that miscarriage of justice. In addition, the actual guilty party goes unpunished and perhaps commits more crime.

Public attention about wrongful convictions in capital cases was spurred by the work of the Innocence Project at Benjamin Cardozo Law School in New York. Some of the organization's most prominent exoneree cases involved using DNA evidence to prove that the defendant could not have committed the crime. Over time, the science and technology of DNA have improved (and are still evolving), and state laws and law enforcement practices have improved in terms of the collection and storing of physical evidence. Popular television programs such as *CSI* and *Law and Order* have dramatized the value of DNA evidence in criminal trials. The initial work of the Cardozo Law School group has proliferated in many states and throughout the world.[23]

It is worth noting that DNA evidence played a relatively small role (18 cases) in the 142 death row exonerations that occurred from 1972 to 2012. More common reasons for exonerations included inadequate legal representation, false eyewitness identifications, confessions coerced by law enforcement agents, the use of confidential informants or "snitches," and prosecutorial misconduct such as withholding exculpatory or mitigating evidence at trial.

The growing awareness of wrongfully convicted persons on death row led some public officials to suspend executions in their states or to seek remedies to problems in the trial process. The U.S. Supreme Court has taken a more cautious approach to potential evidence of wrongful convictions. In *Strickland v. Washington* (1984), the court held 8 to 1 that the right to representation in capital cases had to meet "an objective standard of reasonableness." Justice O'Connor wrote that the defendant had to show that the outcome of the case would have been different but for the unprofessional errors of his or her counsel.

▲ The quality of defense counsel is a significant issue in whether justice is carried out in capital cases.

© Doug Engle/Ocala Star-Banner /Landov

A Texas court overturned the conviction of Calvin Burdine because his attorney was asleep during long portions of the trial. Mr. Burdine had already spent 16 years on Texas's death row at the time of his release.

In a case that still shocks many legal scholars, the Supreme Court in *Herrera v. Collins* (1993) issued a 6-to-3 opinion written by Chief Justice Rehnquist that asserted that the Eighth Amendment does not prohibit the execution of someone who claims to be factually innocent and has new evidence but was denied a federal habeas corpus petition. Leonel Herrera was sentenced to death in 1982 for the alleged murder of two police officers. Over a decade later, Mr. Herrera's nephew filed an affidavit that his father, Raul Herrera, confessed to the crime. There were three other witnesses who claimed that it was Raul—not Leonel—who committed the murders. Texas law permits filing of new evidence within 30 days of the conviction. Leonel Herrera was put to death by the state of Texas in 1993.

▲ Leonel Herrera in 1993.

© Mike Graczyk /Associated Press

Costs of Capital Punishment

The legal and moral imperative to permit exhaustive appellate review of death sentences and the need to provide adequate legal representation for the accused mean that capital punishment is a very expensive part of the criminal justice system. These costs are multiplied by the very long prison stays of death row inmates in super-maximum-security settings. Following are some examples of rigorous and independent analyses of those costs. Plus, the costs of supervising death row inmates are much higher than those for general housing. For example, death row inmates require intensive staff supervision, as they must be under escort any time they leave their cells. In many prisons, the protocol is for a two-guard escort to meals, treatment, outdoor time, library, and visitation.

A study in California by Judge Arthur Alarcon and Professor Paula Mitchell found that California spent over $4 billion on the death penalty between 1978 and 2011.[24] These costs included more than $2 billion for pretrial and trial costs, almost $1.8 billion in automatic appeals and state federal habeas corpus actions, and about $1 billion in incarceration costs. Alarcon and Mitchell concluded that commuting all of the inmates on death row to life without the possibility of parole would produce short-term savings of $170 million per year and would reduce taxpayer costs by $5 billion over the next two decades.[25] LWOP prisoners can be double-celled, do not require escorts, and after their single chance at appeal have no litigation costs.

An earlier report of the California Commission on the Fair Administration of Justice found that the additional cost of housing one inmate on death row, compared with sentencing him or her to LWOP in a maximum-security prison, was approximately $90,000 per year—over $65 million annually for all death row inmates. The commission presented conservative cost projections suggesting that the present California death penalty process costs $137 million per year. Moreover, the commission recommended a series of procedural reforms that would add an additional $233 million to annual death penalty expenditures.

SPOTLIGHT

THE EXECUTIONER

The 35 states that have inmates on death row employ at least one executioner. As a rule, there is a great deal of secrecy around executions and executioners; our society no longer performs these acts in public. Occasionally, however, an executioner comes forward to tell his story. Those who do speak out are often troubled by their work. Many others may view it as a routine task that must be carried out as any other work duty. Some executioners' stories have been laid down in print.

In 2001, journalist Ivan Solotaroff wrote about executioner Donald Hocutt in *The Last Face You'll Ever See: The Private Life of the American Death Penalty*.[1] The author found the executioner severely traumatized by his work. In 1998, Donald Cabana released an autobiography titled *Death at Midnight: The Confession of an Executioner*. Cabana was warden during the 1980s at Mississippi State Penitentiary at Parchman—the same institution where Hocutt worked. In his book, Cabana related being so disturbed by the two executions he had to carry out that he left corrections altogether.

Some executioners confess in these writings to being so troubled by their work that they turn to alcohol or other ways of numbing themselves for protection against the nagging feelings of regret, guilt, and doubt.[2]

For Jerry Givens, the doubts gave way to a complete reversal of belief. Givens was the executioner for the state of Virginia for 17 years. When he began his role as executioner, he believed in the death penalty, and he felt it was simply his duty to carry it out, acting on the behalf of the society that authorized him.[3]

He would kneel down and pray with those men he was about to execute. Givens executed 62 people on Virginia's death row, using educated guesswork to decide how much current to let flow through the body of the condemned person strapped to the electric chair.[4]

The commission asserted that a system in which lifetime incarceration was the maximum penalty would by comparison cost about $12 million annually.[26]

Studies in other states have produced similar cost estimates. The Urban Institute found that Maryland spent $186 million on the prosecution of 162 death penalty cases, over and above what those cases would have cost otherwise. The study determined that a death penalty case costs approximately $3 million—$2 million over the cost of a non–death penalty case.[27] There are studies from Nevada, Washington, New Jersey, Tennessee, Kansas, North Carolina, Texas, and the federal system that have generated rich data on the extraordinary costs encumbered when jurisdiction clings to its death penalty system.[28]

The Problem of Lethal Injection

Although lethal injection has been the most frequent method of execution since the early 1980s, many controversies concerning this method of state-authorized killings persist. Thirty-five states primarily use this method of imposing a death sentence. Lethal injection entails intravenous doses of a three-drug combination or a large dose of a powerful barbiturate. Each state has its own particular method of delivering these fatal doses. The inmate is strapped down in a gurney and connected to an EKG monitor that measures heart activity. Usually, the warden will signal the delivery of the killing drugs. There are often witnesses who observe the process. It is typical that the process involves inducing a state of unconsciousness followed by chemicals that paralyze the entire muscular system and cause the prisoner's heart to stop beating.

But after 17 years, Givens had a change of heart. His conversion was due in part by nearly executing a man who was later found to be completely innocent and was exonerated. Givens also spent time in prison himself for participating in buying a car with money known to be stolen. Givens did four years.

After his release, Givens met with a man named Jonathan Sheldon—the former executive director of Virginians for Alternatives to the Death Penalty (VADP). Givens gradually began attending meetings and giving speeches, including at the Virginia state legislature. Partly due to his dramatic testimony, a proposed expansion of the Virginia death penalty failed to pass. In an interview with the *Washington Post*, Givens says, "People want it done, but they want somebody else to do it."[5] Givens says he wonders if there were any innocent people among the dozens he executed. He understands that he'll never know the answer to that question.

QUESTIONS

1 How should prison administrators choose an executioner?

2 Should there be limits on the number of executions one person can perform?

3 Should an executioner go through regular psychological evaluations? Should he have mental health support?

Notes

1. Cassel n.d.
2. Taylor 2010
3. Avila, Harris, and Francescani 2007
4. Taylor 2010
5. Jouvenal 2013

Physicians in Nazi Germany pioneered this method of execution in the 1930s and early 1940s as part of a euthanasia program aimed at disabled children and adults. The Nazis later abandoned lethal injections for poison gas, which was cheaper and more effective. Proponents of lethal injections in the United States argue that it is a less cruel method of capital punishment than electrocution.[29]

In *Baze v. Rees* (2008), the Supreme Court considered a Kentucky case that challenged whether lethal injection constituted cruel and unusual punishment. The combination of drugs that were used in Kentucky's lethal injections is widely used in other states. The key constitutional question was whether the lethal injection inflicted "unnecessary pain" during the execution process. The Supreme Court rendered a 7-to-2 decision that the Kentucky method of lethal injection did not violate the Eighth Amendment. Thus, most states could legally continue executions using the Kentucky protocol.

The story does not end with *Baze v. Rees*, however. Several of the U.S. manufacturers of the killing drugs began to run low on their supplies, and European pharmaceutical companies were pressured by opponents of the death penalty to close factories that manufactured these drugs or the necessary raw ingredients. Some European states that vehemently opposed capital punishment challenged the companies that were making the lethal chemicals with charges of engaging in illegal international drug trafficking. The U.S. Food and Drug Administration confiscated some of these drugs and found that the existing stock of lethal chemicals was contaminated or of uncertain potency. Several American states such as Alabama, Arizona, Arkansas, Georgia, and South Carolina began buying chemicals from totally unregulated pharmaceutical companies in India. There is

Euthanasia: To kill (a person or an animal) painlessly, especially to relieve suffering.

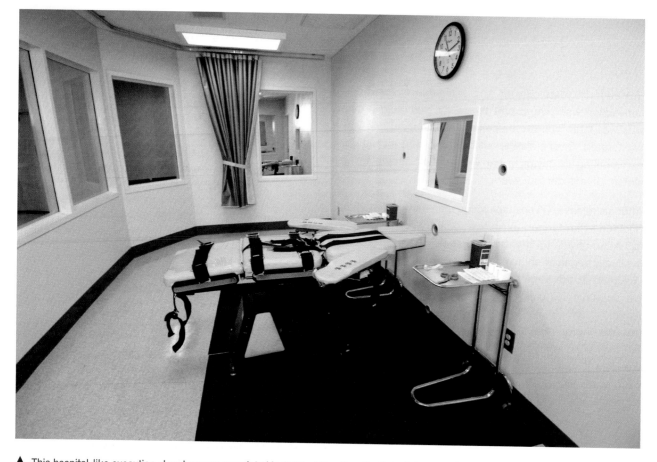

▲ This hospital-like execution chamber was completed in 2010 at San Quentin State Prison as part of a death row retrofit.

California Department of Corrections and Rehabilitation

currently no legal way to obtain some of the component drugs. Other states such as Mississippi, Ohio, Oklahoma, Texas, and Virginia switched to more readily available drugs that were being used to euthanize animals. If the nature of the lethal cocktails had changed, some questioned whether the assumption that there was not "unnecessary pain" infliction was still true. It has been asserted that without appropriate sedation, the executioners are unwittingly engaging in torture. Serious questions have been raised as to whether prison personnel properly follow the lethal injection protocols and if they (as nonmedical professionals) are competent to judge whether the executed inmate is experiencing pain during the execution.

The issue involves a dilemma either way; where medical professionals do not participate, prison staff who are unskilled and untrained in medicine administer the lethal dose of chemicals. Some states have had to loosen the guidelines for the qualifications for administering lethal injection; there are simply not enough doctors or nurses who are willing to perform the task.

As noted earlier, correctional staff actually carry out the executions as part of their regular job assignments. There are anecdotal accounts of prison staff who become the executioners or who witness these state-sanctioned killings and later suffer from enormous guilt, depression, other mental disorders, drug abuse, alcoholism, and even suicide. Wardens such as Jeanne Woodford in California or Allen Ault in Georgia have supervised the imposition of capital punishment and then become strong advocates for its abolition.

This latter issue is extremely thorny and has caused many critics of capital punishment to reflect on the ethical standards of medical professionals who participate in executions.

The American Medical Association (AMA) issued a policy statement prohibiting its members from participating in executions, on the grounds that it violates the hallowed Hippocratic Oath of doing no harm. The American Nurses Association and the American Society of Anesthesiologists have taken similar positions. Only seven states have officially adopted the AMA's code. Only Illinois and Kentucky expressly bar physicians from the execution chamber.[30] More often, medical boards are reluctant to sanction doctors for administering lethal injection.

· ·

SUMMARY

The death penalty exemplifies the unequal and illogical practices of our out-of-control penal system. The social toll of this form of sentencing is significant. The fiscal costs are also high and are even more difficult to justify in tough economic and fiscal times. There is scant evidence that capital punishment actually deters violent crime and plentiful evidence that it does not. The majority of the world's nations reject capital punishment. And traditional supporters of capital punishment among the families of homicide victims and law enforcement are questioning whether the money being spent on rare executions is truly worth it.

Partly because of the high stakes involved in capital cases, the process is fraught with controversy. As in other parts of the criminal justice system, death row inmates are disproportionately poor people of color. There is mounting evidence that innocent people have spent years awaiting execution. Many of them have been exonerated, but there is no telling how many more should be. Furthermore, methods of execution are extremely problematic.

Public support for capital punishment appears to be waning, and its use is becoming more restricted and rare. In recent years, the U.S. Supreme Court has ruled against the death penalty for minors and the developmentally disabled. All indications are that restrictions on the death penalty are likely to increase in the future.

DISCUSSION QUESTIONS

1. What are the basic areas of argument and controversy regarding the death penalty?

2. What are your personal feelings about the fundamental morality of the death penalty?

3. Does your state allow the death penalty? If so, has the number of executions declined in your state during the last 10 years? What are the reasons for that decline?

4. Discuss the linkage between socioeconomic class and the frequency of the death penalty.

5. What are the most critical reasons for the 1972 Supreme Court decision that suspended capital punishment in the United States? What are the reasons and conditions for its reinstatement four years later?

6. Discuss the Baldus study and the issue of race and its relationship to death sentences.

7. Should the death penalty be allowed for the mentally ill? For those who committed their crimes before the age of 18? Do you agree or disagree with key U.S. Supreme Court decisions?

8. Research the case of one person exonerated from death row. Were there reasons beyond any DNA evidence that might have proven sufficient for that person's release?

9. How does wrongful conviction differ from exoneration?

10. Should the cost of death row play a part in legislation and policy, or should costs be considered separately from the issues of morality, deterrence, and victim needs?

11. What is the most humane way of carrying out a death sentence? Why?

KEY TERMS

Double jeopardy, 331

Evidentiary hearing, 335

Exoneration, 337

Euthanasia, 341

NOTES

1. Prejean 1994
2. Krisberg, Baird, and Marchionna 2007, 283
3. Radelet and Lacock 2009
4. Amnesty International 2012
5. Death Penalty Focus 2011
6. American Civil Liberties Union n.d.
7. Amnesty International 2013
8. Wagner and Davis 2013
9. Snell 2014
10. Ibid.
11. Ibid.
12. Hayes 2010
13. Snell 2014
14. The *Furman* case also included *Jackson v. Georgia* and *Branch v. Texas.*
15. This was one of five related cases, including *Jurek v. Texas, Roberts v. Louisiana, Profitt v. Florida,* and *Woodson v. North Carolina.*

16. Baldus, Pulaski, and Woodworth 1990
17. Ibid.
18. Ibid.
19. Paternoster and Brame 2008
20. *Roper v. Simmons* 2005
21. CBS News 2009
22. Death Penalty Information Center 2013b
23. Innocence Project 2013
24. Alarcon and Mitchell 201
25. Ibid.
26. California Commission on the Fair Administration of Justice 2008
27. McMenamin 2008; Roman et al. 2008
28. Death Penalty Information Center 2013a
29. Death Penalty Focus n.d..
30. O'Reilly 2010

$SAGE edge™

Sharpen your skills with SAGE edge at edge.sagepub.com/krisberg

SAGE edge for students provides a personalized approach to help you accomplish your coursework goals in an easy-to-use learning environment. This site includes action plans, mobile-friendly eFlashcards and web quizzes as well as web, audio, and video resources and links to SAGE journal articles.

IV

The Effectiveness and Future of American Corrections

15 The Growth of Privatization in Corrections[1]

LEARNING OBJECTIVES

1. To understand the scope and size of private correctional facilities in the United States.

2. To grasp the kinds of functions fulfilled by private correctional companies.

3. To be able to name at least three private corrections companies, including the two largest.

4. To gain a sense of the relationship between private corrections companies and local economies.

Since their start in the 1980s, private prisons have come to hold 8% of all U.S. state and federal prisoners, including half of federal immigration detainees. Proponents of privatization claim that private prisons can provide a quick response to facility overcrowding, higher-quality and more cost-effective services, improved conditions of confinement, and economic growth in the communities where new facilities are built. These purported benefits are not typically supported by independent research. Scores of private facility incident reports across the country bring into question the safety and quality of these facilities. The primary ways private prisons sustain their profits, including low pay, limited staff training, and other cost-cutting measures, can lead to unmet inmate needs and security issues, heightening the inherent dangers to staff and inmates in secure settings. There are also significant issues with the government's ability to effectively monitor what goes on at private prisons. The expectation that competition for contracts among free-market players would lead to generally improved efficiency, quality, and cost savings has not proved reliable.

Nevertheless, proponents of privatization continue to use these claims as a basis for promoting expansion. Private prison companies spend millions of dollars on lobbying, political campaign contributions, support for legislation favorable to their profits, campaigns to shape public opinion, and research likely to support their practices. These activities lead many to question the prison industry's influence on criminal justice policymaking.

Although the desire for a quick solution to crowding is the most common reason jurisdictions contract for bed space in private prisons, secondary rationales include cost savings and improved services. Also, states and local jurisdictions seek partnerships with prison companies to establish private facilities as a way to boost their economies. There is a shortage of high-quality research to assess the success of these secondary aims.

Secure private facilities designed for adults are the major focus of this chapter, although many of the same issues and potential solutions apply to other types of privatization in corrections. Federal immigration detention and contracted services, such as in-custody health care and programming or postrelease supervision and services, are also briefly discussed here.

History and Functioning of Private Prisons

During the "tough on crime" era beginning in the 1980s, as incarceration rates rose in state and federal institutions, those rates also rose in private, for-profit facilities. Privatization of certain corrections functions, such as health care and other services, was common for some time prior to this, but larger-scale facilities wholly managed by for-profit companies got their start in the mid 1980s.

Privatization: the process of outsourcing traditionally state- or government-run services to private companies.

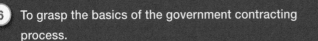

5 To be able to describe how private corrections and public corrections policy may be in conflict.

7 To know how difficult it is to monitor private facilities and why.

6 To grasp the basics of the government contracting process.

The term *private prison* typically refers to secure facilities where all or most of the inmates remain confined at all times, such as prisons, prison farms, penitentiaries, correctional centers, work camps, and reformatories. A large percentage of private facilities are community based, such as halfway houses, residential treatment centers, restitution centers, and prerelease centers, where at least some inmates come and go.

- Of 1.6 million state and federal inmates in 2011, 130,941 were held in private prison facilities (38,546 in private federal facilities and 92,395 in private state facilities).

- Six states held over 25% of their prisoners in private facilities, including New Mexico (41%), Montana (39%), Alaska (31%), Idaho (30%), Hawaii (29%), and Vermont (25%). Nineteen states held no prisoners in private facilities.

- In 2009, U.S. Immigration and Customs Enforcement had an average adult daily population of about 32,606, and about half of these detainees were housed in privately run detention facilities.[2]

- Most of the more than 400 private facilities are minimum or medium security and hold an average daily population of fewer than 500 inmates.[3]

- Some populations, such as women, the mentally ill, and serious offenders, are less likely to be held in private facilities because they are more expensive to house, making it difficult for prison companies to make profits. Almost one third (31%) of juveniles are held in private facilities.[4]

Major Private Prison Companies

Today, two private companies—Corrections Corporation of America (CCA) and the GEO Group—hold the majority of private prison contracts in the country. CCA operates over 60 facilities in 19 states and the District of Columbia and manages more than 50% of the nation's private prison beds. The GEO Group (formerly known as Wackenhut Corrections Corporation and recently merged with Cornell Companies) runs about 60 facilities in

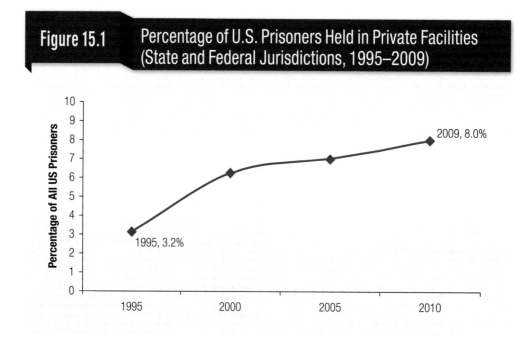

| Figure 15.1 | Percentage of U.S. Prisoners Held in Private Facilities (State and Federal Jurisdictions, 1995–2009) |

The percentage of U.S. prisoners held in private facilities rose from just over 3% in 1995 to 8.0% in 2011.[5]

Sources: Justice Policy Institute (1995); West and Sabol (2010).

▲ These companies all have profit motive in common.

© Tripplaar Kristoffer/SIPA/ Newscom; © iStockphoto.com/ Lya_Cattel; © iStockphoto.com/ Xyno; © iStockphoto.com/ JillKyle; © iStockphoto.com/ Niloo138

17 states. These are publicly traded companies accountable as much to their boards of directors and stakeholders as to the needs of the prison inmates, the prison staff, and the general public. In 2010, the combined revenue of CCA and GEO was more than $2.9 billion. Other large private prison companies include Management & Training Corporation, Emerald Correctional Management, LCS Corrections Services, and CiviGenics/ Community Education Centers, Inc.[6]

How Private Prisons Function

Federal, state, and local governments that seek to privatize correctional services enter into a contractual relationship with a private prison company—"a public–private partnership." Governments seek private prison contracts primarily because of the ability of private prison companies to build or acquire facility space more quickly than government agencies, easing overcrowding and to create a short-term, time- and cost-saving solution compared to the government building its own facilities.

The arrangement can take many forms. Some private facilities hold inmates from a single jurisdiction, while others hold inmates from other states and the federal government. Inmates may be held in a facility owned and operated by the company or in a facility owned by the government and operated by the company. In 2012, the CCA owned 49 facilities and managed another 20 publicly owned facilities.[7]

The company may manage the entire facility, providing for all of the needs of the inmates, or the government may still manage some aspects of the prison, such as medical services or programming. The company may only run certain elements of correctional services such as inmate health care or probation supervision. Those arrangements are largely outside the scope of this chapter.

The government typically announces a request for proposals (RFP), which describes the project it wishes to pursue and all of the issues a prison company will have to address for its proposal to be considered. Once a proposal is accepted, contract negotiations begin. The contract usually stipulates that the government will pay the prison company a daily dollar amount, as low as $30 and up to $80 (or higher) for each inmate. These amounts can vary according to the security level of the inmates; the size and type of facility; and the local costs of services and programming, such as food service, mental and physical health care, recreation, education, vocational training, and the relative contracting and negotiating experience of state representatives.

The development, implementation, and monitoring of private prison agreements is a complicated and fairly unwieldy process—a fact that contributes to the difficulty of regulating and monitoring these contracts. In a facility operated in one jurisdiction but holding inmates from several others, the laws and regulations of several federal, state, and local jurisdictions may be in play. For example, Arizona has three sets of corrections regulations and policies, one for Arizona state prisons, one for private facilities in any state contracted to hold Arizona inmates, and another for private prisons in Arizona not contracted to hold Arizona inmates. The third of these is the least restrictive and specific.

Numerous organizations and individuals are involved. At the state or the local level, a chief executive (governor or mayor) or members of the state legislature, county commission, or city council usually lead the process. State or local justice system officials such as attorneys general, judges, heads of corrections agencies, or law enforcement officers are not typically spearheading the move toward privatization—they may not even support the move—but they and various public employees will play some role in the process. Financiers, attorneys, construction companies, engineers, public utilities, and others will also be involved, especially when a new facility is being constructed.

Prison company executives and staff play a major role as well, not only in representing the prison companies' interests but also in assisting governments in the complicated processes of contracting and implementation. Prison companies often offer to handle much of the paperwork and hoop jumping on behalf of government entities; they are likely to have more experience with the process, and they have a clear interest in the process moving as quickly and smoothly as possible. They also take part in securing project buy-in from other government representatives and community stakeholders.

Administration and oversight of ongoing private prison contracts also involves a variety of public employees. In the federal arena, responsibilities are spread across several wings of the Federal Bureau of Prisons (BOP).[8] In the state context, the task is likely spread across more disparate departments. For example, in Arizona, the Private Prisons subprogram of the state Department of Corrections' Prison Operations Program develops and manages private prison contracts; the Engineering and Facilities Bureau oversees construction and compliance monitoring; the Contract Beds Bureau monitors, evaluates, and supports private prisons; and the Business Administration tracks expenditures.[9]

Other Forms of Corrections Privatization

The privatization of various correctional elements, apart from whole facilities, also continues to grow. In these cases, a government agency will contract with a provider to supply a service such as health care or programming for inmates. The reasons for pursuing these contractual relationships are typically cost savings and improvements in the quality and effective delivery of service through the specialization that private groups can develop.

Privatization of Health Care

A 2005 survey of state corrections departments found that 32 states contracted with private companies for some or all of their prison health care services.[10] Opponents of privatized health care cite concerns that this profit-driven approach may result in insufficient staffing levels; a lack of appropriate treatment for prisoners, such as delays in sending inmates to the emergency room; and oversight issues.[11]

Privatization of Probation

Despite declines in the overall U.S. community corrections population in recent years, many states still have increases, and with state and local budget issues many jurisdictions continue to explore privatization for probation as well as parole. One reason for this shift is growing caseloads for probation officers and limited budgets to address this growth. Recently, for-profit companies have been taking on comprehensive probation functions on behalf of government agencies. With what is called "private probation," private companies fill the role of the probation agency—monitoring clients for meeting the terms of their probation, referring them to services, drug testing, investigating, and imposing sanctions as necessary. Probation violations are reported to the regular probation department or courts, but in some states private probation companies have the authority to toughen terms, raise fees, and file arrest warrants. Not all states use private probation, and not all private probation providers are for-profit. But most *are* for-profit, and questionable practices by these companies—practices often facilitated by state and local governments—have led many to question whether they are successfully and legally serving their intended purpose.

The first state to legalize private probation was Florida in 1975. Federal data do not yet disaggregate private versus public probation, but it is estimated that hundreds of thousands of probationers are now supervised by private, for-profit companies. A 2007 report found that about 10 states contracted with private agencies to provide supervision

Private prisons tend to be far from the homes of prisoners, making in-person visits difficult for family members.

© Marmaduke St. John / Alamy

of an estimated 300,000 clients on court-ordered probation, typically for misdemeanor, low-risk offenses.[12] A 2014 report found jurisdictions in at least 12 states (especially in the Southeast, but also in the Midwest and West) had turned over supervision of some or all of their low-level probationers to private probation firms. It is not clear if these trends will continue, but it is apparent that prison companies recognize supervision services as a growth area.[13] The three largest companies are Judicial Correction Services, Sentinel Offender Services, and Providence Service Corporation. Sentinel Offender Services manages probation supervision only in Georgia, but it has contracts in 48 states for various specialized services, especially administering electronic monitoring for probationers and parolees.[14]

Private probation companies most often serve low-risk clients, while the traditional government-run probation agencies are responsible for more serious offenders. Jurisdictions may have contracts with and pay private probation firms, but most often private probation firms earn their money from fees paid to them by the probationer. In this way, they offer the government a cost-free way to monitor probationers and collect fines. These fees can include a monthly fee of perhaps $30 to $45 and additional service-related fees, such as for drug testing or GPS monitoring. Fees can easily double or triple the cost of the original fine. Nonpayment of fines and fees can lead to additional monetary penalties, additional fines from the court, or restrictions on a driver's license. These sanctions make it hard for a probationer to earn the money to pay fines and fess and avoid revocation.

In many cases, the individual sentenced to probation can pay a fine and avoid probation altogether. An indigent person on probation stands to remain so for months or years as his or her ability to pay the multiplying fees decreases, and as his or her likelihood of incarceration increases. Being unable to attend work, school, treatment services, doctor's appointments, and other commitments makes paying fees even more difficult and increases the likelihood that the probationer will break other terms of probation and end up behind bars.

Georgia uses private probation perhaps more than any other state. There, the effort by county courts to collect unpaid fines was a primary motivator for legalizing private probation for misdemeanors in 2000. For county governments, the potential costs of pursuing payment were often higher than the value of the fines. So, those guilty of public drunkenness, DUI, and traffic violations who are unable to pay fines find themselves on a sort of installment plan, where they have to pay not only the original fine but monthly fees as well. These companies are not required to report on their own finances, but it is estimated that, in 2012, about 40 private probation firms collected almost $100 million in fines, restitution, and court costs, as well as $40 million in additional charges on behalf of Georgia's county courts.[15]

Supporters of private probation hope it expands to include felony offenders. However, critics point out the enormous extra burden, financial and otherwise, that private probation clients endure. They argue that the emphasis by private corrections companies on heavy-handed fee collection rather than supervision, service referral, and general assistance increases the likelihood that probationers will end up behind bars, thereby increasing rather than reducing state correctional costs. There is also concern that states do not adequately regulate and monitor these companies, leading to scores of documented instances of abuse.[16] In lawsuits in Georgia, Alabama, and other states, courts have found that some private probation companies illegally increase fees, extend probation, and land their clients behind bars for nothing more than inability to pay. For instance, in Colorado, large caseloads prompted the use of private probation in 1996 for low-risk offenders, such as those convicted of DUI. There is an apparent conflict of interest when the same private, for-profit probation firms responsible for monitoring DUI individuals, including referring them to services and reporting them to the state when they fail drug tests, also provide substance abuse treatment for additional fees to those same individuals.[17]

Many jurisdictions across the nation have increased the use of both fines and fees to help cover justice system costs, whether those fees are collected directly by the government or by private firms. It is important to note that, while fines are instituted as a means of serving the purposes of corrections, including punishment and deterrence, correctional fees are put in place for a different, essentially administrative, purpose. Fees are a way to defray the costs of the judicial system incurred by the state or, in the case of private probation companies, a way to reap profits. Several states continue the practice of incarcerating those who cannot afford to pay fines and fees despite it being ruled unconstitutional by the U.S. Supreme Court in 1983.[18] Some county and local jurisdictions have been found to abuse their authority to levee fees and to sanction those unable to pay. It is, therefore, not only for-profit companies that face a conflict of interest when revenues are linked to correctional practice.[19]

Furthermore, standards are lacking in many aspects of the industry, which can allow probation officers' compensation to be directly connected to the fees they collect.[20] Recommendations for improving the selection, performance, and accountability of private probation officers include developing more rigorous statewide requirements for the private supervision of probationers, increasing training and educational standards for private agency staff, more stringent agency reporting obligations, and evaluating whether private probation providers have achieved stated performance goals.[21]

Private Prison Performance

Meeting Basic Standards of Humane Treatment

Observers question whether private prisons provide better care and services than public prisons and whether they consistently meet basic standards. Individual studies have found that, compared to publicly managed prisons, private prisons have a higher proportion of inmate-on-inmate assaults; greater likelihood of inmate misconduct, greater likelihood of drug abuse, and higher rate of escapes; lower or unmet standards of care; and "systemic problems in maintaining secure facilities."[22] A review of several previous studies showed that the quality of confinement in public and private prison facilities is often comparable, but with public facilities providing slightly better skills training for inmates and reporting slightly fewer inmate grievances.[23] One of the strongest studies to date on the basic question of reoffending found no difference between the recidivism rates of former inmates of public prisons and of private prisons.[24]

Media accounts have documented numerous incidents of abuse, neglect, violence, escapes, poor conditions, and other alarming events in private facilities.[25] Whether private prisons have more or fewer scandals than their public counterparts is difficult to assess from media reports. However, private prisons do not provide a consistently improved experience for inmates or staff compared to public facilities, and in many cases, the experience can be worse. Immigration detention centers, where different laws and standards often apply, are of particular concern.

Cost Savings to Governments

The cost-effectiveness of private prisons is widely debated, and research on the topic has produced varied results. The verdict is, at best, a draw. Arizona is one of the few states with a law that requires the regular and intensive assessment of private prison performance. The state's study found that private prisons resulted in higher costs compared to public facilities.[26] Other studies have found that privatizing facilities has resulted in minimal or no savings.[27] Some studies, including those by groups affiliated with prison companies or their proponents, have found that privatization can yield modest savings.[28] These findings echo what studies of privatization in other industries have shown: The promise of savings touted by proponents of privatization is elusive.[29]

Research funded by prison companies tends to find that private prisons generate improvements in cost and other factors.[30] However, other researchers caution that costs of public and private prisons cannot be easily evaluated side by side, due to numerous factors such as security level and health conditions of inmates, physical characteristics of facilities, indirect costs, and the large number of parties typically involved in maintaining and paying for both types of prison.[31] Most contracts allow private facilities to house lower-risk and healthier (less costly) inmates than similar public facilities.

Additionally, there are many less obvious costs that arise with private prison practices, such as holding out-of-state prisoners. Two issues that are often overlooked when prisoners are held out of state are the costs of prisoners who commit crimes while incarcerated, and inmate visitation and its impact on recidivism. An inmate who commits a serious crime while incarcerated, or who escapes from prison and then commits a crime, will typically be tried and serve time in the state where he or she was incarcerated, rather than the state of the original conviction, which can result in the host state assuming a significant, long-term financial burden.

Although empirical studies on this subject are rare, the information available does show a positive relationship between inmates who receive visitors while incarcerated and reduced recidivism.[32] Due to the time and costs associated with traveling to visit a friend or family member confined in another state (which are exacerbated by the fact that many prisons are located in rural areas far from airports and with limited public transportation), inmates sent to out-of-state facilities will generally not have many visitors and, upon release, will not have benefited from this rehabilitative influence.

Detainees who are not yet sentenced but are held in distant, privately run jails often must travel to appear in court, which is another issue that impacts safety and costs.[33]

Payment Structures

Many contracts between states and private companies are based on "guaranteed payments." Though the daily population of a prison will vary, such contracts guarantee a minimum occupancy rate, usually 90% or more, and allow private prison operators to overstate costs and maximize revenue. Fees may escalate when the rate is exceeded.[34] There are several kinds of payment structures that may be incorporated into a contract besides the per-bed approach, including a fixed-price, "indefinite delivery/indefinite quantity" approach, which allows contractors to provide prison beds on an as-needed basis.[35]

Performance-based contracting options are relatively new in the public sector and have been encouraged through guidelines such as the Federal Acquisition Regulation. Performance-based contracting allows governments to identify specific outcomes—such as data reporting or successful prisoner rehabilitation—that private prison contractors should achieve, and to link compensation to meeting these goals.[36] One such approach gaining popularity involves guarantees on the part of the contractor that the government will achieve set levels of cost savings, such as a 7% improvement over the costs in public facilities. This particular approach may have its benefits, but it also risks placing still greater emphasis on cost savings. Other performance-based approaches would link payment or incentives to meeting standards for conditions of confinement, successful completion of programming and services on the part of inmates, or a reduction in reoffending after release.

Impact of Privatization on Local Economies

For a number of years, state, county, and municipal jurisdictions have pursued private prison opportunities as a means to generate economic growth and job creation in their communities. Prison companies foreseeing increased need for bed space, but hoping to

Private prisons may offer newer infrastructure than what is found in aging public facilities but their operations are largely out of the public view.

© iStockphoto.com/ Powerofforever; © iStockphoto.com/ PaulFleet

avoid owning expensive facilities, look for local governments who will agree to fund new facility construction through bond sales. These partnerships can appeal to smaller jurisdictions, especially when their traditional local industries have fallen off. Private prison companies often campaign to persuade key leaders and policymakers to help them sell the idea to other government representatives and the public. Much of the early discussion on investment in private prisons takes place behind closed doors, away from opposing viewpoints and the public.[37]

Recent studies have found that growth and expansion of prisons in general (both public and private) have had limited positive impact on economic development at the local level.[38] In fact, communities in which private prisons are located can experience unfavorable economic effects, especially in already depressed economies. A common dynamic is that a small town or county commits most of its limited resources and infrastructure—labor force,

Rural communities can become too dependent on jobs and commercial services associated with rural prisons; when the prison is underutilized or shutdown, local economies suffer.

© Aerial Archives / Alamy

emergency response services, trade services (electricians, plumbers, sanitation)—to supporting the prison, leaving the community dependent on the success of the prison and unable to support other businesses that might want to locate there. Further, local governments that sell bonds to fund construction can find themselves on the hook if the prison company fails to secure sufficient contracts to fill beds. Moreover, the bond rating for the locality is likely to be lowered if it does have trouble repaying the debt, leaving the local economy in worse shape.[39] When the lease is up or abandoned, the aging plant is owned by the government.

Texas, which experienced an immense prison-building boom in the 1990s (much of it related to increases in immigration-related detention), has several examples of public–private partnerships that led to challenges for local jurisdictions. In July 2011, a West Texas 373-bed prison was auctioned off due to a lack of prisoners, a 424-bed facility in Fort Worth (managed by the GEO) has been empty since February 2011, and a new 1,100-bed facility located near Abilene has never housed inmates.[40]

Montana has dealt with similar economic woes tied to private prison construction. Corplan Corrections worked with local officials to build a 464-bed facility in the small town of Hardin. Although the facility was completed in 2007, as of 2014, it held no inmates, due to a lack of in-state or out-of-state prisoners suitable for the minimum-security jail; in fact, Montana prohibits the incarceration of offenders convicted outside Montana. This project has left Hardin to cope with millions of dollars of debt.[41]

Perhaps more importantly from an ethical perspective, jurisdictions that invest in speculative private prison projects can come to the same conflict of interest as prison companies when they find themselves in the contradictory situation of supporting increased incarceration to pay off bonds or bolster their local economy, even if crime and arrests drop and effective and safe alternatives to incarceration are available.

Privatization, Innovation, and Reform

Early proponents of privatization argued that the competition inherent in the private market would spawn innovative processes and practices that would lower costs while improving conditions. It was also thought that public prison officials would themselves pursue innovations, or at least pick up on the techniques of their for-profit counterparts and thereby improve the public system.

Dominated as it is by the CCA and the GEO Group, competition in the privatized corrections market really does not exist. The relative lack of competition in the private prison industry makes it difficult for governments to assemble a pool of qualified candidates and contributes to the likelihood of inadequate performance once a contract is executed. If a particular industry only has a few providers, the government's ability to realize cost savings is considerably lessened, and it is difficult to effectively replace one provider with another, if necessary.[42]

Early on, the rise of private prisons also promised to encourage public prison officials to make improvements in cost efficiencies and to be more open to other reforms.[43] However, it is more likely that the opposite has occurred. When states relieve overcrowding in public facilities through private contracting, state officials, prosecutors, judges, and corrections agencies lose the impetus to seek innovative ways of reducing the reliance on incarceration and to save taxpayer money without threatening public safety. Thus, the prison population continues to grow, as do corrections budgets, at least until the newly contracted beds are themselves full.[44] The speed and flexibility with which private prison companies can acquire bed space provides, in essence, a permanent pressure release valve that squashes what might otherwise be an opportunity for long-term reform.

Importantly (and ironically), the very reforms that are overlooked can serve the same purpose as private prisons, including the quick easing of crowding, cost-savings, and

▲ Students are escorted through the corridors of the Shelby Training Center, a private juvenile detention facility in Memphis owned by Corrections Corporation of America. While walking through the halls, students are required to keep their hands clasped behind their backs. The CCA credits strict discipline for a reduced recidivism rate.

SPOTLIGHT

IN THEIR OWN WORDS: THE CORPORATION PERSPECTIVE

Excerpts from the Corrections Corporation of America (CCA) 2010 "Annual Report" and 2010 "Letter to Shareholders."

2010 "ANNUAL REPORT"

Our growth is generally dependent upon our ability to obtain new contracts to develop and manage new correctional and detention facilities. This possible growth depends on a number of factors we cannot control, including crime rates and sentencing patterns in various jurisdictions and acceptance of privatization. The demand for our facilities and services could be adversely affected by the relaxation of enforcement efforts, leniency in conviction or parole standards and sentencing practices or through the decriminalization of certain activities that are currently proscribed by our criminal laws. For instance, any changes with respect to drugs and controlled substances or illegal immigration could affect the number of persons arrested, convicted, and sentenced, thereby potentially reducing demand for correctional facilities to house them.[1]

Legislation has been proposed in numerous jurisdictions that could lower minimum sentences for some non-violent crimes and make more inmates eligible for early release based on good behavior. Also, sentencing alternatives under consideration could put some offenders on probation with electronic monitoring who would otherwise be incarcerated. Similarly, reductions in crime rates or resources dedicated to prevent and enforce crime could lead to reductions in arrests, convictions and sentences requiring incarceration at correctional facilities.[2]

We are compensated for operating and managing prisons and correctional facilities at an inmate per diem rate based upon actual or minimum guaranteed occupancy levels. The significant expansion of the prison population in the United States has led to overcrowding in the federal and state prison systems, providing us with opportunities for growth. Federal, state, and local governments are constantly under budgetary constraints putting pressure on governments to control correctional budgets, including per diem rates our customers pay to us. These pressures have been compounded by the recent economic downturn. Economic conditions remain very challenging, putting continued pressure on state budgets. . . . We believe we have been successful in working with our government partners to help them manage their correctional costs while minimizing the financial impact to us, and will continue to provide unique solutions to their correctional

improved outcomes. These include alternatives to detention for those awaiting trial or immigration procedures, and alternatives to incarceration such as community corrections, electronic monitoring, day and evening reporting centers, home custody, restorative justice, and intensive supervision. All of these can be used to reduce the demand for new bed space quickly, permanently, and without jeopardizing public safety.[45] These strategies are gaining a foothold in some places. In 2010, legislatures in at least 23 states and the District of Columbia passed laws that have the potential to reduce the prison population while protecting public safety. In fact, some observers suggest that the fortunes of the private prison companies already may be starting to shift because of these reforms and a continuing drop in crime.[46]

Parallel Inadequate Systems

Another key issue in having two parallel approaches to corrections—the public and the private—is that the focus becomes a comparison of the two systems, creating a very narrow perspective from which to assess what works, what doesn't work, and how the overall system can be improved. Certainly, as some state laws specify, private prisons should be

needs. We believe the long-term growth opportunities of our business remain very attractive as insufficient bed development by our partners should result in a return to the supply and demand imbalance that has been benefiting the private prison industry.[3]

2012 "LETTER TO SHAREHOLDERS"

CCA is the largest owner and operator of partnership correctional and detention facilities in the US, with only three states and the Federal Bureau of Prisons operating larger correctional systems. At yearend 2012, we had over 14 million square feet of correctional and detention facilities within 51 owned or controlled facilities. Our owned facilities accounted for about 90% of our $3.6 billion in fixed assets and generated about 90% of our net operating income.[4]

We . . . received a favorable Private Letter Ruling in early 2013 from the IRS, upon which the Board of Directors unanimously approved CCA to elect REIT [Real Estate Investment Trust] status in 2013. Due to our advance planning, we expect to elect REIT status effective January 1, 2013. Since a REIT generally pays no income tax as long as its taxable earnings are distributed to shareholders as dividends, we have a significant tax advantage compared with a traditional "C" Corporation.

We expect the reduction in taxes to contribute to our double digit growth in net income and to enable us to increase the regular quarterly dividend to our investors by 165% in 2013.[5]

QUESTIONS

1 In what ways does the profit motive create potential conflicts of interest for private prison companies?

2 All companies seek to find or create favorable circumstances that increase their potential profits. Are private prison companies justified in finding politicians and laws that will increase the number of people in prison, to increase company profits?

3 Discuss your vision of what a board meeting at this corporation would sound like.

4 Would you invest in a private corrections company? Why or why not?

Notes

1. CCA 2011, 19
2. CCA 2011, 19–20
3. CCA 2011, 34
4. CCA 2013, 3 (para. 3)
5. CCA 2013, 3 (para. 2)

held to at least public prison levels of health and safety, conditions of confinement, service delivery, cost, transparency and accountability, and other factors. However, with this being the limit of expectations, we are simply left with two systems in need of reform. In a sense, the two systems begin to "play down" to each other's level of competence rather than both vying for a truly appropriate and effective response to crime and solutions to the problems that plague both approaches.[47]

The Profit Motive and Conflict of Interest

As previously stated, for-profit corrections companies are beholden to their boards of directors and stockholders. Entrusting prisoner care to companies with such interests is a cause for many concerns.[48] The profit motive may encourage prison companies to use their significant resources to influence corrections laws and policies in ways that increase their profits through more prisoners being held for more types of crimes and for longer sentences, rather than to improve public safety and the outcomes for inmates.

YOU DECIDE

Private Prison Liability for Health Care

While at a private prison, V. R.'s shoulder was injured during a work assignment. He asked to see a doctor, but was escorted back to his cell and told to wait. He didn't see a doctor until two days later, by which time his shoulder was much worse. He needed surgery and physical therapy to regain mobility in his dominant arm. V. R. eventually demanded compensation for the injury and that the state should cover further health care. The private prison had a history of violations of worker safety rules. State officials denied that they knew anything about the inmate's problems and that the private prison company signed a contract to provide all necessary health care services.

V. R. wants to apply federal civil rights laws against state officials, but the state argues that the prisoner has not exhausted all possible remedies and suggests that he attempt to sue the private prison staff in state courts. V. R.'s lawyer points out that inmates are almost never successful in these cases and says it is just a tactic by the state to prolong an expensive process in hopes the inmate will run out of resources and give up.

YOU DECIDE: **What legal safeguards should exist for inmates of private prisons? Should the state be liable for the actions of private prison companies with whom the state contracts?**

Staffing and Services

A critical part of the debate regarding cost savings focuses on staffing and personnel. Because private prisons are generally expected to serve the same function as public prisons but also save public money, prison companies need to make their profit in the small window between their own costs and the costs of public prisons *minus* some percentage of savings to taxpayers. (Some contracts stipulate that this savings will be at least a certain percentage, such as 7%.) The most expensive part of running a prison is staffing; therefore any savings associated with privatization are primarily due to reduced personnel costs.[49] Private prisons tend to employ frontline staff who are non-unionized and low paid, receive few fringe benefits, and lack sufficient experience and training. These circumstances contribute to the high rate of staff turnover and security issues and a lack of mentoring for new employees.[50] Public prison guard unions and private prison companies may have some shared political and policy goals (they both spend millions on lobbying for new prisons and tougher sentencing laws). However, the unions are typically opposed to privatization, as it represents a loss of staff positions, a loss of political influence, and (they argue) increased risk for prisoners due to the loss of experience and quality on-the-job training among the guard staff. Similarly, cost cutting with regard to services, programming, and facility conditions increases inmate–staff tension, grievances, and behavioral issues. This suggests that any cost savings achieved by privatization are at the expense of inmate, guard, and public safety.

When a public facility is replaced by a private prison, public facility staff are often unwilling to work for the private operator for a variety of reasons, including substantially lower pay, poor benefits, and safety concerns. This leads to a loss of seasoned, trained employees who can mentor new staff and establish a culture of professionalism and appropriate treatment of prisoners. Conversely, staff who had worked at a private prison may be ineligible for employment at publicly operated facilities based on factors such as the lack of training and experience mandated by state standards, or failed background checks.

Influence on Length of Stay

Another conflict of interest is the influence prison staff can have on inmates' length of stay. Corrections officers and administrators have discretion in what inmate behavior results in disciplinary action and in the awarding of good-time credits, both of which can impact eventual release dates. Also, parole boards routinely ask for the opinion of prison officials. Individual prison staff are unlikely to have a direct personal financial incentive for pursuing disciplinary action, whereas the private prison company and its shareholders directly benefit from longer prison stays. Several states have enacted laws and policies that address this risk.[51]

The Policy End Run

Privatization raises the risk that policies and practices may be steered by costs alone and put into place without an adequate process of debate and approval. For instance, private prison companies argue that contracts need to give them flexibility to respond to unforeseen challenges or to develop creative practices.[52] In reality, this open-endedness may allow them to implement practices that go against the intentions of the contract or the best interest of the inmates or the public.

Political Influence

Since the modern emergence of private prisons in the mid-1980s, an intricately connected web of political influence has developed alongside the growth of the private prison industry. Because private prisons rely on a steady stream of inmates to fill beds, it is perhaps not surprising that the private prison industry has been pivotal in helping to shape and promote criminal justice policies that favor incarceration as well as putting and keeping proprivatization lawmakers in office.[53]

Prison industry lobbyists also seek to influence sentencing policies as well as the rules and regulations included in government contracts. In 2010, the CCA, the GEO, and Cornell together spent more than $1.5 million on federal lobbying.[54]

Influence on Policy and Law

Private prison companies have been influential in the development and passage of state legislation that increases incarceration, including "three strikes" and "truth in sentencing" laws in the mid-1990s. More recently, and as immigration detention has grown as a

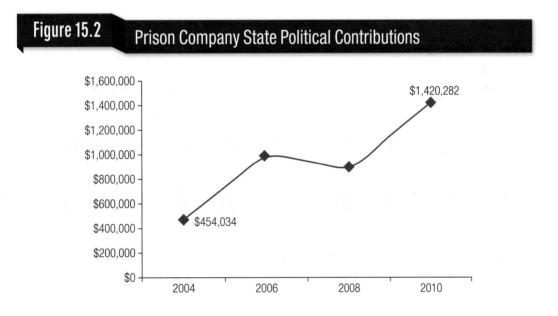

Figure 15.2   Prison Company State Political Contributions

By making financial contributions to individual political campaigns, state political parties, and specific ballot measures, private prison companies exert influence over policymaking that helps ensure the demand for their services and helps to develop and maintain relationships that can aid in obtaining prison contracts. Between 2000 and 2010, the CCA, GEO, and Cornell Companies donated over $800,000 to candidates for federal office and more than $6 million to candidates for statewide office. Additionally, in 2010, these three companies donated more than $1 million to state party committees.[55] The *New York Times* recently quoted a former chief prison inspector—who happens to favor privatization—in Australia as saying, "We have lost control. . . . These big global companies, in relation to specific activities, are more powerful than the governments they're dealing with."[56] *Source: National Institute on Money in State Politics n.d.*

SPOTLIGHT

IMMIGRATION DETENTION POLICY FEEDS PRIVATE PRISON GROWTH

Private prison companies have pursued the area of immigration both in the United States and internationally, with huge monetary success. Accompanying that success are numerous documented cases of abuse and neglect and poor conditions of confinement for detainees, exacerbated by long stays awaiting immigration proceedings.[1] On any given day in 2009, U.S. Immigration and Customs Enforcement (ICE) held an average of 32,606 adults in a total of 178 facilities. Just under half of these detainees were housed in 30 private facilities.[2] Although ICE has developed standards for immigration detention facilities, the standards may not adequately address the conditions and treatment experienced by many immigrant detainees, and in any case, these standards are not followed in all facilities.[3]

One example of immigration detention neglect is the case of Hiu Lui "Jason" Ng, who died in 2008 while being detained in the privately run Wyatt Detention Facility in Central Falls, Rhode Island. Ng suffered from liver cancer that was not diagnosed until just days before his death. A lawsuit filed by the American Civil Liberties Union of Rhode Island, which names officials and employees of both the Wyatt facility and ICE, noted that prison officials not only consistently claimed that Ng was faking his illness but also prevented him from receiving adequate medical care.[4]

QUESTIONS

1   What safeguards should there be to protect detainees in private facilities?

2   How should private facilities be held to those standards?

Notes

1.   American Civil Liberties Union 2010
2.   Detention Watch Network 2011
3.   American Civil Liberties Union 2010
4.   Bernstein 2008

"market" for private prison corporations, the industry has been instrumental in the drafting and enacting of influential state immigration legislation. A key example of this influence is Arizona's SB 1070, which drastically increased law enforcement's options to detain any individual who is perceived to be an undocumented immigrant. This legislation was developed under the auspices of the nonprofit American Legislative Exchange Council (ALEC), whose membership includes lawmakers and powerful corporations such as (until recently) the CCA. An investigation found that the majority of the 36 cosponsors of SB 1070 subsequently received contributions from prison lobbyists or from CCA, the GEO Group, and Management & Training Corporation.[57]

Private prison corporations also mobilize against legislation that would have a negative impact on the industry. This includes the federal Private Prison Information Act, which has been introduced by lawmakers several times in the past decade, including during the 2011–2012 legislative sessions. Reports indicate that the CCA has spent millions of dollars to lobby against this legislation, which would require private facilities that house federal inmates to abide by the same Freedom of Information Act guidelines that apply to public federal prisons.[58]

Friends in High Places

There are many examples of close connections between the major prison companies and current or former government officials. A prison company strategy is to add a corrections

▲ Public officials are accountable to citizens for their roles in negotiating contracts and overseeing operations of private correctional facilities.

http://en.wikipedia.org/wiki/ File:Fullerton_City_Council.jpg; Calwatch

official—in a consultant role—to a prison company's board of directors. Often, the private firm hires the consultant later at a generous salary. A recent case in point is the CCA's 2011 hiring of Harley Lappin, the past director of the BOP, to serve as an executive vice president and chief corrections officer for the company.[59]

The profit incentive has also been known to spawn serious corruption. For instance, in Luzerne, Pennsylvania, agents of a private prison company paid bribes to local judges to encourage them to commit youth to their two local facilities. In Willacy County, Texas, two county commissioners accepted bribes in exchange for favoring certain companies involved in building a new private facility.[60]

Contracting, Oversight, and Monitoring

As described earlier, public–private partnerships hinge on contracts. A contract provides a jurisdiction with a mechanism to clearly identify the contractor's responsibilities and requirements; to prescribe how this work will be accomplished, compensated, and monitored; and to describe penalties that will be incurred if performance is substandard. Contracts need to reflect a jurisdiction's policy and values and need to foresee and forestall as many issues as possible. A comprehensive, sound contracting procedure is a central and crucial feature of an effective prison privatization effort. Lessons can be learned from all types of governmental privatization, not just those in corrections.[61] The experience of various jurisdictions has demonstrated that contracts executed with private prison companies are often poorly drafted and may minimize or omit key provisions, which can lead to numerous problems including inadequate contractor performance, absence of transparency, abuse of prisoner rights, and an overall lack of accountability.[62] Oversight and monitoring have also proved to be difficult and tend to be lax and ineffective.

Penalties for Noncompliance

Contracts can include provisions for levying financial penalties against the contractor if contract terms are breached. In practice, however, these often fail to discourage private prison companies from overstepping. Fines are often set low, such that it may be more cost-effective for a prison contractor to cut corners and pay a fine than to comply with the contract terms. Additionally, the process by which fines may be levied is often not clearly spelled out in contracts nor is it consistently applied and audited.[63]

Monitoring

Another critical feature of a private prison operation is designing, implementing, and maintaining a strong monitoring system. Oversight and monitoring provides a way for the government to measure contract compliance and its success in securing the safety of the public, inmates, and staff. Monitoring can and should address all parts of a contract. Monitoring also provides a basis for contract renewals or terminations and for charging

▲ Governor Arnold Schwarzenegger tours an overcrowded California Rehabilitation Center in Norco. The facility was designed for 2,300 inmates; double bunking helped boost the population to 4,500.

fees and other penalties.[64] It is important to note that monitoring of conditions inside any prison, public or private, is difficult, partly because of the necessarily closed and isolated setting of secure facilities. Privatization, however, adds another level of resistance to transparency and accountability.

Private prison monitors typically use several different methods to assess contract compliance, such as reviews of files, reports, logs, and other records (including spot-checking of records for accuracy); onsite observations; interviews with key stakeholders (managers, staff, and inmates); and statistical comparisons to an analogous publicly operated prison.[68] Monitoring is "a process requiring constant attention and vigilance. Effective oversight of a prison is thus necessarily a labor-intensive endeavor."[65]

Some monitoring plans fail to allow for what most would consider basic requirements, such as unannounced site visits.[66] The monitoring process should also take into account more intangible, unrecorded factors such as a prison's climate, guard-to-inmate communications, staff decision making, and so on, which are described as follows by Collins: "Experienced corrections officials know that a prison may comply chapter and verse with the specifics of a contract and still not be a safe and healthy facility."[67]

As part of the contract between a jurisdiction and a private prison company, the company is typically required to obtain and maintain accreditation from the American Correctional Association (ACA). An important distinction between ACA accreditation and outcome monitoring is that the former focuses on processes and procedures, rather than on outcomes. Experts caution against relying too heavily on ACA accreditation to measure institutional effectiveness and recommend a close linkage between what is called "paper based" accreditation (through ACA or other bodies such as the National Commission on Correctional Health Care) and regular, on-site monitoring of contract compliance, service quality, and outcomes.[68]

Expertise of the Monitor

The monitor's training as well as his or her relationship to the facility is an important concern. The monitor may be a consultant or subcontractor and may be paid by the prison operator, creating a potential conflict of interest. In rural areas, the monitor may be an individual who lives in or is otherwise embedded in the community where the prison is situated, leading to possible tension or bias in pointing out problems that could affect many residents' livelihoods.[69] Also, monitors should have considerable expertise in the area(s) they are monitoring. In the case of prison health care services, monitors should be medical providers who work for the state or county and who can knowledgeably evaluate the quality of services that inmates receive.[70]

Are Private Prisons Necessary?

Privatization is clearly a significant aspect of today's correctional system. As with public corrections, much can be done to improve the current process for planning, implementing, and maintaining private facilities and the various privately run correctional services. Private prison companies and their proponents have the resources and political clout necessary to negotiate highly favorable contracts, influence public perceptions of privatization and corrections policy generally, and otherwise perpetuate current growth trends. It is important that alternative perspectives be allowed to counter these powerful, profit-centered efforts. Beginning with the reduction of demand for private prisons through reduced dependence on incarceration as a response to crime, recommendations range from major changes in corrections policy to local education and organizing activities.

SPOTLIGHT

A PRISON BREAK IN ARIZONA LEADS TO REFORMS TO THE CONTRACTING PROCESS

The 2010 experience of a private prison in Kingman, Arizona, operated by Management & Training Corporation (MTC), illustrates the need for various improvements and additions to standard contracts, including planning related to occupancy and compensation, as well as provisions concerning security and monitoring. After several inmates escaped from Kingman in 2010 and allegedly killed two people, the state transferred more than 200 high-risk inmates from the Kingman facility to another prison and determined that additional prisoners would not be sent to Kingman until MTC complied with identified problems, including retraining of corrections officers. This meant that MTC's guaranteed minimum occupancy rate of 97% was not met for nearly a year. In response to the state's action, MTC filed a "notice of claim" against the state,

seeking approximately $10 million in revenue that was lost when the state stopped supplying Kingman with inmates. This series of events led the state department of corrections to revamp its request for proposal process to include stipulations that private prisons will have to provide additional security regardless of the security level of inmates; state monitors will have continuous, unscheduled access to the facility, inmates, and records; and fines of $25,000 can be levied for certain violations.[1]

QUESTIONS

1 Describe and define public safety standards that private corrections companies should meet.

2 What would be a fair commitment on the part of the government to private companies regarding prisoner population?

Note

1. Ortega 2011a

Sentencing Reform and Regulation

New, tougher, and more specific laws and standards can improve how private prison companies are regulated, monitored, and operated. Some of these would limit power and influence; limit types and scopes of facilities; create standards regarding what laws apply, minimum levels and quality of care, and transparency of company policies and practices; and maximize accountability and responsiveness to issues that arise.

Reducing Demand

A key argument made by private prison proponents is the industry's ability to respond relatively quickly to bed space needs. However, as described earlier, relying on private prisons to ease crowding comes at the expense of reform in the public system.

Detention and sentencing reform is a critical strategy by which the government can reduce its reliance on incarceration and thereby reduce the demand for private prisons. Some states are already pursuing reforms—a continued emphasis on the reduced use of incarceration, increased use of alternatives, and reduced returns to prison after release. These are crucial to reducing the need for prison beds and the reliance on the private prison industry.[71]

Reform of Reentry Strategies

The private prison industry relies on ex-inmates reoffending and returning to prison, and on sentences stemming from probation violations. Offenders can avoid reincarceration if

IN THE COURTS

Minneci et al. v. Pollard et al.
Certiorari to the United States Court of Appeals for the Ninth Circuit

No. 10–1104. Argued November 1, 2011—Decided January 10, 2012

This case involved a federal prisoner being held in a private prison company—Wackenhut Corrections Corporation, which was under contract with the Federal Bureau of Prisons (BOP). Mr. Richard Lee Pollard had two broken elbows but was required by employees of Wackenhut to perform painful actions and was made to complete his prison job without receiving medical attention. He was later denied the splints that were ordered by the prison doctor. Mr. Pollard sued both the individuals and the corporation for federal civil rights and Eighth Amendment violations.

The U.S. Supreme Court denied the claim 8 to 1 (only Justice Ginsburg dissenting) on the grounds that state tort laws were a sufficient remedy for these issues. Pollard's lawyers argued that he was a federal prisoner being held by the BOP and would have been able to apply federal laws if he were in a government-run prison.

The *Minneci* case was decided on fairly narrow legal grounds, but the result shows the reluctance of the Supreme Court to get involved in the regulation of private prisons. This is important as more governments are outsourcing incarceration to private companies. Federal actions have been superior to state tort claims in protecting inmates from abuse.

there are more opportunities for skills training during incarceration, reentry plans, and removing obstacles to services and employment.[72]

Increasing Transparency and Accountability

Private prison contractors, unlike government agencies, are not typically required to report on the inmates housed in privately run prisons, do not make these data easily accessible to monitors, and may not even be aware of the documentation and reporting requirements intrinsic to the operation of public agencies.[73] There is a general lack of tracking, reporting, and accessibility of data on inmates and on private facility operations. Being for-profit corporations, the private prison companies argue that revealing detailed information may give an advantage to their competitors. From a profits perspective, it is in the contractor's best interest to minimize the reporting of data that could provide important information about conditions of confinement, such as the number of assaults that take place in the facility, incident reports, and grievances filed, and about exactly how public monies are being used.[74]

Laws that require full transparency and access to data, stronger contracts, and intensive oversight are keys to improving private prison performance and can help alleviate these concerns. Proposed federal legislation, such as the Private Prison Information Act, would help to shed light on the finances and activities of private prison companies.[75] Another opportunity is in the area of legislation and regulation regarding lobbying, conflicts of interest, and transparency in privatized activities. Also needed is full disclosure of affiliations of those involved in private prison projects, watchdog groups with resources and authority for strong oversight and quick action, and regulations that define the ethics and legality of relationships and conflicts of interest. Better access to private prisons' financial data to track the true costs of running a private prison is also important.

SPOTLIGHT

LEGAL AND GRASSROOTS EFFORTS TO COUNTER PRIVATE PRISONS

Despite the power of privatization proponents, regional, state, and local organizing efforts can provide an effective check on their influence. Advocates can build alliances or coalitions with stakeholder individuals and organizations that have similar goals and work to educate and inform both the officeholders and policymakers making privatization decisions (and signing contracts on behalf of the public with private prison companies) and the community members who will be impacted by these decisions.

Community Organizing. In 2011, Arizona, Florida, Louisiana, and Ohio considered privatizing prison facilities, either for the first time or as a continuing correctional approach. These proposals were met with resistance from community members. In Louisiana, members of the American Federation of State, County and Municipal Employees (AFSCME) protested a proposed plan by Governor Bobby Jindal to sell three state prison facilities to private prison operators. Jindal's proposal was also not supported by the state legislature and did not move forward.[1] In Ohio, a proposal by Governor John Kasich to sell five prisons, opposed by the AFSCME and the Ohio Civil Services Employee Association, was revised to selling one prison to the CCA and turning over operations of two other prisons to Management & Training Corporation.[2]

Legal Action. Some groups and individuals have pursued legal actions to block or influence prison privatization efforts. Recent legal actions have taken several forms, including the following:

- The Florida Police Benevolent Association, representing unionized corrections officers, filed a lawsuit claiming that the legislature violated state law by inserting a directive regarding privatization of corrections department operations in budget language rather than proposing and passing it as legislation.[3] This claim was upheld in state court, with the judge concluding that private prison

Further Research

Objective third-party research on corrections privatization is needed on some of the following areas:

- Rates of abuse, neglect, or victimization and conditions of confinement in private prisons
- The ways the profit incentive impacts facility safety and security and the humane treatment of inmates
- The influence of prison companies on legislation and regulation regarding sentencing, parole and probation, and immigration policy
- The true costs of private prison operation, including indirect costs and costs likely to be borne by public agencies, such as procurement, insurance, emergency services, and case management[76]
- Monitoring efforts and practices in private prisons
- Meaningful responses to contract noncompliance; and privatized correctional services such as medical and mental health care, probation and parole, and programming
- The relative bias of the various sources of information and research on private prisons, including that funded by prison companies

proponents had attempted an end run of the normal legislative process.[4]

- An ethics complaint was filed by the Teamsters union against Florida Governor Rick Scott, claiming his move to privatize prisons in part of the state is compromised due to the fact he received campaign-related contributions from the following CCA and the GEO Group.[5]

- Although they have not held up in court, for the most part, lawsuits have challenged the constitutionality of privatization of functions that are "inherently governmental"—that is, that leave the application of U.S. laws and statues to the discretion of a private contractor.[6]

- Individual lawsuits regarding abuse or neglect of inmates in private facilities can target private prison companies' revenue, although the companies expect and are prepared for a certain number of these suits. The costs of suing private prison companies can be returned to the state or local government in the form of higher contracting fees and overages; however, civil suits are an important means for individual restitution, spotlighting problems, and maintaining checks and balances on prison company practices.

QUESTIONS

1. Do these legal battles seem like fair fights?

2. Is the courtroom the most fitting arena for deciding private prison policy?

3. Are there any advocacy efforts opposing privatization of corrections functions in your state?

Notes

1. Moller 2011a, 2011b
2. Fields 2011
3. Kam 2011a
4. Kam 2011b
5. DeSlatte 2011
6. See Anderson 2009 for a compilation of applicable laws in each state.

SUMMARY

For the most part, the way private prison companies run their businesses—keeping costs down, pursuing favorable contracts, influencing laws, policies and public opinion that most support them, maximizing profits—are not out of line with other for-profit enterprises. What sets them apart is their responsibility for a hugely important and difficult undertaking: ensuring the humane treatment of prisoners, carrying out the rule of law, and preserving safety in the facilities. They serve a crucial government function, yet they approach the task from a strikingly different perspective than the governments and the public they serve.

The presence of private prisons makes true reform of the system less likely. Private corrections companies use financial and political influence to support laws and policies that have further entrenched the overuse of incarceration in this country. Government oversight of private prisons has been inadequate, but contracting can be used to counter the growth of this pervasive but arguably unnecessary part of the U.S. corrections system.

Although it is important not to oversimplify the many factors that contribute to crime and the corrections populations, even the strongest supporters of tough-on-crime policies would agree that the best-case scenario is fewer inmates in custody, as long as public safety is not diminished. The public supports efforts to reduce the use of incarceration when those efforts are shown to be practical and effective. This ultimately leaves only those with a financial interest in private prisons supporting filling more beds in secure facilities.

DISCUSSION QUESTIONS

1. What forms does privatization take in today's corrections system? What areas have been subject to for-profit privatization?

2. What are the primary reasons governments seek out privatization of corrections functions?

3. What are the economic advantages and risks when local jurisdictions invest in speculative private prisons?

4. What are ways private prison companies attempt to influence corrections laws, policies, and decision making? How might these raise ethical challenges?

5. What are the potential advantages and what are the risks when for-profit companies are involved in the policies and politics of public corrections?

6. How are already difficult aspects of public corrections, such as the training of staff, conditions of confinement, inmate discipline, transparency, and holding inmates in out-of-state facilities, exacerbated by privatization?

7. How might serving a term of confinement differ in a public versus a private facility?

8. What is the role of contracting in privatization of corrections, and how can it be used to improve government oversight and monitoring?

9. What avenues for improvement and reform exist in the public corrections system that can help governments avoid privatization?

10. How might the profit motive impact the execution of objective corrections research?

KEY TERMS

Privatization, 347

NOTES

1. This chapter is adapted from Hartney and Glesmann 2012
2. Detention Watch Network 2011
3. Stephan 2008
4. Sickmund et al. 2013
5. Carson and Sabol 2012
6. Ashton and Petteruti 2011
7. Corrections Corporation of America 2012a
8. McCain 2001
9. Davenport 2001
10. LaFaive 2005
11. Bedard and Frech 2007; Joe Goldenson, personal communication, May 5, 2011; Office of Program Policy Analysis and Government Accountability 2009
12. Schloss and Alarid 2007
13. Benzinga Staff 2010
14. Human Rights Watch 2014
15. Ibid.
16. Human Rights Watch 2014; Schloss and Alarid 2007
17. Asmar 2012
18. *Bearden v. Georgia* 1983
19. American Civil Liberties Union 2010
20. Southern Center for Human Rights 2008
21. Schloss and Alarid 2007
22. American Civil Liberties Union of Ohio 2011; Camp and Daggett 2005; Camp and Gaes 2001, 16; Davenport 2001; Hiaasen 2011; McDonald and Carlson 2005; Oppel 2011
23. Lundahl et al. 2009
24. Bales et al. 2005
25. Grassroots Leadership 2009; Private Corrections Working Group 2013
26. Arizona Department of Corrections 2011; State of Arizona, Office of the Auditor General 2010
27. Austin and Coventry 2001; Lundahl et al. 2009; Nelson (2005); Pratt and Maahs 1999
28. Blumstein, Cohen and Seth 2007; Segal and Moore 2002
29. In the Public Interest 2011
30. Corrections Corporation of America 2012b
31. Gaes 2008; Hall and Walsh 2010; U.S. Government Accountability Office 2007
32. Bales and Mears 2008; Holt and Miller 1972

33. Brown 2002

34. Collins 2000; Joint Legislative Committee on PEER 2001; Paul Leighton, personal communication, May 17, 2011; Office of Program Policy Analysis and Government Accountability (2000); Pranis n.d.

35. McDonald and Patten 2003

36. McDonald and Patten 2003; Segal and Moore 2002

37. Gail Tyree, personal communication, September 21, 2011; Frank Smith, personal communication, November 15, 2011

38. Besser and Hanson 2004; Glasmeier and Farrigan 2007; Hooks et al. 2004; Whitfield 2008

39. Chadwell 2009

40. Mitchell 2011; Pinkerton 2005

41. Dawson 2009; Ferguson 2014; Hodai 2010a

42. McDonald and Patten 2003; Mendelson 2009

43. Austin and Coventry 2001

44. Anderson 2009

45. American Civil Liberties Union of Georgia and Georgia Detention Watch 2011; Mendel 2011

46. Ashton and Petteruti 2011; Mitchell 2011; Porter 2011

47. Dolovich 2009; Robert Weiss, personal communication, May 12, 2011

48. Austin and Coventry 2001

49. Ibid.

50. American Civil Liberties Union of Ohio 2011; Sharon Dolovich, personal communication, May 17, 2011; Grassroots Leadership 2009; Frank Smith, personal communication, November 15, 2011; Robert Weiss, personal communication, May 12, 2011

51. Dolovich 2005

52. Segal and Moore 2002; Robert Weiss, personal communication, May 12, 2011

53. American Federation of State, County, and Municipal Employees 2011; Ashton and Petteruti 2011

54. Ashton and Petteruti 2011

55. Bernstein 2011

56. Ashton and Petteruti 2011

57. Archibold 2010; Ashton and Petteruti 2011; Hodai 2010b; Ortega 2011b; Sullivan 2010

58. Hodai 2010c

59. Ashton and Petteruti 2011; Paul Leighton, personal communication, May 17, 2011

60. Associated Press 2011; Pinkerton 2005

61. Collins 2000; Freeman and Minow 2009; Minnow 2005; Selman and Leighton 2010

62. Collins 2000; Sharon Dolovich, personal communication, May 17, 2011; Ortega 2011a

63. Jennings 2011; Paul Leighton, personal communication, May 17, 2011; Ortega 2011a

64. Collins 2000; Crane 2000; Deitch 2006; Pace Law Review 2010

65. Crane 2000; Dolovich 2005, 494

66. Sharon Dolovich, personal communication, May 17, 2011

67. Collins 2000, 36

68. Sharon Dolovich, personal communication, May 17, 2011

69. Dolovich 2005; Paul Leighton, personal communication, May 17, 2011

70. Joe Goldenson, personal communication, May 5, 2011; McDonald and Patten 2003

71. Clear and Austin 2009

72. Kirchhoff 2010; Porter 2011; Solomon et al. 2004

73. Camp and Camp 1987; Mendelson 2009

74. Dolovich 2005

75. Mendelson 2009

76. McDonald and Patten 2003

$SAGE edge™

Sharpen your skills with SAGE edge at edge.sagepub.com/krisberg

SAGE edge for students provides a personalized approach to help you accomplish your coursework goals in an easy-to-use learning environment. This site includes action plans, mobile-friendly eFlashcards and web quizzes as well as web, audio, and video resources and links to SAGE journal articles.

© Jim West / Alamy

16 The Politics and Future of Mass Incarceration

LEARNING OBJECTIVES

1. To gain an understanding of how politics in the broadest sense affects criminal justice policy.

2. To grasp the specific ways that U.S. crime policy has been shaped by electoral politics and the media during the past decades.

3. To become familiar with the rise of mass incarceration in the United States and some of its causes.

4. To be able to discuss how fiscal crises have contributed to changes in political climate and the positions of the left and right political spectrum.

Eight female prisoners are shown sleeping on the floor of an intake cell in the Livingston County Jail in Michigan. The sheriff used this photo to garner support for building a new jail.

© Livingston County Daily Press & Argus and livingstondaily.com/ Associated Press

The enormous growth of incarceration in the United States was not necessarily supported by the will of the public. However, the legislative actions and ballot measures that ratcheted up punishment did not exactly spur a citizen revolt. When the U.S. economy was healthier, and before states and the federal government were facing the severe financial crisis of the 1990s, overt support for prison spending was a safe course for most politicians. Campaigns to scare the public about an impending drug and crime crisis became a fixture of the political landscape. The crime issue has been linked in subtle and manipulative ways and with antipathy toward the social integration of persons of color and unauthorized immigrants. The emerging conservative political leadership demanded loyalty to the dominant view of crime and other policy issues. Prominent and powerful cable networks and talk radio personalities have further politicized the discussion on crime policy.

Sentencing as a corrections policy is usually determined inside government corridors by the executive or legislative branches of government. These deliberations can be heavily influenced by interest-group politics and have less to do with popular opinion. The political class and the media have generally claimed the public wants to get tougher on offenders and will pay whatever it costs to keep them locked up.

Since around the year 2000, measurements of public attitudes appear to reveal disenchantment with corrections. Crime rates have been declining across the country since the

Social integration: Breaking down societal barriers between social groups (racial, ethnic, class, immigrant, etc.) so that minorities and the underprivileged move into the mainstream.

5   To grasp the shift in public opinion regarding appropriate crime policy, especially for low-level crime.

6   To understand some of the data that researchers have been able to provide to the discussion of effective crime control.

7   To name at least three interest groups that have a stake in maintaining a large prison population.

8   To grasp the conflict around determining the power of voting districts.

9   To understand some of the barriers to sentencing reform.

mid-1990s. The chronic economic problems facing the nation have forced a more realistic assessment of how much of public resources are dedicated to prisons and jails. Although the public still believes that crime rates are rising and that there is too much violence, the crime issue is no longer high on the list of worries for voters. On the domestic front, jobs, housing, health care, and the troubled education system are much more salient for the average citizen. It is worth noting that in the 2008 and 2012 presidential elections, the crime issue was seldom the topic of public debates. Republican candidate Ron Paul advocated the legalization of drugs, including heroin—often to an enthusiastic response from conservative voters.

Public opinion polls conducted over the past two decades show that Americans are reassessing the value of imprisonment for nonviolent offenders. The public seems concerned that correctional practices cost too much and may make matters worse. Our citizens appear to believe that prisons make offenders more likely to recidivate and that incarceration should be reserved for violent and dangerous offenders. The previously assumed public support of prisons and jails as a powerful deterrent to crime seems less clear at this point.

Mass Incarceration and Electoral Politics

The fear of being labeled as "soft on crime" has been a major feature of electoral politics at every level of government since the mid-1960s. Paradoxically, the public has generally endorsed harsher penalties even as citizens have been unwilling to support additional funding for building new prisons and jails. In the late 1960s and 1970s, the Republican Party embraced the idea of impeaching U.S. Supreme Court Justice Earl Warren, who symbolized liberal views of racial integration and protection of the constitutional rights of the accused and imprisoned. Similar politics led to the recall of members of the California Supreme Court in the 1986 election—Chief Justice Rose Bird and Justices Cruz Reynoso and Joseph Grodin. Conservatives have attacked the last two California governors—Arnold Schwarzenegger and Jerry Brown—as endangering the public because they reduced the prison population. Governors in New York, New Jersey, Colorado, Louisiana, Florida, Illinois, and Mississippi have faced severe opposition in electoral campaigns for allegedly "soft" crime policies. Bill Clinton lost a race for Arkansas governor due to allegations that he paroled a dangerous inmate. Even Mississippi governor Haley Barbour, having strong conservative bona fides, was nearly impeached for pardoning some prison inmates. In 2012, the Republican National Committee helped Scott Walker win the governorship of Wisconsin by alleging that his opponent, Democratic mayor of Milwaukee Tom Barrett, had lenient attitudes toward corrections. Walker made repeated attempts to discredit Barrett's record on crime and accused him of "fudging" crime statistics.[1]

Being the "law and order" advocate has been a requirement in presidential and congressional contests as well. Criminal justice policies became increasingly politicized after the 1964 presidential election between Lyndon Baines Johnson and Barry Goldwater. The most dramatic example of this strategy was the use of a Massachusetts inmate, Willie Horton, who murdered someone while on temporary prison release. President George H. W. Bush used the scary image of Horton to devastate the campaign of former Governor Michael Dukakis.

The litmus test for elected officials included the unequivocal support for capital punishment, the War on Drugs, three-strikes laws, and mandatory prison sentences. Liberal politicians who feared their electoral demise either went silent on key crime policy issues or—similar to those attacked as communists during the McCarthy era—some liberals

▲ Prison supply is big business.

© Andrew Lichtenstein

overcompensated in an effort to deflect criticism. They tried to show that they were even "tougher" than their challengers. The crime debate was dominated by the media and politicians who either truly believed in cracking down on criminals or did so to avoid critical scrutiny. To use a phrase of President John F. Kennedy about the politics of the day—there were few "Profiles in Courage."

In Whose Interest?

Despite the great power of the issue of crime in the electoral arena, it is important to observe that most correctional policy is significantly influenced by powerful lobbying groups that have a strong vested interest in expanding spending on incarceration. Many in the field refer to these interests as "the prison industrial complex"—the businesses that design, finance, and build prisons and jails. There are for-profit corporations that operate private facilities and others that sell products and services to corrections agencies, including weapons, razor wire, bibles, movies, treatment materials, and uniforms, to name a few. These companies often enjoy monopolies in the correctional market, charging above-market prices, such as the phone services that inmates must use to stay connected with their families. It is also common for companies to receive noncompetitive contracts won through their lobbying efforts with state officials.

Most important are the public employee unions that have grown tremendously in the size of their membership and the dues paid by those members. Prison guard unions and other correctional workers contribute large amounts of money to the same elected

Prison industrial complex: The rapid expansion of the use of prison, mostly as a result of the political influence of private companies that reap financial benefits from that expansion.

SPOTLIGHT

THE "THREE FIFTHS OF A MAN" COMPROMISE

The population count of citizens in a given county or state has various political purposes. Through history, the northern and southern United States have found themselves in contentious debate over this issue.

In 1783 Philadelphia, a committee of delegates drafted a proposal to amend the Articles of Confederation to determine each state's tax obligations based on its population, not its land. The amendment proposed counting slaves as fully as the free among the population. At the time, labor was directly linked to the ability of an area to produce wealth, and slaves were the main labor force in the South. To its authors, the proposal was entirely logical. The North favored counting slaves for the purpose of levying taxes; such an arrangement would create far greater tax contributions from the Southern states. Of course, the Southern states objected for the exact same reason. Eventually, the compromise prevailed of counting three fifths of the slave population toward the total for each state. Despite the compromise, the proposed amendment failed to garner enough support and was defeated.[1]

Ironically, the sides reversed during the Constitutional Convention of 1787, at which time the dominant issues were representation (and votes) in Congress and the Electoral College—in other words, political power. One could argue that this balance gave additional political power to the South to protect and extend slavery. The Northern states favored considering slaves only as property and not as part of the citizen population, thus minimizing the number of Southern representatives in Congress. And the South wanted to count the slave population fully so as to gain the maximum power at the federal level. Once again, the three fifths compromise was invoked. It became part of Article 1 of the Constitution, as follows:

> *Representatives and direct Taxes shall be apportioned among the several States which may be included within this Union, according to their respective Numbers, which shall be determined by adding to the whole Number of free Persons, including those bound to Service for a Term of Years, and excluding Indians not taxed, three fifths of all other Persons.*

The result was that, prior to the Civil War, the Southern states exerted more political influence in federal affairs

officials who decide on the salaries and benefits of the union membership. Moreover, correctional workers have opposed efforts at law reform that would reverse mass incarceration policies.

Private prison companies have also used their ability to contribute to political candidates to influence corrections policies. In 2010, private prisons held 16% of federal prisoners and almost 7% of state prisoners.[2] The GEO Group is the largest private prison corporation in the United States, with 2011 revenue of $1.6 billion.[3] (See Chapter 15.)

Another potent lobbying force that exerted a significant influence on crime policies of the past 25 years were groups that represent the families of murder victims or victims of other crimes, such as driving under the influence (Mothers Against Drunk Driving). Although it is undeniably important that the justice system listen to and respond to the needs of victims, the casualties of the crime problems are not necessarily in the best position to frame effective crime control policies. Some victim groups exist exclusively to push for more incarceration and to defend the death penalty.

Another powerful interest group that supports mass incarceration is elected officials who represent rural, largely agricultural communities, where prisons have been built, in many states.

than if slaves had not been counted at all. Needless to say, it was *not* the interests of the slaves that concerned the Southern legislators. Clearly, the word *slave* was avoided, but everyone knew what the language meant in effect.[2]

After the Civil War, the Fourteenth Amendment, which was ratified in 1868, altered the article's language to read as follows:

> *Representatives shall be apportioned among the several States according to their respective numbers, counting the whole number of persons in each State, excluding Indians not taxed.*

According to one analysis, a consequence of the earlier scheme was that Thomas Jefferson would not have been elected in 1800 without the advantage the South gained with the three-fifths compromise and that John Adams would have been elected instead.[3] Indeed, many things in U.S. history would have played out very differently had the compromise been altered or had it not existed at all.

> *"Much has been said of the impropriety of representing men who have no will of their own. . . . They are men, though degraded to the condition of*

slavery. They are persons known to the municipal laws of the states which they inhabit, as well as to the laws of nature. But representation and taxation go together. . . . Would it be just to impose a singular burden, without conferring some adequate advantage?" —Alexander Hamilton

QUESTIONS

1 What were your assumptions about the "three fifths of a man" compromise prior to reading this Spotlight?

2 Discuss how the three-fifths compromise of 1783 and 1787 is similar to or different from counting prisoners today.

3 Find an example in current politics that centers on the drawing of voting districts.

Notes

1. Claremont Institute 2002
2. Ibid.
3. Banning 2004; Hoover 2004; Wills 2003

As the farming industry faced hard times in the last 20 years due to overseas competition, these rural communities have become increasingly dependent on the corrections industry to provide jobs and to support local business. The closure of a prison could mean that such a community is plunged into a deep economic downturn. In Michigan and New York, citizens from rural communities expressed deep concern over the likelihood of prisons closing.[4]

Until recently, many states and the federal government have counted inmates as part of the population of the cities and counties in which they are located. For example, fully half of the "residents of Susanville, California," are state prisoners. But here is the catch—these "citizens" do not have the right to vote, and so the free residents get extra influence in terms of the number of legislators representing these areas. It is tragically reminiscent of the despicable historic practice of defining an African slave as three fifths of a man for the purpose of increasing the voting power of slave owners. Further, the inmates are counted as local residents in various funding formulas that determine the allocation of federal and state monies. This produces a financial advantage for local government, since corrections departments generally pay for almost all of the costs associated with the inmate residents. In addition, inmate families who visit their incarcerated loved ones add to the local economy by supporting hotels, restaurants, and other local businesses.

Rural areas of north Texas are being transformed as the economy shifts away from traditional agriculture.

© Bob Daemmrich/Corbis

In most states and in Congress, there are legislative districts in which each has an equal vote, regardless of the size of that district's population. This means that rural areas can exert great political influence and can negotiate effectively with the larger jurisdictions. In states in which super majorities are needed to pass budgets or to levy taxes, the rural communities can band together and hold the political process hostage. This helps explain why otherwise liberal urban legislators or governors are reluctant to support policies that reduce the number of prisons or downsize the correctional workforce.

Rural legislators tend to be politically conservative and represent constituencies that are predominately White, although this demographic equation is slowly changing. As noted earlier, criminal justice policies became increasing politicized after the 1964 presidential race between Lyndon Baines Johnson and Barry Goldwater. Over the next five decades, the Republican Party took a tougher stand on crime issues, again attacking liberals as "soft on crime" and portraying them as uncaring about crime victims. "Law and Order" was the catchphrase for most national and state elections.

Criminal justice officials, including statewide associations, have pushed for harsher penalties and have resisted liberalizing reforms. Police, sheriffs, and prosecutors have led the charge. The assertion by law enforcement leaders that a given law or policy change will endanger the public is difficult for politicians to ignore—even if these claims are not based on any facts or research. Further, statewide associations of law enforcement groups who are most likely to lobby in Washington, D.C., or state capitals tend to be dominated by the rural counties and generally reflect a more conservative view than the leadership from urban jurisdictions.

An example of how these forces work together is instructive. A ballot measure in California in 2006 to modestly reform the three-strikes law—basically to require that the third strike be a violent crime instead of any felony—was well ahead in public opinion polling up until one month before the election. A wealthy donor put up a huge amount of funding to pay for television and radio advertisements. The three-strikes reforms had almost no advertising budget and had to rely on "earned media." Next, victims' advocates, the prison guards union, and prosecutors launched a deceptive publicity campaign claiming that fixing three strikes would lead to the release of extremely violent prisoners. Some of the cases that they cited were on death row or serving life terms without the possibility of parole—prisoners who would never get out of prison no matter how the three-strikes law was amended. Then, prominent sheriffs, police chiefs, and prosecutors joined the opponents to sentencing reform. Governor Schwarzenegger appeared on a number of TV spots opposing the reforms, and he rallied all the living California governors to oppose the ballot measure. Within two short weeks, public opposition grew, and the reform measure was soundly defeated. The advocates of progressive reform were outmanned and outgunned.

An Opening to Change

Fiscal crises have forced politicians on both the right and the left to reexamine expenditures on corrections, specifically incarceration. The new economics appears to be compelling a move in many states toward a smarter, less reactive strategy of crime control and offender accountability. This movement is being shepherded in part with interesting alliances among criminal justice officials, advocates, and the faith community.

The unified voice of conservatives on crime issues may be changing, at least in terms of minor drug offenders. An organization called Right on Crime, founded in Austin, Texas, is dominated by leading conservative thinkers and politicians such as Newt Gingrich, Grover Norquist, and Edwin Meese. This group advocates for laws that would divert non-violent and non–sex offenders to probation and other community options. Right on Crime has been active in many red states and appears to have achieved some victories in Texas, but the longer-term influence of the group remains to be seen. Interestingly, Republican governors are beginning to question the huge public expenditures for prisons. They would prefer to reduce state budgets, and they are less beholden to public employee unions in terms of downsizing the corrections workforce.

Those victim advocates that actually provide direct help to crime victims via social services, legal counseling, or monetary compensation are not as likely to side with the tough-on-crime viewpoint. Indeed, there is a growing number of victims' groups that oppose capital punishment or other harsh penalties, preferring to promote restorative justice and reconciliation.[5] The media and elected officials openly defer to victims' groups, and this tends to push the crime debate in a more punitive direction.

An obvious question is "Are there any constituencies for more progressive correctional policies?" Theoretically, these groups could include former inmates, families of inmates, public defender organizations, and other community-based or advocacy groups, but these groups usually have very limited resources, making it difficult for them to contribute to political candidates. They rely more on moral persuasion rather than the tools of political influence such as campaign contributions. With few exceptions, most academics and researchers who possess the data—and can demonstrate the futility and costliness of tougher correctional policies—have traditionally been reluctant to get involved in the political fray.

What the Public Actually Thinks About Corrections Policy

There is a problematic disconnect between the attitudes about incarceration that the public consistently expresses and the policies and laws enacted by their legislative representatives. The latter is driven largely by misinformation and an opportunistic alliance with forces that foster fear of crime in the public mind. As mentioned earlier, several state and national public opinion polls have gauged the public's view of correctional policy. The direction and consistency of the results are quite revealing.

In 2001, Ridder/Braden Inc. surveyed 500 possible Colorado voters for an upcoming election. Fifty-nine percent of the respondents felt that drug addiction should be viewed as a health issue compared with just 11% who viewed drug addicts as criminals. Almost three quarters of the possible voters wanted more funding for drug treatment and drug

SPOTLIGHT

JUSTICE ROSE BIRD

Rose Bird was chief justice of the California Supreme Court from 1977 until 1987. Among other firsts for women that Justice Bird accomplished, she was the first woman to serve in that office. Previously, she was the first woman to serve in a cabinet-level position in the California state government—secretary of agriculture. Then governor Jerry Brown appointed her to both positions. Both Brown and Bird were part of the liberal flank of California politics at that time.

Brown described Bird as very well organized and very intelligent, with excellent skills in evaluating people. When questioned about his appointing a woman, he said that he was looking primarily for integrity and intellectual honesty, ability, and a willingness to work hard for the public interest.[1]

Rose Bird was raised in Tucson, Arizona, by parents who were chicken ranchers. Her father died when she was very young, and her mother, who always emphasized education and encouraged Rose to pursue any vocation she wanted, moved to New York for factory work. Rose excelled at school, and her educational path led her to Boalt Law School at UC Berkeley.[2]

Justice Bird had no prior judicial experience. This and her record in capital cases were the facts that her conservative opponents seized upon. From the very beginning of her tenure, the conservative element labeled her as "soft on crime." During her time on the high court, she voted to overturn death sentences in 61 cases. This single fact proved to be a tool that her political opponents used against her, eventually succeeding in removing her from the court. These opponents included Jarvis and Gann, the authors of a pivotal tax revolt of the day (Proposition 13). Observers have analyzed that the real motivation

▲ California Chief Justice Rose Bird.

© Mark Avery/Associated Press

prevention and education programs instead of the criminal justice system. At the time, 80% of public funding for drug abuse programs was going to the criminal justice system. Eighty percent of surveyed Coloradans believed that treatment was an effective means to reduce drug-related crimes. Fully 60% felt that incarceration was ineffective as a response to people convicted of possession of small amounts of drugs.[6]

In 2001, the American Civil Liberties Union (ACLU) commissioned a national survey of 2,000 adults. Although a slight majority said that people committing nonviolent crimes were not punished harshly enough, 74% favored drug treatment and probation in lieu of prison for nonviolent illegal drug use. Seventy percent agreed that laws should be changed so that fewer nonviolent crimes are punished with prison terms, and 61% opposed mandatory sentences for some nonviolent crimes.[7]

The U.S. Department of Justice published a national survey of 1,300 respondents that showed a range of opinions based on the crime that was committed. For example, 99% wanted those convicted of robbery sent to prison, and 65% wanted those who committed identity theft or counterfeiting to be sentenced to prison. The portion of those favoring incarceration for crimes such as burglary dropped 31%, or for

behind the persistent campaign to oust Rose Bird had to do with other political realities, including property taxes, reapportionment, the Victims' Bill of Rights, and the balanced federal budget amendment.[3]

It was in this political climate that Brown signed into law the "use a gun, go to prison" provision. This legislation removed discretion from judges and mandated prison sentences, even for first-time offenders who had used a gun in the commission of their crime.

The political pressure to be "tough on crime," which undoubtedly influenced Brown and subsequent governors, contributed significantly to the growth of mass incarceration in California. Rose Bird's liberal position and unwillingness to compromise her values, which included being squarely against capital punishment, cost her the bench and her career.

QUESTIONS

1 Does a Supreme Court justice have the right to impose his or her personal views on the decisions made in the course of official duties?

2 Does it matter if these personal views have to do with questions of life and death?

3 Should political coalitions have the right to campaign against justices whose views they oppose?

Notes

1. Endicott 1975, A18
2. Medsger 1983
3. Gughemetti 1985, 46; Brown n.d.

Medicare fraud, which dropped 38%. By contrast, a smaller percentage of respondents favored prison for those convicted for the first time of simple drug possession and illegal immigration (almost 18% and 24%, respectively).[8]

In 2004, a California poll of over 1,000 respondents done for the National Council on Crime and Delinquency (NCCD) found that 56% agreed that "the crime problem would be reduced if fewer individuals were sent to prison and instead were re-educated and rehabilitated out of prison." Two thirds (67%) supported services for nonviolent and drug offenders both in and out of prison.[9] However, willingness to pay for more rehabilitation programs was not universally approved. In 2005, the Public Policy Institute of California reported that 46% of the 2,000 residents that they polled wanted spending on prisons and corrections to be cut, 36% thought spending should remain the same, and 13% thought corrections spending should increase. In most others areas (elementary education, health and human services, and colleges and universities), at least 80% of those polled wanted the state to spend the same or more.[10]

A telephone survey conducted in 2006 by the National Center for State Courts (NCSC) included over 1,500 respondents who expressed optimism that many offenders can turn their lives around (79%), and a slight majority (51%) favored "alternative" sentencing rather than incarceration for nonviolent offenders. As many as 37% thought that alternative sentencing could be tried with some violent offenders, 56% believed that judges should have more discretion in sentencing, and only 36% favored mandatory prison sentences.[11] A later survey commissioned in 2008 by Families Against Mandatory Minimums (FAMM) also suggested that a majority of Americans did not support automatic

▲ What can be done
to ensure that all
constituencies have a
place at the table of
corrections reform?

*© Christian Gooden/MCT/
Newscom*

jail sentences for nonviolent offenders, and 78% felt that judges—not members of
Congress—were better equipped to determine sentences.[12]

NCCD examined attitudes toward system-involved youth in a 2007 national poll that
included over 1,000 people who overwhelmingly favored rehabilitation services (89%)
for incarcerated juveniles. And 81% agreed that spending on treatment services would
save money in the long run. There was nearly unanimous support of increased education
and job skills training or counseling and substance abuse services for youth in the juvenile
justice system (95% and 92%, respectively).[13]

Another NCCD survey published in 2009 of over 1,000 citizens reinforced the notion
that a growing number of Americans are convinced that incarcerating nonviolent and
non–sex offenders was not necessary for public safety. For instance, 79% felt that it was
not absolutely necessary to incarcerate persons who were arrested for public drunkenness, and 86% did not want incarceration to be the primary response to homeless and the
mentally ill on the streets. More than three quarters of those surveyed felt that probation,
community service, restitution, and rehabilitative services were the most appropriate
sanctions for less serious offenders whose crimes did not involve physical harm to

victims or significant property loss. The public views on the value of incarceration were more mixed when it came to punishing those who solicited for prostitution or who violated the terms of their probation or parole (49% and 60%, respectively).[14]

A 2012 national poll commissioned by the Pew Charitable Trusts and conducted by Public Opinion Strategies and the Mellman Group—leading pollsters for Democrats and Republicans alike—showed that Americans now believe that there are too many people in prison and the costs of locking up nonviolent offenders is too expensive. The voters are looking for cheaper and more effective community alternatives to prisons and jails. Even 70% of households that contain crime victims want to see investments shift away from incarceration. The Pew survey also showed vast support for reducing the time that nonviolent offenders must spend behind bars based on completing rehabilitation programs (86%), good behavior (83%), closing budget deficits (78%), and caring for aging and ill inmates (77%).[15]

The Pew study held focus groups nationally and in Georgia, Missouri, and Oregon to determine the arguments that were most persuasive to those who wanted to reduce reliance on incarceration. They found that voters were mostly concerned about protecting public safety; they must be convinced that community alternatives are not "a slap on the wrist" and that individuals will be closely monitored in the community. The public likes new technologies such as global positioning systems (GPS), which promise closer tracking of released or diverted offenders. Voters buy in to the investment-related argument that government needs to become more cost-effective. The citizens agree that job training and substance abuse treatment can help stop inmates from returning to their lives of crime. The public supports the idea of freeing up prison space occupied by the nonviolent inmate so that dangerous and violent offenders can be reliably confined.

This same study also found that crime is not generally a major public concern and that only 2% of voters thought that crime and drug abuse were the most important problems facing their communities. Jobs, the economy, and education are much more salient issues for the vast majority of voters. Those interviewed were persuaded by arguments that emphasized the need for offenders to take responsibility for their actions by paying child support and making restitution to victims. Voters would rather cut spending on prisons than reduce funding for education or increase property and business taxes. Again, cost–benefit arguments were most likely to appeal to those who were open to less incarceration. Concerns about racial injustice in our incarceration policies were not very effective in moving public opinion.[16]

These polling results suggest some openness to reform on the part of the public, but still, a very modest difference of opinion based on one's geographic location, political party affiliation, or ideology. People of color, younger voters, women, and more educated citizens are a bit more likely to endorse alternatives to incarceration than politically conservative older White males, but the difference among groups is relatively small. One recent Florida poll suggests that more conservative Americans are less infatuated with incarceration as a remedy for the crime problem than they have been in the past. In 2012, traditionally Republican groups—Florida TaxWatch, Right on Crime, and the Associated Industries of Florida—sponsored a poll of 800 Floridians who said that they were likely to vote in the Florida Republican primary in 2012. Likely primary voters are considered to be partisan activists and to hold more extreme views than average voters or "swing voters." The results of this Florida poll defy the conventional wisdom that conservative voters still cling to very punitive attitudes and are strong supporters of expanded incarceration. The vast majority of these likely Republican primary voters (86%) did not support transferring nonviolent juvenile offenders to the adult criminal justice system, and 81% wanted evidence-based community alternatives to juvenile prisons. An amazing 86% said that a person who is "tough on crime" can support programs involving community supervision,

Changing Laws Through Ballot Measures

You are an advocate for reducing the reliance on incarceration as the dominant criminal justice response to low-level crime. Despite several public opinion polls suggesting that most voters think that too many minor drug offenders are put in prisons and jails, the governor and the legislature have resisted all efforts to change the applicable laws. Elected officials are heavily lobbied by the unions that represent corrections officers, private prison companies, and criminal justice professionals who benefit from full prisons. Some of your constituents suggest the reform strategy of bringing reform proposals to the voters. Last year the voters were able to modify the state's expansive three-strikes law after the change could not pass the regular legislative process.

Others argue that making crime policy at the ballot box is bad practice, because the results are often determined by whoever has the most money to do television and radio ads. Further, it is clear that most voters do not really understand the content of these measures. The recent past is also filled with examples in which the voters approved very bad criminal justice policies.

YOU DECIDE: **As a reformer, should you spend your energy on an electoral campaign, continue to try to persuade top elected officials, or place a focus on grassroots organizing in the community or on some other strategy?**

mandatory drug testing, and treatment to reduce crime. As many as 81% said that they would support a candidate who advocated for programs of supervised work release and victim restitution, saving taxpayers from having to pay for expensive incarceration for youth. As with earlier surveys, a large proportion of the surveyed Republican activist voters (70%) believed that prisons play an important role in public safety but may have the unintended consequences of creating hardened criminals out of nonviolent, low-level offenders. Sixty percent felt that not every person convicted of minor violent crime should go to prison. Seventy-two percent of the Florida Republican voters wanted the money saved from diverting nonviolent offenders to prison to be reinvested in strengthening probation and parole systems.[17]

Confronting the Politics of Mass Incarceration

Despite the clear shift in public views on the cost-effectiveness of punishment, the media continue to report that voters favor incarceration for most crimes. News coverage, especially on local television, is often dominated by interviews with law enforcement spokespersons or crime victims. The resulting impression is that harsh and punitive opinions are favored in the mainstream. Media representatives are often skeptical of the preponderance of evidence supplied by the polls discussed above. Because elected officials get a good deal of their "data" from media accounts, most politicians have not really responded to the dramatic turn in voter attitudes in the past two decades. Further, the interest groups that live off the "prison industrial complex" have a stake in continued expansion of the incarceration system and derive benefits from fostering fear about the danger posed by community alternatives to prisons and jails. There is a major disconnect between what the public wants, especially for nonviolent offenders, and what politicians assume is the public consensus. The key question is how to get the correct message across in those forums in which sentencing and criminal justice policy are formulated.

Looking at some victories for more enlightened policies is helpful. In California and in other states, voters endorsed ballot measures that reduced penalties for possession and use of small amounts of marijuana, and endorsed a new set of regulations to permit persons to sell and obtain marijuana for medical reasons. These measures were opposed almost unanimously by criminal justice officials and most elected officials in these states. A small number of politicians embraced the reforms.

For example, California's Substance Abuse and Crime Prevention Act of 2000 (Proposition 36) mandated the diversion of minor drug offenders to community-based treatment programs in lieu of jail. Similar laws have been enacted in other states. In these cases, focus groups and polls showed that a large number of voters reported that they knew a close relative who had a substance abuse problem. Further, these voters said that they doubted that jail would help their loved ones. The personal experience of many citizens with substance addiction appeared to counteract the fear tactics employed by criminal justice officials. Moreover, the proportion of voters who have themselves used marijuana grew as the "baby boomers" emerged as a dominant voting group. Media hysteria about the evil of marijuana has cooled, and use of this drug is often portrayed in a humorous or tolerant manner in movies, on television, and on the Internet. The 1950s movie *Reefer Madness*, intended as a cautionary tale about using marijuana, has become a cult classic and is viewed as a satire of the antidrug position. Youthful drug use was seen as a potential disqualification for higher office. However, Americans accepted President Bill Clinton's claim that he "didn't inhale"; they tolerated President George W. Bush's drug and alcohol abuse after he had a religious conversion; and the admissions of drug use in President Barack Obama's autobiography did not appear to concern a majority of U.S. voters.

State marijuana decriminalization campaigns have enjoyed the substantial financial backing of billionaires such as George Soros. Some of these electoral campaigns are no longer underfunded. With the help of these philanthropists, supporters of legalized marijuana have established lobbying groups and conducted educational forums on university campuses and other public venues.

Much less progress has been seen in decriminalizing minor drug use at the federal level, where no executive branch and congressional action has taken place. A national referendum is not possible, and the traditional political dynamic of supporting the views of the federal Drug Enforcement Agency is still strong. This has set up interesting conflicts in which state officials and congressional representatives from those states that have liberalized their local laws are now in active legal battle with the U.S. Department of Justice, which argues that federal drug prohibitions trump any changes in state laws with respect to drug policy.

It is also concerning that voter-approved investments in drug treatment services have never been adequately funded in California and in other liberal states. Lacking any meaningful services, persons with serious addiction problems have gravitated back to jails.

◀ The nation's attitudes and laws are undergoing an undeniable shift with regard to the cultivation and use of marijuana.

© iStockphoto.com/ DaveLongMedia

Referendum: A form of direct democracy, a ballot vote in which the electorate is asked to accept or reject a proposition.

SPOTLIGHT

RIGHT ON CRIME

Its tagline is "The Conservative Case for Reform—Fighting Crime, Prioritizing Victims, and Protecting Taxpayers." The words are well chosen and descriptive of this group's values and agenda.

For the first time in a long time, and as if it were their original idea, prominent conservatives—such as tax reformer Grover Norquist, former Governor of Florida Jeb Bush, and former House Speaker Newt Gingrich—have thrown their political weight behind prison reforms on the basis of the perceived failures of the system to fulfill its promises, citing for example the two-thirds rate of recidivism for Georgia's state prisons. The group's goals are based on fiscal responsibility and the safety of communities.[1] Gingrich, in an op-ed for the *Atlanta Journal-Constitution*, remarked that "just as a student's success isn't measured by his entrance into high school but by his graduation, and a bridge's value isn't measured by its completion but by its long-term reliability, celebrating taking criminals off the street with little thought to their imminent return to society is foolhardy."[2]

It is not too much of a stretch to understand the motivation of "fiscal sanity," because curbing government spending, now even on corrections, has always been a conservative value, as has holding government agencies to account for their performance and efficiency. With regard to both fiscal and programmatic health, prison systems nationwide have been beleaguered and falling behind. What makes this group's outlook surprising from a political perspective is the note of acknowledgment of the social burden on reentering prisoners and an uncharacteristic tone of compassion. Says Gingrich, "They need the help of a community that will rally around them and provide the counseling, encouragement, and love that truly lead to changed behavior."[3]

Right on Crime is a project of the Texas Public Policy Foundation. As stated on its website, the organization is a "research institute in Austin, TX committed to limited government, free markets, private property rights, individual liberty and personal responsibility."

Although it has traditionally touted a "law and order" and "lock 'em up" position, conservative political philosophy apparently can stretch to embrace reforms of the prison system for reasons of fiscal responsibility; it recognizes

---

Criminal justice officials have continued their argument that tougher penalties are needed to coerce chronic drug users into treatment—despite ample evidence that coerced therapy in the drug arena repeatedly fails.

In other cases, law enforcement has modified its approach from a total ban on drug use to one that emphasizes "drug possession in plain view." However, in New York City, there has been a stunning increase in "stop and frisk" arrests for this crime. The vast majority of persons arrested for possession are young people of color, and the New York City Police Department (NYPD) has steadfastly defended its practices. The NYPD has even argued that detaining massive numbers of youth of color has contributed to a major decline in all crimes in the city, although there is no meaningful evidence backing this assertion.[18]

Stop and frisk: A policing strategy that originated in NYC. Officers can stop pedestrians and search them for weapons or contraband. The criteria for what constitutes reasonable suspicion are very loose.

In other locations, such as San Jose, California, police have used the very vague crime category of "public drunkenness" to arrest large numbers of Latino youth. There is not a quick, clear test as there is for alcohol, such as a breathalyzer, to measure public intoxication from drugs, and so enforcement can be highly discretionary. Under intense political pressure from the Latino community, the mayor announced a change in this aggressive enforcement policy. However, even in places where law enforcement has lowered its priority for prohibition of marijuana, persons found with small amounts of the substance have been jailed for violations of the conditions of their probation, parole, or pretrial release.

the legitimate role of the government to protect citizens from public safety threats. However, conservatives still reject the liberal notion that society bears some of the responsibility for creating the conditions that promote crime. Personal responsibility remains the cornerstone of this group's philosophy. Conservatives have consistently pooh-poohed the idea that social factors are relevant to crime causes. Right on Crime cites James Q. Wilson, notable as a stalwart supporter of the idea of incapacitation and as unapologetic in stating that African Americans are "disproportionately likely to commit crimes," for his updated analysis on the possible social causes of crime.[4] They add to their message the critique of past rehabilitation programs that could not justify their cost and effectiveness and the assertion of the voice of victims.

Right on Crime has endorsed juvenile justice reforms in states such as Georgia, for enacting reforms to programming that promises to reduce youth recidivism and save the state millions. Similar reform strategies have also surfaced in the adult systems in these states. The group supports community alternatives to incarceration for low-level offenders, drug treatment, and diverting technical violations of parole and probation to sanctions other than prison—in other words, almost exactly the same message that reformers on the liberal side of the aisle have been promoting for many years.

QUESTIONS

1 Discuss the "meeting in the middle" of the conservative and liberal agendas as they relate to corrections reform. How have the two sides typically differed? Where is the common ground emerging now?

2 Is it a departure for the members of the conservative political spectrum to cite researchers? Why or why not?

3 How does research support the position of Right on Crime?

4 What kinds of cultural shifts have an impact on the crime rate?

Notes

1. Reddy 2013
2. Gingrich and Earley 2010
3. Ibid.
4. Wilson 2011

The good news is that electoral campaigns to decriminalize minor possession of marijuana have been successful and are likely to continue to win; the bad news is that the criminal justice system continues to embrace the War on Drugs. There are still far too many minor drug offenders clogging up overcrowded prisons and jails. Further, efforts to reduce draconian and inequitable penalties for other drugs such as crack cocaine versus powdered cocaine have met with very modest success at the state level. Interestingly, an effort to reduce the 100-to-1 penalties for "crack" versus powder cocaine did pass the U.S. Congress and was signed into law.[19] There are already demands that this reform not be applied retroactively by the U.S. Sentencing Commission, because it would lead to "early release of dangerous felons." In states such as New York, where harsh drug laws have been moderately reduced, a vocal and organized criminal justice leadership continues to question the value of these reforms.

Recent electoral outcomes suggest that the public is very fearful about sex offenders of all types and will support laws that increase punishments and extend state control over these individuals. Chelsea's law and Megan's law are two examples of significant increases in penalties that followed highly publicized sex crimes and murders of young women in California. The concern is that that these laws seek to lengthen the sentences of all persons charged with sex crimes, and that they often contain provisions that have nothing to with sex offenders or victims. Opponents of major court-ordered reforms have used election campaigns to eliminate basic constitutional rights for prisoners and parolees.

▲ Criminal detainees do legal research in the law library at Krome Detention Center in Miami, Florida.

© John Van Beekum/KRT/ Newscom

Is Money the Currency of Reform?

The extraordinary collapse in the banking and financial markets of 2008 plunged nearly every state in the union into a severe economic recession that resembled and recalled the crisis of the American economy in 1929. The sudden drop in the gross national product and the evaporation of credit required urgent government actions including a bailout of major banks, other large financial institutions, and the automobile industry.

An enormous "stimulus package" rapidly infused federal funds into state, county, and city coffers. The steep drop in tax revenues caused a fiscal crisis at all levels of government. Partly because it can control the money supply, the federal government can operate with huge annual budget deficits. However, states and localities cannot print currency, and many are required by state laws to produce a balanced budget each year. In addition, a broad national movement by fiscal conservatives made it very difficult, if not impossible, for state and local governments to raise taxes of any type.

Stimulus package: Steps taken by the federal government to stimulate the U.S. economy and, in particular, to facilitate recovery after the severe recession in the late 2000s, including mortgage assistance to home owners, lowered interest rates, and increased government spending.

Because corrections systems are primarily supported by state and local funds, the fiscal crisis required government officials to either significantly scale back spending on prisons, jails, and local community corrections, or make cuts in more politically popular areas of government operations such as education, health care, policing, and environmental protection. States such as California had little capacity to make these fiscal changes and were on the verge of defaulting on state obligations. Payments to state vendors were delayed, state workers were required to reduce their work hours, and elected officials attempted to renegotiate contracts with public employees over compensation, benefits, and retirement plans. Major savings in corrections required changes in the law to reduce the number of offenders sent to prison, or to cut back on the length of stay in confinement. These sentencing reforms were difficult to implement, due to the entrenched political strategy of stiffening criminal justice penalties. Moreover, as conditions in prisons and jails deteriorated, there were successful lawsuits that required states and localities to increase spending on health and mental health services in prisons and jails, to provide services for disabled inmates, and to reduce severe prison crowding.

This fiscal crisis has led a number of politically conservative elected officials and conservative advocates who are typically opposed to any correctional reform to reassess state capacity to maintain mass incarceration practices. The Texas lobby Right on Crime is notable in this respect, helping the Lone Star State to scale back on prison construction plans. Other states with historically high rates of imprisonment, such as Florida, North Carolina, Virginia, Tennessee, and Mississippi, adopted accelerated release policies, created sentencing commissions to control the size of the state prison population, or increased the frequency of parole grants and pardons. In some instances, states revised sentencing laws for drug offenses to reduce mandatory prison sentences or shorten prison stays. Where the local politics proved too resistant, elected officials pointed to the real or imagined threat of a federal court takeover of the state prison system to motivate for progressive sentencing reforms.

The combination of declining rates of serious crime and arrests, some reduced penalties, and a somewhat more lenient approach to parole and probation violators has led to a decline in state prison populations in many states. As noted earlier, some state facilities have gone from severe overcrowding to empty. The governor of New York, for example, is proposing to close existing state prisons and sell off the property.[20] Even California, which built 22 new state prisons in the late 1980s and 1990s, is now shuttering some of those adult and juvenile facilities. Not unlike the delicate problem of deciding which military bases needed to close because of a shrinking Department of Defense budget, governors and legislators are wrestling with closing rural prisons that are the mainstay of local economies.

The new wave of conservative Republican elected officials who were swept into office in the 2010 midterm election must consider all potential cost-saving measures, including expanded reliance on private for-profit prisons, tough salary and benefit negotiations with the unions that represent prison employees, and layoffs of prison guards. The governors of Ohio and Florida went so far as to propose the complete privatization of state prisons, although these proposals failed to muster sufficient legislative support. However, now that they are required to balance state budgets, the former advocates of unlimited spending on incarceration are open to creative ideas. Those elected officials who are more closely tied to financial contributions and the political help of powerful public employee unions have been much less likely to "think out of the box" on corrections policies and cost-saving measures.

Whether the state fiscal crisis of the early 2010s can propel and sustain more enlightened corrections policies remains an open question. Efforts in the 1970s to save money by closing costly mental health hospitals did not go well.[21] The austerity measures that impacted the mentally ill are thought to have increased the number of homeless on the streets and to have catalyzed an unplanned transfer of mentally ill patients from hospitals to jails and prisons. The idea that governments would invest in high-quality community-based care for vulnerable citizens never materialized. There is concern today that just reducing prison and jail populations without a commensurate investment in high-quality community-based corrections could lead to an even worse public safety crisis. The cost reduction imperative is always subject to the tyranny of the one horrific, high-profile crime committed by a released convict. Public opinion hardens very quickly.

IN THE COURTS
United States v. Deen, United States v. Tapia

Recent cases have added to the movement tending away from lengthy sentences; the courts are deciding cases that perhaps demonstrate a more tempered and constrained use of incarceration than that which led to the mass incarceration that prevails in the United States.

Michael Deen was convicted in Michigan of distributing 5 grams of cocaine and was sentenced to 66 months in state prison. His incarceration was followed by four years of community supervision. A portion of his sentence was reduced, and Deen was released from prison in March 2011. Four months into his term, he was involved in two domestic violence incidents. Those, combined with some problems with alcohol, led his probation officer to recommend a revocation. Even though it was longer than the recommended 10 months, his probation officer recommended a two-year term in prison, which the judge upheld.[1]

The new sentence was that Deen would have to do two more years followed by two years of community supervision. The judge's decision was based on the following reasoning: "It is important to consider whether the goal of rehabilitation, which I think is the endgame in terms of the criminal justice system, can be best achieved through incarceration, and it sounds as though maybe it can."

Effectively, the additional time in prison was imposed, presumably to allow the rehabilitative services in prison to have their effect.

This case decided that the prohibition on lengthening a prison sentence so that the defendant can complete treatment services applies to revocations as well as initial sentencing, which was the decision in the 2011 case of *United States v. Tapia*.[2]

In the *Tapia* case, the judge imposed a sentence that was based in part on the judge's perception of the defendant's need for drug treatment. Alejandra Tapia was eventually able to show that her sentence would have been shorter without this consideration. She also claimed that her initial failure to object to the sentence was a legal error that needed to be corrected. Tapia's sentence was vacated and remanded for resentencing by a unanimous vote of the Supreme Court.

Notes

1. *United States v. Deen*. No. 11-2271. Decided and Filed February 7, 2013. http://www.ca6.uscourts.gov/opinions.pdf/13a0030p-06.pdf, accessed March 1, 2013.

2. *United States v. Tapia*. No. 9-50248, Argued and Submitted November 10, 2011; Filed December 8, 2011. http://cdn.ca9.uscourts.gov/datastore/opinions/2011/12/08/09-50248.pdf, accessed March 1, 2013.

Recruiting New Allies to Corrections Reform

There has never been a sustained and well-funded organizing effort to build a politically potent, multidisciplinary movement to reverse mass incarceration policies. Most advocates have focused on persuading correctional professional and elected officials to change their opinions of the value of mass incarceration. Moral persuasion has been less than effective when matched against powerful and well-financed interest groups that want to maintain the status quo.

It has been difficult to engage in the public policy debate on more cost-effective sentencing policies with those groups and individuals who are not directly connected to the world of

corrections. The general public is still unaware of many key issues, and people have been fed a steady diet of scary images of prisoners on television, the Internet, and the news media. Consuming these stories, one inevitably concludes that our prisons and jails are filled with dangerous, violent offenders, gang members, and sex criminals.

One hopeful exception to this norm has been the growing numbers of members of the faith community who have begun to serve those behind bars by assisting the family members of convicts and aiding prisoners who are returning home. Another small but growing group consists of citizens, especially students, who volunteer their time to offer literacy education and tutoring within prisons and jails. These charitable citizens often are motivated by their real-life exposure to prisoners to support corrections and sentencing reform. Some in-prison workers, in particular those who are involved in the limited educational, vocational, and counseling programs that are still available to convicts, can be strong supporters of sentencing reform and more liberal parole policies. There is a very small but growing number of criminal justice officials including police chiefs, prosecutors, and judges who are openly questioning current corrections policies. Even some law enforcement spokespersons question why prison budgets grow at a time when cities are laying off police officers. The current rhetoric of these progressive criminal justice leaders suggests that being "smart on crime" should replace the knee-jerk stance of being "tough on crime."[22]

In addition, the public has a say in policies that affect incarceration. The public's attitude about decriminalizing or legalizing certain drug use appears to be shifting. Nationwide, support for legalizing marijuana has been trending steadily upward since at least 1990. Responses vary distinctly according to age group, with people younger than 30 largely in support of legalization and those older than 65 largely opposed.[23] A recent poll in California showed a majority of the state's residents favoring legalization.[24] In the 2012 election,

▲ Planning With Purpose is a class offered to inmates inside the Nebraska State Penitentiary by Released and Restored, a Methodist ministry. The class focuses on how to live outside prison after release and is intended to help reduce extremely high recidivism rates.

© Mikael Karlsson / Alamy

SPOTLIGHT

CALIFORNIA'S REALIGNMENT

In 2011, California Governor Jerry Brown signed Assembly Bills 109 and 117, which have come to be known as "Realignment." For years, the state government had been trying to come up with ways to reduce California's prison population. In 2011, the state Supreme Court ruled in *Brown v. Plata* that the drastically overcrowded state of California prisons violated prisoners' Eighth Amendment rights. In so doing, the court provided the political momentum to institute changes in sentencing law.

AB 109 provided that individuals convicted of nonviolent, nonserious, non–sex offenses (and not having a history of such offenses) would be sentenced to time in county, "mandatory supervision," or a combination of both, rather than to state prison. Another major change was that parole violators were to be sent to county jail instead of being returned to state prison. The revolving prison door for parolees (often involving returns to prison for technical violations) had been a key cause of prison overcrowding and a great expense to the state.

Realignment has generated incendiary claims from both its supporters and its detractors, but how it will ultimately impact California is still largely unknown. Realignment opponents have promoted the idea that the legislation allows for sentences to be reduced in length, or for prisoners to be released earlier than they otherwise would have been. However, this is not the case. The way Realignment is designed, judges now have more options for how they sentence individuals for certain crimes, and some of these options help to keep prison populations down by placing more low-level offenders in local jails and under community supervision. But early release is a different issue.

---

two states succeeded in passing legislation to legalize the recreational use of marijuana. Washington and Colorado were the first states to pass legislation that would allow adults over the age of 21 to buy and possess up to one ounce of marijuana and to grow up to six plants for personal use. Massachusetts joined 16 other states as the voters approved the medical use of marijuana. The new laws do not change the illegality of smoking marijuana in public or driving while under its influence. And marijuana use and possession is still illegal under federal law. It remains to be seen what effect, if any, these new laws will have on the prison populations in those states.

Police leaders who are proponents of community-engaged police strategies now suggest that we cannot "arrest our way out of the crime problem." Some law enforcement leaders have suggested that the dominant, military-style model (the War on Crime or the War on Drugs) is misleading and counterproductive. During her tenure as U.S. Attorney General, Janet Reno galvanized progressive law enforcement opinion to support a concentrated focus on prevention, early intervention, and work with vulnerable families. It clearly matters when the nation's top law enforcer articulates a view alternative to the conventional mentality, characterized by the phrase "surveil 'em, nail 'em, and jail 'em." Some law enforcement spokespersons even vocalize the view, once expressed only by prisoner advocates, that America's prisons and jails make the confined become worse and may create even more victimization in high-risk neighborhoods. How to mobilize and enhance the influence of the new law enforcement leaders remains a challenge for the prison reform movement.

The rise of mass incarceration was heavily subsidized by taxpayers and students. Parents and students in elementary and higher education have paid for mass incarceration via larger class sizes, shorter school years, reduced classroom instruction, fewer school counselors, or diminished educational offerings, especially in science, the humanities,

Many supporters of Realignment have said that it will reduce the state's dependence on incarceration and promote a focus on rehabilitation and supportive reentry. However, the extent to which Realignment will impact the rate of incarceration depends on how the new laws are implemented, which varies widely among the 56 counties in the state. Each county has been funded through Realignment to prepare to handle larger numbers and more kinds of offenders. Each may spend this money to support alternatives to incarceration or to build more jails. Additionally, although judges have more sentencing options and thus the ability to incarcerate fewer people, whether they will choose to do so remains to be seen. In spite of the polarized atmosphere of Realignment, its true impact on California has yet to be determined.

QUESTIONS

1 Why would Realignment work to relieve prison overcrowding?

2 Should counties be allowed to devise their own schemes for using Realignment funds?

3 If you were a judge, how would you react to having new sentencing options?

---

arts and music, public libraries, vocational programs, and physical education. The poor and vulnerable have faced cuts in government-subsidized health care and in-home services for the disabled and infirm, as well as food stamps and other social safety-net programs. Timid elected officials of all political stripes have supported savage cuts in almost all domestic programs to, in part, sustain bloated prison and jail funding. Yet, it has been difficult to organize and educate those facing the stark reductions—or their advocates— to join forces with those trying to reverse three decades of mass incarceration policies. Whether future reformers can change this tendency toward isolated single-issue social advocacy is unknown at this point.

. . . .

SUMMARY: THE WAY FORWARD

Pogo, the brilliant creation of New York cartoonist Al Capp, was a nondescript creature that was famous for his satirical insights into political and social life, one classic of which was "We have met the enemy and he is us." The truth that this quip points to is at the heart of the crisis of American corrections. Incipient in the crisis are the potential ways out of the box.

Correctional practices and policy exist within a cultural context that includes loathing and fear of the criminal.

Most people believe that harsh punishments may prevent the convicted from reoffending or potential lawbreakers from committing new crimes. The idea that prisons and jails may spread the societal contagion of violence is not well understood or researched. The hallmark of prisons and jails is "out of sight, out of mind." A significant sector of American society experiences the correctional system directly and personally; a subsector experiences secure confinement. Others come to learn about the corrections system through the experiences of loved ones, coworkers, or neighbors. However, a significant portion of those who are most deeply involved in the system come from a concentrated community; they tend to be poor, people of color, and financially, educationally, and otherwise disadvantaged. Depressed communities are beset with many problems including extreme poverty, deteriorating infrastructure, crowding, homelessness, violence, rampant drug addiction, failing schools, and generally substandard government services. Reforming correctional practices is only one of a dizzying set of challenges to improving these communities.

Well-off Americans tend to know little about the corrections system. They generally learn about it when crises hit the media—murders behind the walls, major riots, escapes, and scandals. Television portrayals of prisons and jails tend to highlight the most dangerous and violent inmates who, in fact, make up a small fraction of the incarcerated population. Our citizenry is grossly uninformed about the facts on who is under correctional supervision, how the numbers have rapidly increased, the prevailing recidivism rates, how long people spend in prison, or the actual costs of corrections. Few if any elected officials or members of the media know the facts about corrections or have personally visited a jail or prison.

As a result of the general ignorance about corrections, the loudest voices or those of well-heeled interest groups tend to control the laws and resources that support current policy. In too many places, corrections has been adversely impacted by voter initiatives that increase the punitive aspects of the sentencing and corrections process without understanding the complex consequences of such legislation. These increases have resulted in the erosion of other basic societal supports— such as education and health care—that make our communities safer.

Solid, factual, and verifiable information is the key to the hopes for meaningful and durable reform. There is growing adoption of evidence-based practice in corrections including improved risk and needs assessment approaches as well as the expanded availability of cognitive-behavioral programs. This is a hopeful direction for corrections, even though the science behind these efforts is still underdeveloped and most of these programs require a major culture shift among correctional workers. It remains a distinct challenge to convince correctional staff that a more empathetic and nonhierarchical system can improve their daily lives as well as the lives of prisoners. Going forward, it will be critical to design reform strategies that can promote this culture change and move out of the "hothouse" environment of pilot programs and be replicated on a massive scale.

As noted earlier, public opinion is beginning to shift in one notable area—the treatment of minor offenders in alternatives to secure detention. There is a strong movement to reduce the incarceration of young people and to divert serious juvenile offenders from prisons and jails. Indicators also suggest that we may be ready to call a truce in the costly and counterproductive War on Drugs. In addition, there are glimmers of hope that Americans will join most of the industrialized world and finally abandon capital punishment.

The economic and fiscal crisis impacting the nation at the community level has weakened the urge to build more prison and jail cells and continue the expansion of the corrections system. However, saving money for its own sake is not the best motivational tool for progressive reforms. A new wave of litigation on violations of the Bill of Rights and other illegal practices in corrections is a growing reality. Lawsuits get the attention of public officials who might otherwise choose to cast a blind eye on problems in the correctional system. How successfully these legal challenges are translated into real reforms remains a mystery.

Certainly, leadership from the very top is an essential ingredient to success. Emboldened during his second term, President Obama has revisited the reformation of criminal justice policy. As part of what he has called "an important first step toward restoring fundamental ideals of justice and fairness," Obama commuted the sentences of eight nonviolent prisoners—a symbolic gesture, to be sure. In clear recognition of racial disproportion, he has supported Attorney General Eric Holder to review the prosecutorial practices that contribute to the problem. He was also quoted as saying that "middle-class kids don't get locked up for smoking pot, and poor kids do."[25] Building on previous legislation to close the gap in sentencing for powder versus crack cocaine, Congress members are cosponsoring a bipartisan bill to allow for the review of more than 8,000 crack cocaine sentences.

Many key questions about sustained reform persist as we go forward. Can gradual and marginal improvements be implemented despite the traditional resistance within corrections to even minor movements toward more humane treatment of prisoners? Should prisons as we know them be abolished? And if this is our goal, what are the alternatives to handling very dangerous and violent criminals? Should we seek to break the public sector dominance of running prisons and rely more heavily on the private sector? Or should we restrict privatization of corrections by favoring much more stringent public regulation of for-profit entities?

Some have argued for a paradigm shift in corrections that moves away from punishment and deterrence and toward "restorative justice." Restorative correctional programs seek to hold lawbreakers accountable to their victims and to the community but in ways that do not disable or destroy them for life. There are also ideas about ramping up the process of helping prisoners reenter society in a positive and supportive way and to do more to educate inmates and promote their employment after release. Other conversations about changing corrections include explorations about "trauma-informed therapy," given the reality that many inmates are themselves victims of severe mental and physical violence. As our public philosopher Pogo observed, "We are facing an insurmountable opportunity." Not since the 1960s has the political and social climate for meaningful reform in the United States been more promising. No one can predict where the corrections system will head in the next few decades. This uncertainty will create "insurmountable opportunities" for those with energy, passion, and the willingness to be part of the transformation process. Hopefully, some of the readers of this text will take up this quest.

It is also worth noting the wisdom of the great American sociologist C. Wright Mills, who reminded us that the personal problems of individuals need to be understood within the political and social structure. As one contemplates the deep personal suffering and anxiety embedded in the correctional system, whether of victims, offenders, family members, or system workers, it is crucial to maintain sight of the political and social structures of race, class, gender, and extreme poverty that underpin the system crisis and lie at the heart of its amelioration.

▲ Open door
© iStockphoto.com/ fhogue

DISCUSSION QUESTIONS

1. Discuss ways in which you see minor drug use more tolerated in society.

2. Design and write a set of poll questions that address the subject of the public's attitudes toward using prison, jail, or community corrections for low-level drug offenders.

3. What is the relationship between correctional policy and electoral politics in your state?

4. What are the political tensions between conservatives and republicans with respect to corrections policy?

5. Discuss the dilemma of rural communities that rely on prisons versus the need to reduce the prison population.

6. Research some of the political alliances of the corrections department in your state. Are there victims' groups involved?

KEY TERMS

Prison industrial complex, 375

Referendum, 385

Social integration, 373

Stimulus package, 388

Stop and frisk, 386

NOTES

1. O'Brien 2012
2. Guerino, Harrison, and Sabol 2011
3. National Prison Divestment Campaign 2013
4. Lydersen 2009; Mann 2008; Santos 2008
5. Death Penalty Focus 2013a
6. Ridder/Braden Inc. 2001
7. ACLU 2001
8. Cohen, Rust, and Steen 2003
9. Krisberg, Craine, and Marchionna 2004
10. Baldassare 2005
11. NCSC 2006
12. FAMM 2008
13. Krisberg and Marchionna 2007
14. Hartney and Marchionna 2009
15. Pew Research Center 2012
16. Lbid.
17. Florida TaxWatch 2012
18. Fagan 2010
19. Ifill 2010
20. Kaplan 2012
21. O'Connor 1973
22. Harris 2009
23. Pew Research Center 2011
24. Field Research 2013
25. Sherer and Rhodan 2014, 32

$SAGE edge™

Sharpen your skills with SAGE edge at edge.sagepub.com/krisberg

SAGE edge for students provides a personalized approach to help you accomplish your coursework goals in an easy-to-use learning environment. This site includes action plans, mobile-friendly eFlashcards and web quizzes as well as web, audio, and video resources and links to SAGE journal articles.

Glossary

abolitionist: A person who favors the abolition of any law or practice they deem harmful to society: for example, there are abolitionists who are opposed to capital punishment (2).

abscond: To fail to appear in court on an appointed day or to fail to report to one's probation or parole officer or to make them aware of a change of residence (4).

accreditation: A formal process to certify competency, authority, or credibility (10).

adjudication: A court's decision regarding the guilt or innocence of a defendant (5).

amicus brief: Arguments presented by "friends" of the court on points of law relevant to the subject of a case, often one of broad public interest (10).

arraignment: A court proceeding to read criminal charges in the presence of the defendant and hear his plea of guilty or not guilty (4).

Auburn System: A 19th-century penal system in which prisoners would perform silent labor in groups by day and be placed in solitary confinement by night (2).

bail: A deposit made to the court in exchange for the release of a defendant from jail and to help ensure his or her appearance at trial. The amount for bail is set by the court (4).

booking: The process by which jail staff register charges against a person held for a law violation (4).

boot camp: A program for juvenile offenders characterized by strict discipline, hard physical exercise, and community labor (2).

case management system: Computer programs that assist caseworkers with many aspects of their work, such as recording and tracking client data (contact information, background, court orders, risk assessment scores, drug test results, GPS monitoring, progress toward meeting conditions, etc.); recording daily work flow notes (i.e., how an officer spent his or her day); integrating client data with information from the court, law enforcement, and other agencies; receiving automated recommendations regarding how best to approach each case; and assistance in meeting agency policies and reporting requirements (5).

caseload: The total body of client cases under a probation or parole officer's care. Also, a probation or parole specialty, such as intensive supervision or domestic violence (5).

chemical and mechanical force: The use of chemical agents, such as pepper spray, or mechanical restraints, such as handcuffs, straitjackets, or shackles, to control behavior or exact punishment (8).

civil rights: Personal liberties granted by virtue of an individual's status as a citizen or resident of a country or community. Most commonly, civil rights refers to those guaranteed by the Constitution, such as freedom of speech and freedom from discrimination (1).

classification system: The grouping of corrections-involved individuals according to their risk of further behavioral problems, which is meant to allow corrections managers to use the most appropriate and cost-effective level of security and supervision (2).

community supervision: Various forms of noncustodial supervision where offenders are allowed to live in the community while remaining under the jurisdiction of the court or corrections agency, similar to and including probation and parole, and usually with the condition that failure will entail time behind bars (1).

commuting: The reduction in the length or severity of a sentence (e.g., the reduction of the death penalty to life in prison), usually by the discretion of a chief executive (governor or U.S. president) or a parole board (7).

compassionate release: The early release of an elderly, terminally ill, or incapacitated inmate so that he or she can receive end-of-life care near family and friends while also relieving the burden of expensive medical care from the corrections department. Sometimes called medical parole or medical furlough, it can also be granted to those with a loved one in need of their care or for other extraordinary circumstances, and it can be subject to conditions of parole including the return to prison if the inmate's health or situation improves (13).

conditions of confinement: The overall terms and conditions for prisoners, derived from the 8th Amendment, including such matters as basic rights and humane physical, medical, and psychological care (1).

conditions of probation: The terms or requirements that an offender must meet to maintain his or her probation status and avoid incarceration. Conditions typically require the offender to keep in contact with a probation officer, maintain employment, avoid criminal behavior, and participate in any court-ordered programming (5).

consent decree: A binding agreement between parties in a lawsuit for the withdrawal of a criminal charge or civil litigation. The decree acknowledges the voluntary cessation of the lawbreaking behavior relevant in the case (6).

contact standards: The prescribed frequency, location, purpose, and processes for meetings between probation or parole officers and their clients (9).

contempt of court: A charge of disobeying or disrespecting the court's authority in the context of a trial or hearing (4).

contraband: Any item that is prohibited. In prison, this could include cell phones or cigarettes as well as drugs or weapons (6).

conviction: When an individual is found by a court of law to be guilty of a criminal offense (3).

corrections: The punishment, supervision, and treatment of individuals suspected or convicted of criminal or delinquent offenses and the various legal and extralegal entities involved in carrying out that function (1).

criminalization: De facto or formal (by law) designation of particular behavior or characteristics as illegal and punishable. Also, a widening of the scope of the types of behavior that are considered criminal or delinquent, including behaviors that the "offender" cannot control, such as acting out on the part of the mentally ill (7).

criminogenic: Tending to give rise to crime or criminality. The factors that generate an individual or group's tendency to commit crime (6).

criminogenic needs: Changeable characteristics and circumstances found in research to be correlated to criminal behavior, especially that place an individual at risk of reoffending during or after correction-systems involvement, such as drug addiction or joblessness (3).

cruel and unusual: The Eighth Amendment of the U.S. Constitution protects Americans against cruel and unusual punishments—those that are unacceptable because they subject a person to undue pain, suffering, or humiliation (6).

cultural competence: An ability to interact effectively with people of different cultural backgrounds. This requires self-awareness of culture, knowledge of the other culture, and an open attitude (11).

custody: Detention in a prison or jail or being held under guard of law enforcement authorities (1).

decriminalization: The process of reducing or abolishing criminal penalties related to a certain action or behavior (3).

dehumanization: Intentional or unintentional treatment of offenders as less than human by ignoring or depriving them of normal human qualities such as respect, compassion, and individuality (1).

deinstitutionalization: The systematic release or removal of offenders from an institution, especially secure residential facilities, for placement and care in the community (8).

delinquency: An illegal offense or misdeed, especially one committed by a juvenile. Also, habitual misconduct by a minor (8).

detention: Holding suspects or defendants as they await court processing prior to trial and a determination of guilt or innocence. More generally, any form of custody or physical control by authorities. In the field of corrections, the term usually refers to pretrial custody, the purpose of which is to ensure the defendant appears in court and does not commit additional offenses (1).

determinate sentence: A sentence to confinement for a fixed or minimum period that is specified by statute (3).

deterrence: The use of punishment, or the threat of punishment, to discourage individuals from committing crime (1).

disciplinary segregation: Placing an inmate in a separate cell for the purposes of punishment and discipline following an incident, a rule infraction, or other disruption (6).

discretionary parole: A term of parole determined by a parole board or other paroling authority. A certain portion of the court's sentence must be served prior to the granting of parole (7).

disenfranchisement: Depriving an individual of the right to vote or, more generally, of full participation in civic life (6).

disparity: A difference in the likelihood that individuals of different race or ethnicity will have some particular outcome, such as being sentenced to incarceration after a drug conviction (3).

diversion: Programing designed to enable law violators to avoid incarceration, criminal charges, or a criminal record (3).

double jeopardy: Prosecuting, trying, or punishing twice for the same instance of a criminal act when the first prosecution led to an acquittal, a conviction, or certain types of mistrial; forbidden by the Fifth Amendment (14).

due process rights: Broadly, due process is an entitlement or legally binding guarantee that established principles and procedures are applied uniformly to each case. Specifically, due process may mean different things in different proceedings, but usually every defendant gets an advance notice of hearings and an opportunity to be present, to be heard, and to defend himself or herself. It also typically includes the rights to legal counsel, to confront and cross-examine the witnesses, to not have to testify against oneself, and to have an offense proven beyond a reasonable doubt (5).

DUI: Driving Under the Influence, also DWI (Driving While Intoxicated), is the crime of operating a motor vehicle with impaired abilities. Measuring blood alcohol level is one way of determining a driver's intoxication status (3).

early release: Release from custody or supervision prior to completion of original sentence, often due to good behavior or to relieve facility overcrowding (5).

Eighth Amendment: Excessive bail shall not be required, nor excessive fines imposed, nor cruel and unusual punishments inflicted (10).

Enlightenment: Refers to a movement that took place primarily in Europe during the 17th and 18th centuries that impacted the arts, sciences, philosophy, and other intellectual fields. Its participants sought to reform society through reason (2).

euthanasia: Painlessly ending the life of a person or animal for the purpose of relieving suffering; mercy killing (14).

evidence-based practice: Practices that have been proved to be effective through rigorous and quantitative analysis (5).

evidentiary hearing: A preliminary hearing after a criminal complaint has been filed by the prosecutor, to determine whether there is enough evidence to require a trial. In the United States, the judge must find it probable that a crime was committed.

exoneration: To clear from suspicion, accusation, or blame (14).

fact finder: In a trial of a lawsuit or criminal prosecution, the jury or judge (if there is no jury) who decides if facts have been proved. Also called a finder of fact (10).

Federalism: The principle of government that defines the relationship between the national government and the states whereby each state owns an exclusive sphere of power and authority, while other powers must be shared (10).

forensics: The use of science and technology to investigate and establish facts in criminal or civil courts of law (9).

Fourteenth Amendment: All persons born or naturalized in the United States, and subject to the jurisdiction thereof, are citizens of the United States and of the state wherein they reside. No state shall make or enforce any law which shall abridge the privileges or immunities of citizens of the United States; nor shall any state deprive any person of life, liberty, or property, without due process of law; nor deny to any person within its jurisdiction the equal protection of the laws (10).

galley slavery: A sentence forcing the convict to work as a rower on a ship. At times, this sentence replaced the death penalty and was used to provide a labor pool for military and merchant ships (2).

gender-responsive: Attentive, aware, and accommodating of the particular needs of women and girls (4).

global positioning system (GPS): Technology used to electronically track the whereabouts of persons under supervision, generally probation or parole, and usually in the form of an ankle bracelet (2).

good-time credits: Time reduction of a sentence length based on the prisoner's problem-free behavior in custody. The number of days taken off the sentence is usually calculated using a specific formula determined by law, such as one day of credit for every two days of "good time" (6).

graduated sanctions: A set of correctional responses to misbehavior that grow in severity as the misbehavior is repeated or becomes more serious (7).

grievance: An official statement of complaint about wrong done to a person. Prisoners may file a grievance with officials about infringements on their rights or unfair or inhumane treatment. Facilities must have a policy and procedure in place for processing and responding to inmate grievances (1).

habeas corpus: A court summons that demands that the custodian present to the prisoner or a representative of the prisoner proof of lawful authority to detain the prisoner. Habeas corpus is intended to prevent the state from detaining individuals capriciously or arbitrarily (6).

halfway house: A residence for newly released prisoners where they can live and gradually reintegrate into their home community while still benefiting from support and supervision. Also known as residential reentry centers (6).

house of corrections: Facilities established in the late 16th century for the punishment and reform of the poor convicted of petty offenses through hard labor. London contained the first house of corrections, Bridewell (2).

House of Refuge: A type of early prison for juvenile delinquents begun in New York, similar to adult houses of correction (8).

incapacitation: A method of preventing crime by removing the offender from the community (1).

indeterminate sentencing: A method of sentencing whereby judges fix maximum and minimum limits to the offender's period of supervision, with the actual release date controlled later by a board of parole. The indeterminate sentence allows judges discretion in consideration of the defendant's behavior, circumstances, and potential for reform (2).

Jim Crow laws: Laws enacted after the end of the Civil War that enforced complete racial segregation and that helped to maintain the subjugation of former slaves (2).

judicial reprieve: An early form of probation where, at the discretion of a judge, lawbreakers could avoid time behind bars if they avoided further criminal behavior (5).

jurisdiction: (1) The authority to make pronouncements on legal matters and administer justice within a defined area of responsibility. (2) The political-geographical region with decision-making authority (5).

jurisprudence: The theory or philosophy of law (1).

Ku Klux Klan: The Ku Klux Klan (KKK) is a White supremacist group founded in 1866. The secret fraternal organization is notorious for acts of terrorism—including murder, lynching, arson, rape, and bombing—to oppose civil rights or any other civic gains for African Americans (11).

litmus test: A pivotal political issue that demonstrates whether a candidate for office or appointment leans far enough conservative or liberal to please his or her target constituency. It is a metaphor taken from a scientific measure of the relative acidity or alkalinity of a given substance (1).

lockdown: Confining inmates to their cells to regain or maintain facility security in response to a fight, a riot, an escape, or other serious disturbance. During a lockdown, which could last minutes, hours, or days, inmate movement about the facility for meals, recreation, classes, or programming is prohibited (6).

Magna Carta: A document that set out a series of laws establishing the rights of the English nobility and limiting the authority of the throne, signed in 1215 (10).

malingering: Exaggerating or faking symptoms of illness to receive special care or avoid duties or work (12).

mandatory parole: A nondiscretionary release mechanism whereby a parole release date is set during sentencing (7).

mug shot: An official photograph taken for an individual's police record, usually when that individual is booked into jail (4).

net-widening: Applying sanctions to individuals who would otherwise have been only warned or released had those sanctions not existed. This can be an unintended consequence of expanding the range of correctional options (4).

noncriminogenic needs: Individual characteristics and circumstances that may be or seem to be related to criminal behavior but which research has not found to be directly correlated to offending or reoffending, such as low self-esteem and depression (3).

paralegal: A person trained to undertake and assist with legal work but not specifically qualified as an attorney (9).

parole: The provisional release to community supervision by a parole officer. The parolee agrees to supervision conditions and serves the completion of the sentence out of custody (4).

parole board: A panel of individuals that decides whether an offender should be released from prison to parole after serving at least a minimum portion of his or her sentence, as prescribed by the sentencing judge (3).

pat search: Also called a frisk or pat down, a pat search is a search of a person's body for weapons or contraband by running the hands over the subject's clothing (13).

penal systems: Methods or approaches relating to, used for, or prescribing the punishment of offenders under the legal system (2).

penology: The study of the punishment of crime and the management of incarceration facilities (2).

Pennsylvania System: A 19th-century penal system advocated by some Quakers, in which prisoners were kept in solitary confinement and expected to repent and reform through contemplation of their sins and God. In practice, many prisoners developed mental illnesses (2).

perjury: Lying in court after vowing to "tell the truth, the whole truth, and nothing but the truth"; to render (oneself) guilty of swearing falsely or of willfully making a false statement under oath or solemn affirmation (11).

petition: A formal application made to a court in writing that requests action on a certain matter (10).

plea bargain: An agreement between the prosecutor and the defendant whereby the defendant pleads guilty to a (usually lesser) charge in return for some concession from the prosecutor (3).

presentence investigation: An investigation of a person convicted of a crime, which is used to produce a presentence investigation report to the court and to inform the judge and the sentencing outcome (3).

pretrial services: Processing, supervising, and providing services to defendants awaiting trial while free in the community, with the purpose of avoiding the unnecessary use of detention while still ensuring the defendant appears in court as required and avoids criminal conduct (4).

prison: Detention facilities operated either by state governments or by the Federal Bureau of Prisons (BOP) that are designed to hold individuals who have been convicted of crimes and who are serving sentences of a year or more (1).

prison industrial complex: Attributes the rapid expansion of the use of prison to the political influence of private companies that reap financial benefits from that expansion through the provision of materials and services (16).

privatization: The process of outsourcing traditionally state- or government-run services to private companies (15).

probable cause: Sufficient reason based upon known facts to believe a crime has been committed or that certain property is connected with a crime (5).

probation: A court-ordered period of conditional correctional supervision in the community, generally served as an alternative to incarceration (4).

prosecutor: The legal party responsible for presenting the case in a criminal trial on behalf of the public against an individual accused of breaking criminal law (4).

prosocial: Actions and behaviors that are beneficial to the larger society (5).

protective custody: In custody situations, this is a means of shielding prisoners from a threat originating outside or inside the prison. It could be simply changing housing units or could involve the use of special cells or solitary confinement (6).

racial profiling: Consideration of race, ethnicity, or national origin by an officer of the law in deciding when and how to intervene in an enforcement capacity. The selection by authorities of certain types of persons they think are more likely to commit crime (11).

random sample: A small part of something intended as representative of the whole in which every element has an equal chance of being selected. Also, the set of participants under study in certain types of highly rigorous research (8).

receiver: A person or entity authorized as a custodian for an agency (or business) when that agency fails to meet its mandated or financial obligations—considered a remedy of last resort (10).

recidivism: The return to criminal behavior after being supervised for a conviction. In research, recidivism is measured over a given period (e.g., 12 months following release from prison) and is defined in various ways, such as arrest, conviction, or incarceration for a new offense (3).

reentry: The process through which incarcerated individuals return to society after serving their sentence (7).

referendum: A form of direct democracy, a ballot vote in which the electorate is asked to accept or reject a proposition (16).

rehabilitation: Restoring or establishing an offender's ability to contribute constructively to his or her individual and community well-being, usually through correctional programming and treatment services targeting the issues that led to his or her criminal behavior (1).

remand: When a case is sent back from a higher court to a lower court for further action or when an offender is returned to custody (4).

residential: Facilities where corrections-involved individuals, especially juveniles, live under 24/7 supervision (8).

restitution: A repayment of money or services to the victim or to society, which may be mandated as part of an offender's sentence (3).

restorative justice: An approach to repairing the harm caused by crime through cooperative practices among victims, offenders, and the community (3).

retributive justice: A theory of justice that sees punishment and exacting just deserts as the best response to crime (3).

revocation: The formal withdrawal of probation or parole status after a court determines the offender has not met the conditions of release, usually resulting incarceration (4).

risk assessment: The process for determining the level of security and supervision corrections-involved individuals require. Risk assessment usually uses a written checklist of weighted criteria (e.g., an assessment instrument or screening tool) that is used to estimate the likelihood that an individual will have disciplinary issues while in custody or will commit offenses after release (12).

risk assessment instrument: A tool used to examine relevant factors to measure an offender's risk of recidivism or risk of violent behavior (3).

risk factors: Individual characteristics and background found by research to be correlated to criminal behavior, especially to reoffending during or after correction-system involvement, such as current offense type and severity, prior offense history and system involvement, and mental health history (3).

secure confinement: Custody or detention that involves locked spaces that are controlled by agency authorities (6).

sentence: The punishment declared by the court to a defendant for being found guilty for a crime, such as a period of incarceration, a period of community supervision, or payment of a fine (3).

sentencing commission: A professional panel charged with determining sentencing options for a given jurisdiction (3).

sentencing guidelines: A set of sentencing minimums and maximums for specific crimes. Guidelines are designed to bring more judicial uniformity to sentencing policy (3).

slave codes: U.S. laws under slavery that governed the relationship between slaves and slave owners and that gave slave owners absolute power over slaves (3).

smart on crime: A buzzword in recent years representing a response to crime that considers such factors as punishments appropriate to offense severity, recidivism reduction, cost-effectiveness, public safety, and equity (1).

social integration: Breaking down societal barriers between different racial, ethnic, and class groups so that minorities and the underprivileged can move into the mainstream (16).

solitary confinement: Special imprisonment where the inmate is isolated from human contact. Solitary is intended as an additional punishment but is sometimes used for protective custody or suicide watch. Solitary confinement tends to create or exacerbate mental illness (1).

special master: A representative of the court appointed to hear a case involving difficult or specialized issues; an expert whose expertise assists the court or who may help administer a claim (10).

stigma: A social or perceived stain on a person's reputation, often suffered unfairly due to the prejudice of others (13).

specialty courts: Courts that focus on a single kind of offense, such as drug offenses. The judge plays the role of intensive supervisor and collaborates with social service agencies to carry out case management and to address underlying issues (7).

status offenses: Behavior that is prohibited only for minors. Status offenses may include consumption of alcohol, tobacco smoking, truancy, breaking curfew, and running away from home. These acts may be illegal for minors, but are legal for all others (8).

stimulus package: Steps taken by the federal government to stimulate the U.S. economy and, in particular, to facilitate recovery after the severe recession in the late 2000s, including mortgage assistance to home owners, lowered interest rates, and increased government spending (16).

stop and frisk: Also referred to as stop, question, and frisk, a program originated in New York City in which officers can stop pedestrians and search them for weapons or contraband. The criteria for what constitutes reasonable suspicion are very loose and has been challenged in the courts (16).

strip search: The search of a person's body for weapons or contraband that requires removal of clothing. Performing such a search requires legal authority (4).

supermax: "Super-maximum-security prisons," which are the most extremely fortified form of incarceration in the United States, and intended to house high-risk individuals convicted of serious crimes (6).

technical violations: A breach of those conditions of probation (or parole) that on their own would not be considered criminal or would not lead to criminal proceedings, such as failing to hold down a job or failing a drug test (5).

terms of supervised release: A sentence of a period of correctional supervision in the community following, as part of the same sentence, a period of incarceration. Violating the terms of supervised release may lead to a new sentence of incarceration and additional supervised release (7).

therapeutic communities: A holistic rehabilitative treatment model emphasizing personal growth and lifestyle change through self-help, positive behavior reinforcement, and group decision making (6).

therapeutic justice: An approach to justice that considers the therapeutic harm and benefits experienced by people engaging with the system (3).

three strikes: Statutes that mandate courts to impose harsher sentences on habitual offenders convicted of three or more serious offenses (3).

training school: A residential facility that offers vocational training to juvenile offenders (8).

transportation: A sentence primarily used in the 17th and 18th centuries in which the convict was exiled and transported, usually by ship, to a penal colony (2).

tribal territories: Also referred to as reservations, these are areas of land managed by the federal government and dedicated to Native peoples (11).

truth in sentencing: Policy stemming from the belief that convicts should serve the period that they have been sentenced to and not be allowed to earn good-time credit toward a parole release (3).

unconditional release: Exit from prison after full sentence completion, so there is no further obligation to the state. These individuals are not subject to any further correctional supervision (7).

U.S. Sentencing Commission: A federal agency created in 1984 to establish guidelines for appropriate sentencing policy and practice in U.S. federal courts and to assist other branches of government in establishing effective crime policy (13).

violation: An act that violates or breaks the law (1).

waiver: A transfer of a juvenile case to the adult criminal court, by the prosecutor, by the judge, or according to statute (11).

War on Drugs: The collective policies, laws, and practices intended to reduce the trade and use of illegal drugs (3).

writ: A court order (10).

wrongful death: A death that results from a wrongful act or from negligence. In the criminal justice system, the execution of an innocent person is a wrongful death (8).

zero tolerance: A policy, usually in schools, of punishing every instance of rule breaking, regardless of any extenuating circumstances such as accidental infractions or first-time offenses. Zero-tolerance policies are often applied to specific infractions, such as fighting or possession of drugs or weapons (12).

References

Abner, Carrie. "Graying Prisons: States Face the Challenge of an Aging Inmate Population." *State News* (2006), 8–11.

Abrams, David S. "Is Pleading Really a Bargain?" *Journal of Empirical Legal Studies* 8 (2011): 200–21.

Acoca, Leslie. "Defusing the Time Bomb: Understanding and Meeting the Growing Health Care Needs of Incarcerated Women in America." *Crime & Delinquency* 44 (1998): 49–69.

Acoca, Leslie, and Kelly Dedel. *No Place to Hide: Understanding and Meeting the Needs of Girls in the California Juvenile Justice System.* San Francisco: National Council on Crime and Delinquency, 1998.

Adams, Jill. "Unlocking Liberty: Is California's Habeas Law the Key to Freeing Unjustly Imprisoned Battered Women?" *Berkeley Women's Law Journal* 19 (2005): 217.

Adams, Kenneth, Katherine J. Bennett, Timothy J. Flanagan, James W. Marquart, Steven J. Cuvelier, Eric Fritsch, Jurg Gerber, Dennis R. Longmire, and Velmer S. Burton, Jr. "A Large-Scale Multidimensional Test of the Effect of Prison Education Programs on Offenders' Behavior." *The Prison Journal* 74 (1994): 443–449.

Administrative Office of the Courts. *A Preliminary Look at California Parole Reentry Courts.* San Francisco: Author, 2012a.

Administrative Office of the Courts. *Reentry Courts: Looking Ahead.* Washington, DC. U.S. Department of Justice Bureau of Justice Assistance, Center for Court Innovation, 2012b.

Alarcon, Arthur L., and Paula M. Mitchell. "Executing the Will of the Voters: A Roadmap to Mend or End the California Legislature's Multi-billion Dollar Death Penalty Debacle." *Loyola of Los Angeles Law Review* 44 (2011): S41.

Aleph Institute. "About." *Prison Programs,* n.d. http://aleph-institute.org/prison-programs.html, accessed April 28, 2014.

Alexander, Michelle. *The New Jim Crow: Mass Incarceration in the Age of Color Blindness.* New York: New Press, 2010.

Alexander, Michelle. *The New Jim Crow.* New York: The New Press, 2012.

American Civil Liberties Union. "Optimism, Pessimism, and Jailhouse Redemption: American Attitudes on Crime, Punishment, and Over-incarceration," 2001. http://www.prisonpolicy.org/scans/overincarceration_survey.pdf, accessed January 14, 2014.

American Civil Liberties Union. *In for a Penny: The Rise of America's New Debtors' Prisons.* New York: Author, 2010. https://www.aclu.org/prisoners-rights-racial-justice/penny-rise-americas-new-debtors-prisons, accessed February 3, 2014.

American Civil Liberties Union. "Reason #2 to Support a National Moratorium on the Death Penalty: Police and Prosecutorial Misconduct Are Common in Death Cases," n.d. http://www.prisonpolicy.org/scans/aclu_dp_factsheet2.pdf, accessed January 6, 2014.

American Civil Liberties Union of Georgia and Georgia Detention Watch. *Securely Insecure: The Real Costs, Consequences and Human Face of Immigration Detention.* Washington, DC: Detention Watch Network, 2011. http://www.georgiadetentionwatch.com/documents/, accessed January 14, 2014.

American Civil Liberties Union of Ohio. *Prisons for Profit: A Look at Prison Privatization.* Cleveland: Author, 2011.

American Correctional Association. *Standards for Adult Local Detention Facilities.* 3rd ed. Lanham, MD: Author, 1991.

American Correctional Association. *Standards and Accreditation.* Alexandria, VA: Author, n.d. https://www.aca.org/standards/, accessed February 14, 2014.

American Federation of State, County, and Municipal Employees. *Making a Killing: How Prison Corporations Are Profiting From Campaign Contributions and Putting Taxpayers at Risk.* Washington, DC: Author, 2011.

American Friends Service Committee. *Struggle for Justice.* New York: Farrar, Straus & Giroux, 1971.

American Probation and Parole Association. *Position Statement: Weapons.* Lexington, KY: Author, 1994. http://www.appa-net.org/eweb/Dynamicpage.aspx?site=APPA_2&webcode=IB_Position Statement&wps_key=e2e8033–bed-4d64-a044-ea98ee53bd17, accessed January 24, 2014.

American Probation and Parole Association. *Peace Officer Status of Probation and Parole Officers.* Lexington, KY: Author, 2006a.

American Probation and Parole Association. *Caseload Standards for Probation and Parole.* Lexington, KY: Author, 2006b. http://www.appa-net.org/eweb/docs/APPA/stances/ip_CSPP.pdf, accessed January 24, 2014.

American Probation and Parole Association. *Probation and Parole FAQs.* Lexington, KY: Author, 2012. http://www.appa-net.org/eweb/DynamicPage.aspx?WebCode=VB_FAQ, accessed September 2, 2012.

Amnesty International. "Not Part of My Sentence: Violations of the Human Rights of Women in Custody." Author, 1999. http://www.amnesty.org/en/library/asset/AMR51/019/1999/en/7588269a-e33d-11dd-808b-bfd8d459a3de/amr510191999en.pdf, accessed November 20, 2011.

Amnesty International. "Death Penalty Facts," 2012. http://www.amnestyusa.org/pdfs/DeathPenaltyFactsMay2012.pdf, accessed May 31, 2014.

Amnesty International. "Death Penalty and Innocence," 2013. http://www.amnestyusa.org/our-work/issues/death-penalty/us-death-penalty-facts/death-penalty-and-innocence, accessed January 6, 2014.

Anderson, Lucas. "Kicking the National Habit: The Legal and Policy Arguments for Abolishing Private Prison Contracts." *Public Contracts Law Journal* 39 (2009): 113.

Andrews, D. A., James Bonta, and J. Stephen Wormith. "The Recent Past and Near Future of Risk and/or Need Assessment." *Crime & Delinquency* 52 (2006): 7–27.

Annie E. Casey Foundation. *Juvenile Detention Alternatives Initiative 2011 Results Report Summary.* Baltimore: Author, 2013. http://www.aecf.org/~/media/Pubs/Initiatives/Juvenile%20Detention%20Alternatives%20Initiative/JDAIResultsReport2011/JDAIResults2011.pdf, accessed December 30, 2013.

Anno, B. Jaye, Camilia Graham, James E. Lawrence, and Ronald Shansky. *Correctional Health Care: Addressing the Needs of Elderly, Chronically Ill and Terminally Ill Inmates.* Washington, DC: U.S. Department of Justice, National Institute of Justice, 2004.

Aos, Steve. *Washington State's Family Integrated Transitions Program for Juvenile Offenders: Outcome Evaluation and Benefit-Cost Analysis.* Olympia: Washington State Institute for Public Policy, 2004.

Aos, Steve, Marna Miller, and Elizabeth Drake. *Evidence-Based Adult Corrections Programs: What Works and What Does Not.* Olympia: Washington State Institute for Public Policy, 2006a.

Aos, Steve, Marna Miller, and Elizabeth Drake. *Evidence-Based Public Policy Options to Reduce Future Prison Construction, Criminal Justice Costs, and Crime Rates.* Olympia: Washington State Institute for Public Policy, 2006b.

Aos, Steve, Polly Phipps, Robert Barnoski, and Roxanne Lieb. *The Comparative Costs and Benefits of Programs to Reduce Crime, v 4.0.* Olympia: Washington State Institute for Public Policy, 2001.

Aos, Steve, Polly Phipps, and Kim Korinek. *Research Findings on Adult Corrections' Programs: A Review.* Olympia: Washington State Institute for Public Policy, 1999.

Arax, Mark. "Guard Challenges Code of Silence." *Los Angeles Times,* January 20, 2004. http://articles.latimes.com/2004/jan/20/local/me-guard20, accessed January 4, 2013.

Archibold, Randall C. "Arizona Enacts Stringent Law on Immigration." *New York Times,* April 23, 2010. http://www.nytimes.com/2010/04/24/us/politics/24immig.html?_r=0, accessed January 14, 2014.

Arizona Department of Corrections. "FY 2010 Operating Per Capita Cost Report: Cost Identification and Comparison of State and Private Contract Beds," 2011. http://www.azcorrections.gov/adc/reports/ADC_FY2010_PerCapitaRep.pdf, accessed January 14, 2014.

Arizona v. United States, 567 U.S. ___, 132 S. Ct. 2492, 2012.

Armstrong v. Wilson, 124 F.3d 1019, 9th Cir., 1997.

Ashton, Paul, and Amanda Petteruti. *Gaming the System: How the Political Strategies of Private Prison Companies Promote Ineffective Incarceration Policies.* Washington, DC: Justice Policy Institute, 2011.

Asmar, Melanie. "Can Private Probation Companies Be Both Monitor and Counselor for Clients?" *Denver Westword,* August 23, 2012. www.westword.com/2012–08–23/news/private-probation-double-dipping/full/, accessed February 3, 2014. Associated Press. "Former Pennsylvania Judge Sentenced in Kickbacks Case." *Wall Street Journal,* 2011. http://online.wsj.com/article/SB10001424053111903791504576589010561506234.html, accessed January 14, 2014.

Atkins v. Virginia, 536. U.S. 304, 2002.

Austin, James. *Findings in Prison Classification and Risk Assessment.* Washington, DC: National Institute of Corrections, Federal Bureau of Prisons, U.S. Department of Justice, 2003.

Austin, James, and Garry Coventry. *Emerging Issues on Privatized Prisons.* Washington, DC: Bureau of Justice Assistance, 2001.

Austin, James, Robert DeComo, Barry Krisberg, Sonya Rudenstine, and Dominic Del Rosario. *Juveniles Taken Into Custody: Fiscal Year 1993.* Washington, DC: U.S. Department of Justice, Office of Juvenile Justice and Delinquency Prevention, 1995.

Austin, James, and Patricia L. Hardyman. *Objective Prison Classification: A Guide for Correctional Agencies* [Library ID 019319]. Washington, DC: National Institute of Corrections, U.S. Department of Justice, 2004.

Austin, James, Barry Krisberg, Karen Joe, and Paul Steele. *The Impact of Juvenile Court Sanctions.* San Francisco: National Council on Crime and Delinquency, 1998.

Avila, Jim, Mary Harris, and Chris Francescani. "Interview With an Executioner." ABC News, December 17, 2007. http://abcnews.go.com/TheLaw/story?id=4015348&page=1, accessed January 14, 2014.

Baldassare, Mark. "PPIC Statewide Survey: Special Survey on the California State Budget, January 2005." Public Policy Institute of California, January 2005. http://www.ppic.org/main/publication.asp?i=584, accessed January 14, 2014.

Baldus, David C., Charles A. Pulaski, and George C. Woodworth. *Equal Justice and The Death Penalty: A Legal and Empirical Analysis.* Boston: Northeastern University Press, 1990.

Bales, William D., Laura E. Bedard, Susan T. Quinn, David T. Ensley, and Glen P. Holley. "Recidivism of Public and Private State Prison Inmates in Florida." *Criminology & Public Policy* 4 (2005): 57–82.

Bales, William D., and Daniel P. Mears. "Inmate Social Ties and the Transition to Society: Does Visitation Reduce Recidivism?" *Journal of Research in Crime and Delinquency* 45 (2008): 287–321.

Banning, Lance. "Three-Fifths Historian." Claremont Institute, August 31, 2004. https://www.claremont.org/publications/crb/id.821/article_detail.asp, accessed January 10, 2014.

Barnes, Harry E., and Negley K. Teeters. *New Horizons in Criminology: The American Crime Problem.* New York: Prentice-Hall, 1943.

Barnes, Harry E., and Negley K. Teeters. *New Horizons in Criminology: The American Crime Problem.* New York: Prentice Hall, 1945.

Barnoski, Robert, and Steve Aos. *Washington State's Drug Courts for Adult Defendants: Outcome Evaluation and Cost-Benefit Analysis*. Olympia: Washington State Institute for Public Policy, 2003.

Bartollas, Clemens, and Stuart J. Miller. *Juvenile Justice in America*. Englewood Cliffs, NJ: Prentice Hall, 1997.

Baze v. Rees, 533 U.S. 35, 2008.

Bazemore, Gordon, and Dennis Maloney. "Rehabilitating Community Service: Toward Restorative Service in a Balanced Justice System." *Federal Probation* 58 (1994): 24–35.

Bearden v. Georgia, 461 U.S. 660, 662–63, 668–69, 1983.

Beccaria, Cesare. *On Crimes and Punishments*. Translated by Henry Paolucci. Englewood Cliffs, NJ: Prentice Hall, 1963. (Original work published 1764)

Beck, Allen J., David Cantor, John Hartge, and Tim Smith. *Sexual Victimization in Juvenile Facilities Reported by Youth (2012)*. Washington, DC: U.S. Department of Justice, Office of Justice Programs, Office of Juvenile Justice and Delinquency Prevention, 2013. http://www.bjs.gov/index.cfm?ty=pbdetail&iid=4656, accessed December 30, 2013.

Beck, Allen J., and Darrell K. Gilliard. "Prison and Jail Inmates at Midyear, 1996." *Prison and Jail Inmates at Midyear Series* [NCJ 162843]. Washington, DC: U.S. Department of Justice, Office of Justice Programs, Bureau of Justice Statistics, January 19, 1997. http://www.bjs.gov/index.cfm?ty=pbdetail&iid=879, accessed January 27, 2014.

Beck, Allen J., Paul Guerino, and Paige M. Harrison. *Sexual Victimization in Juvenile Facilities Reported by Youth, 2008–09* [NCJ 228416]. Washington, DC: U.S. Department of Justice, Office of Justice Programs, Bureau of Justice Statistics, 2010.

Beck, Allen J., and Candace Johnson. *Sexual Victimization Reported By Former State Prisoners, 2008* [NCJ 237363]. Washington, DC: U.S. Department of Justice, Bureau of Justice Statistics, 2012. http://www.bjs.gov/index.cfm?ty=pbdetail&iid=4312, accessed January 10.

Beck, Allen R. "Deciding on a New Jail Design." *Justice Concepts*, 2006. http://www.justiceconcepts.com/design.htm, accessed January 27, 2014.

Bedard, Kelly, and Ted E. Frech. *Prison Health Care: Is Contracting Out Healthy?* Departmental Working Papers, Department of Economics, University of California at Santa Barbara, 2007.

Belknap, Joanne. *The Invisible Woman: Gender, Crime, and Justice*. Boulder, CO: Wadsworth, Cengage, 2007.

Benzinga Staff. "GEO Acquires B.I. Inc. for $415M," 2010. http://www.benzinga.com/news/10/12/720413/geo-acquires-b-i-inc-for-415m, accessed January 14, 2014.

Berk, Jillian. *Does Work Release Work?* Providence, RI: Brown University, 2007.

Berndt et al. v. California Department of Corrections et al. Order by Judge Hamilton granting 528 motion for judgment on the pleadings, filed on August 27, 2013. http://law.justia.com/cases/federal/district-courts/california/candce/4:2003cv03174/236598/566, accessed February 24, 2014.

Bernstein, Nina. "Ill and in Pain, Detainee Dies in U.S. Hands." *New York Times*, August 12, 2008. http://www.nytimes.com/2008/08/13/nyregion/13detain.html?pagewanted=all, accessed January 5, 2014.

Bernstein, Nina. "Companies Use Immigration Crackdown to Turn a Profit." *New York Times*, September 28, 2011. http://www.nytimes.com/2011/09/29/world/asia/getting-tough-on-immigrants-to-turn-a-profit.html?pagewanted=all, accessed January 14, 2014.

Berry, William W. "Extraordinary and Compelling: A Reexamination of the Justifications for Compassionate Release." *Maryland Law Review* 68 (2012): 850–888. http://digitalcommons.law.umaryland.edu/cgi/viewcontent.cgi?article=3396&context=mlr, accessed February 27, 2014.

Besser, T. L., and M. M. Hanson. "Development of Last Resort: The Impact of New State Prisons on Small Town Economies in the United States." *Journal of the Community Development Society* 35 (2004): 1–16.

Bhati, Avi S., John K. Roman, and Aaron Chalfin. *To Treat or Not to Treat: Evidence on the Prospect of Expanding Treatment to Drug-Involved Offenders*. Washington, DC: Urban Institute, Justice Policy Center, 2008.

Bibas, Stephanos. Regulating the Plea-Bargaining Market: From Caveat Emptor to Consumer Protection. *California Law Review* 99 (2011): 1117.

Bilchik, Shay. "Challenging the Myths." *1999 National Report Series*. Washington, DC: U.S. Department of Justice, Office of Justice Programs, Office of Juvenile Justice and Delinquency Prevention, 2000.

Bilchik, Shay. "Juvenile Justice: A Century of Change." *1999 National Report Series*. Washington, DC: U.S. Department of Justice, Office of Justice Programs, Office of Juvenile Justice and Delinquency Prevention, 1999.

Binswanger, Ingrid A., Patrick M. Krueger, and John F. Steiner. "Prevalence of Chronic Medical Conditions Among Jail and Prison Inmates in the USA Compared With the General Population." *Journal of Epidemiologic Community Health* 63 (2009): 912–919.

Binswanger, Ingrid A., Joseph O. Merrill, Patrick M. Krueger, Mary C. White, Robert E. Booth, and Joann G. Elmore. "Gender Differences in Chronic Medical, Psychiatric, and Substance-Dependence Disorders Among Jail Inmates." *American Journal of Public Health* 3 (2009): 476–482.

Bishop, Donna, and Charles Frazier. "Gender Bias in the Juvenile Justice System: Implications of the JJDP Act." *The Journal of Criminal Law and Criminology* 82 (1992): 1162–1186.

Blackburn, Ashley G., Janet L. Mullings, and James W. Marquart. "Sexual Assault in Prison and Beyond: Toward an Understanding of Lifetime Sexual Assault Among Incarcerated Women." *The Prison Journal* 88 (2008): 361–377.

Bloom, Barbara, and Stephanie Covington. "Addressing the Mental Health Needs of Women Offenders." In *Women's Mental Health Issues Across the Criminal Justice System*, edited by R. Gido and L. Dalley. Columbus, OH: Prentice Hall, 2008.

Bloom, Barbara, and Barbara Owen. *Gender Responsive Strategies: Research, Practice, and Guiding Principles for Women Offenders*. National Institute of Corrections, 2002. http://static.nicic.gov/Library/018017.pdf, accessed November 18, 2011.

Blumstein, Alfred. "On the Racial Disproportionality of United States' Prison Populations." *Journal of Criminal Law and Criminology* 73 (1982): 1259–1281.

Blumstein, Alfred, Jacqueline Cohen, Jeffrey A. Roth, and Christy A. Visher, eds. *Criminal Careers and "Career Criminals."* Washington, DC: National Academies Press, 1986.

Blumstein, James F., Mark A. Cohen, and Suman Seth. *Do Government Agencies Respond to Market Pressures? Evidence From Private Prisons.* Law and Economics Research Paper No. 03–16; Public Law Research Paper No. 03–05. Nashville, TN: Vanderbilt University, 2007.

Bonczar, Thomas P. *Characteristics of State Parole Supervising Agencies, 2006.* Washington, DC: U.S. Department of Justice, Office of Justice Programs, Bureau of Justice Statistics, 2008.

Bonczar, Thomas P. *Table 4. New Court Commitments to State Prison, 2006: Offense, by Sex, Race, and Hispanic Origin: Statistical Table* [NCJ 230186]. Washington, DC: U.S. Department of Justice, Bureau of Justice Statistics, 2010. http://bjs.ojp.usdoj.gov/index.cfm?ty=pbdetail&iid=2065, accessed November 19, 2011.

Bonta, James, and D. A. Andrews. *Risk-Need-Responsivity Model for Offender Assessment and Rehabilitation.* Ottawa: Public Safety Canada, 2007. http://cpoc.memberclicks.net/assets/Realignment/risk_need_2007–06_e.pdf, accessed January 27, 2014.

Bor, David H., and David U. Himmelstein. "The Health and Health Care of US Prisoners: Results of a Nationwide Survey." *American Journal of Public Health* 99 (2009), 666–672.

Bosworth, Mary. *Explaining U.S. Imprisonment.* Thousand Oaks, CA: Sage, 2010.

Bowers, William J., and Glenn L. Pierce. "Deterrence or Brutalization: What Is the Effect of Executions?" *Crime & Delinquency* 26 (1980): 453–484.

Braithwaite, John. *Crime, Shame and Reintegration.* Cambridge: Cambridge University Press, 1989.

Bresler, Laura, and Diane K. Lewis. "Black and White Women Prisoners: Differences in Family Ties and Their Programmatic Implications." *The Prison Journal* 63 (1983): 116–123.

Brewster, Dennis R., and Susan F. Sharp. "Educational Programs and Recidivism in Oklahoma: Another Look." *The Prison Journal* 82(2002): 314–334.

Brockway, Zebulon. *Fifty Years of Prison Service: An Autobiography.* Montclair, NJ: Patterson Smith, 1969.

Brown v. Board of Education, 347 U.S. 483, 1954.

Brown, Brian, and Greg Jolivette. *Three Strikes: The Impact After More Than a Decade.* Sacramento: California Legislative Analyst's Office, 2005. http://www.lao.ca.gov/2005/3_Strikes/3_strikes_102005.pdf, accessed February 2, 2014.

Brown, Cathy. "Lawmakers Pore Over Competing Plans for Prisons." *Juneau Empire,* 2002. http://juneauempire.com/stories/030602/sta_legprisons.shtml, accessed January 14, 2014.

Brown, Julie K. "In Miami Gardens, Store Video Catches Cops in the Act." *Miami Herald,* November 22, 2013.

Brown, Patricia Leigh. "Opening Up, Students Transform a Vicious Circle." *New York Times,* April 3, 2013. http://www.nytimes.com/2013/04/04/education/restorative-justice-programs-take-root-in-schools.html?_r=0, accessed February 14, 2014.

Brown, Patrick K. *The Rise and Fall of Rose Bird: A Career Killed by the Death Penalty.* Master's Thesis, Cal State University, Fullerton, n.d. http://www.cschs.org/02_history/images/CSCHS_2007-Brown.pdf, accessed January 14, 2014.

Bufkin, Sarah. "North Carolina General Assembly Votes to Repeal Landmark Racial Justice Law." *ThinkProgress,* November 29, 2011. http://thinkprogress.org/justice/2011/11/29/377897/nc-general-assembly-repeals-landmark-racial-justice-law/?mobile=nc, accessed January 14, 2014.

Bureau of Justice Statistics. *Data Collection: Annual Survey of Jails.* Washington, DC: U.S. Department of Justice, 2012. http://www.bjs.gov/index.cfm?ty=dcdetail&iid=261, accessed January 27, 2014.

Bureau of Justice Statistics. *Mental Health Problems of Prison and Jail Inmates* [Special Report]. Washington, DC: U.S. Department of Justice, 2006.

Bureau of Justice Statistics. *National Correctional Population Reaches New High* [NCJ 188208]. Washington, DC: U.S. Department of Justice, Bureau of Justice Statistics, 2001. http://bjs.ojp.usdoj.gov/content/pub/pdf/ppus00.pdf, accessed January 15, 2014.

Bureau of Justice Statistics. "National Crime Victimization Survey: 2008–2012," May 23, 2013. http://www.bjs.gov/developer/ncvs/, accessed January 15, 2014.

Burgess, Ernest W. "Factors Determining Success or Failure on Parole." In *The Workings of the Indeterminate Sentence Law and the Parole System in Illinois,* edited by Andrew A. Bruce et al., Part IV. Springfield, IL: The Board of Parole, 1928.

Burke, Peggy, Adam Gelb, and Jake Horowitz. *When Offenders Break the Rules: Smart Responses to Parole and Probation Violations.* Washington, DC: The Pew Charitable Trusts, 2007.

Burke, Peggy, Rachelle Giguere, and Leilah Gilligan. *Special Challenges Facing Parole.* Washington, DC: U.S. Department of Justice, National Institute of Corrections, 2011. http://nicic.gov/Library/024200, retrieved May 9, 2014.

Burrell, William. *Caseload Standards for Probation and Parole.* Lexington, KY: American Probation and Parole Association, 2006.

Bush, Evelyn, Susan Poole, Jeff Shorba, and Dona Zavislan. *Women Are Not Men: Operational Practices for Successful Outcomes with Women Offenders.* Presentation at ACA Conference, Winter 2013. http://www.aca.org/conferences/winter2013/WC2013_Presentations/B-2G%20Women%20Are%20Not%20Men-%20Operational%20Practices%20for%20Successful%20Outcomes%20With%20Women%20Offenders.pdf, accessed January 15, 2014.

Bushway, Shawn D., and Anne M. Piehl. "Social Science Research and the Legal Threat to Presumptive Sentencing." *Law and Society Review* 34 (2007): 733–764.

Byrne, Francine, Nancy Taylor, Amy Nunez, Kelly Parrish, and Danielle Tate. *California Drug Court Cost Analysis Study.* San Francisco: Center for Families, Children and the Courts, California Department of Alcohol and Drug Programs, 2006.

California Budget Project. "What Would Proposition 36 Mean for California." Sacramento: Author, 2012. http://

www.cbp.org/publications/publications.html, accessed February 8, 2014.

California Commission on the Fair Administration of Justice. "Report and Recommendations on the Administration of the Death Penalty in California," 2008. http://www.ccfaj.org/documents/reports/dp/official/FINAL%20REPORT%20DEATH%20PENALTY.pdf, accessed January 14, 2014.

California Department of Corrections and Rehabilitation. *Report to the California State Legislature.* Expert Panel on Adult Offender and Recidivism Reduction Programming. Sacramento: Author, 2007. http://sentencing.nj.gov/downloads/pdf/articles/2007/July2007/document03.pdf, accessed January 27, 2014.

California Department of Corrections and Rehabilitation. *Inmates Sentenced Under the Three Strikes Law and a Small Number of Inmates Receiving Specialty Health Care Represent Significant Costs.* Sacramento: Author, 2010.

California Department of Corrections and Rehabilitation. *Annual Report 2011.* Sacramento, CA: Author, 2011. http://www.cdcr.ca.gov/Reports/CDCR-Annual-Reports.html, accessed December 30, 2013.

California Department of Corrections and Rehabilitation. *Prison Census Data as of June 30, 2012: Table 10.* Sacramento: Author, 2012. http://www.cdcr.ca.gov/Reports_Research/Offender_Information_Services_Branch/Annual/CensusArchive.html, accessed February 8, 2014.

California Department of Corrections and Rehabilitation. *Operations Manual.* Sacramento, CA: Author, 2014. http://www.cdcr.ca.gov/Regulations/Adult_Operations/docs/DOM/dom%202014/2014%20DOM.pdf, accessed April 9, 2014.

California Partnership to End Domestic Violence. "Amicus Brief in the Case of *US v. Munguia*," 2011. http://www.law.berkeley.edu/files/MunguiaAmicus(2011)-Final.pdf, accessed January 15, 2014.

Camp, Camille Graham, and George M. Camp. *Guidelines for Correctional Contracting: A Manual for Correctional Administrators.* South Salem, NY: Criminal Justice Institute, 1987.

Camp, Scott D., and Dawn M. Daggett. "Quality of Operations at Private and Public Prisons: Using Trends in Inmate Misconduct to Compare Prisons." *Justice Research and Policy* 7 (2005): 27–51.

Camp, Scott D., and Gerald G. Gaes. *Growth and Quality of U.S. Private Prisons: Evidence From a National Survey.* Washington, DC: Federal Bureau of Prisons, Office of Research and Evaluation, 2001.

Campaign for Youth Justice. "Ten Years and Waiting: A Decade Since the Passage of the Prison Rape Elimination Act," 2014. http://www.campaignforyouthjustice.org/preac.html, accessed December 13, 2013.

Caplan, Joel M., and Susan C. Kinnevy. "National Surveys of State Paroling Authorities: Models of Service Delivery." *Federal Probation* 74 (2010): 1.

Carlton, Sue. "Will Nurse Be Held to a Higher Standard?" *St. Petersburg Times*, October 6, 2007, 1B.

Carson, E. Ann, and Daniela Golinelli. *Prisoners in 2012—Advance Counts.* Washington, DC: U.S. Department of Justice, Office of Justice Programs, Bureau of Justice Statistics, 2013. http://www.bjs.gov/content/pub/pdf/p12ac.pdf, accessed August 29, 2013.

Carson, E. Ann, and William J. Sabol. "Prisoners in 2011." *Prisoners Series* [NCJ 239808]. Washington, DC: Bureau of Justice Statistics, 2012. http://www.bjs.gov/index.cfm?ty=pbdetail&iid=4559, accessed November 1, 2013.

Carter, Madeline. *Evidence-Based Policy, Practice, and Decisionmaking: Implications for Paroling Authorities.* Washington, DC: U.S. Department of Justice, National Institute of Corrections, 2011. http://nicic.gov/Library/024198, accessed January 24, 2014.

Cassel, Elaine. "Why Do People Want to Be Executioners? A Review of *The Last Face You'll Ever See,* by Ivan Solotaroff." *Psych on the Shelves,* n.d. http://college.cengage.com/psychology/resources/students/shelves/shelves_20020504.html, accessed January 14, 2014.

CBS News. "Killer Who Said He Was Jesus Is Executed," 2009. http://www.cbsnews.com/2100-201_162-208099.html, accessed January 14, 2014.

CBSNews.com. "Five-Year-Old Arrested," April 25, 2005. http://www.cbsnews.com/videos/five-year-old-arrested/ accessed January 15, 2014.

Center for Children's Law and Policy. "JJDPA Reauthorization," n.d. http://www.cclp.org/JJDPA_reauthorization.php, accessed January 31, 2014.

Center on Addition and Substance Abuse. *Behind Bars II: Substance Abuse and America's Prison Population.* New York: Columbia University, 2010. http://www.casacolumbia.org/templates/publications_reports.aspx, accessed November 18, 2011.

Center on Juvenile and Criminal Justice. *Juvenile Justice History.* San Francisco: Author, 2013. http://www.cjcj.org/Education1/Juvenile-Justice-History.html, accessed December 30, 2013.

Centers for Disease Control and Prevention. "The National Intimate Partner and Sexual Violence Survey, 2010," February 6, 2014. http://www.cdc.gov/violenceprevention/nisvs/, accessed May 15, 2014.

Chadwell, Sean. "Public Financing of Private Jails." In *Grassroots Leadership: Considering a Private Jail, Prison, or Detention Center? A Resource Packet for Community Members and Public Officials* 2nd ed. Austin, TX: Grassroots Leadership, 2009.

Chase, Robert T. *Civil Rights on the Cell Block: Race, Reform and Violence in Texas Prisons and the Nation, 1945–1990.* Vanderbilt University, 2009. http://xa.yimg.com/kq/groups/16710831/110612865/name/Chase-Final, accessed November 13, 2011.

Cheeseman, Kelly Ann, Janet L. Mullings, and James W. Marquart. "Inmate Perceptions of Security Staff Across Various Custody Levels." *Corrections Management Quarterly* 5 (2001): 41–47.

Chen, Elsa. "In the Furtherance of Injustice? Prosecutorial Discretion and Racial/Ethnic Sentencing Disparities in California Counties." *Conference Papers* [Annual meeting]. Columbus, OH: American Society of Criminology, 2008a.

Chen, Elsa Y. "Impacts of 'Three Strikes and You're Out' on Crime Trends in California and Throughout the United States." *Journal of Contemporary Criminal Justice* 24, no. 4 (2008b): 345–70.

Chesney-Lind, Meda. "Women and Crime: The Female Offender." *Signs* 12 (1986): 78–96.

Chesney-Lind, Meda. *The Female Offender: Girls, Women and Crime*. Thousand Oaks, CA: Sage, 1997.

Chesney-Lind, Meda. *Girls and Violence: Is the Gender Gap Closing?* Harrisburg, PA: VAWnet, a project of the National Resource Center on Domestic Violence/Pennsylvania Coalition Against Domestic Violence, 2004. http://www.vawnet.org, accessed January 15, 2014.

Chesney-Lind, Meda, and Randall G. Shelden. *Girls, Delinquency, and Juvenile Justice*. Florence, KY: Cengage Learning, 1992.

Chui, Tina. *It's About Time: Aging Prisoners, Increasing Costs and Geriatric Release*. New York: Vera Institute of Justice, 2010.

Claremont Institute. "Rediscovering George Washington," 2002. http://www.pbs.org/georgewashington/classroom/index3.html, accessed January 10, 2014.

Clark, Maggie. "Municipal Leaders Resisting Secure Communities in Three Cities." *The Common Path*, June 2012. http://www.marcconline.com/files/newsletter/June-2012-e-newsletter-letter-size.pdf, accessed January 27, 2014.

Clark v. California, 123 F.3d 1267, 9th Cir., 1997.

Clear, Todd R., and James Austin. "Reducing Mass Incarceration: Implications of the Iron Law of Prison Populations." *Harvard Law and Policy Review* 3 (2009): 308–324.

Clear, Todd R., Michael D. Reisig, and George F. Cole. *American Corrections*. 10th ed. Belmont, CA: Wadsworth, 2012.

Coates, Robert B., Alden D. Miller, and Lloyd E. Ohlin. *Diversity in a Youth Correctional System: Handling Delinquents in Massachusetts*. Cambridge, MA: Ballinger, 1978.

Cohen, Mark A., Roland T. Rust, and Sara Steen. *Measuring Public Perceptions of Appropriate Prison Sentences: Final Report*. Washington, DC: U.S. Department of Justice, April, 2003. https://www.ncjrs.gov/pdffiles1/nij/grants/199364.pdf, accessed January 14, 2014.

Collins, William. *Contracting for Correctional Services Provided by Private Firms*. Middletown, CT: Association of State Correctional Administrators, 2000.

Collins, William, C. *Supermax Prisons and the Constitution: Liability Concerns in the Extended Control Unit*. Washington, DC: National Institute of Corrections, November 2004.

Colomy, Paul, and Martin Kretzmann. "The Gendering of Social Control: Sex Delinquency and Progressive Juvenile Justice in Denver, 1901–27." In *Governing Childhood,* edited by A. McGillivray. Aldershot: Dartmouth, 1997.

Columbia Human Rights Law Review. "Chapter 28: Rights of Prisoners With Disabilities." In *A Jailhouse Lawyer's Manual*. 9th ed., 2011. http://www3.1aw.columbia.edu/hrlr/jlm/chapter-28.pdf, accessed January 14, 2014.

Cooper v. Pate, 378 U.S. 546, 1964.

Corrections Corporation of America. "2010 Annual Report on Form 10-K." Nashville, TN: Author, 2011. http://ir.correctionscorp.com/phoenix.zhtml?c=117983&p=irol-reportsannual, accessed January 15, 2014.

Corrections Corporation of America. "2012 Annual Report on Form 10–K," 2012a. http://cca.com/investors/financial-information/annual-reports, accessed January 14, 2014.

Corrections Corporation of America. "Research Findings," 2012b. http://www.cca.com/cca-research-institute/research-findings/, accessed January 14, 2014.

Corrections Corporation of America. "2012 Annual Letter to Shareholders." Nashville, TN: Author, 2013. http://ir.correctionscorp.com/phoenix.zhtml?c=117983&p=irol-reportsannual, accessed January 15, 2014.

Council of Juvenile Correctional Administrators. "Mapping Performance-based Standards and Civil Rights Investigations." *PbS Research Brief,* March 2013. http://pbstandards.org/cjcaresources/158/PbS_CivilRightsInvestigations_201303.pdf, accessed February 14, 2014.

Courtright, Kevin E., Bruce L. Berg, and Robert J. Mutchnick. "Rehabilitation in the New Machine? Exploring Drug and Alcohol Use and Variables Related to Success Among DUI Offenders Under Electronic Monitoring." *International Journal of Offender Therapy and Comparative Criminology* 44 (2000): 20.

Covington, Stephanie. *Women and the Criminal Justice System,* Vol. 17, No. 4. Washington, DC: Jacobs Institute of Women's Health, 2007.

Craddock, Amy. *An Exploratory Analysis of Client Outcomes, Costs, and Benefits of Day Reporting Centers*. Terre Haute: Indiana State University, 2000.

Crane, Richard. *Monitoring Correctional Services Provided by Private Firms*. Middletown, CT: Association of State Correctional Administrators, 2000.

Daugherty, Carmen. *State Trends: Legislative Victories From 2011–2013 Removing Youth From the Adult Criminal Justice System*. Washington, DC: Campaign for Youth Justice, 2013. http://www.campaignforyouthjustice.org/documents/ST2013.pdf, accessed January 31, 2014.

Davenport, Debra K. *State of Arizona, Auditor General, Performance Audit, Private Prisons* [Report No. 01–13]. 2001. http://www.azcorrections.gov/Index.aspx, accessed January 14, 2014.

Davis, Antoinette, Chris Tsukida, Susan Marchionna, and Barry Krisberg. *The Declining Number of Youth in Custody in the Juvenile Justice System*. Oakland, CA: National Council on Crime and Delinquency, 2008.

Dawson, Pat. "The Montana Town That Wanted to Be Gitmo." *Time,* May 3, 2009. http://www.time.com/time/nation/article/0,8599,1894373,00.html, accessed January 14, 2014.

Death Penalty Focus. "Death Penalty Can Prolong Suffering for Victims' Families," 2013a. http://www.deathpenalty.org/article.php?id=56, accessed January 14, 2014.

Death Penalty Focus. *Deterrence*. San Francisco: Author, 2013b. http://www.deathpenalty.org/article.php?id=82, accessed January 2, 2014.

Death Penalty Focus. "Wrongful Conviction and Posthumous Exoneration," 2011. http://www.deathpenalty.org/article.php?id=560, accessed January 14, 2014.

Death Penalty Focus. "Lethal Injection," n.d. http://www.deathpenalty.org/article.php?id=52, accessed January 6, 2014.

Death Penalty Information Center. "Financial Facts About the Death Penalty," 2013a. http://www.deathpenaltyinfo.org/costs-death-penalty, accessed January 14, 2014.

Death Penalty Information Center. "Exonerations by Year," 2013b. http://www.deathpenaltyinfo.org/innocence-and-death-penalty#inn-yr-rc, accessed January 14, 2014.

Death Penalty Information Center. "Women and the Death Penalty," 2013c. http://www.deathpenaltyinfo.org/women-and-death-penalty, accessed January 14, 2014.

Deitch, Michele. *Effective Prison Oversight*. Prepared Testimony for the Commission on Safety and Abuse in America's Prisons, 4th Hearing, Los Angeles, California, 2006.

Deitch, Michele, Amanda Barstow, Leslie Lukens, and Ryan Reyna. *From Time Out to Hard Time: Young Children in the Adult Criminal Justice System*. Austin: University of Texas, 2009. http://www.campaignforyouthjustice.org/documents/NR_TimeOut.pdf, accessed May 20, 2014.

DeMichele, Matthew T. *Probation and Parole's Growing Caseloads and Workload: Allocation Strategies for Managerial Decision Making*. Lexington, KY: American Probation and Parole Association, 2007. http://www.appa-net.org/eweb/docs/appa/pubs/smdm.pdf, accessed February 19, 2014.

DeSlatte, Aaron. "Teamsters File Ethics Complaint Over Prison Privatization Plans." *Orlando Sentinel*, September 14, 2011. http://www.orlandosentinel.com/, accessed January 5, 2012.

Detention Watch Network. "The Influence of the Private Prison Industry in Immigration Detention," 2011. http://www.detentionwatchnetwork.org/privateprisons, accessed January 5, 2014.

Devers, Lindsey. *Plea and Charge Bargaining: Research Summary*. Washington, DC: U.S. Department of Justice Bureau of Justice Assistance, 2011.

DiIulio, John D. 1987. "Prison Discipline and Prison Reform." *The Public Interest* Fall (1987).

DiIulio, John J., Jr. "My Black Crime Problem, and Ours." *City Journal*, Spring 1996. http://www.city-journal.org/html/6_2_my_black.html, accessed January 31, 2014.

DiIulio, John. *Crime and Punishment in Wisconsin: A Survey of Prisoners*. Milwaukee: Wisconsin Policy Research Institute, 1990.

DiIulio, John. "The Coming of the Super-predators." *The Weekly Standard* 1 (1995): 23–28.

Disaster Center. "United States Crime Rates 1960–2012." From FBI, *Uniform Crime Reports*, 2013. http://www.disastercenter.com/crime/uscrime.htm, accessed January 27, 2014.

District of Columbia Department of Corrections. "DC DOC Visitation Eng Final." *Video on Visitation*, July 16, 2012. http://www.youtube.com/watch?v=-PPL6RCzavQ&feature=plcp, accessed February 16, 2014.

Dolovich, Sharon. "State Punishment and Private Prisons." *Duke Law Journal* 55 (2005): 439–548.

Dolovich, Sharon. "How Privatization Thinks: The Case of Prisons." In *Government by Contract: Outsourcing and American Democracy*, edited by Jody Freeman and Martha Minow. Cambridge, MA: Harvard University Press, 2009.

Dotinga, William. "Class of Guards Can't Sue California Prison System." *Courthouse News Service*, March 23, 2012. http://www.courthousenews.com/2012/03/23/44975.htm, accessed January 4, 2013.

Du Bois, W. E. B. *The Souls of Black Folk*. Chicago: A. C. McClurg, 1903.

Douglass, Frederick. "The Convict Lease System." From the third chapter of *The Reason Why the Colored American Is Not in the World's Columbian Exposition*, 1893. http://www.historyisaweapon.com/defcon1/fredouconlea.html, accessed February 16, 2014.

Duncan, Ian, and Jessica Anderson. "Federal Authorities Indict Alleged Gang Member, Jail Guards." *Baltimore Sun*, April 24, 2013. http://www.baltimoresun.com/news/maryland/crime/blog/bs-md-ci-bgf-jail-indict-ment-20130423,0,1619914.story, accessed February 19, 2014.

Eastern State Penitentiary. "History of Eastern State Penitentiary, Philadelphia," n.d. http://www.easternstate.org/sites/default/files/pdf/ESP-history6.pdf, accessed May 7, 2014.

Egelko, Bob. "Court Upholds Female Guard's Harassment Award." *San Francisco Chronicle*, April 16, 2008. http://www.sfgate.com/default/article/Court-upholds-female-guard-s-harassment-award-3287634.php, accessed January 4, 2013.

Eliason, Michelle J., Janette Y. Taylor, and Rachel Williams. "Physical Health of Women in Prison: Relationship to Oppression." *Journal of Correctional Health Care* 10 (2004): 175–203.

Emmanuel, Adeshina. "In-Person Visits Fade as Jails Set Up Video Units for Inmates and Families." *New York Times*, August 7, 2012. http://www.nytimes.com/2012/08/07/us/some-criticize-jails-as-they-move-to-video-visits.html?pagewanted=all, accessed January 27, 2014.

Empey, Lamar. "Juvenile Justice Reform: Diversions, Due Process, and Deinstitutionalization." In *Prisoners in America*, edited by Lloyd E. Ohlin, 13–48. Englewood Cliffs, NJ: Prentice Hall, 1973.

Endicott, William. "Agriculture Chief Is No Farmer: Women's Appointment by Brown Breaks Tradition." *Los Angeles Times*, January 22, 1975.

Estelle v. Gamble, 429 U.S. 97, 1976.

Estes, Adam C. "Colorado Accidentally Releases Man From Jail, Man Allegedly Kills Prison Chief." *The Atlantic Wire*, April 1, 2013. http://www.thewire.com/national/2013/04/colorado-accidentally-releases-man-jail-man-allegedly-kills-prisons-chief/63768/, accessed February 19, 2014.

Evans, Jon. "Who We Are: A Message From Our President." *Good News Jail and Prison Ministry*, 2012. http://www.goodnewsjail.org/who-we-are/, accessed April 28, 2014.

Evans, Paul. "The Americans With Disabilities Act and Inmates With Disabilities: The Extent to Which Title II of the Act Provides a Recourse." *Journal of Law & Policy* 22 (2006): 563–590.

Ex Parte Hull, 312 U.S. 546, 1941.

Fagan, Jeff. "Stop-and-Frisk: Fagan Report Summary." Center for Constitutional Rights, 2010. http://ccrjustice.org/files/Fagan%20Report%20Summary%20Final.pdf, accessed January 14, 2014.

Fair Sentencing Act of 2010. http://www.gpo.gov/fdsys/pkg/BILLS-111s1789enr/pdf/BILLS-111s1789enr.pdf, accessed September 13, 2013.

Families Against Mandatory Minimums. "Compassionate Release." Guideline Amendment Proposed by U.S.

Sentencing Commission, 2013. http://www.famm .org/federal/USSentencingGuidelines/USSentencing GuidelinesUpdates/Compassionaterelease.aspx,accessed January 14, 2014.

Families Against Mandatory Minimums. "Omnibus Survey," 2008. http://www.famm.org/Repository/Files/ FAMM%20poll%20no%20embargo.pdf, accessed January 14, 2014.

Farabee, David. *Rethinking Rehabilitation: Why Can't We Reform Our Criminals?* Washington, DC: AEI Press, 2005.

Farmer v. Brennan, Warden, et al., 511 U.S. 825, 1994, http:// www.law.cornell.edu/supct/html/92–7247.ZS.html, accessed February 14, 2014.

Farrell, Mike. "Ending the Hidden, Savage Routine of Prison Rape." *Huffington Post,* March 17, 2008. http://www .huffingtonpost.com/mike-farrell/ending-the-hidden-savage-_b_91867.html?, accessed February 14, 2014.

Fazel, Seena, and John Danesh. "Serious Mental Disorder in 23 000 Prisoners: A Systematic Review of 62 Surveys." *Lancet* 359 (2002): 545–550.

Federal Bureau of Investigation. *Uniform Crime Report 1993–1997.* Washington, DC: Criminal Justice Information Services Division, 1997.

Federal Bureau of Investigation. *Crime in the United States, 2003: Uniform Crime Reports.* Washington, DC: U.S. Department of Justice, Federal Bureau of Investigation, 2004.

Federal Bureau of Investigation. *Crime in the United States: Variables Affecting Crime.* Washington, DC: Author, 2011. http://www2.fbi.gov/ucr/cius2009/about/variables_ affecting_crime.html, accessed January 15, 2014.

Federal Bureau of Investigation. "Crime in the United States, 2011." *Uniform Crime Reports.* Washington, DC: U.S. Department of Justice, 2012. http://www.fbi.gov/ about-us/cjis/ucr/crime-in-the-u.s/2011/crime-in-the-u.s.-2011/tables/table-1, accessed January 27, 2014.

Federal Bureau of Prisons. *About Us.* Washington, DC: Author, n.d.-a. http://www.bop.gov/about/index.jsp, accessed November 11, 2011.

Federal Bureau of Prisons. *Completing the Transition.* Washington, DC: Author, n.d.-b. http://www.bop.gov/about/ facilities/residential_reentry_management_centers.jsp, accessed February 4, 2014.

Federal Bureau of Prisons. "Merle E. Clutts," n.d.-c. http:// www.bop.gov/about/history/hero_clutts.jsp?i=17, accessed May 13, 2014.

Federal Interagency Reentry Council. *Reentry MythBuster on Public Housing.* Lexington, KY: Council of State Governments, 2012. http://www.nationalreentry resourcecenter.org/documents/0000/1089/Reentry_ Council_Mythbuster_Housing.pdf, accessed January 28, 2014.

Ferguson, Mike. "Job Seekers Stream Into Hardin Prison." *Billings Gazette,* April 16, 2014. http://billingsgazette.com/news/state-and-regional/montana/job-seekers-stream-into-hardin-prison/article_ 1be3c4e6–5aaf-5c32–8695–6ae694053cf0.html, accessed June 2, 2014.

Feucht, Thomas E., and Joseph Gfroerer. *Mental and Substance Abuse Disorders Among Adult Men on Probation or Parole: Some Success Against a Persistent Challenge.* Washington, DC: National Institute of Justice,

Substance Abuse and Mental Health Services Administration, 2011.

Field Research. "Support Legalizing the Sale of Marijuana in California: Strong Backing for State's Existing Medical Marijuana Law," February 27, 2013. http://field.com/ fieldpollonline/subscribers/Rls2442.pdf, accessed January 14, 2014.

Fields, Gary. "As Inmates Age, A Prison Carpenter Builds More Coffins." *Wall Street Journal,* May 18, 2005. http:// online.wsj.com/article/0,,SB111637661650736440,00. html, accessed January 14, 2014

Fields, Reginald. "Ohio Corrections System Sells One Prison to Private Operator, Reorganizes Four Others." *The Plain Dealer,* September 2, 2011. http://www.cleveland. com, accessed January 5, 2012.

Finckenauer, James O., Patricia W. Gavin, Arild Hovland, and Elisabet Storvoll. *Scared Straight: The Panacea Phenomenon Revisited.* Prospect Heights, IL: Waveland Press, 1999.

Fisher, Sethard. "Social Organization in a Corrections Residence." *Pacific Sociological Review* 5 (1961): 89–99.

Florida TaxWatch. "Smart Justice Poll Results," January 2012. http://www.floridataxwatch.org/resources/pdf/ SmartJusticeP01111912.pdf, accessed January 14, 2014.

Fogel, David. *We Are the Living Proof: The Justice Model for Corrections.* Cincinnati, OH: W. H. Anderson, 1975.

Fontaine, Jocelyn, and Jennifer Biess. *Housing as a Platform for Formerly Incarcerated Persons.* Washington, DC: Urban Institute, 2012.

Ford v. Wainwright, 477 U.S. 399, 1986.

Freeman, Jody, and Martha Minow. *Government by Contract: Outsourcing and American Democracy.* Cambridge, MA: Harvard University Press, 2009.

Freiburger, Tina L., and Carly M. Hilinsky. "Probation Officers' Recommendations and Final Sentencing Outcomes." *Journal of Crime and Justice* 34 (2011): 45–61.

Friedman, Lawrence. *Crime and Punishment in American History.* New York: Basic Books, 1993.

Furman v. Georgia, 408 U.S. 238, 1972.

Gable, Robert S. *Electronic Monitoring of Offenders: Can a Wayward Technology Be Redeemed?* Berkeley, CA: Claremont Graduate University, 2007.

Gaes, Gerald. "Cost, Performance Studies Look at Prison Privatization." *National Institute of Justice Journal* 259 (2008):

Gagnon v. Scarpelli, 411 U.S. 778, 1973.

Gatti, Uberto, Richard E. Tremblay, and Frank Vitaro. "Iatrogenic Effect on Juvenile Justice." *Journal of Child Psychology and Psychiatry* 50 (2009): 991–998.

General Accounting Office. *Women in Prison: Issues and Challenges Confronting US Correctional Systems* [GGD-00–22]. U.S. Government Accountability Office, 1999. http://www.gao.gov/archive/2000/gg00022.pdf, accessed January 15, 2014.

Gendreau Paul, Sheila A. French, and Angela Taylor. *What Works (What Doesn't Work).* Ottawa: Public Safety Canada, 2002.

General Accounting Office. *Intermediate Sanctions: Their Impacts on Prison Crowding, Costs, and Recidivism Are Still Unclear.* Washington, DC: Author, 1990. http:// archive.gao.gov/d22t8/142395.pdf, accessed August 19, 2012.

George Washington University. "The Project for Older Prisoners," n.d. http://www.law.gwu.edu/Academics/EL/clinics/Pages/POPS.aspx, accessed January 10, 2014.

Giallombardo, Rose. *The Social World of Imprisoned Girls: A Comparative Study of Institutions for Juvenile Delinquents.* New York: Wiley, 1974.

Gillard, Darrell K., and Allen J. Beck. *Prisoners in 1997* [NCJ 170014]. Washington, DC: U.S. Department of Justice, Bureau of Justice Statistics, 1998. http://bjs.ojp.usdoj.gov/content/pub/pdf/p97.pdf, accessed January 15, 2014.

Gilmartin, Kevin M. *Emotional Survival for Law Enforcement: A Guide for Officers and Their Families.* Tucson, AZ: E-S Press, 2002.

Gingrich, Newt, and Mark Earley. "Cutting Recidivism Saves Money and Lives." *Atlanta Journal-Constitution,* March 23, 2010. http://www.ajc.com/news/news/opinion/cutting-recidivism-saves-money-and-lives/nQdbX/, accessed January 14, 2014.

http://www.emotionalsurvival.com/about.htm, accessed January 5, 2013.

Glaser, Daniel. *The Effectiveness of a Prison and Parole System.* Indianapolis, IN: Bobbs-Merrill, 1969.

Glasmeier, Amy K., and Tracey L. Farrigan. "The Economic Impacts of the Prison Development Boom on Persistently Poor Rural Places." *International Regional Science Review* 30 (2007): 274–299.

Glaze, Lauren E. *Correctional Populations in the United States, 2009* [NCJ 231681]. Washington, DC: Bureau of Justice Statistics, U.S. Department of Justice, 2010. http://bjs.ojp.usdoj.gov/index.cfm?ty=pbdetail&iid=2316, accessed January 15, 2014.

Glaze, Lauren E., and Thomas P. Bonczar. *Probation and Parole in the US, 2008.* Washington, DC: U.S. Department of Justice, Office of Justice Programs, Bureau of Justice Statistics, 2009.

Glaze, Lauren E., and Thomas P. Bonczar. *Probation and Parole in the United States, 2009* [NCJ 231674]. Washington, DC: U.S. Department of Justice, Bureau of Justice Statistics, 2010.

Glaze, Lauren E., and Laura M. Maruschak. *Parents in Prison and Their Minor Children* [NCJ 22298]. Washington, DC: U.S. Department of Justice, Bureau of Justice Statistics, 2008. http://www.bjs.gov/content/pub/pdf/pptmc.pdf, accessed January 15, 2014.

Glaze, Lauren E., and Erika Parks. "Correctional Populations in the United States, 2011." *Bulletin* [NCJ 239972]. Washington, DC: U.S. Department of Justice, Office of Justice Programs, Bureau of Justice Statistics, November 2012. http://www.bjs.gov/index.cfm?ty=pbdetail&iid=4537, accessed February 19, 2014.

Goodstein, Lynne, and Henry Sontheimer. *A Study of the Impact of Ten Pennsylvania Residential Treatment Placements on Juvenile Recidivism.* Shippensberg, PA: Center for Juvenile Justice Training and Research, 1987.

Graham v. Florida, 130 S. Ct., 2011–2010.

Grassroots Leadership. "*Considering a Private Jail, Prison, or Detention Center? A Resource Packet for Community Members and Public Officials.* 2nd ed. Austin, TX: Grassroots Leadership, 2009.

Grattet, Ryken, Joan Petersilia, and Jeffrey Lin. "Parole Violations and Revocations in California: Analysis and Suggestions for Action." *Federal Probation* 73 (2009), 2–11.

Green, Bonnie L., Jeanne Miranda, Anahita Daroowalla, and Juned Siddique. "Trauma, Exposure, Mental Health Functioning, and Program Needs of Women in Jail." *Crime & Delinquency* 51 (2005): 133–151.

Greene, Susan. "Clements Murder Suspect Ebel Was Anxious About Walking Free." *The Colorado Independent,* April 26, 2013a. http://coloradoindependent.com/127596/clements-murder-suspect-ebel-was-anxious-about-walking-free-documents-show, accessed February 19, 2014.

Greene, Susan. "Tom Clements Death: Prison Officials Acknowledge Chief's Death Tied to Solitary Confinement Policies." *The Colorado Independent,* July 8, 2013b. http://www.coloradoindependent.com/128438/co-prison-officials-acknowledge-chiefs-murder-tied-to-solitary-confinement-policies, accessed February 19, 2014.

Greenfeld, Lawrence A., and Tracy L. Snell. *Special Report: Women Offenders.* Washington, DC: U.S. Department of Justice, Bureau of Justice Statistics, 1999. http://bjs.ojp.usdoj.gov/content/pub/pdf/wo.pdf, retrieved May 9, 2014.

Greenholtz v. Nebraska Penal Inmates, 442 U.S.1, 1979.

Greenwood, Peter. *Selective Incapacitation.* Santa Monica, CA: RAND, 1982.

Greenwood, Peter W., Karyn Model, Peter Rydell, and James Chiesa. *Diverting Children from a Life of Crime: Measuring Costs and Benefits.* Rev. ed. Santa Monica, CA: RAND, 1996.

Gregg v. Georgia, 428 U.S. 153, 1976.

Griffin, Patrick, Sean Addie, Benjamin Adams, and Kathy Firestine. *Trying Juveniles as Adults: An Analysis of State Transfer Laws and Reporting.* Washington, DC: U.S. Department of Justice, Office of Justice Programs, Office of Juvenile Justice and Delinquency Prevention, 2011. https://www.ncjrs.gov/pdffiles1/ojjdp/232434.pdf, accessed January 31, 2014.

Guerino, Paul, Paige M. Harrison, and William J. Sabol. *Prisoners in 2010* [NCJ 236096]. Washington, DC: Bureau of Justice Statistics, U.S. Department of Justice, 2011. http://www.bjs.gov/index.cfm?ty=pbdetail&iid=2230, accessed October 2, 2013.

Guerino, Paul, Paige M. Harrison, and William J. Sabol. *Prisoners in 2010.* Washington, DC: U.S. Department of Justice, Office of Justice Programs, Bureau of Justice Statistics, 2011. http://bjs.ojp.usdoj.gov/content/pub/pdf/p10.pdf, accessed January 5, 2013.

Gughemetti, Joseph M. *The People vs. Rose Bird.* San Mateo: Terra View Publications, 1985.

Gunnison, Elaine, and Jacqueline B. Helfgott. "Factors That Hinder Offender Reentry Success: A View From Community Corrections Officers." *International Journal of Offender Therapy and Comparative Criminology* 55 (2010): 287. http://ijo.sagepub.com/content/55/2/287, accessed January 24, 2014.

Guzman, Carolina, Barry Krisberg, and Chris Tsukida. *Accelerated Release: A Literature Review.* Oakland, CA: National Council on Crime and Delinquency, 2008.

http://www.nccdglobal.org/sites/default/files/publication_pdf/focus-literature-review.pdf, accessed February 18, 2014.

Haapanen, Rudy A. *Selective Incapacitation and the Serious Offender: A Longitudinal Study of Criminal Career Patterns.* Sacramento: California Department of the Youth Authority, Program Research and Review Division, 1988.

Hairston, J. Creasie Finney. *Prisoners and Families: Parenting Issues During Incarceration.* Paper presented to the "From Prison to Home" Conference, U.S. Department of Housing and Urban Development, January 30–31, 2002. www.fcnetwork.org/reading/hairston_Prisonersand Families.pdf, accessed February 27, 2014.

Hall, Daron. "Jails vs. Prisons." *Commentary,* n.d. http://www.aca.org/fileupload/177/prasannak/1_1_1_ Commentary_web.pdf, accessed February 25, 2014.

Hall, John, and Kelly Walsh. *Are Florida's Private Prisons Keeping Their Promise?* Tallahassee: Florida Center for Fiscal and Economic Policy, 2010.

Haney, Craig. "Mental Health Issues in Long-Term Solitary and 'Supermax' Confinement." *Crime & Delinquency* 49 (2003): 124–156.

Harkness, Marti, and Lucyann Walker-Fraser. *State's Drug Courts Could Expand to Target Prison-Bound Adult Offenders* (No. 09–13). Tallahassee, FL: Office of Program Policy Analysis and Government Accountability, 2009.

Harlow, Caroline W. *Education and Correctional Populations.* Washington, DC: U.S. Department of Justice, Office of Justice Programs, Bureau of Justice Statistics, 2003.

Harris, Kamala. *Smart on Crime.* San Francisco: Chronicle Books, 2009.

Harris, Maxine, and Roger D. Fallot. *Using Trauma Theory to Design Service Systems.* San Francisco: Jossey-Bass, 2001.

Hart, Peter D. Changing Public Attitudes Toward the Criminal Justice System. New York: The Open Society Institute, 2002.

Hartney, Christopher, and Caroline Glesmann. *Prison Bed Profiteers: How Corporations Are Reshaping Criminal Justice in the U.S.* Oakland, CA: National Council on Crime and Delinquency, 2012.

Hartney, Christopher, and Susan Marchionna. *Attitudes of U.S. Voters Toward Nonserious Offenders and Alternatives to Incarceration.* Oakland, CA: National Council on Crime and Delinquency, 2009.

Hartney, Christopher, and Linh Vuong. *Created Equal: Racial and Ethnic Disparities in the US Criminal Justice System.* Oakland, CA: National Council on Crime and Delinquency, March 2009. http://www.nccdglobal. org/sites/default/files/publication_pdf/created-equal.pdf, accessed January 27, 2014.

Hayes, Kevin. "Utah Firing Squad Execution: Ronnie Lee Gardner Pronounced Dead at 12:17 am." *CBS News,* June 18, 2010. http://www.cbsnews.com/8301–504083_162–20008133–504083.html, accessed January 14, 2014.

Helfgott, Jacqueline. "Ex-Offender Needs Versus Criminal Opportunity in Seattle, Washington." *Federal Probation* 61 (2007): 12–24.

Herrnstein, Richard, and Charles Murray. *The Bell Curve: Intelligence and Class Structure in American Life.* New York: Free Press, 1994.

Herrera v. Collins, 506 U.S. 390, 1993.

Hiaasen, Scott. "Effort to Privatize Florida Prisons Raises Questions of Cost." *Miami Herald,* April 24, 2011. http://www.tampabay.com/news/politics/stateroundup/ effort-to-privatize-florida-prisons-raises-questions-of-cost/1165807, accessed January 14, 2014.

Hodai, Beau. "The Rainmakers: Banking on Private Prisons in the Fleecing of Small-Town America." *In These Times,* March 5, 2010a. http://www.inthesetimes.com/article/5578/the_rainmakers/, accessed January 14, 2014.

Hodai, Beau. "Corporate Con Game: How the Private Prison Industry Helped Shape Arizona's Anti-immigrant Law." *In These Times,* June 21, 2010b. http://www.inthesetimes.com, accessed January 14, 2014.

Hodai, Beau. "Freedom Forum CEO Tied to For-Profit Prisons." *Fairness & Accuracy in Reporting (FAIR),* 2010c. http://www.fair.org, accessed January 14, 2014.

Holland, Jo G. "The Feminization of the Community Corrections Work Force." *Corrections Today* 70 (August 2008): 44–47.

Holt, N., and D. Miller. *Explorations in Inmate-Family Relationships.* Sacramento: Research Division, California Department of Corrections, 1972.

Hoover Institution. "A Slave to the System? Thomas Jefferson and Slavery." *Uncommon Knowledge,* January 19, 2004. http://www.hoover.org/multimedia/uncommon-knowledge/27007, accessed January 10, 2014

Hooks, Gregory, Clayton Mosher, Thomas Rotolo, and Linda Lobao. "The Prison Industry: Carceral Expansion and Employment in U.S. Counties, 1969–1994." *Social Science Quarterly* 85 (2004): 37–57.

Hornberger, Nancy G. "Improving Outcomes for Status Offenders in the JJDPA Reauthorization." *Juvenile and Family Justice Today.* Reno, NV: National Council of Juvenile and Family Court Judges, 2010.

Hope Aglow Ministries. "Introduction," n.d. http://hopeaglow.com/prison_ministry.htm, accessed April 28, 2014.

Howell, Ally W. "A Comparison of the Treatment of Transgender Persons in the Criminal Justice Systems of Ontario, Canada, New York, and California." *Buffalo Public Interest Law Journal* 133 (2010).

Howell, James C., ed. *Implementation Guide for the Comprehensive Strategy for Serious, Violent, and Chronic Juvenile Offenders.* Washington, DC: Office of Justice Programs, Office of Juvenile Justice and Delinquency Prevention, 1995.

Howell, James C. *Juvenile Justice and Youth Violence.* Thousand Oaks, CA: Sage, 1997.

Hoyt, Eleanor Hinton, Vincent Schiraldi, *Brenda V. Smith,* and, Jason Ziedenberg. "Reducing Racial Disparities in Juvenile Detention." *Pathways to Juvenile Detention Reform.* Baltimore: Annie E Casey Foundation, 2001. http://www.aecf.org/upload/publicationfiles/reducing%20racial%20disparities.pdf, accessed January 14, 2014.

Hudson v. Palmer, 468 U.S. 517, 1984. http://www.law.cornell.edu/supremecourt/text/468/517, accessed February 14, 2014.

Hughes, Robert. *The Fatal Shore: The Epic of Australia's Founding.* New York: Vintage Books, 1988.

Hughes, Timothy A., Doris J. Wilson, and Allen J. Beck. *Trends in State Parole, 1990–2000.* Washington, DC: U.S. Department of Justice, Office of Justice Programs, Bureau of Justice Statistics, 2001.

Human Rights Watch. *Ill-Equipped: U.S. Prisons and Offenders with Mental Illness.* New York: Author, 2003. http://www.hrw.org/sites/default/files/reports/usa1003.pdf, accessed November 18, 2011.

Human Rights Watch. *Submission to the Committee on the Elimination of Racial Discrimination.* New York: Author, 2008.

Human Rights Watch. *No Equal Justice: The Prison Litigation Reform Act in the United States.* New York: Author, 2009. http://www.hrw.org/sites/default/files/reports/us0609web.pdf, accessed February 14, 2014.

Human Rights Watch. *Profiting From Probation: America's "Offender-Funded" Probation Industry.* New York: Author, 2014. http://www.hrw.org/reports/2014/02/05/profiting-probation, accessed February 3, 2014.

Hurtibise, Ron. "Juvenile Detainees' Abuse Reports Spike." *Daytona Beach News Journal,* June 30, 2002.

Hutto v. Finney, 437 U.S. 678, 1978. http://scholar.google.com/scholar_case?case=12687903120774416800&q=hutto+v.+finney&hl=en&as_sdt=2006&as_vis=1, accessed February 14, 2014.

Ifill, Gwen. "New Drug Law Narrows Crack, Powder Cocaine Sentencing Gap." *PBS NewsHour,* August 3, 2010. http://www.pbs.org/newshour/bb/law/july-dec10/sentencing_08–03.html, accessed January 14, 2014.

Inciardi, James A., Steven S. Martin, and Clifford A. Butzin. "Five-Year Outcomes of Therapeutic Community Treatment of Drug-Involved Offenders After Release From Prison." *Crime & Delinquency* 50 (2004): 88–107.

Indian Law and Order Commission. "A Roadmap for Making Native America Safer: Report to the President and Congress of the United States," November 2013. http://www.aisc.ucla.edu/iloc/report/files/A_Roadmap_For_Making_Native_America_Safer-Full.pdf, accessed December 13, 2013.

Innocence Project. "Know the Cases," 2013. http://www.innocenceproject.org/know/, accessed January 14, 2014.

Institute for Children, Poverty and Homelessness. *A Home by Any Other Name: Enhancing Shelters Addresses the Gap in Low-Income Housing.* New York: Author, 2012. Retrieved at http://www.icphusa.org/index.asp?page=16&report=100&pg=75, accessed January 26, 2014

International Centre for Prison Studies. *World Prison Brief.* London: Author, 2013. http://www.prisonstudies.org/info/worldbrief/wpb_stats.php?area=all&category=wb_poptotal, accessed February 19, 2014.

In re Gault, 387 U.S. 1, 27, 1967.

In the Public Interest. *Backgrounder Brief: The High Costs of Privatization.* Washington, DC: Author, 2011.

Ireland, Connie S., and JoAnn Prause. "Discretionary Parole Release: Length of Imprisonment, Percent of Sentence Served, and Recidivism." *Journal of Crime and Justice* 28 (2005): 2.

Irvine, Angela. "We've Had Three of Them: Addressing the Invisibility of LBGT and Non-gender Conforming Youth in the Juvenile Justice System." *Columbia Journal of Gender and Law* 9 (2010): 675.

Jackson v. Hobbs, 132 S. Ct. 2455, 2012.

Jalbert, Sarah K., William Rhodes, Michael Kane, Elyse Clawson, Bradford Bogue, Chris Flygare, Ryan Kling, and Meghan Guevara. *A Multi-Site Evaluation of Reduced Probation Caseload Size in an Evidence-Based Practice Setting.* Cambridge: Abt Associates, Inc., 2011.

James, Doris J. "Profile of Jail Inmates, 2002." *Special Report* [NCJ 201932]. Washington, DC: U.S. Department of Justice, Office of Justice Programs, Bureau of Justice Statistics, July 2004. http://bjs.ojp.usdoj.gov/content/pub/pdf/pji02.pdf, accessed January 27, 2014.

James, Doris, and Lauren E.Glaze. *Mental Health Problems of Prison and Jail Inmates.* Washington, DC: U.S. Department of Justice, Bureau of Justice Statistics, 2006.

Jankowski, Louis. "Probation and Parole, 1990." *Probation and Parole Populations Series* [NCJ 133285]. Washington, DC: U.S. Department of Justice, Office of Justice Programs, Bureau of Justice Statistics, 1991.

Jennings, Trip. "Private Prison Staffing Could Trigger Fines." *Santa Fe New Mexican,* 2011. http://www.santafenewmexican.com, accessed January 14, 2014.

JFA Institute. *Unlocking America: Why and How to Reduce America's Prison Population.* Washington, DC: Author, 2007.

Johnson v. California et al., 543 U.S. 03–636, 2005.

Johnston, Norman. *Prison Reform in Pennsylvania.* Philadelphia: The Pennsylvania Prison Society, 2012. http://www.prisonsociety.org/about/history.shtml, accessed January 27, 2014.

Joint Legislative Committee on Performance Evaluation and Expenditure Review (PEER). *Report to the Mississippi Legislature: Cost Analysis of Housing State Inmates in Regional and Private Correctional Facilities* [Report #419]. Jackson, MS: Author, 2001. www.peer.state.ms.us/reports/rpt419.pdf, accessed January 14, 2014.

Jolin, Annette, and Brian Stipak. "Drug Treatment and Electronically Monitored Home Confinement: An Evaluation of a Community-Based Sentencing Option." *Crime & Delinquency* 38 (1992): 158–170.

Jouvenal, Justin. "Ex-Virginia Executioner Becomes Opponent of Death Penalty." *The Washington Post,* February 10, 2013. http://www.washingtonpost.com/local/ex-virginia-executioner-becomes-opponent-of-death-penalty/2013/02/10/9e741124-5e89-11e2-9940-6fc488f3fecd_print.html, accessed January 14, 2014.

Justice Policy Institute. *Gaming the System: How the Political Strategies of Private Prison Companies Promote Ineffective Incarceration Policies.* Washington, DC: Author, 1995.

Kam, Dara. "Corrections Union Sues State Over Prison Privatization Effort." *Palm Beach Post,* 2011a. http://www.palmbeachpost.com, accessed January 5, 2012.

Kam, Dara. "Judge Rules Prison Privatization Plan Unconstitutional." *Palm Beach Post,* 2011b. http://www.postonpolitics.com/2011/09/judge-rules-prison-privatization-plan-unconstitutional/, accessed January 5, 2012.

Kaplan, Thomas. "New York Has Some Prisons to Sell." *New York Times,* May 27, 2012. http://www.nytimes

.com/2012/05/28/nyregion/closed-new-york-prisons-prove-hard-to-sell.html, accessed January 14, 2014.

Karp, David Reed, and Todd R. Clear. *What is Community Justice? Case Studies of Restorative Justice and Community Supervision*. Thousand Oaks, CA: Sage, 2002.

Kennedy v. Louisiana, 554 U.S. 407, 2008.

Kercher, Bruce. "Perish or Prosper: The Law and Convict Transportation in the British Empire, 1700–1850." *Law and History Review* 21 (2003): 527–84.

Kimme, Dennis A., Gary M. Bowker, and Robert G. Deichman. *Jail Design Guide* [NIC 024806]. 3rd ed. Washington, DC: National Institute of Corrections, March 2011.

King, Ryan S., and Marc Mauer. *Aging Behind Bars: "Three Strikes" Seven Years Later*. Washington, DC: The Sentencing Project, 2001.

Kirchhoff, Suzanne M. *CRS Report for Congress: Economic Impacts of Prison Growth*. Washington, DC: Congressional Research Service, 2010.

Kittrie, Nicholas N. *The Right to Be Different: Deviance and Enforced Therapy*. Baltimore: Penguin Books, 1971.

Knochel, Andrew. "Coconino County Jail Adding Sweat Lodge for Native American Inmates." *Arizona Capitol Times,* October 22, 2013. http://azcapitoltimes.com/news/2013/10/22/coconino-county-jail-adding-sweat-lodge-for-native-american-inmates/, accessed January 27, 2014.

Kohli, Aarti, Peter L. Markowitz, and Lisa Chavez. *Secure Communities by the Numbers: An Analysis of Demographics and Due Process*. Berkeley: Earl Warren Institute on Law and Social Policy, 2011.

Krisberg, Barry. *Crime and Privilege: Toward a New Criminology*. Englewood Cliffs, NJ: Prentice Hall, 1975.

Krisberg, Barry. *Reinventing Juvenile Justice*. Thousand Oaks, CA: Sage, 1993.

Krisberg, Barry. "General Corrections Review of the California Youth Authority." Prison Law Office, 2003a. http://www.prisonlaw.com/pdfs/CYA5.pdf, accessed January 14, 2014.

Krisberg, Barry. "Safety and Welfare Review of the California Youth Authority." *Continuing the Struggle for Justice,* edited by Barry Krisberg, Susan Marchionna, and Christopher Baird. Thousand Oaks, CA: Sage, 2003b.

Krisberg, Barry. *Juvenile Justice: Redeeming Our Children*. Thousand Oaks, CA: Sage, 2005.

Krisberg, Barry. "Safety and Welfare Review of the California Youth Authority." In *Continuing the Struggle for Justice,* edited by Barry Krisberg, Susan Marchionna, and S. Christopher Baird. Thousand Oaks, CA: Sage, 2007.

Krisberg, Barry. *Breaking the Cycle of Abuse in Juvenile Facilities* [NCCD Focus]. Oakland, CA: National Council on Crime and Delinquency, 2009.

Krisberg, Barry, James Austin, and Paul Steele. *Unlocking Juvenile Corrections*. San Francisco: National Council on Crime and Delinquency, 1991.

Krisberg, Barry, and James Austin. *Reinventing Juvenile Justice*. Thousand Oaks, CA: Sage, 1993.

Krisberg, Barry, Christopher Baird, and Susan Marchionna. *Continuing the Struggle for Justice: 100 Years of the National Council on Crime and Delinquency*. Thousand Oaks, CA: Sage, 2007.

Krisberg, Barry, Jessie Craine, and Susan Marchionna. *Attitudes of Californians Toward Effective Correctional Policies*. Oakland, CA: National Council on Crime and Delinquency, 2004.

Krisberg, Barry, Robert DeComo, Sonya Rudenstine, and Dominic Del Rosario. *Juveniles Taken Into Custody Research Program: FY1994 Annual Report*. Washington, DC: U.S. Department of Justice, Office of Juvenile Justice and Delinquency Prevention, 1995.

Krisberg, Barry, and Susan Marchionna. *Attitudes of U.S. Voters Toward Prisoner Rehabilitation and Reentry Policies*. Oakland, CA: National Council on Crime and Delinquency, 2006.

Krisberg, Barry, and Susan Marchionna. *Attitudes of U.S. Voters Toward Youth Crime and the Justice System*. Oakland, CA: National Council on Crime and Delinquency, 2007.

Kyckelhahn, Tracey. *State Corrections Expenditures, FY 1982–2010*. Washington, DC. U.S. Department of Justice Bureau of Justice Statistics, 2012. http://www.bjs.gov/content/pub/pdf/scefy8210.pdf, accessed December 30, 2013.

Kyckelhahn, Tracey, and Tara Martin. *Justice Expenditure and Employment Extracts, 2010—Preliminary* [NCJ 242544]. Washington, DC: U.S. Department of Justice, Office of Justice Programs, Bureau of Justice Statistics, 2013. http://www.bjs.gov/index.cfm?ty=pbdetail&iid=4679, accessed February 28, 2014.

LaFaive, Michael D. "Privatization for the Health of It." *Michigan Privatization Report*. Midland, MI: Mackinac Center for Public Policy, 2005

Lundahl, Brad W., Chelsea Kunz, Cyndi Brownell, Norma Harris, and Russ Van Vleet. "Prison Privatization: A Meta-analysis of Cost and Quality of Confinement Indicators." *Research on Social Work Practice* 19 (2009): 383–394.

Langan, Patrick A., and David J. Levin. *Recidivism of Prisoners Released in 1994* [NCJ 193427]. Washington, DC: U.S. Department of Justice, Office of Justice Programs, Bureau of Justice Statistics, 2002. http://bjs.ojp.usdoj.gov/index.cfm?ty=pbdetail&iid=1134, accessed January 24, 2014.

Lawrence, Alison. *Probation and Parole Violations: State Responses*. Washington, DC: National Conference of State Legislatures, 2008.

Le, Thao, Isami Arifuku, Cory Louis, Moishe Krisberg, and Eric Tang. *Not Invisible: Asian Pacific Islander Juvenile Arrests in Alameda County*. Asian/Pacific Islander Youth Violence Prevention Center, Oakland, CA: National Council on Crime and Delinquency, 2001.

Lee, Eumi K. "An Overview of Special Populations in California Prisons." *Hastings Race and Poverty Law Journal* 223 (2010).

Legal Services for Prisoners With Children. "California Habeas Project," n.d. http://www.prisonerswithchildren.org/our-projects/california-habeas-project/, accessed June 1, 2014.

Legislative Analyst's Office. *From Cellblocks to Classrooms: Reforming Inmate Education to Improve Public Safety*. Sacramento, CA: Author, 2008. http://www.lao.ca.gov/2008/crim/inmate_education/inmate_education_021208.aspx, accessed August 2, 2012.

Leiber, Michael, John Reitzel, and Kristin Mack. "Probation Officer Recommendations for Sentencing Relative to Judicial Practice: The Implications for African Americans." *Criminal Justice Policy Review* 22 (2011): 301.

Lemert, Edwin M. *Social Action and Legal Change: Revolution Within the Juvenile Court.* Chicago: Aldine, 1972.

Lemert, Edwin, and Forrest Dill. *Offenders in the Community: The Probation Subsidy in California.* Lexington, MA: Lexington Books, 1978.

Lerman, Paul. *Community Treatment and Social Control.* Chicago: University of Chicago Press, 1973.

Leonard, Jack, and Robert Faturechi. "Code of Silence Among Jail Guards Hinders Abuse Probes, Watchdog Says." *Los Angeles Times,* October 14, 2011. http:// articles.latimes.com/2011/oct/14/local/la-me-jails-code-of-silence-20111014, accessed January 4, 2013.

Levin, Marc. *Work Release: Con Job or Big Payoff for Texas?* Austin: Texas Public Policy Foundation, Center for Effective Justice, 2008.

Liazos, Alexander. "Class Oppression: The Functions of Juvenile Justice." *The Insurgent Sociologist* 5 (1974): 2–24.

Library of Congress. "Bill Summary and Status: S.678." Summary as of December 17, 2009. http://thomas.loc.gov/cgi-bin/bdquery/z?d111:SN00678:@@@L&summ2=m&, accessed January 31, 2014.

Lifesitenews.com. "Canadian Court Orders Federal Prisons to Pay for Sex Change Operations," February 7, 2003. http://www.lifesitenews.com/home/all-stories-on-date/ 2003/02/07/#canadian-court-orders-prisons-to-pay-for-sex-change-operations, accessed January 13, 2014.

Lipsey, Mark. "The Effect of Treatment on Juvenile Delinquents: Results From Meta-analysis." *Psychology and Law: International Perspectives,* edited by Friedrich Lösel, Doris Bender, and Thomas Bliesener, 131–143. Berlin, NY: Walter de Gruyter, 1992.

Liptak, Adam. "Supreme Court Ruling Allows Strip Searches of Any Arrest." *New York Times,* April 2, 2012. http:// www.nytimes.com/2012/04/03/us/justices-approve-strip-searches-for-any-offense.html?pagewanted=all&_r=0, accessed January 27, 2014.

Little, Gregory L., Kenneth D. Robinson, Katherine D. Burnette, and E. Stephen Swan. "Twenty-Year Recidivism Results for MRT-Treated Offenders." *Cognitive Behavioral Treatment Review* 19(1): 1–5. http://www. moral-reconation-therapy.com/Resources/CBTR-%20 19_1%202010GL.pdf, accessed January 27, 2014.

Lombardo, Lucien X. *Guards Imprisoned: Correctional Officers at Work.* New York: Elsevier North Holland, 1981.

Lopez, Mark Hugo. *A Rising Share: Hispanics and Federal Crime.* Washington, DC: Pew Research Center, 2009. http://pewresearch.org/pubs/1124/hispanic-immigrant-crime-report, accessed November 19, 2011.

Lopez, Mark H., and Michael T. Light. *A Rising Share: Hispanics and Federal Crime.* Washington, DC: Pew Research Center, 2009.

Lopoo, Leonard M. and Bruce Western. "Incarceration and the Formation and Stability of Marital Unions." *Journal of Marriage & Family* 6 (2005): 3, 721–735.

Los Angeles Times. "Dysfunction in L.A.'s Jails." Opinion, July 11, 2012. http://articles.latimes.com/2012/jul/11/ opinion/la-ed-jails-los-angeles-20120711, accessed February 19, 2014.

Los Angeles Times. "A Fix for Jail Overcrowding." Editorial, September 5, 2013. http://articles.latimes.com/2013/ sep/05/opinion/la-ed-pre-trial-releases-jails-20130905, accessed January 27, 2014.

Louisiana ex rel. Francis v. Resweber, 32 U.S. 459, 1947.

Lovell, David. "Patterns of Disturbed Behavior in a Supermax Population." *Criminal Justice and Behavior* 35 (2008): 985–1004.

Lowenkamp, Christopher T., Anthony W. Flores, Alexander M. Holsinger, Matthew D. Makarios, and Edward J. Latessa. "Intensive Supervision Programs: Does Program Philosophy and the Principles of Effective Intervention Matter?" *Journal of Criminal Justice* 38 (2010): 368–375.

Lowenkamp, Christopher T., and Edward J. Latessa. *Evaluation of Ohio's Community Based Correctional Facilities and Halfway House Programs.* Cincinnati, OH: University of Cincinnati, Center for Criminal Justice Research, 2002.

Lowenkamp, Christopher T., Edward J. Latessa, and Alexander M. Holsinger. "The Risk Principle in Action: What Have We Learned From 13,676 Offenders and 97 Correctional Programs?" *Crime & Delinquency* 52 (2006): 77–93.

Lowenkamp, Christopher T., Jennifer Pealer, Paula Smith, and Edward J. Latessa. "Adhering to the Risk and Need Principles: Does It Matter for Supervision-Based Programs?" *Federal Probation* 70 (2006): 3.

Lydersen, Kari. "In Rural Michigan, Prison-Closing Blues." *In These Times,* August 7, 2009. http://inthesetimes. com/working/entry/4720/in_rural_michigan_prison-closing_blues/, accessed January 14, 2014.

Mabillon, Jean. "Réflexions sur les prisons des ordres religieux." *Ouvrages posthumes de J. Mabillon et de Th. Ruinard* 3 (1724): 321–35.

MacKenzie, Doris L., and Gaylene S. Armstrong, eds. *Correctional Boot Camps: Military Basic Training or a Model for Corrections?* Thousand Oaks, CA: Sage, 2004.

Madrid v. Gomez, 889 F. Supp. 1146, N.D. Cal. 1995.

Maguire, Kathleen, and Ann Pastore. *Sourcebook of Criminal Justice Statistics.* Washington, DC: U.S. Department of Justice, Bureau of Labor Statistics, 2000.

Males, Mike. *Striking Out: California's Three Strikes and You're Out Law Has Not Reduced Violent Crime: A 2011 Update.* San Francisco: Center on Juvenile and Criminal Justice, 2011.

Mann, Brian. "Prison Closings Trouble Upstate New York." *NPR,* March 4, 2008. http://www.npr .org/templates/story/story.php?storyId=87887743, accessed January 14, 2014.

Marimow, Ann E. "14 More Corrections Officers Charged in Baltimore Corruption Probe Involving Jail Gang." *Washington Post,* November 21, 2013. http://wapo. st/1aU0b1w, accessed February 19, 2014.

Martin, Susan E., and Nancy C. Jurik. *Doing Justice, Doing Gender: Women in Law and Criminal Justice Occupations.* Thousand Oaks, CA: Sage, 1996.

Martinson, Robert. "What Works? Questions and Answers About Prison Reform." *The Public Interest* 35 (1974): 22–54.

Martinson, Robert. "New Findings, New Views: A Note of Caution Regarding Sentencing Reform." *Hofstra Law Review* 7, no. 2 (1979): 243–258.

Martinson, Robert, Douglas Lipton, and Judith Wilks. *The Effectiveness of Correctional Treatment: A Survey of Treatment Evaluation Studies*. Westport, CT: Praeger, 1975.

Maruschak, Laura M. *Medical Problems of Jail Inmates*. Washington, DC: U.S. Department of Justices, Bureau of Justice Statistics, 2006.

Maruschak, Laura M. *Medical Problems of Prisoners*. Washington, DC: U.S. Department of Justices, Bureau of Justice Statistics, 2008.

Maruschak, Laura M., and Thomas P. Bonczar. *Probation and Parole in the United States, 2012*. Washington, DC: U.S. Department of Justice, Office of Justice Programs, Bureau of Justice Statistics, 2013. http://www.bjs.gov/index.cfm?ty=pbdetail&iid=4844, accessed May 19, 2014.

Maruschak, Laura M., Lauren E. Glaze, and Thomas P. Bonczar. *Adults on Parole in the United States, 1975–2012*. Washington, DC: U.S. Department of Justice, Office of Justice Programs, Bureau of Justice Statistics, 2013. http://www.bjs.gov/index.cfm?ty=pbdetail&iid=1997, accessed May 15, 2014.

Maruschak, Laura M. and Erika Parks. *Probation and Parole in the United States, 2011*. Washington, DC: U.S. Department of Justice, Office of Justice Programs, Bureau of Justice Statistics, November 2012. http://www.bjs.gov/index.cfm?ty=pbdetail&iid=4538, accessed February 27, 2014.

Mayer, Judith. *Girls in the Maryland Juvenile Justice System: Findings of the Female Population Taskforce*. Presentation to the Gender Specific Services Training, Minneapolis, MN, 1994.

McCain, Demetria L. "*Malesko v. Correctional Services Corp.* in the Second Circuit: Pursuing Damages for Constitutional Violations by the Private Prison Industry." *Howard Law Journal* 44 (2001): 399.

McDonald, Douglas C., and Kenneth Carlson. *Contracting for Imprisonment in the Federal Prison System: Cost and Performance of the Privately Operated Taft Correctional Institution*. Cambridge, MA: Abt Associates Inc., 2005.

McDonald, Douglas, and Carl Patten. *Governments' Management of Private Prisons*. Cambridge, MA: Abt Associates Inc., 2003.

McMenamin, Jennifer. "Death Penalty Costs Maryland More than Life Term." *The Baltimore Sun*, March 6, 2008. http://articles.baltimoresun.com/2008-03-06/news/0803060171_1_death-penalty-capital-punishment-cost-of-capital, accessed January 14, 2014.

McMurran, Mary. "What Works in Substance Misuse Treatments for Offenders?" *Criminal Behavior and Mental Health* 17 (2007): 225–233.

Mears, Daniel P. "A Critical Look at Supermax Prisons." *Corrections Compendium* 30 (2005): 6–7, 45–49.

Mears, Daniel P., and William D. Bales. "Supermax Incarceration and Recidivism." *Criminology* 47 (2009): 801–836.

Mempa v. Rhay, 389 U.S. 128, 1967.

Medsger, Betty. Framed: The New Right Attack on Chief Justice Rose Bird and the Courts. New York: Pilgrim Press, 1983.

Mendel, Richard A. *The Missouri Model: Reinventing the Practice of Rehabilitating Youthful Offenders*. Baltimore, MD: Annie E. Casey Foundation, 2010. http://www.aecf.org/~/media/Pubs/Initiatives/Juvenile%20Detention%20Alternatives%20Initiative/MOModel/MO_Fullreport_webfinal.pdf, accessed January 31, 2014.

Mendel, Richard A. *No Place for Kids: The Case for Reducing Juvenile Detention*. Baltimore: Annie E. Casey Foundation, 2011.

Mendelson, Nina A. "Six Simple Steps to Increase Contractor Accountability." In *Government by Contract: Outsourcing and American Democracy*, edited by Jody Freeman and Martha Minow. Cambridge, MA: Harvard University Press, 2009.

Menkel-Meadow, Carrie. *Restorative Justice: What Is It and Does It Work?* Washington, DC: Georgetown University Law Center, 2007. http://scholarship.law.georgetown.edu/facpub/583, accessed August 19, 2012.

Mennel, Robert. *Thorns and Thistles*. Hanover: University of New Hampshire Press, 1973.

Messina, Nena, and Christine Grella. "Childhood Trauma and Women's Health Outcomes: A California Prison Population." *The American Journal of Public Health* 96 (2006): 1842–1848.

Metraux, Stephen, and Dennis P. Culhane. "Homeless Shelter Use and Reincarceration Following Prison Release: Assessing the Risk." *Criminal Public Policy* 3 (2004): 201–222.

Miller, Jerome. *Last One Over the Wall: The Massachusetts Experiment in Closing Reform Schools*. Columbus: The Ohio State University Press, 1991.

Miller, Jerome G. "From Social Safety New to Dragnet: African American Males in the Criminal Justice System." *Washington and Lee Law Review* 51 (1994): 479–490.

Miller, Jerome G. *Last One Over the Wall*. 2nd ed. Columbus: The Ohio State University Press, 1998.

Minow, Martha. "Outsourcing Power: How Privatizing Military Efforts Challenges Accountability, Professionalism, and Democracy." *Boston College Law Review* 46, 5 (2005): 989–1026.

Minton, Todd D. "Jail Inmates at Midyear 2010—Statistical Tables." Part of the *Prison and Jail Inmates at Midyear Series* [NCJ 233431]. Washington, DC: U.S. Department of Justice, Office of Justice Programs, Bureau of Justice Statistics, April 14, 2011. http://bjs.ojp.usdoj.gov/index.cfm?ty=pbdetail&iid=2375, accessed January 27, 2014.

Minton, Todd D. *Jails in Indian Country, 2011* [NCJ 238978]. Washington, DC: U.S. Department of Justice, Office of Justice Programs, Bureau of Justice Statistics, 2012. http://www.bjs.gov/content/pub/ascii/jic11.txt, accessed January 27, 2014.

Minton, Todd D. *Jail Inmates at Midyear 2012—Statistical Tables* [NCJ 241264]. Washington, DC: U.S. Department of Justice, Office of Justice Programs, Bureau of Justice Statistics, May 2013.

Mitchell, Mitch. "Texas Prison Boom Going Bust." *Star-Telegram*, 2011. http://www.star-telegram.com, accessed January 14, 2014.

Models for Change. "Racial and Ethnic Fairness DMC," 2014. http://www.modelsforchange.net/about/Issues-for-change/Racial-fairness.html, accessed January 14, 2014.

Models for Change. "Background," n.d. http://www.models-forchange.net/about/Background-and-principles.html, accessed January 14, 2014.

Moller, Jan. "Workers Protest Plan to Sell State Prisons," *Times-Picayune,* March 24, 2011a. http://www.nola.com/politics/index.ssf/2011/03/workers_protest_plan_to_sell_s.html, accessed January 5, 2014.

Moller, Jan. "Gov. Jindal's Plan to Sell State Prisons Is Killed by House Committee." *Times Picayune,* June 6, 2011b. http://www.nola.com/politics/index.ssf/2011/06/house_committee_kills_bobby_ji.html, accessed January 5, 2014.

Montgomery, Ben, and Waveney A. Moore. "For Their Own Good: A *St. Petersburg Times* Special Report on Child Abuse at the Florida School for Boys." *Tampa Bay Times,* April 17, 2009. http://www.tampabay.com/features/humaninterest/for-their-own-good-a-st-peters-burg-times-special-report-on-child-abuse-at/992939, accessed December 30, 2013.

Moore, Shelby A. "Understanding the Connection Between Domestic Violence, Crime, and Poverty: How Welfare Reform May Keep Battered Women From Leaving Abusive Relationships." *Texas Journal of Women and the Law* 12 (2003): 451–484.

Morris, N. "Prisons in the USA: Supermax—the Bad and the Mad." In *Prison Architecture: Policy, Design, and Experience,* edited by L. Fairweather and S. McConville, 98–108. London: Architectural Press, 2000.

Morrissey v. Brewer, 408 U.S. 471, 1972.

Mumola, Christopher J. *Medical Causes of Death in State Prison, 2001–2004* [NCJ 216340]. Washington, DC: Bureau of Justice Statistics, U.S. Department of Justice, 2007.

Mumola, Christopher J., and Jennifer C. Karberg. *Drug Use and Dependence, State and Federal Prisoners, 2004.* Washington, DC: U.S. Department of Justice, Office of Justice Programs, Bureau of Justice Statistics, 2006.

Murphy, Nicole M. "Dying to Be Free: An Analysis of Wisconsin's Restructured Compassionate Release Statute." *Marquette Law Review* 95 (2012): 1679–1741.

Murray, Charles. *Losing Ground: American Social Policy, 1950–1980.* New York: Basic Books, 1984.

Murray, Charles A., and Louis A. Cox. *Beyond Probation: Juvenile Corrections and the Chronic Delinquent.* Beverly Hills, CA: Sage, 1979.

Myrdal, Gunnar. *An American Dilemma: The Negro Problem and Modern Democracy.* New York: Harper and Brothers, 1944.

Nagin, Daniel S., Francis T. Cullen, and Cheryl L. Jonson. 2009. "Imprisonment and Reoffending." In *Crime and Justice: An Annual Review of Research* (Vol. 38), edited by M. Tonry. Chicago: University of Chicago Press.

National Association of State Budget Officers. *State Expenditure Report 2009.* Washington, DC: Author, 2010. http://nasbo.org/LinkClick.aspx?fileticket=w7Rq07411Ew%3d&tabid=79, accessed November 20, 2011.

National Center for State Courts. "The NCSC Sentencing Attitudes Survey: A Report on the Findings," 2006. http://heinonline.org/HOL/LandingPage?collection=journals&handle=hein.journals/indana82&div=59&id=&page=, accessed January 14, 2014.

National Corrections Reporting Program. *Inter-university Consortium for Political and Social Research.* Ann Arbor, MI: U.S. Department of Justice, Bureau of Justice Statistics, 2003.

National Council on Crime and Delinquency. *And Justice for Some: Differential Treatment of Youth of Color in the Justice System.* Oakland, CA: Author, 2007. http://www.nccdglobal.org/sites/default/files/publication_pdf/justice-for-some.pdf, accessed January 27, 2014.

National Immigration Forum. *The Math of Immigration Detention: Runaway Costs of Immigration Detention Do Not Add Up to Sensible Policies.* Washington, DC: Author, 2011.

National Institute of Corrections. *Women as Correctional Officers in Men's Maximum Security Facilities: A Survey of the Fifty States.* Washington, DC: Author, July 1991. http://www.nicic.org/pubs/1991/009504.pdf, accessed January 5, 2013.

National Institute of Corrections and the Moss Group. "Trends From Focus Group Interviews." *Staff Perspectives: Sexual Violence in Adult Prisons and Jails,* Volume 2 [NIC Accession Number 021619]. Washington, DC: U.S. Department of Justice, 2006.

National Institute of Corrections and the Moss Group. "Investigating Sexual Assaults in Correctional Facilities." *Staff Perspectives: Sexual Violence in Adult Prisons and Jails,* Volume 2,[NIC Accession Number 022101]. Washington, DC: U.S. Department of Justice, 2007.

National Institute of Corrections and the Moss Group. "Sexual Violence in Women's Prison and Jails: Results from Focus Group Interviews." *Staff Perspectives: Sexual Violence in Adult Prisons and Jails,* Volume 3 [NIC Accession Number 023064]. Washington, DC: U.S. Department of Justice, 2009.

National Institute of Corrections. *APEX Guidebook Series (Achieving Performance Excellence).* Washington, DC: Author, 2010–2013.

National Institute on Money in State Politics. "Investigate Money in State Politics," n.d. http://www.followthe-money.org, accessed January 14, 2014.

National Judicial Reporting Program. Ann Arbor, MI: U.S. Department of Justice, Bureau of Justice Statistics, 2004.

National Law Enforcement and Corrections Technology Center. *Keeping Track of Electronic Monitoring.* Rockville, MD: Author, 1999.

National PREA Resource Center. "Prison Rape Elimination Act," 2014. http://www.prearesource center.org/about/prison-rape-elimination-act-prea, accessed February 18, 2014.

National Prison Divestment Campaign. "Top Shareholders in CCA & GEO," 2013. http://prison divestment.wordpress.com/campaign-resources/top-shareholders-in-cca-geo/, accessed January 14, 2014.

National Prison Rape Elimination Commission. *Report on Sexual Victimization in Prisons and Jails.* Washington, DC: U.S. Department of Justice, 2012.

National Prison Rape Elimination Commission. "National Prison Rape Elimination Commission Report," 2009. http://

cybercemetery.unt.edu/archive/nprec/20090820154837/
http://nprec.us/publication/report/executive_summary.
php, accessed February 14, 2014.

National Women's Law Center. "Mothers Behind Bars:
States Are Failing," October 21, 2010. http://www.nwlc.
org/resource/mothers-behind-bars-states-are-failing,
accessed January 14, 2014.

National Women's Law Center and the Rebecca Project
for Human Rights. "Mothers Behind Bars: A State by
State Report Card and Analysis of Federal Policies on
Conditions of Confinement for Pregnant and Parenting
Women and the Effect on Their Children,," October 21,
2010. http://www.nwlc.org/sites/default/files/pdfs/moth-
ersbehindbars2010.pdf, accessed January 15, 2014.

Nelson v. Correctional Medical Services, 583 F.3d 529, 2009.

Nelson, Julianne. *Competition in Corrections: Comparing
Public and Private Sector Operations.* Alexandria, VA:
The CNA Corporation, 2005.

Nink, Carl. *Women Professionals in Corrections: A Growing
Asset.* Centerville, UT: MTC Institute, 2008.

Noonan, Margaret, and Scott Ginder. *Mortality in Local Jails
and State Prisons, 2000–2011: Statistical Tables* [NCJ
242186]. Washington, DC: Bureau of Justice Statistics,
U.S. Department of Justice, 2013. http://www.bjs.gov/
index.cfm?ty=pbdetail&iid=4757, accessed October 2,
2013.

North Carolina Coalition for a Moratorium. "NC Racial
Justice Act: Fist Five Death Row Defendants File
Motions Citing Strong Evidence of Racial Bias," August
3, 2010. http://www.bluenc.com/nc-racial-justice-act-
first-cases-filed, accessed January 14, 2014.

Nothstine, Ray. "Angola Prison, Moral Rehabilitation, and the
Things Ahead." *Acton Commentary,* October 10, 2012.
http://www.acton.org/pub/commentary/2012/10/10/
angola-prison-moral-rehabilitation-things-ahead,
accessed January 14, 2014.

Nugent, William R., Mona Williams, and Mark S. Umbreit.
"Participation in Victim-Offender Mediation and the
Prevalence of Subsequent Delinquent Behavior: A Meta-
Analysis." *Research on Social Work Practice* 14 (2004):
408.

O'Brien, Brendan. "Barrett: Walker Is Attacking Cops by
Questioning Milwaukee Crime Stats," 2011. http://
shorewood.patch.com/articles/barrett-walker-is-
attacking-cops-by-questioning-milwaukee-crime-stats,
accessed January 14, 2014.

O'Connor, James. *The Fiscal Crisis of the State.* New York:
St. Martin's Press, 1973.

O'Connor, Stephen. *Orphan Trains: The Story of Charles
Loring Brace and the Children He Saved and Failed.*
New York: Houghton Mifflin, 2001.

Office of Juvenile Justice and Delinquency Prevention. *Dis-
proportionate Minority Contact: Technical Assistance
Manual.* 4th ed. Washington, DC: U.S. Department of
Justice, Office of Justice Programs, 2009.

Office of Juvenile Justice and Delinquency Prevention.
*Upper and Lower Age of Juvenile Court Delinquency
and Status Offense Jurisdiction, 2012.* Washington, DC:
U.S. Department of Justice, Statistical Briefing Book,
2013. http://www.ojjdp.gov/ojstatbb/structure_process/
qa04102.asp?qaDate=2012, accessed January 31, 2014.

Office of Program Policy Analysis and Government Accountability. *OPPAGA Progress Report: Bay and Moore
Haven Private Prison Contracts Renewed; Bay Costs
Increase* [Report No. 99–46]. Tallahassee, FL: Author,
2000.

Office of Program Policy Analysis and Government Account-
ability. *Steps to Control Prison Inmate Health Care
Costs Have Begun to Show Savings.* Tallahassee, FL:
Author, 2009.

Oppel, Richard A., Jr. "Private Prisons Found to Offer Little
in Savings." *New York Times,* 2011. http://www.nytimes.
com/2011/05/19/us/19prisons.html?pagewanted=all,
accessed January 14, 2014.

O'Reilly, Kevin B. "Doctors Who Aid in Executions Unlikely
to Face Sanctions." *Amednews.com,* February 22,
2010. http://www.ama-assn.org/amednews/2010/02/22/
prsb0222.htm, accessed January 14, 2014.

Ortega, Bob. "Arizona Prison Oversight Lacking for Private
Facilities: State Weighs Expansion Even as Costs Run
High," August 7, 2011a. http://www.azcentral.com/
news/articles/20110807arizona-prison-private-over
sight.html, accessed January 5, 2014.

Ortega, Bob. "Arizona Prison Businesses Are Big Political
Contributors." *Arizona Republic,* September 4, 2011b.
http://www.azcentral.com, accessed January 14, 2014.

Ostermann, Michael. "Parole? Nope, Not for Me. Voluntarily Maxing Out in Prison." *Crime & Delinquency* 57
(2011): 686.

Ourdocuments.gov. "13th Amendment to the U.S. Constitution: Abolition of Slavery (1865)," n.d. http://www.our-
documents.gov/doc.php?flash=true&doc=40, accessed
February 14, 2014.

Owen, Barbara. *In the Mix: Struggle and Survival in a Wom-
en's Prison.* Albany: State University of New York Press,
1998.

Pace Law Review. *Opening Up a Closed World: A Sourcebook on Prison Oversight.* New York: Pace University
School of Law, 2010.

Padilla v. Kentucky 130 S. Ct. 1473, 1486, 2010.

Page, Joshua. *The Toughest Beat: Politics, Punishment, and
the Prison Officers Union in California.* New York:
Oxford University Press, 2011.

Palazzolo, Joe. "Judge Orders Sex Change Operation
for Prisoner." *Wall Street Journal Blog,* 2012. http://
blogs.wsj.com/law/2012/09/04/judge-orders-sex-
change-operation-for-federal-prisoner/, accessed January
13, 2014.

Parent, Dale, Jim Byrne, Vered Tsarfaty, Laura Valade, and
Julie Esselman. *Day Reporting Centers* (Vols. 1 and 2).
Washington, DC: National Institute of Justice, 1995.

Partyka, Rhea D. *Stress and Coping Styles of Female Prison
Inmates.* Master's thesis. University of Toledo, 2001.
https://etd.ohiolink.edu/ap:10:0::NO:10:P10_ETD_
SUBID:77671, accessed November 20, 2011.

Paternoster, Raymond, and Robert Brame. "Reassessing
Race Disparity in Maryland Capital Cases." *Criminology* 46 (2008): 971–1008.

Payne, B., and R. Gainey. "The Electronic Monitoring of
Offenders Released from Jail or Prison: Safety, Control,
and Comparisons to the Incarceration Experience." *The
Prison Journal* 84 (2004): 24.

PBS. *Slavery by Another Name*. Official Selection of the Sundance Film Festival, 2012. http://www.pbs.org/tpt/slavery-by-another-name/, accessed February 16, 2014.

Peters, Michael, David Thomas, and Christopher Zamberlan. *Boot Camps for Juvenile Offenders: Program Summary*. Washington, DC: U.S. Department of Justice, Office of Juvenile Justice and Delinquency Prevention, 1997.

Petersilia, J. *When Prisoners Come Home: Parole and Prisoners Reentry*. New York: Oxford University Press, 2003.

Petersilia, Joan. "Probation in the US." *Crime and Justice* 22 (1997): 149–200.

Petersilia, Joan. *Parole and Prisoner Reentry in the United States,* Part I. Lexington, KY: American Probation and Parole Agency, 2000.

Petersilia, Joan. *Parole and Prisoner Reentry in the United States,* Part II. New York: Oxford University Press, 2003.

Petersilia, Joan, and Elizabeth P. Deschenes. "Perceptions of Punishment." *The Prison Journal* 74 (1994): 306–328.

Petteruti, Amanda, Nastassia Walsh, and Tracy Velázquez. *The Costs of Confinement: Why Good Juvenile Justice Policies Make Good Fiscal Sense*. Washington, DC: Justice Policy Institute, 2009. http://www.justicepolicy.org/images/upload/09_05_rep_costsofconfinement_jj_ps.pdf, accessed December 30, 2013.

Pettit, Becky, and Bruce Western. "Mass Imprisonment and the Life Course: Race and Class Inequality in U.S. Incarceration." *American Sociological Review* 59 (2004): 151–169.

Pew Center on the States. *One in 31: The Long Reach of American Corrections*. Washington, DC: The Pew Charitable Trusts, 2009.

Pew Center on the States. *The State of Recidivism: The Revolving Door of America's Prisons*. Washington, DC: Author, 2011a.

Pew Research Center. *Attitudes Toward Social Issues: Increased Support for Legalization of Marijuana*. Washington, DC: Author, 2011b. http://www.people-press.org/2011/03/03/section-3-attitudes-toward-social-issues/, accessed February 27, 2014.

Pew Research Center. *Public Opinion on Sentencing and Corrections Policy in America*. Washington, DC: Author, March 2012. http://www.pewstates.org/uploadedFiles/PCS_Assets/2012/PEW_NationalSurveyResearchPaper_FINAL.pdf, accessed January 14, 2014.

Pickett, Robert. *House of Refuge: Origins of Juvenile Justice Reform in New York, 1815–1857*. Syracuse, NY: Syracuse University Press, 1969.

Pinkerton, James. "Scandal Dims Hopes in Willacy County." *Houston Chronicle Rio Grande Valley Bureau,* February 27, 2005. http://www.chron.com/news/houston-texas, accessed January 14, 2014.

Plata, Coleman v. Wilson, 912 F.Supp. 1282, E.D. Cal., 1995.

Polsky, Howard W. *Cottage Six: The Social System of Delinquent Boys in Residential Treatment*. New York: Russell Sage Foundation, 1962.

Porter, Nicole D. *The State of Sentencing 2010: Developments in Policy and Practice*. Washington, DC: The Sentencing Project, 2011.

Porter, Rachel, Sophia Lee, and Mary Lutz. *Balancing Punishment and Treatment: Alternatives to Incarceration in New York City*. New York: Vera Institute of Justice, 2002.

Potter, Gary. "Crime Control and the Death Penalty." *The Advocate* 19 (1997): 1–4.

Pranis, Kevin. *Cost-Saving or Cost-Shifting: The Fiscal Impact of Prison Privatization in Arizona*. Tallahassee, FL: Private Corrections Working Group, n.d. www.prisonpolicy.org/scans/AZ_PP_Rpt_v4.pdf, accessed January 14, 2014.

Pratt, Travis C., and Jeff Maahs. "Are Private Prisons More Cost-effective Than Public Prisons? A Meta-analysis of Evaluation Research Studies." *Crime & Delinquency* 45 (1999): 358–371.

Prejean, Helen. *Dead Man Walking*. New York: Vintage, 1994.

President's Advisory Commission on Asian Americans and Pacific Islanders. *A People Looking Forward: Action for Access and Partnerships in the 21st Century. An Interim Report to the President*. Washington, DC: Author, 2001.

Prison Mindfulness Institute. "Our Inside Programs." *Projects,* n.d. http://prisonmindfulness.org/projects/ri-doc/, accessed April 28, 2014.

Private Corrections Working Group. *News*. Tallahassee, FL: Private Corrections Working Group, 2013. http://www.privateci.org/news.html, accessed June 1, 2014.

Protalinski, Emil. "Student Goes to Federal Prison for Hacking Sarah Palin's E-mail." *TechSpot,* January 13, 2011. http://www.techspot.com/news/41974-student-goes-to-federal-prison-for-hacking-sarah-palins-e-mail.html, accessed November 18, 2011.

Radelet, Michael L., and Traci L. LaCock. "Do Executions Lower Homicide Rates? The Views of Leading Criminologists." *The Journal of Criminal Law & Criminology* 99 (2009): 489.

Rafter, Nicole H. "Gender and Justice: The Equal Protection Issue." In *The American Prison: Issues in Research and Policy,* edited by Lynne Goodstein and Doris Mackenzie, 89–109. New York: Plenum Press, 1989.

Rafter, Nicole H. *Creating Born Criminals*. Urbana: University of Illinois Press, 1997.

Rapaport, Elizabeth. "Equality of the Damned: The Execution of Women on the Cusp of the 21st Century." *Ohio Northern University Law Review* 26 (2000): 581-600.

Rathbone, Cristina. *A World Apart: Women, Prison, and Life Behind Bars*. New York: Random House, 2005.

Reaves, Brian A. *Federal Law Enforcement Officers, 2008*. Washington, DC: U.S. Department of Justice, Office of Justice Programs, Bureau of Justice Statistics, 2012.

Reddy, Vikrant P. "Striking Visualizations of the National Crime Decline." *Right on Crime,* January 25, 2013. http://www.rightoncrime.com/2013/01/striking-visualizations-of-the-national-crime-decline/, accessed January 14, 2014.

Reilly, Ryan J. "DOJ Threatens to Withhold Grants From States That Aren't Protecting Prisoners From Rape." *The Huffington Post,* February 12, 2014. http://www.huffingtonpost.com/2014/02/12/doj-prison-rape_n_4775411.html, accessed February 14, 2014.

Renaissance Islam. "Ahmadiyya Muslim Prison Ministry USA." *Blog Post,* June 17, 2009. http://ahmadiyyamus

limcommunityusa.blogspot.com/2009/06/american-ahmadiyya-muslim-prison.html, accessed April 28, 2014.

Reynolds, Morgan. *Crime in Texas.* NCPA Policy Report No. 102. Dallas: National Center for Policy Analysis, 1991.

R.G. v. Koller, 415 F Supp. 2d 1129, 1154–1155, 2006.

Rhine, Edward. "Something Works: Recent Research on Effective Correctional Programming." *The State of Corrections: 1995 Proceedings.* Lanham, MD: American Correctional Association, 1996.

Rhodes v. Chapman, 452 U.S. 337, 1981.

Ridder/Braden Inc. "Survey on Drug Abuse and Drug Policy: Summary of Results," 2001. http://www.prisonpolicy.org/scans/Survey_Results.pdf, accessed January 14, 2014.

Ringhoff, Daniel, Lisa Rapp, and John Robst. "The Criminalization Hypothesis: Practice and Policy Implications for Persons With Serious Mental Illness in the Criminal Justice System." *Best Practice in Mental Health* 8 (2012): 1–20.

Riveland, Chase. *Supermax Prisons: Overview and General Considerations.* Washington, DC: U.S. Department of Justice, National Institute of Corrections, January 1999. http://static.nicic.gov/Library/014937.pdf, accessed November 18, 2011.

Robinson, Russell K. "Masculinity as Prison: Sexual Identity, Race, and Incarceration." *California Law Review* 99 (2011): 1309.

Robinson, William I. "The New Global Capitalism and the War on Immigrants." *Truthout,* September 13, 2013. http://www.truth-out.org/news/item/18623-the-new-global-capitalism-and-the-war-on-immigrants, accessed February 25, 2014.

Roman, John, Aaron Chalfin, Aaron Sundquist, Carly Knight, and Askar Darmenov. *The Cost of the Death Penalty in Maryland.* Washington, DC: Urban Institute, Justice Policy Center, 2008. http://www.urban.org/UploadedPDF/411625_md_death_penalty.pdf, accessed January 10, 2014.

Roper v. Simmons, 543 U.S 551, 2005.

Roscher, Sherri L. *The Development of Coping Strategies of Female Inmates With Life Sentences: A Brief Summary of a Dissertation.* Dayton, OH: Wright State University, 2005. http://www.drc.ohio.gov/web/reports/RoscherInternetSummary.pdf, accessed January 15, 2014.

Rosenfeld, Richard, Joel Wallman, and Robert Fornango. "The Contribution of Ex-Prisoners to Crime Rates." In *Prisoner Reentry and Crime in America,* edited by Jeremy Travis and Christy Visher. New York: Cambridge University Press, 2005.

Ross, Helen E., Frederick B. Glaser, and Susan Stiasny. "Sex Differences in the Prevalence of Psychiatric Disorders in Patients With Alcohol and Drug Problems." *Addiction* 83 (1998): 1179–1192.

Ross, Jeffrey I., and Stephen C. Richards. *Behind Bars: Surviving Prison.* Indianapolis, IN: Alpha, 2002.

Ross, Robert, and Elizabeth Fabiano. *Female Offenders: Correctional Afterthoughts.* Jefferson, NC: McFarlane, 1986.

Rothman, David. *The Discovery of the Asylum.* Philadelphia: Little, Brown, 1971.

Ruffin v. Commonwealth, 62 Va. 790, 1871.

Ruiz v. Johnson, 37 F. Supp. 2d 855, S.D. Tex. 1999, rev'd, 178 F.3d 385, 5th Cir. 1999.

Rusche, Georg, and Otto Kirchheimer. *Punishment and Social Structure.* New York: Columbia University Press, 1968.

Samuels, Jocelyn and David J. Hickton. "Re: Investigation of the Pennsylvania Department of Corrections' Use of Solitary Confinement on Prisoner's with Serious Mental Illness and/or Intellectual Disabilities." Washington, D.C.: USDOJ Civil Rights Division, February, 2014. http://www.justice.gov/crt/about/spl/documents/pdoc_finding_2-24-14.pdf, accessed June 20, 2014.

Santos, Fernanda. "Plan to Close Prisons Stirs Anxiety in Rural Towns." *New York Times,* January, 27, 2008. http://www.nytimes.com/2008/01/27/nyregion/27prison.html?pagewanted=all&_r=0, accessed January 14, 2014.

Savolainen, Jukka. *Research Brief No. 2: The Impact of Felony ATI Programs on Recidivism.* New York: New York City Criminal Justice Agency, Inc., 2003.

Scherer, Michael, and Maya Rhodan. "Obama's Legacy Project." *Time,* February 24, 2014.

Schlager, Melinda D., and Kelly Robbins. "Does Parole Work? Revisited. Reframing the Discussion of the Impact of Postprison Supervision on Offender Outcome." *The Prison Journal* 88 (2008): 234–251.

Schloss, Christine S., and Leanne F. Alarid. "Standards in the Privatization of Probation Services: A Statutory Analysis." *Criminal Justice Review* 32 (2007): 233–245. http://www.sagepub.com/hanserstudy/articles/05/Schloss.pdf, accessed February 3, 2014.

Schur, Edwin M. *Radical Non-intervention: Rethinking the Delinquency Problem.* Englewood Cliffs, NJ: Prentice Hall, 1973.

Schwartz, Jennifer, and Darrell J. Steffensmeier. "The Nature of Female Offending: Patterns and Explanation." In *Female Offenders: Critical Perspectives and Effective Interventions,* edited by Ruth Zaplin. Boston, MA: Jones and Bartlett, 2007.

Schwartz, Jennifer, Darrell J. Steffensmeier, and Ben Feldmeyer. "Assessing Trends in Women's Violence Via Data Triangulation: Arrests, Convictions, Incarcerations, and Victim Reports." *Social Problems* 56 (2009): 494–525.

Schwartz, John. "Simulated Prison in '71 Showed a Fine Line Between 'Normal' and 'Monster.'" *New York Times,* May 6, 2004, p. A20. http://www.nytimes.com/2004/05/06/international/middleeast/06PSYC.html?ex=1399262400&en=91f8144cdf7dd44a&ei=5007&partner=USERLAND, accessed January 4, 2013.

Schwartz, Sunny, with David Boodell. *Dreams from the Monster Factory: A Tale of Prison, Redemption and One Woman's Fight to Restore Justice to All.* New York: Scribner, 2009.

Schwarzenegger v. Plata (09–1233).

Scull, Andrew. *Decarceration: Community Treatment and the Deviant.* Englewood Cliffs, NJ: Prentice Hall, 1977.

Sedlak, Andrea J., and Carol Bruce. *Youth's Characteristics and Backgrounds: Findings From the Survey of Youth in Residential Placement.* Washington, DC: U.S. Department of Justice, Office of Juvenile Justice and Delinquency Prevention, 2010. https://syrp.org/images/Youth%20Characteristics.pdf, accessed January 15, 2014.

Sedlack, Andrea J., and Karla S. McPherson. "Survey of Youth in Residential Placement: Youth's Needs and Services." *SYRP Report,* Doc. No. 227660. Rockville, MD: Westat, 2010.

Seeds of Hope Jail Ministry, Inc. "Jail Ministry and Reentry Services," n.d. http://seedsofhopejailministry.org/, accessed May 10, 2014.

Segal, Geoffrey, and Adrian Moore. *Weighing the Watchmen: Evaluating the Costs and Benefits of Outsourcing Correctional Services* (Part 1). Los Angeles, CA: Reason Public Policy Institute, 2002.

Seiter, Richard P., and Karen R. Kadela. "Prisoner Reentry: What Works, What Does Not, and What Is Promising." *Crime & Delinquency* 49 (2003): 360–388.

Sellin, J. Thorsten. *Pioneering in Penology: The Amsterdam Houses of Correction in the Sixteenth and Seventeenth Centuries.* Philadelphia: University of Pennsylvania Press, 1944.

Sellin, J. Thorsten. *Slavery and the Penal System.* New York: Elsevier, 1976.

Selman, Donna, and Paul Leighton. *Punishment for Sale: Private Prisons, Big Business, and the Incarceration Binge.* Lanham, MD: Rowman & Littlefield, 2010.

The Sentencing Project. *Mentally Ill Offenders in the Criminal Justice System: An Analysis and Prescription.* Washington, DC: Author, 2002.

Sexton, Lori, Valerie Jenness, and Jennifer Sumner. *Where the Margins Meet: A Demographic Assessment of Transgender Inmates in Men's Prisons,* 2009. http://ucicorrections.seweb.uci.edu/files/2013/06/A-Demographic-Assessment-of-Transgender-Inmates-in-Mens-Prisons.pdf, accessed January 13, 2014.

Sherbert, Erin. "Female Guards Can't Sue Over Masturbating Inmates." *SF Weekly,* March 23, 2012. http://blogs.sfweekly.com/thesnitch/2012/03/female_prison_guards_cant_sue.php, accessed January 4, 2013.

Sherman, Lawrence W., Denise Gottfredson, Doris McKenzie, John Eck, Peter Reuter, and Shawn Bushway. *Preventing Crime: What Works, What Doesn't, What's Promising* [Report to the U.S. Congress]. Washington, DC: U.S. Department of Justice, Office of Justice Programs, National Institute of Justice, 1997.

Sherman, Lawrence W., and Heather Strang. *Restorative Justice: The Evidence.* London: The Smith Institute, 2007. http://www.restorativejustice.org/10fulltext/restorative-justice-the-evidence, accessed February 14, 2014.

Sickmund, Melissa, T. J. Sladky, Wei Kang, and Charles Puzzanchera. *Easy Access to the Census of Juveniles in Residential Placement.* Washington, DC: U.S. Department of Justice, Office of Justice Programs, Office of Juvenile Justice and Delinquency Prevention, 2013. http://www.ojjdp.gov/ojstatbb/ezacjrp/, accessed December 30, 2013.

Smith, Paula, Claire Goggin, and Paul Gendreau. *The Effects of Prison Sentences and Intermediate Sanctions on Recidivism: General Effects and Individual Differences.* Quebec: Public Works and Government Services Canada, 2002.

Snell, Tracy L. *Women in Prison: Survey of State Prison Inmates, 1991* [NCJ 145321]. Washington, DC: U.S. Department of Justice, Bureau of Justice Statistics, 1994. http://bjs.ojp.usdoj.gov/content/pub/pdf/WOPRIS.PDF, accessed January 15, 2014.

Snell, Tracy L. *Capital Punishment, 2012—Statistical Tables* [NCJ 245789]. Washington, DC: Bureau of Justice Statistics, May 2014.

Solomon, Amy L., Kelly D. Johnson, Jeremy Travis, and Elizabeth C. McBride. *From Prison to Work: The Employment Dimensions of Prisoner Reentry.* Washington, DC: Urban Institute, 2004.

Solomon, Amy L., Vera Kachnowski, and Avi Bhati. *Does Parole Work? Analyzing the Impact of Postprison Supervision on Rearrest Outcomes.* Washington, DC: Urban Institute, 2005. http://www.urban.org/publications/311156.html, accessed January 24, 2014.

Solomon, Amy L., Christy Visher, Nancy G. La Vigne, and Jenny Osborne. *Understanding the Challenges of Prisoner Reentry: Research Findings from the Urban Institute's Prisoner Reentry Portfolio.* Washington, DC: Urban Institute, Justice Policy Center, 2006. http://www.urban.org/publications/411289.html, accessed January 24, 2014.

Sommers, Paul, Bronwyn Mauldin, and Sara Levin. *Pioneer Human Services: A Case Study.* Seattle: University of Washington, Evans School of Public Affairs, 2000.

Southern Center for Human Rights. *Profiting From the Poor: A Report on Predatory Probation Companies in Georgia.* Atlanta, GA: Southern Center for Human Rights, 2008.

Spohn, Cassia, and David Holleran. "The Effect of Imprisonment on Recidivism Rates of Felony Offenders: A Focus on Drug Offenders." *Criminology* 40 (2002): 329–358.

State of Arizona, Office of the Auditor General. *Department of Corrections—Prison Population Growth.* Phoenix, AZ: Author, 2010.

Stephan, James J. *Census of State and Federal Correctional Facilities, 2005.* Washington, DC: U.S. Department of Justice, Office of Justice Programs, Bureau of Justice Statistics, 2008. http://bjs.ojp.usdoj.gov/content/pub/pdf/csfcf05.pdf, accessed January 5, 2013.

Stephan, James J., and Georgette Walsh. *Census of Jail Facilities, 2006* [NCJ 230188]. Washington, DC: U.S. Department of Justice, Office of Justice Programs, Bureau of Justice Statistics, December 20, 2011.

Sterngold, J. "Illiteracy Reinforces Prisoners' Captivity: State Prisons Are Crowded With Inmates Lacking a Basic Education—Their Dismal Job Prospects Mean They're Likely to Land Back Behind Bars." *San Francisco Chronicle,* December 27, 2006. http://articles.sfgate.com/2006-12-27/news/17325943_1_education-illiteracy-vocational-classes, accessed November 20, 2011.

Stinchcomb, Jeanne B., Susan W. McCampbell, and Elizabeth P. Layman. *Future Force: A Guide to Building the 21st Century Community Corrections Workforce* [NIC Accession Number 021799]. Washington, DC: National Institute of Corrections, 2006.

Street, David, Robert D. Vinter, and Charles Perrow. *Organization for Treatment: A Comparative Study of Institutions for Delinquents.* New York: Free Press, 1966.

Streib, Victor L. "Rare and Inconsistent: The Death Penalty for Women." *Fordham Urban Law Journal* 33 (2005): 101–132.

Streib, Victor L. "Death Penalty for Female Offenders, January 1, 1973 through December 31, 2010." Ohio Northern University, 2010. http://www.deathpenaltyinfo.org/documents/femaledeathrow.pdf, accessed January 14, 2014.

Strickland v. Washington, 466 U.S. 668, 1984.

Substance Abuse and Mental Health Services Administration. "Half of Women on Probation or Parole Experience Mental Illness." Rockville, MD: Author, Center for Behavioral Health Statistics and Quality, 2012. http://www.samhsa.gov/data/spotlight/Spot063WomenParole2012.pdf, accessed January 24, 2014.

Sullivan, Laura. "Prison Economies Help Drive Arizona Immigration Law." *National Public Radio,* October 28, 2010. http://www.npr.org/2010/10/28/130833741/prison-economics-help-drive-ariz-immigration-law, accessed January 14, 2014.

Superintendent v. Hill, 472 U.S. 445, 1985. https://supreme.justia.com/cases/federal/us/472/445/case.html, accessed February 14, 2014.

Supreme Court of the United States. *Florence v. Board of Chosen Freeholders of County of Burlington et al.* [No 10-945]. Argued October 12, 2011—Decided April 2, 2012. http://www.supremecourt.gov/opinions/11pdf/10-945.pdf, accessed January 27, 2014.

Swanson, Doug. "Sex Abuse Reported at Youth Jail." *The Dallas News,* February 18, 2007a. http://www.dallasnews.com/sharedcontent/dws/news/texassouthwest/stories/021807dntextycsex.1bd0f05.html, accessed December 30, 2013.

Swanson, Doug. "Complaints Filed Against Guards at All 13 Youth Prisons, Documents Show." *The Dallas News,* March 6, 2007b. http://www.dallasnews.com/sharedcontent/dws/dn/latestnews/stories/030707dnpronutyc.39129f4.html, accessed December 30, 2013.

Syracuse.com. "Transcript of Gov. David Paterson's State of the State Address for 2009," January 7, 2009. http://blog.syracuse.com/indepth/2009/01/transcript_of_gov_david_paters.html, accessed January 15, 2014.

Takagi, Ronald. *Strangers From a Different Shore: A History of Asian Americans.* Boston: Little, Brown, 1989.

Tan, Michael. *The Tragic Costs of Immigration Detention.* New York: American Civil Liberties Union, 2011. https://www.aclu.org/blog/immigrants-rights/tragic-costs-immigration-detention, accessed January 14, 2014.

Tappan, Paul W. "Delinquent Girls in Court: A Study of the Wayward Minor Court of New York." *Psychoanalytic Review* 35 (1948): 97–98.

Taylor, Rupert. "The Difficult Life of Official Executioners," 2010. http://suite101.com/article/the-difficult-life-of-official-executioners-a3163654, accessed January 14, 2014.

Templeton, Robin. "Superscapegoating: Teen 'Superpredator' Hype Set Stage for Draconian Legislation." *Fairness and Accuracy in Reporting,* January/February 1998. http://www.fair.org/index.php?page=1414, accessed January 31, 2014.

Thomas, Jim, Anmarie Aylward, Mary Louise Casey, David Moton, Michelle Oldham, and George W. Wheetley. "Rethinking Prisoner Litigation: Some Preliminary Distinctions Between Habeas Corpus and Civil Rights." *The Prison Journal* 65 (1985): 83.

Thompson, E. P., Douglas Hay, Peter Linebaugh, John G. Rule, and Carl Winslow. *Albion's Fatal Tree: Crime and Society in Eighteenth-Century England.* New York: Pantheon, 1975.

Tollett, T. *A Comparative Study of Florida Delinquency Commitment Programs.* Tallahassee: Florida Department of Health and Rehabilitative Services, 1987.

Travis, Jeremy. *But They All Come Back: Facing the Challenges of Prisoner Reentry.* Washington, DC: Urban Institute Press, 2005.

Travis, Jeremy, and Caterina G. Roman. *Taking Stock: Housing, Homelessness, and Prisoner Reentry.* Washington, DC: Urban Institute, 2004. http://urban.org/UploadedPDF/411096_taking_stock.pdf, accessed January 24, 2014.

Travis, Jeremy, Amy Solomon, and Michelle Waul. *From Prison to Home: The Dimensions and Consequences of Prisoner Reentry.* Washington, DC: Urban Institute, 2001.

Truman, Jennifer, Lynn Langton, and Michael Planty. 2013. "Criminal Victimization, 2012." *Bulletin* (October 2013), NCJ 243389. http://www.bjs.gov/content/pub/pdf/cv12.pdf, accessed January 27, 2014.

Umbreit, Mark S. "Restorative Justice Through Victim-Offender Mediation: A Multi-Site Assessment." *Western Criminology Review* 1 (1998). http://wcr.sonoma.edu/v1n1/umbreit.html, accessed January 27, 2014.

Ulmer, Jeffery T., and Mindy S. Bradley. "Variation in Trial Penalties Among Serious Violent Offenses." *Criminology* 44, no. 3 (2006): 631–70.

U.S. v. Booker, 543 U.S. 220, 125 S.Ct. 738, 160 L.Ed. 2d 621 No. 04–104, 2005.

U.S. Census Bureau. *Annual Survey of Public Employment and Payroll Summary Report, 2010.* Washington, DC: Author, 2012a. http://www.census.gov/prod/2012pubs/g10-aspep.pdf, accessed January 5, 2013.

U.S. Census Bureau. *Federal Government Civilian Employment by Function, March 2010.* Washington, DC: Author, 2012b. http://www.census.gov//govs/apes/historical_data_2010.html, accessed January 5, 2013.

U.S. Census Bureau. "Annual Estimates of the Resident Population: April 1, 2010, to July 1, 2012." *American FactFinder,* 2013a. http://factfinder2.census.gov/faces/tableservices/jsf/pages/productview.xhtml?pid=PEP_2012_PEPANNRES&prodType=table, accessed November 20, 2012.

U.S. Census Bureau. *State and County Quick Facts.* Washington, DC: Author, 2013b. http://quickfacts.census.gov/qfd/states/00000.html, accessed January 27, 2014.

U.S. Census Bureau. *U.S. and World Population Clock.* Washington, DC: Author, 2013c. http://www.census.gov/popclock/, accessed February 19, 2014.

U.S. Department of Justice. "Tribal Law and Order Act," 2010. http://www.justice.gov/tribal/tloa.html, accessed December 13, 2013.

U.S. Department of Justice. "Press Release: Justice Department Releases Final Rule to Prevent, Detect, and Respond to Prison Rape," 2012a. http://www.justice.gov/opa/pr/2012/May/12-ag-635.html, accessed January 14, 2014.

U.S. Department of Justice. "Regulatory Impact Assessment for PREA Final Rule (May 17, 2012)," 2012b. http://www.ojp.usdoj.gov/programs/pdfs/prea_ria.pdf, accessed January 14, 2014.

United States v. Deen. No. 11-2271. Decided and Filed February 7, 2013. http://www.ca6.uscourts.gov/opinions.pdf/13a0030p-06.pdf, accessed March 1, 2013.

U.S. v. Fan Fan, 543 U.S. 220, 125 S.Ct. 738, 160 L.Ed. 2d 621 No. 04–105, 2005.

U.S. Government Accountability Office. *Costs of Prisons: Bureau of Prisons Needs Better Data to Assess Alternatives for Acquiring Low and Minimum Security Facilities.* Washington, DC: U.S. Government Accountability Office, 2007.

"U. S. Government" entryU.S. Immigration and Customs Enforcement. *Secure Communities.* Washington, DC: Author, 2013. http://www.ice.gov/secure_communities/, accessed January 27, 2014.

U.S. Sentencing Commission. *Special Report to the Congress: Cocaine and Federal Sentencing Policy.* Washington, DC: Author, 1997. http://www.ussc.gov/Legislative_and_Public_Affairs/Congressional_Testimony_and_Reports/Drug_Topics/19970429_RtC_Cocaine_Sentencing_Policy.PDF, accessed January 27, 2014.

U.S. Sentencing Commission. *Federal Offenders Sentenced to Supervised Release.* Washington, DC: Author, 2010. http://www.ussc.gov/Education_and_Training/Annual_National_Training_Seminar/2012/2_Federal_Offenders_Sentenced_to_Supervised_Release.pdf, accessed January 24, 2014.

United States v. Tapia. No. 9-50248, Argued and Submitted November 10, 2011; Filed December 8, 2011. http://cdn.ca9.uscourts.gov/datastore/opinions/2011/12/08/09-50248.pdf, accessed March 1, 2013.

Vagins, Deborah J., and Jesselyn McCurdy. *Cracks in the System: Twenty Years of the Unjust Federal Crack Cocaine Law.* Washington, DC: American Civil Liberties Union, 2006. https://www.aclu.org/files/assets/cracksinsystem_20061025.pdf, accessed January 27, 2014.

Vale, Patricia A. "Probation Caseloads Taken Out of Context." Letter to *MarylandReporter.com,* August 11, 2011. http://marylandreporter.com/2011/08/11/probation-caseloads-taken-out-of-context-division-chief-says/, accessed May 14, 2014.

Van Vleet, Russell K., Audrey O. Hickert, and Erin E. Becker. *Evaluation of the Salt Lake County Day Reporting Center.* Salt Lake City: Utah Criminal Justice Center, 2006.

Vera Institute of Justice. *Confronting Confinement: A Report on the Findings of the Commission on Safety and Abuse in America's Prisons.* New York: Author, 2006. http://www.vera.org/sites/default/files/resources/downloads/Confronting_Confinement.pdf, accessed February 14, 2014.

Visher, Christy A., Sara A. Debus-Sherrill, and Jennifer Yahner. "Employment After Prison: A Longitudinal Study of Former Prisoners." *Justice Quarterly* 28 (2010): 698–715. http://dx.doi.org/10.1080/07418825.2010.535553, accessed January 24, 2014.

von Hentig, Hans. *Punishment: Its Origin, Purpose and Psychology.* Montclair, NJ: Patterson Smith, 1973.

Von Hirsch, Andrew. *Doing Justice.* Boston: Northeastern University Press, 1976.

Vuong, Linh, Christopher Hartney, Barry Krisberg, and Susan Marchionna. *The Extravagance of Imprisonment Revisited.* Oakland, CA: National Council on Crime and Delinquency, 2010.

Wacquant, Loïc. "From Slavery to Mass Incarceration: Rethinking the 'Race' Question in the US." *New Left Review* January–February (2002). http://newleftreview.org/II/13/loic-wacquant-from-slavery-to-mass-incarceration, accessed May 20, 2014.

Wagner, John, and Aaron C. Davis. "Md. Senate Panel Approves Measures on Death Penalty Repeal, Tight Gun-Control." *The Washington Post,* February 22, 2013. http://www.washingtonpost.com/local/md-politics/omalley-bill-to-repeal-maryland-death-penalty-clears-senate-panel/2013/02/21/25d54e26–7c53–11e2-a044–676856536b40_story.html, accessed January 14, 2014.

Warner, Tara D., and John H. Kramer. "Closing the Revolving Door?" *Criminal Justice and Behavior* 36 (2009): 89–109.

Warren, Jenifer. *One in 100: Behind Bars in America 2008.* Washington, DC: The Pew Center on the States, 2008. http://www.pewtrusts.org/uploadedFiles/wwwpewtrustsorg/Reports/sentencing_and_corrections/one_in_100.pdf, accessed May 4, 2014.

Warwick, Kevin, Hannah Dodd, and S. Rebecca Neusteter. *Transition From Jail to Community Initiative Practice Brief: Case Management Strategies for Successful Jail Reentry.* Washington DC: National Institute of Corrections and Urban Institute, 2012.

Weis, Joseph G. "Liberation and Crime: The Invention of the New Female Criminal." *Crime and Social Justice* 6 (1976): 17.

Weisberg, Robert, and David Mills. "Violence Silence: Why Nobody Cares about Prison Rape." *Slate,* October 1, 2003. http://www.slate.com/articles/news_and_politics/jurisprudence/2003/10/violence_silence.html, accessed February 14, 2014.

Weissman, Marsha. "Aspiring to the Impracticable: Alternatives to Incarceration in the Era of Mass Incarceration." N.Y.U. *Review of Law and Social Change* 33 (2009): 235.

Wermink, Hilde, Arjan Blokland, Paul Nieuwbeerta, Daniel Nagin, and Nilolaj Tollenaar. "Comparing the Effects of Community Service and Short-Term Imprisonment on Recidivism: A Matched Samples Approach." *Journal of Experimental Criminology* 6 (2010): 325–349.

West, Heather C., and William Sabol. *Prisoners in 2009.* Washington, DC: U.S. Department of Justice, Bureau of Justice Statistics, 2010. http://www.bjs.gov/content/pub/pdf/p09.pdf, accessed January 4, 2014.

West, Heather C., William J. Sabol, and Sarah J. Greenman. *Prisoners in 2009* [NCJ 231675]. Washington, DC: Bureau of Justice Statistics, U.S. Department of Justice, 2010. http://bjs.ojp.usdoj.gov/index.cfm?ty=pbdetail&iid=2232, accessed November 18, 2011.

WFTV.com. "Kindergarten Girl Handcuffed, Arrested at Fla. School," March 30, 2007. http://www.wftv.com/news/news/kindergarten-girl-handcuffed-arrested-at-fla-schoo/nFBR4/, accessed January 15, 2014.

Whitfield, Dexter. *Economic Impact of Prisons in Rural Areas: A Review of the Issues.* Tralee, Ireland: European Services Strategies Unit, 2008.

Wilkinson v. Austin (04–495) 544 U.S. 74 (2005); 372 F.3d 346.

Williams, Alisha, David C. May, and Peter B. Wood. "Lesser of Two Evils? A Qualitative Study of Offenders' Preferences for Prison Compared to Alternatives." *Journal of Offender Rehabilitation* 46 (2008): 71–90.

Williams, Brie, and Rita Abraldes. "Growing Older: Challenges of Prison and Reentry for the Aging Population." In *Public Health Behind Bars: From Prisons to Communities,* edited by Robert B. Greifinger. New York: Springer, 2007.

Williams, William A. *The Contours of American History.* New York: New Viewpoints, 1973.

Wills, Garry. *Negro President: Jefferson and the Slave Power.* New York: First Mariner, 2003.

Wilper, Andrew P., Steffie Woolhandler, J. Wesley Boyd, Karen E. Lasser, Danny McCormick, and David U. Himmelstein. "The Health and Health Care of US Prisoners: Results of a Nationwide Survey." *American Journal of Public Health* 99 (2009): 666–672.

Wilson, David B., Ojmarrh Mitchell, and Doris L. MacKenzie. "A Systematic Review of Drug Court Effects on Recidivism." *Journal of Experimental Criminology* 2 (2006): 459–487.

Wilson, James Q. "Thinking About Crime: The Debate Over Deterrence." *The Atlantic Monthly* 252 (1983): 72–88.

Wilson, James Q. "Crime, Race, and Values." *Society* 30, no. 1 (1992): 90–93.

Wilson, James Q. "Hard Times, Fewer Crimes." *Wall Street Journal,* May 28, 2011. http://online .wsj.com/article/SB100014240527023040665045763 45553135009870.html, accessed January 14, 2014.

Winton, Richard, and Andrew Blankstein. "Lindsay Lohan Sentenced to 90 Days in Jail and 90 in Rehab." *Los Angeles Times,* July 7, 2010. http://articles.latimes. com/2010/jul/07/local/la-me-0707-lohan-20100707, accessed January 27, 2014.

Wolff v. McDonnell, 418 U.S. 539, 1974.

Wolfgang, Marvin. As quoted in *Continuing the Struggle for Justice,* edited by Barry Krisberg, Christopher Baird, and Susan Marchionna. Thousand Oaks, CA: Sage, 2007.

Wood, Peter B., and H.G. Grasmick. "Inmates Rank the Severity of Ten Alternative Sanctions Compared to Prison." *Journal of the Oklahoma Criminal Justice Research Consortium* 2 (1995): 30–42. www.doc.state. ok.us/offenders/ocjrc/95/950725J.HTM, accessed September 10, 2012.

Wooden, Kenneth. *Weeping in the Playtime of Others: America's Incarcerated Children.* New York: McGraw-Hill, 1976.

Woodford, Jeanne, Susan Marchionna, and F. Delgado. *Case Management and the Probation Workforce.* Berkeley, CA: Earl Warren Institute on Law and Social Policy, 2013.

Workforce Associates. *A 21st Century Workforce for America's Correction Profession.* Alexandria, VA: American Correctional Association, 2004.

Worrall, John L., Pamela Schram, Eric Hays, and Matthew Newman. "An Analysis of the Relationship Between Probation Caseloads and Property Crime Rates in California Counties." *Journal of Criminal Justice* 32 (2004): 231–241.

Yahner, Jennifer, and Christy Visher. *Illinois Prisoners Reentry Success Three Years After Release* [Issue brief]. Washington, DC: Urban Institute, 2008.

Yahner, Jennifer, Christy Visher, and Amy L. Solomon. *Returning Home on Parole: Former Prisoner's Experiences in Illinois, Ohio, and Texas.* Washington, DC: Urban Institute, Justice Policy Center, 2008.

Yaroshefsky, Ellen. "Ethics and Plea Bargaining: What's Discovery Got to Do With It?" *Criminal Justice* 23 (2008): 3.

YouTube. "The North Carolina Racial Justice Act." Video uploaded by bythebrook8 on May 11, 2009. http:// www.youtube.com/watch?v=iiCZK7AxUCQ, accessed January 14, 2014.

Zahn, Margaret A., Susan Brumbaugh, Darrell Steffensmeier, Barry C. Feld, Merry Morash, Meda Chesney-Lind, Jody Miller, Allison Ann Payne, Denise C. Gottfredson, and Candace Kruttschnitt. *Girls Study Group: Understanding and Responding to Girls' Delinquency.* Washington, DC: U.S. Department of Justice, Office of Juvenile Justice and Delinquency Prevention, 2008. https://www. ncjrs.gov/pdffiles1/ojjdp/218905.pdf, accessed January 14, 2014.

Zatz, Marjorie S. "The Convergence of Race, Ethnicity, Gender, and Class on Court Decisionmaking: Looking Toward the 21st Century." *Criminal Justice* 3 (2000): 503–552.

Zedlewski, Edwin. *Making Confinement Decisions.* Washington, DC: National Institute of Justice Research in Brief, 1987.

Zedlewski, Edwin W. *Alternatives to Custodial Supervision: The Day Fine* [NCJ 230401]. Washington, DC: U.S. Department of Justice, National Criminal Justice Reference Service, 2010. http://www.ncjrs.gov/pdffiles1/nij/ grants/230401.pdf, accessed August 19, 2012.

Zheng, Eddy, and Helen Zia. *Other: An Asian and Pacific Islander Prisoners' Anthology.* Oakland, CA: Asian Prisoner Support Committee, 2007.

Zimbardo, Philip G. *Stanford Prison Experiment: A Simulation Study of the Psychology of Imprisonment Conducted at Stanford University.* Social Psychology Network, n.d. www.prisonexp.org, accessed May 13, 2014.

Zimring, Franklin. *Perspectives on Deterrence.* Washington, DC: National Institute of Mental Health, Center for Studies of Crime and Delinquency, 1971.

Zimring, Franklin, and Gordon Hawkins. "The New Mathematics of Imprisonment." *Crime & Delinquency* 34, no. 4 (1988), 425–36.

Zimring, Franklin E., Sam Kamin, and Gordon Hawkins. *Crime and Punishment in California: The Impact of Three Strikes and You're Out.* Berkeley, CA: Institute of Governmental Studies Press, 1999.

Index

About the Authors

Barry Krisberg (PhD, University of Pennsylvania) is a Senior Fellow at the Chief Justice Earl Warren Institute on Law and Social Policy at the University of California, Berkeley Law School and a Lecturer in Residence at in the Juris Doctor Program at Berkeley Law. He is known nationally for his research and expertise on juvenile justice and corrections issues and is often called upon as a resource for professionals, foundations, and the media. Dr. Krisberg was appointed by the legislature to serve on the California Blue Ribbon Commission on Inmate Population Management. Past president and fellow of the Western Society of Criminology, he was Chair of the California Attorney General's Research Advisory Committee. Dr. Krisberg was appointed to chair an Expert Panel to investigate the conditions in the California youth prisons. His many books and articles include *Juvenile Justice* and *Continuing the Struggle for Justice*, both published by SAGE.

Susan Marchionna has a varied background in writing, publications, and communications in the criminal justice field. She has most recently consulted with the Earl Warren Institute on Law and Social Policy at UC Berkeley on a number of projects, such as developing evidence-based policy and procedures for the San Francisco Adult Probation Department. Other Warren projects include a probation caseload survey, evaluations of the Juvenile Detention Alternatives Initiative, and brief analyses on policing and crime in California cities. In addition, Susan has worked with the MOSS Group on publications projects related to PREA compliance and sexual safety in institutions, She is serving as the Technical Editor for a new Desktop Guide Series being produced by the Nation Partnership for Juvenile Services in conjunction with OJJDP. Prior to her current consulting work, Susan was the Director of Communication at the National Council on Crime and Delinquency (NCCD). There, she helped develop a series of Focus publications on various research topics. For the NCCD Centennial, Susan edited a collection of essays entitled, *Continuing the Struggle for Justice*. Susan is a graduate of UC Santa Cruz and a long-time resident of the San Francisco bay area.

Christopher Hartney is a senior researcher at the National Council on Crime and Delinquency in Oakland, California. He has worked with the organization since 2001, and has two decades of professional experience in research and statistics. Chris' work at NCCD, funded by various federal, state, and local government agencies and philanthropic foundations, has included the national evaluation of the Juvenile Detention Alternatives Initiative; bed space needs forecasts for youth tried as adults in Baltimore, Maryland and for juvenile justice-involved youth following system reforms in Arkansas; the development of a new approach to prison for young adults emphasizing intensive strengths-based rehabilitative and educational services in small secure facilities; a review of the causes and impacts of the decarceration of youth from California's youth prison system; the national evaluation of Parents Anonymous; the potential cost savings of alternatives to incarceration for non-serious adult offenders; a Structured Decision Making system for the District of Columbia; the interplay of media coverage, public sentiment, data trends, and policy-making with regard to youth violence in major U.S. cities; and a survey of health care access for system-involved youth in 58 California counties. Chris has authored several NCCD publications documenting disproportionate representation of people of color in the justice system and other issues in justice and corrections, including spotlights on women, Native American youth, youth under 18 in the adult system, and international corrections. He is co-author of several peer-reviewed articles and has presented study findings before a variety of professional, governmental, and community groups. Before joining NCCD, his research work included educational assessment and health impacts in communities exposed to industrial accidents. Chris has a B.A. from the University of California at Berkeley and has completed all master's level coursework in experimental psychology at San Francisco State University.

⑤SAGE researchmethods

The essential online tool for researchers from the world's leading methods publisher

Find exactly what you are looking for, from basic explanations to advanced discussion

More content and new features added this year!

"I have never really seen anything like this product before, and I think it is really valuable."

John Creswell, University of Nebraska–Lincoln

Discover **Methods Lists**—methods readings suggested by other users

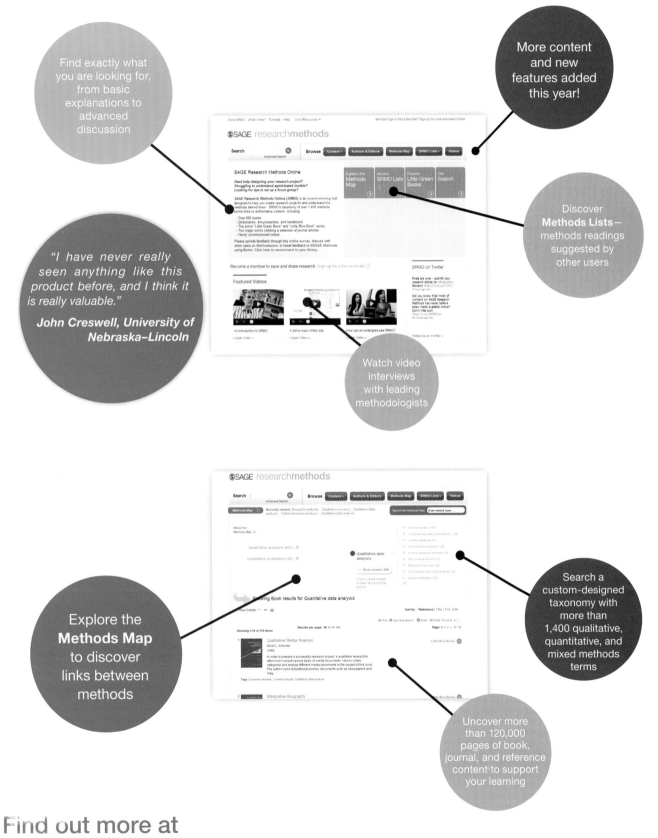

Watch video interviews with leading methodologists

Explore the **Methods Map** to discover links between methods

Search a custom-designed taxonomy with more than 1,400 qualitative, quantitative, and mixed methods terms

Uncover more than 120,000 pages of book, journal, and reference content to support your learning

Find out more at
www.sageresearchmethods.com